THE TOOTH TATTOO

THE TOOTH TATTOO

Peter Lovesey

WINDSOR

PARAGON

First published 2013
by Sphere
This Large Print edition published 2013
by AudioGO Ltd
by arrangement with
Little, Brown Book Goup

Hardcover   ISBN: 978 1 4713 5197 6
Softcover   ISBN: 978 1 4713 5198 3

British Library Cataloguing in Publication Data available

Printed and bound in Great Britain by
T J International Limited

THE TOOTH TATTOO

1

Southbank, London, 2005

Eleven-thirty at night, sweaty in his evening suit and shattered after a heavy night playing Rachmaninov, Mel Farran plodded out of the artists' exit on the south side of the Royal Festival Hall. Good thing his legs didn't need telling the way to Waterloo station and the tube. He'd done it a thousand times. Rachmaninov was said to be the ultimate romantic — miserable old git. The six foot scowl, as Stravinsky called him, had been a pianist through and through. He worked the string section like galley slaves to show off the joanna man, and Mel Farran was a viola-player, so thank you, Sergei.

The moon was up, spreading the shadow of Hungerford Bridge across the paved square called Beacon Market Place.

He was forced to stop. A young woman was blocking his path, one of those situations where each takes a sideways step the same way. It happened twice and they were still face to face.

She said, 'Do you mind?'

Mel took it as a statement of annoyance. He was annoyed, too, wanting to move on, but what's to be gained from complaining?

Then she surprised him by saying, 'Please.'

How dense am I, he thought, not realising she always intended to stop me. Something glossy and flimsy was being waved under his nose. The concert programme. She was holding a pen in the other hand.

Mel forced himself out of his stupor. She wants my autograph, for God's sake. She can't have confused me with the pianist, else why does she think I'm carrying an instrument case?

Quick impression: she was the typical music student, bright-eyed, intense, dark hair in a bunch tied with red velvet. It wasn't all that long since Mel had gone through college himself, passionate about all things musical. He'd queued through the night for the proms, cut back on cigarettes to buy the latest Nigel Kennedy, busked in Covent Garden to pay for a trip to Bayreuth. But he'd never understood the point of collecting autographs, still less the autographs of mere orchestra members.

She pleaded with her eyes. Almond eyes.

8

Nothing remarkable in that. Every college has a large quota of students from the Far East.

He succumbed. 'Are you sure it's me you want?'

'Absolutely.'

'I'm only one of the orchestra.'

'Principal viola. You were wonderful.'

'Get away.'

'Truly.'

Well.

Maybe I was, he told himself, and his self-esteem got a lift. I'm good at what I do and some people appreciate my playing, even when ninety-nine percent are there to hear the pianist. This well-informed young lady knows who I am, so I'd better sign and be on my way.

He tucked the fiddle under his arm to free his hands. 'Where are you from?'

'Tokyo. Have you been there?'

He shook his head. 'One day, maybe. Just my signature?'

'Whatever you want to write.'

That was a facer. At the end of a long concert he couldn't think of two words together. 'May I make it personal and put your name?'

Instead of the gasp of pleasure he was expecting, she curled her lip.

He was thrown. Had he said something wrong?

She gave a laugh — a throaty, mocking laugh, meant to hurt — and took a step back. 'You don't know who I am, dumbo.'

At the same time Mel felt a sharp, strong tug from behind. He flexed his arm. Too late. His viola had been snatched.

He swung round in time to see a young guy on a bike in baseball cap, T-shirt and jeans pedalling away across the square. He was riding one-handed with Mel's instrument case in his free hand. It was a set-up. He must have sneaked up behind while Mel — shit-for-brains — was being soft-soaped by the girl. He'd been mugged.

Life was unthinkable without that viola. It wasn't a Strad. It was not particularly valuable, not even old in instrument-making terms, but it was Mel's voice, his art, his constant companion, his living. You'd need to be a professional musician to understand how he felt.

Hell, he decided, I won't allow this.

He was no athlete, but he started running. Later he realised he should have chased the girl, who was clearly the accomplice. She would have been easier to catch than a bloke on a bike. Instead all of Mel's focus was on his viola and the thief himself, fast escaping

10

along the side of the Festival Hall.

The concert audience had long since dispersed. At that time of night people were keen to get away. The great palaces of culture along the South Bank are locked, impenetrable, but all around — for those who know — are places of refuge, arches, stairwells and underpasses. The whole area becomes a haven for dossers and derelicts.

Mel doubted that the thief was a down-and-out. For one thing, he'd grabbed the fiddle, not his wallet. For another, he was working with the girl, who looked and sounded Royal College of Music. And he was on an expensive-looking bike.

Spurred by a degree of anger he didn't know he possessed, Mel kept up the chase. The thief was faster, but one thing was in Mel's favour: they'd turned left towards the Thames and he couldn't cycle across.

No use shouting. There wasn't anyone else in sight. Taking increasingly shallow gasps, Mel sprinted the length of the building as well as he could, resolved to get the thief in sight again. He turned the corner by the main entrance, already in darkness.

The guy was there, up ahead.

Mel's legs were heavier with each stride and a band of pain was tightening across his chest. He was slowing, for all his strength

11

of will. The buildings were a blur when he started. Now he could see them clearly.

But the thief would have a problem. The riverside walkway was at a higher level and a set of about a dozen steps formed a barrier ahead of him. He'd need to dismount. It wouldn't be easy carrying both bike and viola up there.

Mel urged himself into another spurt.

He was running in the space between the front of the Festival Hall and the side of the Queen Elizabeth Hall. No one was around to help. It's me and him, Mel thought. If I keep going I may catch up before he gets up those steps.

The guy's head turned, checking, Mel guessed, whether he was still in pursuit.

Then he surprised Mel by veering to the right just before the steps, straight towards the QEH. What was he doing? Mel had been assuming the high wall was solid concrete like the rest of the building.

He appeared to cycle straight through and vanish.

Disbelieving, in despair, at the limit of his strength, Mel staggered along the remaining stretch and discovered how it had been done. There was a hidden ramp just before the steps, obviously meant for wheelchair access. The thief must have skimmed up

12

there without breaking a sweat.

Suddenly he was back in view on the walkway, pedalling across Mel's line of vision as if to mock him. But he stopped just to the right of the gated entrance to the Festival Pier, still astride the bike, with his feet on the ground.

He was up against the railing by the water's edge. He swung the viola case back to get momentum. Jesus Christ, Mel thought, he's about to throw it over.

'No!' he yelled. 'For God's sake, no.'

He was powerless to stop it. The thief couldn't hear him this far off.

There was a freeze-frame moment as if he was having second thoughts. Then Mel's precious fiddle was hurled over the edge.

Water is the worst enemy. No stringed instrument will survive immersion. The canvas case wasn't waterproof. It would fill with filthy water. Whether it floated or got dragged down was immaterial.

To Mel, what had just happened was akin to murder. Anyone who has listened to music, who has heard a violin or a viola sing, must know it has life. It's a unique individual with the power to speak directly to the soul, to calm, heal, inspire, uplift the spirit in ways beyond man's capability. Mel would defy anyone not to respond to the purity of legato bowing, the eloquence of the flowing tone. Each instrument has its own voice.

He'd stopped running. His muscles were refusing to function, his brain spinning between disbelief and panic.

Why? What malice drives anyone to such an act?

'Bastard!'

Already the cyclist was moving off left. And now Mel saw he'd get clean away, under the bridge and past the London Eye. All day there is a queue outside the huge observation wheel. But the place closed at nine-thirty. Nobody would be there to stop him at this hour.

In reality his attention wasn't on the thief any longer. He could go. Mel wasn't thinking about justice or revenge. He wanted the impossible: to put the last five minutes into reverse and undo what had happened. Real life isn't like that.

He'd got the shakes now. The shock was consuming him.

He knew he should mount the steps and look over the edge. It was too late to leap over and recover the poor, damaged thing. The only reason for jumping would be suicide. He was almost of a mind to do it.

He forced himself upwards, stiff-legged,

14

still shaking, right up to the railing, and peered over. It was too far down and too dark to spot anything floating there. All the filth of the river spreads to the banks like scum in a sink. The black water caught some ripples of reflected light from the ornate globe lamp-stand and that was all.

Out in the middle there were lights. A small vessel was chugging past the pier towards Waterloo Bridge. A police launch? No such luck. It was more like a powerboat moving sedately because of the conditions. Too far out to hail.

He heard water slurping against the embankment wall below him. The boat's backwash had reached there. He stared down and saw nothing.

Hours later, in his flat, he drank coffee and replayed the scene in his mind. He'd recalled it already for the police, given them such descriptions as he could — the Japanese girl with the red scrunch, the guy on the bike, and his poor, benighted instrument. The constable taking the statement hadn't understood his desolation. He hadn't even promised to pursue the thieves. 'Look at it from our point of view,' he'd said. 'Where would we start? I don't suppose they'll try it with anyone else.'

15

Obviously they had conspired to rob Mel and it wasn't an opportunist crime. There had been planning behind it. But what was the reason? Surely not malice alone? They don't know Mel, so why should they hate him? There was no profit in it. A good, much valued instrument was lost and his livelihood put at risk. They couldn't know if he had other violas.

Senseless.

Or was it? His memory retrieved an image, the powerboat he'd noticed out in the middle of the river. Could it have come close enough for someone aboard to catch the viola as it was slung over the railing? This would provide a cruel logic to what had happened, a well organised plan to rob him.

Now that the finality of his loss had come home to him, he was discovering dark places in his psyche that he didn't know existed. He believed he could kill those two if he met them again.

Would he recognise the girl? He thought so. The light hadn't been good, but he'd seen her up close. He could remember the eyes wide in appeal when they'd first met, catching the light of the streetlamps, yet shot with scorn when she was sure he'd been suckered. He had a clear, raw memory

16

of how her mouth had opened to mock him and most of all he could hear the cruel glissando of her laughter. Was he right in thinking she had been a music student? If so, the mugging was even harder to understand.

Of her partner in crime he could recall only the clothes. He hadn't seen his face.

Did it matter any more? Did he want to hunt them down? He could search the common rooms of all the music colleges in London and maybe find them, but he wouldn't get his viola back.

Anger didn't begin to describe his state of mind.

2

Vienna, 2012

'How much longer does it last?' Paloma Kean asked Peter Diamond.

'Aren't you enjoying it?'

'I'm trying not to breathe.'

Diamond felt in his pocket and produced a tube of peppermints. 'The man who thinks of everything.'

'Thanks, but an oxygen mask would be better.'

There are days when the Vienna sewer tour is more odorous than others. Wise tourists take note of the humidity before booking. Diamond and Paloma, on their weekend city break, had no choice, Saturday afternoon or nothing. It happened that this Saturday in July was warm, with a thunderstorm threatening. Even Diamond had noticed that the smell was not Chanel No. 5.

'After this, you'll appreciate the Ferris

wheel,' he told her.

She was silent. She'd brought this on herself when reminding him that his favourite film, *The Third Man,* was set in Vienna. At the time, she'd congratulated herself for thinking of it. Otherwise they wouldn't have been here.

The adventure had begun back in April with a scratch-card she had found on the floor of his car. Diamond hadn't bothered to check it. He'd said they were giving them away at the petrol station.

She'd revealed three matching symbols and told him he was a winner.

'Everyone is.'

She had insisted on phoning the number on the back of the card.

Deeply sceptical, Diamond had told her, 'That's how they make their money.'

But it had turned out that he really had won a weekend break for two in a city of his choice: Paris, Amsterdam or Vienna. True to form, he'd dismissed Europe's historic capitals with a dogmatic, 'I don't do abroad.'

'Come on,' Paloma had said. 'Lighten up, Peter. This could be so romantic.'

'I'm too busy at work.' Work for Diamond was heading the CID section at Bath police station. There were always matters to be investigated.

Then Paloma had remembered *The Third Man* and whistled the Harry Lime Theme.

'What did you say those cities were?' he'd said, looking up.

And here they were trudging through a reeking sewer with a bunch of elderly tourists carrying flashlights. At intervals everyone stopped to be shown a clip of the film projected on to the brick wall opposite. Paloma could see Diamond's lips move silently in sync with the soundtrack. *'It's the main sewer. Runs into the blue Danube.'* So obviously was he relishing the experience that it would have been churlish to complain.

The day had started agreeably enough in the Café Mozart, another of the film locations. The coffee and *Sachertorte* were expensive, even for a couple used to Bath prices, but Diamond had basked in the ambience and said the experience was worth every Euro and talked about Graham Greene being a regular there in 1947 when he was researching the story. From there they'd moved on to a side street off the Naschmarkt and he'd stressed how fortunate they were to be here on a Saturday, the only day of the week the Third Man Museum opened. Displayed along with countless stills and posters was the actual zither Anton Karas had used to play the haunting theme. You could select from four hundred cover versions of the tune. Paloma had left the place with a headache that Diamond said was surely something to do with the weather. A short walk had brought them to Esperanto Park and the brick-built spiral staircase down to the oldest part of Vienna's sewer system. Proceedings underground had begun with a film explaining how the cholera epidemic of 1830 had made a better sanitation system necessary. Then, after warnings to watch their footing, the guide had led them into the glistening brick-lined drains.

Atmospheric? Paloma couldn't argue with that. She just wished every film clip wasn't punctuated with another head-numbing burst of the zither music.

'Are you enjoying this?' she asked Diamond in the faint hope that he'd had enough.

'Brilliant.'

There was no opting out. This was not the best place to get lost if she tried returning to the stairs.

'How's your head now?' Diamond asked.

'About the same.'

'I think I should warn you that at the end

21

of the tour a man dressed as Harry Lime steps out and fires a gun at us.'

'I can't wait.'

That evening at the Prater they rode the Riesenrad, the giant Ferris wheel that had featured in the film. The worst of the clouds had rolled away to the south and Paloma's headache had departed with them. She was actually enjoying the ride in the rickety old cabin. They were definitely cabins and not pods or capsules. Each was a little room like a railway compartment with a curved roof and windows. They shared theirs with an elderly man in a brown Tyrolean hat with a feather trim who was at the far end surveying the view with a benign smile. Below, ribbons of light stretched to infinity. The wheel itself periodically flashed silver and gold.

'I don't really mind hearing it again,' she told Diamond with a smile.

'What's that?'

'The Harry Lime speech about Switzer-land, five hundred years of brotherly love, democracy and peace producing the cuckoo clock.'

'I was going to spare you that. It wasn't in the original script, you know.'

'You tell me that each time.'

'Orson Welles —'

'That, too.'

He placed a hand over hers. 'You've shown the patience of a saint all day.'

'If I'm honest, I haven't been feeling that way,' she said. 'But I can see how much it means to you, reliving the film.'

'The old black and white movies have got it for me.'

'I know. Giant shadows, sudden shafts of light.'

He took a deep, appreciative breath. 'Like the night scene when Lime appears in the doorway.'

'With a blast of zither music just in case anyone in the cinema isn't paying attention.'

'Er, yes. Well, it is called the Harry Lime Theme.'

'And you grew up with it.'

He baulked at that. 'The film was released before I was born. Orson Welles was old enough to have been my grandfather.'

'Sorry.'

'But that scene gets to me every time.'

'Strange.'

He frowned. 'Why do you say that?'

'Harry Lime was the villain, selling adulterated penicillin. You're supposed to be on the opposite side. You should identify with the Joseph Cotten character.'

'But Welles had all the charisma. The film is clever, playing with your loyalties.'

She tried to see it from his point of view. 'I suppose as a policeman you have to get inside the minds of bad people.'

'Sometimes — but you aren't supposed to admire them. Each time I see it, I really want him to stay at liberty. And today we walked in his footsteps.'

'With great care, watching where we trod,' Paloma said.

There was a movement at the far end of the cabin. The elderly man turned from the window and raised his hat. He may even have clicked his heels. 'Excuse me. I heard what you said. You were talking about the sewers, am I right?'

'You are,' Paloma said. 'We did the tour this afternoon.'

'It wasn't Orson Welles.'

There was an awkward silence.

'Believe me, it was,' Diamond told him. 'I've seen that film more times than I care to count.'

'Mr. Welles took one look and refused to work in such a place,' the old man said.

Diamond was speechless, shaking his head.

'Most of the scenes featuring him were filmed with a double, or in Shepperton

24

studio in England.' The old man seemed to know what he was talking about.

Paloma laughed. 'Do you mean we traipsed through all those dreadful-smelling tunnels for no reason at all?'

'I wouldn't say that,' the old man said. 'They did hours of filming down there, but little, if any, with Orson Welles.'

'Why not?'

'He was being difficult at the time, playing — what is the expression? — hard to get. He had an agreement with Mr. Korda, the producer, to star in three films, but nothing much had come of it and he was annoyed. This was only a cameo role. He is on screen for less than ten minutes of the entire film. I believe he was taken down to the sewer once to see a place where water cascaded from one of the ducts. Harry Lime was supposed to run underneath and get drips running down his face. Welles absolutely refused.'

'You seem to know a lot about it.'

'I'm a Viennese. It's part of our city history.'

'So they built a studio mock-up of the sewer?' Paloma said, and she seemed to be leading him on.

'That is my understanding.'

Determined not to have his day spoilt,

Diamond rubbed his hands and said with conviction, 'Well, at least Orson Welles did what we're doing now — rode the Ferris wheel.'

The old man turned and looked out of the window again. 'Have you heard of back projection? Look carefully next time you watch the film.'

Back in their hotel room, Paloma saw how deflated Diamond was and said, 'We've only got his word for it.'

'He seemed to know what he was talking about. I did read once that they shot parts of the film at Shepperton.'

'Bits, I expect. It was the way they worked. It's still a classic.'

'You're right about that.'

'Silly old man. I bet he rides the damn Ferris wheel for hours on end lying in wait for fans like us.'

'Do you think so?'

'Destroying people's illusions — that's his game. Don't let him ruin our day, Peter. We did the tour. We visited the right places. You'll spot them next time you see the film.'

He was grateful for her words. Paloma was a terrific support. She knew how his pleasure in the day had been undermined. And the weekend hadn't offered much for her to enjoy. He'd been planning to fit in a visit to another of the film locations — the cemetery — next morning and now he changed his mind. 'I'm going to suggest we do something different tomorrow. Our flight home isn't until the evening. Let's make it your day. How would you like to spend it?'

She took off her shoes and flopped back on the bed, hands clasped behind her head. 'That's a lovely suggestion. Let me give it serious thought.'

'There's some wine left. I'll pour you a drink while you decide.'

'Now you're talking.'

But when he returned from the bathroom with the two glasses, Paloma's eyes were closed and she was breathing evenly. It had been an exhausting day.

Over coffee next morning in a small shop near the hotel with a display of irresistible fruit tarts, they debated how to spend their last hours in Vienna. 'Knowing you,' she said, 'and I don't mean to sound offensive, you may not be too thrilled about this. So many great musicians lived and composed their masterpieces here. Could we find Beethoven's house?'

'Why not?' he said, doing his best to sound enthusiastic. 'Where is it?'

They opened their map and asked the waitress, but she didn't seem to understand.

'We need a phrasebook,' Diamond muttered.

From behind them a voice said, 'If it's Beethoven's house you want, you have about forty to choose from in Vienna. He was constantly on the move.'

'Excuse me?' Diamond turned in his chair, peeved that somebody had been eavesdropping.

The speaker wasn't the old man from the Ferris wheel, but he could have been his brother. He had the same gnomish look and a voice like a scraper stripping wallpaper. Probably a Tyrolean hat was tucked under the table on one of the other chairs.

'There are two of any note,' the man went on. 'The first is the Beethoven Memorial House, but you are too late for that. It is closed this month. The other is the Pasqualati House where he composed his fourth, fifth and sixth symphonies and the opera *Fidelio*.'

'That'll do us,' Diamond said. 'Is it open?'

'I believe so.'

'Where exactly is it?'

'Before you dash off, I think I should inform you that Beethoven didn't actually live there.'

28

'I thought you said he did.'

'The rooms open to visitors are furnished to look as if Beethoven was the tenant, but in reality his home was in the adjacent flat — which is privately owned and not open to the public.'

It was like being told Orson Welles hadn't run through the sewers.

'I give up,' Diamond said. 'Where do we go to see something authentic in this city?'

'Some of the exhibits are authentic. The salt and pepper pots unquestionably belonged to Beethoven.'

'Big deal,' Diamond murmured to Paloma.

'You asked where it is,' the old man said. 'You'll find it west of Freyung. This is an old part of the city. You go up a cobbled lane called Schreyvogelgasse to the Mölker Bastei and the Pasqualati House is there. I'll show you.'

'Is it worth it?' Diamond asked Paloma, but she had already passed their map across.

'Here.' A bony finger pinned down the map. 'At the western margin of the Innere Stadt.'

'Some way off, then,' Diamond said. 'Maybe we should choose another composer's house.'

'This is Schreyvogelgasse. As you pass

along, you may wish to glance at number eight. The doorway is famous. It's where Harry Lime first appears in that film, *The Third Man.*'

Diamond's eyes widened.

'It looks as if we'll be going there after all,' Paloma said.

In the taxi, Diamond said, 'I'm beginning to understand. They post little old men all over the city to bring innocent tourists down to earth with a bump.'

'He was trying to be helpful.'

'So was the guy on the Ferris wheel. There are some things I'd rather not be helped with.'

'That's rich — from a professional detective.'

'A secret romantic.'

Her eyebrows popped up.

In the cobbled street she told him to stand in the doorway of number eight for a photo.

'I can't. It's so cheesy.'

'But you want to.'

He didn't need any more persuading. He took up the pose, even giving his straw hat a rakish tilt.

The Beethoven house pleased Paloma. There was a good atmosphere and enough genuine relics to make the old man's criticisms unimportant. 'To think *Fidelio* was created here,' she said.

'Next door.'

'It doesn't seem to matter any more. Are you impressed? I'm sure I can feel his presence.'

'It's not my strongest suit, classical music,' he admitted.

'What is, apart from the Harry Lime Theme?'

'Queen's greatest hits, I suppose.'

'I can see I'll have to work on you.'

'You can try. It's still your day. How shall we spend our last couple of hours here?'

'Let's take a look at the Danube. Is it really blue? We haven't seen it by daylight.'

The nearest bridge wasn't far from their hotel. They packed, cleared their room, left the cases in a storeroom and strolled down Schwedenplatz.

'You're not going to believe this,' Diamond said, studying the map. 'It isn't actually the Danube.'

'Get away.'

'It's the Danube canal. The river is way off to the north-east.'

'Second best as usual, then.'

Blue the water was, under a clear sky. They walked to the centre of the bridge and watched the shipping gliding underneath. A breeze ruffled Paloma's hair.

'This has been a treat,' she said, linking her arm with his.

'All of it?'

'Every minute, now I look back. We got you out of the CID room for a whole weekend. Go on, admit it, you needed the break.'

'It's done me good,' he said.

'And all because of that scratch-card. Next time we shouldn't rely on a piece of luck. I'll try persuading you to look at a travel brochure.'

'Don't push it.'

With more time in hand they bought ice creams and took a walk along the embankment.

'Look, someone's dropped some flowers,' Paloma said as they approached a point where some steps led down to a mooring. A bunch of pinkish-white flowers wrapped in paper was lying on the pavement. When they got closer, they saw more flowers pressed into the lattice mouldings in the wall. Most were dead carnations. 'It must have fallen out.' She stooped to lodge the fresh flowers back into a space in the stonework. They were star-shaped with long, yellow-tipped stamens. 'The scent is powerful. Must be some type of lily. The place has been made into a little shrine. Do you think someone drowned here?'

'Hard to say,' he said, wanting to lighten the mood. 'Where are the little old men of Vienna when we need one?'

'There's a card with one of these dead bunches, some kind of message. But it isn't in German. I think it's Japanese.'

3

Acton, West London, 2012

Temptation arrives in many forms. For Mel, it was cued by the opening notes of Beethoven's Fifth, the ringtone on his phone.

'Yes?'

'Mr. Farran, the viola player?' A male voice, educated, middle-aged and as imperious as Sir Thomas Beecham's in rehearsal.

'That's me.'

'Do you have a moment?'

'Depends. Are you selling something?'

'Certainly not. This is a serious call.'

A rap over the knuckles. Mel should have cut the call immediately and saved himself from the wrecking ball that was swinging his way.

'Who are you?' he asked.

'That's immaterial at this juncture. Call me Ivan, if you wish. I have a proposal massively to your advantage.'

'You *are* trying to sell something.'

'Pay attention, please. This is about your professional career.'

'As a musician?'

'Naturally.'

'A gig?'

A pause. Ivan was plainly unhappy with the expression and considering whether to hang up. 'More than that, much more — if you're prepared to cooperate. But this is too important to discuss over the phone. Are you free tomorrow evening?'

'Free for what?'

'For a drink and a chance to discuss the opportunity. I'll send a car at seven thirty.'

'You know where I live?'

'This isn't spur of the moment, Mr. Farran. I've heard you play, or I wouldn't be bothering.'

Let's admit it — flattery is a sure-fire persuader. 'Where are we having this drink?'

'At my club. There's a dress code, by the way. Lounge suit and tie. You do possess a suit?'

Irritated by the patronising tone, sceptical, yet intrigued, Mel switched off and pocketed the phone. In truth, he was in no position to turn down the invitation. A life in classical music is precarious. His income from orchestral work and teaching was barely a living wage. Yet he was good at what he did. He'd been gifted with perfect pitch and a mother hooked on Mozart. Handed a miniature violin at an age when other kids were learning to tie their shoelaces, he'd mastered the basics within days. He was taught by an elderly Polish maestro and within a year on his advice switched to a miniature viola. Really. They do exist. Violists, the maestro told him, were always in demand, whereas there was a glut of violinists. The old man had been right — to a degree. Mel had never gone for long without ensemble work. He'd survived. However, there wasn't much prospect of advancement. Solo opportunities with the viola were rare. If he'd excelled at the violin — as everyone suggested he could have done — the repertoire is huge and he could have toughed it out with the army of East Asian players who came along at that time. No use complaining now. He could play both instruments to a good level, but it was the viola he was known for. He'd trained at the Royal College and filled in with some of the great orchestras of Europe. Violists are an endangered species. If he'd known just how endangered, he wouldn't have listened to Ivan. But he was an innocent. At twenty-nine, he needed an opportunity and this promised to be it.

Single, hetero, not bad looking, he was originally from Beaconsfield and currently living in a poky first-floor flat in Acton, West London. Fingis Street had never seen the like of the gleaming black limo that drew up outside at seven thirty. Good thing he didn't keep it waiting or the local youths would have unscrewed the Mercedes logo in seconds and scraped a coin along the bodywork to see if it was real.

He was wearing an almost new pinstripe suit from Oxfam. You can bet the original owner had died, but you can't get fussed about stuff like that when you're skint and need to look respectable. All of his work clothes, evening suits, dress shirts and bow ties, black and white, also came from charity shops. Bargains, every one.

'Where exactly are we going?' he asked the driver.

'Clubland, sir. St James's.'

'Which club?'

'I was told it's confidential.'

'Well, I'm being driven there, so I'm going to find out.'

'And I have my orders, sir.'

Mel didn't press him. If Ivan wanted to make a cloak-and-dagger occasion out of the meeting, let it be, he told himself to calm his nerves. He hoped this wouldn't turn out to be a huge let-down.

For all the man-about-town bluster, Mel couldn't say he was familiar with the St James's area of London. He'd never set foot in a gentlemen's club, and when they drew up outside a set of white steps to a shiny black door with brass fittings, he forgot to look for the name.

The doorman had his instructions and waved Mel through when he said who he was. Carpeted entrance hall, grand staircase and oil paintings in gold frames. Mel couldn't say who painted them, except it wasn't Andy Warhol or Francis Bacon. A short, bald man appeared from behind a potted fern and extended his hand. The grip was firm, as if they were old chums.

'So glad you came. There's an anteroom we can have to ourselves. Have you eaten?'

'Yes,' Mel lied, not wanting to be treated to a meal before he knew what this was about.

'In that case, cognac should go down well. Agreed?'

A beer would have been more to Mel's liking, but he didn't have the neck to ask for one. A club servant was sent for the cognac.

Bound copies of *Punch* lined the anteroom. Laughs all round.

'I still don't know your surname,' Mel said when they were seated in leather armchairs either side of a marble fireplace big enough to park a car in.

'Better you don't unless and until we come to an agreement,' his host said. 'You will have guessed I, too, am a musician. Violin. You've heard me play.'

'Have I?'

'Possibly in the concert hall and certainly on disc.'

What do you say to that? If the guy was a soloist, Mel didn't recognise him. He could think of dozens he'd heard in the last eight years.

'In a well-known string quartet,' he added.

'Ah. Am I supposed to guess which?'

'No.'

Be mysterious, Mel thought. See if I care. The cognac arrived in a cut-glass decanter and was poured into balloon glasses. Ivan waited for the flunkey to leave the room.

'There could be a vacancy in the quartet,' Ivan said.

'Could be?'

'Is.'

'For a violist? And you have me in mind?'

'In mind is a good way of putting it.'

Mel waited, but nothing else followed. 'Is this an offer?'

'Not yet. The others will have a say.'

'Are they coming here to join us?'

'No.'

'Who are they?'

'That's not for me to say.'

All this stonewalling was hard to take. Ivan had issued the invitation. He should have been selling the deal. Instead he was swirling the brandy in the glass as if he was reading tea-leaves.

At last, he said, 'It's not straightforward.'

'That's getting obvious,' Mel said.

'The others don't know I've approached you. I believe I can persuade them. We play as a unit, but we're all individuals, which is our strength. A quartet of yes-men would never make fine music. Playing in a quartet is all about dialogue, distinct voices that respond to each other, but not passively. There's question and answer in musical terms, sharp debate, argument even. It isn't all resolution and harmony.'

Mel felt like saying he wasn't a total beginner. He'd played in quartets. 'You said they don't know about me. What if they don't approve?'

'I would expect to persuade them — if I'm persuaded myself.'

'You said on the phone you've heard me play.'

'But can you commit?'

'Commit what — murder?' A cheap re-mark. Something had to be said to lighten the mood.

Ivan didn't smile. 'Commit to a trial period of, say, a year? It would mean total loyalty to the quartet, rehearsals, business meetings, performances, recordings and touring.'

'I'd need to know more.'

'In particular?'

'Who am I replacing?'

'That I can't say.'

'Has he retired — or have you given him the elbow?'

'Neither.'

'Died?'

Silence.

'He's still playing? You're plotting to dump him and he doesn't know?'

A shake of the head. 'We're professionals, Mr. Farran. We have our disagreements, but we're not like that.'

'Speaking of the professional part, how much would I expect to earn? I need to live.'

'Enough for that, and more. We divide all the income equally and that includes our manager. As a new member, you'd take home precisely the same as the rest of us. Not as much as a bank executive earns, but better than you're used to getting.'

'How much approximately?'

'Just under six figures in a good year.'

Yoiks. This was the first thing Mel had heard that he liked. 'At some point soon, you'll have to come clean about who you are, the name of the quartet. If you're earning that money, you must be famous.'

'The fame is immaterial. You're single, yes?'

'I am.'

'So touring shouldn't be a problem?'

'I guess not.'

'We don't live in each other's pockets. There's no sharing of rooms, no forced mingling. All we would insist on is that you are there for rehearsals and concerts. If we take on a residency, as we may, that can involve some teaching. Are you comfortable with that?'

'I've done some. I'd still want to meet the others before deciding.'

'Naturally — and they will insist on meeting you.'

'So will it be arranged?'

Ivan hesitated. 'Possibly. In the fullness of time.'

The 'fullness of time' was presumably how long it would take to dump the current violist, Mel mused, wondering what the unfortunate musician had done wrong. Difficult to feel comfortable about this set-up, but he was willing to stretch a point for a hundred grand a year.

Nothing more of substance was said and he left soon after. It was clearly a 'don't call us' situation.

Three weeks went by before he was contacted again. He was on the sundeck of a riverboat on the Thames playing in a string trio for someone's wedding. This kind of gig was a steady source of income and he didn't think of it as slumming, as some musicians did. The repertoire was undemanding, but the pieces were popular for a reason. Most were from the shows and it was no hardship to play Gershwin and Bernstein along with others who had written damn good tunes and never aspired to the concert hall. In a mid-session break for drinks Mel was cradling a tankard and leaning on the rail watching ducks and moorhens taking refuge in the reeds along the river bank when a nudge from behind almost sloshed the beer out of his glass.

'Careful, chuck. You don't want to wet your Strad.'

He turned and found himself staring into a cleavage threatening to give him vertigo.

He'd noticed this large wedding guest in a lyre-shaped fascinator hat and a wispy, low-cut yellow dress whooping it up with several of the men. The hearty shove in his back had come from her and here she was telling him to be careful.

This lady's had a few, he told himself. People do at weddings. Keep in the spirit of the occasion. 'If this is a Strad,' he said, 'I'm putting it up for sale. What's your best offer?'

'My body,' she said, 'and there's plenty of that, but on closer inspection it looks like a Chinese imitation. The viola, I mean, not me. I withdraw the offer. You're Mel Far-ran, right?'

Caught by surprise, he said, 'I am.'

She drew back a fraction, allowing him to get a wider focus on her physique. She was exceptionally large in all areas. Under the rake of the hat, blonde curls in profusion surrounded a face that was both pretty and pudgy. 'I came specially to see you. I'm the cellist in the quartet you could be joining.'

He took a moment to absorb this. 'Really? Which quartet is that?'

She wagged her finger. 'I may look decks-awash, buster, but you won't catch me as easily as that. I'm more sober than you think and that's restricted information.'

44

'Are you allowed to tell me who you are?'

'I've told everyone else, so I might as well tell you. I'm Cat — known for obvious reasons as Cat with Kitties. Rhyming slang.'

Difficult to follow that. Mel summoned a faint grin.

Cat continued blithely, 'You look the part, anyway, and apparently you can play a bit. Have you ever tried the cello?'

'I know enough not to stick it under my chin.'

'Don't get modest with me. I bet you can play, and I could play yours if you'll pardon the expression. At a pinch I can stand in for anyone.'

'Useful.'

'In the quartet we back each other up.'

'Does that mean you get someone else to carry your cello?'

She laughed and everything wobbled. 'Now you're talking, kiddo. If that's a genuine offer, you could have just sealed your place in the famous foursome. Mind if I handle your instrument?'

She had the knack of giving an innuendo to everything, and she had already picked up his viola.

Mel handed the bow across. Cat gripped the fiddle in a way that showed she was no beginner, tucked the chin-rest into her flesh and played a few bars of Elgar's 'Salut d'Amour', inescapable at events like this.

'Would I get by?'

'You know you would.'

With a sure touch, she segued to the opening solo chords of the Telemann Viola Concerto. Much more demanding.

'You don't need me in your quartet,' Mel said.

'I'm a smart gal, but there's a problem. I haven't yet learned how to play my cello whilst holding the viola.' In yet another smooth change of styles she knocked out some bars from one of the numbers the trio had performed, "Those Were the Days", and did it with gusto. 'Tell you what. Why don't you get yourself another drink and I'll sit in for you? The others won't mind.'

They didn't. She delighted everyone, including Mel's colleagues in the trio, not merely coping with the music, but giving it some welly.

Mel looked on in awe from behind a cluster of guests bobbing to the beat. He was amazed that this boisterous woman belonged to the same quartet as the po-faced Ivan. How on earth did the pair of them relate to each other? Ivan had said something about the members all being individuals, but these two came from different planets. Perhaps the playful Cat was needed as a counter-balance to Ivan's navel-gazing. Mel was in no doubt which of the two he'd rather have for company. What could the others be like? As yet he couldn't picture a rehearsal. String quartets were sometimes known as the "music of friends". His own experiences of ensemble playing told him this could be a long way from the truth, but there was an understanding that discussions must take place and agreement reached on fine points as well as the major issues of interpretation.

He still had no clue as to which quartet they were. He knew of many and had played in some. This wasn't to say he was an expert. String quartets were legion, a surprising number top notch, plenty whose best hope was to get through a concert without people leaving, a humble majority who confined themselves to weddings like this and a few who were just abysmal. The high-flyers literally jetted around the world delighting audiences in distant places, so it was understandable that he'd not heard Cat in concert. He was sure he'd have noticed her.

They'd reached the end of a rendering of *Moon River* that she'd embellished with trills the trio hadn't heard before, all in waltz time, and now she waved the bow for Mel to take over. 'Melly, my dear, I haven't had my second slice of wedding cake. I'm through playing.'

She was given a round of applause and blew kisses to the audience. While changing places with Mel she said with a wink, 'See more of you soon, eh?'

'So I may be in with a chance?'

'Don't push it, ducky. We only met an hour ago.'

'I meant the quartet.'

'Oh, that. Better wait and see. Is this your best instrument?'

'I do have another I keep for concert work.'

'That's a relief. This one isn't fit to use as a doorstop. Promise me you won't show it to any of the others.'

He wasn't going to miss an opening like that. 'I only show mine to girls, really lucky girls.'

'Well, it didn't get my juices going, honey. Keep it hidden.'

'Does anyone else need to vet me?'

'You bet.' She blew a kiss. 'Thanks for today. Wild.'

He didn't see her again that afternoon. At the end of the river trip, when they were packing up, one of the ushers asked him who the woman in yellow had been.

'That was Cat,' Mel said.

'Your girlfriend?'

'D'you mind? We only met today.'

'The reason I asked,' the usher said, 'is that no one seems to know who invited her. The bride's people thought she was one of the groom's family and the groom thought she was on the bride's side. We decided in the end she must have come with you.'

4

Bath, 2012

'It was a suicide,' Diamond told Paloma. 'Want to hear more, or would you rather not know?'

Back in Bath, on an overcast evening with soft rain in the air, they were taking one of their walks along the industrial stretch of the river west of the city, crammed on the south side with warehouses and factories, a far cry from the elegant part of Vienna they'd stayed in, but there was a compensation: they were only five minutes, he judged, from the Dolphin in Lower Weston. Walking wasn't a pleasurable activity for Diamond unless there was a pint and a pie when it finished.

'Every suicide is a tragedy,' Paloma said.

'Of course.'

'It's been on my mind ever since I saw all those flowers people had left. I want to know the details — and yet in a way I don't.'

'Best forget it, then.'

On the opposite side of the river an Inter-City train bound for Bristol enforced a timely pause, long enough for Paloma to come to a decision.

'I'm sorry. I know I shan't stop thinking about it. You'd better tell me what you found out.'

'Then we leave it and move on?'

'Agreed.'

'Okay,' he said. 'I asked Ingeborg. She's a wiz at winkling out information. Even so, it took her a while on the internet. Four years ago the body of a tourist was found in the Danube canal close to those steps. A Japanese woman in her twenties.'

Paloma's sympathy now had more to latch onto. 'A tourist? Poor soul. Was she travelling alone?'

'Apparently.'

'I wonder what drove her to do such a thing. Did they identify her?'

'Months later, through her DNA. She'd been in the water too long to be recognised.'

'How do they do that?'

'DNA is unique to each individual, as you know. They take a sample from the remains and once they know of a missing person they can compare the profiles.'

'What with?'

'Traces found in the home — hair follicles, skin cells, blood, saliva. A comb or a toothbrush will often have DNA attached.'

'I suppose the family reported her missing.'

'Not immediately. She'd been away some time. Her travel arrangements were open-ended.'

Paloma took a sharp, pitying breath. 'So easy to get depressed when you're alone in a strange city.'

'She must have known what to expect.'

'Yes, but things can easily go wrong. You find you're running through your cash, or you lose your credit cards, or you just get ill and there's no one with you to share your troubles and laugh them off. The world can seem a hostile place.'

'It would take more than that to make me jump into a canal.'

She didn't take the remark as lightly as he intended. 'We're not all men of steel.'

'Just trying to keep a sense of proportion.'

'Not always so simple. You said she was Japanese. They think differently about suicide. It's rooted in their culture.'

'What - harry-karry?'

'Hara-kiri, actually. No, that's part of the samurai tradition and too gory to go into. I'm talking about the mass of the people, and the way they think. I'm trying to think of the name of the most famous Japanese dramatist. Anyway, he specialised in plays about lovers who commit suicide, and he was writing over three hundred years ago.'

Paloma's knowledge of international drama had to be respected. She had her own company advising on historical costume for theatre, film and television.

Diamond said, 'I heard somewhere that the Japanese are in the premier league for suicide. If you fail in your job, topping yourself is the honourable thing to do. Politicians, bankers, business managers. It wouldn't happen here. You write a book about your failings and make another fortune.'

His efforts to raise a smile weren't working.

'Did this poor girl leave a note?'

'No.'

'Then how do they know she killed herself?'

'They found something with the body that was almost the same as a suicide note. What are those little carved ivory things people collect? They have some sort of practical function.'

'Netsuke?'

'Right.'

'They go with traditional Japanese costume, fixed to the sash of a kimono so that personal items can be suspended from them.'

'Well, this one was found inside her T-shirt. She may have been holding it to her chest when she jumped. Two embracing figures in snow up to their waists.'

'Chubei and Umegawa.'

His high opinion of Paloma's expertise went up several more notches. 'You know their names?'

'They're well known, almost universal characters. And now I've remembered the name of the playwright: Chikamatsu. He used them in one of his plays. It ends with the lovers going out into the snow to die.'

'You're way ahead of me. The point of this is that the police took the netsuke to be a suicide emblem.'

'Symbolically, it does make sense,' she said. 'I've seen the story represented in woodcuts, paintings and netsuke. This poor woman may have been in love.'

'Not just missing her credit cards, then?'

She finally produced a smile, more in charity than humour. 'Probably not. Had she met someone?'

'Couldn't tell you. I don't suppose the Vienna police could, either.'

'Aren't you interested in why she died?'

'The "how" matters more than the "why". If it happened here and it became obvious she'd killed herself, with no possibility of anyone else being involved, we wouldn't go into all the possible reasons. The inquest will do that. It's not up to the police to find out her state of mind.'

'Peter, you probably don't mean it, but that sounds so uncaring.'

Smarting from that, he justified his statement. 'We're not social workers or psychologists. We'd be wrong to try.'

'But you'd try if she'd been murdered. That's where your argument breaks down.'

He shrugged. 'I didn't think we were arguing. Besides, it's not my case. The Vienna police dealt with it.'

'And decided it was suicide because of nothing more substantial than the netsuke? Didn't they go into it any more deeply than that? Someone could have stuffed the netsuke into her clothes and pushed her in.'

'Murder, you mean?'

'Or manslaughter, horseplay that went wrong.'

'Unlikely.'

'Why?'

'If they used the netsuke to delude the police the killing would be premeditated.

55

But it wouldn't be a very reliable way of going about it. You couldn't guarantee the police would find the thing. It was not much bigger than a walnut.'

'So you agree with the official line - it was suicide?'

'I've no doubt they looked at all the evidence.'

'And this was how long ago? Four years? People still care enough to leave flowers.'

'It's a modern custom.'

'And a nice one. Her family must be devastated. For this to have happened thousands of miles from home — that's heartbreaking.'

He couldn't prevent Paloma identifying strongly with the people involved. He'd hoped she would be satisfied knowing the main facts. She'd spoken of the temporary shrine of flowers several times since returning from Vienna.

He tried one more time to draw a line under the incident. 'Nothing we can do about it. Bad things are happening every day in this world. It's no good letting them get to you.'

She rounded on him with more passion than he expected. 'That's bloody typical of a policeman, if I may say so. Cut yourself off from reality. Develop the hide of a rhinoceros. This was a tragic suicide, a young life sacrificed and probably for love, if the netsuke means anything.'

'Paloma, we didn't know her. I haven't even told you her name.'

'It's the offhand way you said it: "Nothing we can do" — as if she's just a statistic. I know there's nothing we can do. It's up to the Austrian police. But I can't forget we were there and I picked up the flowers. Someone obviously cares about her enough to place a bunch of lilies there four years after the event, even if you want to turn your back.'

He ignored the last remark. 'Japanese friends, I should think, or local people with more sympathy than most of us, like you.'

'There you go again, analysing, looking for explanations. I'm saying it's a personal tragedy. It's real.'

No question: the very thing he'd wanted to avoid was happening. Paloma was reliving the incident and more upset than ever. Worse, it was becoming an issue between them.

She continued, 'We spent most of our time in Vienna tracking that bloody film as if the events actually happened. It was only a story, but you seemed more affected by it than the real human tragedy we stumbled over. I tell you, that scene has been on my mind a lot since we got back.'

'That much is obvious,' he said. 'You don't have to keep telling me. That's why I asked Ingeborg to find out more. Maybe I shouldn't have done.'

She turned her head, as if talking to the river. 'It's better knowing, even if we can't do anything about it.'

They walked as far as Weston footbridge before Diamond spoke again, trying to make peace.

'You had a basinful of *The Third Man*. Selfish of me. I should have given you more choice in what we did.'

'I'm not complaining about that. What I find hard to stomach is that you can get emotionally involved in a film, yet cut off from a real death.'

'My job. Simple as that.'

'Being detached, you mean?'

'Any professional will tell you the same — doctor, paramedic, fireman.'

'Yet you're a softie underneath. I've seen you in tears at the end of the film when the woman walks straight past Joseph Cotten and into the distance.'

'You weren't supposed to notice. I'm just the same in *Casablanca*. She was Anna, by the way.'

'Who was?'

'The woman in the film, played by Alida Valli.'

'For pity's sake, Peter, I despair of you. Yet you won't name the Japanese suicide victim.'

'If it mattered, I would.'

At Twerton, the river divides to accommodate a weir. They followed the towpath along the Western Cut as far as the small humpback bridge that takes its name from the Dolphin.

'This is almost three hundred years old, did you know?' Diamond said with a too-obvious shift in the conversation.

'It can't be.'

'Most of it is. One side was bombed in the Bath Blitz and had to be rebuilt. The pub copped it, too. It's said to be equally old.'

'How do you know this?'

'I live just down the road, don't I? This is one of my locals.'

'One of them. I like that.'

It was too damp to sit in the garden, so they found a table in one of the eating areas inside. He brought a pint from the bar and a glass of Chablis for Paloma.

She was still tetchy with him, as if more needed to be said. He wittered on for a while, explaining that the Dolphin hadn't got its name from a small whale that had strayed up the Avon, but an old word for a mooring post.

Only when their meal arrived did Paloma say, 'When I called you a softie just now, it wasn't meant as an insult. I don't think it's bad if you shed a few tears over a film. It shows you have emotions that are bottled up mostly. You keep them hidden in your working life and I understand why. What I can't work out is why you don't relax enough to let your feelings show when you're off work, such as now.'

'What do you expect? I'm a bloke.'

'There you go again, putting up the shutters.'

At a loss, he stared across the room. He could think of nothing to say. He'd never been comfortable talking about what he thought of as personal. Even with his beloved wife, Steph, he'd rarely opened up and after her sudden and violent death he'd confided in nobody, preferring to endure the unimaginable grief in isolation. The wound would never heal and he was certain that no one, however well-meaning, could assist. He'd put the shutters up — as Paloma had expressed it — for a reason. He couldn't predict how he would react if she were to probe his hidden emotions. Paloma was a valued friend and an occasional lover. Up to now she'd been willing to conduct their relationship on those terms. Unless he was mistaken she seemed this evening to be demanding a change in him that he didn't think he could make.

When it became obvious Diamond wasn't going to speak, Paloma said, 'I know what you're thinking. Let me remind you that we've both got painful areas in our lives — totally different, but hard to bear. My ex-husband, my son. I'll never come to terms with what happened, just as I wouldn't expect you to get over your personal tragedy. We're scarred for life, both of us. But we still *have* a life. Surely it helps to share joys and sadnesses?'

'I prefer to keep my sadnesses to myself,' he said.

She looked surprised. 'But a trouble shared is a trouble halved — or so they say.'

'Claptrap.'

She didn't speak for a moment, but her face drained of colour. 'I beg your pardon.'

'What you just said — it's only a saying and it's rubbish. I'm not discussing my private life with anyone.'

She caught her breath. 'I thought I was a part of your private life.'

'It doesn't mean you're on the inside with a licence to go where you want.'

'You don't know how hurtful you're being.'

'I'll shut up, then.'

He finished the pie and chips in silence. Although rows with work colleagues were his stock-in-trade, this was his first serious difference with Paloma and he knew he was handling it badly. He offered to get another drink.

She was tight-lipped.

'Shall we go, then?' he suggested.

Still silent, she got up from the table and walked to the door. The barman shouted, 'Cheers, folks. Have a great evening.' Neither Diamond nor Paloma answered.

Out on the towpath, something definitely needed to be said. In ordinary circumstances they would head towards his house and she would spend the night with him. But it wasn't as if they were married. These intimacies were occasional and by arrangement — a subtle, consensual understanding.

He said, 'Perhaps it's a sign that we've moved on, having a few strong words with each other.' He meant to say they'd grown closer and could speak their differences without the relationship breaking down.

That wasn't how Paloma took it. 'Moved on? Are you saying you want to end it?' She stopped walking and swung round to face him. 'Are you?'

'Paloma, it's not me making an issue out of nothing.'

'So I'm to blame, am I?'

'I didn't say that.'

'Not in as many words, but that's obviously what you meant. It may sound like nothing to you but I'm not used to being told my opinions are claptrap, especially when I was reaching out to you, doing my best to understand you.'

'I don't want to be understood — not like that, anyway.'

Her face reddened and her eyes filled with tears. 'In that case you don't need me around. Find some other woman to shag, someone who doesn't give a damn about you. You and I are through.'

She turned and stepped briskly away without looking back.

5

Two weeks passed and Mel heard nothing more from the "Famous Foursome," Cat's term for the mysterious string quartet. Thinking they may have decided he wasn't the right choice for violist, he made up his mind not to lose any sleep over it. Sure, the money was tempting, but he didn't care for their methods, acting like Cold War spies, obtaining his address, whisking him off for a secret meeting in a London club, refusing to say who they were and gatecrashing a private wedding party for a second look at him. Out of curiosity he'd Googled string quartets. Would a reputable, high-earning ensemble group be able to exist in the twenty-first century without its own website with pictures of the performers? Even if Ivan was a shadowy figure, the rumbustious Cat was not. He'd found more ensembles online than he had ever dreamed existed, plenty with female cellists and their pictures, too, but none looked like her. If he'd been able to supply a name for the quartet he might have had more success. After numerous tries he decided his time would be better spent practising.

He was starting to think the whole thing could be an elaborate hoax. Classical music wasn't without its jokers, however solemn its reputation. Generally they struck in rehearsal sessions when fooling about was excusable. Most of it was at the level of sabotaging piano stools, music stands and sometimes even the instruments. On occasions the trickery was more sophisticated, involving players being sent wrong instructions. He'd heard of an unfortunate first violin led to believe everyone would be wearing a red bow-tie for a concert of Russian music. Then there was the percussionist tricked into moving his entire set of instruments into the royal box at the Albert Hall for a performance of the '1812 Overture'.

The more he thought about this leg-pull theory, the more plausible it became, but where it was leading? Presumably some kind of humiliation was in store. He'd be notified he was picked for the quartet, turn up somewhere for a rehearsal, open a door and be greeted by all his jeering mates. Was that the sting? It didn't seem enough after such a build-up. Better think again.

There had to be a bigger pay-off.

With a sinking heart he recalled the *Candid Camera* show that had run for so many years taking advantage of unsuspecting members of the public. Surely that had disappeared from TV screens, along with its imitators? They'd spared no expense in staging elaborate cons. What if some crap TV company had decided to dust off the formula and serve it up again?

His comeuppance as mass entertainment? He didn't want that.

Either way, he was obviously the fall guy. Why? He hadn't been getting above himself, had he? He was an even-tempered, unassuming bloke, or so he liked to think. He didn't go out of his way to annoy people.

Maybe he did, and was not aware of it.

Or he was a born sucker. He still recalled with pain the night he'd been robbed of his viola outside the Festival Hall.

If this was a con, he knew musicians were involved. Ivan could have been an actor, but Cat was not. She was a damn good cellist. Someone in the business must have persuaded her to join in the fun.

Next question: who, of all the players he knew, was devious enough to have picked on him? Actually, plenty. In his situation, filling in often for violists in ensemble groups and orchestras, there were hundreds who know him by name. Generally there's some banter when you return to a bunch of people you've met before. A few might want to take it further.

His thoughts veered in another, darker direction. This could be a revenge thing. He'd once had sex with a flautist called Destiny who played for the Royal Opera, a haughty-looking lady with hidden lusts. She'd approached him first, literally put her arm around him and led him below stage at Covent Garden where they'd had a vigorous session on the single-ended sofa normally used for the dying Violetta in *La Traviata*. This didn't inhibit Destiny in the least. Mel was left with soreness amidships and multiple scratches to arms and back. He'd vowed not to repeat the experience, but Destiny had other ideas. For the rest of Mel's stint with the Opera orchestra she made sure everyone knew he'd scored with her and she was up for more. Months afterwards he was still getting phone calls and texts suggesting another session. Everyone in the music world seemed to know. He got weary of being asked when he was planning another date with Destiny.

Could she have hatched this plot? On reflection, probably not: she believed in the direct approach.

But once he'd started on this tack, he thought of other affairs with musicians. Playing in an orchestra tends to encourage close relationships. Sitting for hours in rehearsal with attractive, creative people, you find yourself becoming fascinated by physical details, how her hair is fastened to leave the nape of her neck exposed, or how she crosses her legs at the ankles. The discipline of the music means that in moments between playing, a glance, a smile, a raised eyebrow can convey more than it would outside. With a love of music in common and the shared experience of making it as near to the ideal as possible, responding to the conductor, to the harmonics, you already have everything in place for some flirting when the formalities end.

That was how Mel had scored a number of times. Some romances lasted longer than others, but all had come to an end, almost always with unhappiness on one side or the other. It was not impossible that some of the hurt had lingered. He tried to imagine which former girlfriends were capable of engineering a plot like this, designed to raise his expectations and then humiliate him, and he just couldn't see it. What was happening to him called for a degree of organisation, of bringing in people to help, that didn't square with any of the women he'd slept with.

Currently he was going out with Dolores, the redheaded fount of all knowledge from his local record shop. She didn't play (or wouldn't admit to it), but knew more than he did about all the great artists and ensembles. And while she had a quirky sense of humour that made her approachable, she was most unlikely to be behind what was currently happening to him.

Tonight they were drinking the house Merlot at the Coach and Horses on Kew Green and she looked at him over her rimless specs and said, 'Something bugging you?'

'Why?'

'You're miles away.'

He decided to tell all.

Dolores listened with increasing interest.

'The thing is,' Mel summed up, 'I hate uncertainty. These people could be taking me for a ride, getting my hopes up about a well-paid job in a high-class quartet. If it's a hoax, I need to know. But it's just possible it's on the level and I can't afford to let a good opportunity pass by.'

'How long is it since you met the cellist lady?'

'Couple of weeks.'

'Didn't she give any clue what happens next?'

'She was upbeat. Said something about seeing more of me soon.'

'Suggestive.'

'Just about everything she said was, but she can get away with it. She's big, wall-to-wall. Have you heard of anyone like that?'

'Playing cello in a string quartet? I can't say I have.'

'But you know all the top ensemble groups.'

'On CD, yes. I haven't watched them all perform. Sometimes they're pictured on the cover, but not always. You said her name is Cat. Would that be short for Catherine?'

'She didn't say. Katrina? Kathleen? It may be a nickname.'

'I'm trying to think of cellists,' Dolores said.

He sipped the wine and waited.

She took a different tack. 'You've met two of them. Logic suggests that the third will want to vet you soon.'

He nodded. 'They've got me on a piece of string.'

'Not necessarily. I expect they're as nervous as you are. It's a massive decision. Get someone who isn't compatible and he could destroy the group in a very short time. Did they say what happened to their violist?'

'That's another mystery. I asked Ivan straight out if he died or is being given the push. He more or less told me to back off. He's a hard man, is Ivan. There's some East European in his manner as well as his name — if that is his name.'

'Yet he was the first to approach you, and he told you he'd heard you play, so he must be on your side.'

'You're talking as if this is going to happen.'

'I think it will,' she said.

'But you can't identify the quartet. They've got to be famous if they're earning the money Ivan spoke about.'

'I'm not infallible, Mel. Yes, I may have heard them. I may even recognise their playing, but that doesn't mean I'd know them if they walked in here this minute and bought us a drink.'

'And do the personnel change much?'

'In some groups, yes. Others stay together forever. The same four guys played in the Amadeus for forty years and the Guarneri weren't far behind. Their cellist retired, but the others carried on. Four people coming together to play music can't predict what life will throw at them. Someone gets ill or dies and the others have to decide whether to call it a day or look for a replacement.'

'And is it blindingly obvious when someone new comes in?'

'To me? I can usually hear the difference in a recording of the same piece. To the players I'm sure there are major adjustments.'

'And some resentment, no doubt,' he said, confiding yet another worry that had been gnawing away at his confidence. 'I don't particularly relish being the new boy. Comparisons are going to be made. I wouldn't wish to ape the playing of the previous incumbent just to make the process easy for the others. I doubt if it's possible, anyway.'

'They'll understand,' Dolores said. 'Everything I've heard about string quartets and the way they work suggests that there's debate going on all the time in rehearsal. And sometimes in performance. I don't need to tell you this. You've played in ensembles.'

'Filling in isn't the same as taking over for someone who has left,' Mel said. 'The two people I've met are formidable characters in their different ways. They're not going to give me an easy ride.'

'Would you want one?'

'An easy ride?' He smiled. 'Of course not.'
Then his phone beeped.

'D'you mind if I take this?'

'Feel free.'

'Mr. Farran?' Mel tensed. The voice was
Ivan's, the same Beechamesque tone as if
he was speaking to an audience. 'We spoke
before, about the quartet.'

'Yes.'

'We'd like to arrange an opportunity for
you to play with us.'

'In concert?'

'No, in more of a soirée situation, a private
house, with the three of us and possibly our
manager.'

'Where is this?'

'We will send a car, as before. Would next
Sunday afternoon suit you?'

'I suppose.' His brain was racing. He
almost forgot to ask the basic question:
'What are we playing?'

'Are you familiar with Beethoven's Opus
131?'

He took a deep breath. The Quartet in C
sharp minor is one of the most challenging
in the repertoire, a forty minute master-
piece. He'd have five days to prepare. 'I
wouldn't say familiar. I've played it.'

'That's all right, then,' Ivan said. 'Be sure

to bring your best instrument. We need to hear the sound.'

'Is this an audition, then?'

'Don't think of it as such. Treat it as *an afternoon of making music.* The car will pick you up at two. Do you eat smoked salmon?'

'When I get the chance, yes.'

'We'll have some for tea. Oh, and there's no need to dress up this time. Come in your weekend attire, whatever that may be.' This was Ivan at his most human. Apparently deciding he'd gone overboard, he abruptly ended the call.

'I'm about to find out if this is genuine,' Mel told Dolores. 'Sunday afternoon, Beethoven Opus 131. In at the deep end.'

'You'll be fine,' she said. 'Think of it as —'

'An afternoon of making music?'

'Exactly.'

6

An afternoon of making music?

Some chance.

Mel wasn't treating this lightly. He was about to be put to the test. Each waking hour must be devoted to preparing the piece, learning the seven movements passage by passage in readiness to respond to the other instruments, letting the viola speak, sing, inspire, transform, in harmony with the rest. And of course the difficulty was not being able to predict how the others would interpret their parts. The preparation you can do in isolation is limited.

For encouragement he kept telling himself that this wouldn't be a memory test like a solo performance. Quartet-playing is almost always from the sheet. They'd have the score in front of them with the composer's markings.

Opus 131 is said to have been Beethoven's favourite of all his string quartets. It is also said to be the ultimate in difficulty, in places almost beyond comprehension. Enough to make a nervous player take up drumming.

Yet more than once Mel had filled in for a quartet when the violist had become ill between final rehearsal and concert. He'd gone in cold and performed well enough to get through. Nobody had thrown anything.

Surely these people would make allowance.

Or would they? Ivan was the sort who expected perfection, gritting his teeth at anything less. Cat would treat any false note as hilarious. Hard to say which would be less mortifying. The great unknown was the mysterious third member, the second violin, who hadn't shown any interest yet. Mel tried to put all three out of his mind and steep himself in the work, but he knew in his heart that the personalities in a quartet are fundamental to its performance.

By Saturday he was up with the piece, as well prepared as anyone could expect to be. Sunday morning he went through it twice without fluffing a note. He drank a large black espresso, packed the instrument in its case and started looking out of the window for the black Mercedes.

But it never arrived.

Instead, around ten past two, a red convertible with the roof down rattled the Fingis Street window frames. The driver — not the man he'd met before — got out, gave the house a long look and decided against all appearance to the contrary it must be correct.

Mel saved him the trouble of ringing the doorbell. 'It's me you're picking up, I think. Mel Farran.'

'Good man. Set to go, then?' There was none of the deference of the previous chauffeur. This guy looked and behaved as if he owned the Aston Martin. 'I'm Doug, of Douglas Christmas Management.'

Pause for thought. 'You manage the quartet?'

'Try to — on their more agreeable days. Hop in. We're running late.'

'I need my instrument.'

The driver flashed his whitened teeth. 'Of course.' He took a key from his pocket, pointed it at the car and the boot lid opened.

'Thanks,' Mel said, 'but I'd rather keep it by me.'

'You fiddle players are all the same. Treat them like newborn babies.'

They left Fingis Street behind, roaring through West London, the sound exaggerated by the roof being down. Mel kept the case containing his baby between his knees, deciding this gave more protection in case of a collision. Conversation would have been difficult anyway, and was rendered impossible by rock music at high volume. Doug wasn't a Radio Three man.

Somewhere west of Acton they joined the North Circular and stayed with it as far as Friern Barnet, at which point Mel gave up trying to track the route. Soon they were travelling into an area lush with greenery and golf courses. A right turn, a private road, an electronic gate and they moved up a red-tiled drive and stopped outside a residence like the backdrop to a Gainsborough portrait. Mel shed all doubts about the quartet earning six-figure salaries.

'Whose place is this?' he asked when the engine was switched off.

'Mine, actually. The talent, as I call them, will tell you I'm an extortionist, but that's their little game. In my position you have to have a reasonable lifestyle or people don't believe you're good at what you do.'

'Is this where we're playing?' All week he'd pictured four upright chairs in someone's living room with the other furniture pushed to the walls.

'That's the plan.'

'Are the others inside?'

'And getting stroppy by now.' Doug

marched to the front door, opened it and shouted, 'We made it, musos.'

Mel followed, his knuckles turning white around the handle of his viola case.

The Georgian front of the house was no preparation for the interior, an open-plan conversion, a monument to the possibilities of the rolled steel joist, with several stone pillars where solid walls once stood. The spaces were defined in a conventional way, dining area, kitchen, office, library and a couple of lounges. At the far end three people waited, already seated with stands in front of them in what was evidently the music space. A fourth chair had been put out for the newcomer. Mel spotted Cat first, not unlike Britannia on an old penny coin, her cello leaning against her thigh. She raised her bow.

'Glad you made it, kiddo.'

Ivan was opposite her, checking his watch. His weekend casuals were a three-piece suit and striped tie.

'My fault we're a trifle late,' Doug said. 'Couldn't find the street and ended up on the Hammersmith Flyover.'

Mel was looking at the one musician he hadn't already met, a guy more his own age, with brown hair to his shoulders and dressed in a black shirt and red corduroy trousers, but unwilling, it seemed, to make eye contact.

Doug made the introduction.

'Good to meet you,' Mel said to Anthony and could have saved his breath. The second violin showed no intention of shaking hands or offering any kind of greeting.

Now Doug took a step back. 'I'm going to make myself scarce, people. I'm an unrewarding audience, as you know. Take the hot seat, Mel. They're on pins to know if you'll fit in.'

Thanks for that boost to my confidence, Mel thought.

Cat called out as Doug was leaving, 'Keep your thieving hands off the sandwiches, boyo. I've counted them.'

Heart pumping faster at the ordeal to come, Mel removed his viola and bow from the case and joined the quartet.

'You did tell him on the phone it's Beethoven's Opus 133?' Cat said to Ivan.

Mel's jaw dropped. 'I heard 131.'

'Joke,' she said. 'You'll get used to me, sunshine. We may be tough nuts, but we're not asking you to tangle with the *Grosse Fuge,* not before the first break.'

'Can we be serious?' Ivan said. 'Mr. Farran is our guest for the afternoon. Let's treat him with respect.'

'No need for that,' Mel was quick to tell them. 'I'd rather be informal.'

'Me, too,' Cat said. 'What do you have in mind?'

'I meant –'

'Relax, my pet. You're one of us.'

Ivan gave her a sharp glance. 'Don't be premature. Nothing is decided.' To Mel, he said with a twitch of the lips that was the nearest he would get to cordiality, 'Ready?'

'Of course.'

'We won't treat this as a rehearsal, because it isn't. We'll play the whole quartet as we would if you were our regular violist. No one is expecting a miracle. You'll be adjusting to our tempo and voicing just as we will respond to yours. When infelicities occur —'

'Don't you love that?' Cat broke in. ' "When infelicities occur." He means when someone plays a bum note.'

'We'll make allowance,' Ivan said. 'After all, we're human.'

'Some of us,' Cat murmured. She was doing her best to take the stress out of the situation, even if Ivan didn't care for it.

As for Anthony, he remained expressionless, as if he'd heard all this before.

'Shall we tune the instruments?' Ivan said. 'And by the way, because of the length of the piece and the room temperature it's to be expected that they'll go out of tune before the end. No matter.'

'We'll wing it, bossy boots,' Cat said. 'We always do.'

Ivan lifted the violin to his chin and played a note that acted on Mel's nerves like a thousand volts.

Get a grip, he told himself. You prepared for this all week.

He raised his viola, waited for a lead from the cello, tried the note several times, gave a small twist to the fine tuner, was satisfied, nodded, took a deep breath and waited.

Anthony had come to life and looked a different man tuning his violin. Cat drew her bow several times more across the cello strings and winked. They tried a few chords in the C sharp minor key.

Then it got serious.

The opening movement of Opus 131 is majestic, yet with a sense of foreboding. Beethoven's first mark says 'Adagio ma non troppo e molto espressivo' and presents an immediate test for the first violin. Ivan sounded the first dramatic bars expressing the anguish that mirrored Mel's state of mind. And as Anthony took up the fugal theme on a single up-bow it was apparent how seamlessly the two blended. This was playing of rare quality. The second violin might be a social misfit, but he was a fine musician.

Poised for his entrance in bar nine, Mel knew it had to be spot on. The score called for him to join the playing of the others at precisely the same bow speed. There was no hiding.

His timing was right. He conquered his nerves, launched into the piece and played the crescendo in bar eleven in the knowledge that he needed to top the two violins with the complete fugue subject, a theme that is heard in various guises throughout. A lift of Ivan's right eyebrow signalled satisfaction. Under way and making music as requested.

Now was the moment for the fourth voice, Cat's cello, and she supplied a strong, sonorous note in no danger of being drowned by the others. With all four instruments in play, the harmonics came under scrutiny and to Mel's ear blended well. Even while straining to concentrate he felt lifted by the company he was in. They were spectacularly good. Ivan was a skilful leader, setting the tempo, making way when necessary, yet filling in the harmony with precisely the right strength when required.

Towards the middle of the first movement the violins speak to each other with the last six notes of the fugue motif and then viola and cello take up the dialogue in one of the loveliest passages in the entire quartet repertoire. An immense test, and Mel was equal to it, removing everything from his mind except the purity of the sound. His eyes didn't meet Cat's, yet he felt an emotional affinity with her that only musicians could appreciate.

It was a seminal moment. Performing with such gifted artists was uplifting, however mismatched they were as personalities. I want to be part of this, he thought. I want it more than I ever suspected.

So as movement succeeded movement, he felt buoyed up by the quality of the playing, growing in belief, inspired to new heights. In the jarring transition from the breakneck speed of the scherzo to the poignant adagio of the sixth movement, the viola takes centre stage. All those hours of practice gave him the confidence to play this heart-rending passage from memory, his bowing prolonging the intensity at slow tempo without sacrificing the sense of motion.

The fireworks of Beethoven's seventh and final movement have a huge impact after this. Four instruments in unison from the jolt of the first note on a downward stroke into a rapid pounding rhythm played right at the frog of the bow will startle any audience. With no one else present, not even Douglas, there were only the four musicians to thrill to the vitality of the music, the culmination of all that had gone before. Spells of ferocious playing were separated by those gorgeous lyrical oases. Excited, energised, the quartet performed the finale relentlessly until its sudden, challenging stop.

No one spoke.

After a piece of such range and power, mere words seem crass.

Some seconds passed before Ivan tapped his stand several times with the bow, a gesture of satisfaction. Cat nodded her agreement. Anthony had slumped again, a puppet with slack strings.

At a loss as to how to behave with these people he'd joined intimately through the music but hardly at all as companions, Mel propped the viola in the angle of his lap and waited. He'd raised his level of playing beyond anything he'd achieved before. He was emotionally drained.

Finally, Cat spoke. 'Don't know about you dudes, but that was good enough for me.' She turned to Anthony. 'What do you say?'

'I'm easy.'

'We know that, honey, but what about the

playing?'

'I said — I'm easy.'

Cat turned to Ivan. 'We can take that as affirmative — I think. What's your opinion?'

'Of what?'

'Of the combo.'

'I wish you wouldn't use that expression.'

'Here we go again,' she said. 'Forty minutes of bliss with Beethoven and it doesn't take ten seconds to start another spat.'

'It's unseemly.'

'Give me strength. What do you want us to be known as — the Ivan Bogdanov Players?'

'Now you're being offensive.'

'It would be, stuck with a name like yours.' She raised a hand. 'All right, that was out of order. Sometimes you drive me to it. Back to my question: do we have a future together? I think we do, and Anthony is easy — which coming from him is as good as a twenty-one-gun salute. Are you up for it?'

Ivan sniffed. 'Allowing that Mr. Farran was my suggestion in the first place, I give my consent, but with reservations.'

'What's your problem?' Cat said.

Mel was increasingly uncomfortable. 'Should I go outside while you discuss this?'

'For the love of Mike, no,' Cat said. 'We're talking about reviving the quartet and everyone deserves a say.'

'Then we'd better bring in Douglas,' Ivan said.

'He can go bark at the moon. He'll take his twenty percent whatever we decide. And if we're down to a trio he'll want twenty-five. What's eating you, Ivan?'

'I'm going to propose we agree to a trial period of, say, three months. If, for some reason, it doesn't work as well as we hope, we can review it then.'

'Why? When you and I started there was no trial period or the rest of us would have kicked you out for sure.'

'You don't mean that.'

'I mean the first bit — no trial period. I like equality. If Mel is joining us, he won't want second-class status.'

'Perhaps we should ask him.'

And that was how Mel found himself in the hot seat. He cleared his throat and said, 'If you're serious about inviting me in, I'd like to know more about you.'

This silenced them for a beat or two.

Cat said, 'Such as?'

'What's the name of your quartet?'

Even more hesitation.

Ivan said, 'One matter we must discuss at an early stage is whether to adopt a new name.'

Mel gained in confidence. 'What's wrong with the old one?'

'We had a quartet, a successful one, but it no longer exists.'

'What happened?'

'Our violist left.'

No one added to the bald statement. Mel could hear them breathing.

'Over a disagreement?'

'Not that I'm aware of.'

Finally Cat said, 'You don't have to be so mysterious, Ivan. Harry went missing in Budapest four years ago when we were playing there. Nobody has seen him since. He's a missing person. We've been marking time ever since in the hope he'll walk in one day. It hasn't happened so we faced reality and started looking for a replacement.'

Mel turned to Ivan. 'And you want to buy more time in case he does turn up?'

Ivan reddened.

'He won't,' Cat said. 'We would have heard by now. Something final must have happened.'

'Was he acting strangely?'

'We're all strange, ducky, as you must have worked out for yourself by now. If you want my opinion, Harry was the closest to normal.'

'Was there a disagreement?'

'Disagreements are the stock-in-trade of string quartets. We're strong-minded people, even Anthony, as you'll discover. But there was nothing more than the usual to and fro over the score of whichever piece we were playing. We all bring something to the party and it makes for a more exciting performance.'

'Then you haven't played together for how long?'

'A couple of years, give or take. We tried, but for one reason and another — most of them crap viola players — it hasn't worked out, so we've had to do our own thing — teaching and orchestral work and stuff we wouldn't want anyone else to know.'

Ivan said, 'We haven't made it public that the quartet stopped appearing. We've been fading away.'

'Faded,' Cat said.

'I'd still like to know the name.'

'The Staccati.'

Mel's skin prickled. The Staccati had been an international name. He owned some of their recordings. The only reason he'd overlooked them when he'd racked his brain for likely quartets was that nothing had been heard of them recently. Their great period was five or six years back. They'd been in demand at all the great music festivals

89

across the world. 'I know about you, of course, but never had the pleasure of hearing you in concert.'

'We do most of our playing abroad,' Ivan said. 'You're able to travel, are you?'

'I enjoy it.'

'You won't when it seems never-ending, one hotel after the next.'

'The best deal is a residency,' Cat said. 'A few paid months in one place. Time to chill out, go shopping, get your hair done and find the hottest clubs in town. Heaven.'

'We give a fixed number of concerts and do some teaching,' Ivan said. 'It isn't all about self-indulgence.'

'Listen to him talking,' Cat said. 'Who was always in the park playing chess with the old men?'

Mel said, 'How soon would you want me to make a decision?'

'Yesterday isn't soon enough,' Cat said. 'We need to be concert-ready when Doug swings into action and gets us some gigs. Let's talk about repertoire. Any obvious blind spots?'

'I wish I knew more contemporary music.'

'Put it there, buddy. We stop at Schoenberg.'

'I haven't specialised in quartet music. I had to work hard at this.'

'You think we were playing off the cuff? I haven't watched TV all week. You can play. You should have heard some of the others.'

'Your standard is very high.'

'Bollocks.' She pointed her bow at Ivan. 'What do you say, Rasputin? Do we give it a whirl with Mel on full membership?'

A sigh. 'Very well.'

'Anthony?'

Anthony managed a nod.

'He's easy,' Cat said. 'Why don't we call in Doug and start on the salmon sandwiches?'

The deal was sealed. A verbal agreement would do, Doug said. And, just as Ivan had promised, Mel would earn one-fifth of the profits. The only undertaking he had to give was that the quartet's engagements had priority over everything short of acute appendicitis.

'And what if the original violist turns up?'

'I wouldn't worry about Harry,' Doug said in his nonchalant way. 'He's history. Nice man, wonderful musician, but out of the picture now.'

Years of working in an insecure profession had toughened Mel. 'Sorry. If I'm going to give up all my freelance work I need more of a guarantee.'

91

'I'll speak to the talent.'

'They said full membership. Can I take that as permanent?'

'If they already agreed, yes.'

'Then it has your approval?'

'Let's shake on it.' His grip reinforced the pact.

Mel still felt he had a right to know more. 'Has Harry ever gone missing before this?'

'Missing? No. They all go their own ways in free time on tour. They don't live in each other's pockets. The embassy kept asking us where he was supposed to have gone that evening and nobody knew. Ghastly time. We had to bring in a local musician to play the viola part in the last three concerts and he wasn't terribly good. I was forced to cancel the rest of the tour. Endless wrangling with the Hungarians over breach of contract and compensation claims. Made my life hell. If Harry had turned up at that point I'd cheerfully have shot him. Have another sandwich.'

'So will you make it clear to the others that I'm the permanent replacement?'

'Absolutely.'

Mel raised another concern. 'Won't it be difficult getting engagements after so long?'

A shake of the head. 'The name still has plenty of currency.'

'They want to change the name.'

Doug almost dropped the plate. 'Who does?'

Some inner censor stopped Mel from naming anyone. 'You'd better ask them. Personally, I'd be proud to join the Staccati.'

But Doug wasn't there to hear the last words. He was striding across the room to speak to Ivan.

The clash of wills was won by Doug. They would continue to be known as the Staccati Quartet. Once again, Cat waded in with a wisecrack: 'Staccato is all about sharp, disconnected notes and no four people are more disconnected than we are.' The dynamics of the group were becoming clearer. Ivan was not so dominant as he had first appeared. Cat could undermine him with her streetwise humour. Anthony allowed the others to make all the running, but might yet pounce. For the time being, Doug was the decision-maker.

'How soon will you be up to concert pitch?'

'We need to prepare,' Ivan said with all the earnestness of Noah before the rains came. 'Weeks, maybe months.'

'Why don't you fix up some gigs and tell us?' Cat said to Doug. 'Give some focus to the preparation.'

'I have a few ideas already,' Doug said, and any half-decent manager would have said as much. 'I was thinking of letting you in gently. There are various festivals coming up in this country — Cheltenham, Cambridge, York. Their programmes will already be arranged, but I can't see any of them turning down a chance to slot in the Staccati at short notice.'

Ivan was shaking his head. 'Too soon.'

'Tucson, Arizona? That's an awful long way for a single performance,' Cat said. 'Doug, I think you've got it. Better still, how about trying for a residency? Would you care for that, Anthony?'

Anthony said, 'Cool.'

'That's two of us, then. Mel, are you on board?'

'If there's half a chance, yes.'

'Three.' She turned to Ivan. 'We'd get paid to rehearse in a practice room. Isn't that better than weeks and months squatting in Doug's house?'

He still looked doubtful. 'I suppose if it could be arranged . . .'

'Sponsors, endowments. There's money out there. That's why we employ the best manager in the business.'

Doug almost purred. 'No promises. I'll do

my best.'

With that settled, and the sandwiches all but gone, Ivan suggested they should rehearse another quartet while Doug went off to make phone calls.

Another quartet? Mel's heart sank and it must have been obvious.

'No sweat, kiddo,' Cat told him. 'When we rehearse, we take the thing apart, bar by bar, as if we never played it before. We're all learning together.'

'I didn't bring any other music.'

'You see that printer over there on Doug's computer desk? It's also a photocopier.'

Not long after, they were back with their instruments. They worked on a Schubert quartet familiar to most chamber musicians. Cat's reassuring words on a first rehearsal were borne out. The playing was in fragments, every phrase open to analysis. Strong views were voiced, but the arguing was of a different order from the debates on how the group was managed. These were points of interpretation and nuance, each player speaking with the authority of the score. Anthony found his voice and made clear that the term 'second violin' is misleading. He was not subordinate to Ivan or anyone else. And Mel, for his part, made sure that the viola was given its due.

Quite when Doug returned wasn't clear. By then the concentration was pretty intense. He must have been standing nearby for some minutes waiting for a break. He wasn't fussed. He was like the cat with the cream.

'Sorry to interrupt. Breaking news, as they say. You asked for a residency and I may have got one, a university with a substantial endowment for a series of masterclasses and concerts. They are willing to engage us for six months when the new term starts.'

'Who are?' Ivan said.

'Bath Spa University.'

'Bath.' Ivan spoke the word as if it were Lubianka Prison.

Cat overrode him. 'Not a bad place to spend half a year. Is there enough for us to live on?'

'Approved lodgings, all meals found and twenty grand each plus concert fees.'

'I could survive on that. When do they need to know?'

'I said I'd give them an answer today. It's a fantastic deal. To sugar the pill I said you'd also make a recording in aid of university funds.'

Cat looked at the others. 'Any objections?'

Anthony said, 'How many concerts?'

'You're going to like this,' Doug said. 'What they suggest is a series of soirées, fortnightly musical evenings in private houses, chamber music as it was originally performed. The audiences will be limited to the size of the venue and in most cases this will mean twenty-five to thirty at most. There are some beautiful houses around Bath. I can picture you by candlelight in gracious rooms of the sort the composers themselves must have known.'

'By Jesus, you're a wicked salesman,' Cat said.

'That's what you pay me for.'

'I'm in. How about the rest of you?'

Ivan was straight to where the shoe pinched. 'Fortnightly, I think I heard you say. With a new programme each time? That's a tall order.'

'What I'm suggesting is no more than one string quartet per evening, followed by a champagne interval and then some solo pieces. How does that seem?'

'I could endure that,' Cat said.

'If you like, you can repeat the programmes,' Doug said. 'Your audiences will be different each time, I expect.'

'Presumably they pay for the privilege?' Ivan said.

'The sale of tickets and all profits are

handled by the university. They intend to put it towards the sponsorship — which I may say is very generous.'

'So we perform for nothing?'

'It's all part of the deal, Ivan, as I've tried to explain. Personally, I'd be thrilled to play in such surroundings if I had your talent.'

'You think Ivan plays the fiddle well?' Cat said. 'His main instrument is the cash register. He's a virtuoso.' She turned to Mel. 'Are you up for it, new boy?'

Mel was still in a spin from being admitted to the quartet. Right now, he would have agreed to anything.

Doug asked for a show of hands.

Nobody objected. Ivan seemed to have changed his mind about Bath.

'I'll confirm, then,' Doug said. 'That was a good sound, by the way. What's the piece?'

'That's our manager talking,' Cat said, 'and he doesn't know what we were playing.'

'Schubert,' Ivan said. 'Quartet Number 14 in D minor, better known as "Death and the Maiden".'

7

Ingeborg Smith said, 'Something is up with him.'

The rest of the CID room must have heard, yet nobody else spoke. The central heating was set too high for a mild October afternoon. Lethargy was the prevailing mood.

'He's been out of sorts all week. Longer really.' No one could be in any doubt who she meant. Ingeborg was the Diamond-watcher on the squad.

And on a day like today no one except Ingeborg cared much.

She tried a third time. 'I don't think he's had a civil word for any of us.'

DI John Leaman finally responded with, 'Tell us something new.' Which was rich coming from the misery-guts of CID.

From across the room, Paul Gilbert, the youngest on the team, said, 'It's the trend, isn't it? All those Scandinavian detectives, so depressed you wonder if they'll hold out until the last chapter.'

'What the hell are you talking about?' Leaman said.

'Don't you read?'

'Read what?'

'Some of them get on TV as well.'

'I don't have time for that stuff. I look at science-based series like *CSI* and *Bones*.'

'Be fair, you guys,' Ingeborg said. 'The boss treats us right and he can be amusing when he's on form. You have to tune in to his sense of humour, that's all.'

'My tuning must have gone to pot, then.'

'Bosses come a lot worse than him.'

Gilbert was quick to take her up on this. 'Why do you say that, Inge? Do you know something we don't?'

'I'm wondering if *he* knows something we don't.'

Leaman swung round in his chair. 'Hang about — do you think Diamond's on the way out?'

This possibility galvanised everyone. Keith Halliwell, the most senior man present, said, 'Get away. He's said nothing to me.'

'Whatever is bugging him, he's internalising it,' Ingeborg said. 'With all the government cuts he could be looking at early retirement.'

'Voluntary, you mean?'

'He wouldn't walk,' Halliwell said. 'Not the guv'nor.'

'But he'd take it badly if they forced him out.'

Mental pictures of Diamond being dragged from the building.

'There is another possibility,' Gilbert said.

'Give it to us, then.'

'It could be some of us for the chop. He's been told and he doesn't want to break the news to us.'

Rumours of redundancies had been circulating for months and now something close to panic ensued.

'They can't do that,' Leaman said. 'We're overstretched already.'

'Overstretched when there's a major enquiry,' Halliwell said, 'but that isn't every week of the year. We could be vulnerable.'

'All the public services are taking cuts,' Gilbert said. 'We can't expect to escape.'

Leaman said, 'And it's always last in, first out. So don't look so pleased with yourself, young man.'

By now every head was buzzing with thoughts of unemployment. Some twenty minutes later, Halliwell stood up. 'I'm going to ask him.'

■ ■ ■ ■

Diamond was at his desk with his chin propped on both hands like a medieval gargoyle, but chunkier. He'd discarded his jacket and loosened his tie. 'What is it now?'

'Nothing special, guv. I was wondering . . . do you fancy a cuppa?'

'A cold drink would suit me better. They never get the heating right in this place.'

'Want to slip out for ten minutes?'

'While you mind the shop?'

'Actually I was thinking you might want company.'

'Something on your mind, is there? All right. John can hold the fort. It's not as if we're snowed under. Be better if we were.'

In the Royal Hotel just down the street, Halliwell brought the drinks to the table where Diamond had resumed his chin-in-hands posture.

'Did you want crisps or anything?'

'No. What's your problem?'

'Not mine specially, guv. There were some murmurings in the office about lay-offs.'

'Why? Do they know something?'

'They're thinking maybe you do, and you don't want to tell us.'

Diamond grinned faintly. 'Have I ever shied away from passing on bad news?'

'So we're safe?'

'I wouldn't bet on it, but I haven't heard yet, and if I do I'll fight tooth and nail to keep the squad together, even the layabouts.'

'That's all right, then.'

'What put this into their heads?'

'Nothing really.' Now that the team's concerns were put at rest Halliwell was ready to talk about the weather, or television, or the quality of the beer.

But Diamond wasn't. 'Murmurings, you said. Who was murmuring?'

'No one in particular.'

'Leaman, I bet.'

'To be fair, he isn't the only one, but I didn't come here to tell tales. They study your moods and they reckon you've been under a cloud these last weeks.'

'Study my moods sounds like Ingeborg.'

'So the general opinion is that there has to be something you're hiding from us, such as redundancies.'

'Bullshit.' Diamond rolled his eyes. 'For as long as I can remember, Keith, the politicians have banged on about getting more coppers on the streets. Even now, with all the cuts, they're saying it. How will it be done? By cutting down on the backroom staff. Backroom is the dirty word. That's you and me if we're stuck in the office all day. We need to get out more.'

'Like this?'

He couldn't raise another smile. 'Front-line is the buzzword. If you're front-line you're in no danger of the chop.'

'There hasn't been much serious crime lately.'

'Too true. A major incident would solve everything, keep us in work, get us away from our desks and stop stupid rumours flying around.'

'What do we do — tell the criminal class to step up productivity?'

'Not a bad idea.'

They brooded on this until Halliwell said, 'You do seem more depressed than usual. Is anything wrong?'

'With the CID room? Where shall I start? A DI who likes nothing better than spreading alarm and dissension. A recently promoted sergeant who watches my every move. A DCI who believes all that garbage enough to dump it on me.'

'You once said you wanted to be told if anyone was unhappy.'

Diamond shrugged. 'Fair enough, Keith. I'd forgotten.'

'When I asked if there's anything wrong, I

meant in your life.'

The big man glanced away, across the room. 'If there was, I wouldn't tell you.'

'Your health is okay, I hope?'

'Now you're sounding like the idiot doctor who does the annual medical. Of course I'm okay. I don't make a point of taking my blood pressure or weighing myself, but I'm as fit as you or anyone else. Shall we end this pointless conversation and go back to work in case some of them think I've decided to end it all and jump off Pulteney Bridge?'

He'd had enough of this probing. Well intentioned it may have been, but he wouldn't be telling Halliwell or anyone else about the break-up with Paloma. Months had gone by since that walk along the towpath. Yes, he was unhappy, bloody miserable, and now CID had picked up on it, but he wouldn't be calling Paloma to try and make up. He had his pride and she had hers.

Two days passed before the team was gifted the suspicious death they needed. A couple walking the towpath near Lower Weston — much as Diamond and Paloma had done — spotted a floating object that at a closer look turned out to have arms and legs. They called the emergency number and a patrol car and an ambulance went to the scene.

Normally a dead body is left where it is found so that the police can inspect the scene. This one was moving with the current and there was no telling when or where it had entered the water. A boat was used to retrieve it near Weston Lock and it was stretchered to a waiting van and taken to the Royal United Hospital mortuary.

The first duty of the police was to identify the dead woman, but this was difficult. She was way past the point when anyone would recognise her. A body in water will sink to the bottom and only rises to the surface when decomposition begins and gases form within the stomach and lungs. The time this takes depends on the water temperature. In icy conditions, months. In the Avon in a typical English summer, not much less.

In this case the decomposition was plain to see. Significant areas of the skin and tissue had peeled away.

The deceased was short, at just under five feet, and slight in build. Her hair was natural black, and cut sheer at the back. She had a full set of teeth, with some whitened fillings. The white T-shirt and black jeans she was wearing gave no clue as to her identity. Nothing was in the pockets. She wore no jewellery.

The missing persons register was consulted. Nobody from the local area matched the description, such as it was.

An early decision was taken by the coroner to order an autopsy. It was carried out by one of the hospital's team of clinical pathologists. The police, who provided continuity of evidence, were in attendance. Sometimes new information is discovered at this stage. Not this time.

Identity: unknown.

Cause of death: uncertain.

The pathologist — a man who didn't like wasting time — was unwilling to speculate how this young woman had died. The obvious assumption would have been that she had drowned — difficult to prove in any case and impossible in this one. Drowning is one of the most problematic of all causes of death to diagnose. For one thing, the immersion in water, possibly for a considerable time, rots the body and vitiates the evidence. If the internal organs have deteriorated, as they do in quite a short time, they won't provide confirmation that the victim was struggling to breathe.

In this case, the classic signs, the plumes of froth at the mouth and nostrils, must have dispersed long ago and any internal froth at the trachea and bronchi would have vanished. There were no obvious external marks of injury apart from minor lacerations probably caused by the body being moved with the current and striking submerged rocks and objects. Anyway, the state of putrefaction would have masked anything less than severe wounding. All the pathologist would say was that from the general deterioration she must have been immersed for a minimum of two weeks and probably longer.

He added that a diagnosis of drowning is invariably a best-guess situation and this would be a very inferior guess that he wasn't willing to hazard.

He estimated her age at between twenty and thirty.

As for identification, her own family would not have recognised her. Under water the body assumes a face-down position, with the face, arms and legs dragging along the bottom.

It was only after the post-mortem, when the clothes were being put in a bag for storage, that a medical student assisting the pathologist happened to draw his attention to a faded label on the white cotton knickers.

'Sir, have you noticed this?'

He had not, whatever it was, and he was

not overjoyed to be told. 'Noticed what?'

'I believe this writing is Japanese.'

'Why? Can you read it?'

The student reddened. 'No, but I spent some of my gap year in Tokyo. I can tell the difference from Chinese.'

'So?'

'So if her knickers were made in Japan, isn't there a chance she was Japanese?'

'Unless, like you, she travelled to Japan in her gap year. Or unless Japanese knickers happen to be on sale at Marks and Spencer. Or Tesco. I'm a histopathologist. My expertise doesn't stretch to ladies' underwear.'

'It was just something I noticed.'

'Full marks.' Said with no gratitude.

'Isn't there a way of telling?'

The pathologist gave a long-suffering look to the police witnesses, pulled up his face mask and asked the mortuary attendant to return the body to the table. 'You thought we were through, ladies and gentlemen, and so did I. From the state of her, I wouldn't know if she's Japanese or from up the road, but there is a way of finding out a person's racial origin from the teeth. There's a difference between people of Caucasian origin and the Mongoloid group of Asia and it's known as the shovel tooth — a concavity at the back of the upper incisors.' He leaned over the skull and opened the jaws. 'We don't routinely go into this kind of detail. Can we get a better light on this?' First, he ran his little finger along the back of the teeth. Then he used a dental mirror.

An uncomfortable silence followed.

'Hey ho,' the pathologist said without a glimmer of pleasure, 'this may be significant. These appear to be shovel teeth.'

The student had the sense not to shout, 'Told you so.'

The pathologist said, 'I'd better get one of my colleagues from odontology to confirm this. Sorry, folks, but if you want to follow this autopsy all the way through to the land of the rising sun I must invite you to return next week.'

The following Monday, the remains were brought out again for the dental expert. She was expected to confirm the pathologist's finding, but before starting she announced that she was not confident she could help. 'I know what you're talking about. Shovel teeth are typical of East Asians, but there are all sorts of exceptions and I wouldn't say it's reliable. Native Americans have them and I've seen many examples in Europeans.'

'So you can't tell us if she's Japanese?'

'Frankly, the knickers may be a better guide, but as I'm here, I might as well take a look. Oh dear, she *is* in a sorry state.'

The examination was painstaking, using a magnifier with a halogen light. The odontologist said at one point, 'Plenty of dental work and of excellent quality.' She straightened up and turned to the student. 'Was it you who noticed the label?'

'Yes, ma'am.'

'And you thought she might be Japanese? Well, you could be right. Have you heard of tooth tattoos?'

A frown said the student had not.

'They're the big thing in Japan, like nail art, but for teeth, and she seems to have the residue of one. Didn't anyone spot this?'

Silence from the onlookers and a stony gaze from the pathologist.

'They're not really tattoos at all,' the dental expert explained. 'They're attached. If you fancy yourself with a mouthful of bling you get them applied with a special glue using an LED light to fix them. They can be removed quite easily and there isn't much left of this one, but take a look with my magnifier and tell me what you see.'

The student leaned over and looked through the lens at where the jaw was held apart. The tiny black symbol on one of the upper incisors was chipped in a couple of places, but clearly an embellishment. 'I do see it. Is it a Japanese character? No, I don't think it is.'

'Agreed.'

'It's a music note, isn't it? Looks to me like a quaver.'

'I never even got to first grade, but I'm willing to take your word for it.' The odontologist stood back. 'This all proves nothing, but if you're wanting to find out who she is, I would check for a missing Japanese woman with a possible interest in music.'

'Not my job,' the pathologist said.

At the request of the coroner, the job was passed to the police, but not yet to Diamond's CID team. The Missing Persons Register was checked again. No obvious leads were found. The supposed Japanese connection yielded nothing. Of seventeen young women reported missing in Bath and Bristol since the start of the year, none were from Japan. Fourteen had already been eliminated from the enquiry because of their height and hair colour. The tooth tattoo was thought to be an unlikely decoration for the remaining three.

CID were brought in after a couple of days.

'Any suggestion she was attacked?' Diamond asked the uniformed inspector who had handed over the paperwork.

'Impossible to say, but she did end up in the river Avon.'

'No marks of violence?'

'The body was too far gone to tell.'

'Could be an accident, then, or suicide. Was she fully dressed?'

'The shoes were missing.'

'They could easily have come off in the water.' He glanced through the post-mortem report. 'I've heard of tattoos in weird parts of the anatomy, but a tooth?'

'It's the best clue we've got, apart from the Japanese knickers.'

'Ah — the Japanese knickers.' Diamond rolled his eyes.

'We managed to confirm that the manufacturer doesn't export them. Mind, someone from Britain could have travelled there and bought a few pairs.'

'Someone from Britain or anywhere else on the globe.'

'True. But the tooth tattooing is a Japanese thing. It's popular there.'

'And I'm supposed to work with that?'

'Plus the music connection.'

'One note.'

'What do you expect — the Japanese

113

National Anthem?'

Diamond raised his finger. 'I do the jokes here.'

Back in the CID room, he told the team, 'This is gainful employment, so we're not knocking it. In fact, we're going to make a big production of it. I want a display board with photos of the deceased and all the evidence, a map of the river and anything else you can think of. That's your job, John.'

Leaman beamed. Incident rooms were his speciality.

'Ingeborg, you get a front-line job, checking the two universities and all the private language colleges to see if any Japanese students have stopped attending in the past three months. Sometimes these things don't get reported. And Paul . . .'

'Yes, guv?'

'You're on hotels. Examine the registers for yourself. Don't just ask the reception people. Japanese names are pretty easy to spot. Get the details of all of them who stayed here and when they checked out.'

'Isn't some of that confidential?'

'What do you mean?'

'Data protection.'

'Don't talk to me about data protection. You're in CID, doing a job, trying to trace a missing person.'

John Leaman said, 'Strictly speaking, she isn't missing. We know where she is.'

Diamond didn't appreciate the logic. 'She's missing from somewhere, clever clogs, has to be. It's our job to find out where, college, hotel, tour group. That's how we'll find her name.'

'Precisely,' Leaman said. 'It's the name that's missing, not the person.'

'Any more lip from you, John, and you'll find yourself on knicker duty.' He addressed the team in general. 'Anyone here clued up on music?'

'Depends what sort,' Halliwell said.

'We don't know what sort. We have one musical note.'

'Personally, I like the Big Band sound.'

'Big Band. What's that — Glenn Miller? Duke Ellington? You're just the man to conduct this big band. I need an office manager. It's backroom, I know, but how could we manage without you?'

Halliwell gave the grin of a man who'd spoken once too often.

'Ingeborg?' Diamond said.

'You already gave me a job, guv.'

'Yes, but what's your taste in music?'

'I'm into roots.'

'What on earth . . . ?'

'Folk, Celtic, blues, country and western.'

Paul Gilbert added, 'When it's not rock, jazz or classical, it must be roots. Me, I go for modern rock.'

'This isn't getting us anywhere,' Diamond said. 'I had a weekend in Vienna and visited Beethoven's house, but I wouldn't call myself an expert.'

'We have a wide spectrum, then,' Leaman said. 'I enjoy decent music of all kinds, but for preference I'm a Savoyard.'

'I thought that was a variety of sausage.'

'Gilbert and Sullivan,' Leaman said, not appreciating the laughs.

'The thing is, why did she choose to get a musical note glued to her tooth? Is she a performer? If so, we'd probably have heard. When a musician goes missing, people notice. It gets in the news.'

'She doesn't have to be a musician,' Halliwell said. 'She could be a music lover, just like any of us. I'm not sure if the tooth tattoo is going to help us much more now we know she's almost certainly Japanese.'

Ingeborg had been doing some lateral thinking. 'Guv, is it just a coincidence that you asked me some weeks back to get some background on that Japanese tourist who was found in the canal in Vienna?'

'Must be,' he said to cut her off, wanting

to confine the discussion to what was happening in Bath. 'Better get started on this, boys and girls. Until something bigger comes along, it's the best way to defend our jobs. All the apparatus of an incident room. Computer back-up. Whiteboard. Photos. Action files. Big wheel — that's me. Let's get this show on the road.'

After that, no one had any other option than to look busy. Paul Gilbert remarked to Ingeborg as they headed for the door, 'Looks like the boss is coming out of his Swedish detective phase.'

'We can hope,' she said. 'I wouldn't put money on it yet.'

8

'One more time. She won't be back for ages.' Tippi Carlyle, in her bed facing Mel, ruffled his hair and smoothed her hand across his cheek and jaw. 'She's at Weight Watchers until seven and she always goes for a McDonald's after.'

'It's her house and you're her daughter.'

'The apple of her eye.'

'Okay, which makes it worse if she comes home early and finds me in bed with the apple of her eye.'

She wriggled and her nipples skimmed his chest. 'You can't deny you're up for it.'

'I don't want to upset her and nor do you.'

'Come on, big boy. Have another bite of the apple.'

'And get asked to leave? I like it here.'

She pressed closer. 'This is what you like.'

'I think we should each have a shower — separately — and be in our own rooms when she gets back.'

'You're scared of her.'

'I respect her. She's my landlady.'

'Get real, Mel. She must have guessed about us in — how long? Six weeks? My Mum's not daft. It's not as if I'm under age.'

'Agreed, but she hasn't seen us at it. Let's show respect and leave her guessing.'

'You're terrified she'll kick you out. You prefer her cooked breakfasts to making love to me.'

'Tippi, I want both to continue.'

'Honest? Prove it, then.'

'Not right now.' He kissed her forehead, eased away, rolled over, emerged from under the quilt and started gathering his clothes.

Tippi watched him. 'Tosser.'

'Tomorrow.'

'You must be joking.'

He padded back to his room, closed the door and took that shower. It doesn't get better than this, he thought. A regular income, nice lodgings, a friendly landlady with a dreamboat daughter who can't get enough, and any amount of music. I've hit the jackpot here in Bath.

Two months into the residency, the quartet remained an eccentric bunch, but by mutual consent they stayed apart from each other except when rehearsing and performing. The accommodations office at the university had first offered them a large Victorian house on Lansdown Road to share, and Ivan had behaved as if he was being sent to Siberia. 'That's out of the question, wholly unsuitable,' he'd said. 'Can't you give us separate lodgings?' The others had felt the same way — nothing is more calculated to disturb than overhearing a fellow artist at practice — and said so in unison. Four addresses spread across the city were found. The quartet would need to meet only when music-making. And Douglas, having set up the residency, scarpered back to London.

Part of Mel's contract was giving solo classes for third-year BA music students and postgraduates. The standard was high, the teaching a joy. Little different in method, though, from the lessons he had given at Fingis Road. He had five talented violists not far short of professional standard. In addition, three mornings each week the quartet drove out to the Newton Park campus and attended the Michael Tippett Centre, the university's pride and joy, one of the best locations in the country for ensemble playing. Rehearsals were private at this stage. Later they would allow some undergraduates in.

The first of the "soirées" Doug had negotiated as part of the deal had been held in a beautifully panelled room at Dyrham House, high in the Cotswolds north of the city. In consideration for Mel the ensemble played the Beethoven Quartet in C sharp minor he'd learned for his audition and they delivered its subtle mood changes and breathtaking extravagance with finesse. The audience of thirty or so, including a number of final-year students, received it with shouts of appreciation out of keeping with the surroundings. They seemed to feel mere clapping was not enough.

Everyone agreed that these musical evenings were a good thing. In later concerts, they moved on to Haydn and Mozart. Tickets were hugely in demand. Ivan was annoyed to hear that one had been sold on eBay for £250. 'Doug is hopeless. He should have cut us in on the deal. I could have bought my own Strad with the money we're losing over this.'

'Misery-guts,' Cat said. 'This is the best time we've had since Harry left. Don't knock it.'

At the Michael Tippett Centre, Ivan and Cat gave regular master classes in front of audiences, an ordeal Mel was spared on the grounds that he was still bedding in (as Cat expressed it with a wink); and Anthony because of his poor communication skills ('and he's no fool,' Cat said).

Mrs. Carlyle came home just before nine and knocked on Mel's door with an offer of tea and biscuits. 'You can't spend all evening on your own,' she said. 'Come and watch telly in the lounge with Tippi and me. You'll have to excuse her bathrobe. That girl is always showering.'

When Mel entered, Tippi was on the sofa with her legs curled under her. She didn't look away from the TV screen.

'I lost five pounds today,' Mrs. Carlyle said to Mel.

'Too bad. Where was that?'

'Pounds in weight, silly. I'm not saying where from, but I hope you notice. How was your day?'

'Fine.'

'Giving lessons as usual?'

'Mainly.'

'When's the next concert with the others?'

'The seventh of November.'

'Do you think Tippi and I would enjoy it? We're not highbrow, but we know a good tune when we hear one.'

'Hard to say. Some people obviously enjoy it.'

'Strauss waltzes?'

'Actually, no.'

'Shame. They really get me humming. I dare say you could wangle some tickets. How would you like to see Mel perform, Tippi?'

Tippi may have thought of a rude answer. She didn't give one.

Mel filled the gap. 'Quartet music asks a tad more of the audience than spotting a good tune. There's usually a theme or message that the composer develops in subtle ways. You need to listen — rather than just hearing — and the rewards are there.'

'Not so obvious as Strauss, then?'

'I wasn't going to say so, but yes.'

'I expect at a pinch you can play "The Blue Danube".'

'I can, and I have. I've been a jobbing musician for years, playing all sorts, fitting in where I can. And when I couldn't get work, I did busking down the tube, "The Blue Danube" included.'

'Outside the Pump Room is a good pitch.'

'Thanks. I hope it won't come to that.'

'Or inside. There's a trio playing while everyone scoffs their cream tea. If one of them gets ill, you could help out. Something on the side. We all enjoy something on the side.' She glanced at Tippi, whose eyes didn't move from the TV screen.

Mel said, 'I doubt if the university would approve.'

'It's not slumming, playing in the Pump Room. They have to be good because they get requests. I was told someone asked them to play the "1812 Overture" and they said they'd love to but unfortunately they didn't have the cannon.'

He grinned. 'I like it.'

'A cannon in the Pump Room — that's a laugh. Have you ever played the "1812", Mel?'

'A few times, but not alone. You need an orchestra for that.'

'And a big gun?'

'Ideally, more than one, but it doesn't often happen. There's a story of the Liverpool Philharmonic playing with two cannon mounted at the back of the orchestra. When they fired the first blank the orchestra was deafened and one lady violist fled the stage. Everyone was coated in specks of cordite and the management had to pay the laundry bills.'

'Glory be. What fun.'

'Nothing so dramatic happens in our concerts.'

'I expect you have a few laughs, even so.'

'At rehearsal sometimes. Our cellist has a

sense of humour. She's fun to be with.'

Mrs. Carlyle's eyebrows pricked up. 'She? Did you hear that, Tippi? You'd better listen up. There's a lady in Mel's quartet.'

Tippi didn't even blink.

Her mother hadn't finished. 'Perhaps all three of the others are ladies. I hadn't thought of that. Who's a lucky boy, then?' She put a hand to her mouth and shook with amusement.

'Cat is the only woman,' Mel said.

'It's the other way round, is it? She's the lucky one, with three fellows to choose from. Cat, did you say? Cat with the cream, I should think.'

'Nothing of that sort goes on. We're professionals.'

'Says you.'

He knew she was making mischief, so he grinned, reached for a biscuit and said nothing.

'More tea?' Mrs. Carlyle said. 'Your cup's empty. Tippi can top you up.'

For that remark, she got a glare from her daughter.

'Thanks. I've had all I want,' Mel said, and the words slipped out before he could stop them. 'Busy day coming up. I must read through a score for our next rehearsal, a Mozart I haven't played before.'

'A score sounds like hard work to me,' Mrs. Carlyle said. 'You'll be wanting the usual breakfast, then?'

'Please.' He got up and wished them a joint goodnight.

'She's in a world of her own,' Mrs. Carlyle said. 'I don't know what she does by day to make her so unsociable of an evening. Sleep soundly, Mel. You look tired yourself.'

Musically, he'd moved to a new level since coming to Bath. The musicianship of the others challenged and energised him. He was getting a crash course in the quartet repertoire — already preparing Brahms, Dvoràk, Schubert, Bartók. The learning process was exacting, but so filled with achievement that he didn't begrudge a minute of all the time studying scores. Regularly he would feel he knew a piece and then discover in rehearsal how much more it contained.

Intimate, intense and exhilarating, the fortnightly candlelit concerts made demands on all the players, yet brought coherence to their programme of work. After the Beethoven at Dyrham Park it had come as some relief to Mel to learn some of the more romantic pieces in the repertoire or quartets with exciting cello parts like

Haydn's Opus 20, No. 6, where the viola was more in a supporting role. His musical education was on a sharply rising curve, but it was all immensely satisfying. These were some of the most rewarding evenings of his life.

It was extraordinary how the other members of the quartet were transformed in the white heat of playing. Ivan — old sobersides — inhabited the soul of the composer and became spirited, playful, ecstatic even. Cat stopped being amusing and brought soulfulness from her cello capable of moving anyone to tears. The biggest change was in Anthony, who came alive in the rehearsal sessions, argued with passion for his interpretation and was usually right. Any quartet is only as good as its members and the fusion of their playing. This one was reaching heights rarely scaled.

They knew it of course.

During a break from rehearsal one morning, Mel said to Ivan, 'This is more dynamic than anything I've experienced musically before, the way we all contribute ideas.'

'It's how we've always worked.'

'So creative.'

'Nothing is static in ensemble work. We learn from each other constantly.'

'I'm learning in spades.'

'It isn't one-way. We're responding to you.'

Mel blinked. 'Really?'

'I don't say things I don't mean. So you feel you are benefiting from the experience?'

'Enormously, even though I still hardly know you.'

'Me personally?'

'The group. Anthony puzzles me the most. A sort of Jekyll and Hyde.' He stopped, embarrassed at what he'd said. 'No, that's out of order. Do you know what I mean?'

'Bipolar?'

'I wouldn't want to give it a label.'

'Good — because we don't think he's bipolar. That's about highs and lows, isn't it? Manic-depressive stuff. He's not particularly depressed.'

'There's a personality change when we start rehearsing.'

'The music is paramount to Anthony. It dwarfs everything else. The rest of his life bores him. He can't be bothered with it. Playing in the quartet is his only reality.'

'Isn't that dangerous?'

'There are times when we have to remind him over the most mundane things like getting his hair cut or renewing his passport. He needs someone in his life to chivvy him along. But he's not capable of entering into a relationship, so I don't think he'll find anyone.'

'Not capable? He must have emotional needs.'

'Outside music?' Ivan shook his head. 'I'm not aware of any. The emotion is all channelled into his playing. If his body tells him he requires food, he'll eat. He doesn't read or go to the cinema. When he wants sex, he'll pay for it. All those things are functional, unconnected with intellectual pleasure which comes to him only when he picks up his violin.'

Having said he wasn't giving a label to Anthony's behaviour, Mel passed no comment. Privately he thought this sounded like some form of autism.

'It must have been tough for him when Harry quit.'

'Indescribably tough. We worried over him. He was close to suicide. Douglas got him some work with the Hallé which probably saved his life.'

When the session resumed, Mel watched Anthony's eyes light up. Disturbing, really, to see how addictive music can be. They played a few bars of Schubert's *Rosamunde* and Anthony halted the playing himself. 'It's become sentimental,' he said. 'We're losing the truth of the piece. Can we try this section again from the beginning?'

'Not until we agree what is wrong,' Ivan said.

'The tempo. We've never played it this way. Like treacle running off a spoon.'

'Must be my fault,' Mel said. 'I'm making the difference.'

'I'm not blaming anyone,' Anthony said. 'We can rectify this. Didn't you notice, Cat?'

'Sweetie, I was miles away, trying to remember if I sent my dad a birthday card.'

Anthony swung round to face her, all aggression. 'How can you do that when we're playing?'

'All too easily. Haven't you ever driven a car and thought, I've come this far and I can't remember any of the traffic lights I passed and the turns I made and if I was watching my speed? One part of my brain is doing these things but I'm in another place. The worst is when it happens in a concert. I can see my bow moving and it isn't my hand that's guiding it, can't be, but Jesus, it is. Shit a brick, I'm in Carnegie Hall, playing Beethoven. If it hasn't happened to you, my chick, be grateful.'

Mel knew exactly what she'd described. He'd experienced the same nightmare more than once, although not with this group.

Anthony was lost for words.

Ivan said, 'Let's reconsider. Anthony may

have a point. If I take it with more energy, like so . . .' He played the first bars again. 'What do you think?'

'Still sexless,' Anthony said.

Cat's mouth lifted at the edges, but she said nothing.

'Show us, then,' Ivan said, irritated.

'Your part?' Anthony tucked the violin under his chin and played, and he was right. The section needed a stronger pulse. 'Shall we take it in segments?'

Ivan scowled. 'That won't be necessary.'

They went from the start and the improvement was obvious. Nobody said, 'I told you so.' Rehearsals were like this, with music the only winner.

After the session ended, Ivan said, 'At some stage soon we must decide which piece to record.'

'Who's talking about recording?' Cat said. 'We're still finding our way as a quartet.'

'If you remember, it's part of the deal. A recording for their funds. With downloads and sales of the disc it helps to pay for our residency,' he said and added in a casual tone while fitting his violin into its case, 'I'd like to offer the "Grosse Fuge".'

'That's insane,' Cat said. 'We've only been together six weeks and he wants us to play the most difficult piece in the repertoire.

131

Even with Harry on board, that was always a killer.'

'We made a passable recording,' Ivan said.

'I'm up for it,' Anthony said.

'We all know about you. What about Mel?' Cat said. 'Are you familiar with it? All those fortissimos?'

'I've heard it played and studied the score.'

'With the best will in the world, sunshine, that isn't the same as cutting a disc.'

Ivan said, 'I have confidence in Mel. If we start work immediately, we can be ready in a month or so.'

Cat said, 'We could make life a lot easier for ourselves with a more familiar piece like "Death and the Maiden".'

'We can record that as well,' Ivan said. 'We'll need to offer something else.' He finished fastening the case. 'What's your opinion, Mel?'

Ivan's unqualified support had been unexpected. Mel felt as if he ought to be worthy of it. 'How soon do we have to commit?'

'They want to know soon.'

'*They* want to know?' Cat said. 'How about the players? You just said we must start immediately and for once I couldn't agree more — but only if every one of us opts to go for it.'

Anthony raised his hand.

'He's more than willing,' Ivan said, 'and the second violin part is unbelievably demanding on the fingers. You sound reluctant, Cat.'

'For Mel's sake. What Beethoven asks the violist to do isn't shelling peas, you know. The lad's risen admirably to the challenge, but he's not a regular quartet player.'

'Then we increase the rehearsal sessions.'

'Slave-driver.'

'I wouldn't suggest it if I thought we'd fail.'

'We've come a long way already.' She sighed and shook her head. 'If Mel is willing, then so am I.'

The three original members looked at Mel.

'Let's give it a go,' he said, trying to sound cool.

He shared a taxi with Cat and her cello. There wasn't room for the others.

'I hope you know what you let yourself in for, new boy.'

'I have some idea. I must get a copy of the recording you three made with Harry.'

'It's not bad.'

He tried obliquely to get more on Harry's disappearance. 'He must have been with you some years.'

'Harry? From the beginning. We're not careless. We don't keep losing violists like beads off a string.'

'Did he have family?'

'None he ever mentioned. It's hard on partners, this wandering existence. Like the rest of us, he was self-reliant. Well, I'm saying that and it's not entirely true. Anthony needs mothering, but he's a special case. Sometimes I feel like smothering him. Harry was all man.'

'In what sense?'

She smiled. 'He took his chances when they came.'

'How do you mean?'

'Groupies. We're not much different to pop groups when it comes to fans. In our peak years we had a huge following. Invitations of all sorts flooded in, from billionaires wanting us to play on their Strads to schoolgirls asking us to autograph their bras. Asking the guys, that is. Even they got bored with it after a time.'

'And you think Harry took advantage?'

'Of schoolgirls? No, he wasn't that way inclined. What he got up to was grown-up stuff and he didn't like me asking about it.'

'Was he gay?'

'Harry? No, don't get me wrong. I've seen how pleased he was when women came onto him. The first commandment of quartet life is that you don't pry into each other's goings-on, but laws are meant to be broken and I'm curious by nature, and it sounds like you are, too.'

'He interests me for obvious reasons,' Mel said. 'I've stepped into his shoes.'

'All I can tell you is that he covered his tracks. When we needed to get hold of him at short notice — as you do at times because of a change in arrangements — it was the devil's own job trying to reach him. He was never at his lodgings. But you couldn't fault him for reliability. He turned up at the hall in good time for concerts and rehearsals. Looked a little jaded on occasions, but I guess we all do from time to time.'

'So when he disappeared, it came as a shock?'

'Panic stations. We had to cancel that night's concert with the audience already in their seats. I was all for improvising with some solo numbers, but the others couldn't cope. Ivan was a dead loss. He's no use at all when things go belly up. And Anthony is an ensemble player first and last. Doesn't do solos. I could easily have given them "The Swan" and there are hundreds of pieces for the fiddle that Ivan could have picked from, but no, he insisted we cancel the show. Good thing Douglas was with us. He found a local stand-in for the remaining concerts and we got through somehow, but it wasn't pretty.'

'And you never heard any more from Harry?'

'Nothing. None of us knew where he went in his time off. The embassy found that hard to believe, but it's the way we are. So the local police didn't know where to start looking.'

'Do you think he's dead?'

'I hate to think it, because he was a lovely guy, but what else could have happened? If he'd gone on a bender that night he'd surely have got in touch when he got his head together. He needed the quartet. It was his living.'

'He could have had an accident and lost his memory.'

'Some kind of freak event? We can only hope, but as every day passes . . . You see, being the female in the group, I'm locked in, heart and soul. You guys belong to me, even bossy old Ivan, bless his little cotton socks.'

He was about to say something about the maternal instinct and stopped himself in time. She didn't mean that at all. Behind all the brazen chat was a woman getting emotional — if not sexual — fulfilment from being so close to three men. 'We're lucky to have you.'

She smiled. 'You'd better believe it.'

9

You couldn't have mistaken it for anything else but an incident room. Desks, computers, phones. Graphic photos of the corpse, with a close-up of the tooth tattoo. A large-scale map of the Avon. Lines of enquiry listed on the whiteboard. Plenty of noise and movement from the CID regulars and civilian staff. Presiding over it all, Peter Diamond, much more his old imposing self.

'I've asked for a second autopsy,' he announced to the few members of the team who weren't out of the building on active enquiries.

'Can you do that?' Halliwell asked. 'Isn't it the coroner's call?'

'The coroner isn't God. He's a public servant, same as you and me. I'm not satisfied, and I told him. The medic who did the first one wasn't a forensic pathologist at all. He was a hospital man, a histopathologist. What's that when it's at home?'

'Not sure.'

'Neither am I, not at all sure. He writes a two-sheet report and comes to no conclusion except that the woman had been dead for some time. I could have told him that.'

'He found the tooth tattoo.'

'No, he didn't. He asked some dental expert to look at the teeth and she spotted it. No wonder I don't have any confidence.'

John Leaman looked up from his computer screen. 'Histopathology: the branch of medicine concerned with changes in tissues caused by disease.'

'There you go. It's not disease we're bothered about, it's crime. No use to us at all. I want a proper forensic man like Bert Sealy. Sarcastic swine, but at least he does the job and misses nothing. You don't get short-changed by Sealy.'

'What did the coroner say?'

'He'll look into it. He will.'

'Does the ACC know you spoke to him?'

'She's away on some course, isn't she? Can't reach her. If I could, she'd be the first to know.'

Halliwell grinned.

Energised, Diamond stalked the CID room delegating duties to anyone unlucky enough to catch his eye.

'Haven't we heard back from Paul Gilbert?

He's taking his time round the hotels. What's he doing — testing the beds? You.'

'Me, sir?' some hapless DC said.

'Give Gilbert a call and tell him we need a progress report.'

'Very good.'

'It had better be. And why is Ingeborg so silent? She should have got some names out of the colleges by this time.'

Towards the end of the morning, he used the marker pen to list the hotels Gilbert had visited. 'This is taking too long,' he said. 'We need more manpower. I'll ask for back-up from uniform. The plods are as capable as we are of checking names.'

Ingeborg looked in at lunchtime. 'It isn't easy, guv. Some of the private colleges are hopeless at keeping records. They can tell you who joined and when, but there's no check on day-to-day attendance. As one college secretary said to me, it's the students' loss if they don't put in the hours.'

'And if one goes missing altogether?'

'Could be weeks or months before the system picks it up. Most have personal tutors, but the tutors aren't overly concerned if the students don't appear. There's often a valid reason, they say, like a change of course or a transfer to another college, and they aren't always notified.'

'Sounds like the perfect set-up for absenteeism. It wasn't like that when I went through police college.'

Ingeborg was briefly lost for words, struggling, no doubt, with the thought of Diamond as a police cadet. 'I was told the attendance record for Japanese students is above average.'

He nodded. 'They're a law-abiding race. The Japanese police spend most of their time helping people find their way.'

'Nice work if you can get it,' Halliwell said.

'Foreign students come here on visas,' Diamond said. 'There must be a record.'

John Leaman, the resident know-it-all, said, 'That would be with the UK Border Agency.'

'They decide who gets in, right?'

'Through a points system. All students from abroad need a valid visa letter to say they've been accepted by an approved college. That gets them thirty points. Then they must prove they've got several thousand pounds in the bank for twenty-eight days. That gives them the remaining ten points they need.'

'And you and I know there are loopholes. The money can easily be borrowed.'

'Right. And the letters have been forged on occasions, but not by the Japanese. Like

141

you said, it would be highly unusual to find them fiddling the system. If our young woman was a student, it's more than likely she came officially and her name is known.'

'Along with several thousand others.'

'I'm not sure of the numbers,' Leaman said.

'Let's assume she's on the books. Can the Border Agency tell us if she's dropped out?'

'They'd rely on the colleges informing them.'

Diamond sighed. He'd found the flaw. 'Which they don't.'

Ingeborg said, 'To be fair, guv, some of them do.'

'Why would anyone drop out? Anyone from Japan, brought up to do the right thing, work hard and get results?'

'Can't keep up with their studies. Loss of face.'

He glanced across at the photos of the victim on the display board. 'Can't argue with that.'

No one smiled.

'If the Border Agency doesn't have a grip on this, we're dependent on the colleges,' Diamond said.

'This is the problem I'm finding,' Ingeborg said. 'The colleges are a law unto themselves.'

'Or no law at all?'

'Not much of one, anyway.'

'Haven't they given you any names?'

'Three are being followed up as we speak. It's a matter of contacting the staff concerned and that takes time because the lecturers aren't all in college at one time.'

'Speak to the students. They'll tell you if one of their mates has gone missing.'

Diamond had put his finger on it, as usual. Students would surely cooperate, especially if it was made clear that a body had been discovered. Going through official channels wasn't the only option.

'Thanks, guv. I'll give it a go.'

By the end of the day all the checking had come to nothing. Everyone had been accounted for, even the three Ingeborg had mentioned. She had tried questioning groups of Japanese students. They were keen to help when they heard what she said and there was a useful grapevine of information between different colleges. They had answered the few queries that had come up.

'It's looking more and more as if she was a tourist,' Halliwell said.

'So what did Paul Gilbert find?'

Silence.

'He must be still out there.'

The hotels had been easier to check than the colleges. Registers existed and were reliable. It was just a matter of getting round to them all. The extra help from uniformed officers had lightened the load. There remained a number of bed and breakfast houses that would wait for the morning.

'A day visitor?' Halliwell said.

'In a coach party? They count them back in, don't they?'

'I was thinking she may have been travelling alone — by train, say, from London. Plenty do.'

'There's no way of finding out.'

'Unless her people back in Japan report that she hasn't returned. Have we asked the embassy?'

'One of the first calls I made — and wouldn't you know it, there's a chain of command. It's always the way with bureaucracy. They have to check ten times over before they tell you what day of the week it is.'

'It's in their interest to cooperate.'

'I'm not saying anyone is being obstructive. The people I spoke to were ultra-polite. They'll check with their government and the police and we'll get a response by Christmas.'

'We haven't much to help them apart from

describing the clothes.'

'We emailed the dental record and the all-important tooth tattoo.'

'DNA?'

'DNA as well.'

'Did we send a photo?' Halliwell said.

Diamond tilted his head towards the shots of the corpse. 'That? You wouldn't identify anyone from that.'

From across the room John Leaman had overheard what was said. 'Just a thought, guv.'

'What's that?'

'Something we may be able to do. There are experts who can reconstruct a face from a skull.'

'A decomposing skull?'

'They put it through a CT scanner and get the digital data to produce a computer image, one you can rotate and look at from all angles. From that, they make an exact model in styrene foam with a computer-controlled milling machine —'

'You're losing me,' Diamond said.

'A replica of the actual skull. Then they use wax or clay to add the muscles and tissue.'

'Hold on. How do they know how much wax to add on?'

'I'm not sure. Generally you've got an artist — a sculptor — working closely with a forensic anthropologist.'

'Not the best of combinations.'

'It's not infallible, I grant you.'

'And slow, I wouldn't mind betting.'

'But there is a quicker method.'

'What's that?'

'When it's all done on the computer, using a high-resolution 3D image of the skull. They have a large stock of facial features that they manipulate into place until something fits.'

Diamond gave him a squint. 'Is that more reliable than the wax?'

A pause. 'I couldn't say. I'm not an expert.'

'Sounds like trial and error. Where did you pick up these pearls of wisdom?'

'From one of those CSI shows on TV.'

'Say no more.'

Halliwell came to Leaman's defence. 'Some computer-generated images would look good on the display board.'

Swayed by the suggestion, Diamond tapped the point of his chin. 'D'you think so?'

'Doesn't matter what I think. The ACC would like it.'

'Georgina?' A fleeting smile. He knew exactly what Halliwell was getting at. The Assistant Chief Constable, Georgina Dallymore, had him down as a technophobe. 'On second thoughts, maybe it's worth a try.'

'The computer graphics option?' Leaman said.

'Definitely.' Even Georgina would think a wax head was over the top.

'Why don't you find out some more?' Halliwell said to Leaman.

That evening Diamond walked the towpath alone. He'd heard nothing from Paloma since the bust-up at the Dolphin and his pride wouldn't allow him to call her. She'd dumped him, so it was up to her to get in touch if she still had any regard for him. Actually the speed of her departure had caught him unprepared. A few unguarded words from him and she was off.

You and I are through.

He'd gone over it repeatedly. Maybe she had a point, he had decided as the days went on. He'd treated her as if she was staff. What was the word he'd used when she'd told him a trouble shared was a trouble halved? Claptrap. Not a nice thing to say in the circumstances, and she didn't know she'd touched a raw nerve. He didn't want to share his troubles with anyone.

Yet he knew the seed of the misunderstanding had been sown earlier, in Vienna, when they had come across the little shrine by the canal. It was clear from what she'd said that he shouldn't have distanced himself from the death of the woman. He'd treated the tragedy professionally, as a policeman, sidestepping the sympathy Paloma had obviously felt. Someone had come to a tragic end and he'd not shown the concern expected of him. Paloma had wanted to learn more about the victim while his instinct was to move on and be grateful it was someone else's case.

His bigger misjudgement had been to follow up on the Vienna incident, asking Ingeborg to find out the facts. If he'd been consistent, he would have let well alone. Stupidly, he'd wanted Paloma to be pleased he'd gone to this extra trouble — even allowing that he'd only delegated the duty. He hadn't thought ahead, hadn't sensed that by raising the subject again he was giving her a rerun of the same scene: his professional way of dealing with the fact of death against her heart-felt sympathy.

The outrage she'd kept in check in Vienna had reared up. A moment of turmoil neither of them could have prepared for.

Would she come round?

Women could be every bit as obstinate as men.

Without much to console him, he stopped to watch the steady flow of the river. Recent heavy rain had quickened the current and pieces of driftwood were being carried quite swiftly. Any one of them could have resembled the body when it was first noticed, demonstrating the impossibility of finding exactly where it had entered the water. It must have been submerged somewhere up-river for a considerable time before the internal gases made it buoyant and mobile.

He'd ruled out a search of the river banks.

But there were finites he hadn't taken into account until now. The Avon wasn't free-flowing from source to sea. He should have remembered it had man-made barriers. Only a few hundred metres upstream from here was Pulteney weir, where he'd often seen floating objects trapped by the curved wall. And not far downstream was Weston lock.

The obvious conclusion was that the body had entered the water somewhere below the weir. It had been recovered some way short of the lock, not much over a mile away.

He revised his plan of action. Both river banks along this stretch needed to be searched, a real fingertip search for possible items belonging to the deceased. Her shoes may well have been lost while in the water,

149

but what about her bag, phone, watch or an item of jewellery? Find some object belonging to her and you would almost certainly know where she'd got into the river. Then the sub-aqua team could go to work.

He'd have a search squad make a start in the morning.

With that decided, he resumed his walk and almost immediately his pulse quickened. Ahead on the towpath, approaching from the Saltford direction, was a familiar figure. He recognised the way she walked, her height and the cut of her hair. Coincidence, or had she chosen to walk the towpath knowing he often came here at this time in the evening?

He'd spotted her, so she must have seen him. She continued her approach at the same deliberate rate.

What now? he asked himself. Do I say I behaved abysmally and ask her to forgive and forget? The fact that she's chosen to come this way at this time of day must surely mean she's in a forgiving frame of mind. She's missing me as much as I'm missing her.

Best offer her a drink, but not — for an obvious reason — in the Dolphin, and not the Old Crown, his local, where some of the regulars still remembered Steph. He was still dithering between pubs when he became conscious of a movement by his feet. A small dog, a dachshund, had trotted past and then returned, as if checking if it knew Diamond. It had a confident look, head cocked to the right, although who was the owner of this silky charmer wasn't clear. Having decided, apparently, that Diamond was a disappointment, it turned and scampered off — straight towards the woman he had taken to be Paloma.

Odd.

So far as he was aware, Paloma didn't possess a dog.

He watched the dachshund run the short distance, stop, turn and apparently come to heel — and the woman stooped to fasten the lead to its collar. Now he saw with crushing certainty that she wasn't who he'd supposed. She had the same style of walking, but she was undeniably someone else. He'd superimposed his image of Paloma on to this stranger, a younger woman with lighter-coloured hair.

How pathetic was that? He was as churned up inside as a smitten teenager.

He about-turned and retraced his steps. The world wasn't a romantic novel. Chance meetings don't happen when you need them. If he wanted an improvement in his wretched situation he'd better do something active towards it.

Like what?

Picking up a phone? Ringing her doorbell?

No chance, he told himself.

The search of the river banks got under way in the morning, twelve officers in overalls and boots progressing methodically along both sides below Pulteney weir. As one constable cynically remarked, it was a cheap way for the council to get its rubbish collected. Everything from cigarette stubs to beer cans was painstakingly picked up, and its position noted.

The first stretch as far as North Parade Bridge was deceptively easy. Then the footpath along the west bank came to an end and the footing became perilous. One side of a river is generally easier than another to move along, so they switched duties when possible and everyone was given a share of wrestling with brambles and scrambling along the muddy, uncultivated side. The quality of the finds didn't do much to improve morale. They were the boring throwaway items you would expect and mostly coated in 'grime or slime', as one of the searchers put it.

Diamond put in a mid-morning appearance at Ferry Lane, alongside the cricket ground, and watched the unfortunates making slow progress through the undergrowth. He didn't have much sympathy, especially when he learned that nothing of interest had been found. He'd endured worse in his days as a rookie sifting the contents of a London council tip for bits of a dismembered corpse.

While he was there someone picked up a clay pipe and said it might interest the local historians. The sergeant in charge said it was probably at least a century old and could have been smoked by one of the bargees who once navigated the canal.

'It's a river, not a canal,' Diamond said.

'A waterway,' the sergeant said.

'So what?'

'So it was used by the barges that used the Kennet and Avon canal. To all intents and purposes it's part of the canal. The man-made bit feeds in at Dolemeads. They came down from Reading and linked up with the river for the last stretch to the docks at Bristol.'

The man was right. Never having taken much interest in the canal system, Diamond hadn't given any thought to the river as a waterway. In his mind there was a clear distinction between a river and a canal. A canal was a man-made thing, like the one he'd walked beside in Vienna.

And now that the Danube canal popped into his mind, he thought fleetingly about the woman murdered there.

One dead Japanese woman in a canal in Vienna and another here in the Kennet and Avon.

Coincidence?

Sensible thinking suggested nothing more. It wouldn't be wise or profitable to start constructing theories of an international killer.

'Keep up the good work,' he told the sergeant, 'but tell them I'm not really interested in clay pipes.'

Back in Manvers Street, he found John Leaman practically turning cartwheels in excitement. 'It's all under way, guv.'

'What is?'

'The facial reconstruction. I found a really helpful technician at the Royal United who arranges the CT scans and he knew exactly what I wanted. In fact, he's really chuffed to be helping us.'

'Probably watches CSI on the telly.'

Leaman took this as encouragement. 'He does. So he's already done the scan and emailed it to Philadelphia.'

'Whatever for?'

'I found Professor Hackenschmidt through the internet. He's a world expert in plastic surgery and uses computer imaging all the time. We're hoping he can use his skills to recreate her face. We could have a result in a matter of hours.'

'Let me get this straight,' Diamond said. 'The skull was put through the scanner in Bath and the pictures sent to Philadelphia?'

Leaman's face betrayed some nervousness, as if he knew he'd overstepped the mark. Budgetary considerations were always a worry. 'Correct.'

'Did you ask for any to be sent here?'

'Well, no. We wouldn't know what to do with them.'

'Oh yes we would,' Diamond said. 'You missed the point, John. We'd stick them on our board and look as if we're going places with this investigation. Get on to your friend at the RUH and tell him this is our baby and we need a copy of everything.'

In other respects the progress was less spectacular. All the listed hotels and boarding houses had been checked and there was not a single report of a missing Japanese woman.

'If some of you can't look busier than this,' Diamond said, 'I'll tell the search party on the river bank that reinforcements are on the way.'

After he'd gone into his office and slammed the door, there was a spell of silence. Then Paul Gilbert said, 'Who's that Swedish detective Kenneth Branagh plays on TV?'

Better news came through after lunch. The coroner had reviewed the autopsy report and decided on a second postmortem to be conducted by a Home Office approved forensic pathologist at 8 A.M. next morning. Diamond was invited to attend. He thanked the coroner and said he would do his level best to be there. If, however, something came up, his deputy would attend. After switching off the phone, he called across the room, 'Keith.'

Halliwell looked up. 'Guv?'

'Are you a big breakfast man, bacon, eggs, the full English, as they say?'

'When I can get it.'

'Have a light one tomorrow. Early start for you.'

Autopsies and Peter Diamond didn't mix.

Later in the afternoon came a call from the search squad. They'd found an iPod on the Green Park stretch of river bank between the Churchill Bridge and Midland Bridge.

It looked as if it had been there some time.

Diamond said he would come at once. He asked Ingeborg to join him.

Green Park is a wedge-shaped space on the north side of the river, a piece of land that somehow escaped the builders of centuries past and enjoys some seclusion simply because it borders on the river and is a good distance from the main shops and tourist attractions.

'I lose track,' Diamond said to Ingeborg as they drove along Green Park Road. 'What's an iPod?'

'You really don't know?' she said in disbelief.

'I don't have the patience to keep up.'

'There are iPods and then there are iPods,' she said.

'Now you're poking fun. It's some kind of audio device, right?'

'Or much more. There are touch-screen versions, video versions. Technology moves on.'

'I can use a mobile phone.'

'After much prodding.'

'Am I missing something, not owning an iPod?'

'Depends,' Ingeborg said. 'They can be good if you work out at the gym or go for a jog.'

He looked out of the window instead.

The sergeant from the search team was waiting for them beside a section of the river bank below the towpath now cordoned off with crime scene tape. Alder trees and bushes would have provided a useful screen for anyone up to no good.

'Where is it?' Diamond asked.

A transparent evidence bag was handed over. The object inside was small and square and so coated in mud you couldn't tell what colour it was. A lead with two earpieces was coiled in one corner.

'Good spotting on someone's part,' Diamond said. 'This would have been easy to miss.'

'There's no certainty it belonged to the dead woman,' the sergeant said. 'On the other hand, people aren't in the habit of slinging things like this away.'

'One of the earpieces is broken,' Ingeborg said. 'It looks as if it's been crushed, stepped on, or something.'

'We noticed.'

'The iPod itself looks all right. You might chuck out the earphones, but not that.'

'I agree.'

'The damage could have been done in a struggle.'

Diamond took a closer look. 'Are there

any signs of violence where it was picked up?'

'Hard to tell, sir,' the sergeant said. 'Take a look if you like. We've marked an approach path. I made sure my lads didn't trample all over the scene.'

Diamond could take a hint. His big feet wouldn't aid the investigation. 'We'll get the crime scene professionals out here and have it mapped and photographed. Where are your people now?'

'The other side of Midland Bridge continuing the search.'

Diamond turned to Ingeborg. 'What do you think? Any way we can link the iPod with the victim?'

'The best chance is to find some hair at the scene or match some fibres with her clothes.'

'Put a call through to the men in blue overalls, then. I'll get a sense of where we are and how she might have got here.' He told the sergeant that the search could stop at Windsor Bridge. The body must have entered the water way before there.

If, as he was tempted to suspect, the Japanese woman had been murdered, this little triangle of parkland was as good a spot as any to dump the body in the river. Quiet, well away from houses, with plenty of trees and scrub screening the view, the site had much to commend itself to a killer. You could get a vehicle right to the end of the road known as Green Park, no great distance from the river bank.

And no one would hear the screams.

10

Georgina Dallymore, the Assistant Chief Constable, had spent the past week attending a Home Office course. Rumour had it that the top bananas were being instructed on how to maximise resources, government-speak for cuts. So a collective shudder should have gone through CID when she reappeared. In fact, the team were so busy that Georgina was scarcely noticed.

'What's going on here?' she asked Peter Diamond. 'I wasn't told we had a major incident.'

'You've been away, ma'am.'

'I wasn't away from my BlackBerry, if you know what that is. I expect to be kept informed. What's it about?'

'A body found in the river. We're treating it as suspicious.'

She eyed the display board. 'It looks like a full blown murder investigation. Is all this justified?'

'It is when there's an international dimension.'

She twitched in alarm. 'In what way?'

'The victim — the deceased, I should say — is almost certainly from Japan.'

'A tourist?'

'Possibly. We're working closely with the Border Agency and the Japanese embassy.'

'Do you know who it is?'

He shook his head. 'Female, below average height, twenty to thirty, with a tooth tattoo as the only distinguishing feature.'

'What on earth . . . ?'

Diamond explained. After the dig about the BlackBerry he wasn't missing a chance to let the boss know he was street smart.

Georgina peered at the close-up. 'It looks like a music note.'

'A quaver, actually.'

'I didn't know you read music, Peter.'

'I have hidden depths, ma'am.'

'I've known that for a long time, but music is something else. So is this the only clue?'

'An iPod has been found on the river bank in Green Park.'

'Hers?'

'We can't say yet. I'm having the scene examined for evidence of violence.'

'Was she attacked, then?'

'Unfortunately she was in the water too

long to tell.'

She paused as if to play the statement over. 'I hate to say it, but this has all the hallmarks of an unsolved case.'

He wasn't being goaded into submission. 'You're entitled to your opinion, ma'am.'

'What makes you think this isn't an accidental drowning?'

'In all my time here, I can't recall any accidents below Pulteney weir, where she was found. You don't find swimmers or canoeists there.'

'She could have climbed over the railing,' Georgina said.

'Why?'

'Suicide, obviously.'

'But the iPod was found on the river bank further down.'

'So you're working on the basis that she was murdered and dumped in the river? A pretty big assumption from one lost iPod.'

'We'll know more when the crime scene investigators report.' He decided this wasn't the best time to tell her he'd asked for a second autopsy.

'You *may* know more. Have you checked with missing persons?'

'The first thing we did. Since then we've enquired at all the colleges and hotels.'

'No names yet?'

'So far, no.'

'You've hit the buffers, then. Better scale everything down and get the room back to normal.'

'I haven't told you about Professor Hackenschmidt.'

She blinked rapidly. 'Who's he?'

'The world expert on facial reconstruction using computer imaging. He and his team in Philadelphia are already at work.'

'Did you say Philadelphia?' Georgina was tight-lipped now.

'He works from CT scans.' Another bit of technological jargon coming to his aid.

'Is this coming out of your budget?'

Diamond's way of dealing with awkward questions was to ask one himself. 'I expect you're up with computer imaging, ma'am?'

'I've heard of it, but I didn't expect you of all people to give any credence to it. How much will this cost?'

'I'm told the professor is only too pleased to be involved.'

'Small wonder, if we're paying. I hope you asked for an estimate.'

'One of my team is dealing with it.'

'Who's that?'

'John Leaman.'

'Good. He's no fool.' Having said this, even Georgina seemed to realise Diamond could take offence. 'This is just the kind of outsourcing we've been discussing on the Home Office course. These are tough economic times. We can't employ experts for this and that and go way over budget. We need to make better use of our own resources.'

Diamond wasn't backing down. 'I wouldn't trust this lot to reconstruct a face. We'd end up with something out of *Frankenstein.*'

'Be serious, Peter.'

'I am. You asked if we've hit the buffers and I'm telling you we haven't. It's all in train, if you'll excuse the pun. Can't be stopped now. As soon as the professor sends us a likeness we'll forward copies to Japan and get them on TV and in the papers. Speeds up the whole enquiry. Once the woman is identified we'll get to the truth of it, I promise you. Maximise our resources.' The last words tripped off his tongue so glibly that Georgina was caught off guard. She drew a long, fatalistic breath and returned upstairs to consider her options. Dismantling the incident room might not be the best way forward.

At mid-morning, significant news came in from Keith Halliwell at the mortuary. The second autopsy had been conducted by Dr. Bertram Sealy, as Diamond had hoped.

'And what did he find?'

'He asked me to tell you he was sorry to have missed you, guv.'

'Typical bloody Sealy.'

'But he did find something the first man missed. There's a bone called the hyoid in the throat, above the Adam's apple, quite small and delicate and shaped like a horse-shoe and not attached to any other bones. He removed it and pointed out that it was damaged, fractured at one end.'

'Meaning that violence has been done to the neck?'

'It's the only sign of violence he could find, because of the bad condition of the flesh.'

Diamond whistled. 'Fracturing of the hyoid bone is a common sign of manual strangulation. This could be it.'

'I think it must be. He says it's highly unlikely this was caused accidentally when the body was being recovered from the river, or while it was submerged. To break a young person's hyoid bone you have to exert real pressure on the neck.'

'Is this going into Sealy's report?'

'I asked him. He's a pain. He kept me dangling for about ten minutes while he went through all the other symptoms of strangling: bruising, facial congestion, bleeding into the neck muscles. None of this showed because so much of the flesh had gone rotten in the water. Finally I got it from him. Cause of death: asphyxia by compression of the neck. His words.'

'That's all we need, Keith. We're in business.'

'I thought we were already.'

'Nothing can stop us now, not Georgina, the coroner, Portishead. Tell Bert Sealy he's my hero.'

There are times in police work when nothing goes right. Most days seemed like that to Diamond. Just occasionally there's a break in the clouds and you have to make the most of such moments. Within twenty minutes of the call from Halliwell he heard from the search team at Green Park. Fibres had been found on a bramble bush on the river bank, and there were twin lines in the mud suggesting somebody had been dragged down the slope to the water.

'Heel marks?' Diamond said on the phone to the supervisor of the crime scene team. These days crime scene investigations were farmed out to private firms: outsourcing, as Georgina would put it.

167

'Very likely.'

'If she was wearing shoes, they may be in the water. I'll arrange for the sub-aqua team to take a look. Is it deep there?'

'Don't know. I haven't been for a swim.'

Now Diamond remembered the voice of a man he'd tangled with before, a smart-arse with a liking for sarcasm. 'You're Duckett, aren't you?'

'Who else did you expect? We're a small business, not the Co-op.'

'Surely you can tell at a glance if the river's deep.'

'It shelves steeply.'

'And did you find any shoe prints near these marks?'

'Far too many. We'll need to check what every one of your search team was wearing.'

'You'll be telling me we corrupted your scene.'

'A line of policemen tramping through? Give me a break. And presumably you had a look yourself?'

'Only by the access path.'

'Was there one? It's like a football field here.'

'The fibres,' Diamond said. 'What are they like?'

'Like fibres.'

'Wool, cotton, man-made?'

'We won't know until we get them under a microscope.'

'And I suppose the iPod has gone to the lab as well?'

'Where else?'

After the call had ended, Ingeborg said, 'I heard you asking about the iPod, guv. I wonder if it's still in working order. They're well constructed. It would be good to know what music she liked.'

'How will that help?'

'It kind of brings her alive.'

He gave her a baffled look.

Ingeborg added, 'Well, it tells us more about her. Any new information must be welcome.'

'Give them a call at the lab if you like. I don't fancy discussing music with the guy at the scene.'

Early in the afternoon when America was starting up, John Leaman took a call from Philadelphia. He discussed it with Ingeborg. 'I've just been speaking to one of the professor's team. He wants to know about the dead woman's hair.'

'What about it?'

'The style, I suppose. It doesn't show up in the CT scan, but they'd like to know what we observed. When they send us an image they want the look to be as lifelike as possible.'

'Did you tell him she was in the water for weeks? It doesn't do much for a girl's hair.'

'Can we say anything about the cut?'

'Okay. It's thick, dark hair with a fringe and cut sheer at the back. You can tell him that.'

'I'd be happier if you did.'

She began to laugh 'Aren't you comfortable discussing hairstyles with another guy? I'll speak to them if you like.'

Keith Halliwell was back from the autopsy looking pleased with himself.

Diamond soon altered that. 'Now we know it's murder, we must pull out all the stops. That's a musical expression, in case you weren't aware of it. Try the embassy again for names. They promised to get back to us.'

'Be good if we could send them the computer picture. What's the latest from Philadelphia?'

'Inge was talking to them about hair. They must be close to sending an image.'

'They know she's Japanese, do they? Japanese in our opinion, anyway.'

'They can tell from the shape of the skull, can't they?'

'I was told it isn't obvious.'

Halliwell did his best to reassure. 'I expect they'll give her the almond-shaped eyes.'

'Christ, I hope so.' Diamond had a fleeting vision of a Betty Boop cartoon. 'You're making me worried. I'm less confident now than I was.'

'About the whole case?'

'The picture they're sending.' Diamond vibrated his lips. 'And the whole case, if I'm honest.'

'But the case is keeping everyone busy. Georgina was gobsmacked.'

He raised a smile. 'Yes, that was a nice moment.'

A knock on the door interrupted them. It was Ingeborg. 'Guv, I'm sorry to butt in, but you ought to hear this. The people at forensics found that the iPod was working okay and I asked them to play it for us. Hold on a mo and I'll put it through to your hands-free.' She touched the amplifying phone on his desk and music filled the room — music of an unexpected kind. She stood with arms folded.

Glances were exchanged. This was the first time Beethoven had been heard in Diamond's office, an event about as likely as finding the *Judgement of Paris* on his wall.

'Bit highbrow for me,' he said. 'I was

expecting something Japanese. What is it?'

Halliwell shook his head.

'John Leaman says it's a string quartet,' Ingeborg said. 'At times it sounds like a full orchestra, but four instruments can make a big sound.'

'This is on the iPod?' he said.

'This and a whole lot more. Whoever she was, she was into classical music.'

The heavy notes from the cello were starting to rattle the framed photo of his late wife, Steph. 'Turn it down, will you? I can't think with that row going on.'

She did so. 'The point is that it ties in neatly with the tooth tattoo.'

'Any kind of music would have tied in with that,' he said. 'The Stones, the Beatles.'

'Duke Ellington,' Halliwell said.

Ingeborg smiled. She had to admit that they were right. 'And now we know she had better taste than any of us.'

The computer image from Philadelphia appeared on Leaman's screen towards the end of the afternoon. Everyone got up for a look. Leaman rotated the face through several angles. This was definitely a young woman of Eastern appearance, with high cheekbones, a small cupid-bow mouth and widely spaced eyes topped by well-defined eyebrows. She had the fringe and fine head of hair Ingeborg had described.

'How do they know she wore lipstick?' one of the civilian computer operators said.

'They don't. It's a balance of probabilities,' Leaman said. 'Most Japanese women I've seen use make-up.'

'Wouldn't it be more useful to show her without any?'

'I don't see why. We're issuing this to help people recognise her.'

'The eyebrows are a bit thick.'

'They have to give her some, don't they? We told them she had a good growth of hair.'

Halliwell said, 'It seems to me a lot of this is guesswork.'

Leaman wasn't having that. 'Only the superficial stuff. The bone structure is entirely real.'

'But the fleshy bits can't be. How do we know her nose looked like that?'

'They choose from a bank of features. She's what's known as a Mongoloid type and that means small, flat noses. The Japanese were ahead of most other countries in making a data bank of soft tissues.'

'One thing we can all agree on,' Diamond said. 'This is easier on the eye than the photos taken at the autopsy. Back to work, people. I want a copy emailed to the Japanese embassy now and we'll go public with a press release tomorrow morning.' After the first buzz of interest was over, he said to Halliwell, 'What do you think, Keith? Will it help?'

'To me, it looks like everyone's idea of a Japanese woman. There's not much character you can pick out.'

'It's a proper face. Remember the photofit pictures we used to work with? Compared to this, they were like kids' drawings.'

'But is it reliable?'

'We'll find out. If it isn't, it could do more harm than good.'

He gave his attention to the press release. The tooth tattoo would be featured and so would the clothes the dead woman had been wearing. Until a definite connection was made with Green Park he couldn't mention the iPod and the interest in classical music. He seemed to have spent the best years of his career waiting for forensics to go through their painstaking procedures.

But there was a big plus. The printouts of the computerised face from several angles made a pleasing difference to the display board. He thought about sending copies upstairs to Georgina, but in the end decided to let well alone. With any luck the ACC would be dealing with her backlog of paper work after a week's absence.

That evening he got home to a string of messages on the answerphone. Normally he wouldn't have bothered to play them before supper. Most would be junk calls. He was tired of being told by some fruity voice sounding as if doing him a huge favour, 'This is a free message.' But after all this time he still had hopes of a call from Paloma.

Nothing.

He opened a pouch for the cat and a beer for himself. Put two large potatoes in the microwave. 'What shall I have with it this time, Raffles? Beans, egg or cheese, or all three?'

Paloma had been encouraging him to cut down on the calories and take more exercise. There was a reward system. To earn a pie, he'd had to take a two-mile walk, and she'd come along to make sure. Lately, he'd let himself go again. His ideal had been to look like Orson Welles in *The Third Man,* but he was in danger of ending up like the Welles of the sherry commercials. Did it matter? In his present mood, not a lot.

Baked beans, scrambled egg and grated Cheddar joined the potatoes on his plate.

One of those obsessive Swedish detectives was on the TV. He reached for his DVD of *Casablanca.*

More sensational news greeted him at the office next morning. The forensic lab had got through with an early finding. A hair Duckett's team had picked up at the Green Park river bank site matched the DNA of the drowned woman. All doubt was removed that this was where she had entered the water.

A turning point.

'We can forget about suicide or accident now, guv,' Ingeborg said. 'The heel marks prove she was dragged there and dropped in. You were so right to get us up and running.'

Keith Halliwell said, 'What are we suggesting here — that she was killed before she entered the water and this was the murderer's way of disposing of the body?'

'That's obvious, isn't it?' Ingeborg said.

'Then wouldn't the body have floated, rather than sinking? A person who drowns takes water into their lungs. That's why they go down. A corpse still has some air inside.'

John Leaman joined in with one of his erudite contributions. 'It's not as straightforward as that. Other factors come into it.

176

For one thing, it depends how the body enters the water. Face down, any air in the lungs and airways is trapped and will take time to disperse. But if it gets submerged on its back, the weight of the head bears down and there's more chance of water entering the nose and mouth. And anyway after a corpse has been several hours in the water the airways get filled passively and it will sink. Fresh water is less buoyant than the sea, so the process is quicker in a river.'

Diamond said, 'Where do you learn this stuff?'

'Don't you believe me?'

'Let's deal with what we know for certain. The body was rotting, so it must have been underwater for weeks. We now have a crime scene. With any luck, forensics will give us more information. But we know enough already to get headlines with the press release.'

'Are we going to use the computer image?' Halliwell asked.

'You sound doubtful.'

'I'm not convinced by the science.'

Leaman said at once, 'It's based on a scan.'

'Did you say scam?'

Diamond said, 'Silence in the ranks. The answer, Keith, is yes, I'm going to issue it to the media. A picture is worth a thousand words.'

'And if the picture is nothing like her?'

'There must be some resemblance.'

'May be.'

Ingeborg said, 'People don't expect a computer image to be perfect. There's news value in the fact that we're using this method. And when we finally do get a photo of the victim they'll want to compare it. So we get more publicity, a second bite at the cherry.'

'So speaks our ex-journo,' Diamond said.

Halliwell shrugged and was silent.

The Avon & Somerset sub-aqua team was sent to Green Park.

'Wouldn't it be wonderful if they found her handbag?' Ingeborg said.

'You're joking,' Halliwell said. 'If the killer takes the trouble to dump the body in the river, he's not going to dump her bag in the same place.'

'I was trying to be positive. You're getting as grouchy as the boss. Is it catching?'

Diamond's 11 A.M. press conference was well attended. The Manvers Street media relations manager, John Wigfull, presided. He and Diamond — old adversaries from way back — sat in front of a large projected image of the computerised face. Diamond read his prepared statement and invited questions. It all went well until someone asked about the music on the victim's iPod.

'Classical music, you said, superintendent. The murdered woman liked listening to string quartets, is that right?'

'You'll find a note of it in the release we handed out.'

'Would that be Haydn or Mozart?'

He hesitated. These smart-arse reporters were always trying to put the boot in. 'Beethoven, actually.'

'So you've listened to it. Are you a Beethoven expert, Mr. Diamond?'

'I wouldn't claim that, but I'm not a complete duffer.'

'So was it the Amadeus?'

'Trying to catch me with a trick question?' he said. 'That's Mozart.' He didn't add that he'd seen the film.

'The Amadeus Quartet. I thought every music-loving policeman would have heard of them.'

CID press conferences aren't renowned for laughs, so when they come they are appreciated.

Diamond still wasn't sure if he was being tricked. 'I was *stringing* you along,' he said, and got a satisfying groan for the pun. 'And

179

that's a good *note* on which to finish.'

He asked Paul Gilbert to drive him back to Green Park. Already the cameramen were there in force, lined up behind the tape getting shots of the underwater team in their scuba suits. From now on the press would be tracking every development.

Duckett, arms folded, watched him arrive. Neither needed to treat the other with much deference, and neither did. But to their credit Duckett's firm of crime scene investigators had been prompt this time in reporting the significance of the hair found at the scene.

'Any more discoveries?' Diamond asked after dipping under the 'do not pass' tape.

'Haven't they put you out to grass yet?' Duckett said.

'I was going to ask the same question, but come to think of it you look more at home up to your knees in mud.'

'It may look like mud to you, my friend, but it could be the piece of evidence that gets you off the hook.'

'So what else have you found, apart from the hair and the fibres?'

'We won't know until we get it cleaned up.'

'Have you worked out what happened?'

'You want it in a plate, don't you?' Duckett said. 'What do you do all day in that police station — watch the racing on TV? It's a pig of a scene, this one.'

'Always is.'

'Too many coppers have tramped through in their big boots. It's a wonder we found the hair.'

'Where was it?'

'Caught on a bramble, quite low down. If you really want to know what happened, I reckon she was dead or out to the world before she got here. There's no evidence of a struggle except dragging her to the bank and heaving her in. Have you seen the heel-marks?'

Diamond nodded. 'If she was dead already, would she have floated?'

'Not for long in the current. You see what it's like. She'd have got waterlogged.'

'And after she sank, wouldn't the flow of the river continue to move her along the bottom?'

'In this case it didn't. My opinion is that the body lodged against something deep down. You want to speak to your frogmen. All kinds of stuff gets tipped into the river over time. We're only a few hundred yards from Sainsbury's here. Nothing pleases the yobbos more than heaving trolleys in.'

'It's true the body didn't travel very far,' Diamond said. 'It was spotted at Lower Weston, three or four hundred yards away. But it had been submerged some weeks from the state of it.'

'It will have inflated, as they do, and the pressure finally lifted it clear. The absence of the corpse at the scene is a real pain for me. We're reduced to looking for traces. It's not good for my back.'

'Any traces of the killer?'

'You're an optimist. What do you expect — another hair? We'll examine everything we've got under the microscope and let you know, but I wouldn't hold your breath. Ninety percent of it is going to be rubbish blown across the park.'

'When do you reckon to finish?'

'In a couple of hours if people stop asking damn-fool questions.'

Diamond left him to it. To Paul Gilbert, he said, 'You wouldn't think we're his paymasters, would you, cocky bastard? He's not going to get work from anyone else.'

'He seems to know what he's talking about,' Gilbert said.

'He could say it in a more civil way. Now, I'd like your opinion. Come with me.' They left the crime scene and moved some distance from the press people. 'It's a park, right? You can't drive straight through it.'

'You might with a four-by-four.'

'The tyre tracks would be a giveaway. I haven't seen any. And you wouldn't get any kind of four-wheeled vehicle along the towpath. If you wanted to drop a body into the Avon, how would you get it here?'

'Carry it, I suppose.'

'Where from?'

'Your transport.'

He tried picturing someone burdened with a corpse, stumbling the hundred yards or more from where the road ended. 'You'd need to be strong.'

'She was quite small, guv.'

'True. But it would be easier with some kind of barrow.'

'A supermarket trolley?'

'Maybe, if there was one handy. And this would be done by night, I imagine. Anyway, the killer got her to the bank and dragged her down the last bit, leaving the heels trailing.'

'You'd need to, just to make sure of your footing,' Gilbert said. 'It can't be easy pitching a body into the river.'

'But still a good method of disposal. People are going to assume she fell in, or jumped. It's unlikely any of the killer's DNA will be recovered, even if some was trans-

183

ferred. And he's buying time. Worth the extra effort, wouldn't you say?'

They checked with the sub-aqua team before leaving. Nothing of interest had yet been found. Visibility was a problem and so was the force of the current. A few days of rain had brought extra water off the hills and may well have contributed to the freeing of the corpse from whatever had trapped it. Several days of searching beckoned and the team didn't hold out much hope of more discoveries.

'We got a few unfriendly looks, I thought,' Diamond said as Gilbert drove them back along Green Park Road. 'They volunteer for this work. It gets them out of the office. What do they expect? Diving for pennies in the hot baths?'

His mood improved in the incident room. The excitement was obvious.

'What's happened?'

'We've got a name. That's what's happened, guv,' Ingeborg said.

'Already? Someone recognised the computer image?'

'No,' said Halliwell. 'That's just confusing everyone. The embassy delivered.'

11

'Have you ever done the towpath walk, Mel?' Mrs. Carlyle asked while cooking his breakfast.

'The what?' He was never in the mood for small talk at this time of day and certainly not with his prying landlady.

'The towpath, by the river. You can go for miles. When I was younger, it was the romantic thing to do — if you had someone with you, of course. Mind you, the scenery loses its charm as you go on. Too many factories.'

'I expect so.'

'These eggs are ready now. I'll pop them on the plate with the bacon and tomato. You did say no to fried bread? It's a pity Tippi isn't down yet or I could have cooked hers at the same time. She used to be an early riser. Ever since you arrived she's taken to lying in bed of a morning.'

He didn't want to talk about Tippi's sleep

pattern, especially with her mother. He leaned back and allowed Mrs. Carlyle to put the plate in front of him.

She didn't go away. 'I think she doesn't want you to see her before she gets her face on.'

He shrugged. 'Thanks for this.'

And still she hovered over him. 'The reason I mentioned the towpath is because of something in the paper this morning. A poor young girl was pulled out of the river a few days ago and they seem to think she was murdered. They're appealing for witnesses who saw anything suspicious down at Green Park in the past eight weeks. She was Japanese.'

'Yes?' Spoken in a monotone, to emphasise his lack of interest.

'They know she was put in the river at Green Park because they found her iPod. And this is the part that will interest you. All the music on it was classical, like you play.'

'Classical can mean all sorts.'

'String quartets?'

Now his interest did quicken a little. 'Is that what it says she had on her iPod?'

'You can read it if you like.'

'It's not so remarkable,' he said. 'A lot of people like listening to chamber music.

Could I have my coffee topped up?'

'Need your caffeine, do you? Bad night?' She shuffled towards the kitchen area. 'Or heavy day coming up?

'They're all heavy. I'm learning a difficult piece.'

She returned far too quickly for Mel's liking with the cafetière and the *Daily Mail*. 'You might like to see it. Bath gets in the papers quite often, but unpleasant things like this are rare, thank the Lord.'

'Thanks,' he said, back to his denial of any interest, 'only I don't think I have the time right now.'

'Have a quick look at the picture anyway,' she said. 'One of those artists's impressions, I suppose you'd call it. You wouldn't want to see a dead person's face at breakfast time. I was thinking she could easily have been in the audience for one of your recitals.'

'If she was, I wouldn't have noticed,' Mel said. 'I have to give all my attention to the music.'

She was lingering again, her hand on the back of his chair. 'Or you could have seen her after, hanging about to get your autograph. I've heard that you're famous, you and the Stark Arty Quartet.'

'Staccati. The others may be well known, but I'm not. I'm a late arrival, filling in for someone who dropped out. Nobody wants my autograph.'

'Don't put yourself down, Mel. Plenty of young ladies are dewy-eyed about you when you're playing, I'll be bound.'

The face on the front of the paper lacked any personality. He turned it over and pretended to take an interest in the football. Mrs. Carlyle finally moved away. It crossed his mind that in future he might make a show of listening to his own iPod at breakfast. Would she take the hint? He couldn't depend on it.

The quartet was supposed to be rehearsing Schubert's *Death and the Maiden* at the Michael Tippett Centre, but Cat had phoned to say she had a bad headache and wouldn't be coming in.

Ivan was unforgiving. 'Women and headaches. That can mean anything. If I get a headache I take a painkiller. It's about loyalty to the rest of us. What are we supposed to do — practise our scales?'

Mel said, 'She must be in a bad way to miss a session. Shouldn't we give her the benefit of the doubt?'

Anthony spoke up. 'We can practise without her.'

Ivan shook his head. 'This of all pieces

requires the cello at the centre of things. It's the way it's arranged, with the rest of us responding to her variations. We'll be all at sea.'

'We can do the first variation. That's mine essentially.'

'A few bars and then what?' Ivan said. 'She becomes the soloist in the next. We can't work through it piecemeal, picking the sections that suit us.'

'Why not?' Anthony said in his uncompromising way.

'Because it will do more harm than good.'

'I can't think why.'

'We lose the flow, the unity, the tempo, that's why. It's not just a waste of our time. It's an insult to the composer. What do you say, Mel?'

After that, it was difficult to know what to say. 'I see the difficulty —'

'In that case, I'm not staying,' Anthony said. He slammed his violin into its case and was off like the bishop who woke up in a brothel.

Ivan sighed and said to Mel, 'I was about to suggest we looked for an alternative piece, something with less cello. He wouldn't have agreed. He can't deal with changes of plan.'

'Pity. We needed him. There isn't much

two of us can do.'

'He's a fine player — brilliant, in fact — but as a personality he can be impossible. Well, you just saw. I ought to be used to his ways by now. Cat handles him better than I do. And so did Harry when he was with us.'

'Did you know about this side of him when the quartet formed?'

'Not really. We were so impressed by his musicianship that we overlooked the signs of oddity in his personal dealings with us. You expect eccentricity among musicians and we forgave the occasional outburst.'

'Cat was telling me he doesn't have much of a life outside his music.'

'None at all that I'm aware of — which makes it so much more of a crisis each time anything upsets the arrangements. Shall we go for a coffee?'

In the months so far in Bath, Mel had not spent time alone with Ivan, apart from sharing taxis. He still felt in awe of him. Being told what to wear for that first meeting at the club in St James's had set the tone. A chat over coffee might be a chance to get to know the real Ivan.

Mel made an immediate try to get personal. 'This is my third this morning. All that caffeine. It starts off in my lodgings. Mrs. Carlyle, my landlady, wants to talk in the mornings and I don't. I get through more of this than I should.'

'Are you comfortable where you are?'

'No complaints on that score. How's your place?'

Ivan looked into his cup, taking a moment to decide whether he wanted to open up. 'Adequate. I wouldn't put it higher than that. They say they don't mind me practising, but when I do, they turn up the volume on the television. I can hear it in my room with the door closed.'

'A couple, are they?'

'Civil partners, I think, is the term.'

'Same sex?'

'Gay men, yes. I don't mind that. They keep the house in immaculate order. But they like to economise on the heating so the water is barely warm. I'm not looking forward to the winter.'

'I thought you'd be used to cold winters.'

'Outside, yes, but we were always warm inside. Old-fashioned brick-built Russian stoves are very efficient.'

'Where were you brought up — Moscow?'

'Odessa.'

'So you're Ukrainian now.'

'Always was,' Ivan said with a defiant tilt of the head.

'Not a bad place to be a string player.'

'The only place. Heifitz, the Oistrakhs, Zimbalist, Milstein.'

'What a line-up.'

'There are more I could name. It's a world-wide phenomenon. Do you know the story about Isaac Stern when President Kennedy made him responsible for intercultural exchanges with the Soviet Union? Someone said to Stern that it must be a difficult job. He said, "On the contrary, it's a piece of cake. They send us their violinists from Odessa and we send them our violinists from Odessa." '

An amusing story from Ivan? This was better than Mel could have wished for. 'You started early, no doubt?'

'Didn't we all?'

Mel nodded. He couldn't think of a top violinist who hadn't begun as a child.

Without any more prompting, Ivan launched into his story. 'I was giving recitals at ten years old. My parents were elderly and wanted to see me established as a musician, good enough to make my own way in the world when they passed on, so I mastered the basics early in life. I was accepted by the State Conservatory at fifteen, and there I learned about intonation and phrasing and so on. At seventeen I was playing in the Odessa Philharmonic. A year later I got

192

an audition for the Moscow Chamber Orchestra and was accepted.'

'Leaving your birthplace?'

'I'd already decided to escape from the Soviet system. It was all the things you hear, oppressive, rigid, without a heart. The music we were playing spoke of joy, freedom, spirit and didn't square with the life we were living. So I had this unstoppable urge to leave. To defect, I would need to get a trip abroad. Odessa was classed as a regional city by the State, which meant no orchestra from there was allowed to travel. You had to play in Moscow or Leningrad, as it was known, if you wanted to visit the west.'

'How old were you when you got out?'

'Barely twenty, but old enough to know what I was doing. This was in the mid-eighties. I was friendly with some of the top chess players. I play a good game, up to tournament standard. At that time chess players were defecting regularly and some of them told me how to go about it. The main thing was to get invited to the west as part of a larger unit.'

'Like the ballet stars who came over with the Kirov company?'

'I suppose, yes.' He didn't seem to like the comparison. 'Anyway, I would be well placed with the Moscow Chamber

193

Orchestra.'

'I can understand that. They have a terrific reputation.'

Ivan shrugged. 'More important to me, they often toured abroad. Six months after joining, I travelled with them to Frankfurt, gave the slip to our minders, got in a taxi and paid him over the odds to drive me to another town and stay silent. I asked for political asylum and never saw my parents again. This was 1987. They were dead before the wall came down.'

'That was hard.'

'Life was hard — then and for the next few years. I wasn't a name. I couldn't survive by playing my fiddle, but I had no other trade, so I worked as a hospital porter and mortuary attendant. These hands have performed tasks you wouldn't want to know about.'

'Better than working as a brickie. You wouldn't want to damage your fingers.'

'I would have earned more as a builder or a docker, it's true. You're right. I had to think of my hands.'

'And obviously you got back to playing?'

'I was always playing. Music is therapy. It nurtured my soul.' An extraordinary stillness came over Ivan.

Mel understood why.

'I kept my fiddle through the hard times and didn't change it until I was offered the use of a Strad — practising as often as I could and I also took on some teaching and ensemble work. If you have a talent and you don't neglect it, the opportunities come. I filled in with various ensembles across western Europe and eventually got to England and found an opening with the Bournemouth Symphony. A happy choice.'

'Have you been back to Odessa?'

'Once, with the quartet. I found it much changed, but the music is still of the highest quality. Do you know it?'

Mel shook his head. 'I haven't travelled much.'

'From now on, you will.'

'I still find it hard to believe you took me on.'

'It wasn't a snap decision. We heard a number of others.'

'Will Douglas be looking for more engagements for us?'

'Undoubtedly. He wanted to see if we got along together, if the chemistry was right.'

'It wasn't this morning.'

'Don't worry. We've come through worse. We can all be prima donnas on our day. It's when we're on tour and compelled to travel with each other and not speaking that things get difficult. But I suspect all quartets are like that. It's not as if we've promised to love, honour and obey. We happen to be stuck with each other like four prisoners in a cell.'

Mel grinned. 'I hadn't thought of it like that.'

'Now you know why I didn't want us sharing a house.'

'I guess respect is what we should aim for.'

'Exactly.'

Becoming more confident, Mel asked, 'You chose me for my musicianship alone, is that right? You didn't ask about my temperament.'

'Or if you're an axe murderer?' Ivan said without a flicker of amusement. 'No, we judged you on your playing, first and last, and we expect the same consideration from you.'

'You've got it.'

He added a sly postscript. 'Of course it will be inconvenient if you're picked up by the police.'

'You'll bail me out?'

This prompted a rare smile. 'If we're not in custody ourselves. You have no idea what we're capable of.'

Not a topic to explore, Mel thought. Ivan had mellowed in the last few minutes, but there were limits. 'Will Anthony come round, or does he want some kind of apology?'

'It will be as if nothing happened. An apology is needed and it should come from him, but he won't give one. We'll begin again when Cat is restored to her boisterous best. I hope *your* health is reliable.'

'Usually.'

'I haven't missed a rehearsal or a concert since the quartet was formed, so I feel I have a right to expect high standards of others.'

'What's your secret — vitamin pills?' Mel asked, keen to lighten the mood again.

'A balanced life. I still play chess, these days more on the internet than with a real person across the board, more's the pity. Do you play?'

'You wouldn't find me much of a challenge.'

'Plenty of musicians enjoy the game,' Ivan said. 'I expect you have a life outside music. I'm sure you do.'

Now that the focus switched to Mel, he became ill at ease himself. 'Nothing to speak of.'

'Women,' Ivan threw in. 'I've seen you eyeing up the students in short skirts. Have you dated any of them?'

With his chess-playing skill, Ivan had definitely taken the initiative. Mel felt as defensive as when Mrs. Carlyle was making barbed hints about what went on with her nubile daughter. 'I can't afford the time. I need hours of practice to keep up with you and the others.'

'Hasn't it occurred to you that we're all practising like fury and not telling each other?'

Mel wasn't sure if this was a heavy-handed attempt at humour. 'That would be a comfort.'

But Ivan was serious as usual. 'You may get the idea that because we played the repertoire many times before, we don't need the preparation you do, but you'd be wrong. I practise several hours each evening, however loudly my landlord turns up the volume. For me, the ideal time would be early in the morning, but they'd treat that as an act of war and I can see their point of view. Anthony does nothing else but practise, as we know, and I'm pretty certain Cat will be bowing her cello at this minute, even in the throes of a headache.'

'Thanks. I'll remember I'm not alone when I put in some hours tonight.'

Ivan became the abbot again. 'Don't get distracted by women.'

Mel felt himself blush, as much in annoyance as embarrassment. 'You're reading too much into a few glances at girls.'

'Some of whom come to one-to-one tutorials.'

'You're out of order now. I can honestly say there's nothing going on with any of my students.'

'Keep it that way, then.' Ivan hesitated, realising, possibly, that he needed to justify interfering. 'We don't know for sure if women were Harry's undoing, but they could have been.'

'In Budapest?'

'Budapest, New York, Tokyo. He was always getting out of contact with the rest of us.'

'But you've often said you respect each other's space.'

'Too much, in the case of Harry. He disappeared into a space none of us were aware of.'

'From all I've heard about Harry, he comes across as a likeable guy.'

'He was — or is, I suppose I'd better say. We valued his company as well as his playing.'

But not the playing away, Mel thought. 'As his replacement, I often find myself wondering what he was like. I don't even know his age. I may be wrong, but I get the impression he was one of my generation.'

'A few years your senior.'

'What was his musical background?'

'He started as a violinist, as most viola players do. Went to the Guildhall School of Music and found he preferred the darker tones of the viola. He was with the Birmingham Symphony Orchestra for a short time before joining a talented quartet based in Dublin. There were personality clashes, I believe. The Irish are an excitable nation. They broke up at about the time Cat and I were looking for an experienced violist.'

'Lucky you,' Mel said.

'It wasn't luck.'

'Nice timing, then.'

'As a musician, you should know that timing is ordered and I always make sure it is.'

'Like when you defected?'

'A perfect example. I planned my escape. You don't leave anything to luck when your freedom depends on it. And when it came to forming the Staccati, we were very deliberate.'

'It wouldn't surprise me if you triggered the break-up of the Irish quartet just to get Harry on board.'

Ivan lifted an eyebrow and said nothing. Mel had spoken in jest, but now he was in two minds. This man with his deep-set, unblinking gaze was starting to come across as willing to stop at nothing to get what he wanted from music.

Soon after, Ivan said he needed some time alone. He was giving a master class in the afternoon.

Mel had no students to teach for the rest of the day, so he phoned for a taxi. He rather hoped Tippi would be at the house. After all that pious stuff from Ivan about not letting women distract him he felt like a damn good screw.

He was in the glass-walled foyer looking out for his cab when a small private car came up the drive. A young blonde woman he didn't recognise got out and came inside. She was about ten years older than most students and didn't look as if she was arriving for a lunchtime concert.

She spoke first. 'Are you on the staff, by any chance?'

'Sort of,' Mel said. 'Can I help?'

'I'm police,' she said. 'Ingeborg Smith, Detective Sergeant.'

12

The dead woman was Mari Hitomi, a twenty-year-old from Yokohama. Her father, Kenji, the owner of a sushi bar on Lavender Hill, Clapham, had informed the embassy three days ago that she was missing, having believed for some weeks she was with friends. She should have come back to London at the weekend prior to catch a return flight to Japan. Mr. Hitomi's account of her movements and the tooth tattoo and the interest in classical music had made the identification convincing and a DNA test had confirmed it.

Peter Diamond took Paul Gilbert with him to South London, or, rather, ordered young Gilbert to drive him. Not much was said until they were a few minutes from Clapham. A potential problem was nagging at the big man's confidence. 'Do you eat Japanese food?' he finally asked.

'Why, guv? Do you think we'll be offered some?'

'They're polite people. It's an eating place, a good one, going by the reports.'

'Sushi's okay. I like it.'

'All of it?'

'I can't say I've tried everything.'

'The raw fish?'

'That's all right.'

'Good.' Diamond relaxed. 'If it's offered, I'll pass mine to you when he isn't looking. Between you and me, I prefer my fish cooked in batter.'

'With chips?'

'What else is there?'

With that off his mind, Diamond concentrated on the job. Interviewing a bereaved parent wasn't easy, but at least he didn't have to break the news. The embassy had already done that.

The sushi bar was near enough to Clapham Junction to have a thriving trade from commuters. Every seat was taken at the rotating counter and waitresses in red suits with black bow ties were steadily adding new offerings. Diamond's troubling prospect of questioning Mr. Hitomi over a plate of rice-coated suspicious objects was quickly dispelled.

'We get the hell outta here,' the slight,

silver-haired father of the victim suggested after they had introduced themselves and dipped their heads in response to his courteous bow. 'Better joint across street.'

The better joint was a dimly lit coffee shop without many customers. They carried their mugs upstairs and found a table that was reasonably private. 'Touch base here, no problem,' Mr. Hitomi said. His English sounded as if it was learned mainly from American movies, but the tough talk came in a subdued, husky tone that seemed to show he was still suffering from shock. He was wearing a black tie with a grey pinstripe suit.

'Is your wife here in Clapham?' Diamond asked, wanting to begin as painlessly as possible.

'Yokohama,' Hitomi said. 'Divorce, 2001.'

More of a conversation stopper. It required some sort of respectful response, but 'Ah, so,' wouldn't do. Dive in at the deep end, then. 'And your daughter . . . ?'

'Mari.'

'Was she living at home?'

'Yokohama, also.'

'So Mari was visiting you?'

'Two days only. Then to west country, to hang out with Japanese school buddies. Exeter University.'

'Exeter? But she was found in Bath.'

He nodded. 'Last week I call Exeter, speak to Japanese friends. Mari no show. No call, no text, no letter.'

'Did she say anything to you about visiting Bath?'

'She say zilch.'

'She wanted to be independent?'

'You bet. Independent.'

'We believe she died four to six weeks ago — a long time for you not to have heard from her. Was she in touch with you at all after leaving here?'

Hitomi raised the palm of his right hand in a sort of salute. 'You said it, chum, independent.'

Diamond wished he hadn't said it. Putting words into the mouths of witnesses wasn't good interviewing technique. 'Weren't you worried?'

'Eyeballs out running restaurant. Mari knew the score.'

'She could have texted. You both have phones, I'm sure.'

He gave a sad smile. 'Much to see, many joints to visit. Texting old man no big deal.'

'Joints to visit? Did she say which?'

Hitomi lifted his palm again, on the point of using that word a third time.

Diamond spoke first. 'She was a music

lover, I understand?'

'Check.'

'I mean serious music.'

'From her mother, graduate of famous Kunitachi Music College, Tokyo. Shit-hot violin player.'

'Mari played the violin?'

'Don't get me wrong, man. Mizuki, her mother. But Mari crazy for this music. Boy bands, bluegrass, hip-hop, no chance. Beethoven, Mozart, put it there.'

'I expect you heard there was classical music on the iPod that was found? String quartets.'

'Quartets, sure. Beethoven, Schubert, Haydn since she was a kid this high. Mizuki and me say you dig it, you go for it, babe. Western classical music ginormous in Japan. You seen her phone?'

'We didn't find her mobile, unfortunately.'

'Too bad you miss picture on front.'

Gilbert said to Diamond, 'He means the screen saver.'

'String quartet.'

'She had a quartet as her screen saver? What kind of phone did she have? Do you know which make?'

Hitomi shook his head.

'What was she carrying when she left you? Her clothes — were they in some kind of case or bag?'

'Backpack. Black canvas. Many badges.'

'She had badges attached to it? Places she'd visited?'

He nodded. 'And key-rings.' He made a space between his forefinger and thumb. 'Small violin, clarinet.'

'I understand. In pewter, probably. These were hanging from the backpack, right?'

'You got it.'

'We haven't found the bag. Did she leave anything at your home before going on her travels?'

'Some clothes for laundry. Your guys already took these off.'

'For the DNA testing. Do you have any idea why she would have gone to Bath instead of Exeter?'

This time Hitomi got the word in before Diamond could head it off. 'Independent.'

'She didn't mention friends in Bath, anybody she wanted to visit?'

He shook his head.

'Why Bath?' Diamond said. 'Any clues?'

'Famous place, well known in Japan.'

'She went there as a tourist, then?'

'Tourist, could be.'

'I'd like to ask you about Mari as a person. It may be difficult, even painful, to answer. These are things we need to know. Did she have a boyfriend?'

He rolled his eyes. 'In Yokohama, three, maybe four.'

'And in England?'

'Who knows?'

'If she met someone, was she the sort of girl who made friends easily? Do you understand me?'

'Shack up with guys?'

Diamond hadn't gone as far as that, but now it had been mentioned the answer would be good to get. He raised his eyebrows and waited.

'This is not something Japanese girl speak about to her old man,' Hitomi said and closed the door on that.

'But did she trust men?' Diamond asked, back to his line of enquiry. 'In a strange city, meeting a man for the first time, would she be on her guard?'

'Her guard? Who the hell you talking about?'

'It's an expression — "on her guard" — meaning careful.'

'You've lost me, buster.'

'Would she let a strange man buy her a drink?'

Hitomi pondered the matter. His hand tightened around his mug of coffee. Clearly he was under strain, trying to be frank and remain dignified. 'I guess is possible.'

'Get into his car? I'm trying to understand what happened. Her iPod was found on the river bank in a quiet place away from the city centre.'

'You telling me all this so I figure it must be so. Nobody told me how she died.'

'Because we aren't a hundred percent certain,' Diamond said. 'All we know for sure is that she was in the river still in her clothes. She may have been killed before this. We can't tell how, or why.'

'I'm reading you now.' Hitomi sighed and looked down, no doubt picturing the scene. He took another deep breath before going on. 'Mari is modern young woman, hot chick, twenty years old, straight out of college, degree in higher mathematics. As foreign visitor, in Bath for first time, no buddies, she feels lonesome. Some guy gets friendly, comes on to Mari. This I don't like one bit, but I understand.'

'Me, too,' Diamond said with a glance at Paul Gilbert, 'and all too easily. The unfortunate part is that the guy in question was a murdering bastard and she trusted him.'

'Come again,' the father said. 'Murdering bastard?'

'I was speaking to my colleague.'

Hitomi lowered his head. 'What kind of

jerk am I, not keeping tabs on my own daughter?'

Now Gilbert spoke up. 'Mr. Hitomi, do you by any chance have a picture of Mari?'

'Picture? You bet.' At once, an iPhone was produced. With a couple of touches on the display, Hitomi found not one photo, but a series that he let the phone show as a sequence. He passed it to Gilbert. 'Right here in London town.'

'This visit? That's brilliant.' Diamond was reminded that all the Japanese he'd ever seen were compulsive takers of photographs. He practically snatched the phone from Gilbert. 'Can you show me from the start?'

Hitomi leaned across and touched the screen again.

The shots were sharp and natural, a touching record of a happy young woman in the last hours she had spent with her father, starting with her emerging from the arrivals gate at Heathrow pushing a trolley containing the backpack decorated with badges. Then beside a silver car — presumably Hitomi's — and in the passenger seat. The next was at a front door that must have been his; and indoors at a table, teacup in hand. Several more showed her in the sushi bar, one with her father at her side. There were some street scenes on Lavender Hill,

Mari with arms outstretched, revelling in being in this new setting. The sequence ended at a mainline station that had to be Paddington. She was wearing the backpack and turning to wave as she walked towards a train, still smiling — a poignant final picture that moistened even Peter Diamond's eyes.

'These are just what we need. Can we get copies?'

Gilbert said, 'We can send them to Manvers Street right now if Mr. Hitomi agrees.'

'Did you hear that?' Diamond asked Hitomi. 'These pictures are precious to you, I'm sure, but they'll help us catch her killer. The only likeness we have isn't much of a likeness at all. Show it to him, Paul.'

Gilbert used his own phone to bring up the computer image and turn it through several angles. For all the work that had been done, it didn't bear much resemblance apart from the hairstyle. Comparison with the genuine images they had just examined was a harsh test. The only test more harsh was showing it to her own father.

'My Mari? You got to be joking,' he said, shaking his head.

'You see why your photos are so vital?' Diamond said. 'It's okay to use them, I hope?'

'Be my guest,' Hitomi said.

'In that case, we'll email them to Bath.'

'Sure. Go ahead.'

For all Diamond's battles with modern technology, he couldn't deny that it had simplified parts of his job — as long as someone else was there to press the right keys. Paul Gilbert made sure the complete set of digital images was sent to Bath. A text from Ingeborg with the one word *Magic* confirmed the transfer.

Hitomi's account of his daughter had been priceless information. Up to now he was the only person in Britain known for certain to have seen her. Other witnesses might yet see the photos and come forward, but there was no guarantee that they would.

For all the clichéd tough talk, Diamond could sense the pain this father was suffering, and warmed to him for bearing up so bravely. No question about it: Hitomi had loved his daughter and felt guilty for failing to keep tabs on her.

'I need to be clear about this. Did she know anyone in Britain apart from yourself and the Exeter friends?'

He shook his head.

'Had she visited you before?'

'Here in Britain? No.'

'So we have to assume she was killed by

someone she met here on this trip, or a total stranger. Difficult.'

'But with her picture you find witness, no problem, yes?' Hitomi said.

'We can hope. It won't be easy. But you've given us a chance we didn't have before.'

For the drive back, Diamond bought pasties from a shop further up Lavender Hill, confiding to Paul Gilbert that the smell was so appetising he had to get some, even though he knew there wouldn't be enough meat for his liking. 'I get caught each time. Sniff the cooking and can't pass the shop entrance. And then I regret it later.' He picked up a six-pack of beer for himself and some bottled water for Gilbert, explaining that they couldn't risk being breathalysed.

Not far along the M4, he opened the last tin and said, 'I feel a lot of sympathy for Mr. Hitomi. He was bearing it well, but suffering inside.'

'I expect his ex-wife is having a bad time, too,' Gilbert said. 'Must be worse, being so far away.'

'Tough. Very tough. But Hitomi wasn't just grieving. He felt responsible, guilty even.'

'He wasn't to know what was going to happen.'

'He'll always believe he should have stayed in touch, texting or phoning.'

'She was over twenty, guv. She wasn't a kid. And he was busy with his job. That sushi bar was really humming. It must take most of his time ordering supplies and checking on the kitchen and his waiting staff, taking reservations, being nice to his customers. All these things make a difference in the catering business.'

'But when the job takes you over completely and your nearest and dearest get pushed to the margins, you have to watch out. That's what I'm saying. A lesson for us all.'

Paul Gilbert drove on in silence as if doubtful what to say next.

He needn't have worried. Diamond was deep in thoughts of his own, about Paloma and the conversation on the towpath concerning his bottled-up emotions. Her plea — 'I thought I was a part of your private life' — still pained him. And so did the bust-up that had followed.

13

In the incident room next morning, the whiteboard display was strikingly improved by Kenji Hitomi's photographs of his daughter when alive. Everyone felt the investigation had moved on. The computer-generated images had been removed. Mari the victim didn't much resemble the woman painstakingly assembled in Philadelphia.

'Did they charge us yet?' Halliwell asked John Leaman. 'I don't think we should pay up.'

'Too late. It was fifty percent up front and the rest on receipt. Already went through the bank.'

'Demand a refund.'

'They had a clause to rule it out.'

'You signed an agreement? They'll have lawyers waiting to pounce.'

'Exactly.'

'So how much of our budget was wasted on this?'

'Don't ask. I haven't even told the guv'nor yet.'

'It's Georgina we need to worry about. She's looking for any excuse to downsize us.'

Diamond himself appeared soon after and called for silence. 'We're going public with these pictures of the victim. Someone in the city must have spotted her. She was here in Bath at least one day — the day she was killed.'

'Not necessarily, guv,' Leaman said in the irritating sing-song he used when he knew he was right.

'What do you mean?'

'She could have been murdered in Exeter and brought here by the killer and disposed of in the river.'

'She never reached Exeter.'

'We don't know that for certain. Her so-called friends told her father she didn't reach there, but one of them could have killed her and driven to Bath with the body. We ought to check the Exeter end.'

Diamond backtracked fast. 'You've got a point. Christ, what's the matter with me, not spotting that? The Exeter lot definitely have to be questioned. There could be some falling-out we haven't heard about.' He looked right and left for help, like a floundering swimmer. 'Paul, did we get their names from Mr. Hitomi?'

'He didn't actually name them, guv.'

'Get through to him now. No, better text him. We need the correct spelling.'

'Will do,' Gilbert took out his iPhone.

'Want me to call Exeter CID?' Halliwell asked.

'What — ask them to do the job? We'll handle this ourselves. Even if these friends are innocent as newborn babes it's possible they can tell us stuff about Mari her father doesn't know.'

Leaman couldn't resist rubbing in his small triumph over Diamond. 'Equally she could have been killed in some other place and brought here: Bristol, Swindon, Devizes —'

'All right. We get the drift.'

'Shouldn't we put out a countrywide alert?'

'That'll happen willy-nilly. The press are sure to go national on these pictures. They're quality photos and they tell a story. If she was seen in any place from here to John o'Groats we'll get to hear of it.'

'Better expect some mistaken sightings, then.'

'That's inevitable. I still favour Bath as the location — there was local knowledge at work — but we'll keep an open mind.'

'Why would she have come to Bath?'

'Why do thousands of tourists come every year? You're forgetting this city is known all over the world. Her father said he reckoned she came as a tourist.'

And now, with Diamond shown up once as fallible, Keith Halliwell pitched in. 'He could be wrong. She could have come for some other reason.'

'Such as?'

'Something she didn't want to tell her father about.'

'Go on.'

'Looking up an ex-boyfriend.'

'Japanese?'

'British, American, Japanese — who knows? Someone she knew in Yokohama who is now working or studying in Bath. Mari has set her heart on reviving the relationship. But it turns out he's living with someone else, may have a child as well. Mari is hurt and angry when she finds out.'

'Straight out of *Madame Butterfly,*' Leaman murmured, annoyed that someone had stolen his thunder.

Halliwell wasn't being put off. 'She threatens to tell the new partner about his past. They have a row, it gets violent and he kills her.'

'Quite a theory,' Diamond said.

'You did ask.'

'I'm grateful. And there could be some simple and obvious reason for coming to Bath that nobody has mentioned.'

'What's that?'

An interruption from Paul Gilbert saved him. 'Guv, Mr. Hitomi will be texting the names in the next few minutes.'

'Excellent. While we wait we can decide which of his pictures to release to the press.'

This didn't take long. They chose three: a close-up of Mari in Hitomi's house, a street picture with arms outstretched and the shot of her wearing the backpack looking over her shoulder at the camera.

The names of her friends came through soon afterwards: Taki Kihara and Mikio Nambu. Both were ex-pupils of Yokohama High School studying physics at Exeter University.

'Exeter.' Diamond turned to Ingeborg. 'How long would it take you to drive there — a couple of hours?'

'Probably less. Depends who's sitting beside me.'

Smiles all round. Diamond's dislike of high speeds was well known. Even he managed a twisted grin.

'Tee it up with the physics department.

We'll go this afternoon.' He continued dog-gedly with the briefing. 'One thing Mr. Hi-tomi confirmed is that Mari was into classi-cal music in a big way. We already knew there was Beethoven on the iPod. It now turns out that her mother in Yokohama is a violinist who studied to a high level at some music college in Tokyo.'

'Kunitachi,' Paul Gilbert said.

'Someone give him a Kleenex.'

'The Kunitachi College of Music. I made a note of it.'

Leaman took this as the cue to air more of his musical expertise. 'Suzuki trained.'

The only Suzuki Diamond had heard of was a motorbike and he wasn't being lured into admitting that. 'We'll take your word for it. The point is that Mari's mother taught her to love music and she was keen enough to have miniature musical instru-ments fixed to her backpack. I'm thinking it's possible she was here in Bath for some concert.'

'But we don't know when, so how can we tell?' Halliwell said.

'You want it on a plate. It's a possibility, that's all.'

'The music festival is always at the end of May,' Leaman said, 'but there are concerts of one sort or another all year round.'

'Ingeborg checked all the local music colleges for a missing Japanese student and came up with nothing,' Halliwell said.

'Get with it,' Diamond said with an opportunity to score. 'We're not looking for a missing student now. Mari wasn't living here. That wouldn't stop her looking up some Japanese friend in a music college. The music may be a huge red herring, but it keeps swimming into view.'

Diamond and Ingeborg got on the road after an early lunch. The Exeter University physics department had set up a meeting with Mari's two Japanese friends at 3.30 pm.

'It's a learning experience, this,' he said after they were on the M5 and he'd asked Ingeborg to stay in the slow lane. He believed conversation made the journey go just as quickly as belting along at dangerous speeds. 'Classical music and now physics. Quite a mental leap.'

'Einstein managed it,' Ingeborg said. 'He was a keen violinist.'

'You're starting to sound like John Leaman now.'

'In what way?'

'Trotting out facts. I'm not complaining. John's a useful guy on the team. He was right, saying we must investigate these Exeter friends. I don't know why I didn't think of it. Am I losing my grip?'

'You don't miss much, guv.'

'I'm not sleeping all that well.'

'Any reason?'

'Bit of a crisis in my personal life.' He stared at the back of his hand as if it didn't belong to him. 'You might as well know. I split up with Paloma.'

'Really?' She hesitated before saying with sympathy, 'That's tough.'

'My fault. I came out with one stupid remark too many. Any woman who takes me on is asking for trouble.'

'Would you like to make it up with her?'

'Don't know. We're proud people, both. She gave me an earful.'

'Pity if it's only words that came between you.'

'There's more — my attitude. I can't stop being the hard-nosed cop. She thinks I should lighten up when I'm off duty. I try. Obviously not enough.'

'It goes with the job.' Ingeborg said. 'We're never entirely off duty. We see something wrong and can't ignore it.'

'What started this? You mentioning Einstein, making me feel inferior.'

Ingeborg laughed. 'I'm no Einstein myself.

I failed physics and I can't read music.'

'Too bad. I was hoping you'd be discussing relativity with these undergraduates.'

'And in Japanese?'

'They must be reasonably fluent in English or they couldn't study here.'

'How do you want to deal with them — as a pair or singly?'

'Definitely one by one. Joint interviews don't work. There's always one loudmouth who dominates and it's sod's law that the quiet one has all the information.'

'And we're treating them as suspects?'

'We must. John Leaman could be right. They may have murdered her in Exeter and dumped the body in Bath as a blind.'

'They're supposed to be her friends.'

'They'd need a motive, yes, like some bad blood we've yet to find out about.'

Even in the slow lane, they reached Exeter ahead of schedule. The university complex north-west of the city was easy to locate. Finding a place to leave the car was more of a problem. 'There was a time when most students couldn't afford a motor,' Diamond said.

'It's now,' Ingeborg said. 'They just run up a bigger debt.'

At the physics department they were told

223

that the professor was off the campus all day, so they were given his office to use as an interview room.

'Chair of physics at Exeter will look good on my CV,' Diamond said as he tried the seat. 'Who's first up?'

'It seems to be decided,' the department secretary said. 'We asked them both to be here at the time you stated. Miss Kihara is waiting outside, but the man is late.'

'The *man*?'

'Mr. Nambu.'

'Funny. I assumed they were both female, being friends of Mari. Not obvious from the names.'

'Unless you're Japanese,' Ingeborg said.

'Ask Miss Kihara to step in, will you?'

The student was small and nervous, with powerful glasses that magnified her eyes into a permanent startled look. Being interviewed in the professor's office must have been daunting. She might have been more relaxed in the place Diamond had originally planned to use: the union bar.

'May we call you Taki?'

'Please do.' At once it was clear there would be no problem over the language.

'You knew Mari Hitomi, I believe, and you'll have heard the sad news of her death.'

'It's incredible. A horrible shock.'

'We spoke to her father and he understood she was planning to visit Exeter to see you and Mr. Nambu.'

'That's right. She called me after she arrived in London.'

'Did she fix the visit?'

'She didn't put a date on it. She was going to text us nearer the time. I said she was welcome to stay a few days if she wanted. She could sleep at my place. So we left it flexible.'

'And you didn't receive the text?'

'I wasn't worried. It was a casual arrangement and when weeks went by I thought she must have made other plans. The next thing I heard was when her father phoned. He seemed to believe she'd been coming straight to Exeter. He was very upset when I told him she wasn't with us.'

'It seems she planned a visit to Bath without telling him. Do you know if she had friends there?'

'Nobody I heard of. If they were friends from Yokohama, I'd know. We all keep in touch. There are three in Sheffield, two in Bangor, one in Cambridge.'

'Do you visit any of them yourself?'

She shook her head. 'It's too far on a bike. That's my transport.'

'You don't drive?'

'No.'

If this was true — and it was an instant response, spoken without sign of evasion — one crucial question was settled. She hadn't driven to Bath with a body in the back. 'You've known Mari a long time?'

'We went through school together in Yokohama.'

'What was she like?'

'Very good company. She was open and truthful. Laughed a lot. I was looking forward to seeing her again.'

'We need to get a picture of her as a personality, likes and dislikes, that kind of thing.'

'There was the music, of course,' Taki said. 'She was passionate about that. Serious music. She didn't have time for modern pop.'

'When you say passionate . . . ?'

'I mean it. She'd travel to concerts in other cities. Her bedroom was full of posters of famous musicians, just like some girls go crazy over rock stars. She had a really top-class sound system and hundreds of CDs. Music was her main thing when we were going through school.'

'Did she play an instrument?'

'I never heard that she did. Her mother was a professional violinist and maybe that put Mari off, thinking she could never live up to that standard. She could read music, I know that. She'd buy the score and follow it.'

'She studied maths, her father told me.'

'Sure, in Yokohama University. There's some kind of link between music and maths, isn't there?'

'Do you know if she had boyfriends?'

'I expect so. I haven't seen her for some time.'

'At school, I mean.'

'We all went out with boys. Mari was no exception.'

'Was Mikio a particular friend?'

'Of Mari's?' She blushed a little. 'You mean Mikio at this university? They were seeing each other at one time. You'd better ask him.'

'Are you and he . . . ?' Diamond asked, picking up on the blush.

'Absolutely not.' Her voice shook a little. 'Just because we went through school together it doesn't mean a thing. We happen to be studying in the same department in the same university, that's all.'

The charged quality in her response alerted Diamond. 'Is something the matter between you?'

'This has nothing to do with Mari.'

'But . . . ?'

'We don't get on now.'

'Is that why he wasn't sitting outside when we arrived? To avoid you?'

'It could be.'

'Have you spoken to him at all about Mari's death?'

'We don't speak.'

'But after her father phoned and was so distressed, didn't you ask Mikio if he'd heard from her?'

'No.' She was increasingly tight-lipped. And this interview had started so well.

'It's as serious as that, the rift between you? What's behind it, Taki?'

She dipped her head.

Diamond, at a loss, glanced to his left for assistance.

Ingeborg said to Taki in little more than a whisper, 'We need to know. It may seem personal to you, Taki, but we don't ask questions without a good reason.'

Without looking up, she said, 'My trouble with him has nothing to do with Mari.'

'You don't know,' Ingeborg said. 'It could be important. Did he try it on with you?'

After another long pause, Taki lifted her head and faced them, her eyes red-lidded and tearful. 'At the end of the summer term, he got me drunk. He wasn't dating me, or anything. We were with other students in a pub in the town and everyone was drinking. He kept filling my glass with cider. When I got up to go I was unsteady. I've never been drunk before. I couldn't stand up properly. Everyone except me seemed to think it was funny. Mikio said he'd take me back to my lodgings. He had to hold me up. I remember him at the house helping me upstairs. After that, it's a blank.'

'Do you think he took advantage?'

'I woke up at some time in the night feeling ill. I was alone in my bed and my head was hurting. I managed to get to the bathroom and threw up. Then I realised I was naked.' She twisted her fingers in an agitated way. 'I have no memory of undressing.'

'He stripped you,' Ingeborg said, making it more of a statement than a question. She was always alert to abuse of any sort.

'What else can I think?'

'Were you bruised? Sore? Do you think he raped you?'

'If he did, it wasn't obvious. I was too drunk to know. It's so humiliating. I can't believe I encouraged him, but even that is possible. You'd think I would have some memory of it, only I don't.'

'He could have added something to your drink.'

'I've thought about that. I simply don't know.'

'It happens. If it was just drink, you'd probably have some recollection. Is there any talk of guys here using the date-rape drug?'

'I haven't heard it mentioned.'

'As you say, you could be mistaken,' Ingeborg said, appearing to sense that her outrage was adding to Taki's distress. 'Maybe you undressed yourself. Where were your clothes?'

'On a chair.'

'That doesn't sound like a man intent on rape.'

Taki made a small movement with her shoulders that suggested she'd like to be persuaded, but wasn't. 'I didn't see him again until the new term started and then I was too embarrassed to speak to him. In fact, we haven't spoken since. What makes it worse is that some of the others who were with us in the pub still treat it as a joke.'

'How does he react when they tease you?'

'He doesn't say anything.'

'Does he have a reputation for sleeping around?'

'No. I've heard nothing like that.'

Diamond joined in again. 'Back in Japan, before you came here, what did the girls think of him?'

'Nothing special. He was just another guy.'

'Did you ever go out with him?'

'I don't think he was interested in me.'

'But you said he was interested in Mari.'

'I said they dated a few times. I doubt if it ever got serious.'

'When she spoke to you on the phone about coming to Exeter, did she speak about seeing Mikio as well?'

She gave a nod. 'It was kind of awkward. She asked if I saw him and I said yes because I do in lectures and she said it would be good for the three of us to meet and would I like to tell him she was coming. I didn't want to tell her what happened with Mikio, so I said a better idea was to wait until she arrived and maybe we could fix something then.'

'What did she say to that?'

'She misunderstood me. I must have sounded really cool about her plan, because she jumped to the idea I was dating him and didn't want her to come between us. I insisted that wasn't the case, but I don't know if she believed me.'

'So how did you leave the arrangement?'

'Like I said, we'd keep it loose. She was going to let me know by text when she was coming.'

'Is it possible she called Mikio herself?'

'I don't know.' Taki frowned. Then her eyes became huge behind the glasses as if an appalling scenario was surfacing in her brain. 'I guess it's possible.'

'Did she have his mobile number?'

'We all had contact numbers.'

'We'll ask him,' Diamond said. 'If you didn't tell him Mari was coming, how else would he have known?'

She still looked deeply troubled. 'What I said to you just now — about what happened to me last term — doesn't have to go any further, does it? I'm not accusing him.'

Ingeborg said, 'That's not up for investigation and even if it was, proving anything happened would be impossible so long after.'

'You won't mention it when you interview him?'

Diamond had let the exchange between the two women run on for long enough. Sympathy could only go so far. 'Mari was murdered. Nothing is off limits.'

Ingeborg softened the statement by adding, 'If it comes up, we'll be as discreet as possible.'

After Taki had left the room, Diamond said, 'What did I tell you about the quiet ones?'

'How do we know she's the quiet one?' Ingeborg said.

'We'll get his story presently. Did you believe her?'

'Why shouldn't I?'

'She was quick to tell us she doesn't drive and doesn't speak to the guy. We came here to find out if they combined to murder Mari. Everything this one said absolved her from any part in a possible crime. She told us in effect that if Mikio killed Mari and drove her to Bath, he acted alone.'

Ingeborg's eyes narrowed. 'Are you saying she made all this up?'

'I'm saying she's well and truly stitched up her old school buddy Mikio. Could be true, though. If he's a date rape specialist it's not impossible he drugged Mari and things didn't go to plan. Some of these drugs like ketamine are potentially lethal. He could have given her too much and had a body to dispose of.'

'Manslaughter. I hadn't thought of that.'

'The question is, had Taki?'

The department secretary arrived with tea and biscuits. Switching quickly to his amiable self, Diamond told her he could get used to the academic life. Nobody ever brought tea and biscuits to his office in CID.

'Perhaps you don't treat them right,' the

secretary said with a smile.

'I'm like a favourite uncle to them all,' he said, 'but it makes no difference.'

'Try getting tough, then.'

'Now there's an idea.'

Ingeborg was open-mouthed.

'Mr. Nambu is here now,' the secretary said.

'We'll see him.'

By student standards, Mikio Nambu was improbably well-groomed, in a navy polo shirt and white jeans. He looked as if he couldn't kill a fly, but so did many of the notorious rapists and killers in criminal history, Diamond reflected. As an investigator, you had to accept that wrongdoers aren't necessarily uglier or larger or less presentable than the rest of humanity. Juries were always disarmed by the ordinariness of the people put up before them.

'Sit down, Mr. Nambu. Sorry to take you from your studies. This shouldn't be long. We'll call you Mikio if you don't mind. Is that the way you say it?'

'Mickey will do.'

'We won't get too chummy.' He introduced himself and Ingeborg by rank and surname. 'Do you know why we're here?'

'It's about Mari Hitomi.' His English was at least the equal of Taki's.

'A friend from Yokohama, is that right?'

'She was, yes. I saw the TV news. It's difficult to believe.'

'Always is for the nearest and dearest. Would you call yourself one of Mari's nearest and dearest?'

He shifted in the chair. 'I don't know about that.'

'I'm trying to get a sense of your relationship. You must have dated her. Did you ever sleep with her?'

'We were schoolkids.'

'Is that a no?'

'A definite no.' He leaned back in the chair and said, 'I hope you're not trying to connect me with her murder.'

'You're a witness — or I think you are. She arrived in London and stayed for a short time with her father, who thought she was coming directly here to catch up with old friends from Yokohama — you and Taki Kihara. Did you hear from her?'

He paused. 'There was a text to say she was coming and would get in touch when she knew the date.'

'Is it still on your phone, this text?'

'Deleted. I don't keep everything.'

'When did you receive it?'

'At least two months ago, possibly longer.' He was hesitating before each response, as

235

if expecting a trap.

'And I suppose there's no way of telling if it was sent from London or Bath?'

'It's a mobile phone.'

'Right. So did you see her after the text arrived?'

'She didn't get here.'

'Let's not take anything for granted, Mikio. You don't know if she got here. You're telling me you didn't see her here, is that more accurate?'

'I suppose. I thought she was killed in Bath.'

'Her body was found there. It isn't certain she was killed there, unless you know something we don't.'

He blinked rapidly. 'I don't know what you mean.'

'Do you drive?'

'Yes.'

'Got a car, have you?'

'A Nissan Micra.'

Diamond exchanged a glance with Ingeborg. 'It crossed my mind that you could have arranged to meet her in Bath, in which case you could tell us what she was doing there.'

Mikio shook his head. 'I've never been to Bath.'

'Or some place nearby?'

236

The words came rapidly now. 'I didn't see her. I didn't speak to her on the phone. I received one text and that's all.'

'She could have come to Exeter as she promised,' Diamond said.

'If she did, I didn't see her.'

'Okay, don't panic, Mikio. Where do you keep your car?'

If anything was likely to panic him, it was more interest in his car. He swallowed hard. 'On the street outside my lodgings.'

'Is it there now?'

'Now? It's here on the campus.'

'So would you show it to us?'

They didn't have far to go. The physics department had its own parking area behind one of the labs. Mikio's Nissan Micra, a small, blue hatchback, stood only a few spaces from where Ingeborg had parked.

'I haven't washed it lately,' he said.

'It's all right,' Diamond told him. 'We're not thinking of buying it.'

They walked around the mud-spattered car. The back seat was covered with textbooks and file covers.

'There isn't much room for books where I live,' Mikio said.

'Open up, please.'

A sharp odour was apparent as soon as he unlocked the front door.

237

'What's that — disinfectant?'

'There was a smell I was trying to get rid of. Maybe I should have used something else.'

'What sort of smell?'

'Vomit.'

'Here in the front?'

'That's where it was.'

An insight into student life. Diamond glanced around the interior, which hadn't been cleaned for a considerable time. Forensics would have a field day here if they were ever asked to check it. 'Is the back open?'

Mikio took them around to the rear door. More books, up to a hundred probably, filled the boot space. Diamond sniffed and got the smell of books. Nothing else. This end of the car hadn't been disinfected.

'You can close it. We're done.'

Back in the office, Diamond resumed in a disarming way. 'Tell us what Mari was like when you were going out with her in Yokohama.'

Mikio frowned, still wary of being trapped. 'I already told you we were just schoolkids. Nothing happened.'

'You're on about sex, are you?' Diamond said. 'I'm interested more in her personality, but if you want to tell us what you got up to — or didn't — go ahead.'

A sharp breath. 'No. It's okay. There's nothing to say. Personality. What do you want to know? She was popular, good at her studies, especially maths. She lived with her mother in an apartment in one of the best buildings in Yokohama. It was big, well furnished.'

'You've seen inside, then?'

'Only the hallway and living room.'

'I believe her bedroom was quite a sight, filled with posters,' Diamond said.

More nervous blinking. 'I wouldn't know about that.'

'When you took her out, where did you go?'

'The movies, a couple of times. She didn't like clubs. They had the wrong sort of music. She was into serious stuff.'

'So we are finding out. Did you go to any concerts with her?'

'No, she liked to go alone. She spent all her pocket money travelling around to catch her favourite players. She had all the gigs on her iPad calendar and if I wanted a date I had to fit around them.'

'So did you take her drinking?'

'We were under age. Couldn't afford it, anyway.'

'Was she better off than you?'

'Definitely. She got an allowance from her

dad as well as her mother. But she spent most of it on the music.'

'Tough for you, being second best,' Diamond said. 'How do you make any headway with a girl like that? What did she drink — Coke?'

Mikio reddened. Plainly he saw where this was heading. 'Lemonade actually.'

'Lemonade doesn't have much of a kick.'

'It was her choice.'

'I expect she was drinking stronger stuff these days.'

He was quick to say, 'I wouldn't know. I didn't see her.'

'If she still drinks lemonade, there are ways of pepping it up, aren't there?' Diamond said. 'You know all about getting girls in the mood. Ecstasy, GHB, or whatever the latest is.'

Mikio snapped, his voice rising. 'Look, that's out of order.'

'I wasn't talking about your schooldays. We've moved on. It's a different world here. The girls drink as much as they want of whatever they want and sometimes things get added as well.'

Pushed to the limit, Mikio launched into a defence of his actions. 'Taki's been talking to you about me. If she told you I drugged her at the end of last term, it's a lie. I didn't add anything to her drink. I don't do drugs myself and I wouldn't dream of giving them to girls.'

'What happened, then?' Ingeborg said, fixing him with an uncompromising stare.

'Do you really need to know?'

She didn't answer and neither did Diamond.

'Okay.' Mikio gripped the chair arms. 'There was this end of term booze-up in a pub. We thought it was a laugh when she was getting giggly and I filled her glass to encourage her, but I didn't know she was legless. When it was obvious she couldn't stand properly I felt bloody mean and ashamed. The least I could do was see her home safely, so I drove her back to her place. It wasn't what you're thinking. She threw up in my car. I got her to the house and helped her upstairs. If she told you I did anything else, I didn't. She had vomit down her front. Would you fancy anyone in that state? I opened the door and guided her in and she sat on the edge of her bed and pulled off the smelly top and started unfixing her bra. I decided I'd done my duty and ought to leave fast, so I did. We haven't spoken since.'

The words had come so rapidly and with such strong recollection Diamond found them convincing. None of it sounded rehearsed. 'Did you put disinfectant in the car to take down the smell?'

Mikio needed a few seconds to get over his statement. 'I've given it several goes. Air freshener isn't enough.'

Diamond was ready to move on, whatever Ingeborg had decided. 'What happened between you two isn't my concern unless it touches on the death of Mari. Let's get back to when you were dating her in Yokohama. How did it end? Did you have a row?'

The young man's eyes rolled upwards. 'How did it end? It didn't really. There was never much to it. We stopped seeing each other, but we stayed friends, or she wouldn't have asked to see me on this visit. I couldn't compete with the musicians she idolised, and that's all there is to it.'

'Did she name any of them?'

'I don't remember any names. It was groups mostly, like any pop band, only classical. And you might say she was like any groupie, dead nuts about them.'

'Is that what you really mean?' Ingeborg asked, her feminism challenged yet again. 'A groupie? That's something more than idolising them. It means she was willing to sleep with them.'

'Sorry. I shouldn't have used the word,' he

242

said, on the retreat. 'It's unfair now she's dead. I don't know what was in her mind. The music thing was all a bit obsessive, but that's a stage teenagers go through, isn't it?'

'Who were the groups she liked?'

'They didn't mean much to me.'

'The Staccati?'

He shrugged. 'Don't know.'

'Where did that come from?' Diamond asked Ingeborg.

'Tell you later,' she said. 'But I think we should speak to Taki again before we leave.'

They let Mikio return to his studies. He was out of that office as if a fuse had been lit.

'What did you make of him?' Diamond asked Ingeborg. 'Is this a Japanese crime?'

'If it is, we need to know a lot more about the motive,' she said. 'I was all ready to pin it on him after listening to Taki and how he treated her, but I thought he came across as honest. Jumpy, but truthful.'

Diamond murmured in agreement. 'And the smell of disinfectant in the car definitely came from the floor in front of the passenger seat, which backs his story. When he first opened the door I thought maybe he'd had a corpse in there and tried to clean up, but you wouldn't stick a corpse beside you in the front. The boot area was free of the smell.'

'And he needn't have shown us the car,' Ingeborg said. 'He could have said it was at the other end of the campus.'

Diamond surprised Ingeborg by suggesting she alone should do the follow-up interview with Taki. 'She'll respond better to you. In kindness you should tell her Mikio's version of what happened the night she got drunk. If she's alone with you and more relaxed she may recall something of real importance.'

On the drive back to Bath, he said, 'Well?'

'Well what, guv?'

'Well, you're looking pleased with yourself. How did it go?'

'It was rather sweet. She wept a few tears, but they were tears of relief. She's given herself a hard time these last few months imagining what happened. I think they'll be back on speaking terms soon.'

'And did you get any more from her?'

Ingeborg smiled. 'I did. I asked about the musicians Mari was keen on. We'd talked earlier about the posters in her room, but we didn't get down to names.'

'We asked Mikio and he couldn't remember any.'

'Taki did. She said there was one string quartet that stood out and it was called the Staccati.'

'The name you brought up earlier?'

'Yes — because they're based in Bath.'

'Really?' He turned to look at her, eyes gleaming. 'How do you know about that?'

She played casual. 'Who's been doing the rounds of all the music colleges? I heard the name and remembered it and what's more I've met one of the players.'

14

The four were united again for the next rehearsal at the Michael Tippett Centre. As if to compensate for the day before, they had a spat-free session, rounding off with an hour's bar-by-bar dissection of the *'Grosse Fuge'* and then a run-through.

'The best yet,' Ivan said, resting his instrument on its case. 'We can all improve our intonation, but that will come. Some of your playing was exquisite, Mel.'

'Thanks.'

'Some of it?' Cat said, laughing. 'Good in parts like the curate's egg?'

'I didn't mean that,' Ivan said.

'He can take a joke.' She turned to Mel. 'I liked your sound, too, sunshine, and Anthony won't say a word, but he was quietly purring at those last Arpeggios.'

'Do we have a date for this recording?' Mel asked, to steer the attention away from himself.

'That's up to us,' Ivan said. 'We're not ready yet.'

'The recording studio has its own terrors,' Cat said. 'Personally, I prefer performing in front of an audience.'

'Don't we all?' Ivan said. 'I always find I can bring out something extra.'

'Is that one of your Ukrainian customs, bringing out something extra?' Cat said. 'Do that in public here, comrade, and you'll get arrested.'

Ivan clicked his tongue. 'Isn't it possible to say anything serious in present company?'

Anthony stood up and packed his violin away, indifferent to the banter as usual.

Cat said to him, 'Your turn to share a taxi with me and my cello, right? I'll phone for one now. Want me to order a second one, guys?'

Ivan said he was staying on to teach a student, but Mel said he was ready to leave.

When they reached the foyer only a few minutes later, a cab was already outside.

'Can't be ours,' Cat said. 'It's too quick.'

'I'll check,' Mel said.

The driver lowered his window and when Mel asked who he was waiting for, he said, 'Mr. Farran.'

'That's me,' Mel said, surprised. 'Is the other cab on its way?'

'I wouldn't know, mate. I was asked to pick up Mr. Farran, the viola player.'

'Fair enough.' He gestured through the window to the others that he'd got lucky.

It all happened so fast that the taxi was zooming along the road to Bath before he realised he hadn't given his address. He must have used this driver before, he decided. Often at the end of a rehearsal he felt so wrung out that he wouldn't have recognised his own father in the driver's seat. They were heading in the right direction, so he relaxed and thought about his plans for the rest of the day. He'd need to fit in more practice. In spite of the praise from the others, he knew Ivan was right. His intonation — accuracy of pitch — could be improved. With such latitude possible in their creation of sound, string players had a huge advantage over anyone else in an orchestra, yet there were phases, say in a long legato line with open strings, when the pitch should be suppressed. He'd noted a couple of passages in the Beethoven when he needed to adapt better to the violins. Ivan would certainly speak up if there wasn't an adjustment next time they practised.

The taxi forked left at Park Lane, heading directly north past Royal Victoria Park — an odd decision considering Mel's lodgings were in Forester Road, north-east of the city. Cab drivers were a law unto themselves, so Mel didn't question the route. Maybe the man knew about some obstruction along the way. Or maybe he was putting another half-mile on the clock. If so, it didn't worry Mel, as all the fares went on the quartet's account and were settled by their agent, Doug.

But when they slowed to a crawl for no obvious reason he tapped on the glass. 'Hey, this isn't where I live.'

'All right, mate. It's under control. I'm picking up another fare.'

'What?'

'Just ahead. Your lucky day, by the look of her.'

A woman was waiting opposite the entrance to the Botanic Garden, hand raised for the taxi to stop. People sometimes shared when cabs were in short supply at the station, but this woman was behaving as if she was hailing an empty one. Mel was on the point of objecting before he saw what a dream she was. She could have stepped off the style pages of a weekend magazine. Blonde, in a short white leather skirt and black top, she was smiling as if she knew exactly who Mel was, even though he was sure he'd never met her. She wasn't in any way forgettable.

Mel was a ladies' man. Any lingering thoughts of protest went out of the cab door when it opened and a tidal wave of cleavage almost engulfed him.

'I'm Olga and you must be Mel.'

Distracted, he almost forgot to move his viola case from the seat beside him. 'How do you know my name?'

'Relax. It's all good news if you're up for it.'

'Up for what?'

She laughed. 'Wait and see. It seems a bit cloak and dagger, but from now it's champagne all the way.'

The taxi was already speeding along Weston Road. Mel had abandoned all thoughts of objecting to the extra passenger.

'Heavy practice this morning?' Olga asked. This close, her perfume was overpowering.

'I'm used to it.'

'But you're new to the quartet.'

'Newish. You seem to know a lot.'

'Only the essentials.'

'Where are we going?'

'The Royal Crescent Hotel.'

The taxi took the turn to Marlborough Buildings and was soon rattling over the cobbles in front of Bath's best known thirty houses, a five-hundred foot semi-elliptical terrace faced with Ionic columns. The crescent's position, high above the park with views across lawns and trees to the city, was intrinsic to its glory. Three months into his stay in Bath, Mel hadn't been here before. He was awed.

The famous hotel occupied the space for two houses at the centre, fitting unobtrusively into the architecture. From a distance the only way you could tell it wasn't private dwellings was a pair of ornamental trees in tubs either side of the entrance.

A doorman in dark blue livery stepped forward and opened the cab.

Mel was in such a state that he almost forgot to reach for his viola, an unthinkable oversight ever since he'd been mugged that time in London. He snatched it up and stepped out.

In the front hall, it became obvious Olga knew where to go when she crossed the chequered floor to the staircase. Mel followed his new companion up the stairs as if her undulating bottom had hypnotic powers. Powers of some sort, for sure. Whatever she planned next he was unlikely to object.

The doors along the first floor corridor had the names of well known former residents of Bath. Olga stopped outside the John Wood suite.

251

'We have the use of this for the afternoon.'

Which beat working on the Beethoven, he decided.

She opened the door.

The suite was spacious and honey-coloured, with a padded sofa and armchairs at the centre and walnut furniture. The windows facing the front were elegantly pelmeted and draped in a gold fabric. To the left, discreetly recessed behind a white wooden balustrade, was a kingsize bed.

At full stretch on it was a man.

Mel came to an abrupt halt. A threesome wasn't in his thoughts, and certainly not a threesome in this combination.

Olga said, 'Mel, this is Mr. Hamada. He doesn't speak much English so I'll need to translate.'

'That won't be necessary,' Mel said. 'You've got the wrong idea about me. I'm leaving.' He turned towards the door.

'No, please be reasonable.' She put her hand on his arm.

Something sharp but unintelligible was said from across the room. Mel glanced back.

Mr. Hamada had sat up and removed himself from the bed. He was fully dressed in an expensive-looking suit. He stepped over the little balustrade, bowed solemnly and spoke some words in his own language.

Mel reached for the door handle.

Olga said, 'Wait.'

There was such unexpected force in her voice that he froze.

She went on with more moderation, 'Mr. Hamada apologises for all the inconvenience, the secretive way you were brought here. As a passionate lover of music he has been looking forward to meeting you.'

Mel hadn't supposed this was about music, even though he was holding his viola in its case. After some hesitation he clasped the hand that was offered. Hamada had a strong grip. He was a short man, made shorter because he was in his socks. Mel guessed he was around thirty-five.

'He has a musical matter to discuss with you,' Olga went on, 'but join us first in a drink.'

The bottle was waiting on ice in a silver cooler. The strong grip made short work of the cork. A flute of champagne was placed in Mel's right hand.

'You don't have to hold on to your viola. You're with friends here,' Olga said.

'I won't be staying long.'

Hamada said something to Olga and she said, 'He's asking if he might see your instrument.'

'No chance.'

'He is very knowledgeable about them.'

'Then it won't interest him. It's nothing special.'

'But it plays well, obviously.'

'I'm comfortable with it.'

'Please allow him to see it. He's not fooling. He's a true connoisseur.'

'I don't care what he is. I was brought here under false pretences.'

'Believe me, Mel,' she said. 'It's very much in your interest to cooperate. This could be your lucky day.'

'That's what the taxi driver said before you got in. If this is luck, it's not what I expected.'

She smiled. 'You expected to be here alone with me? That was a little game and I'm sorry. Mr. Hamada is my employer. He has a wife and children. He came to Bath and reserved the suite specially to meet you.'

'I can't think why.'

'Please indulge him. I'll hold your glass.' She must have noted the subtle softening of his protest.

Mel sighed. 'He won't think anything of this.' He unfastened his case, removed the viola and handed it to Hamada, who gripped it by the neck and ran his hand lightly across the soundboard. Then he held it horizontally and examined the rib and the purfling along the edges. He studied the dark wood of the underside before speaking again to Olga.

'He says it's of English manufacture, early twentieth century.'

'He's right about that.'

Mel then heard Hamada say, 'William Hill.'

'Spot on,' Mel said in surprise. 'You do know your stuff.'

Saying you possessed a Hill viola could be embarrassing even among musicians if they weren't specialists in stringed instruments. The name didn't have the cachet of the great Italian instrument makers. Yet William E. Hill of Bond Street produced violins and violas of exceptional quality for fifty years as well as restoring a number of Stradivari instruments.

Nodding his approval, Hamada handed the viola back and spoke more words in Japanese.

'He's asking if you would be so good as to play something,' Olga said.

'I don't think so.'

'Please don't refuse. Just a few bars, to give him the measure of the instrument.'

With reluctance, Mel took the bow from his case, tuned the strings, and played the opening bars of Bach's Chaconne from the Suite in D minor, but a fifth lower, in G minor. Just a snatch of the entire piece was sufficient to demonstrate the timbre of his viola.

Hamada nodded in approval and spoke again. Mel was getting the impression that this little man had a better understanding of English than he was letting on. The translation process kept him at a distance.

'He compliments you on the sound of the instrument and the choice of piece,' Olga said. 'He says he doesn't associate Bach with the viola.'

'It was written for solo violin,' Mel said, 'and transposed by Lionel Tertis, the English master.'

Hamada nodded at the name and spoke some more.

'He says Tertis, more than anyone in the world, raised the status of the viola. He played on an eighteenth century instrument of exceptional quality.' She turned to Hamada to confirm the name.

'Montagnana.'

A distinguished, but lesser known maker. Mel couldn't any longer deny that the man was knowledgeable. 'I wish I'd heard Tertis play. He lived to a great age, but he was before my time.'

Olga was translating for them both with apparent ease. She'd lured Mel here, but he still found her attractive. His playing of the Bach had been aimed more at her than her employer.

'Mr. Hamada says when Tertis because of infirmity could no longer play to the standard he set for himself, he presented his precious viola to his pupil, Bernard Shore.'

'I didn't know that. How generous.'

This time Hamada didn't wait for a translation of Mel's response. He crossed the room to the wardrobe, opened the door and took a bulky object from the top shelf — an instrument case. He brought this to the middle of the room, placed it on the sofa and unzipped it. The case was modern, but the instrument inside was not. It was of viola length, at least the size of his own, but of lighter, thinly varnished wood, almost apricot in colour, obviously antique.

'So is he a player?' Mel asked Olga.

'A collector. What do you think?'

'It looks special.'

Hamada lifted out the viola and handed it to Mel.

The weight was lighter than his own fiddle.

Olga said, 'He is inviting you to play the Bach piece again, using his instrument.'

Not unreasonable, Mel thought. If you own a fiddle, you want to hear it. Aside from that, he was curious to try it himself. He liked the feel. Now that it was in his hands he could tell it was a fraction longer than his own, but about the same weight. He ran his fingertips along the board. Using his own bow, he began the tuning process. Then he started playing another excerpt from the Chaconne.

The projecting power was a revelation, the depth and fullness of tone a joy. He knew at once that this was an experience to be savoured, so he continued moving through the daunting multiple stops of Bach's composition for longer than he intended.

Hamada's serious look had been supplanted by open-mouthed admiration. And when Mel finally lifted the bow away, Hamada clapped and said, 'Bravo.'

His pulse racing from the experience, Mel did his best to appear calm. 'Who is the maker?'

Olga asked the question, listened to the response, turned to Mel and didn't give an answer. Instead she said, 'If you would be so kind, he would love to hear you play some more. We both would.'

No hardship. Mel launched into Kreisler's arrangement of a Tartini fugue written for piano and viola, yet possible to perform as a solo. He gave them the complete piece.

'Now may I know the history of this instrument?' he asked after finishing.

For the second time, Olga put the question to Hamada.

Mel listened keenly to the answer and wondered if he could believe his ears, or had confused the sounds.

Olga translated for him and confirmed the name of the maker. 'It's an Amati, from 1625.'

'Christ Almighty — I thought it was special.'

Four generations of the Amati family of Cremona were making stringed instruments from at least 1560. Nicolò Amati was said to have taught the craft to Antonio Stradivari and Andrea Guarneri. Amati violas were particularly prized because of their rarity compared with violins. Mel had heard of a 1613 Amati selling at auction for half a million pounds.

With reverence he replaced the instrument in its case. 'That was an experience I wouldn't have missed.'

Olga's eyes shone with amusement. 'Twenty minutes ago you were ready to walk out of here.'

'I had no idea what was coming. Any

259

musician worthy of the name would kill to play a fiddle of that quality.'

'I hope not. We don't want bloodshed.'

'Mr. Hamada must be a very rich man as well as a connoisseur.'

'He's both.'

'May I ask what his business is?'

'Shipping, mainly, but he has other companies as well. Your glass is empty.'

'My head is spinning and it isn't the champagne.'

Hamada took this as the cue to refill Mel's glass. He started speaking to Olga and it lasted some time.

She turned to Mel. 'He admires your playing. He says a great instrument needs to be played by a top musician. He arranged for you to come here because he wanted to hear the Amati played by an expert. Now he is certain you must have it.'

'Have it?'

'On permanent loan.'

Mel felt the hairs straighten on his skin. 'That's incredible.' He knew millionaire patrons occasionally presented precious instruments to musicians. This was how rising artists came to play some of the finest fiddles in existence. He'd never imagined such an opportunity would come his way.

'How does Mr. Hamada know about me?'

'He knew you joined the Staccati Quartet. They are respected throughout the world. They wouldn't play with an inferior artist. The instrument is insured, of course, and so well known to connoisseurs that it could not be stolen and sold on for anything like its true value, but he will expect you to take great care of it.'

'I'm still coming to terms with this,' Mel said. 'He's suggesting I take it away today?'

'This was always his intention. Stringed instruments are not meant to be kept in glass cases. If they are not played regularly they can deteriorate.'

'Believe me, this will be played every day if it's in my care,' Mel said.

A smile as thin as a stray horsehair briefly settled on Hamada's lips.

'Of course he reserves the right to reclaim it at any time,' Olga said, and she was speaking without any obvious prompting from her employer. 'But his view is that an instrument of such quality should be played, and by a leading player.'

'What am I supposed to do — sign an agreement?'

She shook her head. 'Mr. Hamada's view is that even if you broke an agreement and failed to return the Amati, nothing you possess could compensate him. He is not interested in financial compensation. This must be a pact of honour. On your side, to value the instrument and play it to its capacity. On his side, to make it available to you free of charge, to treasure and maintain in good condition.'

'That will be my privilege and pleasure.'

'And one more thing must be observed,' she said, still without obvious reference to Hamada. 'The loan is confidential. He doesn't like it known that he collects instruments or makes them available to top musicians. That's why this meeting was arranged in secrecy.'

Mel immediately foresaw a problem. 'Look, the other members of my quartet are sure to notice when I turn up with a new instrument and they'll see at once that it's very special.'

'You can admit that you have it on loan. I dare say you would find if you asked that theirs are not their own. But you are not to tell anyone that Mr. Hamada is the owner. He would take that as a breach of faith.'

'Understood. May I take it to rehearsals — or is it just to be used in the concert hall?'

'I'll ask him.' After more consultation she said, 'He says play on this viola and no other. Put in as many hours as you can. It can take several weeks to adjust to a new instrument.'

'I know that from experience.'

'And in addition the rehearsal process must require you to use the same instrument so that the other players can blend with your sound. Does that make sense musically?'

'Perfect sense. I wanted to get the ground rules clear, so to speak. How will I stay in touch with you? Is there a contact number? Do you have a card, or something?'

'Mr. Hamada will know where the quartet performs and practises. From time to time you may see him in the audience. Should it ever become necessary, we'll contact you.'

'Is there any time limit on this arrangement?'

'None — for as long as you and he stay alive.'

'We look to be about the same age.'

'Stay fit, then.' She added with a long, level look. 'I believe he will.'

Mel faced Hamada again and gave a bow that would not have disgraced a Japanese ambassador. It was the best he could think of to demonstrate his thanks.

The same taxi was waiting in front of the hotel with the door open when Mel emerged carrying the two violas. In his state of unimaginable euphoria he climbed in. He continued to grip the handles, even when seated. He wouldn't dare believe he possessed an Amati until he got the little darling home, took it from its case and played something.

The taxi started over the cobbles.

'I haven't told you where we're going,' he said to the driver.

'It's all right, mate. They know where you live.'

Just for a second it was if a cloud passed across the sun, but he didn't let it trouble him.

15

'The Staccati String Quartet.'

The team stared at their boss as if he'd forgotten to dress. Peter Diamond as a classical music buff was hard to swallow.

'Come on. We already know the murdered woman, Mari Hitomi, was wild about music, and we're not talking reggae and rap. This is the serious stuff that goes on in concert halls. Ever heard of the *Nuns' Chorus,* DC Gilbert?'

'Sorry, guv.'

'This will be an education for some of you.'

John Leaman said, 'The *Nuns' Chorus* as a string quartet will be an education for us all.'

Diamond ignored the sarcasm. 'One of Mari's close friends called her a classical music groupie. I didn't know such things existed, but apparently they do — young girls as devoted to nerdy guys in white tie and tails as most kids are to their pop idols. Mari had posters of this string quartet in her bedroom in Yokohama. And for the past two months the Staccati have been resident in Bath.'

'Teaching and performing at the university,' Ingeborg added.

'I'm surprised you're all looking so open-mouthed,' Diamond said. 'They're world famous. This is the breakthrough, the reason the victim came here. Sergeant Smith will now give us her take on the quartet.'

Ingeborg unfurled a poster and pinned it to the board. 'The Staccati have been performing all over the world for at least fifteen years and this could easily be one of the posters Mari had in her room. To be accurate, only three of these people are currently in the quartet. They changed their viola player recently. We'll get a picture of the new guy soon.'

'Are we treating professional musicians as murder suspects?' John Leaman asked.

'Because they can read music it doesn't make them saints,' Keith Halliwell said. The tension between these two never entirely went away.

'Hold on,' Diamond said. 'All we can say for sure is that the string quartet looks like being the reason Mari came to Bath. She was a fan, so she must have known they were based here. Who killed her and why is another question.'

As if she hadn't been interrupted, Ingeborg said, 'I met the new viola player while I was doorstepping the colleges of music. He's a Brit, thirtyish, friendly enough. We didn't talk long, but he showed me where the quartet do their rehearsals out at the Michael Tippett Centre.'

'Michael who?' Halliwell said.

'Only one of the greatest British composers of the twentieth century,' Leaman said to the rest of the room.

'He lived in Corsham and was a strong supporter of university music,' Ingeborg said. 'But I was telling you about the quartet. They teach a series of master classes and in return for a six-month residency give regular concerts.'

'How regular?' Diamond said.

'Every two weeks.'

'Not bad if you can get it,' Gilbert said.

'It's not a cushy number,' Ingeborg said. 'There are hours and hours of rehearsing. They've got a reputation to keep up.'

'Who are they?'

She tapped the poster. 'The bald guy on the left is the first violinist, Ivan Bogdanov, a Ukrainian and one of the founder members. Lived in the west since he was a young man. Learned his music in the old Soviet Union and played with the Moscow Chamber Orchestra until he decided to defect.'

'And the others?'

'The second violin is Anthony Metcalf, from South Africa originally. There isn't a lot on the internet about him, except he joined about seven years ago and fitted seamlessly into the quartet. A very gifted violinist apparently. Their website suggests he's the quiet one. The guy to the right of him is Harry Cornell, the one they replaced, so we can forget him.'

'When did he quit?' Halliwell asked.

'About four years ago, I gather,' Ingeborg said. 'He was their viola player. They tried a number of replacements, but none of them cut the mustard until Mel Farran came along this summer.'

'The large woman with the cello?'

'Cat Kinsella, said to be among the best in the world and with several recordings of cello concertos to her credit, but prefers ensemble playing to the life of a soloist. She's the other original member of the quartet along with Bogdanov.'

'Those are the players, then,' Diamond summed up, wanting to move on. 'A mix of talented people who make very good music.

268

They've got a strong fan base, which is where Mari Hitomi comes in.'

'You said they give concerts,' Halliwell said. 'Are we assuming Mari came to Bath to attend one of them?'

'Good question,' Ingeborg said. 'These soirées, as they call them, are supposed to be for the university community. They're held in big houses like Dyrham and Corsham Court, and the tickets are distributed among the staff, with some music students included as well. They're not open to the public.'

'So if Mari wanted to hear the quartet . . . ?'

'She'd need to be smart.'

'How?'

'Depends,' Ingeborg said. 'A groupie — if that's what she really was — would find a way. If you were nuts on one of them you'd break any rules to get up close. Slipping through another entrance and posing as one of the music students. Nothing would stop you.'

'Ever go through a phase like that?' Leaman asked Ingeborg.

She gave him a glare that could have pinned him to the display board. 'That's got sod all to do with it.'

'Just trying to understand the female

psyche. You sounded as if you were speaking from experience.'

'My only ambition at her age was to get into CID. Shows how misguided I was.'

'And who was your idol? The guv'nor?'

'John, get back in the knife box,' Diamond said. 'We're doing a job here. We know Mari left London on September twentieth. We believe she took the train to Bath instead of Exeter. There may have been sightings of her. With her picture in the paper we ought to find out soon if she was here long, if she stayed anywhere. But we also need to know what the Staccati people were doing, where they lodge, how they spend their time off, the company they keep and so on.'

'Whether one of their concerts coincided with Mari's time here,' Ingeborg said.

'You think she gatecrashed a concert?'

'Tricky. They're not listed on the website, being private. But if she found out they were performing she could have gone to the venue and waited outside.'

Keith Halliwell said, 'A random killing. Someone sees this young woman hanging around on a dark night.'

'A sex attack?' Gilbert said.

'Who can say?' Ingeborg said. 'The pathologist couldn't tell us. She ended up strangled and dumped in the river, that's all we know for certain.'

'All options are open,' Diamond said. 'Meanwhile, we work with what we know. She was a fan of the Staccati, but was it one of them in particular that she idolised?'

'Not the old Ukrainian guy,' Halliwell said.

'Why not?' Diamond said with a touch of injured pride. 'There's such a thing as a father figure.'

'Sorry I spoke.'

'And if any of you are thinking not the big cello lady, let's remember girl on girl is not out of the question. Okay, to be realistic, the second violinist looks the part.'

'Eye candy,' Ingeborg said.

'Ike who?' Leaman said.

She ignored that. 'And you're right, guv. My mind was wandering. Anthony Metcalf is the good-looking one. Isn't that what you're saying?'

'The pin-up boy.'

'Don't forget the guy who isn't on the poster,' Leaman said. 'The viola player, Mel Farran.'

'He's new,' Halliwell said. 'Mari wouldn't have known about him.'

Ingeborg was quick to correct him. 'Not all that new. These things get written up in music magazines and on the internet. She may well have heard of him and seen his picture. He's nice looking too.'

'Before anyone makes anything of that, here's the game plan,' Diamond said. 'What we've heard from Ingeborg is useful, but basic. Most of it comes from the Staccati website. It's their publicity material. By the end of the day I want the inside story from the people themselves.'

'As soon as that?' Leaman said.

'This afternoon.'

'There's more to discover, that's for sure,' Ingeborg said.

'You're all in on this. Get them talking about themselves. They'll be used to that, so make sure it's not just the standard spiel. Interrupt, question, challenge, get to the truth of how this quartet functions.'

'I thought we were focusing on Mari,' Leaman said.

'You won't get many answers out of her,' Halliwell said, and got a few smiles.

'John's got a point,' Diamond said. 'We'll ask if they had any dealings with Mari before she arrived here and if she approached them in the hours leading up to her death. But that could be a short interview. This is our chance to get to know these people. Be alert to everything they tell you, suspicious incidents, strange goings-on. What they've experienced could be the key to this investigation.'

'So how do we handle this?' Ingeborg asked.

'It's our team taking on their team,' Diamond said. 'Keith, you can tackle Ivan Bogdanov. John, yours is Anthony Metcalf. Ingeborg has already met Farran, so she can deal with him.'

'Does that leave me with the cellist woman?' Paul Gilbert asked.

Diamond was kind enough not to say so, but you only had to look at the poster to see that the youngest member of the squad would be eaten alive by Cat Kinsella. 'I'll take her on myself. You can do some research on the mysterious violist who quit.'

'There's also a manager,' Ingeborg said. 'He seems to work from an office in London.'

'We'll catch up with him later. What's his name?'

'Douglas Christmas.'

Diamond couldn't let that pass. 'I may have sat on his knee. A hoodie with a big white beard? Forget it. You lot are way behind me.'

Ingeborg had checked with the university music department and found that the Staccati would be in rehearsal at the Michael

Tippett Centre the same afternoon.

'Perfect,' Diamond said.

'They may not welcome it,' she said. 'They've got one of their soirées tomorrow night. This could be their last rehearsal.'

'They can do overtime. We have to.'

'Musicians can be temperamental,'

'So can I. Haven't you noticed?' He gave the matter more thought. 'Let them know we're coming and it shouldn't take long. A concert tomorrow night, you said? Where are they playing?'

'Corsham Court.'

'I'm thinking I should hear this lot.'

Ingeborg didn't comment. She had an inkling of what he would say next.

As if he'd just thought of it, he said, 'Care to come with me?'

'Well . . .' she started to say.

'Good, I'll need someone to stop me from clapping at the wrong point. I'd prefer you to John Leaman if you can make it.'

'John knows far more about classical music.'

'But you're better company. Have you got a little black dress? This sounds like a smart occasion.'

Ingeborg didn't pursue the matter of the little black dress. She thought she had another escape route. 'I heard these concerts are hard to get into. There's a long waiting list.'

'Don't worry. I'll get Georgina to pull some strings. She moves in high circles.'

'Perhaps she'd like to partner you.'

'Get outta here.'

The team descended on the Michael Tippett Centre early the same afternoon. They commandeered four practice rooms for interviews before any of the musicians showed up. As a result they were able to separate the quartet as they arrived. A united front might have been difficult to deal with.

Anthony Metcalf was the first. A glaze came over his eyes and he allowed himself to be escorted into a side room by Leaman. As a result, Ingeborg was able to inform Mel Farran when he showed up that interviewing was already under way.

She'd met Mel on her previous visit here. Knowing who she was, he should have been calm, if not relaxed. So it came as a surprise when he appeared startled and on the verge of panic, clutching his violin case to his chest as if Ingeborg was about to snatch it away.

'It's okay,' she said. 'You're not in any kind of trouble. We're looking for help with an ongoing enquiry.'

Still twitchy, he allowed himself to be shown into the woodwind room.

Ivan Bogdanov was difficult in another way. 'It's out of the question,' he told Halliwell. 'We have a performance tomorrow and we need to practise.'

'The sooner we get through, the more time you'll have,' Halliwell said.

'And if I refuse?'

'I arrest you and do it at the police station, ask to see your work permit and proof of identity, take your fingerprints and DNA.'

This put a swift end to Ivan's protest.

Diamond was left to meet Cat Kinsella when she appeared, short of breath, grasping her cello. 'Sorry, young man,' she told him as he brandished his ID. 'No autographs now. I'm late for rehearsal.'

He told her what he was there for. Shaking her head, she allowed him to escort her to the remaining practice room. Once she had rested her cello case against the wall and perched herself precariously on a stool behind a drum kit, Diamond drew up another stool and showed her a picture of Mari.

'Ever seen this young woman before?'

She shook her head.

'She's a major fan. We think she came to

Bath specially to see you.'

'Not me, detective. One of the guys, possibly, but not me. I don't have female fans, nor male, now I think about it. I'm past all that.'

'The passions are on their side. You'd only find out if they threw themselves at you.'

She chuckled at that. 'Get real. I'm a cellist. I don't strut about the stage in skimpy underwear and sequins.'

'But you won't deny there are classical music groupies out there who follow the quartets?'

'There may be a few crazies. Is that really what she was? She looks normal enough in the picture.'

'She could have had a crush on one of you.'

'You'd better find out from the men.'

'We're doing that right now. Have you ever performed in Yokohama?'

'Never.'

'Anywhere else in Japan?'

'Tokyo a few times.' Her face softened as she thought back. 'There's a place called Katsushika Symphony Hills. I remember it because of the Kat bit. Huge. Two halls, one seating over a thousand and the other three hundred. In my innocence I thought they'd booked the small hall for us. I was wrong. Every seat was taken in the thousand-seater, including one in the front row occupied by an urn containing the ashes of a man who'd booked to see us but died a few days before.'

'That said a lot.'

'Actually, no. Not a damn word.'

He smiled. 'So if Mari had come to see you, she'd have had to travel to Tokyo. That's not a vast distance from Yokohama.'

'I'll take your word for that. Geography passed me by when I was in school. Let me tell you something about quartet playing. You have the score on a stand in front of you with a little light over it. If you look up and you can see anything at all above the light, it's rows of identical heads looking faintly like the beads on an abacus. You don't recognise people.'

'Thanks for explaining,' Diamond said, genuinely pleased she was speaking more freely than she had at the start. 'Let's talk about the quartet. You were one of the founders, right?'

'With Ivan, yes. Back in the last century, that was, when I was young and easy, as the poet said. To be truthful, I wasn't easy, I was bloody difficult. Always have been. I'm surprised Ivan ever asked me to join, but the time was right and I jumped at the chance.'

'You were a soloist before?'

'Going right back, I was one of those child monsters, an infant prodigy. We're Liverpool Irish, the Kinsellas, and my dad played the fiddle around the pubs. My mum was red-hot on the squeezebox. They got me started early and pushed me hard. Recorder, flute, piano, violin. I can knock out a tune on almost anything. Don't ask me why, but I was drawn to the cello. There are all kinds of Freudian theories I draw the line at discussing in polite company, or police company, come to that. I started to play when I was nine and must have looked ridiculous wrestling with it. You need to be an athlete. It's easy for a cellist to get musclebound. But I adored it — the sound, the sweet, rich voice was all that I wanted. So at a young age I got through the drudgery of mastering the thing and won a scholarship to music school in Manchester. You must have heard of Chetham's.'

Diamond tried to look as if he had.

Cat was into her story anyway. 'They worked wonders with me and put me in for Young Musician of the Year. Didn't win, but made the final and got noticed. I must tell you — and you won't believe this — in those days I was thin enough to slot into a

279

toaster. Long, blonde hair that I wore in a pigtail. Anyway I learned the repertoire and at fourteen had the cheek to play the Dvorák with a youth orchestra and overnight I was touted as the next Jacqueline du Pré. They wanted me to loosen my hair and record the Elgar looking all frail and angelic. That's what she made her debut with and is mainly remembered for, but of course she could play anything. She was the real deal. Did you see the movie?'

'Somehow it passed me by,' Diamond said.

'Far better to watch some footage of Jackie herself. There's a lovely video of her with Barbirolli. And to think that they wanted me to ape her just to get famous. Catriona Kinsella, aged fourteen and a half, dug her heels in and said she wanted to be herself. Sucks to the Elgar and sucks to wearing a long white dress. It was a teenage rebellion in a music context. Everyone, my parents, the school, the marketing people, bore down on me and said I was flushing a brilliant career down the toilet. The battle went on for almost a year. I started eating, seriously stuffing myself with chocolate, fried foods, pastry, the lot. In a matter of weeks it started showing and in a year I was the lump of lard I am today.'

'Your way of taking control of your life?'

She raised her right thumb. 'Tell that to Weightwatchers. I shaved my head as well in case anyone missed the point. I continued to play, of course. The joy has never gone away. I've played as a soloist with some of the great orchestras. Vivaldi wrote twenty-seven concertos and I've learned almost all of them. What I absolutely refused to do was put myself in the clutches of the popular classical music merchants. If you follow music at all you'll know the process. They take second-rate artists with pretty faces, groom them, call them the voice or the player of the century and turn them into stars, whether they're singers, violinists, pianists. The quality of the sound is crap, they're off-key, and the great gullible public doesn't seem to notice. I could find you literally hundreds of finer voices and better players completely overlooked.' She stopped and shook her head. 'I've lost my thread, haven't I? This is one of my pet beefs.'

'You saw off the vultures.'

A broad smile. 'That sums it up. I might have made millions, but as a musician I'd have been dead meat. When all is said and done, you keep your musical integrity. These second-rate performers know they cashed theirs in. So I scraped away in an orchestra making real music and no money. Gave lessons, did some work on film scores and TV commercials. That's allowed in my scheme of things. I wasn't cheating anyone. This went on for a few years until I met Ivan and he told me he was thinking of forming a string quartet. Ask any string player and they'll tell you that's their dream, to play in a high quality quartet.'

'How did you meet him?'

'Ivan? In the Liverpool Philharmonic. I was temping for a month, but he was the leader. Very solemn, very earnest. I didn't think we'd get along at all, and I was gob-smacked to be asked, but desperate enough to give it a try. Ivan is all right, a bit pompous, only it's not self-conceit. That would be death to any ensemble. He respects the music and his tone quality harmonised with mine from the beginning. That's as vital as technical ability.'

'I expect if he gets too serious you know how to bring him down to earth?'

'I do my best. He doesn't lack emotion. You hear that in his playing. He just finds it difficult to express his feelings in everyday life. We were talking about Japan just now. Ivan used to visit the geisha houses and I always thought that was a perfect arrangement for him, very proper, with clear rules, just like the chess he plays. He'd be waited on and entertained by these gorgeous young women. No hanky-panky at all. Hints of it all around, but the rituals forbid it. He felt secure. He doesn't like surprises.'

'How does he deal with all the success?'

'Of the quartet? He doesn't let it go to his head.'

'The groupies?'

'You're on about them again? Listen, Ivan's not a young man. If he was in danger of making a fool of himself, which isn't likely, I'd tell him. I keep my boys in order.'

Diamond believed her. He was getting a useful insight into how the group functioned. 'Getting back to the time when the quartet was formed, how did you find the others?'

'We needed a second violin and a violist. Ivan knew of a Ukrainian called Yuriy and I remembered Harry from a summer school I did at Dartington. Two totally different personalities. Yuriy was a bear of a man. You'd expect him to have been a percussionist, but he was a red-hot fiddle player. I think there was gipsy blood in him. He'd launch into gipsy music in the middle of a rehearsal discussion just for a laugh, or to take the heat out of an argument, and it always worked. He was great company and a good influence on Ivan, but he did over-indulge with the vodka. I think he got lonely. He had a wife back in the Ukraine and they'd separated on some understanding that they'd stay in touch. Eventually he went back to her. Happy ending for her — I think — and not so happy for us.'

'And Harry?'

She sighed and shook her head slowly. 'Poor, benighted Harry. He was my recommendation, so I still feel responsible. A gifted violist, no question. He adored the instrument and talked it up at every opportunity, which made him an easy target for viola jokes, of which there are many. He was with us a long time, but I never felt I got to know him as well as I wished. On tour, he'd clear off and not say a word about where he was going. We all did our own thing. I hit the shops, Yuriy the bars and Ivan the local chess club.'

'Or the geisha house.'

'When possible. You don't find many of those on the aver tour.'

'So where do you think Harry went?' he prompted her.

'None of us knew and he didn't encourage us to ask. He'd be back for rehearsals and play divinely, so we had no reason to complain until the day he didn't show up.'

'Don't you have any theories?'

'Got into bad company, I suppose, but whether it was of his making or theirs, I don't know. We were in Budapest at the time. He must have had his viola with him, because it wasn't found at the hotel. It was a Maggini worth probably two hundred thousand pounds, and it didn't belong to him. He had it on extended loan from some rich patron. This happens. We poor beggars can't afford instruments of that quality and the owners buy them as investments and want them played. Harry vanished and we found some dreadful stand-in from a local orchestra. We sounded like four cats stranded in the Battersea Dogs' Home. For months after that we were a lost cause. Couldn't fulfil our bookings. We didn't know if Harry would suddenly reappear. It would have been easier if he'd just put a gun to his head. At least we could have looked for a replacement.'

'In the end, that's what you did.'

She pulled a face. 'With mixed results. A series of violists who weren't up to it musically. There's a treacly, sentimental tone — a lingering in the action of the slide — that is death to any quartet. We heard it from the first guy and told him in the nicest way to look for another job. The next stand-in was a woman whose fingering was sloppy.

She couldn't sustain the vibrato and it ruined our tone quality. I think she didn't have the expressive feeling within herself. When we asked her to make the sound continuous it was worse, forced and insincere. God knows, we tried and she did, too, but it was obvious it would never work. She knew it. She walked.'

'Was that when you found Mr. Farran?'

'Mel? After a much longer gap. We'd just about broken up. Anthony — he's our second violin and a whole different story — became so impossible that Doug found him a job with the Hallé. The Staccati was a forgotten group. Quartets are breaking up all the time and everyone in the music world assumed we were finished, but dear old Ivan wouldn't accept it. He's a brilliant player and he could find work anywhere and yet he loves quartet playing and he wouldn't accept that we were through. He used all his contacts to look for a truly gifted player and Mel's name kept coming up. Luckily for us he wasn't committed to any orchestra so we pounced. Good result, too. He's fitted in well.'

'Better than Harry?'

She hesitated. 'It's early days. Harry knew the rest of us and our quirky ways so well. He was a lovely guy and I miss him. The day he disappeared I toured the streets of Budapest looking for him. I still would if there was any realistic hope. But Mel is shaping up nicely.'

'This has been helpful,' Diamond said. 'A real insight into the quartet. The one you haven't said much about is Anthony.'

'Special case,' she said.

'In what way?'

She shook with laughter. 'You name it. I'll say this. Anthony is a terrific violinist. Technically he has the edge on Ivan, but I wouldn't want either of them to know I said that. He could make it as a virtuoso if his head was right.'

Diamond leaned forward and almost fell off the stool. 'What's wrong with it?'

'Not exactly wrong, just out of balance. He sees the world in a different way from the rest of us. Very focused. His power of concentration is amazing. But he has no sense of humour and he makes no allowance for the feelings and opinions of anyone else. Music is all-important to him. His work-rate is phenomenal. He'll master a new score sooner than any of us. It used to worry me that he had no life outside the quartet. Over the years I've come to accept that he found his goal in music and he wants nothing else. Any change of arrange-

287

ments can throw him. That's why Harry going was a major crisis. I seriously feared Anthony would kill himself if we didn't get playing again. It's that essential to him.'

'A personality disorder?'

'I would say so. Have you heard of Asperger's?'

'I don't know a lot about it.'

'It's a form of autism, but the people who get it can still function at a high level.'

'Is that what he's got?'

'It's in that area. They call it the autism spectrum, apparently.'

'How did you recruit him?'

'We needed a second violin to replace Yuriy.'

'Who returned to his wife in the Ukraine?'

'Yes. And almost at once Anthony appeared and asked for an audition. News travels fast in our little world and he'd got word that Yuriy had quit. I'm not even sure Yuriy had actually left. It was obvious at once that this earnest young man was twice the player Yuriy had been. He told us frankly that he'd pulled out of three string quartets and a trio in two years because they weren't up to standard and we looked at each other and wondered if we would make the grade. He was so damn good that we decided to give it a whirl. In the first weeks he was with us it felt as if we were on trial, not Anthony.'

'Did you go on tour with him?'

She laughed. 'It was a hoot. In many ways he's like a baby. The basic things in life pass him by. He forgets to shower, to eat break-fast, to carry money. He can't be relied on to pack. You tell him and he'll do it. Next time you have to tell him all over again. Between us, we cope with him and get a few laughs along the way. Anything you say, he takes as gospel truth so we have to be careful not to speak ironically. Once at rehearsal I had a noisy chair — a regular hazard for cellists — and I said in jest that I'd had baked beans for lunch. "No you didn't," Anthony says. "You had an egg and mayo sandwich. I saw you." Fortunately he's right up with the music, and that's what counts.'

'How is he with the audiences?' Diamond asked.

'I don't think he's aware of them. He's immersed in the music.'

'You meet some of them afterwards, no doubt?'

She pointed at Diamond. 'Hey, this is the groupie question in another guise. You're a sly one.'

'Better answer it, then, in case I turn nasty.'

'The leeches get nowhere with our Anthony.'

'They're going to try. He's good-looking.'

'We know that, but he doesn't. He has no self-image. If they just want an autograph he'll sometimes oblige even if he can't fathom why it's required. If they ask a musical question such as the most common one — "Is your violin a Strad?" — he'll answer. But if they were to ask what he's doing after the concert he'll tell them he's going back to the hotel for a room-service meal and a sleep, which is true. End of conversation. He's got a way of dismissing them with a look.'

'So you don't think it's possible he could end up spending the evening with a woman through some misunderstanding of the sort you mentioned?'

'She'd need to be very devious. And she'd need to understand how his strange logic works.'

'And if he felt he'd been tricked?'

Cat shook her head. 'I don't know. I don't even like to think about it.'

'Doesn't he like women?'

'He isn't capable of liking anyone, male or female. If you're asking me about his love life, there isn't any. He goes to sex workers when he gets randy. Paying for it suits his mentality. No relationship, no affection. And he feels no shame. He'll tell us straight he was with a whore next time we meet. I expect he'd say exactly what happened if we asked. He can be very candid.'

'Yet you say he's a brilliant violinist. Isn't it all about expressing emotion through the way you play?'

'Right on. And communicating emotion to your audience. He succeeds and that's the biggest mystery to me. It's almost as if he comes alive through the instrument. Pathos, tenderness, humour, even love. Where it comes from I can't tell you. His soul, I suppose, finding an outlet that doesn't exist in the locked-up person he is.'

This was getting into areas outside Diamond's competence. 'The only person I haven't asked you about is your manager.'

'Doug? He's normal enough and that's a good thing. He looks after the business side, makes sure we earn enough to survive. All the gigs and recording sessions are down to him. He tells us when and where and we decide what. The musical decisions are ours.'

'So was it his decision to bring you to Bath?'

'We wanted a residency, a chance for the new combination to gel. Being in one place is so much better than touring when you're adjusting to a new member. From what I recall, Doug got on the phone and found out quickly that Bath Spa University were looking for some kind of professional ensemble to teach and play. We agreed the same afternoon.'

'How is it working out?'

'Wonderfully, apart from you lot giving us the third degree.'

'I wouldn't call it that,' Diamond said.

'You're not on the receiving end.'

'These concerts you give. They're small by your standards, aren't they?

'Intimate. They're lovely. That's how quartets were played originally, for small, invited audiences in gracious surroundings.'

'I'm hoping to attend your next one.'

'Really? You don't strike me as a string quartet aficionado.'

He smiled. 'I don't claim to be that.'

'I hope you don't suffer, then.' She glanced at her watch. 'Is the grilling over now?'

'Not yet,' Diamond said. 'You said there are lots of viola jokes. I can't think of one.'

She tilted her head back. 'If I tell you one, am I released without charge?'

'Only if it's a good one.'

'All right. This man walked into a bank carrying a viola case. Why did everyone get nervous?'

'They thought it was a machine gun?'

'No. They thought it was a viola and he might take it out and play it.'

16

'Mine wasn't much help.'

'Mine was an obstacle race, and I don't think I won.'

'Mine was a waste of time.'

'Snap out of it, guys,' Diamond said. 'You're supposed to be professionals.'

Leaman shrugged. 'He refused to talk about anything except the music they're rehearsing.'

'This was Anthony Metcalf, the second violin?'

'I'd get more sense from a talking clock.'

The debrief was taking place in a quiet corner of the senior common room at the Michael Tippett Centre. The team had helped themselves to instant coffee from a jar marked *staff only*. In one of the practice rooms nearby, the quartet had begun their delayed rehearsal

'Anthony thinks of little else except music,' Diamond said. 'I heard that from Cat Kinsella, who was good company once she got warmed up. Even told me a joke.' He put up his hand. 'Later. Did any of you get a reaction when you showed the picture of Mari?'

Leaman and Halliwell shook their heads.

Ingeborg said, 'Mel Farran reacted. He actually calmed down quite a lot when he saw it. Before that he was a different bunny from the one I met here before.'

'Different in what way?'

'Tense. He sat clutching his instrument case across his knees like a barrier. I've seen women hold their handbags like that. It's unusual in a man.'

'Not many blokes have handbags,' Leaman said.

She looked at him as if he was something she'd trodden in. 'I don't know what Mel thought I was going to ask, but I got the impression it wasn't about Mari.'

'Does he have form?'

'No, I ran a check. He's clean.'

'So what did he say when you gave him a sight of the picture?'

Ingeborg's eyes rolled upwards. 'Said he never forgets a pretty face. Then he smirked a bit. He sees himself as God's gift to women.'

'You've changed your tune,' Leaman said.

'He was nice-looking and friendly when we last spoke.'

'He's still nice looking and friendly — and he still thinks he's God's gift.'

'So not one of them appears to have met the victim,' Diamond said.

'Mel did admit Mari could easily have been in the audience at one of the concerts and he wouldn't have known.'

Diamond aired the small piece of expertise he'd learned from Cat. 'Because they have a light on the music stand and they can't see anything over it?'

'No. Because they concentrate on the music.'

He tore open three strips of sugar for his coffee. 'Disappointing, then. No apparent link to our victim. It's only our assumption that she came here to listen to her favourite string quartet.'

'I can't be entirely sure how much Anthony knows, or how little,' Leaman said, and for once he wasn't trying to score points. 'I showed him the picture and he hardly gave it a glance. Wasn't interested.'

'Did you ask him the question?'

'Had he met her? He said he was a musician — as if that said it all.'

'In his case, it probably does,' Diamond said. 'He has some form of autism. People don't interest him.'

Ingeborg took a sharp breath. 'So it's entirely possible Mari spoke to Anthony and he paid no attention.'

Halliwell was some way ahead of her. 'And he killed her and dumped her in the river and blanked it from his mind.'

'I find that impossible to believe,' Ingeborg said. 'Anyway, why would he do such a thing if he's only interested in music?'

Halliwell turned up his palms to show it was mainly guesswork. 'Mari became a nuisance, got in his way.'

'How?'

'She was a groupie, like we said.'

'I get you now.' She nodded. 'He's the poster-boy, the one most likely to have attracted women.'

'Okay,' Diamond said. 'I'd better have a try with Anthony.'

'You won't get anywhere,' Leaman said, blunt, if not actually insubordinate.

Diamond carried on as if no one had spoken. 'I'm not sure if he really can't recall things, or if he just doesn't want to talk about it.'

'Using the autism as a get-out?' Halliwell said.

'That's got to be considered.'

'I said you're on a loser,' Leaman said

'I expect you're right, John, but I'm having a go.' He turned to Halliwell. 'You said Ivan Bogdanov was an obstacle course. What did you mean by that?'

'Treated me as if I was the KGB. Kept talking about his rights and what a waste of his precious time it was and how we ought to be hunting the real killer instead of persecuting innocent musicians.'

Leaman smirked. 'You mean he didn't melt under the Halliwell charm?'

'You slay me.'

Diamond asked, 'Did he respond at all when you showed Mari's picture?'

'Claimed he hadn't seen her. I asked him if the fans ever became a problem and he took the line that people who appreciate good music keep their distance. If he's hiding anything, he's well defended.'

'Ivan is a chess player. I got that from Cat. She respects him. In fact, she spoke well of all of them. Sees herself as the mother hen. She wants the quartet to succeed.'

'They all want that,' Ingeborg said. 'They've got a name, a reputation, a cosy little number here in Bath. It's in their interest to stay together now they've got a good viola player. They'll cover up for each other, I'm sure of that.'

'The question is,' Diamond said, plucking

298

at the lobe of his ear, 'do they have anything to cover up?'

The practice went on for almost two hours before the quartet took a break. When the door of the rehearsal room opened, Diamond was waiting outside. The rest of the CID team had already left for the police station.

Cat emerged at speed and made a beeline for the ladies' room. Her reaction to Diamond was to raise both hands. 'Not now.' Over her shoulder, she added, 'Talk about groupies. You're one of them.'

Diamond stepped into the rehearsal room.

Ivan looked up, but not to welcome the visitor. 'You people have a damn nerve. What is it now? We're in the middle of a practice.'

'A few words with Anthony during your break won't hold you up.'

'Anthony's already answered questions.'

'Not from me.'

'He's within his rights to refuse.'

'If you want to talk about rights, we can take up all of the break before I even start to question him.'

'Intolerable.' Ivan looked across the room to where Anthony was studying the score, apparently oblivious of what was being discussed. 'This policeman wants more time with you. Can you spare him a couple of minutes?'

Diamond said, 'He'll spare me as long as it takes.' He curled his finger at Anthony, turned and left the room, confident that he would follow.

And he did, entering the percussion room and seating himself on the stool behind the drum set.

Diamond looked the young man up and down and understood Ingeborg's remark about the dark good looks. The high, narrow cheekbones and finely shaped mouth were likely to appeal to any woman, however stone-faced Anthony appeared. The unattainable has a strong sexual attraction. A confident woman would expect him to respond to the right signals.

A burly male detective had no such optimism. Getting any kind of response would be a challenge. But there was one thing that might work in Diamond's favour. People with autism generally speak the truth if they say anything at all. They are honest to the point of rudeness.

Start on safe ground, he decided. Get the man talking about what he knows best. 'How's the practice going?'

'Okay.'

Better than no answer at all. 'Preparing for tomorrow's concert, are you?'

This time Anthony settled for a nod.

'Beethoven, wasn't it?' Diamond ventured.

Anthony was supposed to get the idea that Diamond was a fellow lover of music. He didn't show a glimmer of appreciation.

'I couldn't place the piece,' Diamond added, which was true. He was about as capable of placing a piece of Beethoven as he was of riding a Derby winner. 'Do you mind telling me what it was?'

'Opus 59, Number 3,' Anthony said.

'Silly me. I'm a duffer with numbers.'

'In C major.'

'C major.' Diamond raised his thumb as if all had been made clear. 'Any particular part?'

'The fugue.'

'And to me it sounded just as a fugue should.'

'It was too fast.'

'A shade quick, I'll give you.'

Hearing this, Anthony with his care for the truth must have assumed he was in the company of a connoisseur. 'You're right about that. Beethoven's tempo instruction is just about impossible.' Now he wanted to discuss the playing of the fugue, which would be a minefield for Diamond.

'I didn't appreciate that,' Diamond said, 'about the tempo instruction.'

'It's a metronome mark.'

'Does that make a difference?'

'The metronome wasn't invented when the piece was written.'

This was information any self-respecting detective could work on. 'Beethoven added his note at some later date?'

Anthony nodded. 'Much later, when he was stone deaf.'

'So you think he got it wrong?'

'It's meant to be quick and energetic, but —'

'Not so quick as you played it?'

Anthony made a fist and held it up in solidarity with Diamond. 'You're right. Something is lost at the tempo he gives. I keep telling Ivan to slow up a touch. The music is without fault. It can take it. He won't listen. He's implacable. He treats the score as gospel.'

'Don't the others have something to say about it?'

Anthony shook his head.

'Maybe they don't want to make an issue of it,' Diamond suggested. 'Cat is all for peace and harmony and Mel is too new to the quartet to take a stand.'

From Anthony's wide-eyed look this was

an insight he had missed. 'Do you play?'

Diamond shook his head. 'Too busy with other things, unfortunately.'

'But you know Beethoven.'

'I wouldn't go that far.'

'You can speak to Ivan, tell him you were listening to us and it was too quick.'

'Me? He wouldn't take advice from me.'

'For all he knows, you could be one of our audience.'

'With luck, I will be tomorrow night, but I'm in no position to tell a man of his experience how to play.' He was fast running out of musical conversation, but he knew it was the only way to make progress with Anthony. 'Is there an interval?'

Anthony frowned. 'It's full of intervals.'

'Not the music. I mean a break during the concert for people to walk about.'

'That will be too late.'

'I'm not planning to speak to Ivan. I was wondering what comes after.'

'After the interval? Some solo pieces.'

'From you?'

Anthony shook his head. 'The others.'

'All three?'

'All three instruments. Violin, viola and cello.'

'Nice. I can't wait. But what about you? I heard you're a brilliant violinist. Don't you

303

give solos?'

The lips tightened.

'Sorry I asked,' Diamond said. 'You're more of a team player?'

No response. After going so well, this had hit the buffers.

'Do you happen to remember what music you played in the first few concerts the quartet gave?'

'Yes.'

Anthony's precise responses came with the mental condition. They could be a barrier to progress when you expected more. 'I'd like to be told,' Diamond said.

'Beethoven Opus 131, Quartet Number 14 in C sharp minor. Schubert Number 14 in D minor. Haydn Opus 74, Number 3 in G minor. Shall I continue?'

'Wonderful, but no need. And do you also recall where you played?'

Anthony frowned. 'No.'

'I heard you go to some splendid houses, perfect for chamber music.'

'I've forgotten.' The gracious drawing rooms of Somerset and Avon, their Baroque splendour enhanced by candlelight, had already been deleted from this young man's discriminating memory. Only the music counted for anything.

'They don't make an impression?'

304

'I'm not there for the architecture. You can ask one of the others.'

'But you remember every note of the music? Am I right?'

'Not every note. We have the score in front of us.'

'And how was your playing received?'

'All right.'

'Would you happen to remember if one of the audience spoke to you afterwards about your playing?'

'Depends.'

'On what?'

'What they had to say. If it was only praise I wouldn't bother. We get a lot of that.'

'I'm sure it's all well meant,' Diamond said. 'Is there anything you would remember?'

'Intelligent remarks.'

'Intelligent remarks about what?'

'The music.'

One relentless track.

Diamond took a deep breath and tried again. 'Such as?'

'Such as the stress we give to the fourth note in the opening of the Beethoven Opus 131, Number 14. Ivan is the player, not me, and it's a signature moment that sets the tone for all that follows. It can sound disruptive, the transition from G sharp to

A. They're separated by a full bar. He draws it upwards a fraction on the G and then slips back to the same pitch after leaving the A.'

It was about as clear to Diamond as the second law of thermodynamics. 'Thank you for explaining. Did one of the audience raise this with you?'

'Yes.'

'A woman?'

'A man.'

Another hope dashed.

'Can you think of a comment a woman made after one of those early concerts?'

Anthony frowned, as if deciding whether the question came within his span of attention. 'One told me our performance of the Schubert was superior to the recording she has of the original Staccati. Since then I've listened to the piece myself, and she was right.'

'Do you remember who she was, this woman who spoke to you?'

'The wife of the man who owned the house.'

In his long career, Diamond couldn't remember an interview as tough as this. Each door slammed shut before he could get inside. 'Wasn't there another woman who approached you, a younger woman,

Japanese?'

'I don't remember.'

'You would if she had something of interest to say about the music.'

Anthony shrugged as if to say, 'You tell me.'

Now it was Diamond's turn to be logical. 'I can't tell you because I wasn't there. Have you played with the quartet in Japan?'

'Yes.'

'The Japanese like classical music, don't they? I expect some of them are very knowledgeable.'

'Yes.'

'You see, I'm wondering if a certain young woman who heard you play in Tokyo, or wherever it was, loved your playing, came to England this summer and got herself into one of the soirées the quartet gave. She could have introduced herself after the concert and told you she was a fan.'

'Plenty do,' Anthony said.

'Plenty of Japanese women?'

'All sorts. I don't pay attention to fans.'

'But you would pay attention if she made an intelligent comment about the music?'

'I told you that already.'

Diamond decided the only way forward was an appeal to Anthony's better nature. 'Help me, Anthony. Try and remember.

307

Whatever she said may not have seemed worth listening to at the time, but it could be important. She was Japanese and her name was Mari Hitomi and you've seen her picture before.' He took the photo from his pocket.

There wasn't a glimmer of recognition.

'If she didn't have anything to say about the concert, she may have asked a question about your violin, how old it is, how valuable, who made it, whether you have other violins.'

A shrug and a shake of the head.

'She could have asked you to autograph her programme.'

'I wouldn't remember that.' Anthony looked at his watch. 'I must get back. The others will be ready to start again.'

'She had a musical note tattooed on one of her upper teeth.'

'A quaver,' Anthony said at once, 'on the lateral incisor, right hand side. Right to me, left for her.' He didn't add, 'Why didn't you ask?' but Diamond felt as if he had. Even so, it was the breakthrough he'd been working for.

'Did she say anything to you?'

'She must have, for me to notice the tooth.'

'Do you remember what was said?'

'It couldn't have been important.'

'Take another look at the photo. Is this the woman?'

'I don't know. I can't see her teeth.'

'But is the face familiar?'

'I told you I don't remember faces.'

He got no further with Anthony.

Before allowing the quartet to resume their rehearsal, he addressed them as a group. 'You've all been shown a photo of a Japanese woman called Mari Hitomi who was found dead in the River Avon a few days ago. We happen to know she was a fan of the Staccati Quartet visiting Bath about the time you began your residency here. Earlier, each of you claimed you hadn't seen her before, but I have since learned from Anthony that he was approached by a woman of her description after one of the concerts you gave. He spotted the tattoo of a music note on one of her front teeth and this leads me to believe this was Miss Hitomi. Obviously this is significant. We'll need to ask more questions of each of you and I'm advising you as individuals to contact me if you have any more information about her.'

Nobody spoke for several seconds. Then Ivan said, 'Are you telling us we're under suspicion?'

'I was careful with my words,' Diamond said. 'I'm seeking information.'

Cat said, 'You want to be careful about what Anthony tells you. He's a sweetie, but his memory isn't the sharpest when it comes to anything other than music.'

'Thanks, but we'll treat everything we learn from any of you with the same respect.'

'I didn't say he isn't honest. He's the most honest guy you could hope to meet.'

'I'll second that,' Ivan said. 'We trust him totally.'

17

After Diamond had said his piece and left, Ivan stated in a few trenchant words that he wanted to get straight back to work on the Beethoven without any more being said about the Japanese woman. Nobody objected. A surge of energy in the second part of the rehearsal reflected the tension among the quartet. They played Opus 59, No. 3 from the beginning. This time when they reached the fugue they attacked it with a pulsating tempo that almost did justice to Beethoven's impossible metronome mark. The intensity of the task galvanised them all, yet the bowing was crisp and always under control. It was as if they were resolving their own anger through the playing — anger at Diamond, the police and the suspicion hanging over them.

'I think we're in shape,' Cat said after they lifted bows from strings and sat back.

'It was a better rendition, without

question,' Ivan said in a rare expression of satisfaction. 'And this new viola of Mel's has a richness in tone that I, for one, welcome.'

'You should,' Cat said. 'We all should. That's a Cremona fiddle if ever I heard one. 'Fess up, Mel. Where did you nick it from?'

Mel had a powerful urge to put the precious instrument out of sight in its case. He had a lingering disquiet about the way it had come into his possession. 'It's an Amati, from 1625.'

'Then it must be the work of the last and greatest of the family, Nicolò Amati,' Ivan said. 'About that time there was a famine and plague that killed every other violin maker in the city. May I?' He held out both hands.

The request to handle the antique viola was understandable. For Mel, the act of passing it across was a wrench. A mother with her newborn child couldn't have felt more protective. Of course it would be safe in the hands of another musician, he told himself. If you can't trust the members of your own quartet, you shouldn't be one of them.

He steeled himself and placed the Amati in Ivan's hands.

Ivan turned it over and stroked the maple

surface, tracing the grain with his fingertips. 'Exquisite. A thing of wood, hair and gut that can touch the soul and lift the spirit.' One-handed, he raised it by the neck. 'Nice weight.' He tucked it under his chin. 'Good length.'

'Watch out, boys,' Cat said. 'Our first violin is about to change into a violist.'

Mel decided he had better explain how he came to possess such a treasure. 'I was approached by a collector who wants it played.'

'Nothing unusual in that,' Ivan said. 'It would be difficult to name a soloist who didn't at some stage play with an instrument loaned to him.'

'Or her,' Cat said.

'He made me promise not to reveal his name.'

'The super-rich have their reasons, which is why they stay super-rich. Don't be so anxious, Mel,' Cat added. 'You look like the stick insect who found himself in the middle of a rave-up.'

'I can't help it,' Mel said. 'Some years back, when I was starting out as a professional musician, taking any work that came my way, I was mugged outside the Royal Festival Hall and had my viola snatched. They were clever. A girl looking like a student, pretty, East Asian, asked me for my autograph. I had my fiddle in its case under my arm and while I was distracted by this girl some guy on a bike pulled the thing from me and rode off with it. I gave chase all the way down to the river and I thought at first he'd slung it in, but there was a speedboat nearby and they may have collected it and got clean away. I never saw my viola again and I've never forgotten the feeling of loss.'

'You're afraid of someone stealing this?'

He nodded. 'My old fiddle had sentimental value and I was deeply affected, but as a responsibility it doesn't compare with this.'

'A salutary tale,' Cat said, 'but you're safe with us, kiddo.'

Ivan was still holding the Amati. 'I can't resist.' He picked up his bow and played the C string from heel to point, pianissimo, long and slow.

'You've kissed goodbye to it now,' Cat told Mel. 'Is anyone else going to get a try? Anthony is practically wetting himself.'

In the end, they all took a turn at handling the Amati, although no one else played on it. Mel was deeply relieved when Cat handed back the object of so much admiration, if not envy. He stowed it in its case. This should have been the cue to leave, but there was unfinished business.

'So what are we to make of that policeman?' Cat said before they left their seats.

'Nothing,' Ivan said at once. 'We make nothing of him. He's a distraction. He has his job to do and we have ours. The fact that the unfortunate young woman was an admirer of ours is a trivial coincidence. Life is full of chance events.'

'I doubt if Detective Diamond sees it that way, O Wise One,' Cat said. 'He struck me as a man without much faith in chance events. We had enough hassle from the *Polizei* when Harry disappeared. I think we'd better brace ourselves for more. Did he rough you up, sweetie?' she said to Anthony.

'No.'

'Offered you plastic surgery and a safe house in Outer Mongolia?'

'No.'

'Then how did he wear you down?

'Kept asking questions.'

'Well, he's a smart guy if he got an answer. I've known you six or seven years and most times I can't get two words out of you.'

'Will you listen to me?' Ivan said. 'We're musicians and we have a performance tomorrow night. The last thing we need is

315

to get involved in speculation about a death in suspicious circumstances.'

'Too late,' Cat said. 'The big detective means to rub our noses in it.'

'He'll go away if we ignore him.'

Then Anthony announced, 'He said he'll be at the concert tomorrow.'

There was a shocked silence. Ivan chewed at his thumbnail.

'See what I mean?' Cat said. 'Don't kid yourself he's coming to listen to Beethoven. He'll have a pair of handcuffs in his pocket.'

'We've done nothing wrong,' Mel said.

No one spoke.

'Have we?' Mel broke the silence, looking at each of the others.

'You wish,' Cat said finally with a peal of laughter. 'Don't all speak at once. Now let's organise our taxis.'

Mel was to share with Ivan and both taxis were slow in coming. Cat climbed into the first with her cello, assisted by Anthony. Before it drove off, she called out of the window, 'We're hearing over the intercom that your cab went to the tip instead of the Tippett. He's stuck in the garden waste queue. Could be another hour.' Their taxi zoomed away.

'That woman doesn't amuse me,' Ivan

said. 'Never has.'

'Was she making it up?'

'Of course she was. Three-quarters of what she tells you is made up. Ours won't be far behind.'

Mel had spotted a stationary black saloon car parked at the edge of the approach road. Someone was in the driver's seat. 'Could that be it?'

'Where?'

He pointed.

Ivan sniffed. 'It looks to me like a private car. Probably waiting for some student.'

'I might go and ask. Stupid if he's waiting there and we're standing here only thirty yards away.'

'As you wish,' Ivan said. 'I've never known them to park there.'

With his cased viola gripped to his chest, Mel strode towards the parked vehicle. True, he couldn't see any writing on the side or any sign that it was licensed. Some-times it was difficult to tell.

He hadn't gone ten yards when the driver started up, made a screaming U-turn that must have left rubber on the tarmac, and drove off at speed, just missing a student on a bike.

Shaking his head, Mel returned to Ivan's side. 'What was that about?'

317

For once, Ivan had no answer.

'Bloody dangerous,' Mel said. 'Someone could have got killed.'

'Yes,' Ivan said. He'd turned pale.

Their transport arrived soon after, a recognisable cab with a Bath Spa Taxis emblem on the roof.

Most of the journey was in silence. The reckless driving of the car seemed to have affected Ivan. Mel tried saying something about the venue for the soirée and got one-word answers. It was like being with Anthony. 'See you at Corsham tomorrow, then,' he said when the taxi stopped outside his lodgings. 'Early as usual to get ready?'

'Yes,' Ivan said.

Inside the house, Mel closed the front door as quietly as he could, crept upstairs, let himself into his room and slid the precious Amati viola under the bed. Later, he would practise scales, still getting the measure of this marvellous new outlet for his talent. For now, playtime of a different sort was overdue. He stripped to the waist, washed at the hand-basin in the corner, refreshed the deodorant and the aftershave, put on a fresh shirt and checked his hair in the mirror. Then he reached to the back of his sock drawer for two miniatures of gin and a small can of tonic and left his room to cross the passage to Tippi's bedroom. She liked her G&T and Mel liked the result. It took the edge off her sarcasm and made her even more randy.

He didn't knock. They had an understanding. He opened the door and said, 'Better late than never, huh?'

'Late for what?' said a voice he didn't expect.

Tippi's mother, with a crocodile smile, was sitting on the bed.

A better man might have thought of some clever excuse. Mel sighed and said, 'Fair cop.'

This was no bad response, as it turned out, because it avoided an elaborate lie and had a sense of contrition. Mrs. Carlyle must have been expecting some tall story she could lay into. Instead she was thrown off course. Rather than attacking Mel, she started to account for her own behaviour, explaining what she was doing in her daughter's room. 'I came up here to put away some of her washing. She leaves it for days on the clothes-rack in the kitchen if I don't, and she may not mind you seeing her frillies, but I'm old-fashioned enough to think it isn't quite the thing.'

Mel nodded as if he approved every word.

Mrs. Carlyle said, 'Is that gin and tonic you're holding, Mel?'

'Would you like some?' he said, pleased to find anything to say that wouldn't land him deeper in trouble.

'I wouldn't mind, but not here. We don't want Tippi walking in and finding us.'

'True.'

'Heaven knows what she'd think mummy was up to. Bring it across to my room.'

Mel had alarming doubts of his own about what mummy was up to, but he'd offered the drink and he couldn't easily refuse. 'Is she about?'

'Carry the booze across and I'll tell you.'

He felt he had no option.

'Last door on the left,' Mrs. Carlyle said. 'Don't be surprised how bijou it is. When I took a lodger I switched rooms.'

He pushed open her bedroom door. Certainly it was small, and dominated by a double bed that was a nest of pink, with ruched satin along the headboard and sides. The walls, too, were pink, with a design of ribbon and roses.

'Don't stand on ceremony,' Mrs. Carlyle said. 'Make yourself comfortable on the bed. I don't have room for a chair, as you see. I have to perch on the edge of the mattress when I'm using my dressing table.'

Uneasily he lowered himself into the soft-
ness of goose down and foam rubber. He
was facing the window, which was mostly
covered by pink velvet draped in two deep
curves held by tiebacks. He couldn't help
thinking it was the shape of a pair of enormous buttocks.

'There isn't much choice over seating arrangements, is there?' Mrs. Carlyle said. She
took her place beside him and they both
sank a few inches deeper. 'Yours is the
master bedroom, which is right and proper
for a masterful man.'

'I wouldn't say I'm masterful.'

'We'll find out presently. I'm ready for that
snifter now,'

He felt the warmth of her hip against his.
In this new predicament he'd almost forgotten he was still holding the miniatures. 'Do
you have a glass?'

'Not here. Let's be depraved and drink
the gin straight from the bottle and chase it
with the tonic.'

'All right.' He handed her one of the gins.

She unscrewed it and tipped the contents
straight down her throat.

He handed her the tonic and she took a
gulp of that.

'Nice,' she said. 'Next time, we can do it
properly with my Waterford glasses and ice

and lemon, but you made an offer I couldn't refuse. Seize the moment, I say. Do you believe in seizing the moment?'

'I like a drink, if that's what you mean.'

'How old are you, Mel, if you don't mind me asking? And don't say old enough to sit on a lady's bed and sink gin. That's self-evident.'

'Twenty-nine.'

'Are you sure? Not an itsy-witsy bit over thirty?'

'It's the truth.'

'You just appear more mature than that. Far be it from me to complain. The reason I asked is that I was lying here on the bed a couple of nights ago thinking about you — in a totally innocent way, I must add — and it struck me that you must be quite a bit older than Tippi.'

'Tippi?' Mel said as if he hadn't heard of her. 'I've no idea. How old is she?'

'Eighteen last August twentieth. Not quite a Virgo.'

Mel couldn't follow that, so he looked steadily ahead.

'And I had her when I was twenty-one, so I'm thirty-nine, only ten years older than you. Do you realise what that means?'

'Not really.'

'You're closer in age to me than you are

to Tippi.'

'Is that a fact?' he said with all the enthusiasm of a man told that a pit-bull terrier wanted stroking.

'And I was reading in the *Daily Mail* that it's become very fashionable for men to be attracted to women older than they are. It's all about sophistication and experience, on the part of the women, I must add. I'm not saying men aren't sophisticated and experienced about certain things we won't go into — not after only one G&T — but when a knowledgeable woman takes the initiative it enriches the man's enjoyment, and I can understand why.'

Was this a try for more gin? It could be a way of escape if he could leave the room and find some reason not to return. A sudden emergency? A blackout? A coronary?

'The shame of it is that there's this wealth of experience in my generation that men aren't aware of,' Mrs. Carlyle continued while Mel was weighing the options. 'They get distracted by young things who know nothing at all. Surface impressions are so misleading, Mel. A pretty face with a figure to match and they think that's all there is in life. What fools they are. And the biggest fools are the old fools, middle-aged men who chase after girls scarcely out of school.'

Mel wouldn't mind betting Tippi had left school two years ago, at sixteen, the earliest possible opportunity. She wasn't the brightest. But he'd got an opening here. He could take a strong line and get out of this unscathed. 'Are you talking about me, Mrs. Carlyle?'

'Cyn,' she said.

'I don't follow you,' he said, already undermined.

'My first name is Cynthia, but I prefer Cyn if we're getting on closer terms, and you don't need to state the obvious. If I've heard it once, I've heard it a hundred times.'

'Well . . . Cyn . . . I didn't like the drift of what you were saying. I'm not a middle aged predator.'

'Lord love us, Mel, it wasn't you I was talking about. It was the man who parks his car across the street and sits there waiting for her.'

Another surprise. She was full of them. 'Who's that?'

'Don't ask me. I don't know anything about him except he's no spring chicken. Anyone can see that.'

'What's he like?'

'Quite good-looking, dark-haired going grey at the sides. I've been watching him through the binoculars I use when I'm watching the birds on my feeders. He's forty if he's a day.'

'When did he first appear?'

'A couple of days ago.'

'Is he there now?' Mel started to get up.

Mrs. Carlyle grabbed his arm and pulled him down again. 'He'll see you. It's better to look through the lace curtains downstairs.'

'Shall we go down, then?'

'He won't be there now. Tippi went out for a manicure and he'll know that. He's probably parked outside the shop.'

'Are you sure it's Tippi he's interested in?'

She giggled a little. 'What are you suggesting, Mel — that I'm the star attraction?'

This wasn't what Mel was thinking. It was far more likely some crook had got a sniff of the Amati. 'As the man of the house, I'd better go downstairs and check. Where do you keep your binoculars?'

'They'll be where I left them, on the sill in the front room. I'll come with you.'

'No need.'

'I insist.'

Any excuse to be out of here, he thought — and the man in the street interested him as well. He took the stairs fast, with Cyn Carlyle not far behind. He grabbed the binoculars. 'Which direction?'

'A little to your right if he's still there. Oh, I say. That's him, our stalker.'

Mel adjusted the focus and felt his blood run cold. He was looking at a black car, a Megane, and he was pretty sure it was the same car that had raced out of the forecourt of the Michael Tippett Centre.

There was definitely someone in the driver's seat, but in shadow.

'I think it's me he's tailing,' he said, handing the binoculars to Mrs. Carlyle. 'I've seen him before. I'm going out to have a word with him. Shut the door after me.'

'Is that wise?' she said.

Mel was already though the door and crossing the street. He headed straight for the car at a fast step, but the driver was faster. Two massive roars from the engine and the vehicle was in motion.

Mel was about to cross in front of it, to the driver's side. When the car powered away from the kerb, he jerked to a stop and took a step back. Even so, it caught his right leg below the knee, tipped him off balance and threw him onto the road. It was a good thing he wasn't any closer or he would have ended up dead. As it was, his left hand and arm took most of his weight. His shoulder crunched against the tarmac and his head followed.

The driver must have known he'd caused an accident, but he didn't stop. Mel watched the car race to the far end of the street and over the crossroads without a flicker of the brake-lights.

Crazy. It had to be the same fool who'd been at the Tippett Centre. The pity of it was that Mel still hadn't got a sighting of him.

Shaken and angry, he heaved himself into a sitting position. His hand was smarting. There was grazing from the smallest finger to the heel of his palm. Blood was starting to ooze from the flesh. And this was the hand he used for fingering. He didn't think anything was broken, but it could so easily have been. He got to his feet, checked that nothing else was coming up the street, and returned to the house.

The door was opened by Mrs. Carlyle. 'Are you all right?'

'Just about.'

'You're not. You're bleeding.'

He looked at the hand again. 'It's not serious. I'd better run some water over it.'

'That was masterful,' she said.

'Idiotic, in my opinion.'

'You, not him,' she said. 'He could have killed you. He wasn't going to stop. It's a disgrace. I'll call the police right away.'

'Don't do that. I don't want all the hassle.'

'I think I should.'

'It's more trouble than it's worth. I didn't get the number. Didn't even get a proper look at the driver.'

'He shouldn't get away with it, whoever he is.'

'Can I use the tap in the kitchen?'

She followed him along the passage and ran the water for him. 'Look at your hand, you poor dear. Is it painful?'

'It's numb. It just needs cleaning.'

'I'll get some paper tissue. I was so impressed by you, Mel, dashing out there to deal with the stalker. He panicked at the sight of you bearing down on him.'

'Did you get a look at him?'

'No,' she said. 'My eyes were on you alone. You're shaking.'

'I'm not surprised.'

'I'm all of a quiver myself. What we both need is a socking great G&T. Shall we go to the master bedroom and see if the master has any more supplies?'

'My legs wouldn't carry me up there,' Mel said. 'Right now all I want is a strong black coffee.'

18

The only member of CID claiming to know anything about classical music was John Leaman, so next morning he got the job of listing all the Staccati tours and concerts he could trace from the internet. The quartet's website was unhelpful. It had obviously been relaunched recently with all the emphasis on the current players. Whoever had designed it was under instructions to gloss over the problems of the past four years, so there was no detailed log of past performances. A summary of the cities they had visited and concert halls they had played in was provided, but without dates. He had to look for the information elsewhere. By degrees he got there. In their prime they had toured widely and earned rave reviews, but it became obvious that they had done little as an ensemble since 2008.

'When exactly was it formed?' Diamond asked.

'Sixteen years ago,' Leaman said. 'Ivan Bogdanov and Cat Kinsella were founder members. The others are replacements for people who left.'

'And who was Staccati?'

There was some sniggering behind the computer screens.

Leaman studied his boss's face, uncertain if he was being led into a trap. 'It's a musical term for short notes sharply separated from each other, from the Italian, *staccato*, meaning "detached".'

'Strange choice,' Diamond said with an effort to cover up his ignorance. 'It's the opposite of what you want for a team of people. They ought to be called Unison. That's what they should be projecting.'

'It hasn't held them back. They were very successful, up there with the best, doing concerts across the world and making recordings — until the viola player dropped out.'

'Dropped out or dropped dead?'

'He went missing on one of the foreign tours and wasn't heard of again.'

'Ah, yes. Harry . . . ?'

'Cornell.'

'Cat told me about him.'

'It threw them right off course. Big efforts were made to find him. Interpol were notified. The theory seems to be that he gambled heavily.'

'On what?'

'Casino stuff. They think he got on the wrong side of some bad people and was taken out.'

'Gambling doesn't fit my idea of a classical musician.'

'It comes with the territory. Quartets, in particular. Four is the right number for card games. The Budapest were well known for playing bridge, and for high stakes. I think the Amadeus preferred poker.'

'But that's in-house. You're telling me Harry Cornell played with professionals.'

'And rather badly. It's the best guess, that's all.'

'I still can't see it, a serious musician wasting his time gambling.'

'Plenty have, from Mozart to Elgar. It could be to do with calculating the odds. There's a well-known link between music and maths.'

'I'll take your word for it,' Diamond said. 'So when Harry went missing, why didn't they get a quick replacement? They were famous. They could take their pick.'

'It's not so simple. For a long time they expected he would turn up again so they couldn't offer anyone regular work. They performed with stand-ins who didn't cut it for one reason or another. The mix has to be right. Everyone has to blend in. You may find a brilliant soloist who can't work with others. It's as much about temperament and team-building as musical ability. They were unlucky or unwise in their choices and for a time they went their own ways.'

'Broke up?'

'In all but name. Some time last spring they found this new man Mel Farran and he seems to be doing okay. It clinched the residency at Bath for them and soon they'll be touring again.'

'If they aren't involved in a murder trial.' Diamond picked up the printout of Leaman's list. 'Is this their itinerary? They certainly travelled. I heard about the Japan trip from Cat.'

'They've been there a few times.'

'Was this with Anthony on board?'

'The last couple of visits.'

'When Mari was probably in the audience. I'm assuming Anthony was the main attraction.'

'Why him in particular?' Leaman asked.

'Obvious, isn't it? Good-looking, intense and a brilliant violinist. I expect she wasn't the only young girl who lay awake thinking about him.' Diamond continued to study the list. 'Budapest was where Harry went missing. Before that they were touring other European cities. Paris, Rome, Vienna.' He stopped. 'They performed in Vienna in October 2008?'

'A city noted for its music,' Leaman said.

'I know. I was there this summer.' A tingling sensation crept over his face. He called across the room to Ingeborg. 'Remember the Japanese woman you researched for me who drowned in the Danube canal?'

'Miss Kojima.'

'I don't recall the name. I doubt if I even asked you. This was something I didn't want to get involved in for personal reasons.'

'She took her own life.'

'So they reckoned. They found the little ivory thingummy representing suicide.'

'The netsuke.'

'Didn't you tell me this happened as much as four years before I was there?'

'That's right, guv. She wasn't a student, like Mari. She was in her mid-twenties, from Tokyo, and she'd come to Europe as a tourist, apparently alone. Do you think there's a link?'

'I don't know, but I intend to compare dates. If this happened while the Staccati were performing in Vienna, we could be on

333

to something.'

'I'll check right away.'

Images that pained him coursed through his brain. The embankment beside the Danube canal. Paloma spotting the bunch of lilies on the ground and then seeing the other flowers, dead and brittle, forced between the lattice struts of the stone wall. He'd insisted on moving on and she'd refused to treat it as an unknown tragedy that didn't concern them. She'd seemed to think discovering the lilies in their path and replacing them in the pathetic little shrine was significant, a symbolic call to find out the true facts about whoever had died.

Against all his instincts he'd pandered to her superstition, getting Ingeborg to check the story on the internet. The way he'd dealt with it, trying to steer Paloma away from the depressing story once he had related it to her, had led directly to another unhappy waterside encounter, this time beside the Avon, their argument and break-up. In her eyes he was a lost cause, a stony-hearted professional unwilling to open up to sympathy for others or even for himself.

The whole episode still pained him deeply. In an effort to move on, he'd been trying to put it out of his mind, but without much success.

And now it might touch on the case he was investigating.

Ingeborg looked up from her computer screen, 'Found it, guv. The body in Vienna was discovered on the tenth of November, 2008.'

'Yes, but when was she reported missing?'

'I'm not sure if she was.'

'Nobody noticed she'd gone?'

'She wasn't travelling with friends or family. When they found the body, they estimated she'd been in the water three to four weeks, which would make it October.'

Trying to sound calm, he checked the list in his hand. 'When the Staccati were giving a series of concerts in Vienna. A Japanese girl. A canal. The quartet in town. I should have been on to this before now. Was there any evidence that the dead girl, Miss . . .'

'Kojima.'

'. . . was into classical music?'

Ingeborg shrugged. 'I don't recall anything like that. I can access the report again.'

'Where did you find it?'

'In one of the Vienna papers. It wasn't a huge story. I had to read it in translation.'

'Get it on screen again, everything you can. I'm going to call the Viennese police. And the Japanese embassy. They were helpful over Mari, but it always takes longer than you expect to get anything out of these government agencies.' He'd written the name of the Vienna victim and the estimated date of her disappearance on a notepad he'd picked up from one of the desks and he now saw that the top sheet was smeared with black ink. It was all over his hand as well. In his fury with himself he'd squeezed the pen so hard that it had splintered and leaked. 'Okay,' he said, addressing the entire room. 'I want the full life histories of each of the Staccati people — everything we know about them — on my desk before the end of the afternoon. And when I say Staccati I'm including previous members and the manager. What's his name? Christmas.'

'Douglas Christmas,' Halliwell said.

'Yes, he's part of it. He may have an office in London, but he makes the key decisions and I wouldn't mind betting he turns up for the foreign gigs.'

From across the room someone had started humming a tune.

'Who's that?' Diamond said.

Silence shut everything down like a power cut.

'Come on,' Diamond said. 'Share it with us.'

Everyone in the team knew it was best to come clean when the boss was in this sort of mood. The junior member, Paul Gilbert, cleared his throat and started up again with a half-hearted rendering of the old Band Aid number, 'Do They Know It's Christmas?'

'That's more than enough,' Diamond said, flapping his hand. 'You must be older than you look. I was a mere youth when that came out. If that's your take on my comments, DC Gilbert, you'd better investigate Mr. Christmas. Make him your specialist study. Get his background, how he took on the quartet and where he was at the time of these two murders. With your investigative skills we can look forward to finding out if it really is Christmas.'

Gilbert had got off lightly. Humour can be the saving grace of something as grim as a murder investigation, but it has to be well timed. He'd picked the wrong moment.

The evening soirée at Corsham Court had taken on an added importance, a chance to see the four main suspects in performance. Ingeborg collected Diamond from his home in Weston and watched him wedge himself into her Ka.

'You're looking different, Sergeant Smith,' he said when he'd got the belt across his middle.

'Is that meant as a compliment?' She'd fastened the blonde hair high on her head with two glittery combs and was in a burgundy-coloured suit.

'Statement of fact.'

'Now come on,' she said, laughing. 'If we're supposed to appear like a couple enjoying an evening of culture, you'd better start acting the full gent. It's a posh do, this one.'

'Okay, you look like the Queen of Sheba. How's that?'

'Better.'

'Better? It's spot on. It's a musical reference, in case you didn't know. What do you think of my get-up?' he asked.

'Not very different.'

'It's the best I've got. Will it pass?'

'It passed a good ten years ago. If you want a musical equivalent, it's the "Dead March" from *Saul*. Are we quits?'

'But this is my best tie.'

'I'd call that the *Pathétique*.'

'You win,' he said. 'Don't know enough to compete. Seriously, am I dressed right for a soirée?'

'You'll get by, guv — just about.'

'Good enough.'

'If we sit at the back.'

'I didn't get a lot of time for thinking

about my wardrobe. I was still at the office at six, on the line to Vienna.'

'Any joy?'

'They promised full cooperation. This was the police I'm speaking of. They regarded the case as closed, but they're willing to send over everything they have on file. And the Austrian embassy are going to look at their records.'

'It's worth pursuing,' Ingeborg said. 'Too close to our case to be a coincidence.'

'I just wish I'd cottoned on before this.' He checked for the crease in his trousers and found two. Should have been more careful before hanging the suit last time he put it away. 'Is there much socialising at these things?'

'I couldn't tell you. I haven't been to one.'

'There's got to be some. You do the chat and I'll drink the bubbly and watch the action.'

Corsham Court, off the A4 to Chippenham, is a grandiose hotchpotch of English architecture, originally Elizabethan and home over the centuries to the elite of Wiltshire families, the Hungerfords, the Thynnes and the Methuens. They all brought in builders, with mixed results. Even the illustrious Capability Brown had a go. As well as landscaping the grounds and extending the building he converted the East Wing into a magnificent picture gallery, and this was the setting for the Staccati concert.

The guests were assembling in the ante-room, where it soon became obvious that most of them knew each other. Diamond spotted several who could be numbered among the great and the good of Bath society.

'Forgot to wear my chain of office,' he muttered to Ingeborg as they faced each other on the fringe of the gathering.

'What's that, linked handcuffs?'

'Where are the musicians?'

'They'll be tuning up. Can't expect them to circulate.' She froze.

'What's up?'

'Don't look round. Someone you know just came in. Keep talking to me.'

'Who is it?'

'Your friend Paloma.'

His voice went up an octave. 'Paloma? Here?'

'She's with someone. I don't think she's seen you. They're on the opposite side, near the fireplace.'

'Who? Who's she with?'

'A guy in an expensive suit. Can't say I recognise him.'

Diamond's above-average blood pressure soared to well above average. Who was this dog's dinner Paloma was partnering? The prospect of her taking up with someone else hadn't entered his head. He glanced over his shoulder. 'Which side of the fireplace?'

'This side. They're being served drinks. You could look now.'

Paloma was in an outfit he hadn't seen before, black, with a wispy blue scarf or pashmina. She looked taller. New shoes. Extra high heels. She was laughing at something, clearly enjoying herself.

The dog's dinner was taller than Diamond — allowing Paloma to wear the high heels without towering over him. He was also slimmer and younger. Certainly had more hair and it was only slightly silver at the sides. In a dove grey three-piece suit, he exuded privilege and class. Even had a pink tie.

Diamond had no idea who he was.

'Take it easy, guv,' Ingeborg said.

'I'm okay,' he said through clenched teeth.

'You're staring.'

He took a deep breath and looked away. 'When everyone goes in, we'll hold back and let them find seats. Then we can make sure we're not too close. I need another drink.'

The champagne was coming round on

silver trays. He reached for a glass, downed it fast and took another.

'You might need to get to a seat earlier than you think,' Ingeborg told him.

'She's had her hair done differently.'

'I wouldn't let that bother you, guv.'

Someone in a pinstripe and purple shirt who seemed to be acting as host approached them with another man in tow. 'Here am I, doing my best to introduce people and I don't even know your names.'

'Ingeborg Smith.'

It took a nudge from Ingeborg to get Diamond to speak his name. Mentally he was over by the fireplace.

'Bathonians both?' the host man said.

'Locals, yes,' Ingeborg said.

'This is Mr, em . . .' The host turned to the other man.

'Christmas. Doug Christmas, the manager of the quartet, down from London.' Dark, with longish hair brushed back, he flashed a smile, but more at Ingeborg than Diamond. 'I do my best to smooth the way for them.'

'Did you arrange all this, then?' Ingeborg asked Christmas after the host had moved on to make more introductions. Diamond, still in a state of shock, plainly wasn't up for polite conversation.

'Not tonight's concert. That's down to the

university. They have the use of some offices here, so they have a foot in the door, so to speak. Have you heard the Staccati before, Ingeborg?'

'Not like this, not live,' she said. 'We're looking forward to it, aren't we?' She turned to Diamond. 'Looking forward to it,' she repeated as if to a deaf man.

'Can't wait,' he said after a pause.

Ingeborg turned back to Douglas Christmas. 'Do you go on tour with them when they perform abroad?'

'Not for the entire tour. Can't spare the time, more's the pity,' he said. 'I make a point of visiting them at various concerts. Bring them a few treats from home, new shirts, the latest paperbacks, music magazines, a large box of chocs for Cat the cellist. It keeps up their spirits. You can get depressed living in foreign hotels for long periods.'

'I expect you're in regular touch with them.'

'Daily. Hourly, if there's a crisis.'

'What can go wrong?'

'You name it. No one to meet them at the airport. Sub-standard hotel. Cock-ups over the concert programme. There was even one horrible tour when our violist went missing. A very gifted musician, too. I had to drop everything and take the first flight to Budapest to sort things out.'

'What happened?'

'They cancelled the concert. I arrived in a murderous mood, after Harry's blood, and I still feel bad about that, because the poor fellow stayed missing. No one has seen him or heard anything to this day. It was a massive setback. We muddled through for a time with substitute players, but it wasn't the same. We've only recently got back to some kind of normality.'

Part of Diamond's brain had been taking in what was said. He dragged his attention back to this side of the room and turned to Christmas. 'Was he scared of you?'

This brought a frown and raised eyebrows. 'Who?'

'The violist who disappeared.'

'Harry? Good Lord, no.'

'You said you were in a murderous mood.'

'A turn of phrase, no more.' He laughed. 'I may be known in the trade as Jaws, but I treat the quartet like my own kids. I'm still broken up about Harry.'

'What could have happened?'

'I wish I knew. He was a loner. I suppose they all are in their different ways, only he was always more secretive than the others and always strapped for cash, asking me for something ahead of payday. I discovered he was a compulsive gambler, off to the casino each time they arrived in a new city. He didn't tell the others, as far as I know. He was always back in good time for each rehearsal and performance and always played divinely. You can't do that if you're high on something.'

'So he got on all right with them?'

'No problem I ever heard of. There are always tensions between talented people and we have strong characters in the Staccati, but Harry dealt with personal relationships in an adult way.'

'Was he depressed?'

'He didn't appear so. We went through all this at the time with the Budapest police.'

'I'm sure,' Diamond said. 'Have any of the quartet told you about their current problem?'

'Problem?' His face turned a shade paler. 'What's that?'

'Here in Bath.' Diamond pitched his voice lower. 'I'll be straight with you, Mr. Christmas. Ingeborg is a detective sergeant and I'm the head of CID. We're investigating the suspicious death of a young Japanese woman who seems to have come to Bath because she was a keen fan of the quartet. She was found in the river some days ago.'

'You don't think my clients have anything to do with it?' Christmas said in an appalled tone. 'They're not going to kill fans. They need them.'

'There may be a connection with a case in Vienna four years ago. Another Japanese woman. She went missing at the same time the Staccati were performing there. She was found in the Danube canal.'

'I know nothing of this.'

'But you know they were in Vienna in 2008?'

'True. They played several nights at the Konzerthaus. I was there for one of them and it was a perfectly normal gig. This is the first I've heard about a missing woman and it's outrageous to suggest such a thing has any connection with the quartet.'

'The body wasn't found until after you'd all left. So you were in Vienna yourself?'

'It's one of my favourite cities.'

'Mine, too,' Diamond said as if he was a world traveller. 'Was this visit prior to the Budapest engagement when your violist went missing?'

The manager's face creased in alarm. 'By God, it was. All part of our 2008 European tour. How extraordinary. It's got to be a ghastly coincidence.'

Diamond didn't need to comment on

that. A voice from across the room announced, 'The concert will begin shortly.
Kindly proceed into the picture galley and
take your seats.'

'Are you going in?' Christmas said.

Diamond nodded. 'Wouldn't miss it for
the world.'

'Better not delay.' He was off.

Diamond's gaze returned to the opposite
side of the room, where Paloma and her
partner were in conversation with some
other people. 'They're in no hurry,' he said
to Ingeborg. 'Why don't they bloody move?'

'Cool it, guv.'

The anteroom was emptying fast. His plan
to hold back would misfire if he and Ingeborg were left there, conspicuous.

'We'd better go in,' Ingeborg said.

Still he hesitated.

And then Paloma turned her head and
saw them. Her brown eyes held Diamond's
briefly and widened in shock. Of all the
people she might have expected to see at a
chamber music recital, he would not have
been high on the list. Clearly embarrassed,
she swung away, grasped her partner's
forearm and almost tugged him towards the
door.

'Did you see that?' Diamond said to
Ingeborg. 'She was holding his arm. Do you

347

think they're an item?'

'Guv, I've no idea.'

He was hurting. 'The body language says everything, doesn't it? They're more than just friends.'

'Don't let it get to you. It may be quite innocent.'

'What's she doing here anyway?'

'I expect she's saying exactly the same about you. We'd better go in.'

They took the end seats in the last row but one. Paloma and her escort were closer to the front, in the middle of the second row. Capability Brown's gallery was seventy-two feet by twenty-four and the seating had been arranged lengthwise, but in a shallow arc facing a white marble fireplace. Chairs and music stands for the performers were positioned in front.

Diamond's police career had put him in some unlikely places. This, by his standards, was among the most alien. Classical art was not his thing any more than music was. The pictures were hung in the style of the early nineteenth century, when the objective was to use as much wall space as possible. Large gilt-framed paintings from the Methuen family's collection were suspended one above the other in twos and threes. To his eye the pictures looked sombre and repellent. He had no confidence that the music would be any more congenial.

A ripple of applause started and grew in volume. The quartet made their entrance. Ivan Bogdanov led them in, violin and bow in hand, a squat, bald figure in a white jacket and white bow tie that was their uniform. Even Cat Kinsella had a jacket over a white top and wore dark trousers like the others. Her waist size was probably more than twice Ivan's. But she walked well and had no difficulty carrying her cello. Anthony Metcalf was the tallest, handsome, expressionless, indifferent to the audience. Finally came Mel Farran and he was definitely interested in the sea of faces, taking nervous glances as he moved towards the music stands. A strip of white bandage covered the outer edge of his left hand.

'Pick your killer,' Diamond said to Ingeborg and the woman in front of them stopped clapping and turned to see who had spoken.

The musicians took their places and spent a moment adjusting the lights on their music stands.

'What are they going to play?'

'It's on the sheet,' Ingeborg said out of the side of her mouth.

'What sheet?'

'On the chair when we came in.'

'Ah.' He'd been too interested in Paloma to notice. He shifted his weight to the left, delved under his thigh and retrieved it.

Beethoven, Opus 59, No. 3 in C major.

The quartet must have tuned their instruments off stage. Ivan gave a nod, put bow to string and they were straight into it.

19

'Is that it?' Diamond asked. The clapping had finished and everyone was moving.

'Only the interval,' Ingeborg said.

'God help us.'

'Be thankful for small mercies.'

He stood up to get the feeling back into his legs. The seats weren't the most comfortable. At the same time he looked across to where Paloma had been.

She'd gone.

He'd spent much of the concert debating with himself whether to go over and speak to her. She had definitely spotted him. It seemed churlish to go through the evening without saying anything. Yet weeks had passed with no contact and the last words she'd spoken had been about as final as you can get between people in a relationship. He wasn't good at peacemaking.

And yet . . .

If she'd come here alone, he told himself,

he would have seized his chance. She might well have given him the frost, but at least the pain would be private to the two of them. The new companion — or whatever he was to her — made any approach a minefield. Diamond knew for sure that if the dog's dinner pitched in with backchat or sarcasm he'd give him more than a mouthful, and what use was that? Paloma would side with her new man and a bad situation would get massively worse.

'I'll be back presently,' Ingeborg said.

'Oh, sure.'

Needing to get his head straight as well as pumping some blood into his legs, he stepped over to the nearest wall and stood in front of the pictures. They held as much interest for him as outdated copies of *Country Life* in a dentist's waiting room. Reynolds, Romney and Rubens weren't his choice of painters. The Diamond theory of art required scenes and figures that looked real, as these did, but not so laboured over that they lost all vitality. He preferred the style of Hockney, fresh, bold and cheerful.

'Didn't expect to find you here.'

He swung round and there she was. Give Paloma her due: she wasn't letting their recent history stop her from speaking to him.

No problem now with circulation. Heart thumping, he managed to say, 'Likewise. How's it going?'

'Fine. And you?'

'Soldiering on.'

Something was different about her, apart from the hair colour. He realised her eyes were level with his. Those crazy heels made her taller.

But the eyes weren't angry, as he'd seen them last. Her mouth curved upwards. 'In all the time I've known you, string quartets were never mentioned.'

'That's for sure. I'm no expert.'

'But it's nice you're giving it a try. The Staccati are about as good as it gets. Did Ingeborg persuade you to come?'

She'd spotted Ingeborg, then. What did she think — that he was dating one of his team? 'No. I invited her in case I made a fool of myself clapping in the wrong places.'

'Is she into classical music?'

'Not really. As an ex-journo, she's done most things.' He'd skirted around the real reason for his presence here. Paloma seemed so encouraged that he was doing the cultural bit that he didn't want to disillusion her and admit he was on police business.

'Invitations to these soirées are hard to come by,' she said.

'I got ours through Georgina. She's well connected.'

'Through her choral singing? Of course. So did you enjoy the Beethoven?'

'I'd have enjoyed it more if I hadn't got pins and needles in my legs. The seats aren't the most comfortable.'

'I know what you mean. I wanted to stand up halfway through. I expect they hired them specially for the concert.'

'Those look better.' He was eyeing the long row of padded chairs ranged along the wall below the pictures.

'They're Chippendale,' Paloma said, 'and not for sitting on. Not these days, anyway. I'll tell you something that will amuse you. See the fabric they're covered with? What do you notice about it?'

'Matches the walls?'

'Right. It's exactly the same stuff, crimson silk damask. At some point the original chair coverings got worn to shreds and needed replacing. Unfortunately the same fabric couldn't be got for love nor money, so some bright spark came up with the idea of cutting out patches of the wall-covering from behind the pictures and using them on the chairs. If you took the pictures down, you'd see a lot of large square holes. It means they can't change the arrangement, so they're stuck with this crowded display that was okay two hundred years ago, but looks all wrong now.'

'How did you find out?'

'I know the house well. It's sometimes used for period dramas. *Northanger Abbey. The Remains of the Day.* They usually get my help.'

'Should have realised. Seeing you here, I didn't think of that. Is the business thriving?'

'Doing okay. And yours? Still keeping the crime rate down?'

He smiled. 'Mostly.'

'How's Raffles?'

'The same, running the house the way he likes.'

The small talk would run out soon. Diamond hadn't found out for certain if she was in a new relationship.

'People seem to be returning to their seats,' Paloma said.

'Where exactly are you?' he asked as if he hadn't been watching her all evening.

'Over there. Third row back. You haven't met Mike, have you? The tall guy in the light grey suit. He'll be wondering where I am. Better get back to him. Enjoy the rest of the music.'

She was away. A civilized exchange had been ruined for him by the way she spoke about the dog's dinner: Mike — not Michael, but the shorter, more familiar name, suggesting a closeness that hit Diamond like a low punch. The very fact that she'd left the guy alone for the whole of the interval indicated that they'd passed the stage of dating. *He'll be wondering where I am.* She could have been talking about her husband.

Diamond slunk back to his seat.

Ingeborg was already looking at the programme. 'The cellist is doing a solo next.'

'Ah.'

' "Salut d'Amour".'

Cat Kinsella's arrival was warmly applauded. The confident way this woman with the girth of a sumo wrestler carried in her cello and positioned it between her knees spoke volumes for her temperament. She began playing with a clear, strong note.

Elgar's bittersweet music was never going to lift Diamond out of his low mood, but he was here for a reason and by degrees he forced himself to give all his attention to Cat. What was it that made her prefer playing in the quartet to giving solo performances like this? By all accounts she was in the first rank as a cellist, capable of any of the great concertos in the repertoire. She could be a virtuoso, a top name in her own right.

There are people who think of themselves as team players. Mostly they relish the support of those around them. He wasn't sure if this was true of the Staccati. They were more like talented individuals who tolerated each other. Of the four he'd met, Cat had the most regard for the others. She spoke well of them all, even the nitpicking Ivan. With her sharp wit, she was good at defusing tensions between the men. As the solitary female, did she see her role as a peacekeeper or something more? Were they a foster family for a woman without children of her own? Or was she living the dream that she had three lovers? Who could say what her sexual fantasies might be — or what actually happened.

Out here alone, the focal point of the entire room, interpreting Elgar with skill and sensitivity that even Diamond could appreciate, she still left him puzzling how it could be that she was happier when performing with the men around her.

The piece came to a plaintive end. She stood and dipped her head as the audience responded. Seated again, and as if to demonstrate that there was another side to Cat Kinsella, she launched into the 'Ritual Fire Dance'. The audience had its passions well stirred and quite forgot that it was middle class in middle England in midwinter.

'How about that?' Ingeborg said over the cheering at the end.

'Best I've heard tonight.'

'Me too.'

Difficult to follow a turn as gripping as that. Next on was Mel Farran, the new member. He looked even more ill at ease than when he'd made his original entrance with the others. He knocked one of the music stands with his foot and almost tipped it over. Some of the bandage on his hand had come unstuck and he had to press it back into place. Mel clearly wasn't comfortable in this situation. Before he played the first note he seemed to be scanning the rows as if he expected a gunman out there. Diamond watched, intrigued. *All right, chum. The worst you'll see is a couple of detectives you've already met, and they ought to give you confidence. If you've done nothing wrong, that is.*

Mel played two pieces by Fritz Kreisler. Once under way, he became calmer and so did the audience. Difficult for Diamond to tell whether he was playing well. More out of relief than anything else the audience gave him a generous reception, after which he was joined by Ivan Bogdanov for an arrangement for viola and violin of Handel's

358

Harpsichord Suite No. 7 in G minor. The two blended well.

While the piece was being played, Diamond's concentration wasn't total, or even partial. He'd heard almost as much of this stuff as a man could take in one evening — a man whose musical education hadn't up to now stretched beyond Freddie Mercury and Montserrat Caballé singing 'Barcelona'. His attention wandered to the huge painting over the mantel-piece, a particularly gruesome hunting scene. People mostly on horseback were slaughtering wolves and foxes with clubs and spears. Dead and dying animals testified to the success of the day's sport. A strange backdrop for a musical soirée. How ironic if one of the quartet turned out to be a killer.

All four returned to play the last piece on the programme, *Andante Festivo,* by Sibelius. At this stage of the evening the term 'strung out' summed up Diamond's condition in more senses than one. But the piece was mercifully over in about five minutes. Then to his despair the audience demanded an encore. They wouldn't stop clapping.

Ivan led the musicians off.

'Thank God,' Diamond said to Ingeborg.

She said, 'Hang about, guv. They're coming back.'

Diamond's buttocks flexed. Amazing any life was left in them.

Ivan stepped forward to speak. 'We would like to offer you a piece neglected by many ensembles: the Sibelius String Quartet in D minor, Opus 56.'

Huge applause.

The buttocks went into spasm. Another entire quartet.

As if he was a mind-reader, Ivan continued, 'But it's late and unfortunately we don't have time for the entire composition, so with apologies to Sibelius we'll pick it up at the start of the fifth and final movement. Thank you for being such a splendid audience.'

The quartet knew what they were doing. Whatever it was that made the Sibelius a neglected quartet, its climax was a sure-fire audience-pleaser, the Allegro, dynamic, demanding and impassioned. When the bows were lifted from the instruments a standing ovation followed. Diamond was among the first to rise. He needed no prompting.

'I've become a fan,' Ingeborg told him. 'Wasn't that awesome?'

'Yes, but don't overdo the clapping.'

'Such talent. It's almost impossible to

believe one of them could be . . .'

'I can believe it, no problem,' he said.

20

'What's the matter with you?' Ivan asked.

'My hand, you mean?' Mel said. 'It's not serious.'

'Your whole performance. You were pathetic. Timing, intonation. And don't blame the new instrument. You were perfectly good in rehearsal.'

The quartet were using the gothic library in the West Wing at Corsham Court as a base. Their manager Douglas had joined them. Tired and drained from the performance, they were supposed to be unwinding before travelling home. This wasn't unwinding; it was winding up.

Cat came to Mel's defence as if she was shaping a passage with her cello, a stabilising counterpoint. 'Ivan, that's way over the top. He wasn't that bad. He was a damn sight better than most of the so-called violists we've played with, and I never heard you slag one of them off.'

'Because we know he can do better.' Ivan turned on Mel again. 'Are you a drinker? If you are, we have a right to be told.'

With the musicians almost squaring up to each other, Douglas tried his old-school best to calm the situation. 'Steady on, old man.'

Mel decided the others deserved an explanation. More than anyone, he knew his playing hadn't been up to standard. 'Ivan is right. I was rubbish. I had a fall today. Well, to be honest, I was knocked down by a car.'

Douglas said, 'Stone the crows!'

'And it wasn't due to drink, not on my part, anyway.'

'Where did this happen?' Cat asked.

'In the street outside my lodgings. My landlady spotted this stationary car with someone seated inside staring at the house. He'd been there a long time and she thought we had a stalker. She has a rather attractive daughter. I went over to speak to the guy. When he saw me coming he drove off fast. I don't think he meant to hit me. He just wanted to be away, but the side of the car brushed against me and sent me flying.'

'So he *was* a stalker?' Cat said.

'He wasn't staying to talk about it, whoever he was.'

'That's how you did your hand?'

363

'It was grazed and bled a bit. My arm is the problem. It's stiff today and I bashed my head on the road as well.'

'And still turned up tonight and gave a performance?' Cat said. 'Played your solo pieces and the duet as well as the Beethoven and the Sibelius? That's heroic.' To Ivan, she said, 'I hope you're about to apologise for the snide remarks you made.'

'I do.'

'In all humility?' Cat said with a stare worthy of a headmistress.

Humility was an alien concept to Ivan, but he mumbled something that wasn't a denial.

'Your left hand is the one you use for fingering, isn't it?' Douglas said to Mel. 'I don't know how you got through the evening.'

'All those vibratos,' Cat said, her face creasing in sympathy.

'The fingers weren't damaged, I'm glad to say. I'd have let you know if I thought I was going to mess up. More than anything, my state of mind was the problem.'

'Listen, darling, you weren't pathetic, as Joe Stalin over there so unkindly put it. I don't suppose any of the audience noticed.'

Douglas said, 'I certainly didn't. And from the reception you were given there's no doubt Cat is right. Nobody was any the wiser.'

'I wouldn't count on it,' Mel said.

'Get a grip, people,' Cat said. 'This was one evening in front of twenty or thirty rich punters who think the only good note is a banknote. The bigger picture is that Mel's playing has raised our game. We're better now than at any time since we formed. Isn't that a fact, Anthony?'

The laconic second violin gave a nod.

'He says bang on, back of the net, hole in one,' Cat said.

Douglas shifted the focus back to the accident. 'Didn't the driver stop?'

Mel shook his head.

'Hit and run, the bastard,' Cat said.

'Did you get a look at him?' Douglas asked.

'My landlady did. She said he was in his forties, going grey and quite good looking. Not much of a description, I know, but she'd probably know him if she saw him again.'

'Did you call the police?'

Mel shook his head. 'Didn't get the number. And I don't think he meant to knock me over.'

'It was dangerous driving, whatever you may think.'

'Aside from the fact that the man's a menace to women,' Cat said.

'We can't be certain he was a stalker,' Douglas went on. 'Has it occurred to you, Mel, that this may have nothing to do with your landlady's daughter — that he was spying on you?'

'What for?' Ivan said.

'It crossed my mind, I have to say,' Mel said. 'I've been over it a few times. I wondered if he was interested in the Amati, waiting for a chance to break in and steal it.'

Cat was frowning. 'How would he know about the Amati? You've only had it a couple of days.'

'I've no idea.'

'It's not as if it was written up in lights. Only a handful of people know and most of them are in this room.'

'Well, it's news to me,' Douglas said. 'An Amati viola? That's a rare beast, isn't it? Where did you get it?'

'He's not at liberty to say,' Cat said. 'A secret millionaire. They never come my way.'

Ivan was still brooding over the mystery. 'There's some other explanation. Must be.'

'Wait a mo,' Douglas said, raising a finger. 'Have any of you thought this may be connected to Harry's disappearance?'

'Someone targeting violists?' Cat said. 'Come off it, Doug. Lightning doesn't strike twice.'

'We never discovered the reason.'

'That was four years ago in Budapest. It's history now and we're in England in case you haven't noticed. We've moved on. Don't put scary ideas into Mel's head. The poor lad has suffered enough.'

'Even so, we must take care of him. How are you getting back to Bath?'

'Taxis as usual,' Ivan said.

'I'll give Mel a lift in the Aston Martin. I'm still thinking we should report this incident to the police. Did you know they were here tonight? I met two of them before the concert.'

'A big guy called Diamond?' Cat said.

'Yes, and a blonde with a foreign-sounding name.'

'We knew they were coming,' Cat said. 'It's all about this unfortunate Japanese girl.'

'The police said something about this,' Douglas said. 'There's so much to catch up on.'

'She was found dead in the river, murdered apparently. They're saying she was a fan of ours.'

'Doesn't mean you're responsible.'

Ivan said, 'A point we all made clear. Once

the police get a sniff of something they think is suspicious, watch out. They're well capable of planting evidence. What's the term?'

'Stitching us up?' Cat said.

'That might be true in your country,' Douglas said. 'I can't believe the British bobby would stoop to anything so low.'

Ivan rolled his eyes. 'It's quite possible that the man who knocked Mel down was a plain clothes policeman keeping him under observation. Maybe we're all being spied on. There was a suspicious-looking car outside the Tippett Centre yesterday and he drove off fast when we spotted him. Mel saw it, too.'

'I'm totally confused now,' Douglas said.

'So am I,' Mel said. 'Some of these theories must be wrong. A sex pest, an instrument thief, a kidnapper of violists and a police spy? Let's try and keep a grip on reality.'

Douglas turned to Mel and smiled. 'Well said. This seems as good a moment as any to announce some good news.'

'We could certainly use some,' Cat said. 'What is it?'

He rubbed his hands. 'News travels fast these days, as we all know. There's a real buzz among concert managers around the world that the Staccati have re-formed. The enquiries are coming in thick and fast and I'm now in a position to offer you a five-week South American tour as soon as you've completed your stint here in Bath. You'll be going to some wonderful places — Rio de Janeiro, São Paulo, Montevideo, Buenos Aires, Santiago, Lima and Bogotá. Some of these cities have facilities you wouldn't believe, amazing concert halls that will sell out within hours. Five star hotels all the way.'

'And fees?' Ivan said.

'The best I've ever negotiated for you. South Americans adore their music and they're passionate about the chance of hearing you. I know it's a lot of travelling, but, believe me, you get well rewarded.'

'I'm tempted,' Cat said. 'As you know, I prefer longer stays, but this will be new territory, new shopping opportunities.'

'And a new market for your backlist,' Douglas added. 'A huge boost to your CD and video sales. Already several of them are talking about press calls and TV appearances.'

'What do you say, boys? Are we up for it?' Cat said.

After the build-up, the decision was low-key, a matter of looks, shrugs and nods, but no one disagreed.

'Super,' Douglas said. 'I'll confirm it all when I get back to London tomorrow.' At a stroke he'd removed all the negative feelings after the concert. 'And on that high note, I recommend a well-earned sleep. I'll bring the car round to the front entrance. I can find room for one more.'

It was agreed Ivan would travel with Douglas and Mel, leaving Cat to share a taxi with Anthony.

Mel and Ivan walked together to the main entrance, an opportunity for Mel to raise a point that had caused him some concern. 'I didn't say anything back there because everyone seemed to be getting paranoid, but there's something I should tell you about the car you and I saw out at the Tippett Centre.'

'What's that?' Ivan's tone was as friendly as a January night in Riga.

'I'm almost certain it followed my taxi home. It was the same car that knocked me down.'

'Unlikely,' he said. 'Talk about paranoid. You're sounding paranoid yourself.'

'You saw it. What make do you think it was?'

'A Megane.'

'That's the car that hit me.'

Ivan was silent a moment. Then he said, 'They're a common make. They're everywhere.'

'I'm telling you this because it seemed to me at the time you were visibly shaken just by the sight of that car. You went silent. You scarcely said a word all the way back to Bath.'

'I was tired from the rehearsal.'

Mel said no more. In this sour mood, Ivan was giving nothing away.

Shortly after midnight he let himself into the house. In darkness he removed his shoes and left them by the door. Clutching the Amati to his chest he crept up the stairs fearing each creak of the boards might waken the household. The last thing he wanted was a late night meeting with Mrs. Carlyle in her night-clothes. On tiptoe he moved along the landing to his room and let himself in, closing the door with stealth. He didn't risk turning on the light. In this small house the click of a switch was audible everywhere.

He slid the Amati safely under the bed next to his other viola. Then he stripped to his Calvin Kleins, leaving the clothes heaped on the floor. No bathroom visit tonight.

He'd give his teeth an extra go in the morning.

Relieved to have made it and more than ready for sleep, he eased himself under the quilt, turned on his side and found he wasn't alone. His chest was in contact with a warm, bare back. His pelvic area had come to rest against the divide of a chunky pair of buttocks, also bare.

She made a not unwelcoming murmuring sound. She was nine-tenths out to the world.

For the next few seconds Mel stayed still and silent, considering his options. From the shape and smell of her, this was unmistakably Tippi. She'd sneaked into his bed naked and ready for his return. Warmed by the quilt, she'd fallen asleep. Normally he'd not think twice what to do next. Tonight he had a sore left arm and his head was aching. He'd psyched himself up for the concert and now fatigue had caught up with him.

The bed was pleasantly warm. Would it be any use easing back from her and hoping she would drift off again?

He made the attempt.

Without success.

'Mel?'

He tried breathing evenly.

She turned right over and reached unerringly for his Calvin Kleins. 'You're late, but not too late.'

'It over-ran,' he said.

'Never mind,' Tippi said, giving the elastic a tug. 'Get 'em off.'

'Can I have a raincheck?'

'What?'

'It's an American expression. Means: could we make it another time?'

'You're joking.' She explored the front of his pants and then said with less certainty, 'Aren't you?'

'I've had a rough day, Tippi. Got knocked down by a car.'

'Mummy told me.'

'Yes. She saw it all.'

'She says you were like Superman charging across the street. She's got it into her head that the driver was a stalker, stalking me. To be honest I haven't noticed him myself.'

'It was the first I'd seen of him.'

'But as you did it for me I decided to give you this nice surprise.'

'I'm touched,' Mel said.

'I wouldn't know it yet,' Tippi said, checking again.

'The thing is, I hurt my arm and it's still quite sore.'

'Your arm?'

'Yes.'

'Nothing further down?'

'Oh, no. I'm fine in that department.'

'Prove it, then.'

'I can't, because of the arm.'

'Come again.'

'The arm. That's why I suggested a raincheck.' Just in case that hadn't settled the matter, he tried giving her something else to think about. 'The man in the car may not be stalking you. He may be interested in a new viola I've been given to play. It's a valuable item, extremely valuable actually.'

'He shouldn't have driven the car at you, whoever he is.'

'I agree, but I reckon he was trying to drive past me.'

'Mummy doesn't think so. She told the cops he meant to hit you.'

'What did you say?' he said in alarm. 'The cops?'

'Keep your voice down,' Tippi said. 'You'll wake her up. She called in at the police station in Manvers Street tonight and told them what happened. She said it's her public duty to report him.'

'For Christ's sake why?'

'Well, he was stalking me and he almost killed you.'

'I wish she hadn't,' Mel said.

'Too late now. I expect they'll want to hear

374

from you.'

'I was never in any danger.'

'Your arm's hurt. You just said.'

'Aches a bit. I wouldn't want to put any weight on it. That's the problem.'

'No problem at all.' Tippi grabbed his pants and yanked them down his thighs. 'Move into the middle. This'll be fun. Me on top.'

Tired as he was, he felt himself responding.

At breakfast, he waited for Mrs. Carlyle to raise the matter of the police. He was keen to hear what they'd said, but he couldn't turn back the clock. What was done was done. And this morning he *was* done. It had taken a superhuman effort to get downstairs.

'You were late coming in last night,' she said while she was cracking the eggs.

'I hope I didn't disturb you,' he said, meaning every word.

'Not really. I may have heard something. If you disturbed anyone, it was my Tippi. I heard her moving around in the small hours. I'm not expecting her down for breakfast.'

'I took my shoes off.'

'Very considerate.'

'I mean when I first came in.'

'I believe you. I saw them when I came down this morning. So was it a good concert?'

'Not really. I was a bit off.'

'Played some wrong notes, did you?'

'It was more a matter of rhythm and tempo. You need to be on top of your form to respond to the other players, and I wasn't and it showed — not all the time, but enough to shake my confidence and theirs.'

'Maybe you should have cancelled after all you went through. You're still looking pale.'

'It has to be something drastic to call off a concert. People were going to turn up. It was too late to let them know.'

'If they were told what happened to you and why, they'd be sympathetic. How's your arm today?'

'Improving.'

'They say exercise is the best remedy. Are you up for it?'

For a moment, he was unsure what she meant. Then the plate of bacon and eggs arrived in front of him.

'Get your knife and fork working on that,' Mrs. Carlyle said. 'I told the police you're a superhero. It's all on tape. They took me into a special interview room. This was yesterday evening. I decided it was my duty as a mother to report what happened, so I went down to Manvers Street and saw this nice young man in plain clothes called Paul. Far too young to be a copper, in my opinion, but he knew how to treat a lady. Tea and a biscuit, I got. He told me to take as long as I wanted and I had a wicked thought that I can't repeat to a gentleman like yourself. Anyway, I said what happened, how brave you were and everything, having a go like that.'

'I wouldn't call it having a go,' Mel said. 'I only went over to speak to the guy.'

'You got knocked over and injured for your trouble. He's a danger to the public and I told them so. I don't want him across the street ogling my Tippi. I know she dresses to attract the men but that's no reason to have them sitting outside the house like tom cats. You don't know what they're thinking. Well, you do, and you don't want it. He wasn't her age. He was out of the ark compared to her. I gave them a description, as much as I could.'

'Are they going to do anything about it?'

'I don't expect so, but they'd like a statement from you and I think you ought to go along and volunteer like I did.'

'They'll have got as much as they need

from you. I didn't get a proper look at the guy.'

'But you saw his black Renault Megane, rather too much of it, in fact.'

'It's a common make. They'll never trace it.'

'That's not the point. He could be back today. Show them your injuries and they'll get him for dangerous driving and attempted murder.'

'I don't think so. They're minor injuries.'

'He needs to be locked up, Mel. If he doesn't come after my Tippi you can be sure he'll pick on some other young girl and it could be far worse next time. You don't want that on your conscience. Besides, they know your name and where you live and what you do for a living. I told them.'

'Oh, thanks.'

She missed the sarcasm. 'A mother's instinct, caring for her young. Under all that make-up is an innocent child.'

21

'I won't be making a habit of it,' Diamond said of the soirée.

Ingeborg was more positive. 'It was really good in parts.'

'The part that matters is that we met the manager,' Diamond said. 'We weren't there for the music.'

'What did you make of him?' Keith Halliwell asked.

'Douglas Christmas?' Ingeborg said. 'A smooth operator. I guess you need someone like that fronting a cultural group. He'd make a good impression abroad with his old-world charm.'

'Rather less with you?' Halliwell said.

'Charming people always have a hidden agenda.'

He grinned. 'If you're a blonde.'

The CID team were all present and there was a sense of anticipation. Diamond's case conferences tended to be informal, for whoever happened to be around. This one had been scheduled in advance as not to be missed.

'Listen up, people,' he said. 'Yesterday as you know an international dimension was added to the case. It emerged that another Japanese woman went missing in a city where the Staccati were performing — in this case, Vienna, in 2008 — and was found dead some time after in the Danube canal. We can't be certain of a link, but it has to be investigated.'

While Diamond was speaking, Ingeborg pinned a new photo to the display board. Posed against a whitewashed wall, a woman's face making no effort to please stared forward from the centre of the frame. This was no family snap. Everyone in the room knew a mugshot when they saw one.

Diamond continued, 'Points of similarity. One, her nationality, of course. Two, the body was recovered from a city waterway. Three, she was submerged too long for a cause of death to be determined. Four, no obvious injuries. Five, she was clothed. Six, there was no great alarm when she went missing. And seven, she died at about the time the Staccati were in town.'

He waited for that to take root.

'And these are the differences. One, this

woman, Miss Emi Kojima, was about five years older than Mari Hitomi. Two, she'd been out of touch with her family for rather longer. Three, she was found with a netsuke under her T-shirt. That's a small antique ornament of a particular design that led the Viennese police to deduce she took her own life.'

'But it could have been planted by her killer,' John Leaman said, keen as always to chip in.

'Goes without saying.' Diamond folded his arms and lulled everyone into thinking there was little else to report. 'Nothing we don't know already, you're telling yourselves. But I asked Ingeborg to run a search on the Vienna victim and she's discovered some background that I'm sure you'll agree is new and significant.' He turned to Ingeborg. 'Over to you.'

'Getting straight to it,' she said, 'from an early age Emi Kojima attended one of the famous Tokyo violin schools.'

Murmurs of interest rippled through the room.

'Music again?' John Leaman said.

'She was said to have been an exceptionally gifted player. They take them young and get them up to an amazing standard. But at seventeen she was caught in possession of cocaine and asked to leave the school. After that she seems to have left home and drifted into petty crime and prostitution. She lived in one-room in a notorious Tokyo slum. The picture you see was taken after an arrest, one of many. Her family despaired of getting her back to some kind of normality. A sad story, but far from uncommon.'

Most eyes had returned to the photo on the display board. Emi Kojima's jaded look seemed to confirm that she had been pulled in and charged so often that it had no meaning for her.

'So,' Diamond said, 'we can add one more point of similarity: an interest in classical music. And one difference: this woman had a police record.'

'How did she make it to Vienna if she was in poverty?' Halliwell asked.

'Three guesses. She wasn't there on a city break.'

'Are we talking organised crime?'

'We could be.'

'Trafficking?'

'That's well possible.'

'To work as a hooker in Europe?'

'What do you think?'

'Excuse me,' Paul Gilbert said, 'but how would this link up with the string quartet? None of them are Japanese.'

'Doesn't stop one of them paying for sex with her,' Ingeborg said. 'Guys on tour for weeks on end.'

'Classical musicians?' Gilbert said in disbelief.

'They need to get their rocks off, same as you, ducky,' Ingeborg said.

Young Gilbert turned puce and everyone else enjoyed the moment.

'He's right to ask the question,' Diamond said. 'It comes down to this: did one of the Staccati pick up Miss Kojima in Vienna and kill her, and also Miss Hitomi in Bath?'

'Someone who fancies Japanese girls?' Halliwell said.

'Or hates them.'

Paul Gilbert was still grappling with the concept. 'Something doesn't add up. If she was working as a prostitute in Vienna and got picked up and killed by one of the Staccati, the fact that she went to violin school is neither here nor there. That was all in the past.'

Ingeborg looked as if she was in free fall. In her eagerness to join up the dots she'd missed this basic flaw in the logic. 'Now you put it like that, the music link may be a red herring. It must be what she was doing in Vienna that got her killed.'

'That makes sense to me,' Diamond said,

moving smoothly on. 'Let's stay with it.'

'If we're talking about the Staccati in Vienna,' Halliwell said, 'this was before Mel Farran joined. There are only two males in the frame, the old guy and the silent one.'

' "Old" is a relative term,' Diamond said. 'He could be my age.'

No one else spoke a word.

'Losing some of his hair doesn't make him decrepit. But as you say, either of these might have gone looking for paid sex. And we shouldn't ignore the third man.' Diamond stopped and looked around the room. 'Do I hear someone whistling?'

A few heads turned towards the source of the Harry Lime Theme.

Caught again.

Paul Gilbert seemed to shrink within himself.

Diamond could have hung the young man out to dry. Instead he gave a disarming comment. 'It sounds better on a zither.'

Relief all round.

Diamond wasn't departing from his script. 'The third man — Harry Cornell — known to go off on missions he discussed with nobody. He's in the frame with the others. It's possible he was with this woman and killed her. The next city they visited was Budapest and he went missing there.'

Leaman was encouraged to develop the scenario. 'He dumped her in the canal in Vienna and he expected the body would be discovered any time soon, so he went into hiding.'

'Yeah, down the sewers,' Halliwell said.

'Don't try me,' Diamond said. 'The joke's been done.'

Halliwell clearly wasn't impressed by the third man theory. 'For this to make any sense, Harry would have stayed in hiding for four years and turned up again in Bath and killed another Japanese woman. For Christ's sake, why?'

Ingeborg said, 'We haven't discussed the motive.'

Leaman agreed. 'All we have is the vague idea that some nutter has a kink about Japanese women.'

'Two very different women,' Ingeborg added.

Gilbert said, 'Should we be checking all the cities the Staccati have visited for unsolved murders of Japanese women?'

'Speak for yourself,' someone murmured.

'A serial killer?' Diamond said.

Gilbert hesitated. 'That's possible, isn't it?'

'Fair point. Do that, would you, Paul? We have a list of all their gigs for sixteen years, thanks to John Leaman.'

Gilbert looked as if he'd just grown older by all of those years. 'Me? How would I do that?'

'Interpol. That's why they exist, for something like this.'

The young man's face relaxed. 'Thanks, guv.'

'Then if they're unable to confirm anything it's a matter of trawling through the international press.'

The appeal of teasing Gilbert was that every emotion was as vivid on his face as if he was a silent film actor.

'Don't despair. A lot of it's digitised.'

'The Japanese papers should be helpful,' Halliwell said.

Ingeborg said, 'This is getting mean. You'd better come clean, guv. Are we seriously looking at a serial killer?'

'Personally, I think it's unlikely,' Diamond said. 'A series of killings would have shown up on the radar before now. The Japanese police are no slouches. So it won't be necessary to go back all those years, Paul. But it's not impossible some maniac has just started on a psychopathic career, and I'm serious about checking for a similar case in the past five years. Meanwhile for the rest of us it's back to the nitty-gritty of probing the secret lives of our musicians. And I'm not ruling out their manager. He flew out to Vienna while they were performing there.'

'Is Mel still in the frame?' Ingeborg said. Her tone suggested he ought not to be. Mel had made a favourable impression on her when she interviewed him. 'He wasn't around when the first girl was killed in Vienna.'

'You saw him at the concert,' Diamond said. 'Of the four, who looked the most nervous?'

'He *is* the new boy, guv.'

'He's had several months to settle in. This wasn't the first concert they've played.'

She nodded. 'Okay. I'll keep digging.'

Paul Gilbert still hadn't been silenced by the drubbing he'd received. 'There could be a reason why Mel was nervous.'

'Better tell us, then,' Ingeborg said before any of the others could inflict more punishment.

'It's in the copy of the message log I put on the guv'nor's desk.'

A show-stopping moment followed. Everyone in the room except young Gilbert knew Diamond was a word-of-mouth man who rarely went near his desk.

'Message about what?' Diamond asked.

'The statement I took yesterday evening

from a Mrs. Carlyle.'

Diamond drew a sharp, impatient breath. 'Never heard of her. Is it relevant?'

'It could be.'

'Go on, then.'

'She came in and made this voluntary statement. Only the thing is she happens to be Mel Farran's landlady and it was all about a hit and run incident outside the house yesterday afternoon. Mel was knocked down.'

The old blood pressure rocketed. 'And you wait until now to tell us?'

'It was in the message. I thought you must have seen it by now, guv. If you want to listen to the statement it's all on tape.'

Diamond managed to contain himself. Strictly speaking, the lad had acted correctly. Not sensibly, with the way things were done in CID, but correctly. 'We'll do that. Fetch it in and play it to us.' While Gilbert went off to retrieve the cassette, Diamond told the rest of the team, 'This may have nothing to do with our investigation, but we can't take that chance.' He frowned. 'How come Gilbert interviewed this woman? A voluntary statement about a traffic incident ought to be dealt with downstairs.'

No one knew why, so he asked the young

DC when he reappeared with the cassette player.

'When she first came in she wasn't talking about the car accident, guv. She was on about a sex maniac stalking her daughter. Uniform said it was a CID matter and I happened to be the only one here.'

'We'd better hear this.'

He switched on.

They listened enthralled to Mrs. Carlyle's melodramatic account of the stalker and his all-too-obvious lust for the innocent Tippi. They heard how her gallant lodger Mel went to investigate and was almost killed by the escaping car.

Diamond was gracious enough to say at the end of it, 'Difficult interview. You handled her well, finally got to the real facts.' He pressed his forefinger against his chin. 'Why didn't Mel report this himself, I wonder?'

'Too busy with the concert, I expect,' Ingeborg said.

'Maybe.'

'Perhaps what actually happened wasn't as dangerous as the woman described it,' Leaman said. 'She sounds hyper on the tape.'

'Mel did have a plaster on his left hand,' Ingeborg said. 'And at the soirée he was looking every which way as if he expected someone to attack him.'

'But he didn't report the driver,' Diamond said, refusing to excuse the omission. 'I want to know why. And if the mountain won't come to Mohammed . . .'

Mel's lodgings were in Forester Road, north-east of the city centre. Diamond asked Ingeborg to drive him there since she was the member of CID who knew the violist best and had a good rapport with him. In his twitchy state Mel would probably appreciate some female reassurance. Which wouldn't stop Diamond putting the boot in when required.

It was best to call unannounced, so they'd made no appointment. This was still before mid-day. The quartet rehearsed mainly in the afternoons. Mel shouldn't have left the house.

'What was the make of the stalker's car?' Diamond asked as they cruised up the road looking at house numbers.

'A Renault Megane. Black.'

'Haven't noticed one along here, have you?'

'In view of what happened he'd be an idiot to come back the next day,' Ingeborg said.

They stopped outside a house with a

crimson door and gleaming metal fittings.

'You must be Tippi,' Diamond said when their knock was answered by a young woman in a bathrobe with her hair colour matching the door.

She gave him a suspicious look. 'How do you know? And what's it to you anyway?'

'Police,' he said, showing his ID. 'Your mother reported an incident yesterday and we're following up on it.'

'Mum's out.'

'Good. We'd like to speak to Mel if he's in.'

'He's out, too.'

'Any idea where?'

'He walks in the park sometimes.' She pointed along the road in the direction of Sydney Gardens.

'Your mother seems to believe you have a stalker,' Diamond said. 'Has he troubled you before?'

'Who — me?'

'That's what I'm asking, Tippi.'

'A stalker? Give me a break.'

'What's that meant to mean? Don't you believe your own mother?'

'I wasn't here, didn't see him.'

'And nothing like it has happened before?

'Dunno, do I? If he's any good at it, I wouldn't notice him.'

■ ■ ■ ■

They drove down to Sydney Gardens, originally an eighteenth century pleasure garden that suffered a major assault soon after its opening when the Kennet and Avon canal was driven through. And forty years later it was sliced through a second time by the track of the Great Western Railway. But thanks to deep cutting and the building of ornamental bridges and a parapet, the worst horrors were averted. Jane Austen walked there often in its heyday and remarked that one of the advantages was that it was wide enough to get away from the music. These days the gardens are a haven of quiet in a busy city. Helpfully for Diamond, it wasn't the sort of park where you had no chance of finding anyone. There is a central path almost from end to end with views to either side.

They spotted Mel Farran near the Temple of Minerva, the faux Greek structure of Corinthian columns at the centre of the gardens. Clearly he saw them coming and seemed undecided whether to make an about turn, but thought better of it.

'How are you doing?' Diamond said when they got close enough. 'You had a run-in with a Renault Megane yesterday, I was told.'

Mel was quick to dismiss. 'It was nothing. My landlady got excited, but I'm fine.'

'Any idea who was driving?'

'It all happened too fast. As much my fault as his, I reckon. I don't want to make a complaint.'

'How was it your fault?'

'I was dead set on speaking to him and I kept going when he started the car. Walked right into it.'

'When you say "dead set" —'

'I thought I recognised the car. Saw one just like it the same day outside the Tippett Centre, some idiot who drove off fast and almost knocked down a student. But I could be mistaken.'

Diamond didn't let that pass. 'You think you saw him twice the same day?'

'I didn't get the number or anything. I'm not a hundred percent sure.'

'Can you think of any reason why anyone is tailing you?'

Mel hesitated. 'No.'

'Just that you seemed nervous at the concert last night, as if you were looking out for him.'

He pulled a disbelieving face, as if somebody else was being discussed, and then seemed to remember and gave a shrill laugh. 'That's nothing to do with the driver of the Megane. I was playing a new instrument in public for the first time and I thought the owner might be in the audience.'

'Don't you own your viola?'

'I couldn't possibly afford an Amati. They're worth a fortune. This sometimes happens with professional players — if you get lucky. We get offered top quality instruments by the people who own them. In a few cases they're gifts, but mostly they're on extended loan.'

'I guess that would make anyone nervous.'

'Especially as I once had my own instrument stolen.'

'When was this?'

'Years ago, when I was doing orchestral work.' Mel related the story of the mugging outside the Royal Festival Hall and it was obvious that the experience had deeply affected him. Even at this distance in time his voice broke up a little in telling it.

'That's so cruel,' Ingeborg cried out suddenly.

'Mean,' Diamond said. 'What would they want with a viola that had very little value?'

'Maybe they thought it was worth more,' Mel said. 'For me, it was valuable.'

'A young musician, trying to earn a living?' Ingeborg stressed in sympathy. 'I should think it was irreplaceable.'

'So who does your Amati belong to?' Diamond asked.

Mel vibrated his lips and became cagey again. 'I'm not allowed to say. The owner likes to remain anonymous. That's a condition of the loan.'

'From what you were saying, you only acquired it recently. Can I infer that he lives in Bath?'

'No, you can't.'

'Meaning he doesn't live here — or I shouldn't be asking?'

'No comment.' Followed by a twitchy grin.

'We've heard those words a few times before, haven't we?' Diamond said with a glance at Ingeborg. 'Let's walk a bit, Mel.'

They crossed the bridge over the railway and headed through a wooded area towards Sydney House, a large private building at the eastern end of the gardens, but screened by another pseudo-classical folly known as the Loggia, a semi-circle of Ionic columns and pilasters fronting a cement wall.

'Tell us about your background, how you came to join this quartet — or is that another secret?'

'Not at all.' Mel seemed to welcome the

change of emphasis. 'It was a phone call from Ivan. They needed a violist and they'd got to know about me and came to some recital to hear me play. I met them by stages, Ivan first, then Cat, and they called me in to do an audition, playing with them. I was in a blue funk but it seemed to go well and I was welcomed in.'

'Did you have any qualms about joining?'

'I jumped at the chance.'

'And now you're fully signed up.'

'Yep.'

'For how long?'

'Indefinitely.'

'Foreign tours?'

'They're planning one for South America as soon as we finish our stint in Bath.'

'Up the Amazon?'

He smiled. 'I hope not.'

'Have you played abroad before, Mel?'

'Heaps of times, filling in with orchestras and ensembles.'

'Europe?'

'Paris, Warsaw, Berlin, Vienna, Amsterdam.'

Trying not to reveal that every neuron in his brain was transmitting at peak capacity, Diamond threw in a question that could have passed for small talk. 'So you've been to Vienna? Who was that with?'

'You name it. I must have played there a dozen times. The first was with the London Symphony Orchestra. Last winter guesting with the Vienna State Ballet.'

'When you say "guesting" . . . ?'

Mel grinned. 'I wasn't dancing. They needed a violist at short notice and one of the orchestra remembered me from a previous visit. In the music business it's who you know.'

While the two were in conversation, Ingeborg had left them to it. They appeared to have hit it off without any input from her. But she'd noticed something Diamond had not. Her difficulty was finding how to tip him off without Mel knowing. She touched Diamond's arm. 'Guv.'

He ignored her, still high on the discovery that Mel had worked in Vienna. 'So when were you first there?'

Mel was still talking in a relaxed way. 'With the LSO? That was a shorter trip. Two or three concerts as far as I remember. Mahler, I think. As you approach the stage there's a bust of the composer staring at you. Slightly unnerving.'

'Yes, but when?'

'Two thousand and eight, if my memory is right.'

'Weren't the Staccati performing in Vienna

in two thousand and eight?'

'Don't know. I wasn't following their progress at the time.'

'I believe they were.'

'Coincidence, then. But Vienna is a stop-off on most of the European tours, so it's no big deal if we overlapped.'

Diamond was like a sniffer dog in a cannabis plantation. His list of strong suspects had increased. 'Which part of Vienna were you in?'

'Now you're asking,' Mel said. 'Must have been Karlsplatz. We played at the Musikverein.'

'The Staccati were at the Konzerthaus. That's a different location, is it?'

'I didn't run into them, if that's what you're asking. There are several concert halls.'

Ingeborg caught up with them and gave Diamond a nudge. 'Guv, can I have a word?'

'Presently.' He continued to question Mel. 'Can you recall what time of year you were there with the LSO?'

'At this distance in time?'

'I can check with their management, I expect.'

'Why do you need to know?'

'It's all part of our investigation into the death of the Japanese girl,' he said, not wanting to give more away at this stage.

They were crossing the white-painted cast-iron bridge over the canal, more than a mile from where Mari's body had been recovered, but still a reminder of why they were there. Ahead, the path would end at the Loggia in front of Sydney House.

Ingeborg refused to be sidelined any longer. 'Guv, we're being watched.'

'What?'

'I noticed this hooded guy standing among the trees by the temple where we first met Mel and he's been trailing us ever since, using the trees as a cover.'

'Where is he now?'

'Not sure. I just caught glimpses through the bushes.'

'Why didn't you say?'

She didn't answer.

'He'll have to cross the bridge if he's coming after us.' Diamond said. 'He'll be out in the open then. Wearing a hoodie, you said. What colour?'

'Dark blue.'

'I'll walk on with Mel. Why don't you double back and see if you can catch him and find out what his game is.' For Mel's benefit he added, 'Parks are favourite places for weirdos.'

Ingeborg did as she was asked. On the

other side of the bridge she left the path and headed into the undergrowth to the right.

'Will she be all right?' Mel asked.

'He's the one who should be worried,' Diamond said, glancing back. 'She's a black belt.'

They stopped to look. A minute or two went by. They'd lost sight of Ingeborg. The scene was peaceful. People were playing tennis on the courts to the left. A light breeze rustled the leaves.

'There he is.'

A dark figure broke from cover and sprinted through the trees with Ingeborg in pursuit. At first the hoodie appeared to be heading across the open ground towards Beckford Road. Then Ingeborg cut the angle to intercept him and he veered in their direction again.

'She'll trap him,' Mel said. 'He won't get over the canal.'

'Dead right,' Diamond said. 'He's had it.'

22

The hooded man was less fit than his pursuer. And unfortunately for him, he'd picked the wrong direction.

'He doesn't know he's heading straight for the canal,' Mel said. 'You can't tell from where he is.'

Diamond just folded his arms and watched.

At the end of the eighteenth century when the canal had been dug through Sydney Gardens the main demand of the committee was that it should be invisible to the promenaders, so it was sited at a depth of twelve feet. From where Diamond and Mel stood, its sinuous route was obvious, but you had to be really close.

'Does *she* know it's there?' Mel asked.

'Ingeborg? She was on the bridge with us.'

Gasping and flailing like a marathon runner in sight of the finish, the hoodie was no more than thirty yards ahead of Ingeborg.

He covered the last uneven stretch and reached the stone parapet that was there for safety purposes. Now he would see the sheer drop.

Instead of giving up, or turning to fight, he didn't hesitate. He bent low, gripped the top of the wall, heaved himself over, swung his body down and held on with his finger-tips. For a moment he hung there. Then he dropped the remaining six feet or so to the towpath. He could have broken both ankles, but he didn't. He bent his knees as he hit the ground, staggered a few steps and straightened up. Then he was up and running again, jogging along the towpath towards the north end.

Diamond put his hands to his mouth and yelled to Ingeborg. 'Don't try it. Let him go.'

She would have followed, but had the sense to obey instructions. Hands on the wall, she leaned over to see where her quarry had gone.

He was about to disappear into the long tunnel beneath Beckford Road.

'It's not worth it,' Diamond called out. He'd walked that tunnel more than once with Paloma and he knew it wasn't far short of a hundred yards.

He grabbed the mobile from his pocket

and called Bath Central. He couldn't really expect a patrol team to be close enough to arrest the stalker as he emerged at the other end, but it had to be tried. And even as Diamond was doing his limited best to describe the suspect, part of his brain was asking what crime the guy had committed. Threatening behaviour? Resisting arrest?

Not too convincing.

'Who was he?' Mel asked when Diamond finished the call.

'If you don't know, I'm sure I don't. It's you he was following.'

'How do you know?'

'It can't be us. We only came into the gardens because Tippi told us you were here.'

'D'you think he's the Megane driver?'

'I can't think of anyone else.'

Ingeborg crossed the bridge and joined them, in a foul mood. 'He was slowing up, for God's sake. I could have caught him.'

'You did okay,' Diamond told her.

'I'm not feeble.'

'Whatever gave you that idea?'

'Yes, but —'

He knew better than to get into an argument about her physical ability. 'It's taken care of. I told control, asked for assistance.'

And she had the good sense not to persist.

'What can we do him for?'

'I want to know what he's up to, that's all.'

'Me, too,' Mel added. He appeared genuinely mystified by all the attention he had been getting.

They made their way back through the gardens to Forester Road, where Ingeborg's car was parked. Diamond questioned Mel closely about the company he kept and whether he'd made any enemies recently.

'I don't have time to go out,' he said. 'It's all rehearsals and tutoring.'

'Who do you tutor?'

'Music students. It's part of our deal.'

'Female?'

'Some are.'

'Could anyone be jealous?'

'I can't think why.'

'Come on, Mel,' Diamond said. 'Even I know students get crushes on lecturers. It wouldn't be unheard of for a man of the world like you to get his leg over.'

Mel shook his head. 'No chance.'

'Oh, yeah?'

'Look, if I want sex it's on tap at my lodgings.'

There was a pause for thought.

'It crossed my mind, I have to say,' Diamond said, 'but her mother seems to think she's Snow White.'

'Have you met her mother?'

'No, I got that second-hand, but I've met Tippi.'

A nod from Mel was enough. No elaboration was needed.

'Just a thought here,' Diamond added. 'Does Tippi have a boyfriend who might suspect you have home advantage, so to speak?'

'She's never mentioned one.'

'She wouldn't, would she?'

'A jealous lover?' Mel said, as if surprised by the idea.

'It's you he's following now, not Tippi.'

Mel scraped the hair back from his forehead. 'I hadn't really thought about that.'

'Better be on your guard. Up to now he seems content to watch you, but that could change.'

They were approaching the house and Diamond hadn't finished with Mel. 'What time are you leaving for the rehearsal?'

He looked at his watch. 'In just under an hour.'

'Because I'd love to see this valuable instrument of yours.'

'All right.'

Mel had his own key. There was no need to bring Tippi to the door again. She wasn't about when they went in. Probably getting dressed, Diamond decided. But he was mistaken. After they'd gone upstairs and Mel opened the door of his room, they found Tippi sitting on the bed with her feet up.

'Wrong room,' Mel said.

'You don't mind?' she said coolly. 'I was checking my nails. The light's so much better in here.'

'I've got visitors,' Mel told her.

'See you later.' In the act of wriggling off the bed to leave the room, she treated them to a view that was more page three than Snow White. Diamond thought she winked at him as well.

Mel wasn't embarrassed. He'd explained the situation already. He reached under the bed and withdrew the instrument case.

'I still can hardly believe this,' he said as he unzipped it and opened up. 'Four hundred years old, near enough.'

The Amati was a beautiful object regardless of its antiquity, the glazed wood almost orange in colour, the finger board and pegs darker.

Mel lifted it one-handed from the case. 'Isn't the graining superb? Would you like to hold it? Mozart himself could have played this. He was a viola player, you know.'

Diamond, congenitally clumsy and fearful of doing damage, put both arms underneath and cradled the precious thing Mozart may have handled.

'Compare it with my own, and see the difference.' Mel fished under the bed and came out with another case and opened it. This second viola was in a darker wood, but to an inexpert eye looked similar. 'Mine is a William Hill, and pretty well regarded.'

Diamond occasionally placed a bet with William Hill, but doubted if there could be any connection.

'It can't live with this, can it?' Mel said.

'Well it has to, under the bed. Is that the best place?'

'As good as any if it isn't locked in a bank vault, and that's not what the owner wants.'

Diamond handed the Amati back to Mel with the same sense of relief as the vicar at a christening. 'What about the bow? Is that special?'

'Oh, yes. It came with the instrument. The very best bows sell for about a hundred grand. I can't tell you the maker of this one. I was so staggered to be presented with the viola that I forgot to ask. To be honest I'm not using it. Tough enough getting used to a new viola, so I still play with my old Tourte. If it's comfortable and gives the

407

sound you want, why switch?'

'And the case?'

'That isn't special.'

'I'll take a look, if you don't mind.'

Diamond picked the case up and turned it over. He was checking for clues to the true owner's identity. He found none. Maybe ultra violet would have picked up some security marking you couldn't see with the naked eye.

'I thought Stradivari was the great violin man,' Ingeborg said.

'He made only about ten violas that survive, compared to five hundred violins and fifty cellos,' Mel said. 'He was said to be a pupil of the guy who made this. Nicolò Amati was the third generation of instrument makers in their family, and the greatest. Sadly most early violas have been mutilated.'

'In what way?'

'Cut down in size to something not worthy of the name viola. This one escaped, fortunately. I was told it dates from 1625 and that's of interest because for some reason every almost other Amati you hear about is said to have been made in 1620 and some are fakes, so the date itself has to be regarded with some suspicion. To find one from 1625 gives it a touch more credibility.'

'But there's no question that this is the real thing, is there?' Ingeborg asked.

'Not to my mind. Listen.' He picked up his bow and played a snatch of something neither of them recognised, but with a golden tone, warm and soul-stirring. 'Can that be a fake sound? I don't think so.'

'Beautiful,' Ingeborg said. 'Will you ever go back to your other one?'

'Not while I have the use of this. I don't really feel it's mine. But in a sense you never truly own a fiddle. It's passed down over the centuries from one musician to the next, so you're a caretaker.' He replaced the Amati in its case.

'Forgive me,' Diamond said. 'I know nothing about musical instruments. It's hollow, of course?'

'For the sound,' Mel said with a tentative smile, uncertain if he was being sent up.

'But it has these S-shaped holes.'

'Known as f-holes,' Mel corrected him. 'The old-fashioned f looked like an S. The Amati family perfected the shape. It's remained the same ever since.'

'What if some small object was dropped inside — a cigarette, say, or a coin, or a ring. Would it affect the sound?'

Mel looked surprised by the question. 'A hard object like a ring would rattle. I'd know as soon as I picked the instrument up. In fact I think I'd know if something as light as a cigarette was in there.'

'My distorted way of thinking,' Diamond said, continuing to play even more clueless than he was. 'If someone wanted to ship drugs through customs, the inside of a violin or viola might be a good place to stow it. Mind you, a cello would be better still.'

Mel gave a prim response. *'Drugs? That's too far out for me.'* 'The holes are too small,' Ingeborg said.

'Just a thought, that's all,' Diamond said.

Like Mel, she didn't think much of Diamond's theory. 'It wouldn't fool a sniffer dog.'

'Probably not.'

'I can tell you something for sure,' Mel said. 'I wouldn't let anyone interfere with this instrument.'

'Good for you,' Diamond said.

'I'm not in the business of drug-running, anyway.'

'And I don't suppose you've ever indulged.'

'No chance.'

'Not while you're stuck in Bath,' Diamond said. 'But the South American tour might be a different story. Put that in your fiddle and smoke it. Are any of your fellow musicians drug users, would you say?

Mel grinned. 'Can you picture it?'

'They get their highs from Beethoven and Brahms, do they?'

'And why not?'

'Well said,' Ingeborg murmured, confirming her high regard for Mel.

'Is Colombia on the itinerary?' Diamond asked. He wasn't leaving this.

'Not that I've heard.'

'If a fellow in a sombrero called Speedy Gonzales offers to carry your case, don't let him.'

'I get the message,' Mel said with a forced smile.

'But in the meantime — and this is serious — if you get another sight of the stalker, let us know at once. No heroics.'

In the car on the way back to Manvers Street, Ingeborg said, 'What was all that about drugs, guv? You don't seriously think they're a factor, do you?'

'Testing the ground,' he said. 'There's an extra element in this case that I doubt is music.' He fished in his pocket. 'I'm going to call control, see if they picked up our hooded man.' He wasn't yet managing one-handed, but he used the mobile more often these days.

After exchanging a few words with the communications room he told Ingeborg, 'No joy. Not even a sighting.'

'What description did you give them?' she asked.

'Average height and build, wearing a hoodie, dark blue or black. Dark trousers and shoes.'

'It's not a lot, especially if he has the sense to take off the hood or tuck it out of sight.'

'I suppose. What do you think his game is? Have we covered all the angles?'

'All the obvious ones. Anything else would be stretching it.'

'And you still think Mel is on the level?'

'Don't you?' She gripped the wheel so hard that the steering shuddered.

In the CID room a surprise awaited them in the shape of a young blonde woman with plaited hair coiled on top of her head. In a houndstooth suit and white blouse, she was sitting on the edge of Keith Halliwell's desk drinking coffee from the machine.

'Guv, this is Dagmar,' Halliwell said, as if Diamond should know all about Dagmar.

'Right,' Diamond said, with an enquiring glance towards Ingeborg, who amazed him by saying, 'Dagmar? How did you manage this?' She turned to Diamond and said,

'Dagmar is my contact in the Vienna Police. I never expected to meet her in person.'

Dagmar eased herself off the desk, which involved a small jump. She was not much taller than the three-drawer filing cabinet. She formally extended a hand and addressed Diamond in a voice so deep that it more than compensated. 'Pleased to meet you, Detective Superintendent. I am Detective Inspector Aschenberger of the Bundespolizei, Vienna District.'

'We didn't know they were sending anyone,' Diamond said, impressed by the strength of her grip.

'I flew in this morning.'

'That was quick.'

'But you are not my reason for coming.'

'No?' He scratched his chin, uncertain where this was leading.

'I am here for a course in forensics at Bristol University, but I volunteered to make a special visit to Bath after we heard from you yesterday.'

Ingeborg said, 'You're a star.'

Diamond said, 'So why are you here — apart from meeting Ingeborg?'

Dagmar stooped and picked her backpack off the floor and made a startling noise ripping open the Velcro flap. 'As you know, most of the material you requested was sent electronically, but there is a piece of evidence that by law we must keep in the possession of our police service.'

'The netsuke?' He felt like picking Dagmar up and kissing her on both cheeks. He had become increasingly curious about the strange little ornament found with Emi Kojima's body. 'You brought it with you?'

'I can allow you to examine it as long as I am present. This way, we observe the letter of the law.'

'Understood.'

Dagmar produced from the backpack a transparent evidence bag and handed it across. It contained an object not much bigger than a table tennis ball, but less white. It was intricately carved.

'May I take it out?' Diamond asked.

'No problem. Many people have handled it since it was found.'

'Not many as clumsy as me, I bet.' With care, he tipped the netsuke into his palm. It weighed very little. 'Nice carving!' He held it up with his left hand. Two figures, male and female in traditional costume, formed the upper portion, with hands joined around the rim, exquisitely detailed. The doomed lovers were finely worked by the sculptor, but only to waist level. The lower half of the piece had been left as a mainly flat surface representing fallen snow, giving the impression they were half submerged in a drift.

'Do you know the story?' Dagmar said.

'The lovers who commit suicide by going into deep snow?'

'Chubei and Umegawa. We learned about this when we consulted Japanese experts to find out whether the netsuke had some significance.'

'As an emblem of suicide?'

'Exactly.' She brought her small hands together in a gesture of finality. 'With their advice we reached the conclusion that the victim meant it to symbolise her choice of death.'

'So we heard. And did the evidence back this up?'

She shrugged. 'There were no obvious signs of . . . what do you say?'

'Foul play?'

'Yes. No foul play.'

Diamond didn't relish challenging the Bundespolizei, Vienna District, interpretation, but it had to be done. 'The body had been in the water for some time, right?'

'Correct.' Dagmar looked at him with all the respect she would show to a man who had arrived at her door to sell double-glazing.

'So it was difficult to be certain?'

415

'We don't claim it is certain. These questions had to be decided by a jury and they could have been mistaken.'

'They wouldn't be the first. And who carried out the autopsy?'

'A hospital doctor.'

'Not a forensic pathologist?'

'She was a qualified pathologist.'

'Not a forensics expert. We had two autopsies done on our victim. The second revealed that she was strangled. A small bone in her throat fractured. Unless your pathologist was looking for it . . .'

Dagmar said, 'Nothing like this was in the report of our autopsy. But even if there was damage to the throat and it wasn't discovered, it is too late now. The body was returned to Japan for disposal.'

He didn't press the point any more. He wanted to stay on speaking terms. 'Did you discover where this netsuke came from? They're collectors' pieces, aren't they?'

'Usually they are, particularly if they are antique. They can be extremely valuable. We had this one valued by an expert and he said the workmanship was of high quality.'

'Even I can see that,' Diamond said holding the ivory piece up to the light. 'It's obviously handmade, not cast.'

'That is true,' Dagmar said, 'but the value

416

is not especially high. It's not antique. There are craftsmen working with modern precision tools who make these as copies of ancient designs.'

'Forgeries?'

'If they are traded as antiques, yes. But if they are sold as what they are, modern artefacts, you can't call them forgeries. They have some intrinsic value for the workmanship.'

Ingeborg came in on the conversation. 'But if they're ivory, they're illegal. Ivory products have been banned since 1989, and rightly so, in my opinion.'

'That is true and no right-minded person would argue with you,' Dagmar said in a tone suggesting she was about to do exactly that. 'True of elephant ivory. But this netsuke is not elephant ivory.'

'What is it, then?'

'Mammoth.'

'Get away,' Diamond said.

Dagmar continued in her solemn voice, 'Don't you know about this? The melting of the ice-cap has revealed large quantities of mammoth remains in the Russian tundra. The tusks are workable as ivory and can be traded within the law. They are not particularly valuable.'

'Yet this thing I have in my hand is actually thousands of years more ancient than the netsuke that are so prized. That's weird.'

'Weird, but true. Mammoth ivory netsuke are increasingly being worked and traded, and not just by Japanese.'

An awed silence had descended. Visions of mammoths roaming the Siberian wastes half a million years ago were pretty remote from the CID room in Bath.

It took Paul Gilbert to bring everyone back to the twenty-first century. 'So how does this affect the case?'

'It doesn't,' Dagmar said. 'The symbolism would still be just as valid if it was made from plastic.'

'Where would she have got it from?' Diamond asked for the second time.

'In Vienna? From some private source. You don't find these in good antique shops.'

Diamond said, 'We may sound ungrateful, Dagmar, but we're not. We're looking at it from the perspective of another case.'

'I know about this. Your Japanese woman.' Even so, her lip curled slightly as she added, 'But if I understand correctly there was no netsuke found with her.'

'Yet there are other things in common.'

'But your woman was strangled, you said.'

'And we must decide if we agree with that jury of yours that Emi Kojima committed suicide.' Back to confrontation, but it had to be said.

Dagmar shot him a withering look.

He refused to blink. 'Just now you said there were no obvious signs of foul play. I noted your words. Might there have been something you wouldn't classify as obvious?'

'Have you read the autopsy report?' Dagmar asked.

'It only landed on my desk this morning.'

'We provided a translation.'

'Thank you. I haven't got to it yet. Is there anything we should know about?'

Keith Halliwell said, 'I've been through it. Some of the fingernails on both hands were broken. She had quite long nails.'

Dagmar said, 'It all depends on your interpretation. This may have happened when the body was underwater, or being recovered.'

'Or when she was fighting an attacker,' Halliwell said.

Dagmar shrugged in a dismissive way.

'You went to some trouble finding out about her background in Tokyo,' Diamond said. 'The drugs and the prostitution.'

'That was all provided by the Japanese authorities.'

'Before, or after, the autopsy?'

'After. But we had it in time for the

419

inquest.'

'Did you discover why she came to Vienna? Was she selling herself there?'

'We had no reports that she was.'

'It's hard to understand how a woman who used drugs and traded in sex managed to get herself to Europe.'

'Maybe,' Dagmar said, 'but it happened.'

'Perhaps there was trafficking going on.'

'Quite possibly, giving her a reason to kill herself.'

'Or be killed. Is there much of a Far East influence on organised crime in your city?'

'There is some for sure, just like the mafia, into all kinds of illegal money-making. They are the yakuza, a network of Japanese gangs with international connections, increasingly in Europe.'

'I know a little about them,' Ingeborg said. 'They're rooted in tradition and go back a long way, but it comes down to the usual rackets like drugs, loan-sharking, gambling, protection and prostitution. They had a stake in a large swathe of Japanese industry, but the authorities have cracked down hard in recent years and they're starting to make inroads elsewhere. This poor young woman could have been part of the process.'

Diamond sensed the discussion slipping away from the investigation. 'There's a point you may not be aware of,' he said to Dagmar. 'Both of these victims had a grounding in classical music. Emi was trained to a high level in a Tokyo violin school. And Mari's mother was also a product of one of those schools and Mari inherited the passion for it. I don't think she performed, but she spent all her pocket money on concerts. We believe she came to Bath specially to hear a string quartet called the Staccati. She had them as a screensaver on her phone.'

'Three of them,' Ingeborg was quick to correct him. 'The fourth is a late addition.'

'True,' he said, 'but all four were in Vienna in 2008 when Emi ended up in the canal.'

'Not Mel,' Ingeborg insisted, her face flushing.

'He happened to be there with the London Symphony Orchestra,' Diamond informed her. 'I don't think you heard him telling me in Sydney Gardens. You were keeping tabs on the stalker at the time.'

Now Ingeborg went white. 'I didn't know this. You didn't tell me.'

'Probably just coincidence,' he said to pacify her. There was a bigger issue here than Ingeborg's cosying up to Mel.

Dagmar asked, 'Have you interrogated these people?'

' "Interrogated" is putting it too strongly.

We're talking to them. We have it confirmed by one of them that Mari Hitomi attended the first concert they gave. She wasn't seen alive after that.' He let that sink in before saying, 'Now do you understand our interest in what happened in Vienna?'

She said tersely, 'We are not aware of any link between this quartet and the death of Emi Kojima.'

Diamond lifted the netsuke high. 'I'm thinking this could be it.'

23

If Diamond had thought of catching up on some paper work (unlikely) or making peace with Ingeborg (more likely) or going for a pie and chips (the best bet), none of it happened. As soon as Dagmar hoisted her backpack and left, there was a call from downstairs to say a gentleman had arrived and wanted to see him urgently.

A gentleman? That endangered species was not often sighted in Manvers Street nick.

Douglas Christmas was waiting in the front hall. The pinstripe suit, MCC tie and dolphin smile would without question have impressed any desk sergeant, as would the voice like a BBC newsreader from seventy years ago. 'Remarkably decent of you to see me at short notice,' Douglas told Diamond. 'The car's outside, being guarded by one of your obliging chaps.'

'I wasn't planning a drive.'

'But you'll change your mind if I treat you to a strawberry tart and a proper cup of tea, served in a pot. There's a charming place up the street.'

Now that food was mentioned, Diamond's stomach groaned. He hadn't had a bite since breakfast.

Douglas knew he was onto a winner. 'If you prefer, there are gateaux to die for. Don't you agree with me that tea in the afternoon is the highest expression of life, liberty and the pursuit of happiness? And I do have that small matter to raise with you.'

The red Aston Martin convertible was illegally parked in the street at the front of the police station. A uniformed constable was in the act of directing a bus around it. How Douglas had negotiated this was a mystery. Diamond made a mental note never to underestimate the man.

'Hop in,' Douglas said.

'If the place you have in mind is Patisserie Valerie, it isn't worth taking the car,' Diamond said. 'It's a five-minute walk.'

'I'm not much of a walker, old boy.'

'There's nowhere to park in the High Street.'

'What do I do with the jalopy, then?'

'I can tell you one thing. I'm not being party to a parking offence.'

'Look the other way, then.' Douglas solved the problem by slipping a banknote into the top pocket of the officer doing duty for him.

In the teashop, Diamond studied the menu. He was a newcomer here, but he'd heard Paloma sing its praises more than once. He asked the waitress if the breakfast was still available. She said in the nicest way that it was too late in the day, whereupon his go-getting companion switched on the heat of his charm. First Douglas asked the waitress her name. He then introduced himself and said he was a regular at the Soho branch in Old Compton Street, which had been opened by Madame Valerie herself as a replacement for her Frith Street shop bombed during the war. He said his guest, Mr. Diamond, was a food expert who had come specially to sample the quality of the service. Sadly — he continued without pause — the lovely Madame Valerie had long since baked her last croissant but he was confident she was with them in spirit, delighted that all these years later this splendid shop bearing her name existed in Bath and that a waitress called Jeannie was willing to speak to the chef about a special request from a VIP customer.

After all that, what else could Jeannie say

except that she would see what could be done?

'Food expert?' Diamond said.

'Everyone is, my dear fellow. You know what you like, don't you?'

'God knows who she thinks I am.'

'The food critic of the *Sunday Times,* I expect,' Douglas said. 'You'll get your breakfast.'

First he got the chef in person saying he would be delighted to cook a breakfast and would the gentleman care to sample his eggs benedict with salmon?

'A simple fry-up, thanks,' Diamond said.

It had been a telling demonstration of Douglas's persuasive talent.

'So what's the small matter?' Diamond asked him.

Douglas poured the tea. 'I'll be heading back to London shortly and I promised my clients I'd speak to you about all the interest you and your people have been showing in them. They're artists, you see, sensitive plants, not men of the world like you and me. I can see a real danger that their music-making will suffer.'

'They've been onto you, have they?'

'I noticed it myself. The new man, Mel, is very jumpy. You put him under the cosh, this morning, I gather.'

426

'That's overstating it,' Diamond said. 'A few civil questions.'

'But deeply alarming to a chap who lives a sheltered life.'

'I needed to get at the facts about an incident his landlady reported to us. A man in a car was stalking him yesterday and actually knocked him over.'

'I heard about this. Very bizarre.'

'Did Mel use those words, about being put under the cosh?'

'Not directly. Ivan acts as their spokesman.'

'Ivan? I can hear him saying it.'

'Yes, a wonderful artist and a difficult personality. Ivan is waspish in his better moods and positively rebarbative when he feels there is an issue to pursue. He lived in a police state for much of his youth, so anything that smacks of authority gets him going. He feels the quartet are being persecuted.' Douglas then softened the statement with all the polish of a professional negotiator. 'You and I know this isn't true. You're just doing your job. I did my best to explain. I can't remember a time when Ivan was so agitated.'

'Maybe something else is agitating him.'

'Is there anything else?'

'The stalker, I suggest,' Diamond said.

'Ivan was present at the Michael Tippett Centre when they first noticed the car and saw it drive away at speed. He's heard from Mel what happened later. Something is going on there, and Ivan knows it.'

'Did you see this stalker yourself?'

'A bloke in a hoodie running away.'

'Pity you didn't catch him.'

'He took a risk, jumping from a dangerous height. He was able to leg it through a canal tunnel and away.'

The breakfast arrived soon after.

'That looks a treat,' Douglas said. 'I almost wish I hadn't asked for the raspberry tart.'

'What about the other two, Cat and Anthony?' Diamond asked. 'Are they agitated as well?'

'To a degree. Anthony doesn't say a lot, but he picks up the vibes when the others are in a flap.'

'Does he ever get violent?'

Douglas hesitated. 'He's a single-minded chappie, is our Anthony. It's not a good idea to cross him, but I don't think it's ever come to blows, if that's what you're asking.'

'And Cat? How is she behaving?'

'On the surface, no different. She makes light of everything in the interest of harmony. She's a good balance for Ivan, a positive force. However, I do detect some real concern underneath all the levity. There's a look in her eye I haven't seen since Harry went missing.'

'No one is threatening her. I haven't spoken to her for days.'

'Yes, but any threat to her boys, as she calls them, makes her anxious. The quartet is her lifeline.'

'Would she fight to defend it?'

'Like a tigress.'

'I'll watch out, then,' Diamond said as he took another mouthful. 'This is good. The chef gets five stars from this critic.' He looked straight into Douglas's brown eyes. 'And what's in it for you, apart from your twenty percent?'

For a moment, Douglas was lost for words. He wasn't used to such bluntness. 'The quartet are my friends, for one thing, and immensely talented for another. They need a manager, and I do my humble best for them.'

'Isn't there ever a time when you wish you were one of them?'

'Not in a million years. I don't have a musical bone in my body. Between you, me and the blessed Valerie, it's an ordeal sitting through their concerts, but I have to show the flag.'

'Yet you know the music business.'

'From top to bottom. That's my job.'

'Your talent.'

Douglas smiled. 'Kind of you to say so, but I don't think one should confuse the gift of the gab with the gift of the gods. What they have is genius.'

More than a hint of envy lay behind those words, in spite of what had been said, Diamond decided. 'Are they your biggest earners?'

'I shouldn't really say, in fairness to my other clients, but it's blindingly obvious. Yes, they keep the wolf from my door, bless them.'

'If they stopped performing for any reason, you'd feel the draught?'

'And I'd know the door was open and the wolf was coming in. It happened, of course, when Harry went AWOL. Quite a crisis, that was.'

'What's your theory about what happened?'

Douglas leaned so far across the table that he had to stop his tie from straying onto his raspberry tart. 'This is strictly between you and me. Not even the sainted Valerie should be a party to it. He played a heck of a lot of poker, rather badly. You know what they say? If you're invited to join a game, look around the table and if you don't see a sucker, get up and go, because it's you.'

'He lost badly?'

'Catastrophically badly and the sort of people he played with let the debts run up to a ridiculous level and then called them in. Several times he asked me for payment in advance for concerts that weren't even in rehearsal yet. I did my best to help him out, poor fellow, because I could tell he was terrified.'

'Under threat?'

'No question.'

'Do you think his creditors killed him?'

'Sadly, I do.'

'How would that have helped them?'

'*Pour encourager les autres.* You don't mess with the mafia.'

'Is that who they were?'

'He called them the mob. "The mob have called time on me," were almost the last words he used to me. When I told the Budapest police, they seemed to take it as a reason to drop the case.'

'When exactly did he speak these words?'

'On the phone shortly after they arrived in Budapest.'

'Did the others know he was in hock to the mafia?'

'It's hard to tell. The group dynamic is

complex. They appear to respect each other's privacy, but they spend so much time together on tour that they must have an idea of everyone's comings and goings. I'm in a privileged position because I hold the purse-strings. Occasionally they need bailing out. I'll get a call asking if I can transfer some funds urgently.'

'Which of them have called you?'

'All, from time to time.'

'What does Cat spend her money on?'

'You name it. She's a shopaholic. You should see the luggage she brings back.'

'And Anthony?'

Douglas gave the benign smile of a father figure. 'The poor boy is hopeless with money. He'll give it away. He visits call-girls and the smart ones get the measure of him and demand gifts of jewellery and exorbitant fees. It's happened in several cities. Cat tries to keep tabs on him, but it's not possible all the time and she can't follow him into all the sordid addresses he visits. I wouldn't ask her to.'

'Which brings us back to Ivan,' Diamond said. 'He strikes me as the sort of guy who looks after number one. I can't imagine him going to you for help.'

'You're right in a way,' Douglas said. 'There's never an emergency. When he

432

requires an advance it's as an investment.'

'In what?'

'Hasn't he told you? He's a chess player.'

'That much I know. Does he play for high stakes?'

'I doubt it. No, he deals in chessmen. When the quartet are on their travels, Ivan always has a few beautiful handcrafted chess sets with him. He sells them to the people he plays with — at a handsome profit. If you're fanatical about the game, these gorgeous carved figures are irresistible, I'm told.'

'I see. So the investment you mentioned is to stock up with chess sets?'

'Exactly.'

'Who is his supplier?'

'Someone from Russia or the Ukraine he knows from years back. Must be Russia, come to think of it, because he wants his cash in roubles. It's the black economy, I'm sure. None of this nonsense over VAT, or whatever tax they operate there. I turn a blind eye.'

'And it's big money, is it?'

'Pretty impressive. And of course he's paid in the local currency.'

'There's a chess club here in Bath, but I doubt if the members are in that league financially.'

'He has contacts all over the world and some of them are very rich men. They tend not to be the sort who join the local chess club. But you'd have to ask Ivan if he's done any business locally.'

'I don't want him to get the idea I'm in league with the taxman.'

'Do you play chess yourself?' Douglas asked.

'A bit. I know the moves.'

'Offer him a game. Give him a chance to show you how good he is. He never ducks a challenge. He's a chess junkie.'

'And do you think he'll talk as we play? I'd like to ask him about the Russian connection.'

'Be sure to get your question in early, then. He doesn't take long over a game.'

The afternoon session at the Michael Tippett Centre should have felt flat, coming, as it did, the day after the concert at Corsham Court. But Ivan suggested they were ready to play the *Grosse Fuge* in its entirety and, strange to relate, the challenge energised them all. The Everest of quartet music was written originally as the finale of String Quartet Opus 130 in B flat major, but Beethoven's publisher persuaded him later to substitute a less demanding movement, and the *Fuge* was republished as a stand-alone work. Unlike anything else Beethoven created for strings, incomprehensible to many of his contemporaries, this overwhelming piece leaps forward musically into dissonance. Stravinsky famously called it "an absolutely contemporary piece of music that will be contemporary forever." Strident, tempestuous, uneven, it makes huge demands on each player. Only in the fifth and final part does the composer relent a little and show harmony emerging from the skewed rhythms and variations.

They finished exhilarated, their spirits lifted.

'I've got the shakes,' Mel said.

'Tell me about it,' Cat said. 'This must be an electric chair I'm sitting on. Hey, no one ever got a better sound out of the Amati than you did just then. Listen. I swear it's purring.'

'Thanks.'

'And you guys on the end weren't rubbish, either. What do you say, Anthony? Was that the best yet?'

'I was playing, not listening,' Anthony said.

'Not waving, but drowning.'

'What?'

'Ignore me, sweetheart. Just something that popped into my head as you spoke. I

435

know exactly what you mean. I wish we'd recorded that. Personally, I think the composer himself would have clapped. D'you think God has fitted Beethoven with a hearing aid? I hope so. Ivan, have you taken a vow of silence? We're all waiting for your verdict.'

'You're right. We should record it,' Ivan said.

'Do you mean that?'

'It's a step on from the recording we made with Harry. A significant step.'

'Count me in.'

'If only for ourselves we should do it,' Ivan said. 'I can book the studio and the technical people. Let's go for it tomorrow.'

'All agreed?' Cat said.

The others nodded.

'Better call those taxis, then. I'm getting an early night. I suddenly feel bushed.'

The unexpected sound of a cough came from above them. They all looked up. The rehearsal studio had a gallery. Nobody was in sight, but they heard a door closing.

'Someone was up there,' Cat said. 'Damn cheek, listening in.'

'Students, I expect,' Mel said. 'You can't blame them. After all, it is a music department.'

Ivan was out of his chair and across the

floor to the door.

'Where are you going?' Cat said.

He didn't answer. They heard him running along the corridor towards the stairs.

'He's getting more paranoid by the day,' Cat said.

Mel stowed the Amati in its case and said with what he hoped was a voice devoid of urgency, 'I'll just take a look out the front.'

'You're no better than he is,' Cat said. 'All right. Leave it to Big Momma to fix the transport.'

The entrance hall was crowded with students when Mel got there. After threading his way through to the plate-glass front he checked the open area where cars drew up. Nothing was parked there. But a black hatchback was speeding away along the drive and might just have been the Renault Megane. Difficult to be certain from that distance.

He returned to the others. Ivan was back with them, fussing with his music sheets, clearly frustrated. 'Where have you been?' he asked Mel.

'Out front.'

'Did you see anything?'

'Only a load of students. How about you?'

'Negative.'

Cat folded her arms and emitted a sharp,

437

displeased breath. 'What's happening here? You guys are as jumpy as toads in a thunderstorm. Isn't it time you let me in on the secret?'

Ivan busied himself returning his violin to its case.

The focus shifted to Mel. As the new man, he'd received nothing but friendship from Cat. He felt he couldn't ignore her. 'I told you about my little accident,' he said. 'What I didn't say is that I'm pretty certain the car that knocked me down outside my lodgings was here the same afternoon, waiting out front. When Ivan and I took some interest, he drove off fast. I just went to check in case he was back today.'

'And he wasn't?'

'I saw a car disappearing into the distance. It could have been the same one.'

Ivan looked up. 'You didn't say that when I asked.'

'Because I don't know for certain.'

Any of the others could have seen that a struggle was going on in Ivan's mind. His cavernous Slavic eyes held Mel's for a moment and then moved to Anthony and finally fixed on Cat. 'I've been keeping something to myself because I didn't think it was helpful for any of you to know. I can't explain it. I don't like to think what it means. I recognised the man in the car the other day, the man who is stalking us. I'm absolutely certain it's Harry.'

24

Just when he'd scaled the heights, Mel was in free fall. His place in the Staccati had seemed secure, the *Grosse Fuge* mastered, the South American tour confirmed. His magnificent new instrument was producing sound of such purity that his soul rejoiced each time he put bow to strings.

And now this.

For all the amazement everyone had voiced, Ivan had insisted he was not mistaken. He wasn't given to exaggeration. Precision was innate to his character, a Slavonic insistence on stating the facts with accuracy. No question: he had seen Harry Cornell sitting in that car.

So if Harry was alive and secretly watching the quartet, what was his game? It seemed obvious to Mel. The man had decided he wouldn't muscle in right away and demand his place back. He'd chosen to play it cautiously and get a sense of what was going on. His musicianship wasn't at issue. He was a brilliant violist who had served the Staccati well, toured with them, played concerts, made recordings. They'd always spoken of him warmly. They'd surely welcome him back.

After Ivan's shock announcement, they had all made a point of saying it was the best news possible that Harry was alive. What else could anyone say? As to taking him back, they had the tact to stay silent while Mel was there. But there's only one violist in a string quartet.

Shocked and depressed, Mel sat in his room brooding on what would happen next. Without difficulty he could see himself back to the grind of playing for weddings and anniversaries, filling in when orchestras needed a stand-in for one of their regulars.

Worse still, he'd be stuck with his old William Hill. Mr. Hamada would want the Amati back as soon as word reached him. What a wrench that would be. Mel had fallen in love with his new viola. It was a deeply emotional attachment. With that superbly crafted fiddle he experienced fulfilment, a richness of experience he hadn't dreamed was within his capacity. He'd felt ready to join the company of the masters.

Depression simmered for a while and

turned to anger. Where had Harry bloody Cornell been for the past four years? He'd let his fellow musicians down, allowed them to think he was dead. They'd gone through a grim period when the quartet was in decline and virtually defunct. Now they were on the brink of success again, he expected his place back, all forgiven.

Selfish git.

Mel turned his left hand and looked at the graze-mark, still obvious. A great way to get back into favour, driving your car straight at your replacement on the team. And now he began to see the hit-and-run in a different light. Harry had followed him home, checking where he lived and waited for him to appear again. When the opportunity came he'd revved the car and sent him flying. Immediately after, Mel had been of a mind to dismiss the knockdown as partly his own fault. Now he was telling himself it was more sinister.

Harry had deliberately tried to injure him.

Or kill him.

His first assumptions had been mistaken. Harry wasn't playing the waiting game. He'd had long enough to get to know the quartet and their moods. They were a contrary bunch of people. Considering how shabbily he'd treated them, they may have decided he didn't deserve a second chance. And if so, his remedy was to make certain they needed him by removing his replacement.

It was a grotesque idea, but Mel had a sore arm to prove it.

What was to stop Harry from trying again?

Mel got up and stared out of the window. The street lights were on, but it was difficult to tell one parked car from another. Fear crept over him.

Behind him he heard the door handle being turned.

He swung round.

'Only me,' Mrs. Carlyle said. 'You've got a visitor downstairs and he looks awfully like the stalker, but he's an absolute charmer and he seems to know you, so I said I'd see if you're in.'

Typical, Diamond thought.

Ivan's lodgings were at one of the best addresses in Bath, Great Pulteney Street, palatial, quiet and only five minutes from the city centre. If anyone in the quartet was going to get the best digs, it would be their wily spokesman.

Diamond wanted this to seem like a social call. He'd even thought about letting Ivan know in advance, but decided against that.

Control freaks always change arrangements to suit themselves. He decided a surprise visit at about eight in the evening was best.

The man wearing eye-shadow who answered said he was sorry but Mr. Bogdanov had made it crystal clear that he wasn't at home to visitors tonight.

'It's all right,' Diamond said. 'I'm family.'

Well, he was — to his sister Jean in Liverpool.

Quite a few flights of stairs to the top flat. What a good thing it was, Diamond thought, that Ivan had only a violin to lug up there. A double-bass would have put him at risk of a coronary.

It was dark on the top landing. Diamond couldn't find a bell. He knocked with his knuckles, heard a movement from inside, and was ignored.

'Ivan?'

No response.

'This is only Peter Diamond.' He knocked harder. 'From the Bath police . . . Are you all right in there?'

He gave it a few seconds before upping the ante. 'I know you're in there.'

He was getting impatient.

'I don't want to kick it in unless I have to.'

He heard a safety-chain being slotted in. The door opened a couple of inches. 'Didn't they tell you downstairs? I'm not to be disturbed.'

'Well, it's happened, so you might as well see me.'

'What do you want?'

'Just a few minutes of your time. I'm not here officially. May I come in?'

'About what?'

Some flattery was wanted here. 'I'm looking for some expert advice.'

'From me?'

'Who else? No one is better placed to help me.'

After some hesitation: 'Are you alone?'

'Absolutely.'

Ivan released the chain and admitted him. In a silk dressing-gown, pyjamas and leather slippers, he could have been a character out of a Noël Coward play. It seemed right for a flat in Great Pulteney Street.

'Were you practising?' Diamond asked.

'No, but I'm busy.'

They were in a large sitting-room with an Afghan carpet, three-piece suite, music-stand and TV set. A violin in its case lay on one of the armchairs. Some foreign newspapers were scattered over another.

'Is this what you're busy at?' Diamond had spotted a chessboard on a nest of tables, the pieces spread, as if in mid-game.

'It's a match that was played many years ago between two grand masters you won't have heard of,' Ivan said.

'Try me.'

After a beat a different note entered his voice. 'Do you play?'

'To a modest level. Care for a game?'

'I thought you were here for advice.'

'We could talk as we play.'

'All right.' Ivan didn't need any more persuading. He crossed to a sideboard, picked up a box and another board. Then he reached under the unfinished game and drew out a second table. He opened the board. 'You can be white.'

'I'd rather draw for it.'

'Very well.' Ivan picked out two pawns, enclosed them in his hands behind his back and allowed Diamond to make the choice.

White.

Red and white rather than the more usual black and white, the pieces were housed in a velvet-lined box.

'These look special,' Diamond said as they started setting up.

'Ivory.'

'The red as well?'

'Stained.'

'It's a magnificent set.'

'This is the Staunton design everyone has.

I could show you better.'

'You trade in them, don't you?'

Ivan shrugged. 'Only as a sideline.'

'But they're not antique.'

'No,' Ivan said. 'Are you going to start?'

Diamond pushed his king's bishop's pawn forward two squares.

'Bold.' In the offhand manner born of long experience Ivan advanced his king's pawn two squares.

Diamond made an early pause in the play. 'You're safe with me as someone who enjoys the game, but isn't ivory banned these days?'

'It's not elephant. It's the ethical alternative, mammoth ivory, from northern Siberia.'

Hey ho, Diamond thought, this sounds familiar. 'Perfectly legal, then.'

'It's down to global warming. More and more skeletons are being uncovered each year as the tundra melts.'

'So you still have contact with the old country?' Diamond nudged his king's bishop's pawn one square forward.

'You must be bluffing,' Ivan said.

'Not at all.'

'Then I've got you checkmate in two.' He slid his queen on the diagonal as far as it would go. There was no escape. Diamond's king was trapped. Ivan gave him a glare

447

worthy of the customs hall at Heathrow. 'Fool's mate, supposedly, but I believe you're making a fool of me.'

'It's not in my interest to do that.' Diamond said. 'Well done. I'd offer you another game, but it wouldn't last much longer. How much do you charge for these?'

'The going rate for a Staunton set is ten thousand dollars, something over six thousand pounds sterling.'

'And you said you have other designs?'

'Knights on horseback and so on. They cost rather more. But I don't think you came here to buy.'

'How does it work? Are the sets carved in Russia?'

'Why are you so interested?'

'This is where I need your advice. There may be a connection with the case I'm investigating. An ivory netsuke was found on the victim in Vienna and proved to be mammoth ivory.'

Ivan showed no reaction.

Diamond asked, 'Do you know anything about the trade in Japanese ornaments?'

'I don't deal in them, if that's what you're thinking,' Ivan said.

'I know you don't,' Diamond said, 'and even if you did, I wouldn't expect you to tell me. I'm still keen to know where these beautiful chess sets are made.'

'In Archangel, by a master carver. It's a business arrangement. I buy from him. I travel with the quartet to some of the great cities of the world and I play a lot of chess. From time to time I am asked about the sets and I will sell at a reasonable profit.'

'Guilt-free ivory.'

Ivan nodded.

Diamond took a photo from his pocket. 'This is the netsuke that was found. It's definitely carved from mammoth ivory. As a connoisseur of these things —'

'Not of netsuke. I don't trade in netsuke,' Ivan interrupted him.

'That isn't what I meant. You appreciate Japanese culture.'

He flushed deeply. 'No more than the next man.'

'I was told you like to visit the geisha houses when in Japan.'

'Who told you that?' Ivan said in a clipped, angry tone.

'I forget,' Diamond said. 'Must have been one of the quartet. It's the truth, isn't it?'

'What if I do?'

'Nothing to be ashamed of,' Diamond went on. 'Traditional Japanese dancing and music and the famous tea ceremony. All highly respectable, isn't it? Highly expensive, too.'

'The way I choose to spend my time and money is no concern of yours,' Ivan said. 'I have a long-standing interest in the geisha. As a musician, I have studied the shamisen, the three-stringed instrument they play with the plectrum.'

'So the music is the pull, and not the young ladies?'

If looks could kill, Diamond would have been ashes ready for scattering. 'Geisha is an aesthetic experience. This isn't some catchpenny tourist attraction. I go to the genuine okiya in the geisha district in Kyoto.'

'Don't get me wrong, Ivan. I'm not accusing you of anything. It's your advice I came for. The geishas wear traditional dress, I'm told, and this would surely include at least one netsuke on the sash.'

'I'm not an expert on the costume.'

'But it's part of that aesthetic experience you mentioned.'

'Correct.'

'I was going to ask what you think of this particular example.'

'I wouldn't have a view. Anyway, it's only a photograph. You can't tell.'

'I've held it in my hands,' Diamond said,

'and it's a marvellous piece of carving. Would you happen to know where objects like this are created?'

'In Japan, I should think.'

'Of Siberian mammoth ivory?'

'I expect it gets shipped there.'

'Might there be craftsmen working in Eastern Europe?'

He gave a shrug. 'Conceivably.'

'But you wouldn't know any? The man in Archangel who makes the chess sets doesn't have a second line in Oriental objects?'

'Not to my knowledge.'

'Has anyone ever discussed this with you before?'

Ivan swayed back as if Diamond had thrown a punch. He didn't answer, but he didn't need to.

'One of the quartet?' Diamond pressed him.

The conversation had hit the buffers.

'I'm sure this is difficult for you,' Diamond said. 'They're friends and fellow artists, but I'm investigating two suspicious deaths and I can't allow your loyalty to obstruct me. They all know about your sideline selling the chess sets and one of them may have taken a particular interest in where they came from.'

'Douglas Christmas knows more about

my business than any of them,' he said finally. 'He assists with the finance.'

'Providing you with the roubles. He told me.'

Ivan tensed. 'That's confidential. He had no right.'

'Don't worry,' Diamond said. 'Tax evasion isn't my department. Leaving Douglas aside, which of the others has talked to you about the trade?'

'I really think you should leave now.'

'One of them saw an opportunity of branching out on his own. It's Harry, isn't it?'

Although Ivan didn't speak a word, his face had turned deathly white.

'I need to know, Ivan. You're a frightened man. Anyone can see that. You could be in need of my protection. This isn't chess, this is life and death.'

Frightened he certainly was. His lips gave an involuntary twitch before he got control. 'I only learned about this through a mistake. Seven or eight years ago we were performing in Paris and I was stupid enough to invite a potential client to the hotel. There was some kind of mix-up at the desk and they sent him to Harry's room instead of mine. Of course Harry wanted to know everything. He questioned me repeatedly until I told him the truth about the dealing I did. He was deeply in debt from his gambling.'

'And saw this as a way out of his troubles?' Diamond said.

'Exactly.'

'Except that he chose to deal in netsuke?'

'It's more profitable than chess sets.'

'The Japanese woman who was found dead in Vienna had a netsuke in her T-shirt. They took it to be a suicide emblem. Convenient.'

Ivan shrugged and didn't comment. He seemed to feel he'd said enough already.

'One more thing,' Diamond said. He took out the photo of Emi Kojima. 'On the evening of your last concert in Vienna, did you see this woman?'

It was obvious from Ivan's eyes that he recognised Emi at once. He made a performance of studying the photo to take time to prepare an answer. 'She was in the audience.'

'Did she speak to you afterwards?'

Another silence followed. This was being played like the serious chess match they could have had.

'She spoke to us all,' Ivan said. 'You might as well know.'

'And did she end the evening in Harry's

453

company?'

A nod. 'We saw them in the hotel bar together.'

'When you say "we" . . .'

'Anthony, Cat, Douglas and me. After a time they walked to the elevator. The bar was on the ground floor. They could only have been going up to Harry's room.'

Diamond gave a voice to the conclusion he's been heading towards for days. 'And now Harry is alive and here in Bath secretly watching you all.'

25

The man in Mrs. Carlyle's front room was instantly familiar to Mel from posters of the Staccati, the sort of well-proportioned, rugged face that attracted women and put men at ease, yet now looking creased with fatigue or strain. He couldn't have shaved for days. He was in some kind of padded jacket with the hood turned down. Far from threatening, he was obviously ill at ease.

'Hope you don't mind me calling. I really do need to meet you. I'm Harry Cornell.'

The educated voice did not match the unkempt appearance. It was all so disarming that Mel reached for the hand that was offered. 'Mel Farran.'

'Can we talk here without being overheard?'

Mel thought about the Carlyle women and their interest in everything he did. 'Probably not. We can go out if you want.'

'I'd rather not. How about your room?'

They went upstairs. Mel sat on the bed and allowed Harry to use the chair.

'I hate this cloak and dagger stuff,' Harry said, 'but I can't take chances. What I have to say is for you alone.'

'Okay. Want to take your coat off?'

He shook his head. He kept his hands buried in the pockets. 'First, I want to say how sorry I am for knocking you down the other day.'

'That was you in the Megane?' Mel said more as a statement than a question, confirming what he had already worked out for himself.

'You weren't seriously injured?'

'More shocked than hurt.'

'I know you played in a concert that evening. It was unforgivable of me. I'm truly sorry. I panicked when it was obvious you were coming towards the car to speak. I wasn't ready to meet you then. All I could think was I had to get the hell out of there.'

'Why were you there at all?'

'Making sure.'

'Of what?'

'Where you lived. I'd already followed a taxi as far as the street, but I didn't see where you went in. If nothing else, I got that confirmed.'

'What exactly do you want?'

456

'You're a fine musician,' Harry said. 'I heard you playing today. You bring out the best in the others.'

'Thanks, but —'

'What's your instrument?'

'I thought you knew.'

'The maker, I mean.'

'Nicolò Amati.'

Harry's eyes widened. 'I thought it sounded out of this world. May I see it?'

A firm line was needed here. The man's behaviour had done nothing to engender confidence. 'Sorry, but no.'

'You don't think I'd damage it?'

'It doesn't belong to me.'

'Ah.' A short silence from Harry. 'This is something I wanted to ask you about.'

No, no, no, a voice screamed in Mel's head. 'I can't say any more.'

'A very rich man owns your viola and wants it played to a high standard. Am I right?'

'Shall we talk about something else?'

'Soon after I joined the Staccati, I was given a Maggini to play,' Harry said, smoothly overriding Mel's request. 'From 1610. Any of us would go through fire to own a fiddle like that. Extraordinary workmanship and a wonderful tone. You must have heard it on one of our recordings.'

'I have,' Mel said, 'and I know exactly what you mean.'

'None of us in the quartet owned our instruments,' Harry said. 'We were all indebted to the super-rich, but that's the way things have been for as long as music has been played. Fat cats buying antique instruments as investments.'

'I know.'

'And then they're horrified to discover the damn things need to be played to preserve their sound quality. Paganini presented his own Guarnerius to his native city of Genoa and they kept it in a glass case in the municipal palace and buggered the tone. To be fair, my patron may have been a fat cat, but he actually knew a lot about fiddles. He had an amazing collection from what I could gather. I don't know if he owned an Amati.'

Mel didn't rise to the bait.

'A Japanese guy who didn't speak much English,' Harry went on. 'I never discovered how he made his millions. You don't like to ask, do you? Anyway, I was offered the little beauty on indefinite loan and I played it all the years I was in the quartet. I didn't even get a chance to kiss goodbye to it.'

'You had to return it?'

'It was collected.' His look was so bleak

that he could have been saying a knife had been thrust into his gut.

Mel didn't like the way this was heading. 'So what do you play now?'

'I don't play at all.'

Difficult to believe. 'Why? Did you take against it, or something?'

'Long story,' Harry said. 'I don't know how much the others told you.'

'They don't know anything. They thought you were dead.'

'I might as well be.'

Mel didn't comment. How can you follow a remark like that?

'I'm constantly on the run,' Harry said. 'I sleep in the back of my car, never in the same place twice. That's okay. I've lived on the streets and survived, but I can't feel safe anywhere.'

This was all so alien to Mel's idea of the life of a top musician that the best he could do was try to appear sympathetic.

'Do they ever talk about me?' Harry asked.

'The quartet? Occasionally.'

'What do they say?'

'They have good memories of you.'

'All of them?'

'In their different ways, yes. They still have huge respect for your playing — and your company.'

'That's nice.'

'After you went missing, they were devastated. Cat roamed the streets of Budapest looking for you. Anthony went all to pieces. They had to find work for him with the Hallé.'

'And Ivan?'

'He's more philosophical, as you'd expect. He seems to think women were your problem. He saw me eyeing up some students in short skirts the other day and gave me quite a lecture about it.'

'Using me as an example?'

'Actually, yes.'

It was difficult to tell whether the twitch of Harry's lips was a smile or a grimace. 'But they think I'm dead?'

Mel avoided the direct answer. 'As time went on . . .'

'The other day,' Harry said, fixing Mel with a steady, questing look, 'out at the Michael Tippett Centre, I wasn't sure, but I thought Ivan looked at the car and recognised me.'

This was a minefield. 'I wouldn't know. We're all a bit jumpy now. Was that you in Sydney Gardens running away along the canal?'

A nod.

The conversation seemed to have ground

to a halt. Mel felt more comfortable when Harry was talking. 'What is the story?'

'All right, I'll tell you,' Harry said after a pause. 'Some of this you'll have heard already. I used to play poker. Fancied I was a red-hot player. Whichever city we fetched up in, I'd seek out the casino, or, better still, a private game without the house edge. But most serious players these days use casinos. We earned good money on tour so I could play big games. It turned out I wasn't the wiz I thought I was. I was too much of a bloody optimist. Wouldn't fold when I should have. I won a few times and then lost big. Started stacking up debts. In the end, it got silly. You must have heard some of this from Cat or Ivan.'

'Hardly anything.'

'I never borrowed from the others. Sometimes I'd ask Doug for a bit on spec.'

'They weren't sure if it was poker or women taking up your time.'

He smiled. 'There were a few one-night stands, I admit. You know how they come onto you after a concert? Sometimes you're in the right mood. But no, I wouldn't say women are my weakness. Anthony is the one for that. Even before we'd check in at the hotel he'd ask the bellman where the red light district was. How's the old goat doing

461

these days?'

'All right, I think.'

'I like Anthony. Terrific fiddler. Better than Ivan, which is saying a lot. I was telling you about my poker debts. They got worse than serious. I was blacklisted in several of the major casinos. They're syndicated, you see. They wouldn't let me play, but they still chased me for what I owed, and some of the debts are collected by gentlemen who call themselves family.'

'The mafia?'

'You don't mess with those guys. I needed another source of income — and fast. You may not know this, but Ivan, the crafty old bugger, has a nice little earner in hand-carved chess sets.'

'That's news to me.'

'He wouldn't tell you unless you asked. It's all cash in hand, no tax. I only found out accidentally when the hotel in Paris sent one of his customers to my room by mistake. This French guy didn't have much English, but he had a stack of Euros with him. He was waving them at me and talking about *les échecs.* I thought he was telling me cash is better than a cheque. Finally he produced a card with Ivan's name on it and I sent him to the right room. In my cash-strapped situation, I was more than a little curious what all this was about, I can tell you. I asked the concierge the meaning of *échecs*. When I put it to Ivan he was tight-lipped, as you'd expect, but I wormed out the truth. He has an arrangement with some craftsman in Archangel, that Russian port right up near the Arctic Circle.'

'Making chess sets?'

'Ivory chess sets.'

'Isn't that illegal?'

'Mammoth ivory isn't. They're digging it out of the permafrost in Northern Russia when the snow melts. It's a huge resource. They believe millions — literally millions — of woolly mammoth skeleton remains are waiting to be uncovered. It's cheap and legal and every bit as good as elephant ivory.'

'Is Ivan selling it as elephant ivory?'

Harry shook his head. 'He wouldn't take the risk. He's straight with his customers. He still has a sizeable mark-up on the chess-sets, hawking them everywhere the quartet goes on tour.'

'And did you ask for a stake in it?'

'Ask Ivan? No chance. You couldn't black-mail him. What he's doing is legal. Well, he's paying no tax, but I wouldn't shop him to the revenue. No, I thought a lot about it, how I might turn a few honest pennies. There are all sorts of ivory products in short

463

supply because of the ban on killing elephants. The trading still goes on, obviously, and thousands of elephants are shot each year. The main market is the Far East. Decorative combs, chopsticks, fans, all that stuff. And netsuke. You know what they are?'

Mel nodded.

'I decided to branch out on my own as a mammoth-ivory netsuke dealer. The idea wasn't totally new. Netsuke were already being created and supplied. I just had to find my own carver and eventually I did. We gave a concert in Vladivostok and had two days to ourselves. I don't know how good your geography is. Vladivostok is the last station on the Orient Express run, only a boat trip from Japan. It has a thriving Japanese quarter. I found a whole street of shops selling ornaments, mostly antique. There were a few new netsuke for sale there, quite highly priced. By this time I'd read up about ivory and how you identify it, which is quite a study in itself. Basically, in a cross-section you look at the graining, called Schreger lines, and how narrow they are. I wasn't an expert by any means, but I managed to convince the shopkeeper I was. With the help of a magnifying glass and some bluffing I let him think I was some kind of inspector from the Environmental Enforcement Agency. He was bricking it. He assured me his netsuke were legitimate mammoth ivory and produced the paperwork with the name and address of his carver. Just what I needed.'

'Was the carver local?'

'Three or four blocks away. I looked up my guy the same afternoon and did a deal. He was Japanese born, a sensational carver, and of course apart from the quality of the workmanship the beauty for me was that the product was small, light in weight and just about unbreakable — ideal for travel. Much more cost-effective than Ivan's chess sets, which take up a lot of space in his luggage.'

'Did you tell Ivan what you were up to?'

'No. He's a prickly character, as you must know by now.'

'Then why are you telling me?'

'I'll come to that. My netsuke business really took off in Europe. I'd seek out the upmarket shops and sell at profit of more than a hundred percent. Even better, it was becoming a hobby, weaning me off the poker. I got a real kick out of having a product everyone admired and coveted. I was paying off my casino debts. I thought nothing could go wrong — which, as anyone knows, is exactly when you're due for a kick where it hurts most.'

'What happened?' Mel asked.

'I was green as owl-shit. Should have realised if there was money to be made this way, then someone else would already be doing it.'

'Who was it?'

'A Japanese syndicate. I didn't know they were already trading in ivory objects in just about every capital city in Europe and Asia. But their trade was the illegal kind, ivory from slaughtered elephants. Ten tonnes a year. That represents around a thousand elephant deaths.'

'That's horrible,' Mel said.

'There's still a huge demand for the stuff. People don't seem to make the connection with a noble, giant creature that has a time-honoured right to exist. But you don't need a lecture from me. You obviously feel the same disgust I do. Okay, I was profiteering, too, but from fossilised material. As it turned out, this was my undoing. Some alert member of the syndicate got to know about me and decided to act. But they believed I was in direct competition, trading in elephant ivory. They decided to take a close look at my carver's work, so they set a honey-trap.'

'A woman?'

'In 2008, the Staccati gave a concert in Vienna, at the Konzerthaus. We were at the top of our form that night, playing the Debussy in G minor — all those restless harmonies — followed by Mendelssohn's charming A minor with its quotations from Beethoven. I was elated when we finished, fair game, I suppose, for the young Japanese woman from the audience who came up afterwards and spoke to us, thanking us in turn for enchanting her with our playing. You'll know yourself that some fans just gush and you wish they'd go away. It became obvious that this woman was a scholar of music. She talked about the closing bars echoing the ending of the Cavatina from Beethoven's Opus 130 and how our interpretation of those final four quavers had brought the homage to a perfect conclusion. Do you know the piece?'

'I do. We've played it and Ivan likes to give a special emphasis to each note.'

'It works a treat, doesn't it? Anyway, this lady was spot on with her comments. She charmed us all. While I was packing up she said — just to me — that she was staying at our hotel and would like to talk music if I wasn't too exhausted. I knew from the look in her eyes that there was more on offer than conversation.'

As a self-confessed soft touch for the ladies, Mel sympathised.

'I suggested we have a drink back in the hotel, but warned her I was tired and couldn't stay long. As hotel bars go, this one was okay, with a fountain and some nice lighting. The others were in there with our manager Doug having a nightcap a few seats away. When you're on tour it's just about impossible to make a move without everyone knowing.'

'You have to be thick-skinned.'

Harry grinned. 'Speaking from experience? Anyway, believe it or not, when she came to my room we continued to talk music intelligently for a bit, about the Debussy, that fantastic passage near the end of the first movement when second violin and viola play together. She'd noticed how Anthony was leading because he had the upper voice and she appreciated how I was reacting to him. A musician's observation. It brought us closer together and the sex, when it came, was all the more satisfying because of it. This wasn't "Bang-bang, thank you, ma'am" as I'd rather expected. Afterwards I offered her a drink from the mini-bar and we talked about my touring. And since she was Japanese, it seemed natural to mention the netsuke and show her some samples from my suitcase.'

'She appreciated them?'

'God, yes. She almost had another orgasm. She said the carving was the best she'd ever seen, and she may have been telling the truth, because my guy in Vladivostok was a genius in his way. I could tell she would have loved to own one. I don't know if it was the champagne or the nice things she'd said about my playing, but in a rush of generosity I offered her one as a memento of the evening. She was thrilled. Yes, it was a valuable gift, but I told myself I could have lost three times as much in one session at the poker table. So it was a happy evening. She left my room some time after midnight and I slept well.'

Mel had listened to all this with mounting concern. He knew the police were investigating the murder of a young Japanese woman in Vienna at the time the Staccati had been performing there four years ago. She'd been dumped in the canal. If Harry had slept with her, he had to be the prime suspect. Why was he admitting so much unless it was to shift the blame elsewhere?

There was more. 'Our next concert was in Budapest and we moved on the next day. I gave no more thought to Emi, my Japanese fan. We were flat out rehearsing a new programme. I barely found time to do my rounds of the shops that sold ivory objects. A pity I did, because when I got to one of the last I was invited into the back room. This was normal for doing business. But the way I was treated certainly was not. I was grabbed from behind, thrown to the ground and held there. I thought I was being mugged by at least two strong men. I had quite an amount of cash in my wallet and there were still a few unsold netsuke in the case I carried. You're outnumbered, I thought. Best not to fight. So I lay still. Next I felt my jacket being grabbed off my shoulder and my shirt ripped open to expose my arm. Out of the corner of my eye I caught sight of a syringe poised to inject me with something and that's all I remember until I regained consciousness in total darkness doubled in a foetal position with my hands cuffed behind me. From the bumping I was getting and the engine noise I guessed I was imprisoned in a car-boot.'

'Incredible,' Mel said.

'Well, it happened to me, I promise you. I had no idea how long I'd been unconscious or what this was about. I thought of the concert we were supposed to be giving and my precious Maggini back in the hotel. It was a nightmare. Hours went by, or so it seemed, before we stopped. The boot opened and two young Japanese guys were looking down at me. One had a bottle of water and a straw and I was allowed to sit up and take some liquid. I tried asking questions, but there was no communication. He shoved me down again, slammed the lid and I was left for a while, I suppose while they were eating. More hours of driving followed. I had no way of telling where we were headed.'

If this is an invented alibi, it's an elaborate one, Mel was thinking. 'So where did you end up?'

'No idea,' Harry said. 'When I was finally allowed out of that bloody car-boot, I was blindfolded, taken into a building and thrown into a cellar. It could have been anywhere. I was given the basics, bucket, water and some kind of bread.'

'What did they want from you?'

'I didn't find out for days. Finally a little guy in a suit arrived to interrogate me.'

'Japanese?'

'Definitely. He knew all about Emi coming to my room in the hotel and he knew I traded in netsuke. But he didn't seem to know they were mammoth ivory or where they were made. Gradually it got home to me that my selling around Europe had got

471

up their nose. They had a good thing going trading in ivory objects, illegal elephant ivory, and they viewed me as unfair competition. My netsuke were getting a reputation as superior work and they weren't happy. They wanted a closer look at some of my merchandise and Emi had been instructed to sleep with me and beg, borrow or steal a piece.'

'Which she'd done successfully.'

'Right. But she hadn't reported back. She'd disappeared. And he wanted to know what I'd done with her. I couldn't tell him where she was. I had no idea she was dead. In this situation I had no reason to hold back, so I told him what happened that night. He didn't believe me. He talked about codes of behaviour and certain penalties prescribed by the organisation he belonged to.'

'Which organisation?'

'Have you heard of the yakuza?'

'No.'

'You'd better know. They're the Japanese mob. A network of huge syndicates making money out of crime. Their roots go back to the 1800s and they had a peculiar privileged status in Japanese society, allowed to bear weapons in return for helping the police to keep order. They still command some respect, even though they're the biggest managers of organised crime. Like the mafia, they have their tentacles into just about every institution, banking, the stock exchange, the media. You name it. Like you, I knew nothing about them. I picked this up gradually.'

'You were down in the cellar some time, then?'

'Weeks. They were in no hurry. I lost weight and went into a deep depression. Then one morning the guards came in and made it clear I was being moved again. I allowed myself to hope they might be returning me to Budapest. Some hope. I won't bore you with all the discomforts of the journey. We ended up in Vladivostok.'

'That's a huge distance.'

'Tell me about it. I was taken there to be questioned by someone else from the organisation. And this guy didn't mess about. He told me I was a murderer, that Emi's body had been found in the Danube canal in Vienna and she had one of my netsuke tucked inside her clothes. I denied knowing anything about it, of course, but I wasn't believed. He talked about honour and punishments. He was definitely out to scare me. It was only at the end of this grilling that I realised what they really wanted was the name and address of my carver.'

'Hadn't you told them?'

'It hadn't come up before, but now I was in Vladivostok I sensed that the guy interrogating me was the local yakuza don. He was miffed because he'd lost face from not knowing who had been carrying out this beautiful work in his own backyard. He expected me to volunteer the name and address of my carver, but he was too proud to ask in front of his henchmen. You have to understand that dignity is paramount to these people. The thing was, it gave me something to bargain with, or so I told myself. So I kept shtum. There were two more sessions and I let him know my terms. If I supplied the name, I expected to get my freedom. They would have no reason to keep me.'

'What was his reaction?'

'Inscrutable, to say the least. He wasn't going to grovel for sure. No promises were made. But one afternoon I was blindfolded and taken out of my cell by two of his thugs and driven a short distance. They removed the blindfold and I knew exactly where they'd brought me. It was the Japanese quarter in Vladivostok. At first I thought they were about to release me. Ever the optimist.'

'They wanted you to take them to your carver.'

'You've got it. And of course there was a slight ethical dilemma. Did I want to lead the mob to my obliging little helpmate? You wouldn't wish that lot on your worst enemy. But I'd gone past the point of behaving honourably. I figured they wouldn't kill him. The worst they would do was pressure him to work for them, using elephant ivory instead of mammoth. He was my ticket to freedom. So, driven by desperation, I led them to his address.'

'And was he there?'

'Gone. No sign. Another family had moved in. It was a different business altogether, run by women selling silk fabrics. I was shocked. I definitely had the right building. I knew the houses on either side. Yet the women there claimed to know nothing about my guy or where he'd gone. Of course the heavies who were with me took a poor view of this. They talked to the women in Japanese and still got no help. Then they turned on me, accusing me of taking them on a wild goose chase.'

'Did you make a run for it?'

'No chance. It may have crossed my mind, but they each had a hold of one of my arms. I was marched back to the car and blindfolded again and taken back to my prison. That was a low point, believe me. I'd played my ace and lost. I'd had my first glimpse of freedom in weeks and now I was back in captivity having angered my captors.'

'Do you think your carver had got wind that he was about to be visited?'

'He must have. He would surely have let me know if he was changing his address. I was his best customer. Maybe the women with the silks were his own family, covering for him. Whatever it was, I was shafted.'

'What happened then?'

'It gets worse. The guy I called the don came back next day with his helpers. He said I was a murderer and a liar and his organisation had a time-honoured way of dealing with such people, to warn others what to expect. It was known as *yubitsume*. Do you know about it?'

'No.'

'It's a form of penance or apology and generally the offender is expected to carry out the punishment himself. In my case, the don said, I couldn't be trusted, so they would do it for me. They placed a square of white cloth on a table and grabbed me by the wrist and held my hand over it. Then the don himself took a knife from his pocket and cut off the end of my left little finger just below the top joint.'

Mel felt a crawling sensation along the length of his spine. 'God — that's cruel.'

'Painful, anyway,' Harry said. 'The original idea of *yubitsume* was that it weakened your ability to use a sword. In Japanese martial arts the bottom three fingers are used to grip the hilt. So you become more dependent on your yakuza brothers defending you. And of course everyone who saw your maimed hand knew you had disgraced the family in some way. If you transgressed a second time they cut it to the next joint, leaving you with a stump . . . like this.'

He removed his left hand from his pocket and held it up. He had a thumb and three fingers. The mangled end testified to the truth of his story.

'They took the second joint?' Mel said in horror.

'A few days later. I was considered a serious offender.'

'But it means . . .' Mel's voice trailed away.

'I can't do the fingering on the viola. I won't be asking for my job back.'

The cruelty of the punishment would have been savage enough for anyone. On a professional musician it was the loss of his life's work. Mel understood why Harry had said earlier that he might as well be dead. There

477

was no way he could ever play again. A few times in the last few minutes Mel had wondered if he was being strung along. This ugly stump was proof of Harry's integrity.

'When did they let you go?'

'I escaped. I think they were planning to take the finger on my right hand. Certainly they showed no sign of letting me go. I pretended the wound had gone septic and asked to see a doctor. They drove me out to see one of their own doctors in the city. I was acting as if I was weak and delirious from blood poisoning. This put them off their guard and between the car and the surgery I made a run for it. They chased, but I managed to escape through the side streets. So there I was, a free man again, but with no money, no form of identity, and on the run from the yakuza, who were not going to hand me the keys of the city if they found me. Not much use throwing myself on the mercy of the Russian police either.'

'What did you do?'

'Lived rough, begged for food, joined the homeless community. Vladivostok is already full of beggars and not the best place to be a vagrant. I spent a few nights in jail, got ill drinking bootleg vodka, survived two Russian winters. I'm not proud of some of the things I did to survive.'

'You were there as long as that?'

'A broken man. Psychologically, it took a long while to get over the shock of not being able to play the fiddle any longer. If I got back to the west I couldn't foresee any future. From all I'd been told by my captors, I was the number one suspect for Emi's murder in Vienna. The Brits would hand me over to the Viennese police. I didn't have the strength to face all that. In the end I got some money — don't ask how — and smartened up enough to travel again. Worked my way slowly across Europe. Actually passed through Vienna and visited the place where Emi's body was found. Bit of a risk, but I wanted to do it. I know she wasn't totally truthful with me, but she was under duress as well and she was sweet.' He shrugged. 'And here I am.'

'Why? Why seek us out again?'

'I saw in the papers about the Japanese girl murdered here in Bath and thrown in the canal. The tooth tattoo. The interest in music. It seemed to link up with Emi's murder and I want to find out the truth.'

Mel was trying to think how he could get rid of Harry. 'I wish I could help, but . . .'

Harry shook his head. 'I'm not looking for help from you. I'm here to warn you of what you could be getting into.'

Mel did his best to make light of it. 'Good thing I don't trade in ivory.'

'I'm talking about that,' Harry pointed under the bed. He'd spotted the viola case.

'My instrument? Thanks, but I'm being ultra-careful with it, as you appreciate.'

'I'm thinking about who owns it. I don't know for certain that the guy who presented me with the Maggini is the same who owns your Amati. I don't know for certain that he's a high-up in the yakuza. All I can tell you is that I've looked online at the press accounts of when I was first reported missing in Budapest. They all say that when my hotel room was searched, my two Tertis Model violas were found. Not one of them mentions the Maggini. It must have been collected. For this to have happened so quickly, before even the police got there, someone must have known about my abduction — someone with inside knowledge of the yakuza, someone acting on behalf of the owner, Mr. Hamada.'

Mel felt a definite tingling sensation at the tip of his left little finger.

'So, my friend, you've heard my story,' Harry said, 'and now it's time for some straight talking from you.'

Mel shook his head. 'I don't have anything to say.'

'I'm serious,' Harry said. 'This is how serious I am.'

The right hand had come out of his coat
pocket holding a handgun, an automatic.

26

'It's bloody frustrating,' Keith Halliwell said to those of the team who were listening, 'but there's no point in us buzzing around Bath like blue-arsed flies. The boss has put out an all-units call. Wait for the shout. It'll come. Then we can reel him in.'

'Is he dangerous?' Paul Gilbert asked.

'Lethal when DCs ask daft questions.'

'I mean Harry Cornell.'

'Anyone on the run has to be considered dangerous. After four years he's probably got himself a shooter.'

'He must know he's taking a risk coming here. What's he doing it for?'

'How would I know? He's the one you want to ask. Old scores, maybe. If he's stalking the people he used to know, he must have something to settle with them.'

'Could it be sour grapes that they replaced him in the band and he's a forgotten man now?'

'The *band*?'

'Quartet.'

'You could be right. These performers have inflated egos.'

'The guy who replaced him had better watch out, then. I wouldn't want to be in his shoes.'

Diamond treated himself to a later start. He'd worked over-time the evening before, not only visiting Ivan, but making a late trip to Manvers Street to set up the dragnet for Harry. He phoned in early. No news. It was too much to hope for a quick arrest.

He caught himself talking to the cat again as he put down food, a sure sign of stress. Raffles ignored him, and after a sniff ignored the pieces of salmon squeezed from the pouch and sat by the plate waiting, a way of informing a dim-witted owner that rabbit, lamb or beef were preferable every time. Cat food in packets of twelve always included some flavour Raffles rejected.

'You're too picky for your own good, Mr. Cat,' Diamond said. 'A contented mind is a continual feast. It's a lesson in life.'

A short lesson. Ten minutes later he softened and put out a plate of lamb. Raffles had been Steph's cat and he could almost hear her urging him to open another packet.

So the cat got the continual feast and the contented mind.

The big man pottered around, making tea and toast until he noticed the message light winking on the kitchen phone. A call must have come in while he was shaving. He pressed *play* in case it was Manvers Street to say they'd found Harry Cornell.

The voice was Paloma's.

He stopped everything, stood still and listened.

'Peter, this is me. I expect you're still hard at work on the case of those poor Japanese women. Well, I was thinking back to our Vienna trip and that little shrine of flowers we found by the canal. It may mean nothing at all, but on the other hand . . . Listen, I've been doing some research of my own and I ought to speak to you about it. Is there any chance we could meet? Let me know if you think I could be helpful.'

If you think I could be helpful.

No need to think. This was Paloma wanting to meet again. He called her mobile.

She had switched it off. Nothing is ever simple. So he left a voicemail message saying he'd be grateful for any help she could give and would call her again to fix a time and place.

He'd not slept well. His brain had kept

484

returning to Harry Cornell, asking why the missing violist had resurfaced after so long. Was the man dangerous, as Ivan believed? Almost certainly.

Emi Kojima had last been seen alive in Harry's company late at night in October 2008, in the bar of their hotel in Vienna. She was a Tokyo prostitute who had mysteriously arrived in Vienna and turned up at one of the Staccati concerts. Working girls don't make expensive trips to Europe. Someone must have funded her, and for a reason. She had some knowledge of classical music so she'd been chosen for this job. What was the job? Surely to learn more about Harry's trading in netsuke — a lucrative private enterprise that was upsetting the big boys. Some criminal syndicate had arranged for Emi to sleep with Harry and get the truth about his dealings. She was later found dead with one of Harry's netsuke hidden in her clothing. This suggested she'd stolen it as a sample of his wares, but was killed before she could report back and deliver the goods — which made Harry the prime suspect.

Any of the quartet, or Douglas Christmas, could testify in court that they'd witnessed the pair drinking together and stepping into the lift. It wasn't too much to surmise that the action moved from the hotel bar to Harry's room.

Harry, already deeply in debt to the mafia, needed his second income. He would have been alarmed when Emi got interested in his business activities.

Alarm, panic, violence. A deadly sequence.

The hotel where all this had happened backed onto the Wienfluss, which fed into the Danube canal, where the body was found.

Then Harry went missing in Budapest, the next stop on the quartet's tour. With the mafia calling in his gambling debts and the yakuza closing in on his netsuke dealings, and the Vienna police likely to discover the body, his only sensible option had been to disappear.

As it turned out, Emi's death was assumed to have been suicide and no one made the connection with the quartet. They had never been questioned about their enthusiastic fan and who she slept with.

Four years on, the quartet had re-formed and were based in Bath. If Harry took the slightest interest in his fellow musicians, he'd have looked at the website. Curiosity may have brought him here, or envy, or the pull of the quartet-playing he loved and missed. Whatever the reason, he was in the city and a second Japanese woman had been strangled. By now, Harry would be desperate to know if there were fresh suspicions about the Vienna death and if his old companions had been questioned and how much they remembered.

This would explain the stalking.

Diamond tried putting himself in Harry's situation. There was a limit to what he could learn from a distance. He needed to speak to one of the Staccati. Who would he approach? Not the prickly old Soviet defector, Ivan. Not Cat, who would blab to everyone and think it a huge joke. And certainly not Anthony whose tunnel vision recognised little else but music.

Which left Mel, the new man, an unknown quantity for Harry, but without direct knowledge of what had happened in Vienna. As a fellow violist Mel ought to be a twin soul. And well placed to report on what the others were saying these days. This explained why Harry's car had been seen outside Mel's lodgings. And why Mel had been followed into Sydney Gardens. It was even possible Harry had been on the point of approaching Mel that morning in the gardens — neutral ground — when Diamond and Ingeborg had appeared.

At the cost of a decent night's sleep,

Diamond had a better grasp of events. A meeting with Mel was next on his agenda.

But not quite.

As he was about to leave the house, his phone rang. He snatched it up and heard Paloma's voice: 'Peter? I was in the shower when you called. Any chance we could meet?'

'Every chance,' he said. 'Can I come now?'

Her Georgian house in Lyncombe Vale doubled as home and business premises. Maybe it was understandable after their recent history that she chose to see him upstairs in her office with her mahogany desk between them and her personal assistant Judy in the same room working on the computer. Once in Vogue was a thriving international company that supplied period illustrations for television and stage designers. Two large bedrooms had been knocked into one to store the prints, books, bound magazines and newspapers. It was a huge archive, yet you had the sense that everything had its place and Paloma knew exactly where each item was to be found.

'Coffee?'

'Too early, thanks,' he said. 'It's not my caffeine rush hour yet. But don't let me stop you.'

'How's work?' Her unease was obvious. They were both as stiff-backed as guests at a state dinner. And Judy's presence didn't help.

'Hectic, as usual. Yours?'

'Much the same. You look tired.'

'Do I? It must be all the clubbing.'

He wasn't going to ask how her personal life was going. All too painfully he was minded of the tall guy he'd seen her with at the concert, the one he had dubbed the dog's dinner.

'I got your message about Vienna,' he prompted her.

'Oh, yes. Vienna,' she said with obvious relief. 'The little shrine of flowers by the canal. I've been thinking about them. The woman who died was Japanese, you discovered?'

'Yes, and we thought she committed suicide, but we now believe she was murdered.'

'Like the woman found in Bath?'

'Strangled, yes. That's the theory.'

'Don't you know for certain?'

'The body was returned to Japan and cremated. Our suspicions are based on circumstantial evidence, a growing amount of it.'

'You sound confident.'

'I am. She'd been working as a prostitute in Tokyo. Then she turned up in Vienna at one of the Staccati concerts. We reckon she was employed by the Japanese mafia.'

'Doing what — apart from the obvious?'

'Basically, spying. One of the quartet — the one who later went missing — was dealing in netsuke made from mammoth ivory. It got up the noses of the mob because they wanted the monopoly on the netsuke trade. So they ordered Emi to find out more.'

'Who was the dealer?'

'The violist. Not the one we heard at Corsham. He's new. This was a man called Harry Cornell.'

'And he was in Vienna?'

'In two thousand and eight, when all this happened.'

'Did he murder her?'

'It looks a strong bet.'

'Was he a Brit?'

Diamond nodded. 'Why do you ask?'

'Let me tell you about the flowers. Do you remember the bunch I found lying on the pavement and pushed back into the wall?'

'The lilies.'

'We called them lilies and it's true they are a variety of lily. There was no message with them that I could see. Most of the dead flowers were bunches of carnations, some with cards attached, with Japanese writing. I assume they were put there by Japanese people who knew the woman.'

'I expect so.'

'The Japanese like carnations. But I was more interested in the living flowers, the long-stemmed ones we called lilies. Do you remember them, with the pinkish-white star shapes and long yellow-tipped stamens?'

'Just about,' he said.

She opened a book that she'd marked with a Post-it note and handed it across the desk. 'They were asphodels.'

He remembered them now. 'I wouldn't have known. Is it important?'

'I don't know. You must decide. They have a strong association with death. In Greek mythology, the underworld, where dead souls went, had asphodel meadows. The best place to find yourself in was the Elysian fields, where the blessed went. The asphodel meadows were a stage lower, for indifferent and ordinary souls. You'd probably sinned a bit if you ended up there.'

'Just a bit?'

'Let's say you weren't considered a total write-off.'

'I think I know where the write-offs went.'

'Happily it doesn't concern us.'

'Yet.'

She conjured up a smile. 'Speak for yourself. Do you know about the language of the flowers?'

'I've heard there is one,' he said. 'All Greek to me.'

'No, this isn't Greek. This is English. The asphodel has a meaning all its own, a precise message that hasn't changed in two hundred years. You'll find it in pre-Victorian books and even today on the internet. It's this: "My regret follows you to the grave".'

He needed a moment to take it in. 'Strange. Like a message to a dead person?'

'All the main flowers have significance according to this system and most of the sentiments are pretty bland, like snowdrops meaning hope, campanulas gratitude.'

'Roses for love?'

'Red roses. But this one is specific. It may be pure chance that someone settled on asphodels, but if they were using the language of the flowers intentionally, they were making a statement that was very suitable for a shrine.'

' "My regret follows you to the grave." Are you thinking this could have been left by the murderer?'

'That's why I phoned you. It sounds like someone with a guilty conscience.'

'I suppose,' he said. 'But let's not forget

all the carnations already left there by Japanese friends or family. They knew Emi back in Japan and wanted to pay respect while they were in Vienna.'

'So you're thinking friends or family must have left the asphodels?'

'Don't you?'

'I would,' Paloma said, 'except that the Japanese have their own language of the flowers and it doesn't include the asphodel. This is a peculiarly British thing.'

'I get it now,' he said. 'You're thinking some Brit must have left them because of what they're supposed to mean. Harry?'

'They were not more than a day old when we found them. They could only have been placed there while we were in Vienna ourselves. If it was Harry, he'd have needed to be in Vienna in July.'

'That's not impossible,' Diamond said. 'We don't know where he disappeared to after Budapest. I suppose he could have come through Vienna. He'd need to know the symbolism.'

'He's a musician,' she said. 'An intelligent, sensitive person, one assumes.'

And not a yob like me, he thought, who couldn't tell an asphodel from an asparagus. 'Maybe I underestimate these musicians.'

'It may be a long shot, Peter, but once I

started checking it seemed to make sense. Isn't there something about murderers returning to the scene of the crime?'

'That's a myth. Only if they're taken there in handcuffs to show where they buried the body.'

'Have you checked whether any flowers have been left by the Avon in memory of the other girl?'

He shook his head. Checking bunches of flowers wasn't part of the investigation process.

'Might be worth your while,' she said.

'Possibly.' He didn't say it with much conviction.

'Anyway,' Paloma said with a trace of annoyance, 'I decided it was my duty to bring it to your attention.'

Her *duty*? With that short, uncompromising word the gulf between them had grown into Death Valley. He'd kidded himself this was about something more than obligation. 'Thanks. You've obviously done some homework.'

The disappointment must have been written all over his face. He felt himself reddening.

'I didn't phrase that very well,' she added.

'That's okay.'

'It's strange,' she said. 'When I saw you at

the concert the other evening I was flabbergasted. I wouldn't have expected to meet you there in a million years.'

'There you go.'

'But now I understand. The link with the Staccati. Peter, I do hope one of them hasn't killed these women. I can't believe they're capable of such dreadful crimes. They're fabulous musicians. Even you must . . .' She clapped her hand to her mouth. 'Sorry. That's so patronising.'

'True, even so,' he said. The earlier remark had wounded him more. 'A lot of what we heard was way above my head. I recognised the "Ritual Fire Dance".'

'Enjoyed it?'

'Always have.'

'Perhaps we should do another concert some time. Quartet music is an acquired taste.'

It sounded like a peace offering, but he couldn't tamely accept it. Too much had come between them. The real issue hadn't been faced. Impulsively, he blurted it out. 'I'd spoil your enjoyment. You're better off with someone who knows this stuff, like your latest man.'

At her computer in the background Judy the PA continued to gaze at the screen, but her ears must have been flapping.

Paloma frowned. 'My what?'

'Your tall friend in the grey suit.'

'That was Mike.'

'Yes, you told me.'

'My brother Miguel. I must have mentioned him before now. He likes to be known as Mike.' Now it was her turn to blush. 'Oh my God, you didn't really think I was seeing someone else. Peter, I know we had our difference of opinion, but I'm not so angry with you that I'm going out with other men.'

The relief surged through him. He was speechless, far more emotional than he expected.

She filled the silence with more explanation. 'Mike lives in London. He's a Beethoven fanatic, and I was offered tickets through my connection with Corsham Court, so I thought of him.'

He blinked and his eyes moistened.

Paloma said, 'Why don't I walk downstairs with you? Judy can look after the office.'

They left the PA in charge.

'This hasn't been a total waste of your time if it's cleared up that misunderstanding,' Paloma said as they went down her grand, crimson-carpeted staircase.

'Far from it,' he said. 'Far from it.'

She linked her hand under his arm. 'I'm glad you came.'

'You could be onto something with the asphodels.'

'Stuff the asphodels. I've missed you, Peter.'

'If I'm honest, it hasn't been much fun for me.'

'Truce?' she said when they reached the front door. She offered her lips and they kissed lightly.

'Truce,' he said. 'Sorry — and not just for jumping to the wrong conclusion. Sorry for being an oaf on the towpath that evening.'

'And I'm sorry for being such a grouch. Can we start over?'

'That would be good.'

They kissed again and held each other before he got into the car and drove away.

Mrs. Carlyle came to the door of the house in Forester Road. 'You're the policeman.'

Diamond didn't deny it.

'You want to speak to Mel?'

'That's the general idea. Is he out in Sydney Gardens again?'

'Definitely not. He had a phone call from one of his musical friends and ordered a taxi straight away. He was in a bit of a state if you ask me.'

497

'Which friend?'

'How would I know? But it seemed to be an emergency. Something about a cat.'

'Cat? She's the cellist. Has something happened to her?'

'I couldn't tell you. Funny name for a cellist.'

27

Cat was living south of the river in a two-up, two-down terraced house, a relic of Bath's industrial past. Compared with Ivan's grand address in Great Pulteney Street, Sydenham Buildings was a slum, bordered by the railway, the main road and the cemetery, but there was an advantage in that Cat had sole use of the furnished house. There are definite compensations in living apart from one's landlord.

All the curtains were across when Diamond arrived. He was getting wise to the lifestyle of musicians. Used to working late, they were in the habit of lying in. He rang twice and stepped back to see if the bedroom curtains moved.

He rang again.

Nothing.

He put his ear against the door and couldn't hear anything from inside.

If Cat wasn't at home, who was Mel visiting?

Another of the quartet — Anthony, the second violin — was in lodgings a short walk away. As the member most in need of day-to-day assistance he'd doubtless been housed close to Cat so that she could keep a sisterly eye on him. His digs were at the bottom of Westmoreland Street, parallel with Sydenham Buildings.

Still seized with the urgency he'd got from Mrs. Carlyle, Diamond drove the car round there instead of walking.

His ring was answered and it was Cat who opened the door. She was looking distressed. Faint lines of mascara marked the paths of tears down her cheeks. 'Man, do we need you!' she said, opening her arms. 'Come in. They're all inside.'

He sidestepped her embrace.

The other three members of the quartet were standing in the living room facing the window as if something of surpassing interest was happening in the street.

'Relax, guys. The Old Bill are on the case,' Cat told them with an effort to be cheerful.

When the three musicians turned, it was obvious they were anything but relaxed. Anthony had the shakes. Mel looked ten years older. Ivan could have passed for

Hamlet's father.

'What's up?' Diamond asked.

'What's up?' Cat said. 'Harry's out there in a car with a bullet through his head, that's what's up.'

She was a natural jester, and you couldn't take much she said at face value.

'Oh, yes?' Diamond said, preparing to grin.

'Fact,' she said and took a big tearful sniff. The men weren't smiling either.

He was forced to accept that she probably meant what she'd said. 'Where exactly?'

'The other side of the street, opposite your car.'

He went to the window. Some detective I am, he thought. Drove up and never noticed.

Harry's black Megane was out there with a man slumped over the wheel.

'Anthony found him, poor lad,' Cat said. 'Imagine the shock.'

'Have you called the police?'

'Of course.' She gave Diamond as disbelieving a look as he'd just given her. 'That's you, isn't it?'

'I didn't get the shout. They must be on their way. Stay here, all of you. Don't leave this room.'

Harry dead, when everyone had barely

501

adjusted to the surprise that he was alive.

When Diamond opened the front door, the two-tone wail of the first response car soared above the growl of morning traffic. His grasp of events could be faulted, but his timing couldn't. He'd beaten the emergency service.

He ran across the road.

The man with his head flat to the steering wheel was unmistakably dead, with a neat, star-shaped red hole below his right ear. Hardly any blood had been shed. Never having got a full sight of Harry Cornell, Diamond couldn't identify him except from a general likeness to photos he'd seen. But the jacket was similar to the one the runaway had been wearing in Sydney Gardens except that the hood was now drawn back from the head.

From the nearside he saw that a handgun, a black automatic, was wedged in the space between the seats. Both of the dead man's hands hung limply over his left thigh above the weapon. The fourth finger of the left was missing.

He knew better than to touch any of the car doors, all of which were unlocked. Quite an array of food packets and cans littered the back seat. A blanket was on the floor. Harry must have been using the car as his home. Forensics would have a field day.

The police siren had been getting louder and was joined by others, and now two blues and twos in quick succession swung off the Lower Bristol Road and powered towards him. He raised a hand in greeting in case some idiot failed to recognise him and used a taser.

Fortunately he was well enough known. 'You got here fast. How did you manage it, sir?' the driver of the first asked.

'I'm Superman. Tell control we have a man here shot through the head who answers to the description of Harry Cornell, the guy we've all been looking for. We need forensics, a police surgeon to certify that death has occurred and enough tape to secure the scene. Then it's a matter of doorstepping for witnesses. You know the drill.'

'Has he topped himself?'

'Unlikely, but that's not a question for you or me. For the present we try to keep an open mind. Get on with it, would you? I'll be in the house opposite when I'm needed.'

The response teams were trained to deal with incidents like this. No two scenes were ever the same and there was much to be done, yet Diamond's priority had to be with the living, the people with a link to the dead man.

He called Manvers Street and told Keith Halliwell and Ingeborg Smith to get to Westmoreland Street fast to assist with the questioning.

Back in the house he asked the shocked members of the quartet to be seated. In the small front room this was only possible with Mel and Anthony perched on the arms of a two-seat sofa shared by Cat and Ivan. They could have been posing for a group photo, and a strange one it would have made, fit to be a Charles Addams cartoon. 'Right you are, people. I need to know the sequence of events. Anthony, when did you raise the alarm?'

Cat said, 'His landlady called me —'

Diamond stopped her. 'Thanks. He's got a voice of his own. We'll come to you shortly.' He wanted particularly to hear from the one steadfast truth-teller of the group.

Anthony said, 'Seven forty-five.'

'Good. How did you come to discover the body?'

'Looked out the window.'

'And saw?'

'Harry's car.'

'So you knew what he was driving?'

'We all knew.'

There were murmurs of confirmation.

'Could you see from the window that he was dead?'

'No.'

The previous interview with Anthony at the Michael Tippett Centre had taught Diamond to take one-word answers as encouragement, better than silence.

'Tell me what you saw.'

'Harry's car.'

'Sorry,' Diamond said, mindful of the logical process of Anthony's thinking. 'I already asked you that. Could you see anyone inside?'

'Harry.'

'And what was he doing?'

'Leaning forward, against the wheel.'

'What did you do about it?'

'Went out for a better look.'

This was the only way with Anthony, patiently prising out information. The brain that was so expressive with music had to be helped to make a connected narrative in words. 'What did you see?'

'The bullet-hole in his head.'

'What did you do next?'

'Went back to the house.'

'And?'

'Told Mrs. Oliphant to phone Cat.'

'Mrs. Oliphant being your landlady, I suppose. Is she around?'

'No.'

'Where is she?'

'The corner shop.'

'Shopping already?'

'She works there.'

'But she found time to call Cat before she left? You did the right thing, Anthony.'

Anthony didn't register any emotion.

Diamond put one more key question to his truth-teller. 'Do you know how Harry was shot?'

A shake of the head.

'That's no, is it? I want to hear you say it.'

Anthony, expressionless, said, 'No.'

Ivan said, 'Isn't that obvious? He wasn't there when it happened. None of us were. We know Harry was carrying a gun and he put it to his head and took his own life.'

'Did I hear right?' Diamond said. 'You knew he was in possession of a gun?'

'He showed it to Mel and Mel warned us all last night on the phone.'

Mel cleared his throat. 'I decided everyone had a right to be told.'

'I'm obviously missing something here,' Diamond said, turning to Mel. 'Did you have a meeting with Harry?'

'Last night. He came to see me at my lodgings.' Mel launched into an account of almost everything Harry had told him, about the poker debts; the mammoth ivory; the netsuke carver he had found in Vladivostok; the sex with Emi Kojima in Vienna; the gift to her of the netsuke piece; his capture by the yakuza in Budapest; the long, uncomfortable journey by car to Vladivostok; the mysterious disappearance of the carver; the refusal of the yakuza to believe Harry knew nothing about Emi's killing; the amputation of his finger joints; his escape; and his eventual return to Britain.

A short silence followed, time required to absorb the extraordinary sequence of events.

Diamond couldn't see any way Mel had invented such an elaborate story. Nothing in it conflicted with his own discoveries. Moreover it was evident from Ivan's twitchy reactions that each mention of his personal influence on events touched raw nerves.

'The one thing you haven't spoken about is the gun,' Diamond said.

'He only produced it after he'd said all this,' Mel said. 'I was shocked.'

'Who wouldn't be?' Cat said. 'None of us slept last night wondering if Harry would come knocking — or without knocking.'

'Did he threaten you with it?' Diamond asked Mel.

'Not at any point. He made enough of an impact by simply producing it. He held it out in the palm of his hand. It scared me.'

'What did he want from you?'

'An update on what the others were saying about him.'

'Did he say why?'

'No, but it was clear he was feeling insecure.'

'How did you answer?'

'With the truth as I understood it. I told him straight there had been the full range of feelings from annoyance that he failed to turn up for the Budapest concert to concern when he went missing, to resignation after years went by that he could well be dead. He asked if the quartet really believed he'd killed Emi and I said nobody had ever suggested he was a murderer.'

'It didn't cross our minds,' Ivan said, 'but in view of what's happened this morning . . .'

Cat said, 'What are you trying to tell us, Comrade Bogdanov? Do you think he shot himself because of a guilty conscience?'

Ivan spread his hands. 'We'll find out, presumably.'

'There's more, isn't there?' Diamond pressed Mel. 'What else did he want to know?'

'The name of the person who supplied my new viola. I didn't tell him. I'm strictly bound to keep that a secret.'

'Even at gunpoint you held out?' Ivan said.

Mel clicked his tongue in impatience. 'I told you he didn't once point the gun. He had no intention of shooting me. He told me the gun was for his own protection and I believed him. He'd escaped from the yakuza, as I told you, and he thought they were still after him.'

'Not to mention the mafia wanting their poker debts settled,' Cat said. 'If that wasn't a rock and a hard place I don't know what is. Poor old rascal didn't know where to turn.'

'And then the second girl was strangled and the two cases were linked,' Ivan said. 'He became a suspect for the first, if not the second. We don't know how long he's been in England, do we?'

'He didn't say,' Mel said.

'Could Harry have murdered Mari Hitomi?' Cat asked, big-eyed. 'I can't think why.'

'Maybe she also was working for the yakuza,' Ivan said.

She took a sharp breath. 'I hadn't thought of that.'

The speculation wasn't helping Diamond. He'd run through similar possibilities in his own mind already. He picked up the last point Mel had made. 'Why was he interested in your viola?'

'It's a beautiful instrument, an Amati,' Mel said, nodding. 'As a fellow violist, he wanted to handle it, but I didn't let him. He didn't insist. He knew the owners of these fabulous instruments set strict conditions about their use.'

Cat said, 'Harry knew that. He had a Maggini on loan to him. None of us can afford the beautiful toys we play with.'

Diamond asked Mel, 'Was anything else said that might help me to understand Harry's mind-set?'

'I've covered it,' Mel said. 'He acted more like someone on the run than a threat to me or anyone else. I know he had the gun, but in the end he put it away and left quite tamely.'

'Would you say he was suicidal?'

'Under stress, for sure. He did make one remark.' Mel put his hand to his head and scraped it through his hair. 'I'm trying to think back to how it came up. Yes, I was telling him that while he was missing for so long we gave him up for dead and he said, "I might as well be." '

'Poor lamb!' Cat said.

'Did he say where he was going next?' Diamond asked.

'No. It was getting late by then. After ten, anyway.'

'But you phoned each of the others to let them know?'

'Because they had a right to be told Harry was around, and armed. And if I'm honest, I was shaken up by the visit. I felt I wanted to speak to someone who would understand.'

Diamond glanced out of the window. A forensic tent was being erected around Harry's car. The police surgeon had arrived and was struggling into a blue protective overall.

'And this morning,' Diamond said, turning back to the group, 'what happened after Anthony's landlady got on the phone?'

'I phoned the others and we met here and decided the right thing to do was call 999,' Cat said.

'Who was first here?'

'I was,' Ivan said. 'I took a taxi. Cat wasn't long after me. She came on foot, living nearby, as she does. We were outside looking at the car when Mel's taxi arrived.'

'Did you touch anything?'

'Naturally we did,' he said as if the question shouldn't have been asked. 'We looked inside to see if he was still breathing. When it was obvious he wasn't, we shut the door and came in here and made the emergency call.'

Cat had a better idea what Diamond was thinking. 'You don't even need to say it. Our prints are all over the car. If there's anything dodgy about the suicide theory, Ivan and I are going to be the prime suspects, but what else could we have done? We had to check whether life was extinct. Don't they always say the first few minutes are critical?'

'Do we know when he died?' Mel asked.

'We may get an estimate from the doctor,' Diamond said, 'but times of death are difficult to pin down. If someone heard the shot we'll have a better idea. We'll ask at all the houses.'

'Could have been last night, I was thinking.'

'What would he have been doing here last night?' Cat asked.

'What was he doing here at all? Visiting Anthony, obviously.'

'Except he stayed in the car and shot himself.'

Diamond glanced outside again and saw that Ingeborg's car had arrived on the other side of the taped-off section. 'I'll be needing statements from each of you.'

Ivan folded his arms in a defiant way. 'It had better not take long. We're booked for a digital recording session this afternoon.'

'Where?'

'At the Michael Tippett Centre. The technicians are expecting us.'

Mel said, 'In view of what's happened, maybe we should cancel out of respect.'

'Not at all,' Ivan said. 'Harry would have wished us to go ahead. And I asked Douglas to come back for it.'

'You're right for once,' Cat said. 'We've got to do this for Harry, we really must. He loved the *Grosse Fuge*, for all its challenges.'

This was getting a momentum that Diamond would find difficult to stop. For the moment he said, 'We'll see how long it takes to get those statements.'

'You can't hold us indefinitely,' Ivan said. 'Besides, we have very little to make statements about.'

'Apart from Mel,' Cat said. 'His will take the rest of today and tomorrow, I should think. All that stuff Harry told him last night. Can he record it?'

Diamond shrugged. 'It still has to be written down and signed. A statement is a document.'

'Best get started, then.'

Ivan was at his most crotchety. 'I really don't see the urgency of this. The man is dead. He shot himself. It's not as if anyone

513

else was involved. We could take all week and it wouldn't make a jot of difference.'

'You're wrong,' Diamond said. 'It's clear to me that Harry was murdered.'

28

Out in the street, Ingeborg Smith and Keith Halliwell were awaiting instructions.

Diamond was chirpier than he had been for weeks. 'Top of the morning to you. Raring to go, are you?'

All he got was puzzled looks.

'I need statements from all four, an account of their movements from nine last night until I arrived this morning. They'll probably tell lies and I want it as evidence.'

'All of them will lie?' Ingeborg said.

'Maybe not. Anthony may not say anything at all.'

'Really?'

'The little he does say is going to be true. He'll need drawing out, though. I'm not sure how much he knows.'

'Is it a conspiracy then?' Halliwell asked.

'It could become one. This is like nothing else I've come across, four strikingly different individuals who don't mind sniping at each other, but in reality are as close as atoms in a nucleus. They must stick together to survive as performers and their music-making matters more to them than morality or law-breaking. They're not comfortable going it alone, any of them. They have no family commitments. The Staccati is their family and quartet-playing is what they do. One goes, and it's curtains for all of them.'

'A few mixed metaphors there, but we get the point,' Ingeborg said.

Diamond gave her a pained look. 'Do you want to go through it with a red pen?'

She bit her lip. 'Sorry, guv.'

'Are they as good as they think they are?' Halliwell said to defuse the tension.

'Musically as good as it gets. Morally, the jury are out,' Ingeborg said, diplomatically picking up Diamond's theme.

'Better dive in, then,' he told them. 'Who's going to be first to split the atom?'

With that, he lifted the Do Not Cross tape and entered the secure area.

He was handed a package wrapped in polythene.

'XL for you,' the crime scene woman said.

'I'm taking that as a compliment.' He stepped to one side and started the undignified process of stepping into the protective suit. These things weren't designed for people with more flesh than figure. A well-cut suit hides a lot.

Inside the forensic tent three similarly clad crime scene officers were at work. He had to squeeze around the open doors of the car and step over legs and equipment to make his presence known to the police surgeon, who was standing over Harry Cornell's corpse.

'Anything I should be told, doc?' Diamond asked.

'I can tell you one thing.'

'What's that?'

'You need a forensic pathologist for this, not a family doctor. They've sent for Bertram Sealy. He knows his stuff, whatever you and I may feel about his corpse-side manner. I've done my bit. Life is extinct. I'm off to see someone who really needs me.'

'Before you go, did you look at the bullet hole?'

'I did, and the bullet passed right through the head,' the doctor said. 'But don't expect any CSI stuff from me.'

The body was still in the position Diamond had first seen, head against the steering wheel with only the right side of the face visible. 'Would this be the exit wound?'

'We can agree on that, going by the stellate shape,' the doctor said, ignoring his own injunction. 'I believe that's due to bone fragments being forced out by the action of the bullet. If you lift the head to look at the other side, you'll find a neat round hole where it went in. Is that what you wanted to know?'

'Thanks. It confirms what I thought.' He paused. 'No chance you could estimate the time of death?'

'Yes.'

Diamond's eyes opened wide. 'You can?'

'I mean yes, there's no chance.'

Still wearing his forensic jumpsuit, Diamond returned to the house. Ivan and Cat remained in the sitting room, sombre and silent. They each gave his mode of dress a long look, but passed no comment.

'Are we under way with the statement-taking?' he asked.

Cat nodded. 'They're limited by the poky accommodation. The young woman is in the kitchen with Anthony, and Mel is upstairs with the man. We were just saying it could take a while.'

Ivan made a point of looking at his watch. 'We'd better be through before lunch, all of us. We're due in the recording studio at two.'

'What are you hoping to record?' Diamond asked.

'There's no hoping about it. The session is fixed. The *Grosse Fuge.*'

'Can't say I know it,' Diamond said. 'Can you whistle a few bars?'

Ivan scowled.

'Beethoven,' Cat said. 'It's in our contract to cut a disc in aid of the university.'

'If you get there I may listen in.'

Ivan stared through him. Obviously anyone who hadn't heard of the *Grosse Fuge* was a waste of space.

Dr. Bertram Sealy arrived within the hour holding his trademark flask of coffee and the case he called his guts-bag. Diamond watched from a distance, allowing him to make some progress before going out to join him, wondering what insult Bath's least congenial pathologist would have for him.

Clad in his own rather superior pale blue overall, Sealy was on his knees by the car studying the victim's hands. Without looking up, he said, 'Right up your alley, this, Peter Diamond. Grotty little backstreet tucked away between the railway and the cemetery. Home from home for you with your charity-shop suits. Are you enjoying yourself?'

'I always enjoy seeing a genius at work,' Diamond said. 'Where did you buy your

Andy Pandy outfit? The pound shop?'

Sealy stood up. Ever prepared with all the comforts, he'd been kneeling on a rubber cushion. 'The deceased isn't much of a fashion plate either. Do we know who he is?'

'A viola player who was once in a famous quartet.'

'He wouldn't have played too famously with a digit missing from his left hand,' Sealy said.

'It hadn't passed me by.'

'I presume he was like Charlie Chaplin.'

Diamond frowned. 'How does Chaplin come into it?'

'Played the fiddle left-handed, didn't he? You want to sharpen up your observational skills. What I'm saying is that this fellow must have done the same, used his left hand to hold the bow, so as to do the fingering with his right.'

'That isn't so,' Diamond said. 'He played the orthodox way. Couldn't play at all after losing the finger.'

'Should have been more careful, then.'

'It wasn't an accident. Have you looked at the head wound yet?'

Sealy was not ready to move on. 'Are you one hundred percent certain he was right-handed?'

'I've seen pictures of him playing.'

Sealy tapped his chin with his surgical-gloved finger. 'That's odd.'

'The exit wound being on the right side of the head?' Diamond said.

'Well, yes.'

'I thought so, too.' Diamond aired his new bit of expertise. 'It *is* the exit wound because it's stellate, agreed?'

'Swallowed a forensic manual, have we?' Sealy said. 'This is the problem. The bullet entered the head from the left side. Did a right-handed man put the gun to his left temple? Or use his left hand to fire with? Difficult and unlikely. Ergo if he really was right-handed he didn't fire the gun himself. It was murder.'

'From close range?'

'Look at this.' Sealy grasped the hair on the dead man's head and pulled it back far enough to display the circular hole on the left side. 'It's too neat for a contact discharge and there's no muzzle stamp, but there is what we call an abrasion collar caused by friction, heating and dirt. That's close range.'

'Right.'

'The burning and powder tattooing wouldn't be present if the gun was fired from a distance of more than, let's say, a metre. Do you have any suspects?'

'Several.'

'Better look for GSR, then.'

'You've got me there.' Diamond had a blind spot for acronyms and abbreviations.

'Gunshot residue. The thing was fired in a confined space. And don't just check the hands and clothes. It can get into nostrils, ear canals, places you wouldn't think of.'

Diamond wasn't ignorant of forensic procedures, but he didn't look forward to literally getting up the noses of the quartet without arresting them. He'd only just confirmed that murder had been committed and any evidence he had against the four was circumstantial. They wouldn't think it a privilege to be asked for swab samples.

Sealy was still talking about the gun. 'I wonder where the bullet ended up if it didn't smash the window.'

'He may have ducked,' Diamond said, 'in which case the angle could have been downwards and we'd find it lodged in the bodywork.'

One of the CSI team spoke up. 'We already found it in the offside door, sir.'

'Where is it, then?'

'In an evidence bag with my boss. It's a nine millimetre. Fits the Glock 17 that you see between the seats.'

'Thanks.' Diamond turned back to Sealy. 'Is it too much to ask for an estimate?'

'Of what? My fee?'

'Time of death.'

'Has any pathologist *ever* given you an accurate time of death? If so, he was either a bloody good guesser or the killer.'

'Thanks for nothing, then.'

'If I could give you an answer, believe me I would triple my fee.'

Diamond exited the tent and squirmed out of the protective suit. He'd formed a pretty clear picture of the killing. At some point last evening or early this morning Harry had parked the car opposite Anthony's lodging with the intention of visiting him. His proven method was to sit in the car and observe before doing anything else. He may have spent the night there. The gun, his protection, would be kept somewhere handy, in a pocket, or the glove compartment, or lying on the passenger seat.

The killer had approached the car and seen Harry sitting behind the wheel. They knew each other, so it was not immediately a conflict situation. Harry hadn't apparently wound down his window to speak. He must have reached across and opened the door on the passenger side, allowing the killer to lean inside or sit beside him and talk. At some point Harry must have mentioned the gun, as he had when speaking to Mel. The moment it was produced was the opportunity for the killer to grab it and fire at point blank range.

An impulsive killing.

The short period following the shot was critical. Had anyone in the nearby houses overheard? Quite likely. But if they went to their windows and looked out, what was there to see? Just the usual line of parked cars. The killer would wait five or ten minutes before quitting the scene. And there was time for a decision. Take the murder weapon away, or leave it close to Harry's hand to suggest suicide? Maybe attempt to wipe it clean of prints and DNA first. Press it against Harry's hand before placing it between the seats, and then slip quietly away.

But in the pressure of the moment basic errors had been made. The most obvious had already been made clear: a right-handed man doesn't put a gun to the left side of his head. Suicide was never an option.

Firing the shot inside the car was another mistake. Sealy was right about gun shot residue, but in addition there would be DNA from the killer deposited on and around the passenger seat. It was a maxim of forensic science that every contact leaves a trace. Wiping the gun wouldn't work either. These weren't sterile conditions. Traces would remain.

All very encouraging for the investigation.

But there's always a snag. The snag here was the familiar one that bedevilled modern detectives. Forensic science won't be hurried. This was a complex scene. The car had been lived in for days, if not weeks. Talk about traces: it teemed with traces, of skin particles, hair, food, blanket fibres and all the other droplets and driblets that are deposited in a car every time it is used.

The evidence would be agonisingly slow in emerging. Weeks, probably.

Diamond needed a swifter result. He returned to the house.

Ivan and Cat were still waiting to have their statements taken. Ivan was like a corked volcano.

'Can't you speed this up? You're supposed to be in charge.'

This was a helpful opening. 'All right,' Diamond said. 'We can make a start right away.'

'On what?' Ivan said. 'My statement as to where I was last night? It comes down to one sentence. You visited me yourself and I didn't leave my lodgings until this morning when I got the call from Cat.'

Cat said, 'Mine is a one-sentence statement, too. A seven forty-five call from Anthony's landlady.'

'Before we go into that,' Diamond said, 'I need some help from you both about what happened four years ago in Budapest.'

'Budapest?' Ivan said as if Diamond had named Timbuktu.

Cat was faster onto it. 'Where Harry went AWOL? Not much we can help with there, your honour. It was a mystery at the time and I'm not much clearer now.'

'You told me you searched the streets for him.'

'It was panic stations. Ivan can tell you. We had a concert to give. Brilliant and talented as we are, we haven't yet discovered how to play a string quartet without a violist.'

'Was it unusual for Harry to let you down?'

'Unheard of,' Cat said. 'Ivan will bear that out.' She almost had to nudge him to speak up.

'That is true,' Ivan said after a pause for thought. 'He would go off alone for hours on end — and we now know where — and always be in time for concerts and rehearsals. He had a playboy streak, but there was a responsibility there as well.'

'And a sensitive side,' Cat said.

'Sensitive in what way?'

'Whenever we performed in Vienna, he would visit Beethoven's grave in the Central Cemetery and place a single sprig of rosemary there, for remembrance.'

'The language of flowers?' Diamond said with an upsurge of interest.

'It is, isn't it? I don't know all the meanings, but Harry must have.'

He tucked that away in his memory. 'What interests me in particular is what happened to his viola after he disappeared.'

'The Maggini?'

'Going by what he told Mel, it must have gone missing from his hotel room before the police made their search. A valuable antique instrument.'

'A thing of beauty,' Ivan said.

Cat asked Diamond, 'What are you getting at? Do you think he took it with him?'

'Highly unlikely,' Diamond said. 'He was doing the rounds of the shops trying to offload the ivory netsuke when the yakuza kidnapped him.'

'Well now. That is a point,' Cat said. 'Of course he wouldn't take the Maggini with him. He had it on trust and he looked after it. We're all using priceless pieces of wood and gut to make music, including Mel. My cello is a Strad. Are you thinking our instruments are behind these crimes?'

'People are behind them,' Ivan said.

'Of course, O Wise One,' she said, 'but people can be motivated by greed.'

Ivan snorted in impatience.

Diamond turned to him. 'Don't you agree?'

'The instruments have nothing to do with any of this,' Ivan said emphatically.

'You sound confident.'

'Because I am.'

'So was it you who removed the Maggini from Harry's room?'

Ivan flushed scarlet as if the suggestion was monstrous. He took in a deep breath. Then he sighed, his shoulders sagged and he admitted, 'I took it into safe-keeping as a precaution. It was eventually returned to the true owner.'

'I wish you'd told me earlier.'

'There was an issue of confidence. The same owner presented me with the Guarnerius I play. He pledges us to secrecy.'

'Who is the owner?'

'I'm not at liberty to say.'

'You won't be at liberty much longer if you don't say.'

Another sigh. For all his tough talk, Ivan's resistance was habitually paper-thin. 'His name is Hamada and he is a Japanese collector of rare and beautiful instruments. He heard of Harry's disappearance and asked me to make sure that the viola was safe. I gave a generous tip to one of the chambermaids and she let me into the room knowing I was a colleague of Harry's.'

'When you say "heard of Harry's disappearance" it begs a question.'

'Was Mr. Hamada a party to the kidnapping? Definitely not,' Ivan said. 'He's a powerful man who guards his privacy, but his intentions towards us are wholly supportive.'

Diamond wasn't convinced. 'He knew about the kidnapping before the police were on the case. He must have links to the yakuza.'

'That's not impossible,' Ivan admitted. 'But yakuza isn't a unified group. It's a generic name given to more than twenty Japanese gangs who compete for the best pickings from organised crime. Their codes and traditions, including the amputation of fingers, may be similar, but they rival each other. Mr. Hamada's interest in the quartet has been positive from the start. I've known him for years and he wants his instruments played by the best musicians and in the world's top concert halls. Not long ago he came to Bath and presented our new member Mel with a priceless Amati viola. That isn't a man who would be party to the kidnapping of one of us.'

This was a new insight for Diamond, and believable. A super-rich man might well keep tabs on the yakuza to know what crimes were committed by some of its many factions.

'You say you've known him years.'

'I've only met him a few times, but we keep in touch. I delivered the Maggini to him personally in London some months after recovering it. He entrusted me with it until I could place it into his hands.'

'You didn't tell the rest of us,' Cat said.

Ivan shrugged. 'You know what he's like.'

Cat turned to Diamond. 'If it's any help, I can also vouch for Mr. Hamada. He's on our side. I'm sure if he'd had the power to stop them kidnapping Harry, he would have done so.'

'It was a disaster for us all,' Ivan said. 'Harry should never have got into so much financial trouble.'

'If we'd known the full facts, we would have rallied round,' Cat said. 'We suspected he was into something flaky at the time, but none of us guessed it was so serious.'

Ivan said with a shake of the head, 'The idiot.'

'Too late in the day to chuck insults after him,' Cat said. 'The poor boy's had a hellish time ever since and now he's dead.'

'We all had a huge stake in the quartet's existence,' Ivan said, addressing Diamond. 'Our professional lives were bound up in it. We tried to look out for each other. I was usually the spokesman and leader. Cat was like a mother to us all and kept us in good spirits. Anthony with his focused brain is like a child in some ways and needs practical help. And Harry with his laid-back manner kept us from getting too intense about our music or anything else. It was a nice balance.'

This touching tribute to the Staccati came to an end just as Ingeborg emerged from the kitchen with Anthony.

'All done?' Diamond asked.

Ingeborg nodded and ran a hand through her blonde hair. The session had obviously been stressful.

'Anything I should be told?'

She shook her head.

Then Keith Halliwell came down the stairs followed by Mel.

'We could murder a coffee,' he said.

'They did it!' Cat said at once. 'Take them down to the nick and throw the book at them.'

'Do you want one?' Halliwell asked Ingeborg.

She shook her head. 'Why do you think I picked the kitchen for my interviewing?'

Diamond said, 'The last two statements shouldn't take long.'

Ivan said, 'After that, are we free to go?'

'I'll need you all to read them through and sign them, but that can be done at the end of this afternoon's recording.'

There were smiles of relief from three of the musicians. Even Anthony managed a nod.

29

'What's the boss up to now, letting them record their party piece?' Ingeborg asked on the drive to Newton Park.

'Don't ask me,' Halliwell said. 'We had all four in that house this morning. We could have pulled them in and got to the truth.'

'There's a change in him today. He's more like he used to be.'

'Cocksure and pushy?'

'I was going to say frisky, but I guess it's much the same.'

'As if he knows something we don't.'

'By the way he's behaving, anything is possible. Only it could be down to something else,' Ingeborg said. 'His love life is looking up. He came in wearing aftershave this morning.'

'Doesn't he usually?'

'Only when he's seeing Paloma.'

They parked behind the Michael Tippett Centre and zig-zagged around clusters of gossiping students on their lunchbreak towards the two digital recording studios. Diamond was waiting outside, still unmistakably frisky. 'Don't look so hard done by,' he said. 'I've asked and this lasts only sixteen minutes.'

'For one take,' Halliwell said. 'They're never satisfied with one.'

Diamond hadn't thought of that. 'Today, they have to be.'

'Have they all turned up?' Ingeborg asked.

He nodded. 'And so has Douglas Christmas.'

'I'd almost forgotten him.'

'He's in there already. Shall we join him?'

Extra seats had been placed at the rear of the narrow control room. The technical team were already manning the digital audio workstation, headphones on, testing the controls. Through the glass the Staccati were seated in the usual formation, violinists to the left and Mel and Cat right. Deep in concentration, they were fine-tuning, obtaining the A from Ivan and making their own small adjustments. In addition Cat and Mel would compare C strings, a wise check for accuracy allowing that the pitch of the instruments was an octave apart. There was an air of anticipation, that mix of excitement and nerves that is the dynamic of any

534

performance.

Diamond took the chair beside Douglas. 'Glad you made it here.'

The manager nodded. 'I support them whenever I can. After all, they're my breadwinners.'

'Enjoy your last meal, then.'

Douglas clearly missed the point but registered with a grin that it must be humorous. In fact, he followed with a quip of his own. 'And what are you chaps doing here — making an arrest?'

Diamond said straight-faced, 'All in good time.'

'Are you familiar with the piece?'

'That would be an overstatement.'

'I'd better warn you, then. It can be difficult to the untrained ear, even brutal.'

'Up my street, then.'

Everyone smiled.

'Ghastly news about Harry,' Douglas said. 'A sad end to a fine musician. I'm going to suggest they dedicate this to his memory.'

'Difficult and brutal?'

Douglas was lost for words. Clearly he wasn't on Diamond's wavelength.

The producer touched a switch on the console and spoke through his mic to the artists. 'How are we doing, folks? Almost ready to go?'

In the studio Ivan turned to the others and got their agreement. He raised his bow towards the window.

'In your own time, then. We're running now.'

The players took their cue from Ivan and began.

The overture, as the composer termed it, of the *Grosse Fuge,* made no concessions. It demanded attention to what amounted to snatches of unrelated music separated by long pauses that would only have relevance as the piece developed. Eventually they would be identified as a kind of running order for what was to come, but perversely Beethoven had turned the whole thing on its head and started with the finale.

Fair warning.

The sound was relayed to the control room for the benefit of the little audience. The technicians in their headphones concentrated on getting the ideal mix, oblivious of any conversation from behind them. There *was* a voice speaking. At the back, Diamond had begun a performance of his own.

'While this goes on I'm going to explore the evidence and see if we can agree what actually happened. We have three unexplained deaths, three murders as it turns out, with the Staccati featuring in some way in each one.'

'The common factor,' Halliwell said, rather like the second violin developing the theme.

'Let's start in reverse order,' Diamond went on. 'Why was Harry killed? On impulse, apparently. The opportunity presented itself and the killer snatched the gun and shot him. If you're planning a murder you can't expect your victim to supply the loaded weapon. So it was unplanned. A crude attempt was made afterwards to suggest it was suicide. Crude and poorly executed.'

'There must have been a reason for the killing,' Ingeborg said.

'There was. Harry had to be silenced.'

'Why?'

'It goes back a long way. He had unfinished business with the quartet. He naively supposed he could return and get their support in proving he was innocent of Emi Kojima's murder in Vienna in 2008. The Austrian police had been led to believe she drowned herself, but the yakuza knew better. They knew the netsuke she was carrying in her clothes — a suicide emblem — wasn't a statement of intent, but a sample obtained on their instructions and for their inspection. She had been working for them, brought to Vienna to get the inside story of the trade in ivory objects, and they were angry. They decided, rightly, that she had been murdered. Harry was the obvious suspect and they removed two of his finger joints to try and extract a confession. But Emi's death was a mystery to Harry. He couldn't say who killed her, or why.'

'What a nightmare,' Ingeborg said. 'It's bad enough being tortured for information, but when you don't have the information to give, that's too horrible to imagine.'

Diamond was trying to keep imagination out of it. 'Harry remained in terror of the yakuza. He'd escaped and gone into hiding, but he lived in constant fear of being caught again and put through more agony, or executed. When he learned that the Staccati were fully functioning again and were in Bath with a new violist he decided to visit his former colleagues and ask if they knew the truth of what happened in Vienna in 2008. He returned to Britain, rented a car, drove to Bath with the idea of observing them first, armed with a gun for his own protection. After so much had gone wrong in his life he was cautious.'

'Can't blame the guy, after all he'd gone through,' Ingeborg said.

Diamond continued the story. 'But first came the shock of Mari's body being discovered in the canal, another Japanese woman murdered and disposed of in the same way. What was he to make of it? Could one of his old colleagues be the killer? He wasn't sure which of them he could trust.'

'Mel,' Halliwell said. 'Mel was the new man. And he thought Mel hadn't been in Vienna.'

'As we later discovered, he had, playing with the London Symphony Orchestra, but Harry didn't know that. To Harry, Mel was clean, the new man, his replacement as viola player. So Harry tracked him down to where he was living and after watching the house for a time and nearly getting caught at it, he plucked up courage and visited there to find out from Mel how things currently stood. A calculated risk. Fortunately they got on well, particularly because there was no threat of Harry claiming back his place in the quartet. After the loss of his finger he would never play again. The meeting passed off peaceably and Harry planned his next move. He would make an approach to Anthony.'

'Why Anthony?' Ingeborg asked.

'Because he could rely on him to tell the truth. There's no sophistry with Anthony. He gives it to you straight if he gives you anything at all. That's a symptom of his condition. So if Anthony knew what really happened in Vienna — even if he had killed the woman himself — Harry had a chance of extracting a truthful account. He drove to Westmoreland Street last night and waited for the right moment.'

The quartet were already into the second section and it was complex. The essence of any fugue is that a melody or theme known as the subject is introduced and then taken up by each of the other players until all four are weaving an elaborate mesh. Connective passages lead on to other variations of the theme. That can be demanding enough. Here, Beethoven had a double fugue in play from the start, a remorseless deluge of counterpoint, savage in its intensity. The term 'brutal' that Douglas had used was not unwarranted. Fingering too quick for the eye to follow, frenetic bowing and faces taut with concentration testified to the severity of the journey through this jungle. The players were at the limit of what was musically possible.

Diamond, too, was developing a difficult new subject. The music wasn't entirely lost on him; he expected to evoke moods of disquiet and dissonance that matched. 'For the moment let's leave Harry sitting in his car outside Anthony's place. I want to return to the night Emi Kojima was murdered in Vienna. Remember she was a talented musician herself. She'd been chosen by the yakuza as the honey trap for Harry, to get the lowdown on his ivory trading. She attended the recital at the Konzerthaus and made a point of approaching the artists afterwards and talking intelligently about the music. She was there to pull Harry, and she did. Later in the evening the other players were drinking in the hotel bar and saw Harry get into the lift with Emi, the last time she was seen alive.' Diamond turned to Douglas. 'You were there that night.'

Douglas jerked as if he'd been punched. Up to now he'd been staring through the glass, obviously trying to give the impression he wasn't listening to Diamond. 'Aren't you interested in the music?'

'It's over my head,' Diamond said. 'You'll be able to hear it on disc later. I'm asking about Vienna, what was said in the hotel bar.'

'I hope you're not suggesting I had something to do with these tragic events.'

Diamond smiled. 'I don't mind telling you I've had my suspicions. You seemed to be around at the critical times.'

'It's my job. I'm their manager.'

'Yes, and just to be certain, I made a call before coming here to check if you were in London this morning, and you were. You couldn't have shot Harry.'

'I'm glad that's clear, then. I don't kill my own clients, even ex-clients. What did you just ask?'

'What was the talk about Harry in the Vienna hotel bar?'

'It was a long time ago,' Douglas said. 'I think we passed a few remarks. He was up to his old ways with the ladies, that sort of thing. He had a spicy reputation.'

'Anything else?'

A shrug and a sigh. 'We were all quite relaxed about it, as I recall. We recognised the young woman as the music buff who came up after the concert. Someone — it may have been me — laughingly suggested she might have been trying to lure Harry away to the Tokyo Quartet. Good violists, you see, are much in demand. And Vienna is the place where musical wheeling and dealing is done.'

'It wasn't a serious remark?'

'Not from me, of all people. I didn't want anyone to defect.'

'Would the others have taken it lightly?'

Douglas tilted his head one way and the

other like a parrot under scrutiny. 'Cat will have laughed it off, or topped it with something more outrageous. You never know how Ivan or Anthony will react. They can get far too uptight and obsessive about the quartet, but I don't think they rose to the bait. I honestly can't remember how it was left. Soon after, we all went to bed ourselves.'

As if on cue, the quartet had started the third part, a more accessible sequence at a slower tempo, tender by contrast with what had just gone before. The players' faces reflected the lyrical nature of the theme. The lines of anxiety had gone from Ivan's brow. Beside him, Anthony's lips had formed into something near a smile. Mel was leaning back as he played. And Cat had time to brush away a wayward strand of hair.

Diamond resumed. 'Emi didn't remain all night with Harry. She left after they'd had sex and she'd persuaded him to part with the netsuke. Earlier, she'd given the impression she was a guest at the hotel, but this wasn't true. She was under instructions to report back to the yakuza with the netsuke. She took the route beside the river Wien that links to the canal and she must have been followed. Someone was deeply alarmed about her.'

'Harry?' Halliwell said. 'He'd worked out

what this was all about?'

'Unlikely. He wouldn't have dropped her into the canal without recovering the netsuke. After all, it linked her to him. But someone attacked her and almost certainly strangled her and dumped the body in the canal. The reason, the motive, is the key to this whole mystery.'

In the studio, a dramatic change in the music sent the players careering into the fourth part. The jarring fugal themes returned at full pitch, outrageous in complexity, skewed into ever-changing variations, playing havoc, twisting, reversing, rollercoasting into dissonance and darkness. Eyes wide, the musicians strove to stay with it, the strain as extreme as it gets.

'We can't consider the killing of Emi without leaping forward to Mari Hitomi,' Diamond said. 'The deaths are related. We know for certain that Mari was strangled and thrown into the Kennet and Avon canal. The same method of disposal. And why? Because up to this time the killer appeared to have got away with the first murder this way. A rotting corpse recovered after weeks in water doesn't yield many clues. If she hadn't been identified from the tooth tattoo we might never have made the connection. Once we had the facts, the parallels were striking. Two Japanese women with knowledge of classical music who attended Staccati concerts and approached the players afterwards as fans. Two women who ended up murdered in canals. What can we get from that?'

'The killer had a thing about Japanese women?' Halliwell said.

Ingeborg rounded on him. 'What do you mean — a "thing"?'

'I don't know what psychologists would call it. A love-hate complex? All his sexual fantasies revolve around Japanese women.'

'Ivan,' Ingeborg said at once.

'I've been thinking hard about Ivan,' Diamond said. 'He's a regular visitor to the geisha houses. He told me himself that he visits Kyoto and plays the three-stringed instrument with the geishas. These aren't knocking-shops. They're highly respectable places controlled with long-established rules. It's genuinely about traditional culture. But with my suspicious mind I wondered what really motivates Ivan. Is he secretly wishing he could have sex with these unattainable women? And when a Japanese woman says she's a fan and wants to hang out with the quartet, does it start an adrenaline rush in Ivan? Is he transferring all those pent-up desires to these hapless women? It's not difficult to see how it could get nasty if, for example, they reject the advance.'

'How would it have happened?' Ingeborg said.

'He'd see Emi going up to the hotel room with Harry and he'd wait for her to come out. Something similar with Mari. He thinks because the geishas dance attendance he's got a special way with all Japanese women. With these two it doesn't work out and he turns violent.'

'Is that it?' Ingeborg said. 'Ivan is the killer?'

Behind the glass they could see Ivan's piston movement with the bow, ferociously rising to the demands of the score while the fingers of his left hand kept a continuous vibrato in play.

'He seemed more shaken than anyone else when Harry reappeared this week,' Diamond went on. 'He recognized him in the car and kept the knowledge to himself. When I called on him at his lodgings he was fearful that I was Harry. I had to threaten to knock the door down.'

'Did Harry know Ivan was the killer?' Halliwell asked.

'Harry knew nothing. Ivan was in a state of near-panic because he thought Harry wanted reinstating as the Staccati violist. He didn't know about the missing finger. Ivan can't take disruption. He wants the quartet to stay as it is. After four years in the wilderness they had only just got back to peak performance again. He had no strategy for dealing with Harry. As a chess player that alarmed him.'

'So the panic wasn't because Harry could turn him in?'

In the studio, the ferocious drive of the violins reached a pitch of intensity that caused Diamond to break off.

There was a difference of tone when he resumed. 'When all is said and done, these crimes aren't down to Ivan,' he said with certainty. 'Remember he's the controlling one, the chess expert. There was too much left to chance, too many mistakes, too many unknowns. Do I have to go over them again? He wouldn't dream of attempting a murder without a master plan. Ivan would make sure he committed the perfect crime.'

'I can agree with that,' Douglas said. 'He covers every angle.'

'Is it Anthony, then?' Ingeborg said.

'What's the case for Anthony?' Diamond said. 'The ball's in your court.'

'Pretty straightforward,' she said. 'He's obsessive, autistic, liable to tantrums. Yet

547

he's no child. He has a sex drive and visits prostitutes. He's been around when each of the killings took place. Harry was murdered right outside the house where he lives.'

'Why would he have killed these women?'

'Because he has no ability to relate to us,' she said, as if speaking for all women. 'He can't form relationships. We're sex objects, and that's it. The tragic irony is that he's a young, attractive-looking guy who is going to appeal to women. But when they show interest he assumes it's sex they want and if they don't immediately respond he kills them.'

'Simple as that?' Diamond said.

'Issues are simple for Anthony.'

'So you're saying he murdered Harry as well?'

'Harry made the mistake of parking outside Anthony's lodging and sitting there. Anthony went out to him and asked what he wanted. Harry started asking awkward questions about what happened in Vienna and Anthony grabbed the gun and pulled the trigger.'

'Do you know this for sure? You interviewed him.'

Assertive as Ingeborg liked to appear, she was sometimes betrayed by a blush and it happened now, spreading with the speed of a flash fire. 'I didn't in fact get much from him. I've told you my theory.'

'You think he shot Harry because questions were asked about the killing of Emi?'

'Awkward questions.'

Diamond was shaking his head. 'Awkward questions aren't awkward for Anthony. What's done is done. He gives it to you straight. He told us what happened this morning, how he went out and saw the bullet-hole in Harry's head and how he told his landlady and she phoned Cat.'

'Yes,' she said, still pressing her theory, 'but what he didn't say is what matters. He didn't say he'd gone out to the car and shot Harry last night, which I believe is what happened. You didn't ask him, so he didn't tell you.'

'In fact I put the question to him when I first got to the scene before you came,' Diamond said. 'These were my actual words to Anthony: "Do you know how Harry was shot?" He shook his head and I insisted on a verbal answer and got one. He gave me a clear "No". Are we all agreed that he speaks the truth?'

Douglas said, 'Every time. Even when it's uncomfortable for other people.'

Halliwell said to Ingeborg, 'You took his statement. Did he say anything about speaking to Harry last night?'

Her gaze slipped away to the musicians pounding out a fortissimo passage in great sobs of sound, and then came back to Diamond. 'All right, guv. I agree with you. Anthony is in the clear.'

There would have been a pause for thought if thought was possible in a maelstrom.

When the volume decreased a little, Halliwell said, 'That leaves the least likely.'

'Mel?' Ingeborg said, mystified. 'He's only just joined them. Anyway, he's not violent. He's a normal, well-adjusted guy.'

'We all know how you feel about Mel,' Halliwell said.

'That's below the belt. If you remember, I commented after first meeting him that he thinks he's God's gift to women.'

'So we've got that clear,' Diamond said to get some order in the ranks. 'Shall we examine the case for Mel being the killer? You say he only just joined them, Inge, and that's true. However, we discovered he was in Vienna performing with the London Symphony Orchestra in 2008, in the month Emi was killed. Coincidence, or evidence of guilt?'

'Pure chance. There's nothing to connect him with Emi or the Staccati at that time,'

Ingeborg said.

'But he does act like God's gift,' Halliwell couldn't resist quoting her. 'From all we hear, he shags anything that moves — his landlady's daughter and probably his landlady as well. We know what Emi's profession was and we know she was a musician herself. He could have coupled with her. We can't rule it out.'

'What — strangled her and dumped her in the canal? Mel?' Ingeborg said with scorn.

Diamond said, 'There's a story about Mel that may have some bearing on this.' He turned to Ingeborg. 'About his viola being stolen outside the Festival Hall. You were there with me. You heard him tell it.'

'I know. A really mean trick on somebody's part,' she said, 'but I don't see the relevance, guv.'

'Can you recall the details? You and I heard it, but Keith hasn't and it may be new to Douglas.'

In a slightly mystified voice Ingeborg started repeating the tale. 'He was on his way home from a concert at the Festival Hall one night and this student stopped him and asked for his autograph.'

'Stop there,' Diamond said. 'You've missed the point. She was from the Far East.'

'Why does that matter?' She put her hand

to her mouth. 'Oh. He's got a thing about Asian women. He was tricked by this one and never forgot it.'

'Finish the story.'

For the benefit of the others, she told it to the end. 'It didn't strike me as important at the time,' she added. 'I suppose it could have turned his mind.'

'Let's move on,' Diamond said. 'Mel joins the quartet. They recruit him. He doesn't go looking for the job. But here in Bath he's as likely as anyone else to have met Mari at the concert she attended.'

'He claimed to have no memory of her,' Halliwell said.

'He would, wouldn't he?' Diamond said. 'I don't see that as significant. He could have fixed to meet her later, on some pretext like a walk along the towpath.'

'And strangled her because she reminded him of the girl who set him up for the mugging?' Ingeborg said. 'It still seems far-fetched.'

'Unless you can think of a better motive.'

Halliwell returned to the point he'd made already. 'He's a letch. These women came onto him and he responded.'

'You mean a murdering letch,' Diamond said. 'In other words, a psychopath.'

'We don't know if either victim was killed

as part of a sex act, but they could have been. The bodies were too far gone to show any signs.'

'They were dressed,' Ingeborg said, contemptuous of Halliwell's theory.

'Doesn't mean nothing happened,' Halliwell said.

Diamond wanted to move on. The sixteen-minute fugue was at least two-thirds through. 'I'm willing to look at that. But what would have caused Mel to shoot Harry, a totally different kind of killing?'

'We agree Harry knew too much for the murderer to allow him to live,' Halliwell said.

'Or was too curious and likely to find out the truth,' Ingeborg chimed in. 'Harry had visited Mel earlier the same night. Something he said caused Mel to panic. He knew where to find him. It was obvious Harry would try and see Anthony next.'

'What's all this? Are you warming up to the idea of Mel as the killer?' Diamond said to her, faintly amused at the U-turn.

'He knew Harry was carrying the gun. He may have thought he could fake a suicide.'

'Hang on a minute,' Diamond said. 'Let's inject some reality into this. The reason Harry called on Mel last night is that he felt safe with him. He'd get the updated story from him. If he'd thought for a moment that Mel was the killer he wouldn't have gone near him. They had their conversation and he left in peace. And even supposing Mel *is* the murderer, how would Harry know? At the time Emi was murdered, Harry wasn't around. He was in bed in his hotel room. We all agree Emi had sex with him and left the hotel alone after midnight. And as for Mari, if Mel had some kind of date with her in Green Park, we don't even know if Harry was in the country by then. The first time he was spotted was less than a week ago. Mel had no reason to kill Harry. Mel is innocent.'

A crescendo from the Staccati appeared to salute this conclusion.

There was another short period when nothing was spoken and the control room was filled only with the dissonant wail of the strings.

'We've eliminated them all,' Ingeborg said. 'Except one.'

The fifth and final part of the *Grosse Fuge* restores sanity. It picks up and develops the transparent, tuneful theme that was briefly employed in the second part. It is recognizable Beethoven, a coda in pianissimo that pacifies and pleases.

'To quote a smarter sleuth than any of us,'

Diamond said, ' "When you have eliminated the impossible, whatever remains, however improbable, must be the truth." '

30

'If you mean who I think you do,' Ingeborg said in a voice that was calm, but challenging, 'women are not stranglers. It's not a woman's crime.'

'Have you seen her hands?' Diamond said.

Everyone looked to where Cat was still pressing the strings with strength and mobility, extracting trills from the cello that matched anything the three men were producing. Fleshy they may have been, but they were long-fingered, workmanlike hands. Given a slender neck to grip, they could have ended a life, no question.

'Both female victims were petite,' Diamond reminded them.

Ingeborg tried reasoning with him. 'You don't want to go down this route, guv. She's a caring person. She keeps the men from getting quarrelsome. She's quick, witty, takes the heat out of any argument.'

'Why on earth would she want to kill

anyone?' Halliwell said, finally finding a common cause with Ingeborg.

'All will be revealed,' Diamond said. 'I'm pulling her in for questioning.'

The *Grosse Fuge* came to its serene conclusion, a sense that a mountainous journey had been completed and the travellers were safe. The quartet lifted their bows and lowered them. Relieved smiles all round.

'Terrific,' the voice of the producer penetrated the studio. 'I don't think you'll better that.'

Ivan gave a nod. 'Shall we settle for it?' he asked the others.

'Even Anthony is satisfied,' Cat said. 'Somebody please collect me from cloud nine.'

In the control room, Diamond said, 'We'll give them ten minutes.'

It was fully two hours later when a solicitor had been found and Cat was seated beside her in Interview Room One at Manvers Street.

'What's all this about, then?' she said, arms folded defiantly, after the formalities had been gone through and the tape was running. This wasn't going to be one of those 'no comment' sessions.

Diamond had asked Halliwell to sit in with him. Most of the others would be on the other side of the one-way observation window. 'It's about what you've been up to, and why,' Diamond said.

'Recording the *Grosse Fuge,*' she said with gusto, 'and you were there to be blown away by it, lucky man.'

'It would have blown anyone away. But I want to ask you about Vienna in 2008. Your quartet was equally brilliant then, but with a slightly different combination.'

'Harry on viola.'

'Before he went missing.'

'Before he was kidnapped, poor lamb.'

'You know about the kidnapping, then? That's a good start.'

'Mel filled us in this morning. Harry called at his house yesterday evening. What a horror story it was, too.'

'You were the originals, you, Harry and Ivan.'

Cat remarked to her solicitor, 'He wants us to know he's done his homework.'

'You've always been the mainstay of the Staccati,' Diamond said. 'Be they alcoholic, autistic or exiles, you mother them all.'

'Is that what they told you?'

'It's what you repeatedly tell everyone. The first time we spoke at any length, you

558

told me you keep your boys in order.'

She said to the solicitor, 'He doesn't miss a trick.'

'I'm sure they appreciate it,' Diamond said. 'In their different ways, they all need mothering, don't they? They're your family. You told me how, after Harry went missing, you wandered the streets of Budapest searching for him.'

'Where are you going with this?' Cat's long fingers beat an impatient rhythm on the table.

'I'm thinking a single woman like yourself found an ideal outlet for her strong maternal instincts.'

'I thought you were a policeman, not a shrink.' Her tone was less playful now.

'We have to understand people's motives,' he said. 'Let's talk about the music, then. You're one of the best cellists in the world, I'm told. You could have a solo career, but you prefer playing in the quartet.'

'There's nothing criminal in that. I'm a team player, an ensemble person through and through.'

'You've said it for me,' Diamond said. 'You keep the Staccati going. It's your personal mission, creative and fulfilling.'

'I won't argue with that.'

'But if anyone threatens its existence, you

see red. I was told you're like a tigress then.'

'Who said that?'

'If it's true, does it matter? There was that evening in Vienna when you were having a drink after the concert in your hotel bar with the others.'

'Most concerts end like that.'

'This one was different because Harry wasn't drinking with you. He was in another part of the bar with a Japanese woman you'd all met.'

'Harry was like that. Never known to refuse an offer.'

'You were all discussing the two of them and Douglas remarked that this woman — who knew a lot about music — could be out to persuade Harry to join another quartet.'

'Douglas said that?'

'He tells me he did.'

She arched her eyebrows in a show of surprise. 'I have no recollection at all.'

'Harry took the woman, whose name was Emi Kojima, to his hotel room.'

'Tell us something new, sunshine. Stuff like this has been going on since Adam and Eve.'

'But you were deeply suspicious of her motives. You considered Emi a serious threat to your beloved quartet and, let's face it, your personal and professional life. You waited on the same hotel floor for her to leave. She was alone and you followed her along the river bank towards the Danube canal. I'm guessing now, but I reckon at some point you caught up with her and challenged her to say what her intentions were. She was terrified of you. She tried to get away, but she was small, no match for you. You may have simply pushed her, or you may have put your hands around her throat. Either way, she ended up dead in the canal. She wouldn't be found for some weeks. You returned to the hotel shaken by what you'd done, but thinking you'd stopped her from poaching Harry. The tour continued, but unfortunately in the very next city, Budapest, Harry went missing.'

'The last part is correct,' Cat said to her solicitor.

The solicitor said, 'I'm advising you not to comment.'

'I'm only agreeing that we lost Harry. Of course we did. The rest, about me attacking the woman, is up there with UFOs and little green men.'

Diamond wasn't put off. Cat had clearly decided to bluff her way through this and he hadn't expected her to tell all after the first salvo. 'So in spite of all the risk you took,' he continued in the same steady manner, 'the quartet was in trouble. All credit to you and Ivan for trying to keep it going.'

'Desperate times.' She took up the narrative as smoothly as if nothing had passed between them. 'I had Anthony throwing tantrums because he wanted work. You've no idea how childish he can be. And Ivan had to be stopped from jumping ship. I kept reminding them both that we had a brand name and a fan base and a backlist of recordings.'

The solicitor touched her arm to silence her, but Cat wasn't of a mind to underplay her achievement. 'You've no idea how much competition there is among quartets. All these pushy kids coming out of Eastern Europe and the Far East were only too keen to fill the vacuum.'

'And you didn't know at the time that Harry had been kidnapped by the Japanese mafia?'

'We thought he was dead. What else could we think after so long? That's why we hired Mel to replace him — eventually. Years had gone by. We weren't even history. We were forgotten. We needed to build our reputation all over again.'

'So you got the residency here.'

'Thanks to Doug. He kept the faith. Top man.'

'And everything was coming up roses until you gave your first concert and a small Japanese woman said she was a fan and started cosying up to the men. To you it must have seemed like a rerun of Vienna in 2008, except that this time Anthony was getting the attention. She talked intelligently to him about the music. She'd played the violin to a high level herself. Do you remember the shock this gave you, Cat?'

White-faced, she was about to say she didn't, but Diamond added, 'Anthony does, and he's selective in his memories. He particularly noted her tooth tattoo.'

Again, the solicitor put a restraining hand over Cat's forearm.

She wouldn't be silenced. 'Anthony wouldn't stitch me up. He needs me. He can't function without me.'

'His mind doesn't work like that,' Diamond said. 'He takes each day as it comes. He didn't stitch you up, as you put it. You stitched yourself up. You were incensed. You weren't going to allow Mari Hitomi to threaten the Staccati after the tough times you'd been through. I don't know what went through your mind, whether you believed she was trying to recruit Anthony for another quartet, or if it was pure jealousy that she was young and pretty and might sleep with him. You weren't having it. You spoke to her yourself and offered some kind of lure — perhaps a private meeting with the quartet. She was to meet you after dark at Green Park, that remote patch of ground just across the river from where you live.'

'This is the biggest load of horse hooey I've ever heard,' Cat said.

The solicitor said, 'Miss Kinsella, in your own best interest —'

'I'm not giving anything away, darling,' Cat said with an effort to sound unconcerned. She looked Diamond squarely in the eye. 'On with the fairy story, matey. We're dying to hear what the wicked witch did next.'

'I prefer the image of the tigress,' Diamond said. 'You had your cubs to protect.'

'Oh, give me strength.'

'Your boys, then. This unfortunate young woman — who simply came to that concert as a fan wanting to meet the musicians she adored — was grabbed and strangled and dragged to the river and dropped in. You'd got away with it in Vienna, you figured, so why not a second time?'

She gave no sign of caving in. 'You can do better than this,' she said, trying to bait him.

564

'What about the hundreds of other fans I killed because they came on strong with the boys? It's farcical when you think about it.'

'There was another victim, and that was Harry.'

'I knew we'd get around to him,' she said, rolling her eyes upwards. 'And how are you going to slot dear old Harry into this catalogue of slaughter? He was one of my boys, a Staccati player and a lovely guy in spite of all his demons.'

'No longer a Staccati player.'

'Because of his missing finger? True, but that doesn't mean he wasn't family.'

'Yes, I believe you really liked Harry,' Diamond said, 'but he made the fatal mistake of trying to find out the truth of what happened in Vienna, and how Emi Kojima's murder linked up with Mari Hito-mi's. If he could discover who killed Emi he'd have an answer for the yakuza if they caught up with him again. Harry wasn't behaving as family should. He was poking the tigress with a pointed stick.'

'God help us,' Cat said. 'I'm getting weary of this *Jungle Book* stuff.'

'Yesterday evening you and Anthony shared a taxi home and when it stopped outside Anthony's lodging you saw Harry's car there with Harry waiting inside. It was obvious what he intended. He reckoned if he spoke to Anthony about what was going on, he'd get honest answers. Anthony might not be capable of putting two and two together and identifying you as the killer, but Harry was. You had to act quickly.'

'Oh, yes?'

'You live only two or three minutes away. After the taxi dropped you at your house, you returned to Westmoreland Street to speak to Harry yourself. He was still in his car, waiting. You sat beside him in the passenger seat and listened to his story. To show how desperate he was, he showed you the gun. You seized your chance, grabbed it and shot him dead.'

Cat sighed and shook her head. 'Are you for real?'

'It was an impulse killing and a big, big mistake. Suddenly you had a corpse sitting beside you and this time there was no easy way of disposing of it. Panic. The best you could think to do on the spur of the moment was rig it up to look like suicide. You wiped the gun, pressed it into Harry's hand to get his prints on it and let it drop between the seats. Then you walked home and showered and washed all your clothes. Next morning when the call came through from Anthony's landlady, you made sure you weren't the first on the scene. Ivan got there first. By the time I arrived, you were inside the house with the others weeping crocodile tears.'

'Pardon me,' she said. 'The tears were genuine. I was heartbroken Harry was dead.'

'Heartbroken because you couldn't put the clock back. What a mess you made of it — a so-called suicide on the left side of the head from a right-handed man.'

'You keep going on about this as if it was me, but you're wrong,' she said, but on a shrill, petulant note. 'You're way off the mark and I can sue you for false arrest.'

'No chance,' Diamond said. 'Don't you know about gunshot residue? When a gun is fired the explosive gases and particles escape and cling to the hands, clothing and hair of the person who fired the gun as well as settling on anything else in the vicinity. While you were cutting your disc this afternoon, a forensic team was going through your flat collecting evidence. Yes, you showered and washed everything, but you can't prevent these tiny particles being scattered over the floor of your bedroom and bathroom. We have enough to prove you fired the fatal shot.'

'You're bluffing,' she said in a fierce, combative voice.

'Why do you think I let you go ahead with the recording? We needed time to get a warrant and search your house.' He reached under the table and held up an evidence bag containing the murder weapon. 'And if you think you wiped this clean, think again. We'll be taking your prints and DNA presently after I've formally charged you with Harry's murder.'

'You can't do that,' she said. 'I've admitted nothing, nothing at all.'

'Doesn't matter when we've got the evidence,' he said with all the authority he could muster, allowing that forensics would take weeks to produce enough for a prosecution. He was banking on this effusive woman talking her way into proof of guilt. 'You could say nothing at all and still go down with a recommendation that life means life.'

The solicitor was on her feet. 'That's enough. You're trying to elicit a statement by the use of oppression. You're in flagrant abuse of the Police and Criminal Evidence Act.'

'Oh, shut up,' Cat said. 'I need to know the worst that can happen, don't I?'

It was a seismic moment.

To Diamond, she said, 'What are the chances of a lighter sentence if I plead guilty to all three?'

'It wouldn't be up to me,' he said evenly, 'but an admission of guilt is always taken into account.'

'I'm up for it, then,' she said with some of her former bounce. 'Where shall we start? Vienna, 2008?'

The following weekend, Diamond took Paloma for a candle-lit dinner at the Hole in the Wall in George Street. No awkwardness lingered between them. He felt relaxed after bringing the Staccati case to a successful conclusion. And Paloma had landed a contract to be the costume consultant on a new TV series set in the 1940s.

'So you obtained a confession?' she said.

'We did.'

'Without violence, I hope.'

'She sang like a blackbird on the first day of spring.'

'Is that usual?'

'No. Their brief generally makes sure they don't, but in this case Cat insisted, and when that woman insists, no one had better stand in her way.'

'She'll get a long sentence, I expect.'

'Life. For three murders, that will be seriously long.'

'So the Staccati is no more?'

'Not necessarily. Ivan is looking for another cellist.'

She looked wistful. 'Pity if they have to break up. What will that poor autistic man do?'

'Anthony? He'll join another ensemble. I don't have any worries over him.'

'He'll miss all the mothering from Cat.'

'I doubt if he will,' Diamond said. 'A lot of it was more about Cat's need to feel wanted. Anthony is such a good musician that people will put up with his strange ways.'

'I hope you're right.' She smiled. 'Cat will keep the prison entertained. She'll probably form an all-girl quartet.'

'I'm sure of it. We're doing the prison service a favour, sending them someone as chirpy as her.' He poured more wine into her glass. 'But let's talk about your new project. It's a bit more modern than the shows you've been dressing lately, isn't it?

'Yes, I may even ask to see some of your old black and white movies.'

'You know you're always welcome.'

'And I was thinking before you get wrapped up in another case that it might be good to fit in another city break.'

'I'm all for that,' Diamond said at once.

'You are?' She couldn't hide her surprise.

'I enjoyed Vienna — probably more than

you did.'

She laughed. 'I had some fun out of it, too. A lovely city. Where shall we go next?'

'That could be difficult.'

'Why?'

'I don't know if I've seen it in the brochures.'

'Which city do you have in mind?'

'Fits in with your new project.'

'Don't keep me in suspense.'

'I was thinking *Casablanca.*'

580 BEST-SELLING

home plans

MetroBooks

MetroBooks

An Imprint of the Michael Friedman Publishing Group, Inc.

First MetroBooks edition 2001

ISBN 1-58663-322-8

Jan Prideaux/Editor in Chief
Morenci Wodraska/Associate Editor
Tina Grijalva/Plans Editor
Jennifer A. Lowry/Plans Editor
Ashleigh Muth/Plans Editor
Jeanine Newsom/Proofreader
Jay C. Walsh/Mac System Administrator
Matthew S. Kauffman/Graphic Designer
Peter Zullo/Graphic Designer
Teralyn Morriss/Graphic Production Artist

Photography Credits

*Front Cover: Design HPU040404, page 324 by Donald A. Gardner
Photo by Riley & Riley Photography, Inc.*

*Back Cover: Design HPU040359, page 289 by Donald A. Gardner
Photo by Riley & Riley Photography, Inc.*

First Printing, July 2001

Printed in the United States of America

10 9 8 7 6 5 4 3 2 1

For bulk purchases and special sales, please contact:
Michael Friedman Publishing Group
Attention: Sales Department
230 Fifth Avenue
New York, NY 10001
212/685-6610 o FAX 212/685-3916

Visit our website:
www.metrobooks.com

TABLE OF CONTENTS

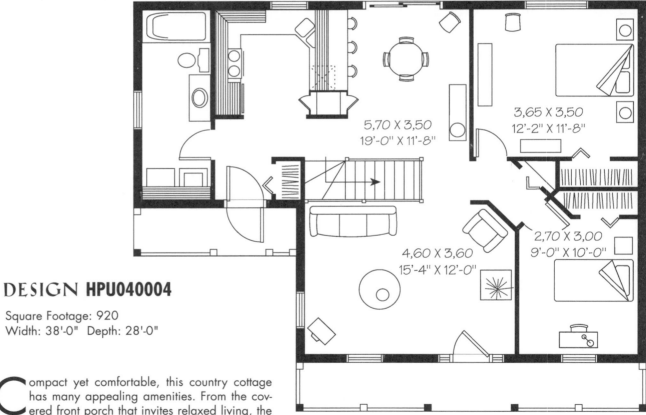

5,70 X 3,50
19'-0" X 11'-8"

3,65 X 3,50
12'-2" X 11'-8"

4,60 X 3,60
15'-4" X 12'-0"

2,70 X 3,00
9'-0" X 10'-0"

DESIGN HPU040004

Square Footage: 920
Width: 38'-0" Depth: 28'-0"

Compact yet comfortable, this country cottage has many appealing amenities. From the covered front porch that invites relaxed living, the entrance opens to the living room with access to the dining room and snack bar at the rear. Two bedrooms are secluded to the right of the plan with the kitchen and bathroom/laundry facilities located on the left side. A second porch off the kitchen provides an opportunity for more relaxation, casual dining and quiet moments. This home is designed with a basement foundation.

DESIGN BY
©Drummond Designs, Inc.

4

DESIGN HPU040005

Square Footage: 1,079
Width: 34'-0" Depth: 34'-0"

This house plan is rich in efficiency and cottage-style living. A quaint covered porch charms visitors and offers an enchanting glimpse into the spacious living room through a beautiful front window. Kitchen counter space is in abundance for the family chef. The kitchen is open to a dining area, which accesses the rear of the home. The opposite side of the home is dedicated to the family sleeping quarters. The master bedroom enjoys twin windows overlooking the backyard. An additional bedroom has a window viewing the front of the property and shares a full hall bath with the master bedroom. This home is designed with a basement foundation.

DESIGN BY
©Drummond Designs, Inc.

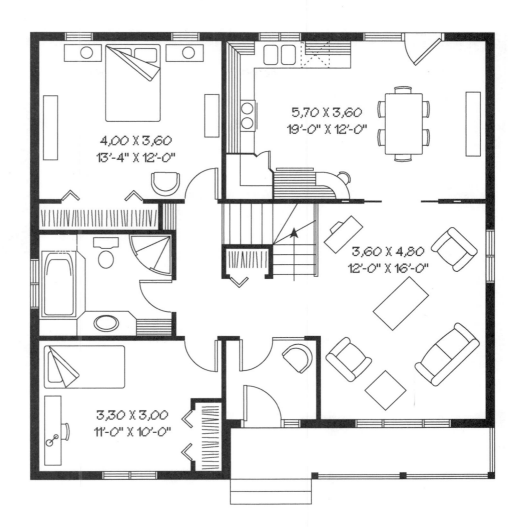

4,00 X 3,60
13'-4" X 12'-0"

5,70 X 3,60
19'-0" X 12'-0"

3,60 X 4,80
12'-0" X 16'-0"

3,30 X 3,00
11'-0" X 10'-0"

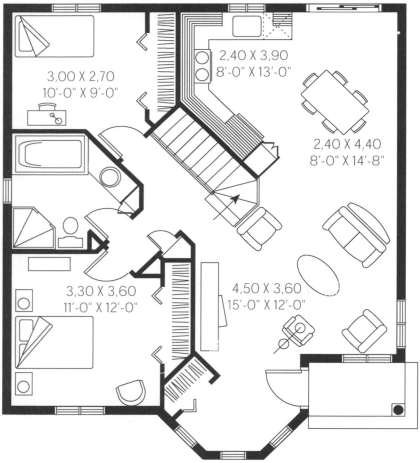

3,00 X 2,70
10'-0" X 9'-0"

2,40 X 3,90
8'-0" X 13'-0"

2,40 X 4,40
8'-0" X 14'-8"

3,30 X 3,60
11'-0" X 12'-0"

4,50 X 3,60
15'-0" X 12'-0"

This sweet Folk Victorian cottage, decorated with a bit of gingerbread trim, features a unique bay-windowed foyer with a generously sized coat closet. Additional windows—the elegant arched window in the front bedroom and four tall windows in the family room—fill this design with natural light. The family room adjoins a skylit kitchen, which provides a compact pantry and opens to a dining room with sliding glass doors to the backyard. Two bedrooms, both with long wall closets, share a bath that includes an angled vanity, corner shower and comfortable tub. This home is designed with a basement foundation.

DESIGN HPU040006

Square Footage: 958
Width: 30'-0" Depth: 35'-4"

DESIGN BY
©Drummond Designs, Inc.

An exciting floor plan and an attractive exterior with side panels and a display of muntin windows make this home a great starter. Upon entry, a coat closet resides to the left. On the right is the living area well lighted by the bayed windows under the turret and open to the dining area. A sliding door in the dining room leads to the backyard. An angled kitchen counter provides plenty of work space and features a window sink. An owners bedroom shares a full hall bath with one family bedroom. This home is designed with a basement foundation.

DESIGN HPU040007

Square Footage: 972
Width: 30'-0" Depth: 35'-0"

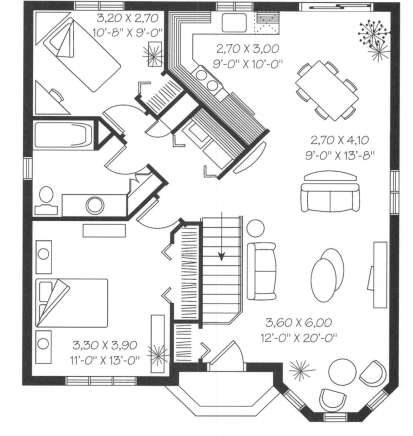

3,20 X 2,70
10'-8" X 9'-0"

2,70 X 3,00
9'-0" X 10'-0"

2,70 X 4,10
9'-0" X 13'-8"

3,60 X 6,00
12'-0" X 20'-0"

3,30 X 3,90
11'-0" X 13'-0"

DESIGN BY
©Drummond Designs, Inc.

This cottage, complete with sweeping rooflines, is dazzled with country allure. The covered front porch is perfect for rocking chairs on cool summer nights. Enter into the foyer, which features a coat closet. To the right, the dining room connects to an island-cooktop kitchen. To the left, the spacious living room overlooks the front yard. A laundry room is located at the rear of the plan, near a secondary coat closet and a back door to the outside. Upstairs, the master bedroom contains a large walk-in closet and a private bath. Two additional bedrooms share a hall bath. This home is designed with a basement foundation.

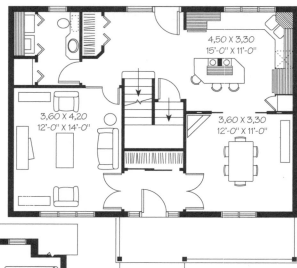

4,50 X 3,30
15'-0" X 11'-0"

3,60 X 4,20
12'-0" X 14'-0"

3,60 X 3,30
12'-0" X 11'-0"

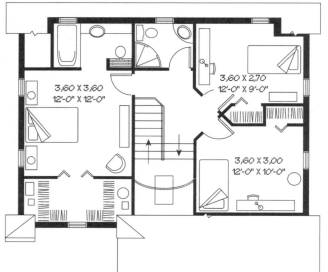

3,60 X 3,60
12'-0" X 12'-0"

3,60 X 2,70
12'-0" X 9'-0"

3,60 X 3,00
12'-0" X 10'-0"

DESIGN HPU040008

First Floor: 768 square feet
Second Floor: 726 square feet
Total: 1,494 square feet
Width: 32'-0" Depth: 24'-0"

DESIGN BY
©Drummond Designs, Inc.

3,60 X 4,40
12'-0" X 14'-8"

4,80 X 4,20
16'-0" X 14'-0"

3,30 X 4,20
11'-0" X 14'-0"

3,70 X 3,80
12'-4" X 12'-8"

3,60 X 3,90
12'-0" X 13'-0"

DESIGN HPU040010

Square Footage: 1,387
Width: 44'-0" Depth: 34'-0"

DESIGN BY
©Drummond Designs, Inc.

Pillars and nested gables add style and charm to this one-story home. An open and airy floor plan allows for great versatility and creativity. Lots of windows bring sunshine in and expand the interior with wonderful views in every direction. Two bedrooms with huge closets reside on the left; the living spaces occupy the right side of the plan. A well-equipped kitchen serves the dining area with ease. A full bath sits to the left of the entry. This home is designed with a basement foundation.

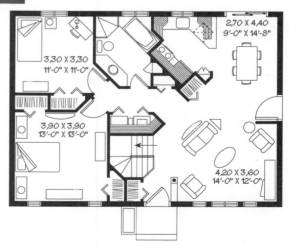

DESIGN HPU040009

Square Footage: 1,064
Width: 38'-0" Depth: 28'-0"

DESIGN BY
©Drummond Designs, Inc.

Brightly lit by multiple windows, this petite home is a sunny haven for any family. Traditional siding graces the exterior. The kitchen opens to an eating area and family room. Two family bedrooms share a full hall bath that includes a tub overlooking the backyard. A side entrance to the home opens between the eating area and family room. This home is designed with a basement foundation.

2,70 X 4,40
9'-0" X 14'-8"

3,30 X 3,30
11'-0" X 11'-0"

3,90 X 3,90
13'-0" X 13'-0"

4,20 X 3,60
14'-0" X 12'-0"

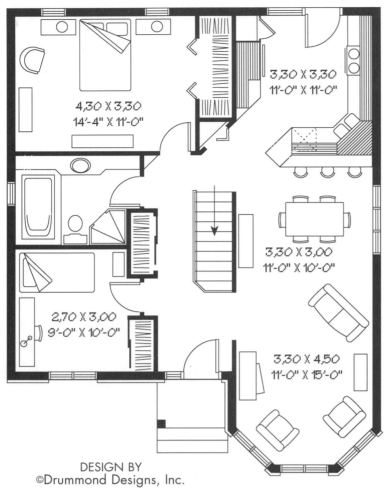

4,30 X 3,30
14'-4" X 11'-0"

3,30 X 3,30
11'-0" X 11'-0"

3,30 X 3,00
11'-0" X 10'-0"

2,70 X 3,00
9'-0" X 10'-0"

3,30 X 4,50
11'-0" X 15'-0"

DESIGN BY
©Drummond Designs, Inc.

An alluring quaint, brick exterior creates a cozy ambience inside this traditional family plan. Petite yet efficient, this plan is designed for the young family. Surrounded by brightly lit windows, the bayed sitting area is perfect for a living room setting. The dining area views the side yard, while the kitchen accesses the rear yard. The master bedroom features roomy closet space. An additional bedroom shares a full hall bath with the master bedroom. This home is designed with a basement foundation.

DESIGN **HPU040011**

Square Footage: 994
Width: 30'-0" Depth: 38'-0"

This design promises sunlit mornings with the panel of windows on the front bedroom, the lovely etched-glass front door and sidelights, and the sunburst on the garage. Inside, this adorable European cottage offers a generous amount of living space and well-thought-out plan. The right side of the plan is occupied by one of three family bedrooms, the living room and an L-shaped kitchen with a pantry and sliding glass doors to the backyard. A full hall bath, with a tub and separate shower, is just around the corner from the two additional bedrooms. This home is designed with a basement foundation.

DESIGN **HPU040012**

Square Footage: 1,089
Width: 32'-0" Depth: 45'-0"

DESIGN BY
©Drummond Designs, Inc.

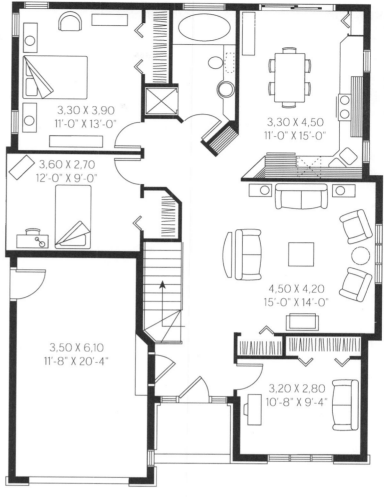

3,30 X 3,90
11'-0" X 13'-0"

3,30 X 4,50
11'-0" X 15'-0"

3,60 X 2,70
12'-0" X 9'-0"

4,50 X 4,20
15'-0" X 14'-0"

3,50 X 6,10
11'-8" X 20'-4"

3,20 X 2,80
10'-8" X 9'-4"

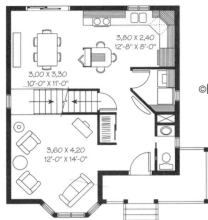

This country classic boasts a traditional siding exterior, plus a two-story bay window area. Downstairs, the bay windows illuminate the living room, while upstairs they brighten the master bedroom. An open kitchen/dining area and a laundry room complete the first floor. Two additional family bedrooms share a full bath with the master bedroom and reside on the second floor. This home is designed with a basement foundation.

DESIGN **HPU040013**

First Floor: 643 square feet
Second Floor: 643 square feet
Total: 1,286 square feet
Width: 24'-0"   Depth: 30'-0"

DESIGN **HPU040014**

First Floor: 759 square feet
Second Floor: 735 square feet
Total: 1,494 square feet
Width: 22'-0"   Depth: 36'-0"

The charming front porch and the two-story turret welcome guests to this lovely home. The turret houses the living room on the first floor and the owners suite on the second floor. The dining room is open to the living room and provides a box-bay window. The L-shaped kitchen features a breakfast room accessible to the backyard. A curved staircase next to the powder room leads upstairs to three bedrooms and a bath. Each family bedroom contains a walk-in closet. This home is designed with a basement foundation.

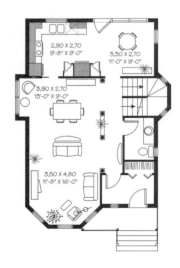

DESIGN HPU040015

First Floor: 681 square feet
Second Floor: 623 square feet
Total: 1,304 square feet
Width: 28'-0" Depth: 40'-0"

DESIGN BY
©Drummond Designs, Inc.

4,20 X 6,00
14'-0" X 20'-0"

3,80 X 4,70
12'-8" X 15'-8"

3,60 X 5,70
12'-0" X 19'-0"

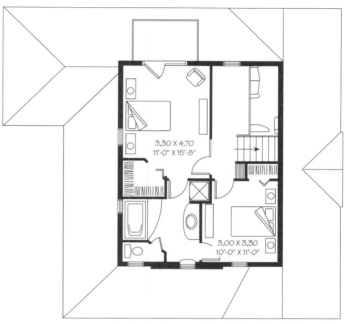

3,30 X 4,70
11'-0" X 15'-8"

3,00 X 3,30
10'-0" X 11'-0"

A glass-door entrance welcomes visitors into the picturesque charm of this countryside home. A large wraparound porch leads to a relaxing outdoor lounge area—perfect for summer afternoons. The island kitchen opens to an eating area, across from the living room. A powder room, laundry area and the one-car garage complete this floor. Upstairs, two family bedrooms are linked by a full bath. This home is designed with a basement foundation.

13

DESIGN HPU040017

Square Footage: 1,253
Width: 44'-0" Depth: 34'-0"

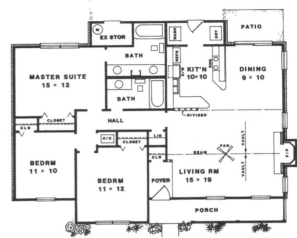

Rustic and efficient, this home is packed with family appeal. Enter through the foyer into the vaulted living room. This room features a ceiling fan and a fireplace. The L-shaped kitchen opens to the dining room, which overlooks the rear patio. The spacious master suite includes a private bath, while two additional bedrooms share a full hall bath. An optional two-car garage is also available.

DESIGN HPU040016

Square Footage: 1,036
Width: 37'-0" Depth: 45'-0"

DESIGN BY
©Vaughn A. Lauban Designs

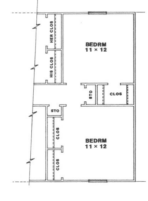

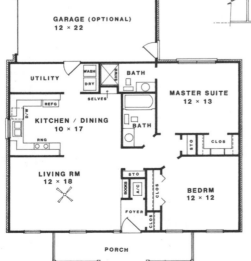

This quaint Victorian cottage offers beautiful detailing and the possibility of adding on later. Enter the spacious living room and then continue to the dining area and U-shaped kitchen. A utility room is located just off the kitchen. On the right, a family or guest bedroom is steps away from a full bath. The master suite features a full bath and walk-in closet. The future expansion offers two more secondary bedrooms and provides the owners suite with two closets instead of a walk-in for a total addition of 392 square feet. The garage is optional.

DESIGN HPU040018

Square Footage: 1,463
Width: 54'-0" Depth: 60'-0"

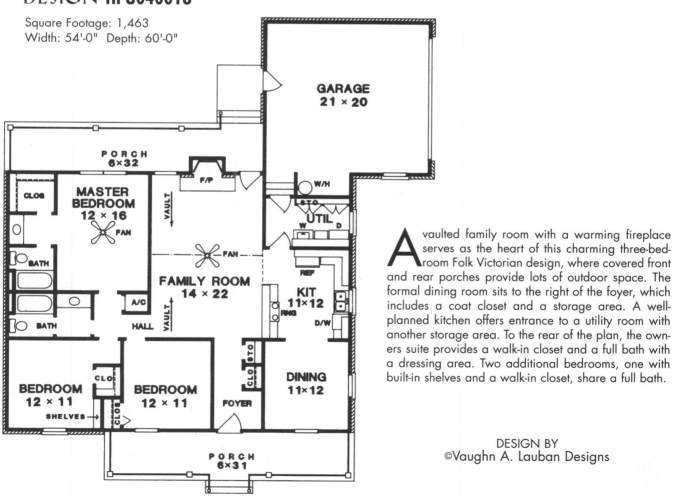

A vaulted family room with a warming fireplace serves as the heart of this charming three-bedroom Folk Victorian design, where covered front and rear porches provide lots of outdoor space. The formal dining room sits to the right of the foyer, which includes a coat closet and a storage area. A well-planned kitchen offers entrance to a utility room with another storage area. To the rear of the plan, the owners suite provides a walk-in closet and a full bath with a dressing area. Two additional bedrooms, one with built-in shelves and a walk-in closet, share a full bath.

DESIGN BY
©Vaughn A. Lauban Designs

15

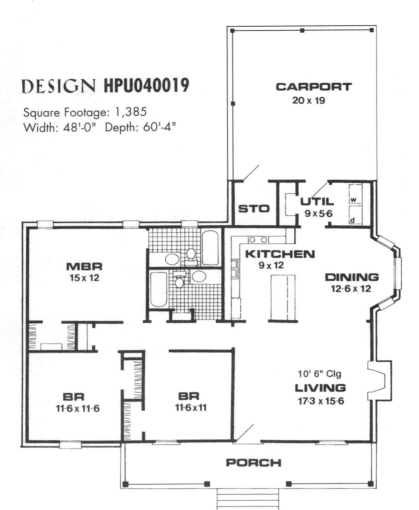

DESIGN HPU040019

Square Footage: 1,385
Width: 48'-0" Depth: 60'-4"

CARPORT
20 x 19

STO

UTIL
9 x 5·6

KITCHEN
9 x 12

DINING
12·6 x 12

MBR
15 x 12

10' 6" Clg
LIVING
17·3 x 15·6

BR
11·6 x 11·6

BR
11·6 x 11

PORCH

This awesome exterior starts with wide front steps under a gabled roof that lead to an extended covered porch. The brilliant floor plan provides a generous amount of space in the living room (with fireplace) and the island kitchen adjoined by a bayed dining area. Just past the kitchen is a utility room with a washer and dryer plus a utility storage area. The master bedroom features a private bath and a walk-in closet, while two additional family bedrooms share a full hall bath and a linen closet. The carport and storage room are located in the rear of the home. Please specify basement, crawlspace or slab foundation when ordering.

DESIGN BY
©Larry James & Associates, Inc.

DESIGN HPU040020

First Floor: 720 square feet
Second Floor: 203 square feet
Total: 923 square feet
Width: 32'-0" Depth: 38'-6"

DESIGN BY
©Larry James & Associates, Inc.

This compact design offers a host of extras beginning with its charming exterior. Wide country-style porches grace both the front and back of this cozy home. The focus of the interior centers on the open living area with a vaulted ceiling. Split into a great room and dining room, this area includes a large warming fireplace and lots of windows for outdoor viewing and increased natural lighting. The fully equipped kitchen is located near the rear porch for convenient outdoor dining. The owners bedroom finishes the first floor. An extra bedroom upstairs includes two closets. Storage space is located in the eaves. Please specify basement, slab or crawlspace foundation when ordering.

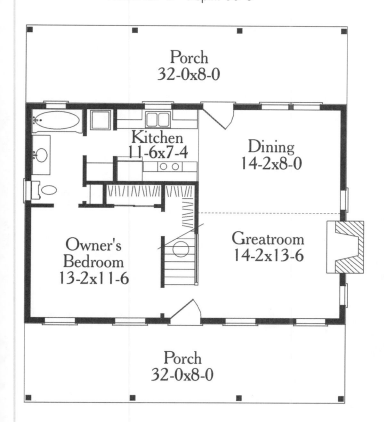

Porch
32-0x8-0

Kitchen
11-6x7-4

Dining
14-2x8-0

Owner's
Bedroom
13-2x11-6

Greatroom
14-2x13-6

Porch
32-0x8-0

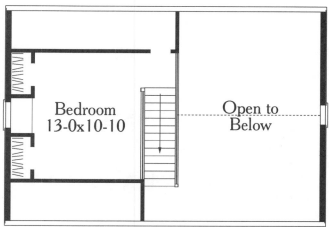

Bedroom
13-0x10-10

Open to
Below

17

DESIGN **HPU040022**

First Floor: 772 square feet
Second Floor: 411 square feet
Total: 1,183 square feet
Width: 32'-0" Depth: 28'-7"

DESIGN BY
©R.L. Pfotenhauer

This petite Gothic Revival cottage, with a steeply pitched roof, dormers and pointed-arch windows, would be perfect as a vacation or starter home. A large covered front porch is available for entertaining and relaxing, while the living room, warmed by a fireplace, offers access to a covered side porch. The U-shaped kitchen shares space with a cozy dining area. A boxed window allows natural light in to the front bedroom, which is conveniently close to a bath. Upstairs, another bedroom, this one with a walk-in closet, accesses a full bath and overlooks the living room.

DESIGN **HPU040021**

First Floor: 688 square feet
Second Floor: 559 square feet
Total: 1,247 square feet
Width: 27'-8" Depth: 30'-8"

Steep, soaring gables embellished with band-sawn ornamentation heightens the drama of this Gothic Revival gem. The heavy carved brackets on the front porch invite the curious into the entry foyer. The living room features a fireplace and plenty of light that filters through the casement windows. For effortless entertaining, the kitchen opens to the dining room. Upstairs, there are two bedrooms including the master bedroom and a full bath. The master bedroom features sloped ceilings and tie beams.

DESIGN BY
©R.L. Pfotenhauer

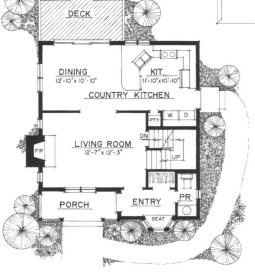

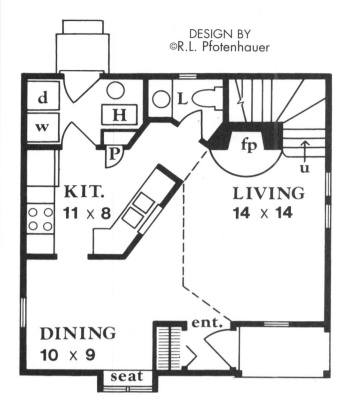

DESIGN BY
©R.L. Pfotenhauer

KIT.
11 × 8

LIVING
14 × 14

fp

u

d

w

H

L

P

DINING
10 × 9

ent.

seat

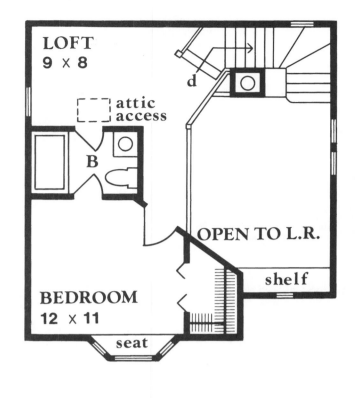

LOFT
9 × 8

attic
access

d

B

OPEN TO L.R.

shelf

BEDROOM
12 × 11

seat

Graceful, curving, gingerbread trim transforms this cozy cottage into a Carpenter Gothic-style confection. From the steep gable roof and appropriately detailed ornamentation on the outside, to the snug yet well planned interior, this design is packed with vintage charm. A soaring two-story living room with a balcony overlook dominates the first floor. The fireplace and stair are combined into one unique architectural feature. The dining room has a cozy window seat; the kitchen offers a handy pass-through to the living area. Upstairs, the master bedroom enjoys an elaborate bay window, a twelve-foot ceiling and a walk-in closet. The sleeping loft, which can be enclosed for a second bedroom, shares a bathroom with the master bedroom.

DESIGN HPU040023

First Floor: 547 square feet
Second Floor: 418 square feet
Total: 965 square feet
Width: 24'-0" Depth: 25'-4"

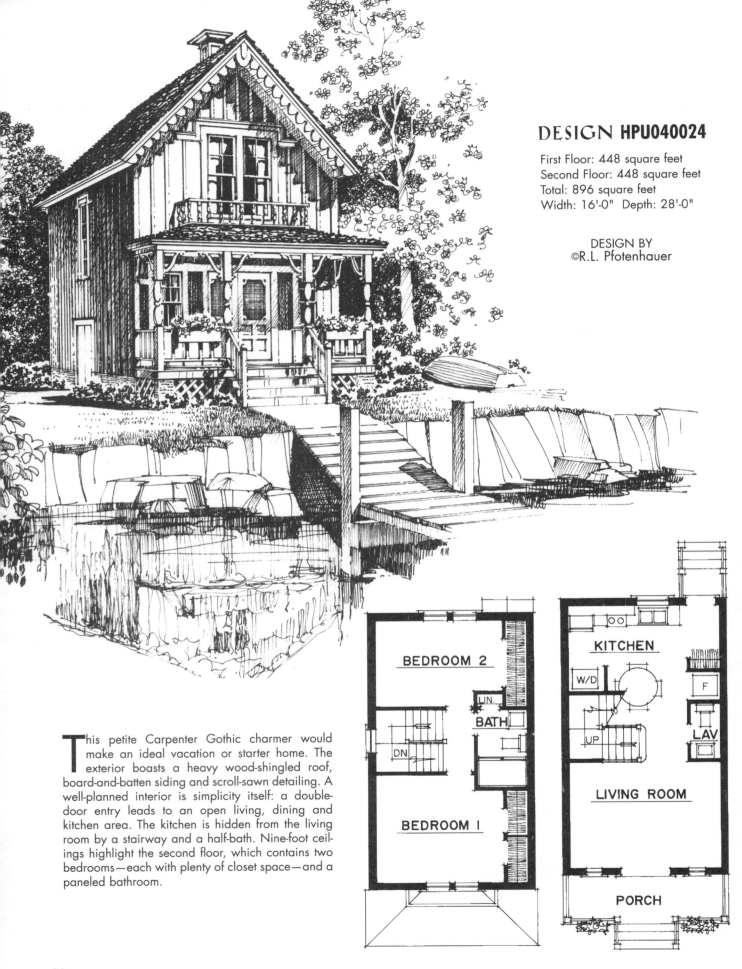

DESIGN HPU040024

First Floor: 448 square feet
Second Floor: 448 square feet
Total: 896 square feet
Width: 16'-0" Depth: 28'-0"

DESIGN BY
©R.L. Pfotenhauer

BEDROOM 2

LIN.

BATH

DN

BEDROOM 1

KITCHEN

W/D

UP

F

LAV

LIVING ROOM

PORCH

This petite Carpenter Gothic charmer would make an ideal vacation or starter home. The exterior boasts a heavy wood-shingled roof, board-and-batten siding and scroll-sawn detailing. A well-planned interior is simplicity itself: a double-door entry leads to an open living, dining and kitchen area. The kitchen is hidden from the living room by a stairway and a half-bath. Nine-foot ceilings highlight the second floor, which contains two bedrooms—each with plenty of closet space—and a paneled bathroom.

DESIGN HPU040025

First Floor: 448 square feet
Second Floor: 448 square feet
Total: 896 square feet
Width: 16'-0" Depth: 41'-6"

Perfect for a lakeside, vacation or starter home, this two-story design is sure to be a favorite. A large railed porch on the first floor and the covered balcony on the second floor are available for watching the sunrise. Inside, on the first floor, the living room is spacious and convenient to the kitchen and dining area. A powder room finishes off this level. Upstairs, the sleeping zone consists of two bedrooms, each with roomy closets, and a full hall bath with a linen closet. The front bedroom accesses the balcony.

BEDROOM 2
13'-0" x 9'-0"

DN

LINEN

BATH

BEDROOM 1
13'-0" x 11'-4"

COVERED BALCONY
16'-0" x 10'-0"

KITCHEN
15'-2" x 9'-0"

W D

DINE

HVAC

UP

PR

LIVING ROOM
15'-2" x 11'-3"

PORCH
16'-0" x 10'-0"

DESIGN BY
©R.L. Pfotenhauer

DESIGN BY
©The Sater Design Collection

DESIGN **HPU040026**

First Floor: 1,342 square feet
Second Floor: 511 square feet
Total: 1,853 square feet
Width: 44'-0" Depth: 40'-0"

Amenities abound in this delightful two-story Floridian home. Behind the extravagant exterior, the foyer opens directly to the fantastic grand room, which offers a warming fireplace and two sets of double doors to the rear deck. The dining room also accesses this deck and a second deck shared with Bedroom 2. A convenient kitchen and another bedroom also reside on this level. Upstairs, the master bedroom reigns supreme. Entered through double doors, it pampers with a luxurious bath, a walk-in closet, a morning kitchen and a private balcony.

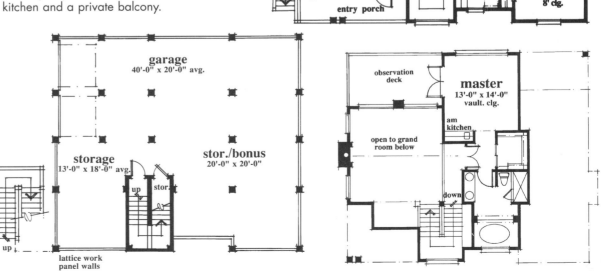

deck
17'-0" x 9'-0"

dining
12'-8" x 11'-0"
8' clg.

deck

grand room
20'-0" x 18'-0"
vault. clg.

kitchen
11' x 12'

br. 2
12'-0" x 11'-8"
8' clg.

fireplace

up **down**

foyer

br. 3
12'-0" x 10'-0"
8' clg.

down

entry porch

garage
40'-0" x 20'-0" avg.

observation deck

master
13'-0" x 14'-0"
vault. clg.

open to grand room below

am kitchen

storage
13'-0" x 18'-0" avg.

stor./bonus
20'-0" x 20'-0"

up **stor.**

down

up

lattice work
panel walls

DESIGN HPU040027

Square Footage: 1,288
Width: 32'-4" Depth: 60'-0"

Welcome home to casual, unstuffy living with this comfortable Tidewater design. Asymmetrical lines celebrate the turn of the new century, and blend a current Gulf Coast style with vintage panache brought forward from its regional past. The heart of this home is the great room, where a put-your-feet-up atmosphere prevails, and the dusky hues of sunset can mingle with the sounds of ocean breakers. French doors open the master suite to a private area of the covered porch, where sunlight and sea breezes mingle with a spirit of bon vivant.

DESIGN BY
©The Sater Design Collection

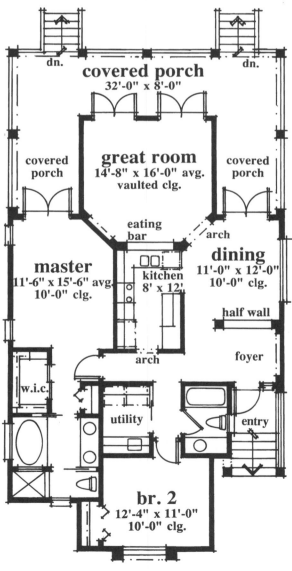

dn.

covered porch
32'-0" x 8'-0"

covered porch

great room
14'-8" x 16'-0" avg.
vaulted clg.

covered porch

eating bar

arch

master
11'-6" x 15'-6" avg.
10'-0" clg.

kitchen
8' x 12'

dining
11'-0" x 12'-0"
10'-0" clg.

half wall

foyer

arch

w.i.c.

utility

entry

br. 2
12'-4" x 11'-0"
10'-0" clg.

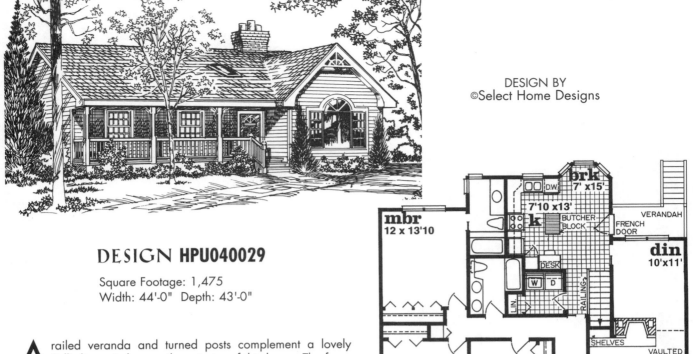

DESIGN BY
©Select Home Designs

DESIGN HPU040029

Square Footage: 1,475
Width: 44'-0" Depth: 43'-0"

A railed veranda and turned posts complement a lovely Palladian window on the exterior of this home. The foyer is brightly lit by a skylight, and leads to the living room with a vaulted ceiling, fireplace and bookshelves. The dining room overlooks a covered veranda that opens from the breakfast room. A well-organized kitchen features a butcher-block island. Sleeping quarters include a master suite and two family bedrooms that share a full double-vanity bath.

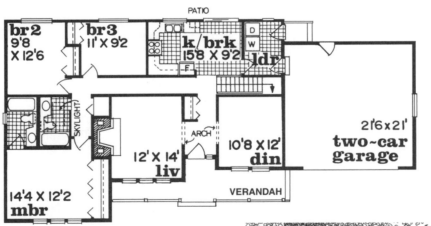

DESIGN HPU040028

Square Footage: 1,399
Width: 69'-0" Depth: 35'-0"

DESIGN BY
©Select Home Designs

Classic floor planning and a worthy exterior dominate this one-story starter home. The exterior features a Palladian window and multi-pane windows. The central foyer is flanked by the living room with a fireplace and the formal dining room. Across the hall are the U-shaped kitchen and the breakfast room with sliding glass doors to the rear terrace. A laundry area accesses the two-car garage and the backyard. Two family bedrooms share a full skylit bath. The master bedroom boasts a large wall closet and private bath. A full basement can be developed at a later time, if needed.

W hat an appealing plan! Its rustic character is defined by cedar lattice, covered columned porches, exposed rafters and multi-pane, double-hung windows. The great room/dining room combination is reached through double doors off the veranda and features a fireplace towering two stories to the lofty ceiling. A U-shaped kitchen contains an angled snack counter that serves this area and loads of space for a breakfast table—or use the handy side porch for alfresco dining. To the rear resides the master bedroom with a full bath and double doors to the veranda. An additional half-bath sits just beyond the laundry room. Upstairs, two family bedrooms and a full bath finish the plan.

PORCH

D
W

COATS

mbr
12'9x13'4

k
10'x10'

DN
UP

LINE OF
FLOOR OVER

**din/
great rm**
21'x13'6

LINE OF
FLOOR OVER

VERANDAH

DN
DN

DESIGN HPU040030

First Floor: 995 square feet
Second Floor: 484 square feet
Total: 1,479 square feet
Width: 38'-0" Depth: 44'-0"

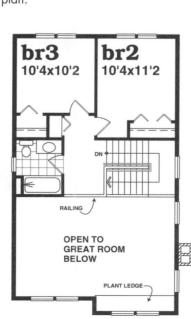

br3
10'4x10'2

br2
10'4x11'2

DN

RAILING

**OPEN TO
GREAT ROOM
BELOW**

PLANT LEDGE

QUOTE ONE®
Cost to build? See page 502
to order complete cost estimate
to build this house in your area!

DESIGN BY
©Select Home Designs

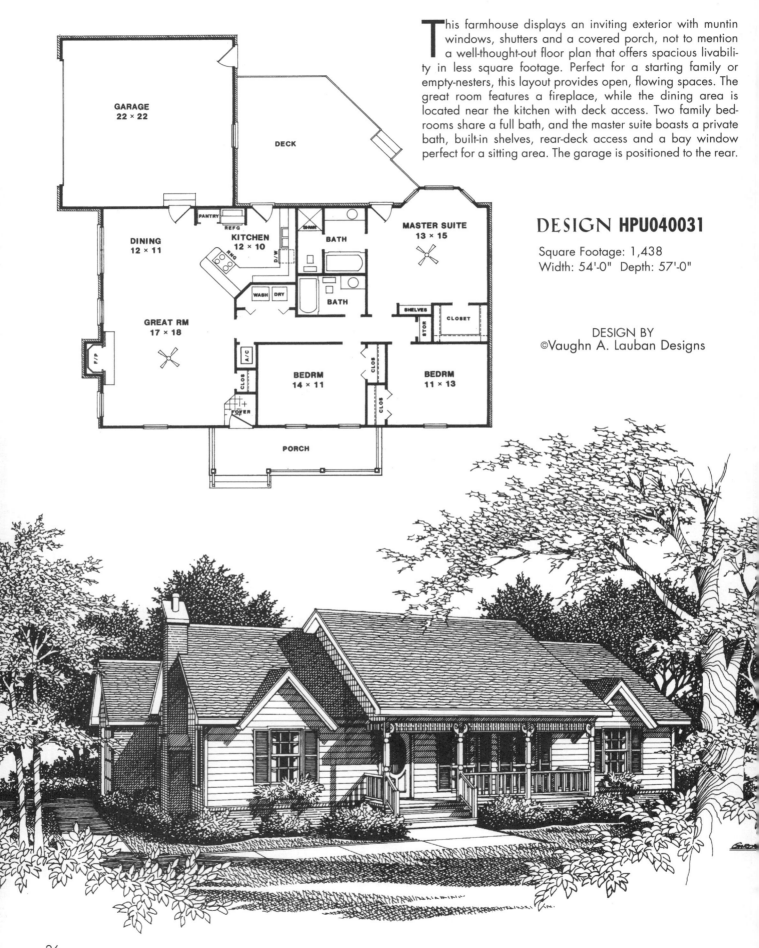

GARAGE
22 × 22

DECK

PANTRY

REFG

DINING
12 × 11

KITCHEN
12 × 10

RNG

D/W

SHWR

BATH

MASTER SUITE
13 × 15

WASH DRY

BATH

GREAT RM
17 × 18

F/P

SHELVES

STOR

CLOSET

A/C

CLOS

BEDRM
14 × 11

CLOS

CLOS

BEDRM
11 × 13

FOYER

PORCH

This farmhouse displays an inviting exterior with muntin windows, shutters and a covered porch, not to mention a well-thought-out floor plan that offers spacious livability in less square footage. Perfect for a starting family or empty-nesters, this layout provides open, flowing spaces. The great room features a fireplace, while the dining area is located near the kitchen with deck access. Two family bedrooms share a full bath, and the master suite boasts a private bath, built-in shelves, rear-deck access and a bay window perfect for a sitting area. The garage is positioned to the rear.

DESIGN HPU040031

Square Footage: 1,438
Width: 54'-0" Depth: 57'-0"

DESIGN BY
©Vaughn A. Lauban Designs

T he details of the exterior of this small, attractive Colonial-style home include wood siding, shuttered windows, a gabled room and a stunning entry with sidelights. At the front of the house, the family room offers a fireplace to warm the cold night air. Beyond lies the dining room and U-shaped kitchen, which share a door to the sun deck. Two family bedrooms located at the middle of the home share a bathroom that contains a laundry. To the left of the house is the master bedroom with two closets, an optional plant shelf, and a bathroom with dual sinks and a linen closet.

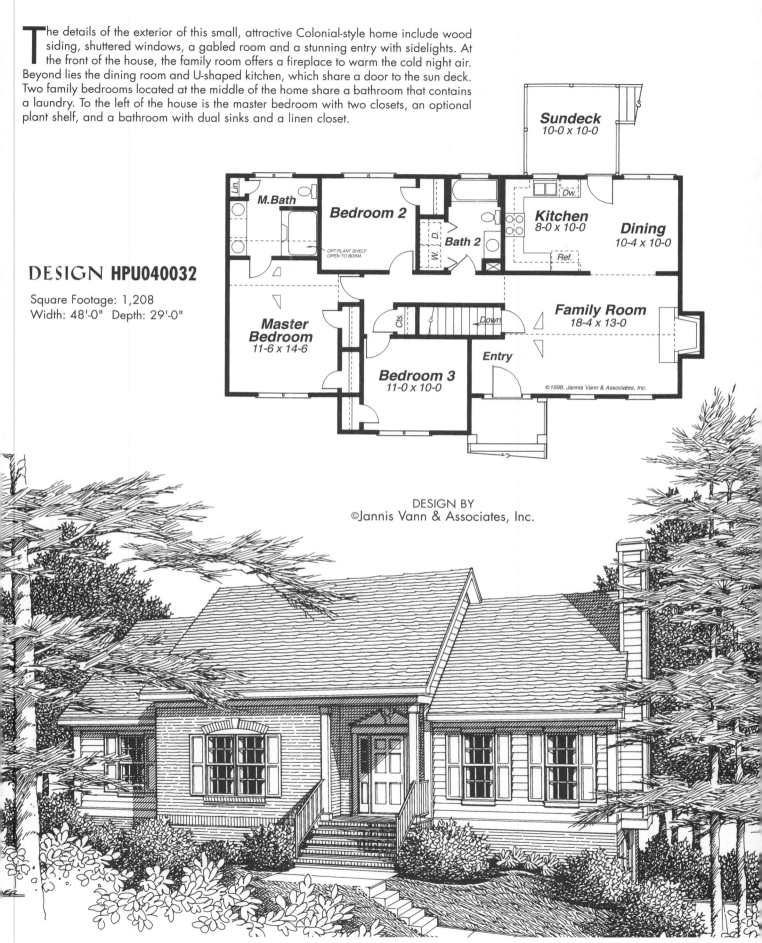

Sundeck
10-0 x 10-0

Lin.

M. Bath

Bedroom 2

Kitchen
8-0 x 10-0

Dw.

Dining
10-4 x 10-0

OPT. PLANT SHELF
OPEN TO BDRM.

W. D.

Bath 2

Ref.

DESIGN **HPU040032**

Square Footage: 1,208
Width: 48'-0"   Depth: 29'-0"

Master Bedroom
11-6 x 14-6

Cls.

Down

Family Room
18-4 x 13-0

Bedroom 3
11-0 x 10-0

Entry

©1998, Jannis Vann & Associates, Inc.

DESIGN BY
©Jannis Vann & Associates, Inc.

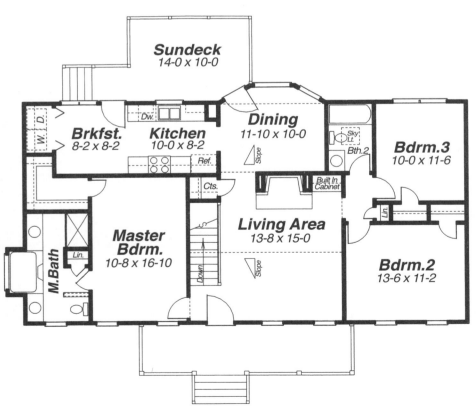

Sundeck
14-0 x 10-0

Brkfst.
8-2 x 8-2

Kitchen
10-0 x 8-2

Dining
11-10 x 10-0

Bdrm.3
10-0 x 11-6

Dw.

Ref.

Slope

Bth.2

Sky. Lt.

Built In Cabinet

Cts.

W. D.

Lin.

Master Bdrm.
10-8 x 16-10

M.Bath

Living Area
13-8 x 15-0

Down

Slope

Lin.

Bdrm.2
13-6 x 11-2

DESIGN BY
©Jannis Vann & Associates, Inc.

DESIGN HPU040033

Square Footage: 1,345
Width: 52'-0" Depth: 32'-0"

This home, with its gabled roof, covered front porch and columns with arched beam support, offers a practical floor plan. The front door opens to the living room, which has a sloped ceiling, a fireplace and built-in cabinetry. To the left is the master suite with a walk-in closet, dual-vanity bathroom, separate shower and garden tub set in a bayed window. Two more bedrooms on the other side of the house share a bathroom that includes a skylight. The dining room, kitchen and breakfast area at the back of the house enjoy views of the sun deck and backyard. The dining room features bayed windows as well as a door leading to the sun deck.

A brilliant display of windows decorates the siding exterior of this traditional design. Walk onto the covered front porch—perfect for stargazing at night. Inside, the living room features a ceiling fan and a fireplace. The kitchen opens to the dining area and is conveniently located near the two-car garage, which is connected by a patio. Two family bedrooms share a full hall bath. The master suite overlooks the rear deck and features a ceiling fan, private bath and spacious closet.

DESIGN HPU040034

Square Footage: 1,247
Width: 43'-0" Depth: 60'-0"

DESIGN BY
©Vaughn A. Lauban Designs

DESIGN HPU040035

Square Footage: 1,395
Width: 44'-11" Depth: 50'-1"

A combination of muntin windows with lintels, side paneling and brick add flavor to this traditional home. Surrounding the foyer is a full hall bath separating two family suites. The master bedroom is located to the rear of the plan and boasts a private bath, linen closet and a huge walk-in closet. The self-sufficient kitchen includes plenty of work space, a breakfast bar and a pantry. Adjacent to the dining room, the family room provides an area for an optional fireplace. The garage entrance is conveniently placed near the laundry room and the kitchen.

DESIGN BY
©Living Concepts Home Planning

DESIGN HPU040036

Square Footage: 1,395
Width: 44'-11" Depth: 50'-1"

DESIGN BY
©Living Concepts Home Planning

B eyond the luminous exterior of hipped and gabled roofs, you can enter this traditional home through a covered porch with a railing—perfect for a rocking chair to sit and enjoy the weather! The master suite includes a vast walk-in closet and a master bath with two linen closets. A full hall bath is available to the occupants of the two additional suites; each suite presents angled entries and wall closets. The kitchen provides a serving bar, an entire wall of cabinet space and direct access to the laundry room and garage. A fireplace is optional in the family room. The dining area includes sliding glass doors to the rear patio.

DESIGN HPU040037

Square Footage: 1,204
Width: 43'-1" Depth: 47'-1"

A welcoming porch leads to an entry that features a sidelight and transom. Inside, the foyer carries guests past a utility closet and niche, to the island kitchen with a snack bar. The kitchen opens to the eating area and the family room (with an optional fireplace) accessible to the rear patio. The secluded master suite provides privacy and features a master bath and walk-in closet. Suites 2 and 3 are separated from the living area and share a full hall bath. The well-placed garage entrance opens to the foyer.

DESIGN BY
©Living Concepts Home Planning

MASTER SUITE
12'-0" x 12'-0"

FAMILY ROOM
15'-0" x 15'-4"

PATIO

EATING AREA
7'-0" x 8'-0"

BATH

NICHE

KITCHEN
12'-0" x 10'-0"

SUITE 2
9'-8" x 9'-10"

FOYER

PORCH

GARAGE
20'-0" x 20'-0"

SUITE 3
9'-8" x 9'-0"

31

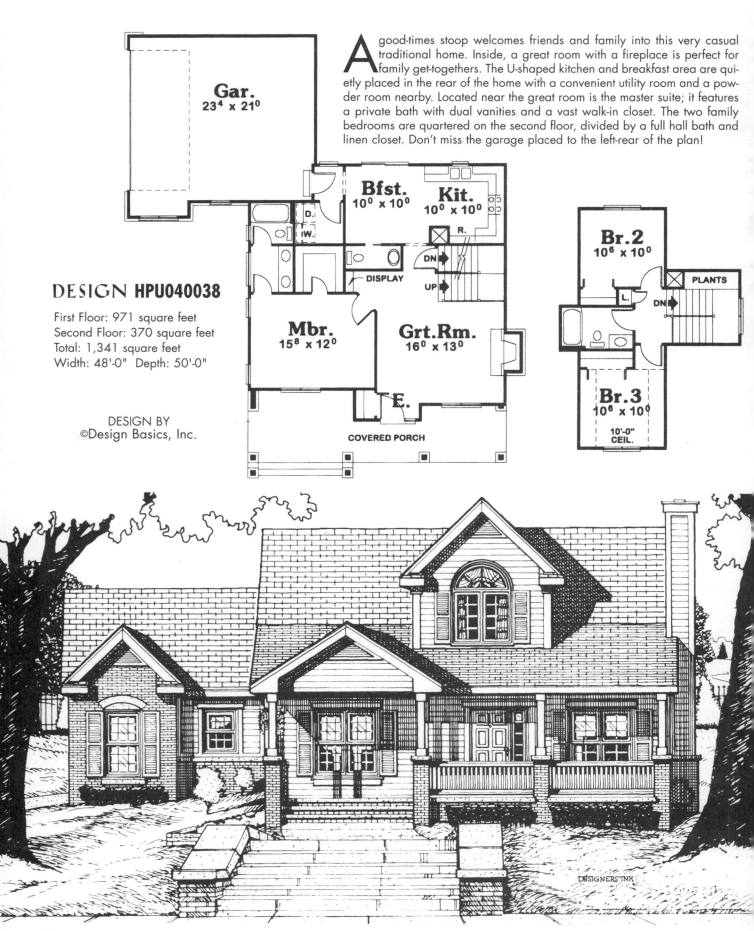

Gar.
23⁴ x 21⁰

A good-times stoop welcomes friends and family into this very casual traditional home. Inside, a great room with a fireplace is perfect for family get-togethers. The U-shaped kitchen and breakfast area are quietly placed in the rear of the home with a convenient utility room and a powder room nearby. Located near the great room is the master suite; it features a private bath with dual vanities and a vast walk-in closet. The two family bedrooms are quartered on the second floor, divided by a full hall bath and linen closet. Don't miss the garage placed to the left-rear of the plan!

Bfst.
10⁰ x 10⁰

Kit.
10⁰ x 10⁰

D.
W.

R.

DN

UP

DISPLAY

Br.2
10⁶ x 10⁰

L.

PLANTS

DN

DESIGN **HPU040038**

First Floor: 971 square feet
Second Floor: 370 square feet
Total: 1,341 square feet
Width: 48'-0" Depth: 50'-0"

Mbr.
15⁸ x 12⁰

Grt.Rm.
16⁰ x 13⁰

E.

Br.3
10⁶ x 10⁰

10'-0"
CEIL.

DESIGN BY
©Design Basics, Inc.

COVERED PORCH

DESIGNERS INK

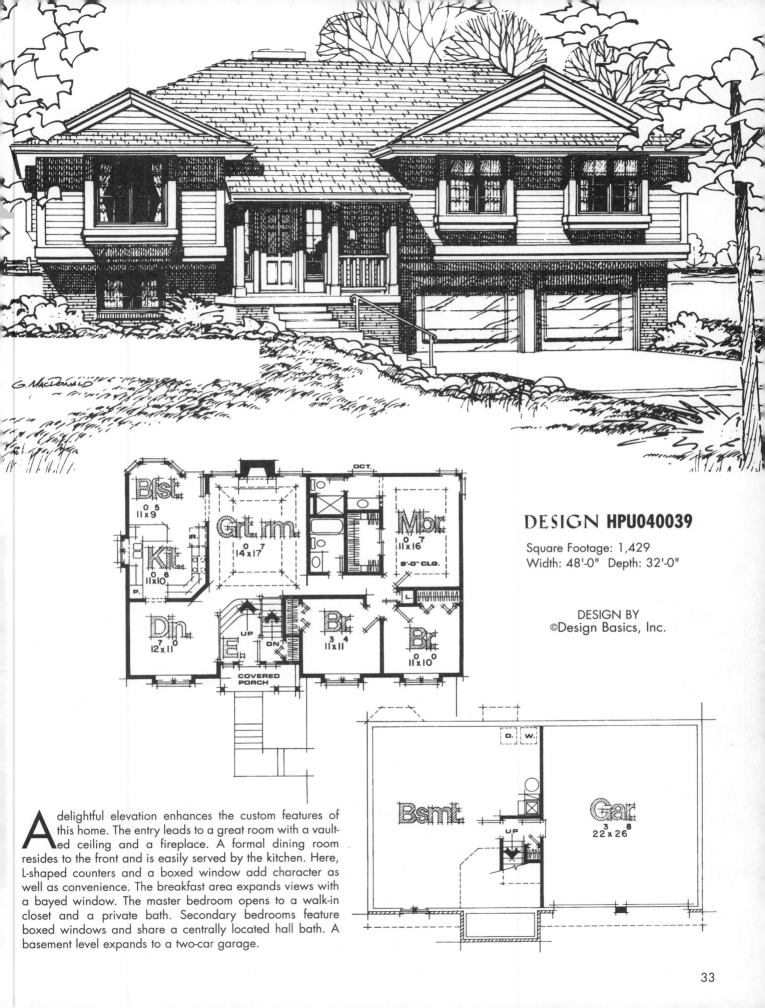

DESIGN **HPU040039**

Square Footage: 1,429
Width: 48'-0" Depth: 32'-0"

DESIGN BY
©Design Basics, Inc.

Bfst
11x9

Grt. rm.
14x17

Mbr
11x16
9'-0" CLG.

Kit
11x10

Dn
12x11

Br
11x11

Br
11x10

COVERED PORCH

Bsmt

Gar
22x26

A delightful elevation enhances the custom features of this home. The entry leads to a great room with a vaulted ceiling and a fireplace. A formal dining room resides to the front and is easily served by the kitchen. Here, L-shaped counters and a boxed window add character as well as convenience. The breakfast area expands views with a bayed window. The master bedroom opens to a walk-in closet and a private bath. Secondary bedrooms feature boxed windows and share a centrally located hall bath. A basement level expands to a two-car garage.

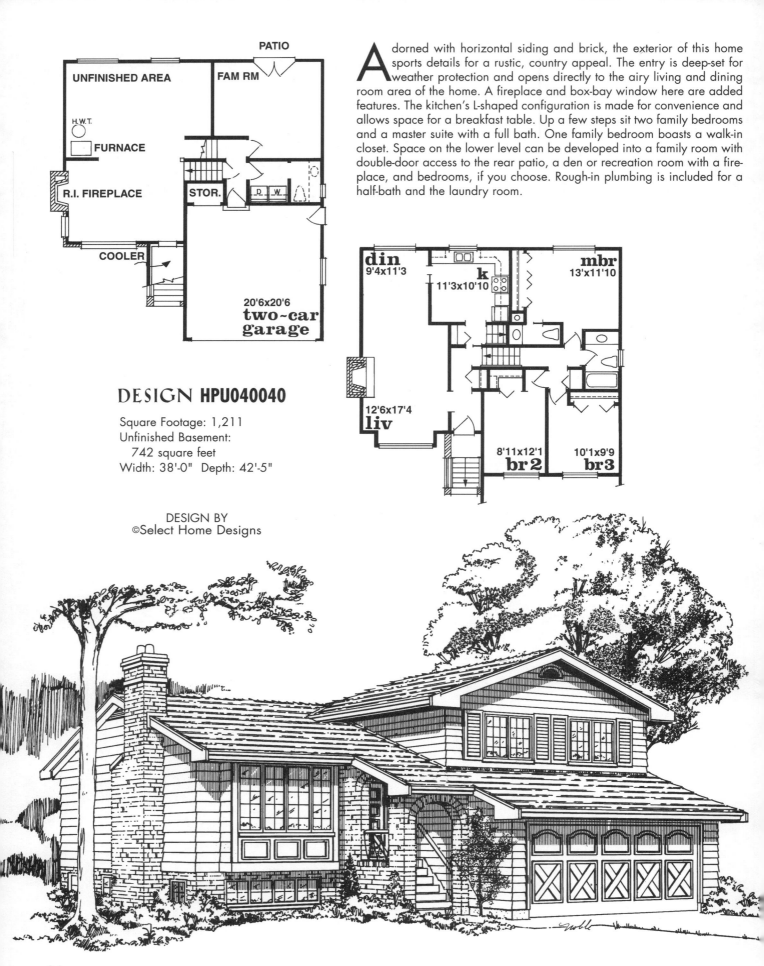

UNFINISHED AREA

PATIO

FAM RM

H.W.T.

FURNACE

R.I. FIREPLACE

STOR.

D W

COOLER

20'6x20'6
two-car
garage

DESIGN HPU040040

Square Footage: 1,211
Unfinished Basement:
742 square feet
Width: 38'-0" Depth: 42'-5"

DESIGN BY
©Select Home Designs

din
9'4x11'3

k
11'3x10'10

mbr
13'x11'10

12'6x17'4
liv

8'11x12'1
br 2

10'1x9'9
br 3

Adorned with horizontal siding and brick, the exterior of this home sports details for a rustic, country appeal. The entry is deep-set for weather protection and opens directly to the airy living and dining room area of the home. A fireplace and box-bay window here are added features. The kitchen's L-shaped configuration is made for convenience and allows space for a breakfast table. Up a few steps sit two family bedrooms and a master suite with a full bath. One family bedroom boasts a walk-in closet. Space on the lower level can be developed into a family room with double-door access to the rear patio, a den or recreation room with a fireplace, and bedrooms, if you choose. Rough-in plumbing is included for a half-bath and the laundry room.

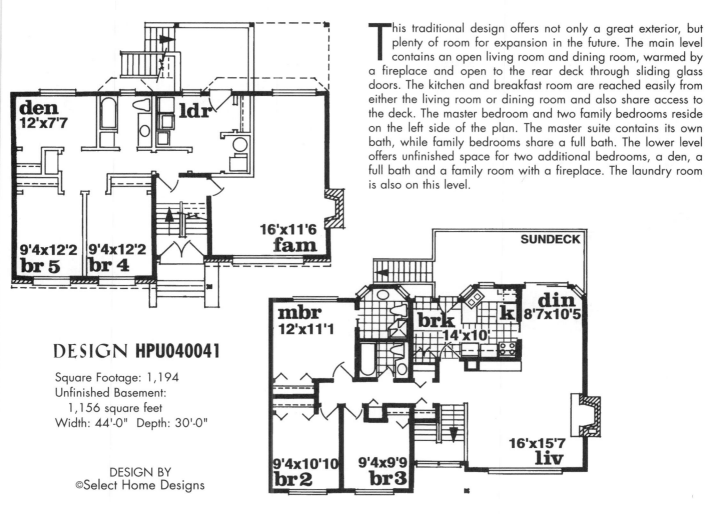

den
12'x7'7

ldr

9'4x12'2
br 5

9'4x12'2
br 4

16'x11'6
fam

This traditional design offers not only a great exterior, but plenty of room for expansion in the future. The main level contains an open living room and dining room, warmed by a fireplace and open to the rear deck through sliding glass doors. The kitchen and breakfast room are reached easily from either the living room or dining room and also share access to the deck. The master bedroom and two family bedrooms reside on the left side of the plan. The master suite contains its own bath, while family bedrooms share a full bath. The lower level offers unfinished space for two additional bedrooms, a den, a full bath and a family room with a fireplace. The laundry room is also on this level.

SUNDECK

mbr
12'x11'1

brk
14'x10'

k

din
8'7x10'5

DESIGN HPU040041

Square Footage: 1,194
Unfinished Basement:
1,156 square feet
Width: 44'-0" Depth: 30'-0"

DESIGN BY
©Select Home Designs

9'4x10'10
br2

9'4x9'9
br3

16'x15'7
liv

DESIGN HPU040042

Square Footage: 1,458
Bonus Room: 256 square feet
Width: 47'-7" Depth: 46'-5"

A multitude of windows fills this home with an abundance of natural light. The foyer leads you and your guests into the inviting living room, which can be furnished with an optional warming fireplace and built-ins. A short hallway to the left of the living room takes you to the family sleeping quarters where a full bath is shared by two suites. The master suite is secluded for privacy on the far right. The private bath here includes a walk-in closet and Hollywood tub. Additional space above the garage can be developed at a later date.

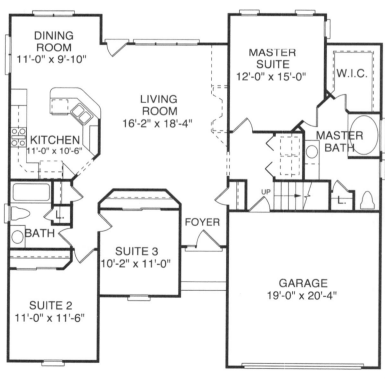

DINING ROOM
11'-0" x 9'-10"

KITCHEN
11'-0" x 10'-6"

BATH

LIVING ROOM
16'-2" x 18'-4"

SUITE 3
10'-2" x 11'-0"

SUITE 2
11'-0" x 11'-6"

FOYER

MASTER SUITE
12'-0" x 15'-0"

W.I.C.

MASTER BATH

UP

GARAGE
19'-0" x 20'-4"

DESIGN BY
©Living Concepts Home Planning

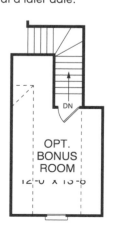

OPT. BONUS ROOM
12'-0" x 13'-6"

DN

DESIGN HPU040043

Square Footage: 1,395
Width: 44'-11" Depth: 50'-1"

A double-gabled roof and garage lead you to admire the welcoming porch and front muntin window with shutters. Inside, two bedroom suites are divided by a full hall bath. The L-shaped kitchen includes a pantry and snack bar and opens to the family room with an optional fireplace. The dining area provides sliding glass doors to the rear patio. The master suite boasts a vast walk-in closet and a grand private bath. The garage entrance is located in the utility room.

DESIGN BY
©Living Concepts Home Planning

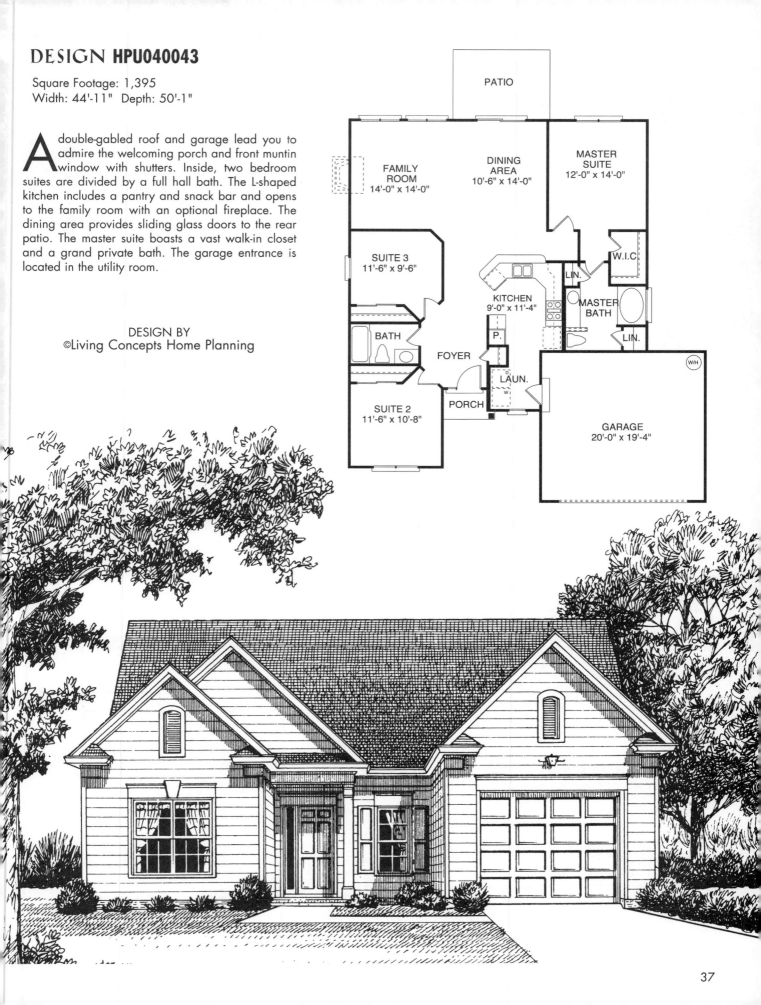

PATIO

FAMILY ROOM
14'-0" x 14'-0"

DINING AREA
10'-6" x 14'-0"

MASTER SUITE
12'-0" x 14'-0"

SUITE 3
11'-6" x 9'-6"

W.I.C

LIN.

BATH

KITCHEN
9'-0" x 11'-4"

MASTER BATH

LIN.

FOYER

P.

LAUN.

W/H

SUITE 2
11'-6" x 10'-8"

PORCH

GARAGE
20'-0" x 19'-4"

© 1995 Donald A. Gardner Architects, Inc.

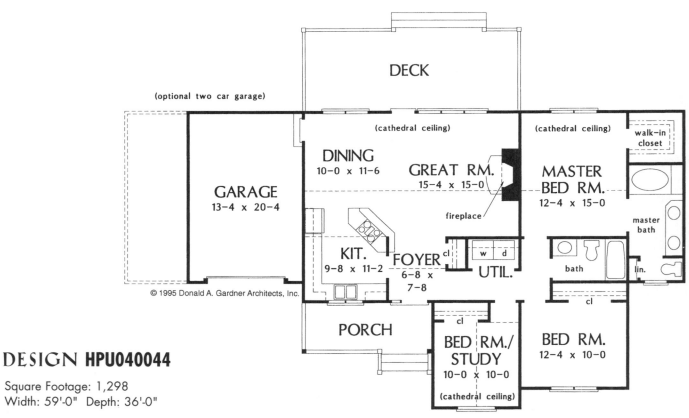

(optional two car garage)

DECK

(cathedral ceiling)

GARAGE
13-4 x 20-4

DINING
10-0 x 11-6

GREAT RM.
15-4 x 15-0

fireplace

(cathedral ceiling)

walk-in closet

MASTER
BED RM.
12-4 x 15-0

master bath

KIT.
9-8 x 11-2

FOYER
6-8 x
7-8

cl

w   d

UTIL.

bath

lin.

cl

© 1995 Donald A. Gardner Architects, Inc.

PORCH

cl

BED RM./
STUDY
10-0 x 10-0

(cathedral ceiling)

BED RM.
12-4 x 10-0

DESIGN HPU040044

Square Footage: 1,298
Width: 59'-0" Depth: 36'-0"

This design possesses plenty of curb appeal. From its gable roof and covered front porch, to its large rear deck, this home will brighten any neighborhood. Inside, open planning is the theme in the dining room/great room area, with a cathedral ceiling combining the two areas into a comfortable unit. The kitchen contributes to the openness with its snack bar/work island. Three bedrooms—or two bedrooms and a study—complete this attractive second home.

DESIGN BY
Donald A. Gardner Architects, Inc.

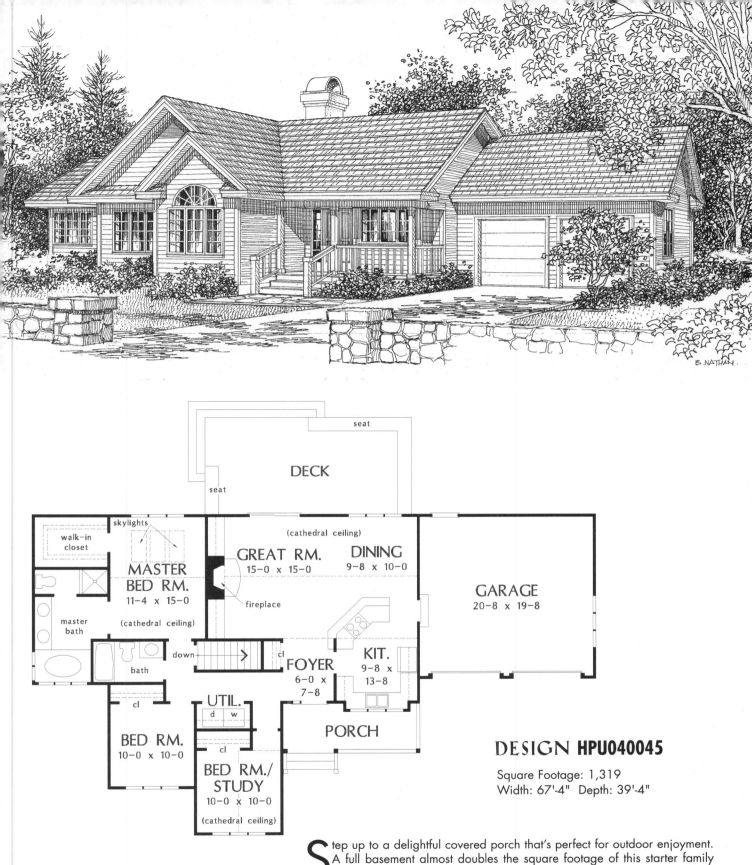

DECK

seat

seat

skylights

walk-in closet

MASTER BED RM.
11-4 x 15-0

(cathedral ceiling)

master bath

bath

(cathedral ceiling)

GREAT RM.
15-0 x 15-0

fireplace

DINING
9-8 x 10-0

GARAGE
20-8 x 19-8

down

cl

FOYER
6-0 x 7-8

KIT.
9-8 x 13-8

cl

UTIL.

d   w

cl

BED RM.
10-0 x 10-0

PORCH

BED RM./
STUDY
10-0 x 10-0

(cathedral ceiling)

B. NATHAN

DESIGN HPU040045

Square Footage: 1,319
Width: 67'-4" Depth: 39'-4"

DESIGN BY
Donald A. Gardner Architects, Inc.

Step up to a delightful covered porch that's perfect for outdoor enjoyment. A full basement almost doubles the square footage of this starter family home, which is as efficient as it is attractive. The floor plan features a cooktop-island kitchen, which opens to the great room with a fireplace and the dining area. French doors lead from the master bedroom to a deluxe private bath with a double-bowl vanity, separate shower and garden tub. The master bedroom also boasts skylights and a walk-in closet. One bedroom and a bedroom/study each include spacious closets and share a full hall bath.

DESIGN BY
©Design Basics, Inc.

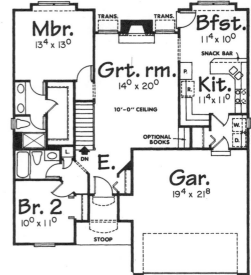

DESIGN HPU040048

Square Footage: 1,212
Width: 40'-0" Depth: 47'-8"

Attractive and uncomplicated, this two-bedroom home is perfect for first-time or empty-nest builders. Living, eating and cooking areas are designated as the center of activity in an open and unrestricted space. The master bedroom offers plenty of closet space and a private bath. Other features include a front coat closet for guests, a closet in the laundry room and, in the great room, a fireplace flanked by transom windows.

The wide, covered stoop is substantial enough for a chair. The great-room fireplace is flanked by transom windows and shares its warmth with the adjacent breakfast room. The kitchen, open to the breakfast room via a snack bar, also accesses the laundry room that leads to the garage. On the other side of the plan, two family bedrooms share a hall bath, and the master suite enjoys the luxury of a walk-in closet and a private bath with a double-bowl vanity and separate tub and shower.

DESIGN BY
©Design Basics, Inc.

DESIGN HPU040047

Square Footage: 1,360
Width: 52'-0" Depth: 46'-0"

DESIGN HPU040049

Square Footage: 1,400
Width: 39'-4" Depth: 50'-0"

Look closely at this smaller plan, and you'll be amazed at the livability it contains. Three bedrooms, two with a shared bath, are separated by the common areas. The family room and dining room form one open area with a sliding glass door to the rear for patio access—or choose the fireplace option for this area. The L-shaped kitchen has an attached nook with another sliding glass door to the patio. A well-appointed master suite contains a walk-in closet and full bath. The bath may be reconfigured to include a spa tub and separate shower. A laundry room connects the main house to the two-car garage.

DESIGN BY
©Lucia Custom Home Designers, Inc.

OPT. MASTER BATH

FIREPLACE OPTION

PATIO

NOOK

KITCHEN

PAN

DW   REF

FAMILY ROOM

13'-4" x 22'-0"

DINING

MASTER SUITE
12'-0" x 15'-0"

M. BATH

W.I.C.

BEDROOM #2
12'-0" x 10'-2"

PLANT SHELF

W   D

LIN.

FOYER

LAUN

BATH

A/C

WH

ENTRY

GARAGE
20'-0" x 20'-0"

OPT. DOOR

BEDROOM #3
11'-4" x 10'-0"

W.I.C.

M. BATH

DESIGN HPU040050

Square Footage: 1,392
Width: 42'-0" Depth: 54'-0"

With an unusually narrow footprint, this one-story home will fit on most slender lots and still provide a great floor plan. The entry is graced with a handy coat closet and leads back to the spacious great room (note the ten-foot ceiling here) and to the right to two family bedrooms and a full bath. Stairs to the basement level are found just beyond the entry hall. The breakfast room and kitchen dominate the left side of the plan. Separating them is a snack-bar counter for quick meals. Pampered amenities in the secluded master bedroom include a walk-in closet, windowed corner whirlpool tub, dual sinks and separate shower. A service entrance through the kitchen to the garage leads to a convenient laundry area and broom closet.

DESIGN BY
©Design Basics, Inc.

Mbr.
14^8 x 13^0

Bfst.
12^0 x 10^0

SNACK BAR

Grt. rm.
14^0 x 20^0

Kit.
12^0 x 11^2

LIN.

10'-0" CEILING

Br. 3
11^3 x 10^0

DN

E.

Gar.
19^4 x 22^3

COVERED
STOOP

Br. 2
11^3 x 10^0

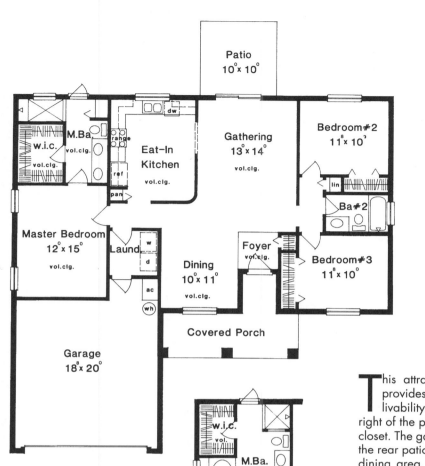

Patio
10⁰ x 10⁰

M.Ba
w.i.c.
vol.clg.
vol.clg.

Eat-In
Kitchen
vol.clg.

range
ref
pan
dw

Gathering
13⁰ x 14⁰
vol.clg.

Bedroom #2
11⁸ x 10⁹

lin

Ba #2

Master Bedroom
12⁰ x 15⁰
vol.clg.

Laund
w
d
ac
wh

Dining
10⁰ x 11⁰
vol.clg.

Foyer
vol.clg.

Bedroom #3
11⁸ x 10⁰

Covered Porch

Garage
18⁸ x 20⁰

DESIGN HPU040051

Square Footage: 1,390
Width: 50'-0" Depth: 48'-0"

w.i.c.
vol.

M.Ba.
vol.clg.

Master Bedroom
12⁰ x 14⁰
vol.clg.

Optional
Master Suite

This attractive bungalow with multi-pane windows provides three bedrooms and an awesome plan for livability. The two family bedrooms reside to the far right of the plan and share a full hall bath and hall linen closet. The gathering room features sliding glass doors to the rear patio, and easily accesses the eat-in kitchen and dining area. On the far left of the plan is the laundry room and the master suite. The master suite features two options for a private bath; each option includes dual vanities, a walk-in closet and separate shower.

DESIGN BY
©Lucia Custom Home Designers, Inc.

© 1995 Donald A. Gardner Architects, Inc.

DESIGN **HPU040052**

Square Footage: 1,246
Width: 60'-0" Depth: 60'-0"

This one-story home offers tremendous curb appeal and many extras found only in much larger homes. A continuous cathedral ceiling in the great room, dining room and kitchen gives a spacious feel to an efficient plan. The kitchen, brightened by a skylight, features a pantry and a peninsula counter for easy preparation and service to the dining room and screened porch. The master suite opens up with a cathedral ceiling, walk-in and linen closets, and a private bath that includes a garden tub and a double-bowl vanity.

DESIGN BY
Donald A. Gardner Architects, Inc.

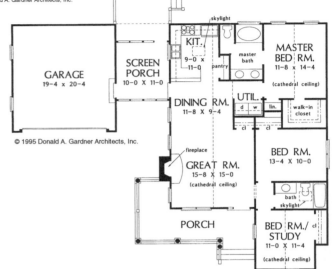

© 1995 Donald A. Gardner Architects, Inc.

DESIGN **HPU040053**

Square Footage: 1,246
Width: 60'-0" Depth: 48'-0"

Open living spaces allow an easy flow in this gracious country cottage, and vaulted ceilings add volume. The front porch wraps slightly, giving the illusion of a larger home, while a cathedral ceiling maximizes space in the open great room and dining room. The kitchen features a center skylight, breakfast bar and screened-porch access. Two bedrooms share a bath up front, while the master suite enjoys a private location at the back of the plan.

DESIGN BY
Donald A. Gardner Architects, Inc.

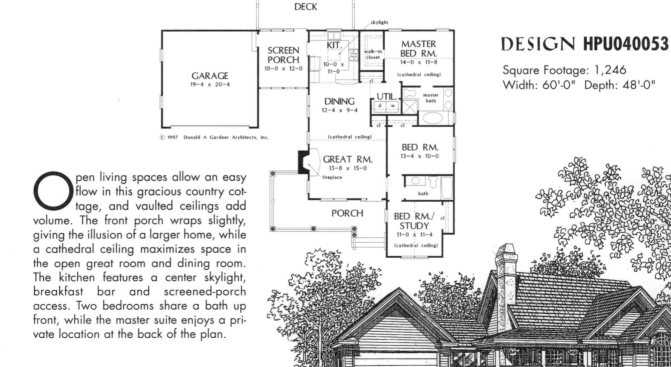

© 1997 Donald A. Gardner Architects, Inc.

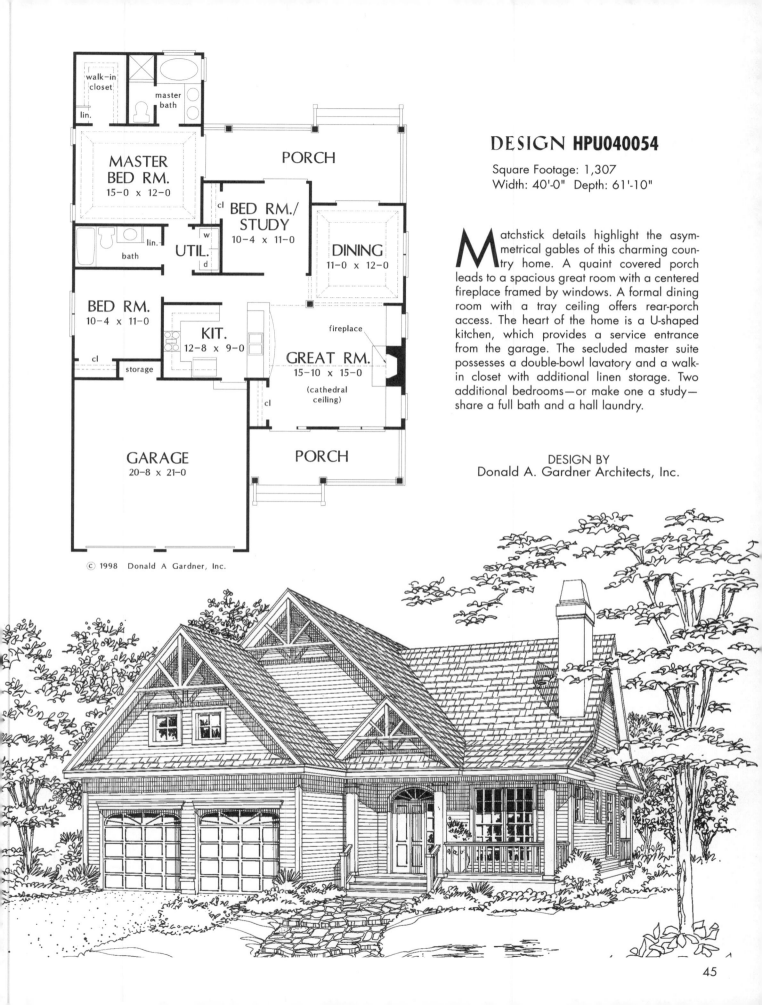

walk-in closet

lin.

master bath

MASTER BED RM.
15-0 x 12-0

bath

lin.

UTIL.
w
d

cl

BED RM./ STUDY
10-4 x 11-0

PORCH

DINING
11-0 x 12-0

BED RM.
10-4 x 11-0

cl

KIT.
12-8 x 9-0

storage

fireplace

GREAT RM.
15-10 x 15-0

(cathedral ceiling)

cl

GARAGE
20-8 x 21-0

PORCH

© 1998 Donald A Gardner, Inc.

DESIGN HPU040054

Square Footage: 1,307
Width: 40'-0" Depth: 61'-10"

Matchstick details highlight the asymmetrical gables of this charming country home. A quaint covered porch leads to a spacious great room with a centered fireplace framed by windows. A formal dining room with a tray ceiling offers rear-porch access. The heart of the home is a U-shaped kitchen, which provides a service entrance from the garage. The secluded master suite possesses a double-bowl lavatory and a walk-in closet with additional linen storage. Two additional bedrooms—or make one a study—share a full bath and a hall laundry.

DESIGN BY
Donald A. Gardner Architects, Inc.

© 1996 Donald A. Gardner Architects, Inc.

DESIGN HPU040056

Square Footage: 1,306
Width: 43'-0" Depth: 49'-0"

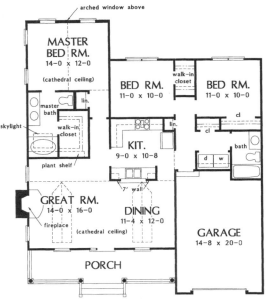

arched window above

MASTER
BED RM.
14-0 x 12-0
(cathedral ceiling)

master bath

skylight

plant shelf

walk-in closet

lin.

BED RM.
11-0 x 10-0

walk-in closet

BED RM.
11-0 x 10-0

cl

lin.

cl

bath

KIT.
9-0 x 10-8

d w

GREAT RM.
14-0 x 16-0

fireplace

7' wall

DINING
11-4 x 12-0
(cathedral ceiling)

GARAGE
14-8 x 20-0

PORCH

© 1996 Donald A. Gardner Architects, Inc.

A central kitchen acts as the focal point for this country ranch home. It includes a snack bar and is conveniently close to both the living and the sleeping areas. The great room and dining area are combined, offering a fireplace, a cathedral ceiling and access to the front porch. Notice that the washer and dryer are handy to the kitchen as well as the family bedrooms and the shared full bath. The master bedroom and bath include a cathedral ceiling, a walk-in closet and a skylit whirlpool tub.

DESIGN BY
Donald A. Gardner Architects, Inc.

A spacious cathedral ceiling expands the open great room, dining room and kitchen. The versatile bedroom/study features a cathedral ceiling and shares a full skylit bath with another bedroom. The master bedroom is highlighted by a cathedral ceiling for extra volume and light. The private bath opens up with a skylight and includes a double-bowl vanity, garden tub and separately located toilet. A walk-in closet adjacent to the bedroom completes the suite.

DESIGN BY
Donald A. Gardner Architects, Inc.

DECK

KIT.
11-0 x 10-10

walk-in closet

(cathedral ceiling)

MASTER
BED RM.
13-4 x 14-2

w d

UTIL.

DINING
13-4 x 9-4

cl

master bath

skylight

cl

GARAGE
15-8 x 20-4

fireplace

GREAT RM.
15-8 x 15-4

(cathedral ceiling)

sto.

BED RM.
13-4 x 10-0

bath

skylight

lin.

cl

PORCH

BED RM./
STUDY
13-4 x 11-4
(cathedral ceiling)

© 1995 Donald A. Gardner Architects, Inc.

B. NATHAN © 1995 Donald A. Gardner Architects, Inc.

DESIGN HPU040055

Square Footage: 1,302
Width: 47'-0" Depth: 50'-4"

B. NATHAN

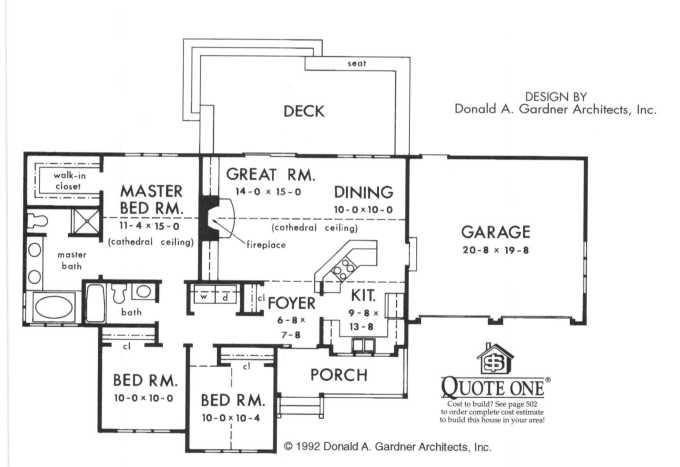

DECK

seat

DESIGN BY
Donald A. Gardner Architects, Inc.

GREAT RM.
14-0 × 15-0

DINING
10-0 × 10-0

(cathedral ceiling)

MASTER BED RM.
11-4 × 15-0
(cathedral ceiling)

walk-in closet

master bath

fireplace

GARAGE
20-8 × 19-8

w   d   cl

FOYER
6-8 ×
7-8

KIT.
9-8 ×
13-8

bath

cl

BED RM.
10-0 × 10-0

cl

BED RM.
10-0 × 10-4

PORCH

QUOTE ONE®
Cost to build? See page 502
to order complete cost estimate
to build this house in your area!

DESIGN HPU040057

Square Footage: 1,287
Width: 66'-4" Depth: 48'-0"

This economical plan makes an impressive visual statement with its comfortable and well-proportioned appearance. The entrance foyer leads to all areas of the house. The great room, dining area and kitchen are all open to one another, allowing visual interaction. The great room and dining area share a dramatic cathedral ceiling and feature a grand fireplace flanked by bookshelves and cabinets. The owners suite has a cathedral ceiling, walk-in closet and bath with double-bowl vanity, whirlpool tub and shower. Two family bedrooms and a full hall bath complete this cozy home.

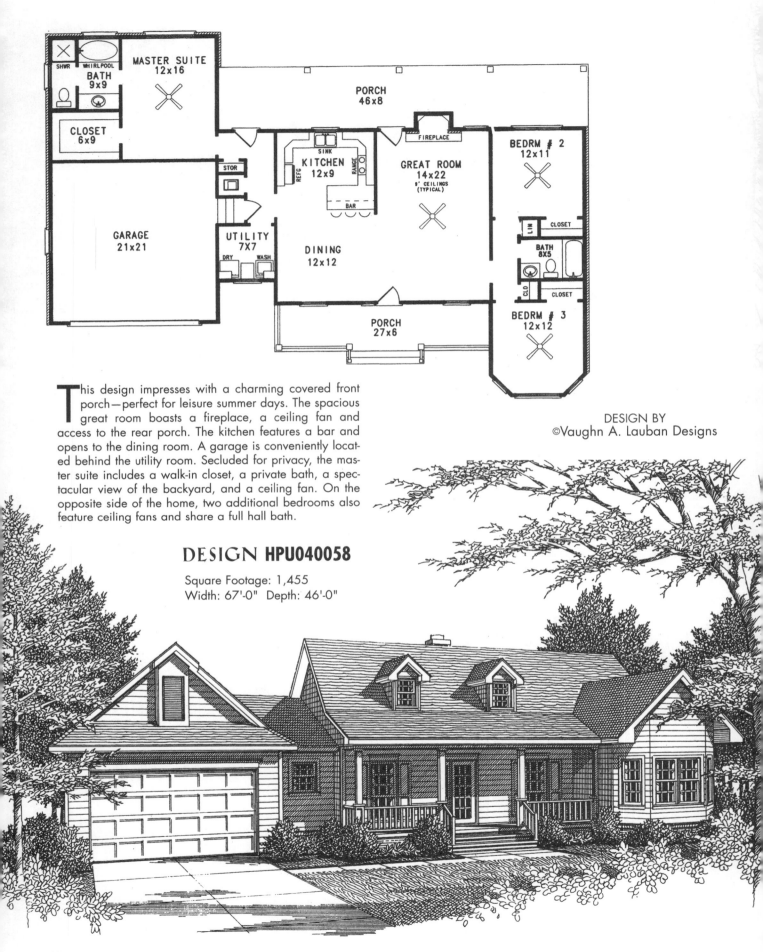

MASTER SUITE
12x16

BATH
9x9
SHWR WHIRLPOOL

CLOSET
6x9

GARAGE
21x21

STOR

UTILITY
7X7
DRY WASH

PORCH
46x8

KITCHEN
12x9
SINK
REFG RANGE
BAR

DINING
12x12

FIREPLACE

GREAT ROOM
14x22
9' CEILINGS
(TYPICAL)

BEDRM # 2
12x11

LIN CLOSET

BATH
8X5

CLO CLOSET

BEDRM # 3
12x12

PORCH
27x6

This design impresses with a charming covered front porch—perfect for leisure summer days. The spacious great room boasts a fireplace, a ceiling fan and access to the rear porch. The kitchen features a bar and opens to the dining room. A garage is conveniently located behind the utility room. Secluded for privacy, the master suite includes a walk-in closet, a private bath, a spectacular view of the backyard, and a ceiling fan. On the opposite side of the home, two additional bedrooms also feature ceiling fans and share a full hall bath.

DESIGN BY
©Vaughn A. Lauban Designs

DESIGN HPU040058

Square Footage: 1,455
Width: 67'-0" Depth: 46'-0"

DESIGN HPU040059

Square Footage: 1,372
Width: 38'-0" Depth: 65'-0"

Petite and efficiently impressive, this home is perfect for any average-sized family. A covered front porch welcomes visitors into the foyer. The living room is cooled by a ceiling fan in the summer and warmed by a corner fireplace in the winter. The kitchen, which features a utility room, is conveniently located between the garage and the dining room. A porch located off the dining area is perfect for outdoor grilling. The master suite is also cooled by a ceiling fan, and features a private bath and a walk-in closet with shelves. Two additional bedrooms share a full hall bath between them.

DESIGN BY
©Vaughn A. Lauban Designs

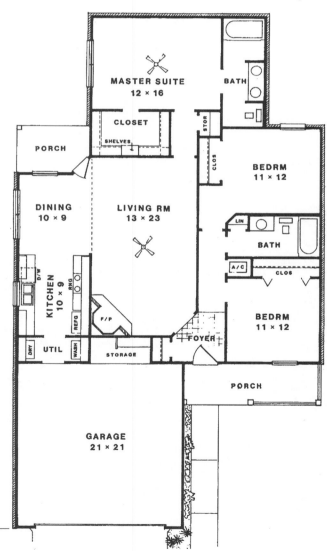

MASTER SUITE
12 × 16

BATH

CLOSET
SHELVES

STOR

CLOS

BEDRM
11 × 12

PORCH

DINING
10 × 9

LIVING RM
13 × 23

LIN

BATH

A/C   CLOS

KITCHEN
10 × 9

D/W

RNG

REFG   F/P

BEDRM
11 × 12

DRY

UTIL

WASH   STORAGE

FOYER

PORCH

GARAGE
21 × 21

DESIGN HPU040060

Square Footage: 1,345
Width: 56'-6"
Depth: 62'-2"

A dormer above the great room and a round-top window add special features to this cozy traditional plan. The great room also contains a fireplace and a sloped ceiling. Elegant round columns define the dining and kitchen areas while creating an openness with the great room. Ceilings in the dining room, kitchen and great room all slope up to a ridge above the columns. A bedroom adjacent to the foyer can double as a study. The master bedroom has a fine bath which includes a double bowl vanity, shower and whirlpool tub. The garage is connected to the house with a breezeway for flexibility. The plan is available with a crawlspace foundation.

DESIGN BY
Donald A. Gardner Architects, Inc.

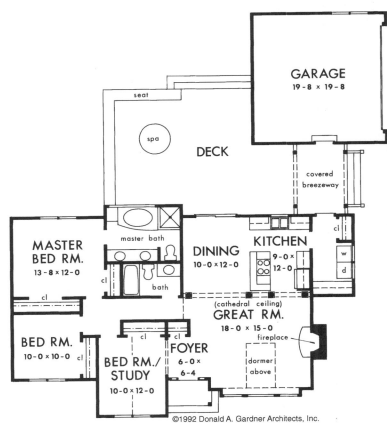

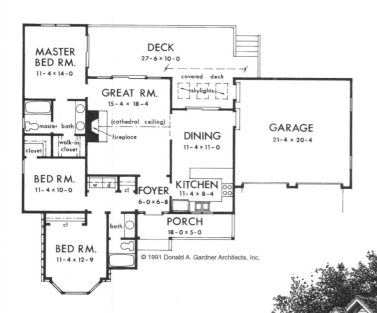

MASTER BED RM.
11-4 x 14-0

DECK
27-6 x 10-0

covered deck
skylights

GREAT RM.
15-4 x 18-4

(cathedral ceiling)
fireplace

master bath

walk-in closet

closet

GARAGE
21-4 x 20-4

DINING
11-4 x 11-0

BED RM.
11-4 x 10-0

w d

cl

FOYER
6-0 x 6-8

KITCHEN
11-4 x 8-4

bath

PORCH
18-0 x 5-0

cl

BED RM.
11-4 x 12-9

A multi-pane bay window, decorative dormers and a covered porch dress up this one-story cottage. The entrance foyer leads to an impressive great room with a cathedral ceiling and fireplace. The U-shaped kitchen, adjacent to the dining room, provides an ideal layout for food preparation. A large deck offers shelter while admitting sunlight through skylights. A luxurious master bedroom takes advantage of the deck area and is assured privacy from two additional bedrooms. These family bedrooms share a full bath.

DESIGN HPU040061

Square Footage: 1,310
Width: 61'-0" Depth: 51'-5"

DESIGN BY
Donald A. Gardner Architects, Inc.

DESIGN HPU040062

Square Footage: 1,322
Width: 56'-8" Depth: 63'-4"

Small doesn't necessarily mean boring in this well-proportioned, three-bedroom country home. A gracious foyer leads to the great room through a set of elegant columns. In this living area, a cathedral ceiling works well with a fireplace and skylights to bring the utmost livability to the homeowner. Outside, an expansive deck includes room for a spa. A handsome master suite has a tray ceiling and a private bath. Two additional bedrooms sit to the left of the plan. Each enjoys ample closet space, and they share a hall bath.

DESIGN BY
Donald A. Gardner Architects, Inc.

GARAGE
20-4 x 20-4

seat

spa

DECK

covered breezeway

skylights

BED RM.
11-4 x 10-0

GREAT RM.
14-0 x 14-8

skylights

fireplace
(cathedral ceiling)

DINING
10-8 x 14-0

w d

master bath

MASTER BED RM.
12-8 x 13-0

walk-in closet

cl

bath

cl

cl

FOYER
6-7 x 6-0

KIT.
10-8 x 12-4

BED RM.
11-4 x 10-4

PORCH

DESIGN HPU040063

Square Footage: 1,142
Width: 48'-10" Depth: 35'-8"

This one-story traditional home caters to family living. The efficient, U-shaped kitchen opens to an adjacent bayed breakfast area. The family room features a corner fireplace and access to the rear yard. Two family bedrooms share a full bath, while the master bedroom offers a private bath with a walk-in closet. Please specify slab or crawlspace foundation when ordering.

DESIGN BY
©Larry E. Belk Designs

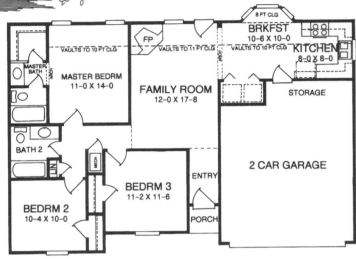

8 FT CLG
BRKFST
10-6 X 10-0
KITCHEN
8-0 X 8-0
VAULTS TO 10 FT CLG
VAULTS TO 11 FT CLG
VAULTS TO 10 FT CLG
FP
MASTER BEDRM
11-0 X 14-0
FAMILY ROOM
12-0 X 17-8
STORAGE
MASTER BATH
BATH 2
2 CAR GARAGE
MECH
BEDRM 3
11-2 X 11-6
ENTRY
BEDRM 2
10-4 X 10-0
PORCH

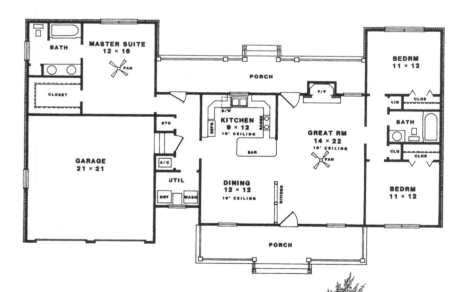

BATH
MASTER SUITE
12 × 16
FAN
CLOSET
STO
KITCHEN
9 × 12
10' ceiling
REFG
RANGE
D/W
BAR
A/C
GARAGE
21 ·21
UTIL
DRY
WASH
DINING
12 × 12
10' ceiling
DIVIDER
GREAT RM
14 × 22
10' ceiling
FAN
F/P
PORCH
BEDRM
11 × 12
LIN
CLOS
BATH
CLO
CLOS
BEDRM
11 × 12
PORCH

Well suited for the countryside, this rustic design features a multitude of amenities within. The covered front porch welcomes visitors inside to the great room, which offers a fireplace and ceiling fan. The master suite also features a ceiling fan and, in addition, a walk-in closet and private bath. Two other family bedrooms are located on the opposite side of the home.

DESIGN HPU040064

Square Footage: 1,458
Width: 67'-0" Depth: 40'-0"

DESIGN BY
©Vaughn A. Lauban Designs

DESIGN HPU040065

Square Footage: 1,267
Width: 52'-0" Depth: 49'-0"

This design is rich in traditional American appeal. Enter from a charming covered porch. A vaulted ceiling, a fireplace and a ceiling fan enhance the great room. Straight ahead, the dining room accesses the rear patio. The kitchen features a snack bar and a side utility room with a door to the master bath. The master suite is secluded for privacy and includes a private bath, a walk-in closet and a wide view to the backyard. On the other side of the home, two additional bedrooms share a hall bath. A two-car garage with storage space completes the plan.

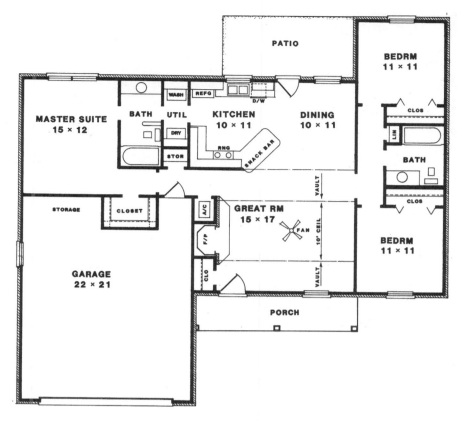

DESIGN BY
©Vaughn A. Lauban Designs

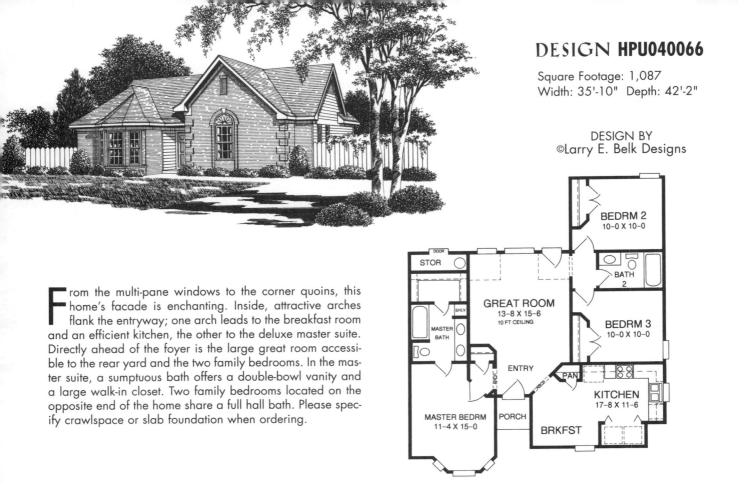

DESIGN HPU040066

Square Footage: 1,087
Width: 35'-10" Depth: 42'-2"

DESIGN BY
©Larry E. Belk Designs

From the multi-pane windows to the corner quoins, this home's facade is enchanting. Inside, attractive arches flank the entryway; one arch leads to the breakfast room and an efficient kitchen, the other to the deluxe master suite. Directly ahead of the foyer is the large great room accessible to the rear yard and the two family bedrooms. In the master suite, a sumptuous bath offers a double-bowl vanity and a large walk-in closet. Two family bedrooms located on the opposite end of the home share a full hall bath. Please specify crawlspace or slab foundation when ordering.

STOR

DOOR

BEDRM 2
10-0 X 10-0

BATH 2

GREAT ROOM
13-8 X 15-6
10 FT CEILING

MASTER BATH

SHLV

BEDRM 3
10-0 X 10-0

ENTRY

PAN

KITCHEN
17-8 X 11-6

MASTER BEDRM
11-4 X 15-0

PORCH

BRKFST

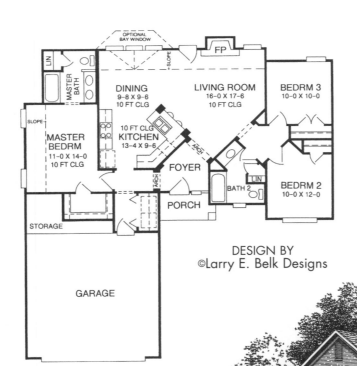

OPTIONAL BAY WINDOW

FP

SLOPE

LIN

MASTER BATH

DINING
9-8 X 9-6
10 FT CLG

LIVING ROOM
16-0 X 17-6
10 FT CLG

BEDRM 3
10-0 X 10-0

SLOPE

MASTER BEDRM
11-0 X 14-0
10 FT CLG

10 FT CLG
KITCHEN
13-4 X 9-6

FOYER

BATH 2

LIN

BEDRM 2
10-0 X 12-0

PORCH

STORAGE

GARAGE

DESIGN BY
©Larry E. Belk Designs

Brick detailing and corner quoins lend charm to this traditional exterior. Inside, a graceful arch announces the living room, complete with a fireplace and a French door to the back property. The angled kitchen is conveniently positioned to offer service to the dining room, and provides a snack counter for easy meals. Split sleeping quarters offer a private wing to the sumptuous master suite, which has a twin-lavatory bath. Please specify crawlspace or slab foundation when ordering.

DESIGN HPU040067

Square Footage: 1,282
Width: 48'-10" Depth: 52'-6"

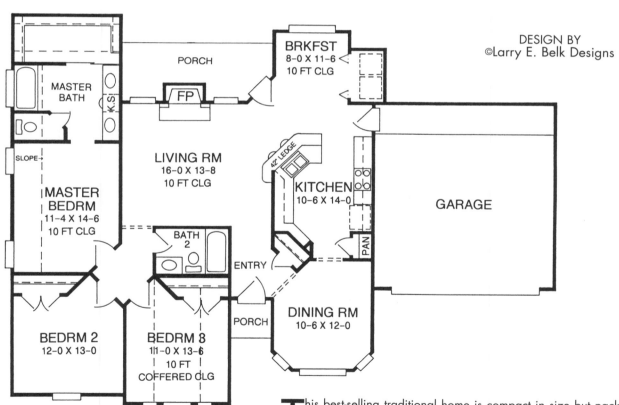

DESIGN BY
©Larry E. Belk Designs

BRKFST
8-0 X 11-6
10 FT CLG

PORCH

MASTER BATH

FP

LIVING RM
16-0 X 13-8
10 FT CLG

42" LEDGE

KITCHEN
10-6 X 14-0

GARAGE

PAN

SLOPE→

MASTER BEDRM
11-4 X 14-6
10 FT CLG

BATH 2

ENTRY

BEDRM 2
12-0 X 13-0

BEDRM 3
11-0 X 13-6
10 FT COFFERED CLG

PORCH

DINING RM
10-6 X 12-0

DESIGN HPU040068

Square Footage: 1,500
Width: 59'-10" Depth: 44'-4"

This best-selling traditional home is compact in size but packed with all of the amenities you'd expect in a larger home. The foyer opens to a formal dining room with a classic bay window. The adjacent kitchen opens to a breakfast nook and shares an angled eating bar with the living room, which offers a cozy fireplace flanked by picture windows. The master suite features His and Hers vanities, a whirlpool tub/shower combination and a walk-in closet. Ten-foot ceilings in the major living areas as well as in two of the bedrooms contribute an aura of spaciousness to this plan. Please specify crawlspace or slab foundation when ordering.

DESIGN HPU040070

Square Footage: 1,405
Width: 40'-0" Depth: 60'-8"

This traditional brick home flaunts a touch of European flavor with its corner quoins. It also presents great curb appeal from the wide muntin window to the sidelight and transom in the entry. The spacious living room includes a warming fireplace. The dining room and U-shaped kitchen are connected by the snack bar and easily access a covered patio. Two family bedrooms reside along the extended hallway. At the end of the hall is the master bedroom, which presents a deluxe private bath and a walk-in closet. The utility room acts as a passage to the two-car garage.

DESIGN BY
©Fillmore Design Group

DESIGN HPU040069

First Floor: 748 square feet
Second Floor: 705 square feet
Total: 1,453 square feet
Width: 49'-8" Depth: 28'-4"

DESIGN BY
©Studer Residential Designs, Inc.

This two-story brick features siding accents and gabled rooflines. The front porch is perfect for welcoming guests or spending an evening on a porch swing. Inside, a long great room is a wonderful space for multiple uses. With access to the rear yard, the great room provides outdoor interaction. A breakfast bay accompanies the roomy kitchen, which features plenty of work space. Upstairs, two family bedrooms share a hall bath. The master bedroom features a walk-in closet and a private bath. This home is designed with a basement foundation.

DESIGN HPU040071

Square Footage: 1,285
Width: 32'-10" Depth: 52'-10"

This traditional-style home with decorative brick begins with a ten-foot entry ceiling and a closet. The living room also features a ten-foot ceiling as well as a warming fireplace. The U-shaped kitchen and dinette area highlights a sloping ceiling. The master bedroom opens to a patio and includes a sloping ceiling, a bath with a skylight and a walk-in closet. A second bedroom also includes a sloping ceiling.

DESIGN BY
©Fillmore Design Group

57

DESIGN HPU040072

Square Footage: 1,317
Width: 45'-0" Depth: 52'-4"

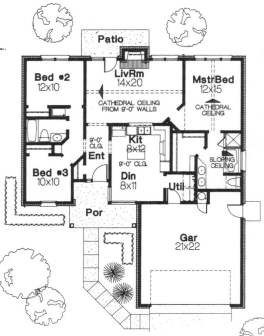

This unique home has many attractive features, including a sidelight and sunburst. The living room offers a cathedral ceiling with a wood-burning fireplace. The kitchen boasts an island counter and a dining area, which then leads to the utility room. The master suite enjoys a cathedral ceiling, garden tub, walk-in closet and separate shower. Two bedrooms share a bath on the opposite side of the house.

DESIGN BY
©Fillmore Design Group

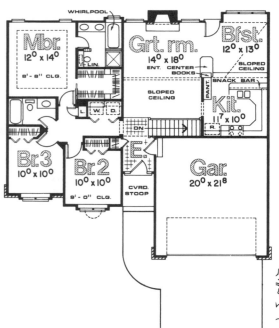

For great livability, this one-story home places its living areas to the back of the plan. The foyer leads directly to the great room and its focal-point fireplace. Extras include a built-in entertainment center and bookcase in the great room and a snack bar separating the sunny breakfast room from the U-shaped kitchen. The master bedroom includes a large walk-in closet and a pampering bath with a whirlpool tub, separate shower and dual-bowl vanity. Two front-facing family bedrooms share a full hall bath.

DESIGN BY
©Design Basics, Inc.

DESIGN HPU040073

Square Footage: 1,341
Width: 47'-4" Depth: 45'-8"

DESIGN **HPU040074**

Square Footage: 1,451
Width: 50'-0" Depth: 50'-0"

A bright volume entry with a transom opens to the great room with a fireplace and tall windows. The kitchen features a generous pantry and a snack bar adjoining the breakfast room. The spacious master bedroom contains a large walk-in closet, a boxed ceiling and a delightful master bath filled with amenities such as dual vanities and a whirlpool tub. The private second bedroom features a boxed window. Note how the angles used throughout the home enhance architectural interest. A versatile front room with an optional transom and second entrance from the foyer may be used as a living room or third bedroom.

DESIGN BY
©Design Basics, Inc.

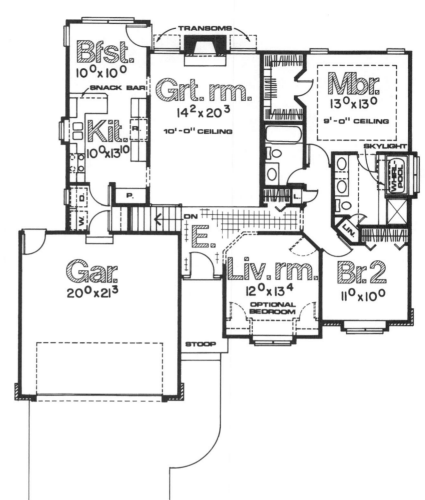

DESIGN HPU040075

Square Footage: 1,310
Width: 49'-10" Depth: 40'-6"

DESIGN BY
©Larry E. Belk Designs

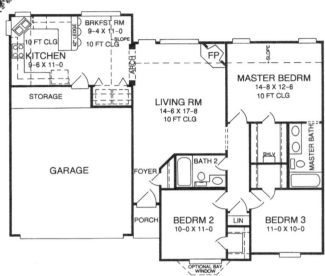

This charming plan is perfect for families just starting out or for the empty-nester looking to pare down. Every room is designed for maximum livability, from the living room with a corner fireplace to the efficient kitchen with a snack bar and hidden washer and dryer. The master bedroom is fashioned with a dual-vanity bath and a walk-in closet equipped with shelves. Two additional bedrooms each have a walk-in closet and share a hall bath. Please specify crawlspace or slab foundation when ordering.

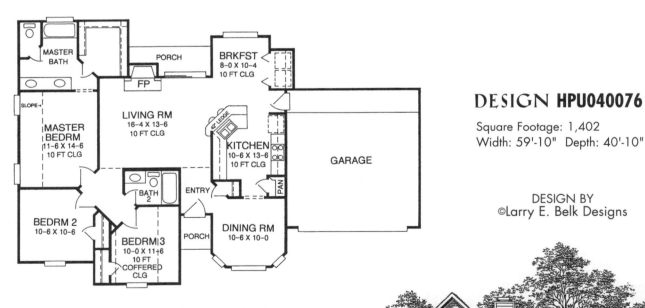

DESIGN HPU040076

Square Footage: 1,402
Width: 59'-10" Depth: 40'-10"

DESIGN BY
©Larry E. Belk Designs

Fine detailing and multiple rooflines give this home plenty of curb appeal. A large living room with a fireplace is the focal point for this lovely home. The dining room and sunny breakfast room provide complementary eating areas. The master bedroom features a large walk-in closet and a bath with a combination whirlpool tub and shower. Two additional bedrooms and a full hall bath complete this livable plan. Please specify crawlspace or slab foundation when ordering.

DESIGN HPU040077

Square Footage: 1,453
Width: 48'-8" Depth: 44'-0"

With two gables, a hipped roof and a covered front porch, this petite three-bedroom home is sure to please. A spacious great room features a warming fireplace flanked by transom windows. In the kitchen, an island counter is available for added space to prepare meals. A large breakfast area sits adjacent to this room. Two secondary bedrooms share a full bath as well as easy access to the laundry room. The master bedroom offers a walk-in closet and a private bath. Note the option for a second closet in this bedroom.

DESIGN BY
©Design Basics, Inc.

Optional Master Bedroom

Mbr.
14⁰ x 12⁰

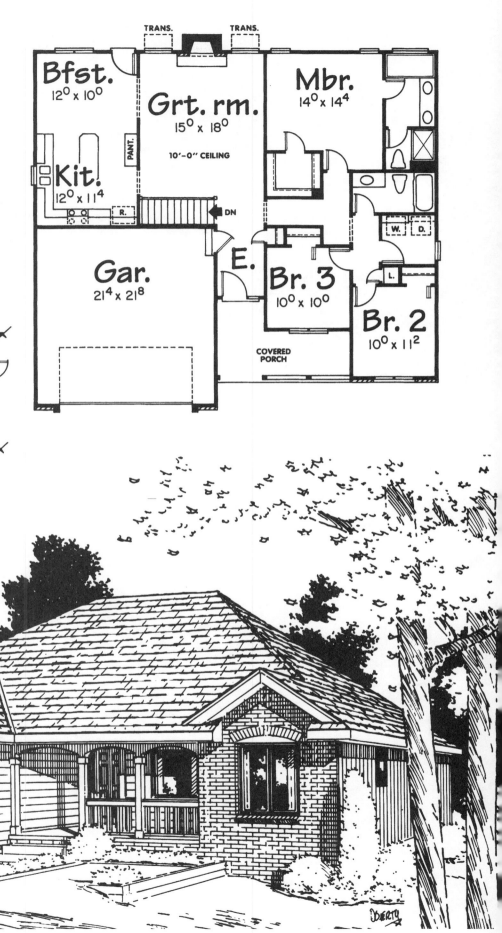

TRANS.   TRANS.

Bfst.
12⁰ x 10⁰

Grt. rm.
15⁰ x 18⁰

10'-0" CEILING

Mbr.
14⁰ x 14⁴

PANT.

Kit.
12⁰ x 11⁴

R.

DN

W.   D.

Gar.
21⁴ x 21⁸

E.

Br. 3
10⁰ x 10⁰

L.

COVERED
PORCH

Br. 2
10⁰ x 11²

DESIGN HPU040078

Square Footage: 1,434
Width: 70'-0" Depth: 44'-0"

With the exterior facade of a large elegant home, this super-efficient design creates not only an exterior that looks much larger than it is, but the room sizes are impressive too! The isolated and spacious master suite provides a grand bath and a walk-in closet. The secondary bedrooms are located at the far right of the plan; each features walk-in closets, and they share a full hall bath. The living room opens to porches via French doors to the front and back. The kitchen is the heart of the home and includes a pantry. Please specify crawlspace or slab foundation when ordering.

DESIGN BY
©Breland & Farmer Designers, Inc.

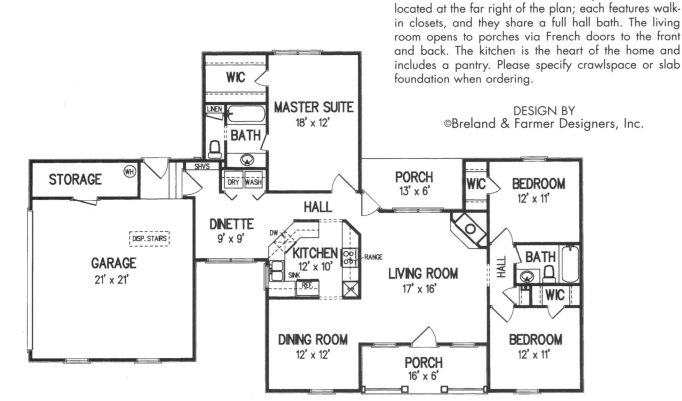

SPECIAL DETAILS

Smart designs that shine with brilliant benefits

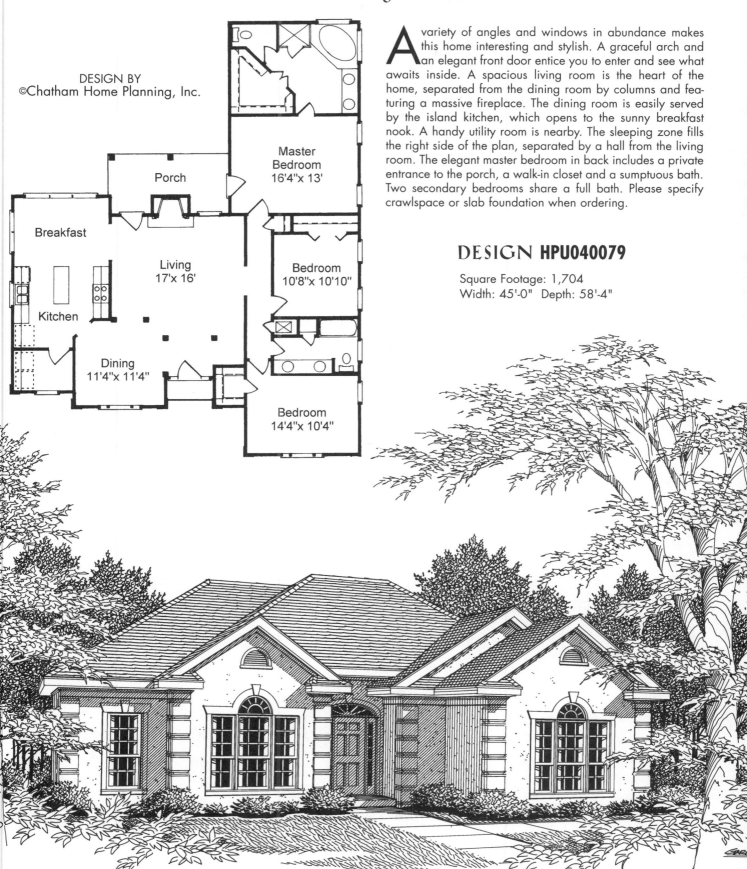

DESIGN BY
©Chatham Home Planning, Inc.

Master Bedroom
16'4"x 13'

Porch

Breakfast

Kitchen

Living
17'x 16'

Bedroom
10'8"x 10'10"

Dining
11'4"x 11'4"

Bedroom
14'4"x 10'4"

A variety of angles and windows in abundance makes this home interesting and stylish. A graceful arch and an elegant front door entice you to enter and see what awaits inside. A spacious living room is the heart of the home, separated from the dining room by columns and featuring a massive fireplace. The dining room is easily served by the island kitchen, which opens to the sunny breakfast nook. A handy utility room is nearby. The sleeping zone fills the right side of the plan, separated by a hall from the living room. The elegant master bedroom in back includes a private entrance to the porch, a walk-in closet and a sumptuous bath. Two secondary bedrooms share a full bath. Please specify crawlspace or slab foundation when ordering.

DESIGN HPU040079

Square Footage: 1,704
Width: 45'-0" Depth: 58'-4"

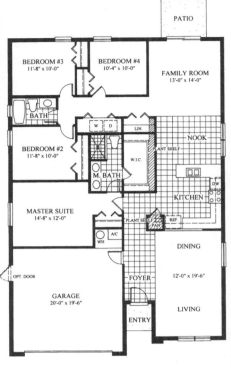

The unique exterior of this home presents a volume entry with a transom. The floor plan is designed in a symmetrical pattern, arranged around a center hall. The formal areas, the kitchen, the breakfast nook and the family room are aligned along the right side of the plan. A patio to the rear of the plan is accessed through a sliding glass door in the family room. Or, if you choose, install the fireplace instead. Three family bedrooms share a full hall bath, while the master suite enjoys its own private bath with a walk-in closet.

DESIGN HPU040080

Square Footage: 1,855
Width: 39'-4" Depth: 59'-4"

Optional
Master Bath

DESIGN BY
©Lucia Custom Home Designers, Inc.

Though only just over 1,600 square feet, the choices you have with this design are astounding. The master bedroom suite includes optional sliding glass doors and a private bath configuration. At the heart of all these spaces is a U-shaped kitchen with an adjoining breakfast nook. A laundry room and a hall bath separate the two family bedrooms. A door to the side yard is optional in the garage.

DESIGN HPU040081

Square Footage: 1,666
Width: 39'-4" Depth: 56'-8"

DESIGN BY
©Lucia Custom Home Designers, Inc.

Optional
Master Bath

MASTER SUITE
12 × 16

BATH

LIN

SHWR

STO STO

CLOS

SHELVES

STORAGE

UTILITY

WASH DRY A/C

GARAGE
20 × 22

PORCH

KITCHEN
11 × 11

D/W

REFG

RNG

F/P

DINING
12 × 14

DIVIDER

PORCH

NOOK
10 × 12

CLOS

CLO

LIVING RM
18 × 15

TRAY CEILING

BED RM
11 × 12

BATH

STO

CLOS

BED RM
11 × 12

DESIGN BY
©Vaughn A. Lauban Designs

DESIGN HPU040082

Square Footage: 1,646
Width: 59'-0" Depth: 48'-0"

This design embraces French accents with a Southern feel. Corner quoins, a covered porch and a hipped roof define elegance. The open living room enjoys a tray ceiling and easy flow to the breakfast nook and kitchen. A fireplace is perfect for cozy evenings with guests. The dining room is just a few steps from the super-efficient kitchen. Two family bedrooms share a full bath and are split to the right. The master suite is secluded to the left and is pampered with a private bath and walk-in closet. A two-car garage completes this design.

DESIGN HPU040083

Square Footage: 1,920
Width: 38'-10" Depth: 74'-4"

The entry courtyard creates an impressive introduction to this lovely European-style home. Double doors lead to the foyer, which opens through decorative columns to the formal dining room. A view of the enchanting rear garden and fountain enhances the heart of the home and invites guests to linger. Casual living space includes a breakfast nook with a view of the rear courtyard, and a family room with a fireplace and access to a private porch. A secluded master bedroom offers a whirlpool tub.

DESIGN BY
©Andy McDonald Design Group

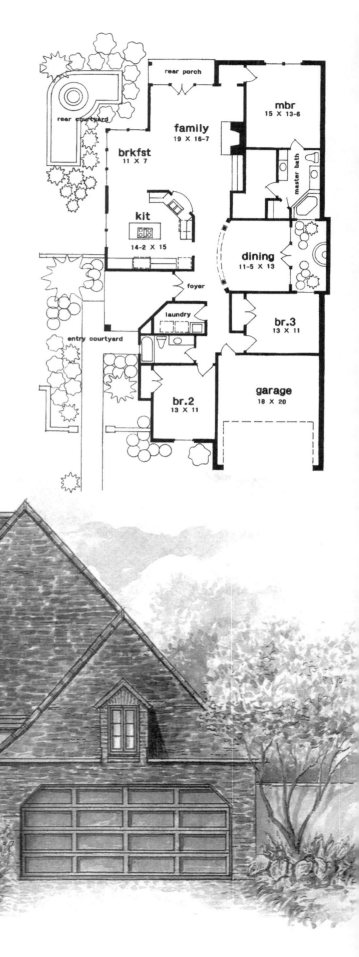

DESIGN HPU040084

Square Footage: 1,804
Width: 49'-10" Depth: 74'-9"

Extraordinary rooflines complement this brick-and-stucco home. Through the foyer, the family room enjoys a central position with a fireplace—the warm spot in the house. The family room provides rear views through double doors and windows. The dining area is conveniently located near the island kitchen and adjoining breakfast room, which is surrounded by natural light and accesses the rear covered porch. Two family bedrooms can be found to the front right of the plan and share a full bath. The master bedroom features a walk-in closet, compartmented toilet and accommodating bath. A two-car garage completes this design.

DESIGN BY
©Andy McDonald Design Group

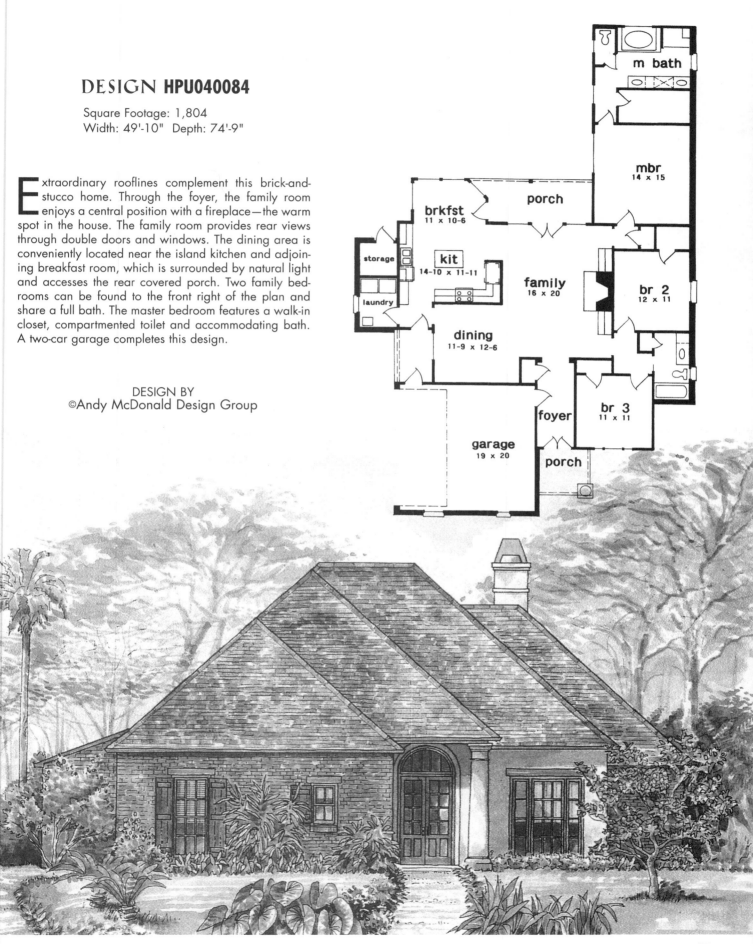

m bath

mbr
14 x 15

porch

brkfst
11 x 10-6

storage

kit
14-10 x 11-11

family
16 x 20

br 2
12 x 11

laundry

dining
11-9 x 12-6

foyer

br 3
11 x 11

garage
19 x 20

porch

Floor plan labels:

Master Bedroom 18⁰·13⁸

Covered Patio 20⁴·14⁰

w.i.c.

M.Bath

Dining 29⁴·19⁴

Great Room

Kitchen

ref

Foyer

Nook 9⁰·9⁴

Bedroom #3 /Den 12⁰·11⁴

Bath #2

Entry

Bath #3

Bedroom #2 12⁰·14⁴

Utility

a/c

Garage

DESIGN HPU040085

Square Footage: 1,992
Width: 44'-0" Depth: 92'-0"

A bit of the Southwest and a tad of the Mediterranean is offered in this lush design. A tiled roof and unique windows make this facade truly attractive. Inside, the tiled foyer opens to an open layout. The great room flows into the dining room, and both enjoy the corner fireplace, rear-porch access through double French doors, and side views. The kitchen boasts an island work center and a breakfast nook surrounded by windows. Two bedrooms—or make one a den—can be found to the left. Bedroom 2 enjoys a private bath. The master bedroom opens up to the rear patio through French doors and pampers with a luxurious bath and walk-in closet.

DESIGN BY
©Lucia Custom Home Designers, Inc.

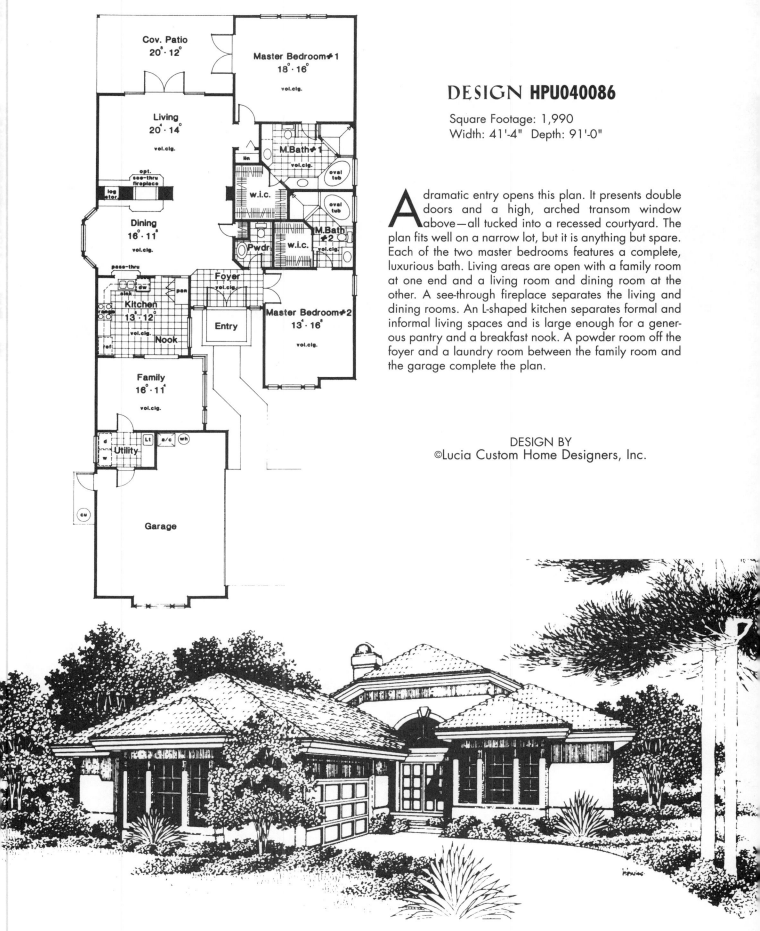

Cov. Patio
20⁰·12⁰

Master Bedroom≠1
18⁰·16⁰
vol.clg.

Living
20⁴·14⁰
vol.clg.

M.Bath≠1
vol.clg.

oval tub

opt.
see-thru
fireplace

log
tor.

w.i.c.

oval tub

Dining
16⁰·11⁰
vol.clg.

M.Bath
≠2

pass-thru

Pwdr.

w.i.c.

Foyer
vol.clg.

Kitchen
13⁰·12⁰

sink

dw

pan

vol.clg.

Nook

Entry

Master Bedroom≠2
13⁴·16⁰
vol.clg.

range

ref.

Family
16⁰·11⁴
vol.clg.

d

Lt

a/c

wh

Utility

w

cu

Garage

DESIGN **HPU040086**

Square Footage: 1,990
Width: 41'-4"   Depth: 91'-0"

A dramatic entry opens this plan. It presents double doors and a high, arched transom window above—all tucked into a recessed courtyard. The plan fits well on a narrow lot, but it is anything but spare. Each of the two master bedrooms features a complete, luxurious bath. Living areas are open with a family room at one end and a living room and dining room at the other. A see-through fireplace separates the living and dining rooms. An L-shaped kitchen separates formal and informal living spaces and is large enough for a generous pantry and a breakfast nook. A powder room off the foyer and a laundry room between the family room and the garage complete the plan.

DESIGN BY
©Lucia Custom Home Designers, Inc.

DESIGN BY
©Chatham Home Planning, Inc.

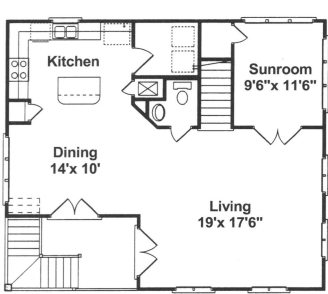

Kitchen

Sunroom
9'6"x 11'6"

Dining
14'x 10'

Living
19'x 17'6"

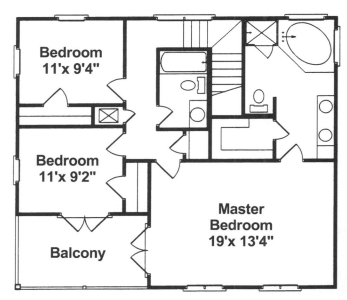

Bedroom
11'x 9'4"

Bedroom
11'x 9'2"

Master Bedroom
19'x 13'4"

Balcony

DESIGN **HPU040087**

First Floor: 907 square feet
Second Floor: 872 square feet
Total: 1,779 square feet
Width: 34'-0" Depth: 30'-0"

Two stories and still up on a pier foundation! A covered front porch leads to two sets of French doors—one to the spacious living room and one to the dining area. An L-shaped kitchen features a work island, a nearby utility room and plenty of counter and cabinet space. A sun room finishes off this floor with class. Upstairs, the sleeping zone consists of two family bedrooms—one with access to a balcony—a full bath and a master bedroom. Here, the homeowner will surely be pleased with a walk-in closet, a corner tub and a separate shower, as well as balcony access.

DESIGN BY
©Chatham Home Planning, Inc.

Kitchen

Living
14'2"x 19'6"

Dining
11'4"x 12'

Porch

Bedroom
11'x 10'

Bedroom
10'6"x 10'6"

Study
9'x 7'3"

Master Bedroom
13'x 14'

Balcony

With a pier foundation, this two-story home is perfect for an oceanfront lot. The main level consists of an open living area that flows into the dining area adjacent to the kitchen. Here, a walk-in pantry and plenty of counter and cabinet space will please the gourmet of the family. A full bath and a utility room complete this floor. Upstairs, the sleeping zone is complete with two family bedrooms sharing a linen closet and a full hall bath, as well as a deluxe master bedroom. Features here include a private balcony, a walk-in closet and a dual-vanity bath.

DESIGN HPU040088

First Floor: 912 square feet
Second Floor: 831 square feet
Total: 1,743 square feet
Width: 34'-0" Depth: 32'-0"

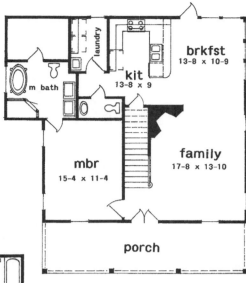

This adorable abode could serve as a vacation cottage, guest house, starter home or in-law quarters. The side-gabled design allows for a front porch with a "down-South" feel. Despite the small size, this home is packed with all the necessities. The first-floor master bedroom has a large bathroom—with a clawfoot tub!—and a walk-in closet and is ideal for older guests or family members. An open, functional floor plan includes a powder room, a kitchen/breakfast nook area and a family room with a corner fireplace. Upstairs, two additional bedrooms share a bath. One could be used as a home office.

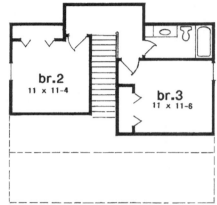

DESIGN HPU040090

First Floor: 1,050 square feet
Second Floor: 458 square feet
Total: 1,508 square feet
Width: 35'-6" Depth: 39'-9"

DESIGN BY
©Andy McDonald Design Group

Run up a flight of stairs to an attractive four-bedroom home! With a traditional flavor, this fine pier design is sure to please. The living room features a fireplace and easy access to the L-shaped kitchen. Here, a work island makes meal preparation a breeze. Two family bedrooms share a full bath and access to the laundry facilities. Upstairs, a third bedroom offers a private bath and two walk-in closets. The master suite is complete with a pampering bath, two walk-in closets and a large private balcony.

DESIGN BY
©Chatham Home Planning, Inc.

DESIGN HPU040089

First Floor: 1,056 square feet
Second Floor: 807 square feet
Total: 1,863 square feet
Width: 33'-0" Depth: 37'-0"

DESIGN HPU040091

First Floor: 1,189 square feet
Second Floor: 575 square feet
Total: 1,764 square feet
Width: 46'-0" Depth: 44'-6"

L

An abundance of porches and a deck encourage year-round indoor/outdoor relationships in this classic two-story home. The spacious great room, with its cozy fireplace, and the adjacent dining room both offer access to the screened porch/deck area through French doors. The private master suite accesses both front and rear porches and leads into a relaxing private bath complete with dual vanities and a walk-in closet. An additional family bedroom and a loft/bedroom are also available.

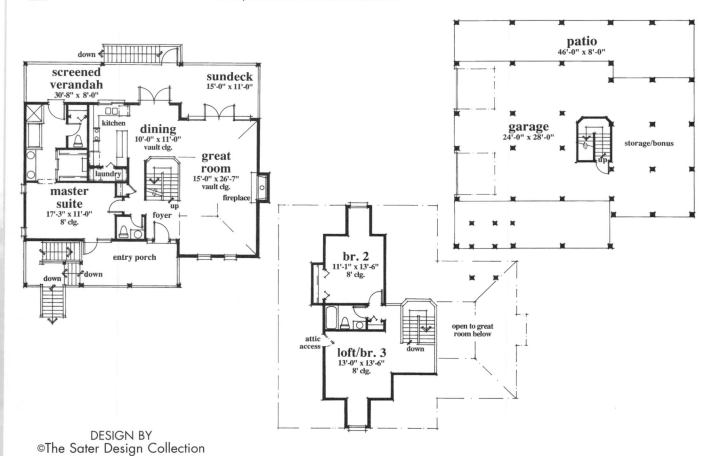

DESIGN HPU040092

First Floor: 1,007 square feet
Second Floor: 869 square feet
Total: 1,876 square feet
Width: 43'-8" Depth: 53'-6"

An enchanting center gable announces a graceful, honest architecture that's at home with the easygoing nature of this coastal design. A columned porch and romantic fretwork lend balance and proportion outside. The great room, featuring double doors, arches, a built-in entertainment center and a warming fireplace, is the heart of this home. The kitchen is adjoined to the dining room (with French doors) by an eating bar and provides a walk-in pantry. The foyer stairs lead to a master suite with a spacious bedroom and a lavish private bath.

DESIGN BY
©The Sater Design Collection

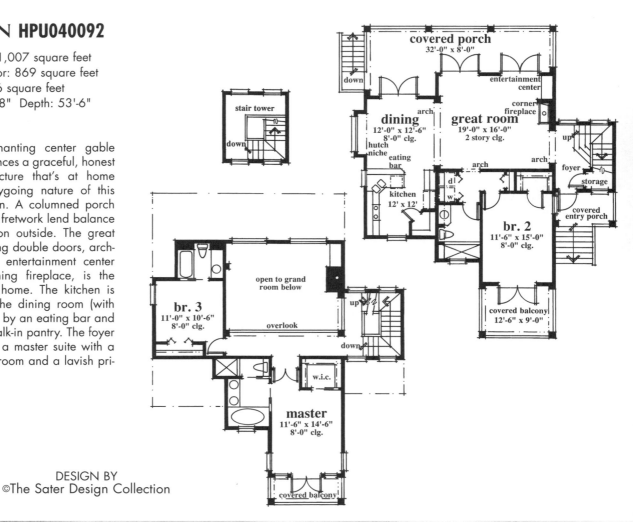

This cozy retreat offers bright and airy living areas and covered porches. Built-ins and a media niche frame the great-room fireplace. Four sets of French doors in the great room access the covered wraparound porch. The gourmet kitchen shares an eating bar with the great room and is open to the dining room through a hallway with arches. A first-floor bedroom with a built-in desk easily accesses the full hall bath. The second floor contains an observation deck, the master suite with a grand private bath and walk-in closet, plus a third bedroom with a private bath and window seat.

DESIGN HPU040093

First Floor: 1,046 square feet
Second Floor: 638 square feet
Total: 1,684 square feet
Width: 25'-0"   Depth: 65'-6"

DESIGN BY
©The Sater Design Collection

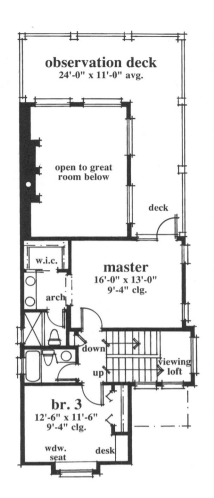

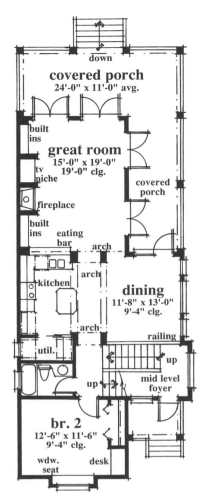

DESIGN HPU040094

First Floor: 938 square feet
Second Floor: 1,034 square feet
Total: 1,972 square feet
Width: 30'-0" Depth: 74'-0"

The wide steps of this inviting farmhouse greet all who approach with a warm welcome. Encircled by sidelights and a transom, the front door leads to an extra-spacious great room. Just beyond, a secluded rear porch also touches the breakfast room, providing a convenient transition to the backyard. Any accomplished cook would deeply appreciate the long angled kitchen with its abundant counter space and storage capabilities. A covered cooking porch will protect those who want to grill outdoors despite inclement weather conditions. In the bedroom area above, the master suite has an interesting nook for either a desk or a sitting area. A garden tub is well placed away from the double vanities, to give the couple who share the bath a spacious area in which to dress. All bedrooms contain large walk-in closets. Each bedroom enjoys its own long, private vanity area.

DESIGN BY
©Authentic Historical Designs, Inc.

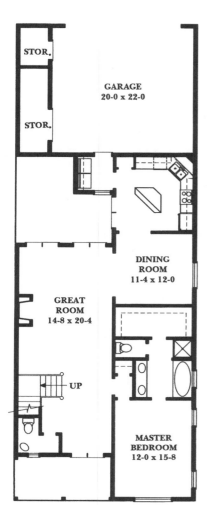

STOR.

STOR.

GARAGE
20-0 x 22-0

DINING
ROOM
11-4 x 12-0

GREAT
ROOM
14-8 x 20-4

UP

MASTER
BEDROOM
12-0 x 15-8

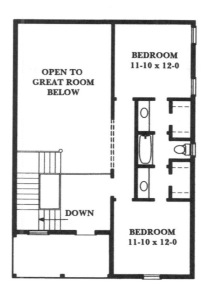

OPEN TO
GREAT ROOM
BELOW

BEDROOM
11-10 x 12-0

DOWN

BEDROOM
11-10 x 12-0

DESIGN HPU040095

First Floor: 1,270 square feet
Second Floor: 630 square feet
Total: 1,900 square feet
Width: 28'-0" Depth: 76'-0"

DESIGN BY
©Authentic Historical Designs, Inc.

Possessing an irresistible charm, this electric French design will elicit accolades from all who pass by. The double front porch provides a shady spot for a cool drink and a moment of relaxation. A spacious foyer, ample enough for a cherished antique, greets those who enter. Just beyond, the great room with its soaring ceiling gives additional flair to this open and inviting plan. An open-railed stairwell leads to a dramatic landing that overlooks the great room below. Access the second-floor porch easily from this landing. Two spacious bedrooms share a compartmented bath; each has a separate vanity and a walk-in closet.

DESIGN HPU040096

First Floor: 1,340 square feet
Second Floor: 651 square feet
Total: 1,991 square feet
Width: 30'-0" Depth: 74'-0"

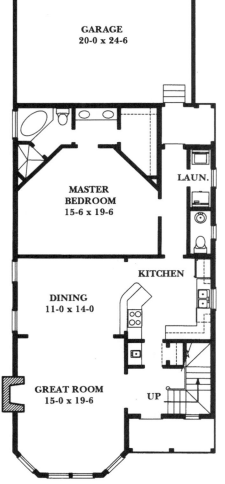

GARAGE
20-0 x 24-6

LAUN.

MASTER BEDROOM
15-6 x 19-6

KITCHEN

DINING
11-0 x 14-0

GREAT ROOM
15-0 x 19-6

UP

This pleasing Victorian design, with its double-stacked front bay, will meet your requirements. A multitude of windows admits the sun into this glittering home, drenching the house with light. The handsome great room showcases an old-fashioned fireplace and leads into a semi-formal dining room. The kitchen is partially separated from the dining room by a raised breakfast bar. A separate wet bar will assist in entertaining and could open to the great room, if desired. The first-floor master bedroom, with its intriguing angles, repeats the bays on the front facade of the house. A step-in laundry room is conveniently located near the master bedroom and is also in close proximity to the kitchen. A graceful, open stairway rises to the well-apportioned family bedrooms above.

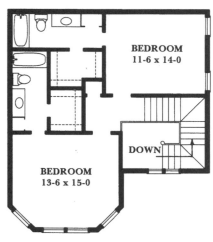

BEDROOM
11-6 x 14-0

DOWN

BEDROOM
13-6 x 15-0

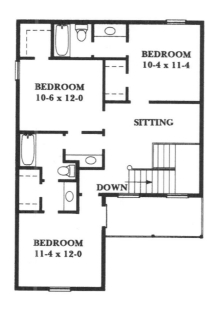

DESIGN HPU040097

First Floor: 978 square feet
Second Floor: 820 square feet
Total: 1,798 square feet
Width: 29'-0" Depth: 75'-0"

GARAGE
21-6 x 25-0

DINING

GREAT
ROOM
13-8 x 17-6

UP

MASTER
BEDROOM
12-0 x 13-8

BEDROOM
10-4 x 11-4

BEDROOM
10-6 x 12-0

SITTING

DOWN

BEDROOM
11-4 x 12-0

DESIGN BY
©Authentic Historical Designs, Inc.

The clapboard siding and double-stacked porches of this simple Victorian residence give warmth and appeal to this inviting design. Fish-scale shingles provide additional architectural ornamentation. Inside, an open-railed stairway rises from the foyer. The first-floor master suite is located off a vestibule adjacent to the foyer, providing privacy from family activities. The master suite has a roomy bath and a large walk-in closet. The L-shaped kitchen makes space for a dining table, which will be the center of family activities. The great room, with a wood-burning fireplace, opens to a large covered porch. Above, the open stairs rise to a sitting area, perfect for a computer or play center. Each of the three ample family bedrooms has a walk-in closet. Additionally, each bedroom also accesses to its own private vanity. One of the bedrooms opens directly to the second-floor porch; this bedroom could also serve as a second-floor den, if desired.

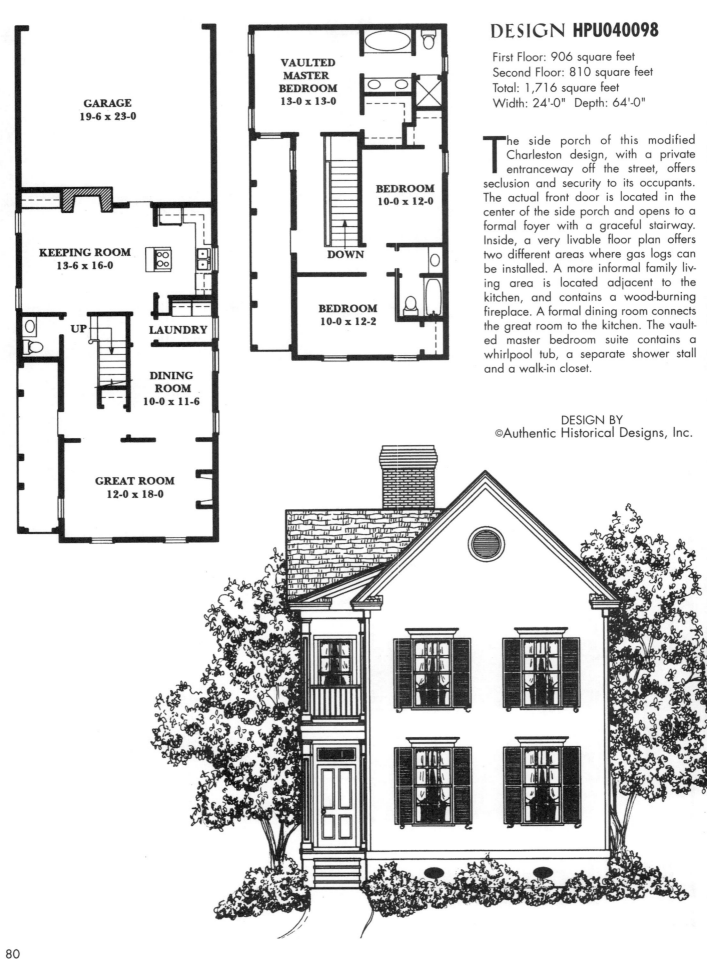

GARAGE
19-6 x 23-0

KEEPING ROOM
13-6 x 16-0

UP

LAUNDRY

DINING ROOM
10-0 x 11-6

GREAT ROOM
12-0 x 18-0

VAULTED MASTER BEDROOM
13-0 x 13-0

BEDROOM
10-0 x 12-0

DOWN

BEDROOM
10-0 x 12-2

DESIGN HPU040098

First Floor: 906 square feet
Second Floor: 810 square feet
Total: 1,716 square feet
Width: 24'-0" Depth: 64'-0"

The side porch of this modified Charleston design, with a private entranceway off the street, offers seclusion and security to its occupants. The actual front door is located in the center of the side porch and opens to a formal foyer with a graceful stairway. Inside, a very livable floor plan offers two different areas where gas logs can be installed. A more informal family living area is located adjacent to the kitchen, and contains a wood-burning fireplace. A formal dining room connects the great room to the kitchen. The vaulted master bedroom suite contains a whirlpool tub, a separate shower stall and a walk-in closet.

DESIGN BY
©Authentic Historical Designs, Inc.

DESIGN HPU040099

First Floor: 900 square feet
Second Floor: 1,081 square feet
Total: 1,981 square feet
Width: 26'-0" Depth: 66'-0"

There is not an area in this country where this classic Greek Revival home would not feel instantly at home. A friendly front-facing gable with an elegant spider-web window accentuates the openness of the front facade. The double tier of galleries proclaims a house that will play a predominant role in a vibrant urban streetscape. Transom-topped windows lend additional grandeur to the ample great room. The bayed dining room can be handled with as much or as little formality as the owners desire. An adjacent breakfast bar provides a more casual setting for sandwiches and snacks. Conveniently located, a covered porch is readily accessible for a summer barbecue. The large walk-in laundry has a separate sink and pantry for the cook who likes to stock up on both staples and gourmet items. The sleeping quarters reside upstairs.

DESIGN BY
©Authentic Historical Designs, Inc.

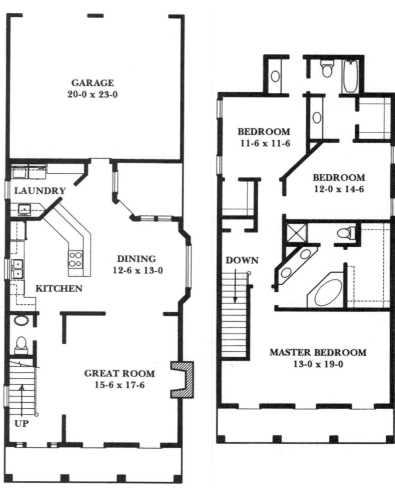

GARAGE
20-0 x 23-0

LAUNDRY

DINING
12-6 x 13-0

KITCHEN

GREAT ROOM
15-6 x 17-6

UP

BEDROOM
11-6 x 11-6

BEDROOM
12-0 x 14-6

DOWN

MASTER BEDROOM
13-0 x 19-0

DESIGN HPU040101

First Floor: 802 square feet
Second Floor: 802 square feet
Total: 1,604 square feet
Width: 28'-0" Depth: 32'-0"

Here's a sophisticated country design with a few gently European details and a wrap-around porch. A stylish interior starts with a separate entrance hall with a closet. The breakfast nook features a sitting area, brightened by windows and served by an L-shaped kitchen. Sleeping quarters include a master bedroom with a walk-in closet, plus two additional bedrooms. The second-floor bath has a corner tub and a separate shower. This home is designed with a basement foundation.

DESIGN BY
©Drummond Designs, Inc.

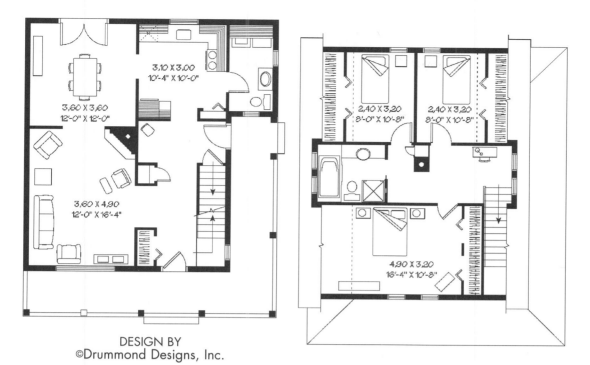

DESIGN BY
©Drummond Designs, Inc.

Quaint details give this country home a lemonade and porch swing feel. The foyer leads to the living room with a corner fireplace. Just steps away is the dining room with double French doors to the rear yard. The kitchen provides plenty of space to prepare for large or intimate parties. The laundry room and a half-bath are placed near the kitchen for making chores easier. Upstairs, the master bedroom features plenty of closet space. Across the hall, two secondary bedrooms and a loft round out the upper level. This home is designed with a basement foundation.

DESIGN HPU040102

First Floor: 781 square feet
Second Floor: 720 square feet
Total: 1,501 square feet
Width: 29'-4" Depth: 30'-0"

Farmhouse fresh with a touch of Victorian style best describes this charming home. A covered front porch wraps around the dining room's bay window and leads the way to the entrance. To the right of the entry is a living room that features a wet bar and a warming fireplace. At the rear of the plan, an L-shaped kitchen is equipped with an island cooktop, making meal preparation a breeze. Casual meals can be enjoyed in a dining area that which merges with the kitchen and accesses the rear patio. A powder room and utility room complete the first floor. Sleeping quarters contained on the second floor include a relaxing master suite with a large walk-in closet, two family bedrooms and a connecting bath.

DESIGN HPU040103

First Floor: 1,082 square feet
Second Floor: 838 square feet
Total: 1,920 square feet
Width: 66'-10" Depth: 29'-5"

DESIGN BY
©Fillmore Design Group

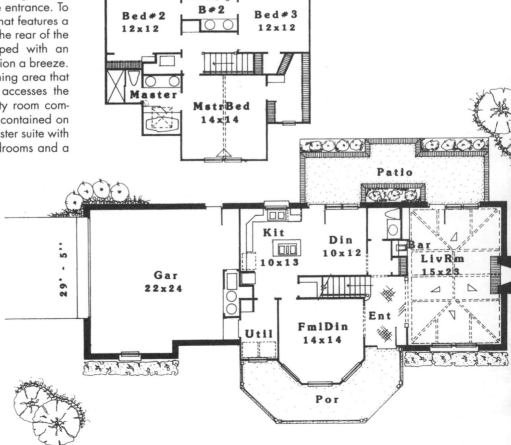

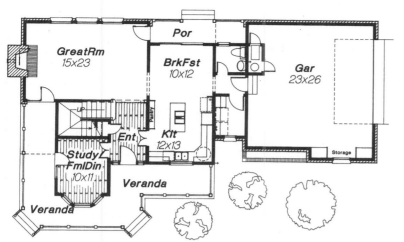

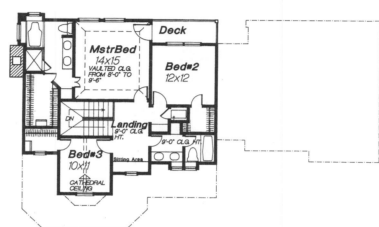

F ish-scale shingles, a weather vane, a cupola and a covered wraparound veranda complete with Victorian touches make this farmhouse a truly memorable sight. The great room includes a fireplace for those chilly evenings and accesses the porch—perfect for warmer nights. The island kitchen and breakfast area access the great room, entertainment area and a passage to the garage. All three bedrooms reside on the second floor. The master suite has a vaulted ceiling, private bath, walk-in closet and access to a private deck. A unique sitting area is located on the landing between Bedrooms 2 and 3. A full hall bath with dual vanities is also shared between the two bedrooms.

DESIGN HPU040104

First Floor: 1,024 square feet
Second Floor: 904 square feet
Total: 1,928 square feet
Width: 65'-0" Depth: 35'-5"

DESIGN BY
©Fillmore Design Group

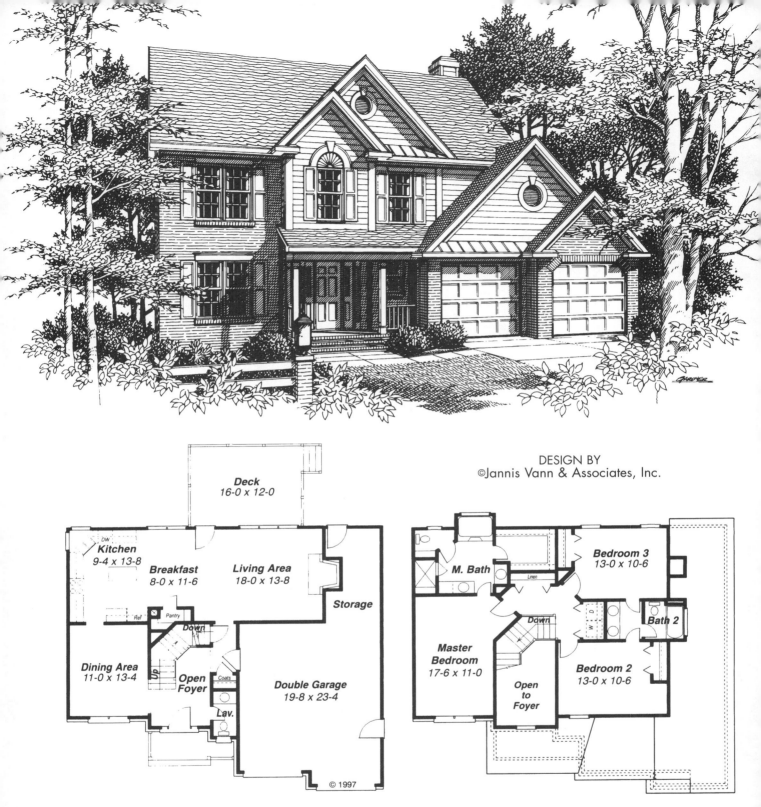

Deck
16-0 x 12-0

DESIGN BY
©Jannis Vann & Associates, Inc.

Kitchen
9-4 x 13-8

Breakfast
8-0 x 11-6

Living Area
18-0 x 13-8

Storage

Ref.

Pantry

Down

Dining Area
11-0 x 13-4

Open Foyer

Coats

Lav.

Double Garage
19-8 x 23-4

© 1997

M. Bath

Linen

Bedroom 3
13-0 x 10-6

Down

W D

Bath 2

Master Bedroom
17-6 x 11-0

Open to Foyer

Bedroom 2
13-0 x 10-6

DESIGN HPU040105

First Floor: 869 square feet
Second Floor: 963 square feet
Total: 1,832 square feet
Width: 44'-0" Depth: 38'-0"

Under this quaint covered porch resides an inviting entry with sidelights and a six-panel door. Inside, the openness of the rear rooms—the living area, breakfast area and island kitchen—provide a feeling of spaciousness. The kitchen serves a formal dining room as well as the breakfast room. A rear sun deck is accessible from the main living area. Upstairs, secondary bedrooms share a vanity area that opens to a private toilet and tub room. A comfortable master suite offers a walk-in closet and a lavish bath with separate vanities.

The livability of this narrow home is great. Well worth mentioning is the veranda and the screened porch, which both highlight the relaxing outdoor design. The foyer directs traffic to the far rear of the home, where open living and dining rooms can be enjoyed. The U-shaped kitchen easily services both the dining room and the breakfast room. Three bedrooms reside on the second floor. The master suite features a private bath and walk-in closet. The third floor provides storage space.

DESIGN BY
©Home Planners

DESIGN HPU040106

First Floor: 911 square feet
Second Floor: 861 square feet
Total: 1,772 square feet
Attic: 884 square feet
Width: 38'-0" Depth: 52'-0"

L

Quote One®

Cost to build? See page 502
to order complete cost estimate
to build this house in your area!

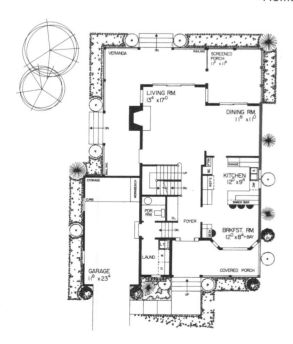

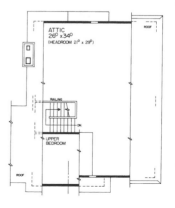

87

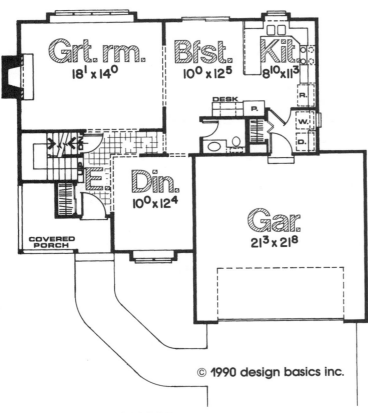

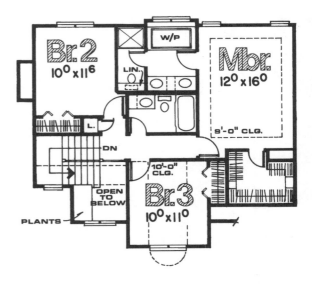

© 1990 design basics inc.

DESIGN HPU040107

First Floor: 891 square feet
Second Floor: 759 square feet
Total: 1,650 square feet
Width: 44'-0" Depth: 40'-0"

DESIGN BY
©Design Basics, Inc.

This modest-sized home provides a quaint covered front porch that opens to a two-story foyer. The formal dining room features a boxed window that can be seen from the entry. A fireplace in the great room adds warmth and coziness to the attached breakfast room and the well-planned kitchen. Sliding glass doors lead from the breakfast room to the rear yard. A washer and dryer reside in a nearby utility room, where a closet provides ample storage. A powder room is provided nearby for guests. Three bedrooms are on the second floor; one of these includes an arched window under a vaulted ceiling. The deluxe owners suite provides a large walk-in closet and a dressing area with a double vanity and a whirlpool tub.

DESIGN **HPU040108**

First Floor: 1,421 square feet
Second Floor: 578 square feet
Total: 1,999 square feet
Width: 52'-0" Depth: 47'-4"

DESIGN BY
©Design Basics, Inc.

Victorian details and a covered veranda lend a peaceful flavor to the elevation of this popular home. A volume entry hall views the formal dining room and luxurious great room. Imagine the comfort of relaxing in the great room, which features a volume ceiling and abundant windows. The kitchen and breakfast area includes a through-fireplace, snack bar, walk-in pantry and wrapping counters. The secluded master suite features a vaulted ceiling, luxurious dressing/bath area and corner whirlpool tub. Upstairs, the family sleeping quarters contain special amenities unique to each.

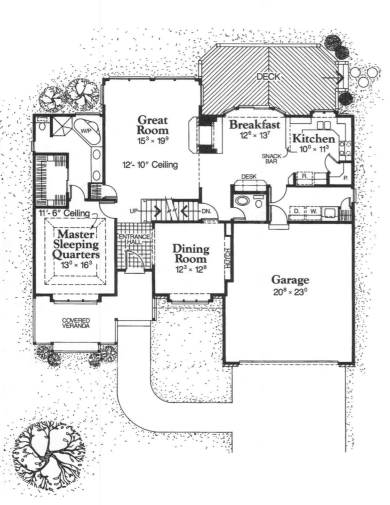

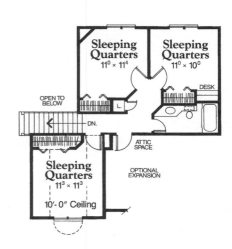

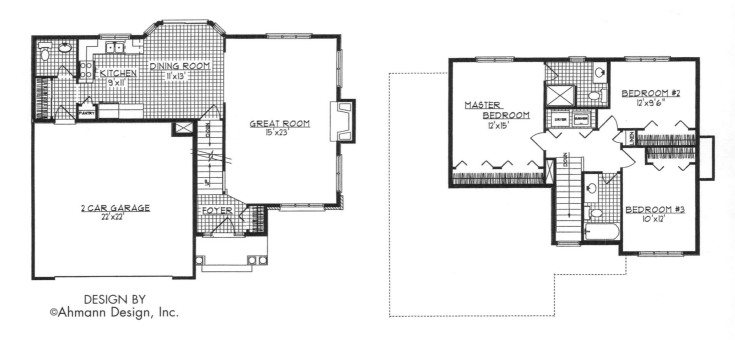

KITCHEN
9'x11'

DINING ROOM
11'x13'

PANTRY

GREAT ROOM
15'x23'

DOWN

2 CAR GARAGE
22'x22'

UP

FOYER

MASTER
BEDROOM
12'x15'

DRYER WASHER

BEDROOM #2
12'x9'6"

LINEN

DOWN

BEDROOM #3
10'x12'

DESIGN BY
©Ahmann Design, Inc.

DESIGN HPU040109

First Floor: 811 square feet
Second Floor: 741 square feet
Total: 1,552 square feet
Width: 44'-0"   Depth: 36'-0"

This two-story home features traditional details blended with a touch of contemporary flare. With three bedrooms on the second floor, this home becomes the perfect choice for a family's first home. Enjoy cozy evenings in the great room in front of the fireplace. The large windows on the front of this home allow plenty of sunlight to stream in, making this a warm and inviting place on most any day. The three bedrooms upstairs include a master bedroom with two closets.

DESIGN HPU040110

First Floor: 760 square feet
Second Floor: 742 square feet
Total: 1,502 square feet
Bonus Room: 283 square feet
Width: 39'-1"   Depth: 36'-9"

Made for a narrow footprint or in-fill lot, this home offers traditional lines with a farmhouse flavor. A welcoming porch ushers family and guests into the foyer. The large U-shaped kitchen is just to the right with a nearby laundry room for convenience. The dining area is found to the rear and enjoys rear views and porch access. The family room is perfect for a fireplace and entertaining guests or spending a quiet night at home. The master suite features a coffered ceiling, walk-in closets and a full bath. Two family suites share a full bath, and a bonus room is found just across the hall.

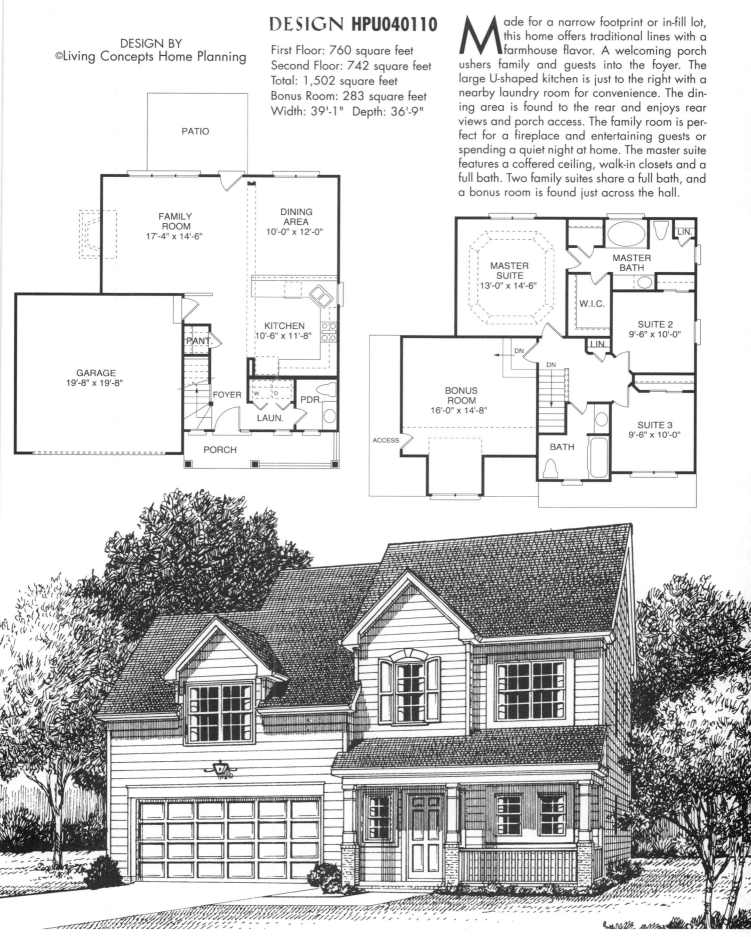

PATIO

FAMILY ROOM
17'-4" x 14'-6"

DINING AREA
10'-0" x 12'-0"

KITCHEN
10'-6" x 11'-8"

PANT.

GARAGE
19'-8" x 19'-8"

FOYER

W   D

LAUN.

PDR.

PORCH

MASTER SUITE
13'-0" x 14'-6"

MASTER BATH

LIN.

W.I.C.

SUITE 2
9'-6" x 10'-0"

DN

DN

LIN.

BONUS ROOM
16'-0" x 14'-8"

BATH

SUITE 3
9'-6" x 10'-0"

ACCESS

Garage
19'-2" X 23'-8"

Stor.

Cov.
Porch

Patio

Utility

Breakfast
13' X 8'-8"

Living
20' X 12'-6"

Bath

Ba.

Kitchen
11' X 10'-6"

Master
Bedroom
13' X 16'

Foyer

Dining
11' X 11'-6"

Porch

This perfectly charming country home features amenities to complement both quiet and active family lifestyles. The foyer opens to the warmth and hospitality of the expansive living area, complete with a fireplace and double doors leading to the rear patio. A convenient U-shaped kitchen easily serves both the formal dining room and the informal bay-windowed breakfast area. The main-floor master suite sports a plush private bath and a great walk-in closet. Two large bedrooms upstairs each have their own access to a uniquely designed full bath with twin lavatories—separated by a compartmented toilet and tub. Please specify crawlspace or slab foundation when ordering.

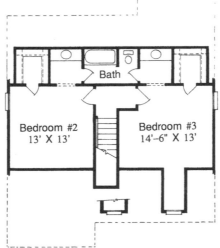

Bath

Bedroom #2
13' X 13'

Bedroom #3
14'-6" X 13'

DESIGN HPU040111

First Floor: 1,185 square feet
Second Floor: 617 square feet
Total: 1,802 square feet
Width: 36'-6" Depth: 69'-9"

DESIGN BY
©Chatham Home Planning, Inc.

DESIGN HPU040112

First Floor: 844 square feet
Second Floor: 875 square feet
Total: 1,719 square feet
Bonus Room: 242 square feet
Width: 45'-0" Depth: 37'-0"

DESIGN BY
©Living Concepts Home Planning

A Palladian window adds interest to the modified-gable roofline of this livable three-bedroom design. Columns and tall glass panels flank the covered entryway. A hall closet and a powder room line the foyer. The great room includes a warming fireplace, and the kitchen and the breakfast area with patio access sit across the back. The master suite with a deluxe private bath and walk-in closet, plus the two family bedrooms, resides on the second floor. Please specify crawlspace or slab foundation when ordering.

93

© 1998 Donald A. Gardner, Inc.

DESIGN HPU040114

Square Footage: 1,544
Bonus Room: 320 square feet
Width: 63'-0" Depth: 24'-6"

DESIGN BY
Donald A. Gardner Architects, Inc.

This home would look good in any neighborhood. From the covered front porch to the trio of gables, this design has a lot of appeal. Inside, the Craftsman styling continues in the manner of built-in shelves and a warming fireplace in the great room and plenty of windows to bring in the outdoors. The U-shaped kitchen offers easy access to the formal dining area. Expansion is possible with an optional bonus room, adding a second level. A tray ceiling adorns the owners suite and the owner will enjoy a His and Hers walk-in closets and a pampering bath complete with a twin-sink vanity and a separate shower and garden tub.

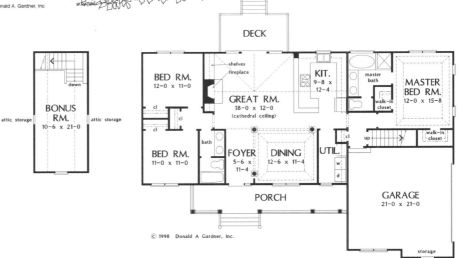

© 1998 Donald A Gardner, Inc.

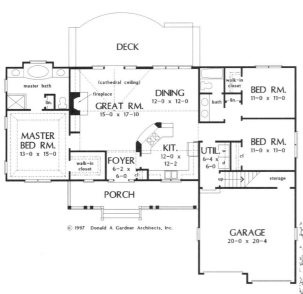

© 1997 Donald A Gardner Architects, Inc.

DESIGN HPU040113

Square Footage: 1,517
Bonus Room: 287 square feet
Width: 61'-4" Depth: 48'-6"

DESIGN BY
Donald A. Gardner Architects, Inc.

The foyer opens to a spacious great room with a fireplace and a cathedral ceiling in this lovely traditional home. Sliding doors open to a rear deck from the great room, posing a warm welcome to enjoy the outdoors. The U-shaped kitchen features an angled peninsula counter with a cooktop. A private hall leads to the family sleeping quarters, which includes two bedrooms and a full bath with a double-bowl lavatory. On the other side of the house, the master bedroom enjoys a tray ceiling and spacious bath. Sizable bonus space above the garage provides a skylight.

© 1997 Donald A. Gardner Architects, Inc.

94

© 1994 Donald A. Gardner Architects, Inc.

The intricate window treatment and stately columns give this home magnificent curb appeal. Inside, the columns continue from the foyer into the spacious great room. A fireplace is flanked by windows with a view to the rear deck and the spa. The great room opens to the large island kitchen and the formal dining room. The master suite is to the left of the foyer. The remaining bedrooms, a shared full bath and a conveniently placed utility room are located in the right wing of the house.

DESIGN HPU040115

Square Footage: 1,537
Width: 59'-2" Depth: 55'-0"

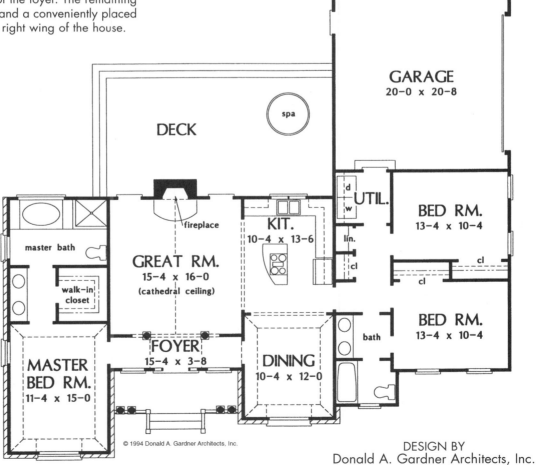

© 1994 Donald A. Gardner Architects, Inc.

DESIGN BY
Donald A. Gardner Architects, Inc.

95

DESIGN HPU040116

First Floor: 1,330 square feet
Second Floor: 496 square feet
Total: 1,826 square feet
Width: 48'-0" Depth: 54'-10"

DESIGN BY
©Fillmore Design Group

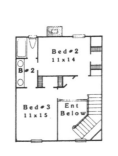

A brick exterior with wooden lap-sided gable accents proves that tradition and custom design blend nicely in this unique home. A covered porch with old-fashioned woodwork precedes an entry that offers a view of the stairs and balcony above. The first floor features a beautiful formal dining room with cedar posts and an enormous living room with a brick fireplace flanked by tall windows. The split sleeping arrangement locates the two family bedrooms upstairs, away from the secluded master bedroom downstairs.

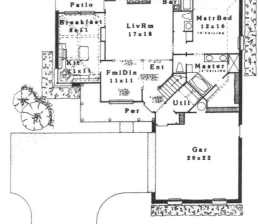

Twin dormers and double gables adorn the exterior of this pleasing three-bedroom home. The foyer opens to the formal dining area and arches leading to the great room, which offers a warming corner fireplace. Add the optional greenhouse to the kitchen-sink window for a beautiful glass display or herb garden location. Keep household records and dry goods well organized with the desk and pantry room just off the galley kitchen. The vaulted breakfast room is brightened by three lovely windows. A lovely master retreat features a whirlpool tub, separate shower and knee-space vanity. Two additional bedrooms share a full bath. Please specify crawlspace or slab foundation when ordering.

DESIGN BY
©Larry E. Belk Designs

DESIGN HPU040117

Square Footage: 1,725
Width: 56'-4" Depth: 72'-8"

DESIGN HPU040118

Square Footage: 1,654
Width: 54'-10" Depth: 69'-10"

Twin dormers perch above a welcoming covered front porch in this three-bedroom home. Inside, a formal dining room on the right is defined by pillars, while the spacious great room lies directly ahead. This room is enhanced by a fireplace, plenty of windows, access to the rear yard, and a forty-two-inch ledge looking into the angular kitchen. Nearby, a bayed breakfast room awaits casual mealtimes. The sleeping zone consists of two family bedrooms sharing a full hall bath and a luxurious master bedroom suite with a huge walk-in closet and a sumptuous private bath. Please specify crawlspace or slab foundation when ordering.

DESIGN BY
©Larry E. Belk Designs

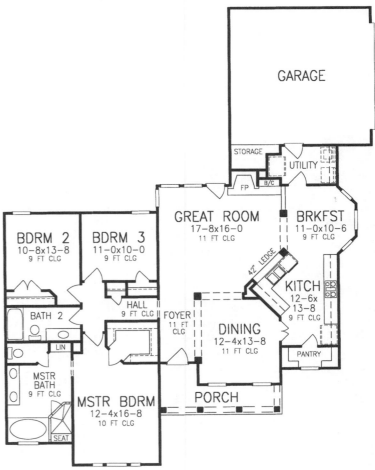

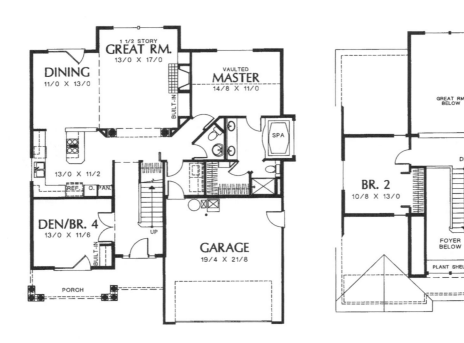

DESIGN HPU040119

First Floor: 1,396 square feet
Second Floor: 523 square feet
Total: 1,919 square feet
Width: 44'-0" Depth: 51'-0"

L

Double pillars herald the entry to this charming design. They are offset from the front door and introduce a porch that leads to the den (or make it a fourth bedroom). Living areas center on the casual life and include a great room, with a fireplace, that opens directly to the dining room. The kitchen is L-shaped for convenience and features an island cooktop. The master suite on the first floor sports a vaulted ceiling and bath with spa tub and separate shower. The upper floor holds two secondary bedrooms and a full bath. The open staircase is decorated with a plant shelf that receives light from double windows over the foyer.

DESIGN BY
©Alan Mascord Design Associates, Inc.

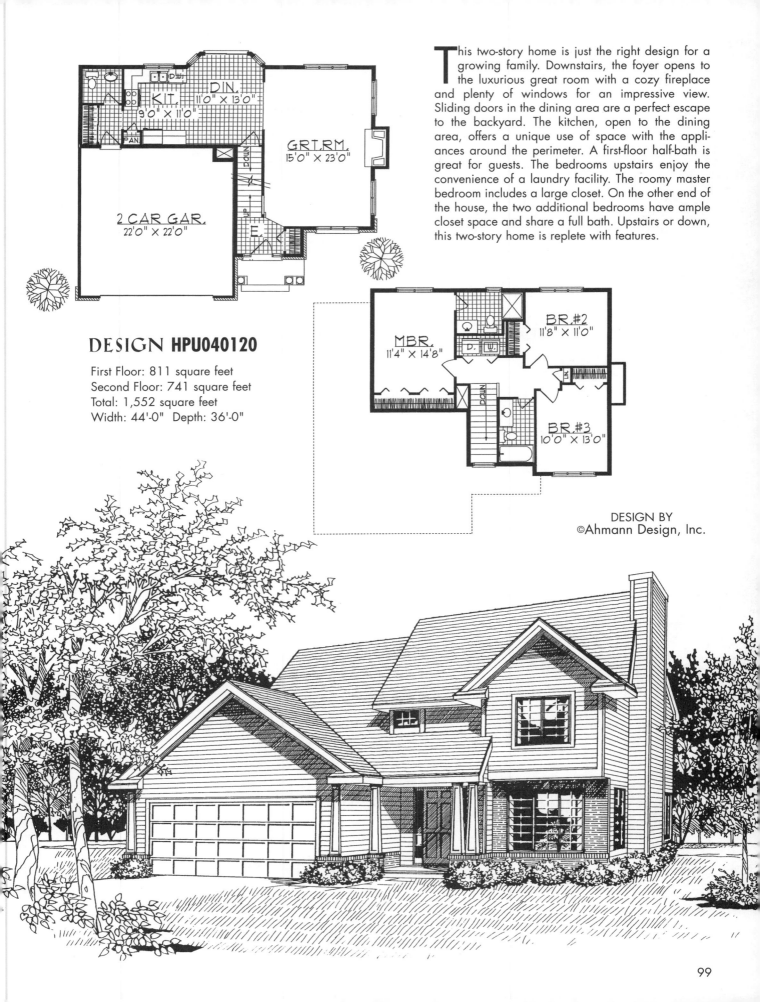

KIT.
9'0" X 11'0"

DIN.
11'0" X 13'0"

GRT.RM.
15'0" X 23'0"

2 CAR GAR.
22'0" X 22'0"

DOWN

UP

PAN

This two-story home is just the right design for a growing family. Downstairs, the foyer opens to the luxurious great room with a cozy fireplace and plenty of windows for an impressive view. Sliding doors in the dining area are a perfect escape to the backyard. The kitchen, open to the dining area, offers a unique use of space with the appliances around the perimeter. A first-floor half-bath is great for guests. The bedrooms upstairs enjoy the convenience of a laundry facility. The roomy master bedroom includes a large closet. On the other end of the house, the two additional bedrooms have ample closet space and share a full bath. Upstairs or down, this two-story home is replete with features.

DESIGN HPU040120

First Floor: 811 square feet
Second Floor: 741 square feet
Total: 1,552 square feet
Width: 44'-0" Depth: 36'-0"

MBR.
11'4" X 14'8"

BR. #2
11'8" X 11'0"

BR. #3
10'0" X 13'0"

DOWN

DESIGN BY
©Ahmann Design, Inc.

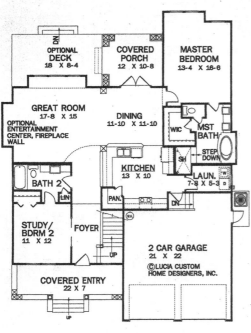

This floor plan offers a modern approach to today's needs. The study to the left of the foyer could be a third bedroom with an adjoining bath. The great room, dining room and kitchen make up the central open area. An entertainment center and fireplace are optional. From this area, access a covered porch and an optional deck through French doors. A bedroom and bath reside on the second floor, along with a loft area and an overlook to the great room below. There's also an optional closet and unfinished bonus space, perfect for future expansion.

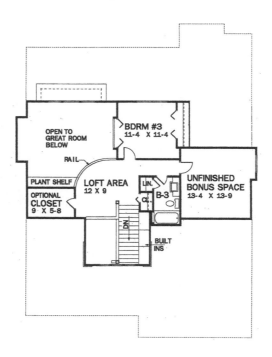

DESIGN **HPU040121**

First Floor: 1,553 square feet
Second Floor: 391 square feet
Total: 1,944 square feet
Bonus Room: 183 square feet
Width: 44'-0" Depth: 62'-8"

DESIGN BY
©Lucia Custom Home Designers, Inc.

100

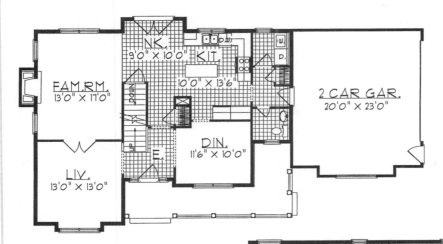

B rick-and-siding, dormered windows, open gables and circle-top windows highlight this modern farmhouse design. The tiled entry leads to the dining room on the right and the breakfast nook and island kitchen straight back. The laundry and half-bath are nearby for convenience. The family room can be found at the left rear and features a cozy fireplace and rear views. The formal living room enjoys a bumped-out bay and double doors that open onto the family room. Upstairs, two family bedrooms share a hall bath—one bedroom features a tray ceiling. The master bedroom boasts a cathedral ceiling, walk-in closet, dual vanities and separate tub and shower.

DESIGN HPU040122

First Floor: 1,065 square feet
Second Floor: 921 square feet
Total: 1,986 square feet
Width: 60'-0" Depth: 34'-0"

DESIGN BY
©Ahmann Design, Inc.

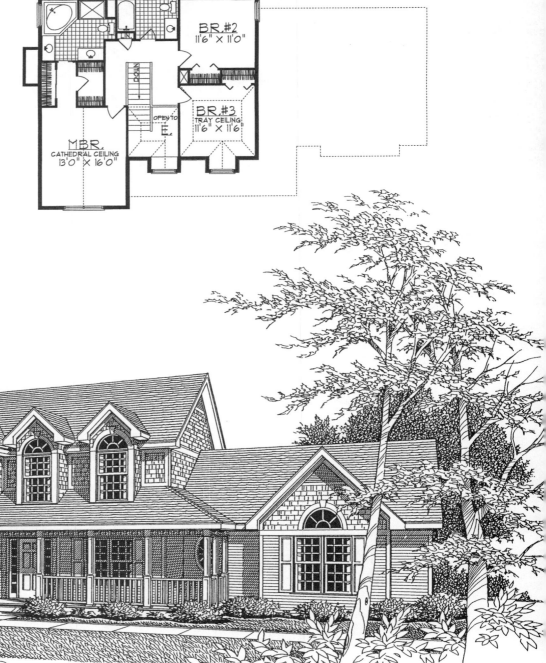

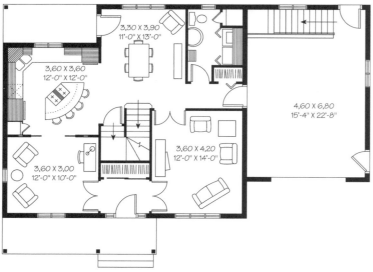

3,30 X 3,90
11'-0" X 13'-0"

3,60 X 3,60
12'-0" X 12'-0"

4,60 X 6,80
15'-4" X 22'-8"

3,60 X 4,20
12'-0" X 14'-0"

3,60 X 3,00
12'-0" X 10'-0"

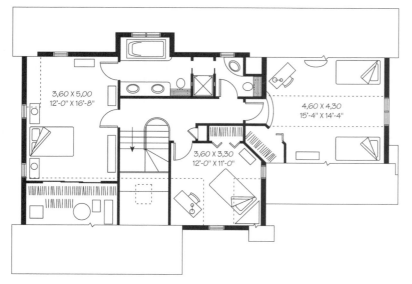

3,60 X 5,00
12'-0" X 16'-8"

4,60 X 4,30
15'-4" X 14'-4"

3,60 X 3,30
12'-0" X 11'-0"

DESIGN HPU040123

First Floor: 866 square feet
Second Floor: 998 square feet
Total: 1,864 square feet
Width: 48'-0" Depth: 29'-0"

A beautifully offset double-gabled dormer adds a playful touch to this Craftsman home. With open gables and a covered porch, an inviting atmosphere takes family and guests into the foyer. Double doors flank the entry; to the left is the media room with pocket doors to the island kitchen. On the right, a living room features double doors to the dining room. A laundry and half-bath complete this level. Upstairs, the master suite is pampered with a private bath. Two secondary bedrooms share a hall bath. This home is designed with a basement foundation.

DESIGN BY
©Drummond Designs, Inc.

A sturdy and attractive design, this fine three-bedroom home will look good in any neighborhood. The raised foyer overlooks a spacious living room, where a through-fireplace and a wall of windows add to the already abundant charm. In the L-shaped kitchen, a cooktop work island/snack bar benefits from the through-fireplace, while the adjacent dining room offers access and views to the rear yard via sliding glass doors. Upstairs, a small balcony overlooks the living room. Three bedrooms—one with a walk-in closet—share a lavish bath. This home is designed with a basement foundation.

DESIGN BY
©Drummond Designs, Inc.

DESIGN HPU040124

First Floor: 760 square feet
Second Floor: 752 square feet
Total: 1,512 square feet
Width: 48'-0" Depth: 30'-0"

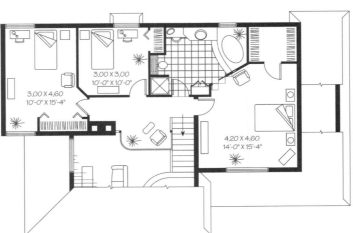

DESIGN HPU040126

Square Footage: 1,656
Bonus Room: 427 square feet
Width: 52'-8" Depth: 54'-6"

DESIGN BY
©Larry James & Associates, Inc.

Sit and watch the sunset on this relaxing front porch, or go inside for intimate conversations by the fireplace in the great room. A bay window in the dining area will adorn any meal with sun or moonlight. A spacious owners bedroom has a large walk-in closet and a full bath. Two secondary bedrooms share a full bath with the main living areas. A bonus room upstairs allows room for expansion later. Please specify basement, crawlspace or slab foundation when ordering.

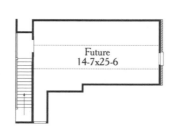

Future
14-7x25-6

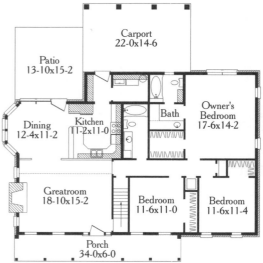

Carport
22-0x14-6

Patio
13-10x15-2

Dining
12-4x11-2

Kitchen
11-2x11-0

Bath

Owner's
Bedroom
17-6x14-2

Greatroom
18-10x15-2

Bedroom
11-6x11-0

Bedroom
11-6x11-4

Porch
34-0x6-0

DESIGN HPU040125

First Floor: 1,159 square feet
Second Floor: 711 square feet
Total: 1,870 square feet
Width: 44'-4" Depth: 38'-0"

DESIGN BY
©Jannis Vann & Associates, Inc.

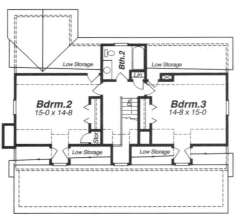

Low Storage

Bth.2

Lin.

Low Storage

Bdrm.2
15-0 x 14-8

Bdrm.3
14-8 x 15-0

Stor.

Low Storage

Low Storage

Wherever you live, this country-style home will be a winner! Dormers and an inviting covered porch lend this home enormous appeal. Inside, the main living area offers a cheery fireplace. To the rear of the plan, a dining area overlooks the sun deck. The adjacent kitchen and sunny breakfast area are just a step away. Master-bedroom luxury awaits on the other side of the plan. The large bedroom is complemented by a roomy bath with a corner tub, walk-in closet and twin vanities. Upstairs, two family bedrooms with dormer windows share a bumped-out full bath.

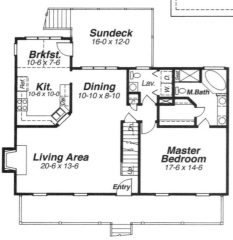

Sundeck
16-0 x 12-0

Brkfst.
10-6 x 7-6

Kit.
10-6 x 10-0

Dining
10-10 x 8-10

Lav.

M.Bath

Living Area
20-6 x 13-6

Master
Bedroom
17-6 x 14-6

Entry

A beautiful half-circle window tops a covered front porch on this fine three-bedroom home. Inside, the main-level amenities start with the large, open great room and a warming fireplace. A uniquely shaped dining room is adjacent to the efficient kitchen, which offers a small bay window over the sink. The deluxe master suite is complete with a cathedral ceiling, bay sitting area and a private bath with laundry facilities. On the lower level, a two-car garage shelters the family fleet, while two bedrooms—or make one a study/home office—share a full hall bath.

DESIGN BY
©Jannis Vann & Associates, Inc.

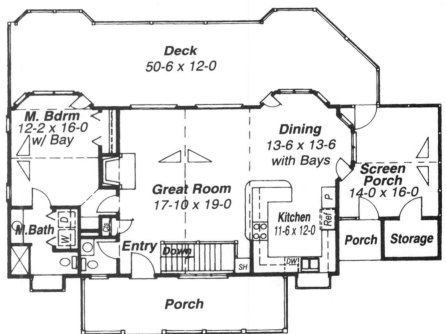

Deck
50-6 x 12-0

M. Bdrm
12-2 x 16-0
w/ Bay

Dining
13-6 x 13-6
with Bays

Screen
Porch
14-0 x 16-0

Great Room
17-10 x 19-0

Kitchen
11-6 x 12-0

M.Bath

Entry

Down

Porch Storage

Porch

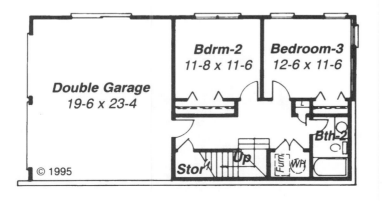

Double Garage
19-6 x 23-4

Bdrm-2
11-8 x 11-6

Bedroom-3
12-6 x 11-6

© 1995

Bth-2

Stor

Up

Furn

WH

DESIGN HPU040127

Main Floor: 1,128 square feet
Lower Floor: 604 square feet
Total: 1,732 square feet
Width: 59'-0" Depth: 46'-0"

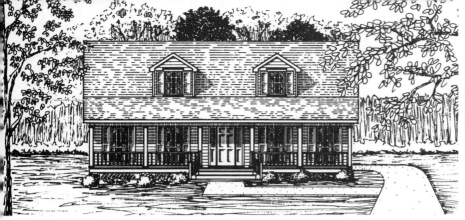

DESIGN HPU040129

Square Footage: 1,704
Width: 47'-0" Depth: 66'-0"

Old-fashioned Southern style is offset by the innovative floor plan of this charming home. Full-height windows line the front porch, drawing natural light and generous views into the front rooms. The foyer leads past the formal dining room on the right to the spacious living room with a sloped ceiling and fireplace. The large galley kitchen is open to the bay-windowed breakfast area and serves the dining room. The owners suite features an octagonal tray ceiling, His and Hers walk-in closets, a garden tub and separate shower. Please specify crawlspace or slab foundation when ordering.

DESIGN BY
©Chatham Home Planning, Inc.

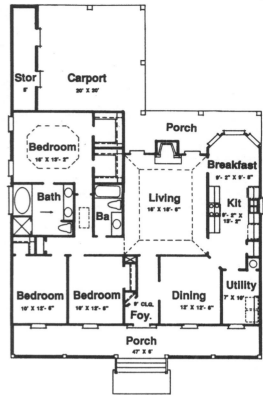

DESIGN HPU040128

Square Footage: 1,689
Width: 67'-0" Depth: 43'-0"

Southern country comfort is at its finest in this three-bedroom home. The great room features a central fireplace and built-ins—perfect for entertaining friends and family. The dining room boasts double French doors to the rear patio and enjoys natural light streaming through surrounding windows. Two family bedrooms to the right share a full bath. The owners bedroom finds privacy on the left and is complemented with a full bath and walk-in closet. Please specify basement, crawlspace or slab foundation when ordering.

DESIGN BY
©Larry James & Associates, Inc.

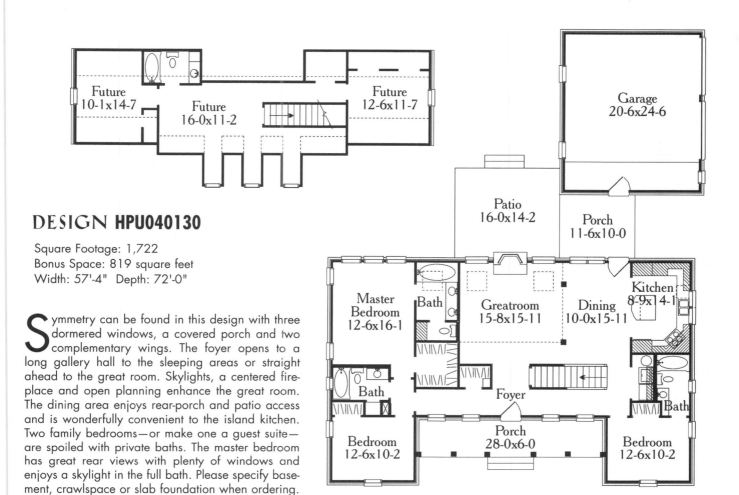

DESIGN **HPU040130**

Square Footage: 1,722
Bonus Space: 819 square feet
Width: 57'-4"   Depth: 72'-0"

Symmetry can be found in this design with three dormered windows, a covered porch and two complementary wings. The foyer opens to a long gallery hall to the sleeping areas or straight ahead to the great room. Skylights, a centered fireplace and open planning enhance the great room. The dining area enjoys rear-porch and patio access and is wonderfully convenient to the island kitchen. Two family bedrooms—or make one a guest suite—are spoiled with private baths. The master bedroom has great rear views with plenty of windows and enjoys a skylight in the full bath. Please specify basement, crawlspace or slab foundation when ordering.

DESIGN BY
©Larry James & Associates, Inc.

DESIGN HPU040132

Square Footage: 1,751
Width: 64'-0" Depth: 40'-6"

This raised-porch farmhouse holds all the charisma of others of its style, but boasts a one-story floor plan. A huge living area dominates the center of the plan. It features a vaulted ceiling, built-ins and a warming fireplace. The formal dining room across the hall opens to the foyer and the living area, which is defined by a single column at its corner. Casual dining takes place in a light-filled breakfast room attached to the designer kitchen. A spectacular master suite sits behind the two-car garage. It has a tray ceiling, walk-in closet and well-appointed bath. Family bedrooms at the other end of the hallway share a jack-and-jill bath that includes a separate vanity area.

DESIGN BY
©Archival Designs, Inc.

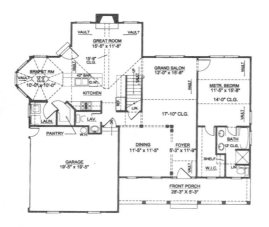

DESIGN HPU040131

First Floor: 1,296 square feet
Second Floor: 468 square feet
Total: 1,764 square feet
Bonus Room: 169 square feet
Width: 49'-0" Depth: 46'-0"

DESIGN BY
©Archival Designs, Inc.

This tidy Southern cottage design opens with a covered front porch that protects the entry and adds a touch of downhome flavor. A central foyer is defined by columns that separate it from the formal dining room and the grand salon. In the vaulted great room, note the fireplace and the snack bar, which it shares with the kitchen. The master bedroom on the first floor features a vaulted ceiling and a bath with a separate tub and shower. Two family bedrooms on the second floor share a full bath. One of the bedrooms has a dormer window. Bonus space can be developed later to include a home office or an additional bedroom.

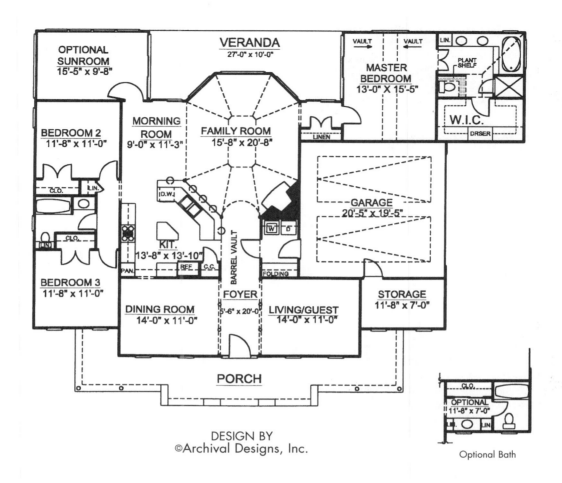

OPTIONAL
SUNROOM
15'-5" x 9'-8"

VERANDA
27'-0" x 10'-0"

VAULT ← → VAULT

MASTER
BEDROOM
13'-0" X 15'-5"

PLANT
SHELF

W.I.C.

BEDROOM 2
11'-8" x 11'-0"

MORNING
ROOM
9'-0" x 11'-3"

FAMILY ROOM
15'-8" x 20'-8"

LINEN

GARAGE
20'-5" x 19'-5"

KIT.
13'-8" x 13'-10"

BARREL VAULT

BEDROOM 3
11'-8" x 11'-0"

DINING ROOM
14'-0" x 11'-0"

FOYER
5'-6" x 20'-0"

LIVING/GUEST
14'-0" x 11'-0"

FOLDING

STORAGE
11'-8" x 7'-0"

PORCH

DESIGN BY
©Archival Designs, Inc.

OPTIONAL
11'-8" x 7'-0"

Optional Bath

Stately arches topped with a pediment make this home a comfortable fit into an elegant lifestyle. The foyer is flanked by the formal dining and living rooms. A hall with a barrel-vaulted ceiling leads to the vaulted family room, which features a corner fireplace and convenience to the kitchen, morning room and rear veranda. This area provides a spectacular space for family get-togethers. Two secondary bedrooms with a full bath can be found to the left of the kitchen. An optional sun room is a delight just off the morning room. The master suite accommodates the discerning homeowner. It highlights a vaulted ceiling, dual vanities, a separate tub and shower, and an oversized walk-in closet.

DESIGN HPU040133

Square Footage: 1,928
Bonus Room: 160 square feet
Width: 58'-0"   Depth: 47'-0"

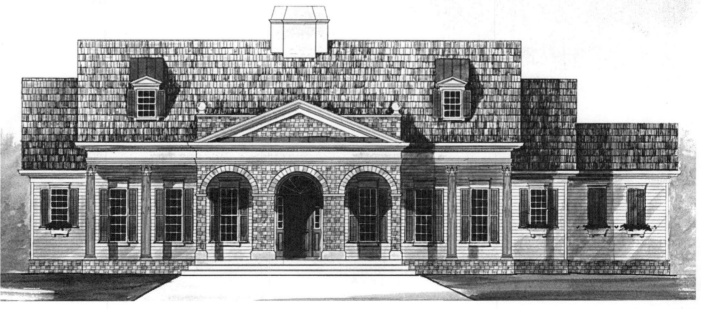

DESIGN BY
©Chatham Home Planning, Inc.

This Creole cottage possesses the feel of a much bigger house. Natural light streams through the full-length windows that span the entire front wall. This home has the convience of two full baths and one powder room. The master bedroom includes a walk-in closet and a deluxe bath with an oversized tub and separate shower. Two bedrooms and a balcony—that opens to the living area—occupy the second floor. Please specify crawlspace or slab foundation when ordering.

DESIGN HPU040135

First Floor: 1,247 square feet
Second Floor: 521 square feet
Total: 1,768 square feet
Width: 36'-6" Depth: 57'-0"

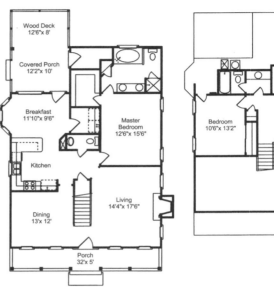

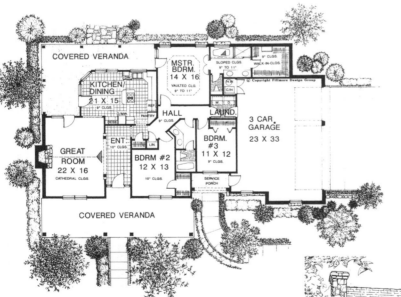

DESIGN HPU040134

Square Footage: 1,830
Width: 75'-0" Depth: 52'-3"

DESIGN BY
©Fillmore Design Group

A lovely front porch and decorative cupola give this home extra sparkle. Characteristics that include the cupola, shutters, arched transoms and an exterior of stone and lap siding mark this as a Colonial design. To the left of the entry, the great room is complete with a cathedral ceiling and fireplace. A hall leads to sleeping quarters that include two secondary bedrooms and a luxurious master bedroom.

A deep wraparound porch trimmed with square pillars, a wood balustrade and traditional lattice adds character and interest to this Cape Cod design. Floor-to-ceiling double-hung windows with true divided glass light the downstairs, while dormers upstairs complete the rustic look. The main floor includes a fireplace in the living room, a bay window in the dining room and a master suite with a walk-in closet. The dining room and kitchen are divided by a peninsula with seating for informal dining. The peninsula contains the sink, in keeping with one of the latest trends in kitchen design. There is also a powder room off the kitchen. Upstairs, two bedrooms, each with a walk-in closet, share a bath. Please specify crawlspace or slab foundation when ordering.

Kitchen
13'6"x 12'

Dining
11'8"x 12'

Master
Bedroom
12'x 16'

Living
14'2"x 16'

Porch

Bedroom
10'x 13'2"

Bedroom
14'x 13'2"

DESIGN HPU040136

First Floor: 1,046 square feet
Second Floor: 572 square feet
Total: 1,618 square feet
Width: 44'-0" Depth: 39'-0"

DESIGN BY
©Chatham Home Planning, Inc.

DESIGN HPU040138

Square Footage: 1,770
Width: 64'-0" Depth: 48'-0"

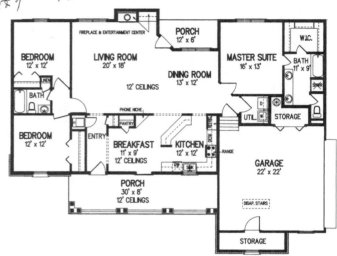

This traditional design boasts a large entry porch and free-flowing interior spaces. The spacious living room is open to the adjacent dining room and offers a built-in fireplace and entertainment center. The entry, breakfast area, kitchen, and dining and living areas have twelve-foot ceilings. The master suite is secluded for privacy and conveniently located only steps away from the kitchen. Please specify crawlspace or slab foundation when ordering.

Utilizing wood and stone for the exterior facade, this home boasts a large receiving porch and free-flowing interior spaces. The spacious living room opens to the dining room and offers a built-in fireplace and entertainment center. The entry, breakfast area, kitchen and the dining and living areas all enjoy twelve-foot ceilings, while other rooms have traditional eight-foot ceilings. The master suite is secluded for privacy and features a bath with a separate tub and shower and a walk-in closet. Please specify crawlspace or slab foundation when ordering.

DESIGN HPU040137

Square Footage: 1,770
Width: 64'-0" Depth: 48'-0"

PORCH
20' X 8'

DESIGN BY
©Breland & Farmer Designers, Inc.

BEDROOM
12' x 12'

WIC

LIVING ROOM
24' X 16'
SLOPED CEILINGS

MASTER SUITE
16' X 16'

DRESS. RM.

BATH

WIC

STORAGE
9' X 9'

BOOKS

FIREPLACE

SHWR.

LINEN

UTIL.
8' X 7'

BATH

C-A/C

HEAT & A/C

STOR

STOR

DRY WASH

GARAGE
23' X 22'

HALL

LINEN

EATING AREA
10' X 10'

SHVS.

FOYER

DINING ROOM
12' x 12'

PANTRY

KITCHEN
12' x 12'

RANGE

REF

SHVS.

BEDROOM
12' x 12'

DW   SINK

BALCONY
10' X 6'

SHVS.

WORK BENCH

SHVS.

PORCH
44' X 8'

DESIGN HPU040139

Square Footage: 1,925
Width: 78'-0" Depth: 52'-0"

This three-bedroom farmhouse offers classic style and an up-to-date floor plan. The slope-ceilinged living room offers a fireplace and French-door access to a covered rear porch. The kitchen features a large pantry and is located between the casual eating area and the formal dining room. Two family bedrooms, one with built-in bookshelves and a walk-in closet, share a full bath to the left of the living room. To the right, the owners suite includes a dressing room and a full bath with a walk-in closet. Please specify crawlspace or slab foundation when ordering.

DESIGN HPU040140

First Floor: 1,230 square feet
Second Floor: 477 square feet
Total: 1,707 square feet
Bonus Room: 195 square feet
Width: 40'-0" Depth: 53'-0"

L

With sunny windows throughout and a wonderfully open living space, this plan appears larger than its modest square footage. The great room is highlighted with a corner window, a fireplace and a soaring ceiling. The dining room continues the open feeling and is easily served from the kitchen. A bayed nook complements the island kitchen that also has a stylish wraparound counter. The owners bedroom suite has a lofty vaulted ceiling. Upstairs there are two family bedrooms that share a full hall bath—plus a bonus room that can be developed as needed.

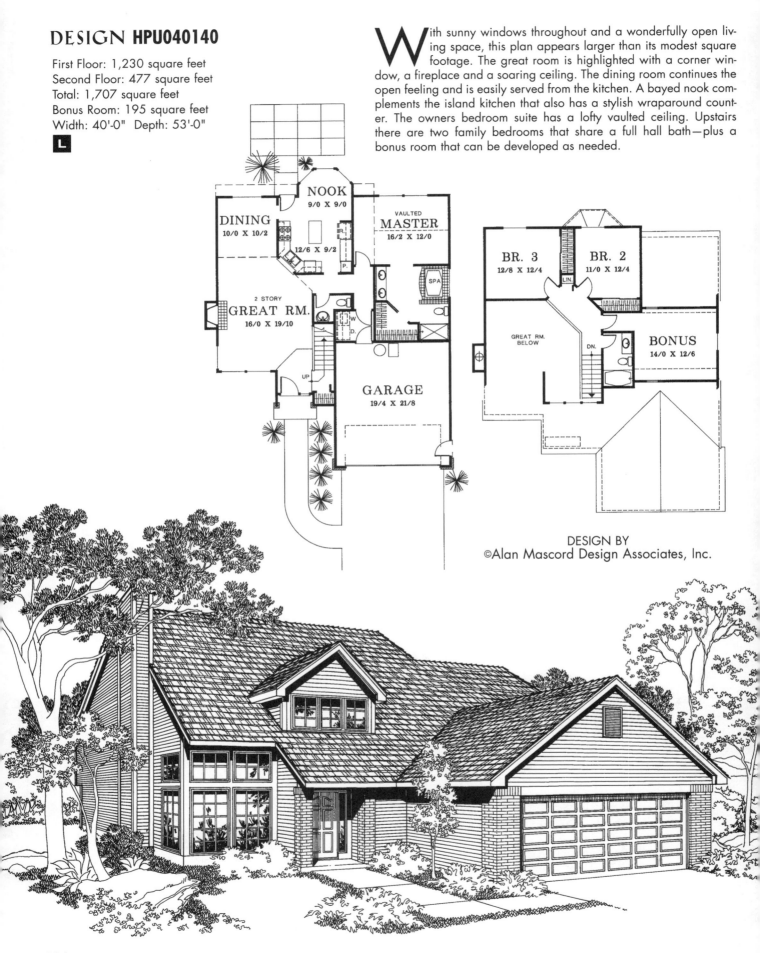

NOOK
9/0 X 9/0

DINING
10/0 X 10/2

VAULTED
MASTER
16/2 X 12/0

12/6 X 9/2

2 STORY
GREAT RM.
16/0 X 19/10

SPA

W
D.

UP

GARAGE
19/4 X 21/8

BR. 3
12/8 X 12/4

BR. 2
11/0 X 12/4

LIN.

GREAT RM.
BELOW

DN.

BONUS
14/0 X 12/6

DESIGN BY
©Alan Mascord Design Associates, Inc.

DESIGN HPU040141

Square Footage: 1,687
Width: 50'-0" Depth: 52'-0"

L

Intriguing rooflines create a dynamic exterior for this home. The interior floor plan is equally attractive. Toward the rear, a wide archway forms the entrance to the spacious family living area with its centrally placed fireplace and bay-windowed nook. An island counter, mitered corner window and walk-in pantry complete the efficient kitchen. This home also boasts a terrific master suite complete with a walk-in wardrobe, spa tub with corner windows, and a compartmented shower and toilet area. Two family bedrooms share a hall bath.

DESIGN BY
©Alan Mascord Design Associates, Inc.

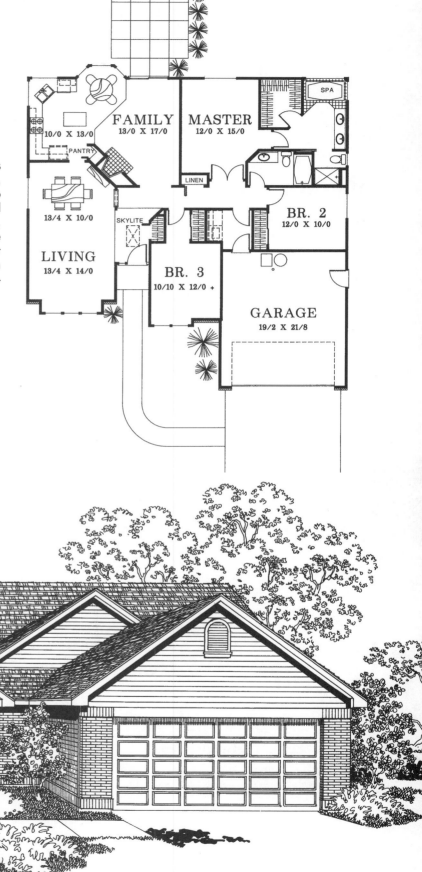

FAMILY
13/0 X 17/0

MASTER
12/0 X 15/0

SPA

10/0 X 13/0

PANTRY

LINEN

13/4 X 10/0

SKYLITE

BR. 2
12/0 X 10/0

LIVING
13/4 X 14/0

BR. 3
10/10 X 12/0 +

GARAGE
19/2 X 21/8

DESIGN HPU040143

Square Footage: 1,915
Width: 46'-0" Depth: 60'-2"

A sunny bay window and a shady recessed entry create an elegant impression in this lovely design. The sleeping quarters are arranged for privacy along the perimeter of the spacious living areas. The kitchen provides generous work space, and the dining room is open to the gathering room with fireplace. To the rear, a covered veranda is accessible from the dining room and the master suite. Note the lavish bath and huge walk-in closet in the master suite.

DESIGN BY
©Living Concepts Home Planning

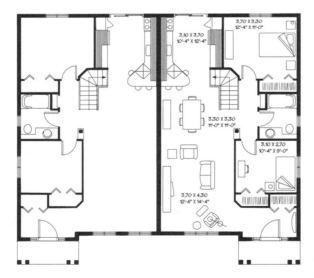

DESIGN HPU040142

Total: 1,893 square feet
Width: 48'-0" Depth: 40'-0"

DESIGN BY
©Drummond Designs, Inc.

E legant living can be found in this duplex home. Enhanced with columns and a lovely pediment just above the entryway, this design offers slight differences in facade and window treatments. One side enjoys a circle-top window and an open gable, while the other is understated with a gable roofline. Inside, the floor plans are identical. The open living area provides space for a dining area and entertaining space. The kitchen features a breakfast bar and plenty of counter space. Two bedrooms and a full bath complete this efficient design. This home is designed with a basement foundation.

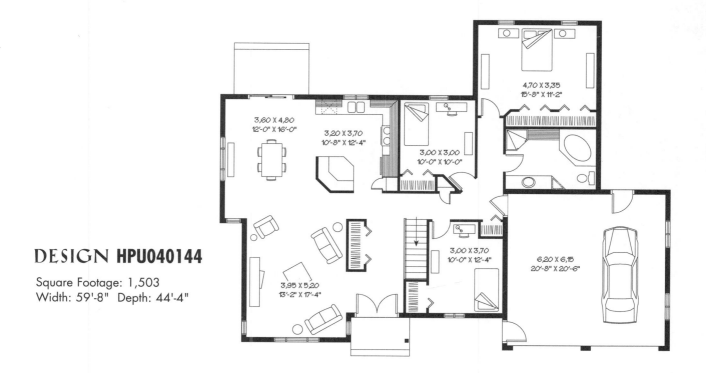

DESIGN HPU040144

Square Footage: 1,503
Width: 59'-8" Depth: 44'-4"

Traditional lines and an elegant double-door entry give this home curb appeal. In front, a large picture window is accented by a slight arch and keystone. The living room just to the left of the foyer is open to the dining room, which features a bumped-out bay flooding the area with natural light and ambience. The L-shaped kitchen boasts an island and services the dining and living rooms with ease. Two family bedrooms are down the hall. The owners suite enjoys plenty of closet space. The spacious full bath features a separate tub and shower. This home is designed with a basement foundation.

DESIGN BY
©Drummond Designs, Inc.

Garage
20-6x21-0

Stor.
6-7x5-11

Laun.
7-11x6-2

Kitchen
13-0x12-0

Dining
14-9x12-0

Porch
15-2x8-8

Owner's
Bedroom
13-5x17-1

Bedroom
10-1x13-0

Bath

Greatroom
16-0x16-4

Bath

Foyer

Bedroom
13-10x11-1

Porch
22-3x7-2

Future
19-4x16-2

Future
16-3x13-7

Future
13-4x10-6

A lovely front porch invites family and friends into the great room that features a fireplace and open, flowing planning. The dining area enjoys an open view of the great room and the rear porch—perfect for entertaining. An island kitchen serves both areas with ease. The owners suite is positioned at the rear with a walk-in closet, dual vanities, compartmented toilet, and separate tub and shower. Two family bedrooms to the left share a full bath. Please specify basement, crawlspace or slab foundation when ordering.

DESIGN HPU040145

Square Footage: 1,709
Bonus Space: 710 square feet
Width: 54'-6" Depth: 62'-8"

DESIGN BY
©Larry James & Associates, Inc.

©1999 Donald A. Gardner, Inc.

B. NATHAN

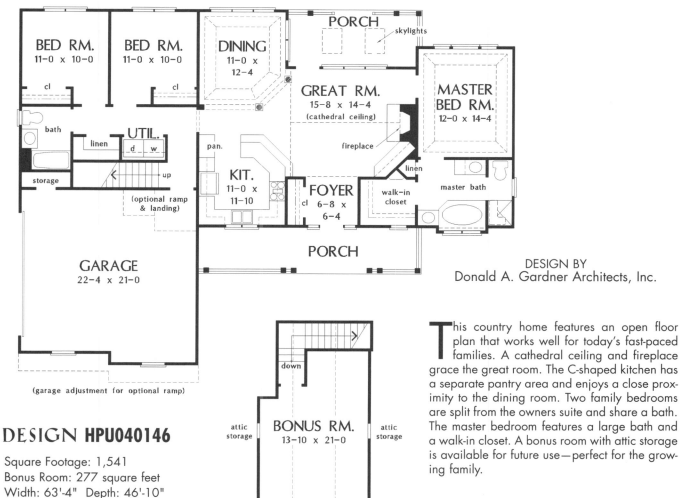

BED RM.
11-0 x 10-0

BED RM.
11-0 x 10-0

DINING
11-0 x
12-4

PORCH

skylights

GREAT RM.
15-8 x 14-4
(cathedral ceiling)

MASTER
BED RM.
12-0 x 14-4

cl

cl

bath

UTIL.

linen

d   w

pan.

fireplace

linen

master bath

storage

up

KIT.
11-0 x
11-10

FOYER
cl 6-8 x
6-4

walk-in
closet

(optional ramp
& landing)

GARAGE
22-4 x 21-0

PORCH

DESIGN BY
Donald A. Gardner Architects, Inc.

(garage adjustment for optional ramp)

DESIGN HPU040146

Square Footage: 1,541
Bonus Room: 277 square feet
Width: 63'-4"   Depth: 46'-10"

down

attic
storage

BONUS RM.
13-10 x 21-0

attic
storage

This country home features an open floor plan that works well for today's fast-paced families. A cathedral ceiling and fireplace grace the great room. The C-shaped kitchen has a separate pantry area and enjoys a close prox-imity to the dining room. Two family bedrooms are split from the owners suite and share a bath. The master bedroom features a large bath and a walk-in closet. A bonus room with attic storage is available for future use—perfect for the grow-ing family.

DESIGN BY
Donald A. Gardner Architects, Inc.

DESIGN HPU040147

Square Footage: 1,506
Width: 71'-0" Depth: 42'-4"

A lovely facade, adorned with multi-pane windows, shutters, dormers, bay windows and a covered porch, gives way to a truly livable floor plan. The living room, with a cathedral ceiling, fireplace, paddle fan, built-in cabinets and bookshelves, directly accesses the sun room through two sliding glass doors. Sleeping accommodations include a master bedroom with ample closet space and two family bedrooms. Note the split-bedroom plan configuration—providing utmost privacy.

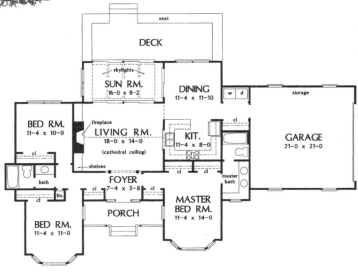

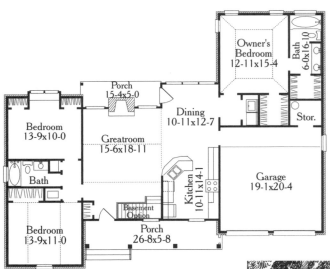

Two covered porches lend a relaxing charm to this ranch home. Inside, windows frame the focal-point fireplace. The vaulted ceiling in the great room adds spaciousness to the adjoining kitchen and dining areas. A tray ceiling decorates the owners suite, which also sports two walk-in closets and a full bath with two vanities. Two family bedrooms sit on the other side of the plan and share a full bath. Please specify basement, crawlspace or slab foundation when ordering.

DESIGN HPU040148

Square Footage: 1,643
Width: 62'-2" Depth: 51'-4"

DESIGN BY
©Larry James & Associates, Inc.

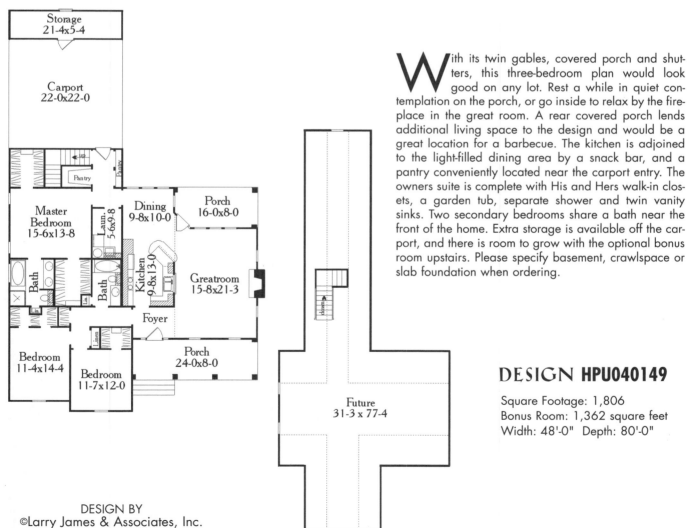

Storage
21-4x5-4

Carport
22-0x22-0

Master
Bedroom
15-6x13-8

Bath

Bath

Laun.
5-6x9-8

Pantry

Kitchen
9-8x13-0

Dining
9-8x10-0

Porch
16-0x8-0

Greatroom
15-8x21-3

Foyer

Bedroom
11-4x14-4

Bedroom
11-7x12-0

Linen

Porch
24-0x8-0

down

Future
31-3 x 77-4

With its twin gables, covered porch and shutters, this three-bedroom plan would look good on any lot. Rest a while in quiet contemplation on the porch, or go inside to relax by the fireplace in the great room. A rear covered porch lends additional living space to the design and would be a great location for a barbecue. The kitchen is adjoined to the light-filled dining area by a snack bar, and a pantry conveniently located near the carport entry. The owners suite is complete with His and Hers walk-in closets, a garden tub, separate shower and twin vanity sinks. Two secondary bedrooms share a bath near the front of the home. Extra storage is available off the carport, and there is room to grow with the optional bonus room upstairs. Please specify basement, crawlspace or slab foundation when ordering.

DESIGN HPU040149

Square Footage: 1,806
Bonus Room: 1,362 square feet
Width: 48'-0" Depth: 80'-0"

DESIGN BY
©Larry James & Associates, Inc.

DESIGN HPU040151

First Floor: 1,168 square feet
Second Floor: 498 square feet
Total: 1,666 square feet
Width: 44'-0" Depth: 44'-0"

DESIGN BY
©Ahmann Design, Inc.

To begin this home, the foyer opens to the luxurious living room with a cozy fireplace surrounded by built-in cabinets. Sliding doors in the dining area are a perfect escape to the backyard. A first-floor master bedroom is ideal for privacy. Two additional bedrooms occupy the second floor; they have ample closet space and share a full bath. Upstairs or down, this two-story home is packed with features.

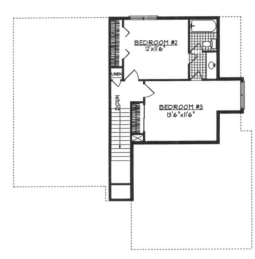

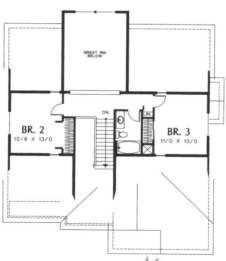

DESIGN HPU040150

First Floor: 1,396 square feet
Second Floor: 523 square feet
Total: 1,919 square feet
Width: 44'-0" Depth: 51'-0"

A covered porch flanked with double columns provides special interest for this lovely traditional home. A separate entry through the den creates a perfect opportunity for use as an office or home-operated business. The foyer leads to all areas of the house, maximizing livability. The split bedrooms, with the master suite on the first floor and two secondary bedrooms upstairs, make this an ideal design for empty-nesters or active retired couples.

DESIGN BY
©Alan Mascord Design Associates, Inc.

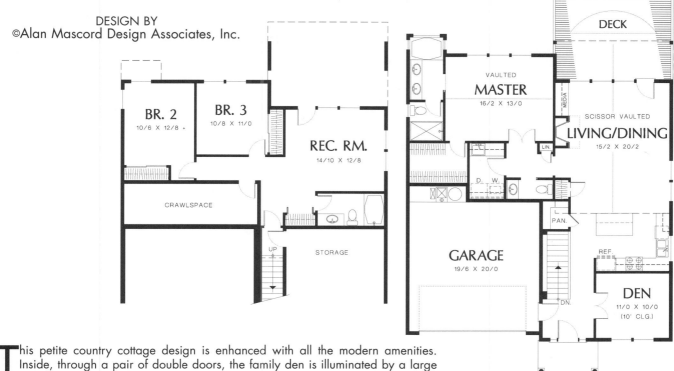

BR. 2
10/6 X 12/8 +

BR. 3
10/8 X 11/0

REC. RM.
14/10 X 12/8

CRAWLSPACE

UP

STORAGE

VAULTED
MASTER
16/2 X 13/0

MEDIA

DECK

SCISSOR VAULTED

LIVING/DINING
15/2 X 20/2

LIN.

D. W.

PAN.

GARAGE
19/6 X 20/0

REF.

DN.

DEN
11/0 X 10/0
(10' CLG.)

This petite country cottage design is enhanced with all the modern amenities. Inside, through a pair of double doors, the family den is illuminated by a large window. The kitchen, which features efficient pantry space, opens to the living/dining area. This spacious room is highlighted by a scissor vaulted ceiling, and features a warming fireplace and nook space. The living/dining room also overlooks a large rear deck, which is accessed through a back door. Secluded on the ground level for extra privacy, the vaulted master bedroom includes a private full bath and a walk-in closet. A laundry room, two-car garage and powder room all complete this floor. Downstairs, two additional family bedrooms share a hall bath. The recreation room is an added bonus. Extra storage space is also available on this floor.

DESIGN HPU040152

Main Level: 1,230 square feet
Lower Level: 769 square feet
Total: 1,999 square feet
Width: 40'-0" Depth: 52'-6"

DESIGN HPU040153

Square Footage: 1,550
Width: 62'-8" Depth: 36'-0"

DESIGN BY
©R.L. Pfotenhauer

A handsome porch dressed up with Greek Revival details greets visitors warmly in this early American home. The foyer opens to the airy and spacious living room and dining room with vaulted ceilings. The secluded master bedroom also sports a vaulted ceiling and is graced with a dressing area, private bath and walk-in closet. Two decks located at the rear of the plan are accessed via the master bedroom, kitchen and living room. A full bath serves the two family bedrooms.

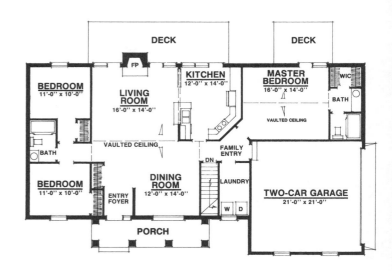

E nter through a beautiful arched entrance into the enchantment of modern American tradition. Straight beyond the foyer, the great room is spaciously enhanced by a cathedral ceiling and features a fireplace and an illuminating arched window. The island kitchen/breakfast area is open to the dining room, which overlooks a large rear deck with a spa. A complete master suite and two other bedrooms are accommodating sleeping areas for the family.

DESIGN HPU040154

Square Footage: 1,542
Width: 52'-8" Depth: 65'-2"

DESIGN BY
Donald A. Gardner Architects, Inc.

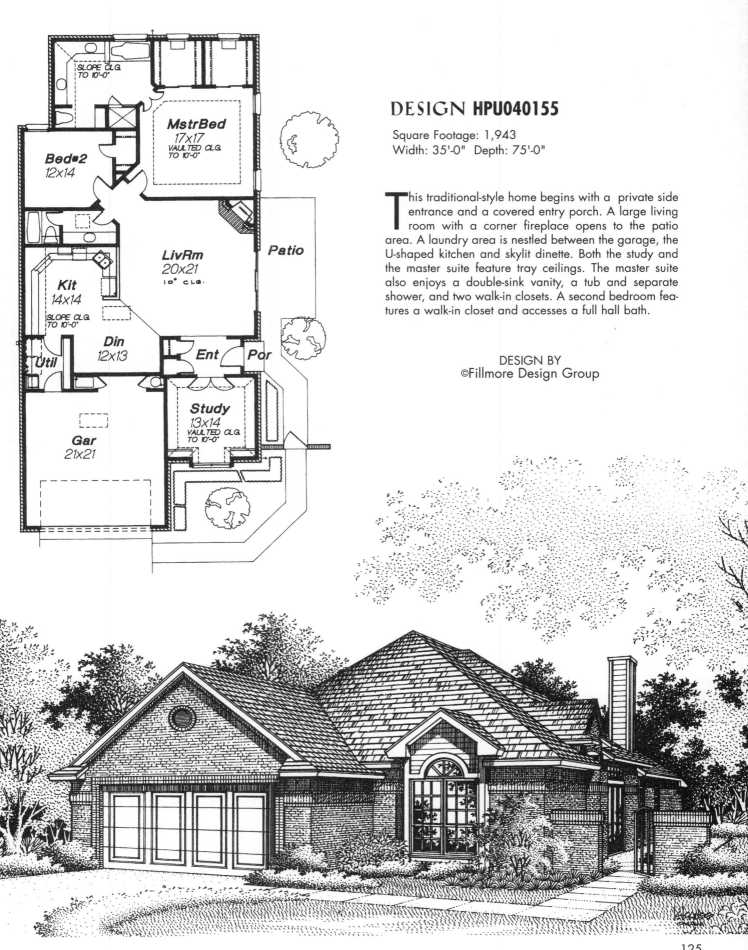

DESIGN HPU040155

Square Footage: 1,943
Width: 35'-0" Depth: 75'-0"

This traditional-style home begins with a private side entrance and a covered entry porch. A large living room with a corner fireplace opens to the patio area. A laundry area is nestled between the garage, the U-shaped kitchen and skylit dinette. Both the study and the master suite feature tray ceilings. The master suite also enjoys a double-sink vanity, a tub and separate shower, and two walk-in closets. A second bedroom features a walk-in closet and accesses a full hall bath.

DESIGN BY
©Fillmore Design Group

SLOPE CLG. TO 10'-0"

MstrBed
17x17
VAULTED CLG
TO 10'-0"

Bed#2
12x14

LivRm
20x21
10° CLG.

Patio

Kit
14x14
SLOPE CLG. TO 10'-0"

Din
12x13

Ent

Por

Util

Study
13x14
VAULTED CLG
TO 10'-0"

Gar
21x21

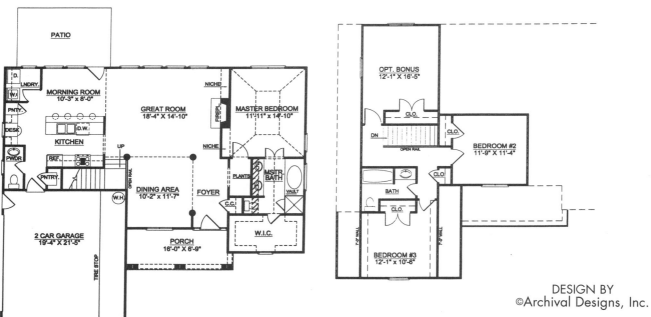

DESIGN BY
©Archival Designs, Inc.

DESIGN HPU040156

First Floor: 1,234 square feet
Second Floor: 458 square feet
Total: 1,692 square feet
Bonus Room: 236 square feet
Width: 48'-6" Depth: 42'-4"

With New England charm, this early American Cape Cod is a quaint haven for any family. Enter from the porch into the foyer, which opens to the dining area and great room. The great room is illuminated by a wall of windows, and features a fireplace with two built-in niches on either side. An efficient kitchen is brightened by the morning room, which accesses an outdoor porch. The opposite side of the home is dedicated to the master suite, which includes a vaulted master bath and a spacious walk-in closet. A two-car garage completes this floor. Two secondary bedrooms reside upstairs and share a full hall bath. An optional bonus room can be used as a fourth bedroom, a playroom or a home office.

DESIGN HPU040157

First Floor: 1,638 square feet
Second Floor: 1,763 square feet
Total: 3,401 square feet
Width: 74'-0" Depth: 46'-0"

DESIGN BY
©Archival Designs, Inc.

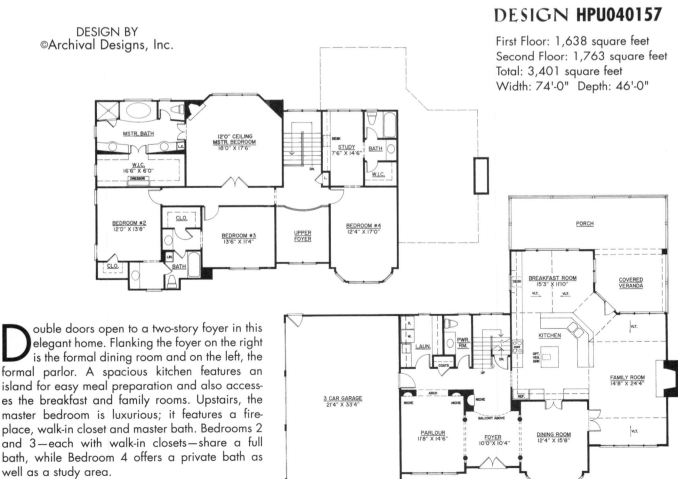

Double doors open to a two-story foyer in this elegant home. Flanking the foyer on the right is the formal dining room and on the left, the formal parlor. A spacious kitchen features an island for easy meal preparation and also accesses the breakfast and family rooms. Upstairs, the master bedroom is luxurious; it features a fireplace, walk-in closet and master bath. Bedrooms 2 and 3—each with walk-in closets—share a full bath, while Bedroom 4 offers a private bath as well as a study area.

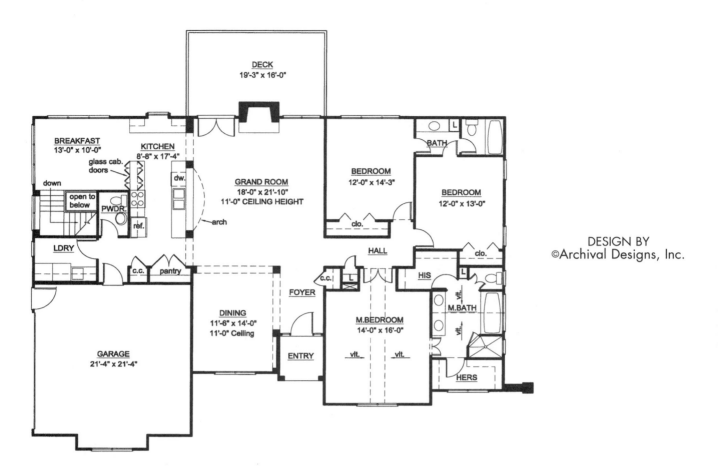

DESIGN BY
©Archival Designs, Inc.

DESIGN HPU040158

Square Footage: 1,751
Width: 64'-0" Depth: 40'-6"

Fine detailing gives this European home a classic exterior. Beyond the foyer, columns define the dining room, and the grand room includes a fireplace and French doors accessible to the rear deck. The kitchen is filled with amenities such as glass cabinet doors, a large pantry and a view of the grand room over the sink. Easily accessible from the kitchen is the breakfast room, laundry room and powder room. Three spacious bedrooms reside on the right side of the plan. The master suite features a deluxe master bath with His and Hers closets, a whirlpool tub, separate shower and dual vanities. The two additional family bedrooms each include private access to a full compartmented bath.

DESIGN HPU040159

Square Footage: 1,670
Width: 50'-0" Depth: 45'-0"

With an offset entrance, this home adds interest and charm to any neighborhood. Enter into a spacious family room, with a galley kitchen nearby offering easy access to the sunny breakfast room. Bedrooms 2 and 3 each have walk-in closets and share a full hall bath. Bedroom 2, which opens off the family room, could also be used as a den. The formal dining room separates the master bedroom from the rest of the home, providing pleasant privacy. The master suite features many amenities, including a walk-in closet, a private bath and access to a private courtyard.

W.I.C.
plant shelf above

M. BATH

MASTER BEDROOM
16'-11" x 13'-5"
11'-0" CEILING

built in table

BREAKFAST
8'-0" x 7'-11"
11'-0" CEILING

FAMILY ROOM
15'-11" x 21'-9"
11'-0" CEILING

KITCHEN
8'-0" x 10'-1"
11'-0" CEILING

arch w/ plant shelf above

COURTYARD
12'-2" x 11'-0"

DINING ROOM
13'-1" x 11'-0"
11'-0" CEILING

pantry

BEDROOM 2
12'-6" x 11'-2"
10'-0" CEILING

BATH

PORCH
12'-0" x 22'-4"

GARAGE
19'-5" x 19'-5"

c.c.

linen

LNDRY.

BEDROOM 2
13'-6" x 11'-0"
8'-0" CEILING

W.I.C.

W.I.C.

DESIGN BY
©Archival Designs, Inc.

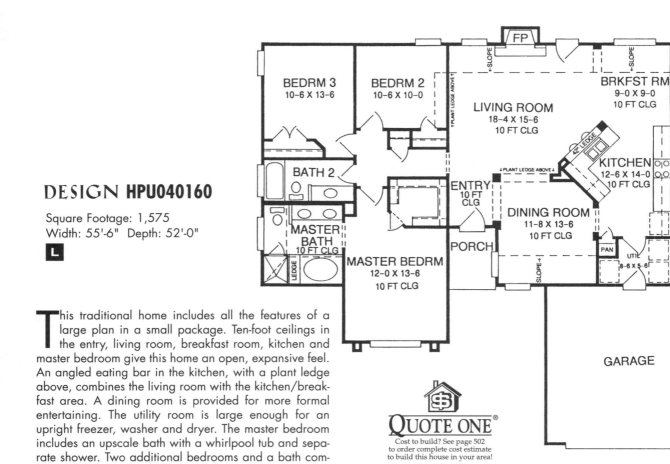

DESIGN HPU040160

Square Footage: 1,575
Width: 55'-6" Depth: 52'-0"

L

This traditional home includes all the features of a large plan in a small package. Ten-foot ceilings in the entry, living room, breakfast room, kitchen and master bedroom give this home an open, expansive feel. An angled eating bar in the kitchen, with a plant ledge above, combines the living room with the kitchen/breakfast area. A dining room is provided for more formal entertaining. The utility room is large enough for an upright freezer, washer and dryer. The master bedroom includes an upscale bath with a whirlpool tub and separate shower. Two additional bedrooms and a bath complete this comfortable home.

QUOTE ONE®
Cost to build? See page 502
to order complete cost estimate
to build this house in your area!

DESIGN BY
©Larry E. Belk Designs

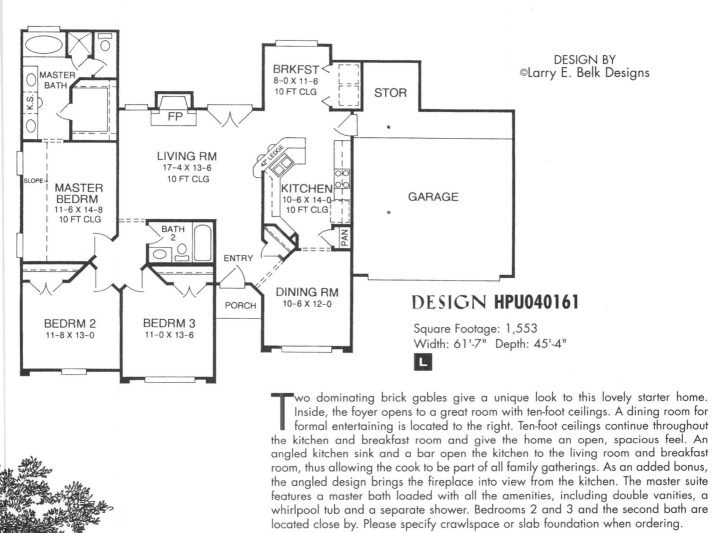

MASTER BATH

K.S.

MASTER BEDRM
11-6 X 14-8
10 FT CLG

SLOPE

FP

LIVING RM
17-4 X 13-6
10 FT CLG

BRKFST
8-0 X 11-6
10 FT CLG

STOR

BATH 2

42" LEDGE

KITCHEN
10-6 X 14-0
10 FT CLG

PAN

GARAGE

BEDRM 2
11-8 X 13-0

BEDRM 3
11-0 X 13-6

ENTRY

PORCH

DINING RM
10-6 X 12-0

DESIGN BY
©Larry E. Belk Designs

DESIGN HPU040161

Square Footage: 1,553
Width: 61'-7" Depth: 45'-4"

L

Two dominating brick gables give a unique look to this lovely starter home. Inside, the foyer opens to a great room with ten-foot ceilings. A dining room for formal entertaining is located to the right. Ten-foot ceilings continue throughout the kitchen and breakfast room and give the home an open, spacious feel. An angled kitchen sink and a bar open the kitchen to the living room and breakfast room, thus allowing the cook to be part of all family gatherings. As an added bonus, the angled design brings the fireplace into view from the kitchen. The master suite features a master bath loaded with all the amenities, including double vanities, a whirlpool tub and a separate shower. Bedrooms 2 and 3 and the second bath are located close by. Please specify crawlspace or slab foundation when ordering.

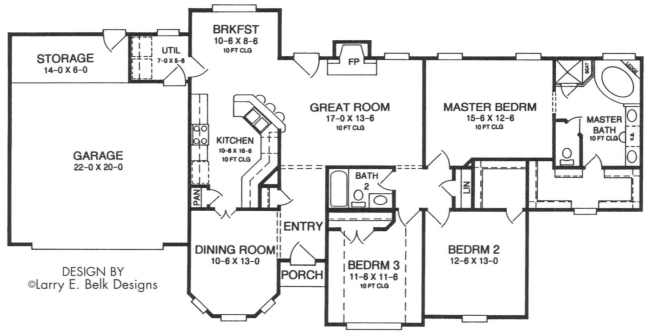

STORAGE
14-0 X 6-0

UTIL
7-0 X 5-6

GARAGE
22-0 X 20-0

DESIGN BY
©Larry E. Belk Designs

BRKFST
10-6 X 8-6
10 FT CLG

FP

KITCHEN
10-6 X 16-6
10 FT CLG

PAN

DINING ROOM
10-6 X 13-0

GREAT ROOM
17-0 X 13-6
10 FT CLG

ENTRY

PORCH

BATH
2

BEDRM 3
11-6 X 11-6
10 FT CLG

MASTER BEDRM
15-6 X 12-6
10 FT CLG

LIN

BEDRM 2
12-6 X 13-0

MASTER
BATH
10 FT CLG

DESIGN HPU040162

Square Footage: 1,742
Width: 78'-0" Depth: 40'-10"

This traditional design warmly welcomes both family and visitors with a delightful bay window, a Palladian window and shutters. The entry introduces a beautiful interior plan, starting with the formal dining room, the central great room with a fireplace, views and access to outdoor spaces. Ten-foot ceilings in the major living areas give the home an open, spacious feel. The kitchen features an angled eating bar, a pantry and lots of cabinet and counter space. Comfort and style abound in the distinctive master suite, offering a high ceiling, corner whirlpool tub, knee-space vanity and compartmented toilet. An ample walk-in closet with a window for natural light completes this retreat. Nearby, Bedrooms 2 and 3 share a hall bath, and Bedroom 3 offers a raised ceiling. Please specify crawlspace or slab foundation when ordering.

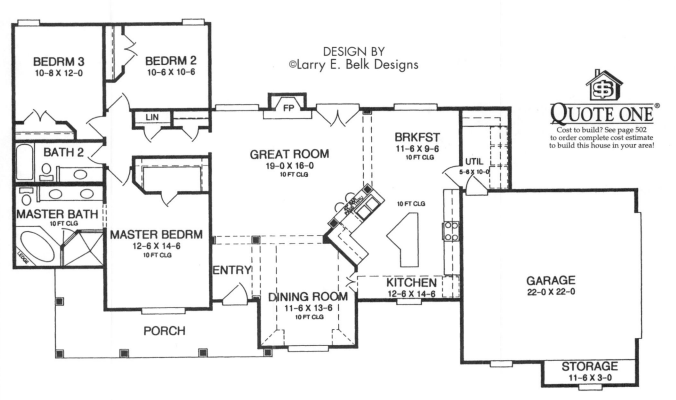

DESIGN BY
©Larry E. Belk Designs

BEDRM 3
10-8 X 12-0

BEDRM 2
10-6 X 10-6

LIN

BATH 2

MASTER BATH
10 FT CLG

LEDGE

MASTER BEDRM
12-6 X 14-6
10 FT CLG

ENTRY

PORCH

GREAT ROOM
19-0 X 16-0
10 FT CLG

FP

DINING ROOM
11-6 X 13-6
10 FT CLG

BRKFST
11-6 X 9-6
10 FT CLG

UTIL
5-6 X 10-0

10 FT CLG

KITCHEN
12-6 X 14-6

GARAGE
22-0 X 22-0

STORAGE
11-6 X 3-0

Quote One®
Cost to build? See page 502
to order complete cost estimate
to build this house in your area!

A traditional brick-and-siding elevation with a lovely wraparound porch sets the stage for a plan that incorporates features demanded by today's lifestyle. The entry opens to the great room and dining room. The use of square columns to define the areas gives the plan the look and feel of a much larger home. The kitchen features loads of counter space and a large work island. The angled sink features a pass-through to the great room. Washer, dryer and freezer space are available in the utility room along with cabinets and countertops. The master bedroom includes a walk-in closet with ample space for two. The master bath features all the amenities: a corner whirlpool tub, a shower and His and Hers vanities. Bedrooms 2 and 3 are located nearby and complete the plan. Please specify slab or crawlspace foundation when ordering.

DESIGN HPU040163

Square Footage: 1,789
Width: 78'-0"   Depth: 47'-0"

L

DESIGN HPU040165

First Floor: 1,250 square feet
Second Floor: 534 square feet
Total: 1,784 square feet
Width: 42'-0" Depth: 49'-0"

From the foyer to the breakfast nook and formal dining room, this two-story home has it all. To the left of the foyer sits an elegant formal dining room. Straight ahead is the great room with a central fireplace and two large rear-facing windows to bring the outdoors in. The master suite located on the main floor offers a large walk-in closet and a private bath with a double vanity. Upstairs, two additional spacious bedrooms share a full bath.

DESIGN BY
©Ahmann Design, Inc.

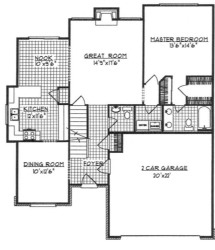
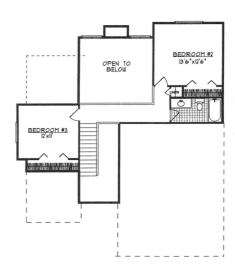

This spacious two-story home is designed for the family who needs functionality but doesn't want to sacrifice the eye-catching design. On the main floor, an open great room invites you to evenings around the fireplace. The open plan on this floor allows free circulation of guests and family from the great room to the nook to the island/snack-bar kitchen. Upstairs, the master suite is spacious and the master bath has His and Hers vanities. Two additional bedrooms share a full bath. No matter which room is your favorite, this stunning home is sure to be the home of your dreams.

DESIGN HPU040164

First Floor: 1,026 square feet
Second Floor: 726 square feet
Total: 1,752 square feet
Width: 60'-4" Depth: 43'-0"

DESIGN BY
©Ahmann Design, Inc.

HOLZHAUER INC. 92

DESIGN BY
©Fillmore Design Group

DESIGN HPU040166

First Floor: 1,368 square feet
Second Floor: 492 square feet
Total: 1,860 square feet
Width: 50'-0" Depth: 47'-1"

This narrow-lot, two-story home shows an abundance of exterior charm. Of particular note is the transom above the front door with glass sidelights. The two-story brick gable in front creates a massive appearance. Inside, the foyer opens directly to a formal dining room and a large great room that offers windows to the rear and a fireplace and built-in TV shelf. The family dining area features a cone ceiling and fantastic view of the rear yard. The first-floor master suite has a cathedral ceiling and two walk-in closets in the bath area. There is a covered patio off the master suite and also off the casual dining room. Two family bedrooms and a full bath complete the second floor.

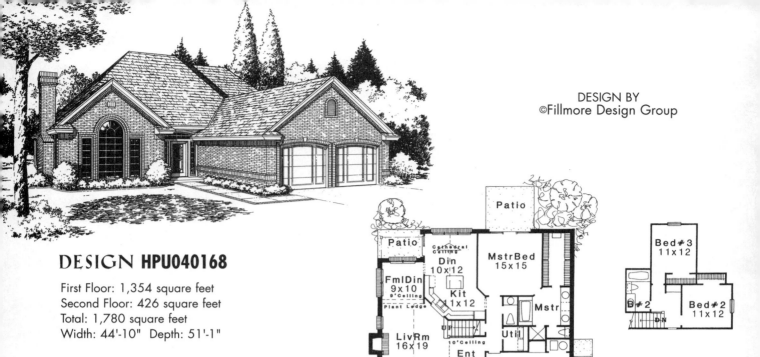

DESIGN HPU040168

First Floor: 1,354 square feet
Second Floor: 426 square feet
Total: 1,780 square feet
Width: 44'-10" Depth: 51'-1"

A dramatic Palladian window attracts passersby to this traditional design with its brick detailing. The living room enjoys a cathedral ceiling and wood-burning fireplace and is separated from the formal dining room by a lovely plant ledge. The nice master suite features private-patio access, a large walk-in closet, and a separate tub and shower in the master bath. Two bedrooms are located upstairs with a full bath.

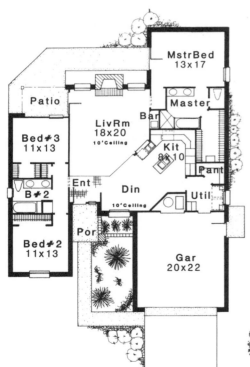

DESIGN HPU040167

Square Footage: 1,664
Width: 48'-0" Depth: 63'-1"

Soaring round-top windows lend excitement to the brick exterior of this traditional design. A spacious living room, with a grand fireplace flanked by windows, opens to the kitchen and dining areas on the right and an appealing covered patio on the left. The large master bedroom features a double-vanity bath and an oversized walk-in closet. The utility area directly accesses the garage and a walk-in pantry.

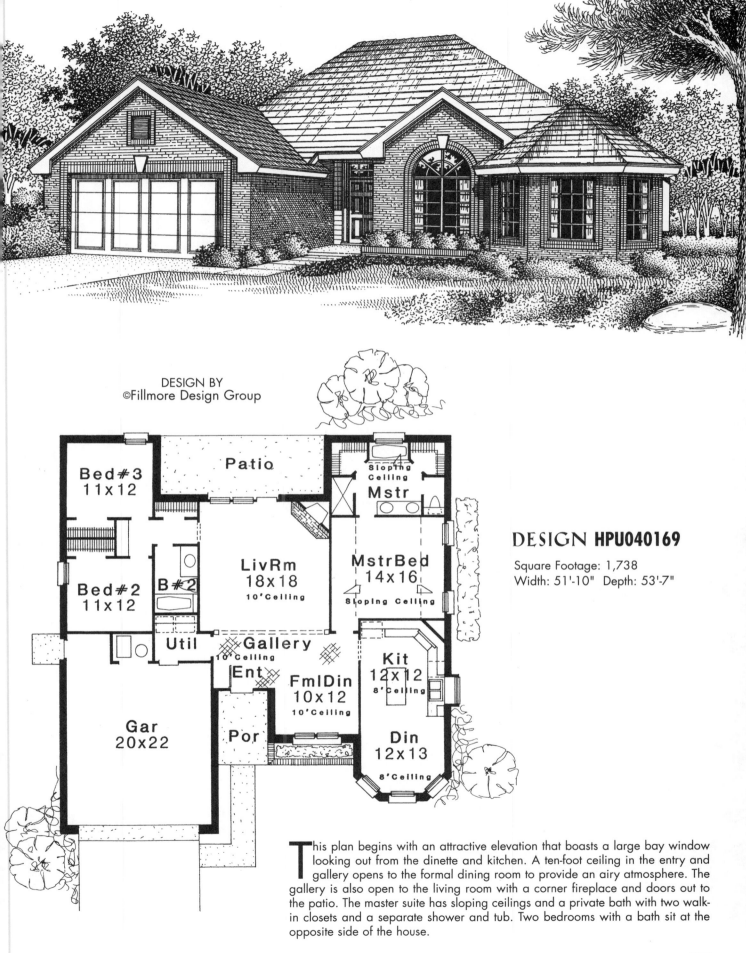

DESIGN BY
©Fillmore Design Group

Bed#3
11x12

Patio

Sloping
Ceiling

Mstr

Bed#2
11x12

B#2

LivRm
18x18
10'Ceiling

MstrBed
14x16
Sloping Ceiling

Util

Gallery
10'Ceiling

Kit
12x12
8'Ceiling

Ent

FmlDin
10x12
10'Ceiling

Gar
20x22

Por

Din
12x13
8'Ceiling

DESIGN HPU040169

Square Footage: 1,738
Width: 51'-10" Depth: 53'-7"

This plan begins with an attractive elevation that boasts a large bay window looking out from the dinette and kitchen. A ten-foot ceiling in the entry and gallery opens to the formal dining room to provide an airy atmosphere. The gallery is also open to the living room with a corner fireplace and doors out to the patio. The master suite has sloping ceilings and a private bath with two walk-in closets and a separate shower and tub. Two bedrooms with a bath sit at the opposite side of the house.

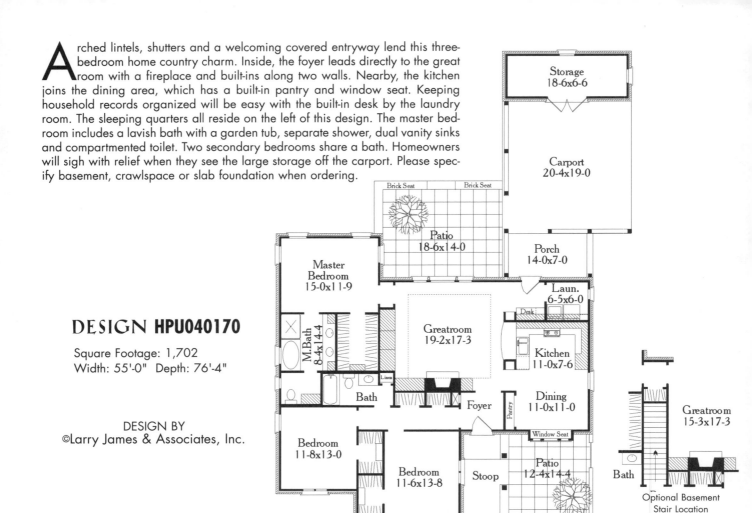

Arched lintels, shutters and a welcoming covered entryway lend this three-bedroom home country charm. Inside, the foyer leads directly to the great room with a fireplace and built-ins along two walls. Nearby, the kitchen joins the dining area, which has a built-in pantry and window seat. Keeping household records organized will be easy with the built-in desk by the laundry room. The sleeping quarters all reside on the left of this design. The master bedroom includes a lavish bath with a garden tub, separate shower, dual vanity sinks and compartmented toilet. Two secondary bedrooms share a bath. Homeowners will sigh with relief when they see the large storage off the carport. Please specify basement, crawlspace or slab foundation when ordering.

DESIGN HPU040170

Square Footage: 1,702
Width: 55'-0" Depth: 76'-4"

DESIGN BY
©Larry James & Associates, Inc.

Storage
18-6x6-6

Carport
20-4x19-0

Porch
14-0x7-0

Brick Seat   Brick Seat

Patio
18-6x14-0

Master
Bedroom
15-0x11-9

M.Bath
8-4x14-4

Bath

Bedroom
11-8x13-0

Bedroom
11-6x13-8

Greatroom
19-2x17-3

Linen

Foyer

Stoop

Laun.
6-5x6-0

Desk

Kitchen
11-0x7-6

Dining
11-0x11-0

Pantry

Window Seat

Patio
12-4x14-4

Greatroom
15-3x17-3

Bath

Optional Basement
Stair Location

138

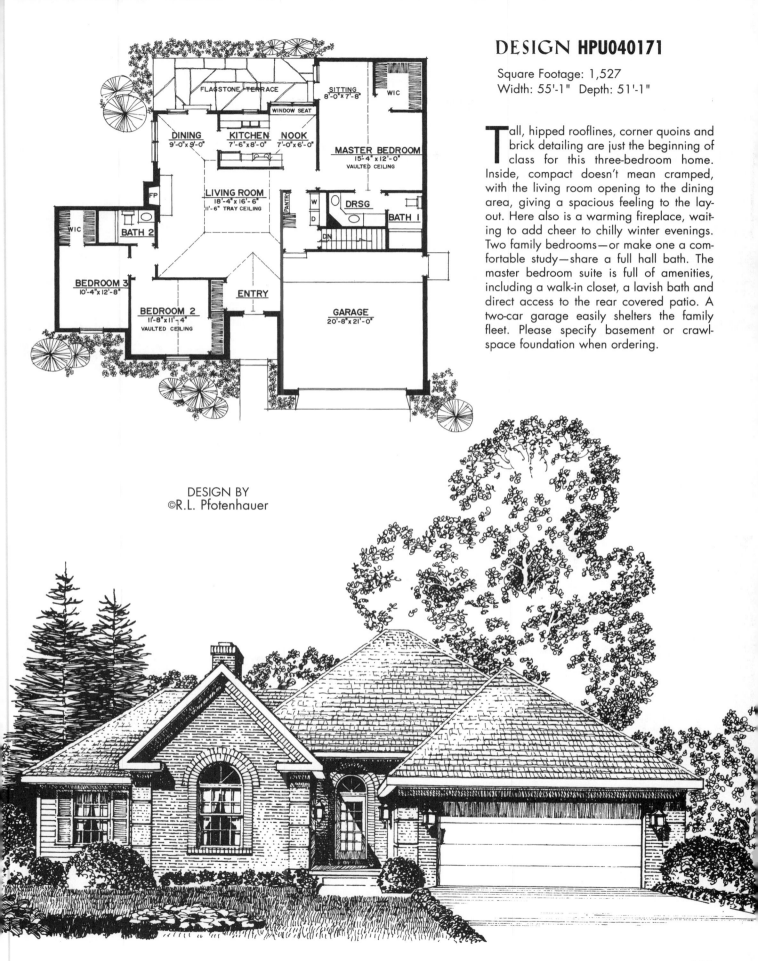

DESIGN HPU040171

Square Footage: 1,527
Width: 55'-1" Depth: 51'-1"

Tall, hipped rooflines, corner quoins and brick detailing are just the beginning of class for this three-bedroom home. Inside, compact doesn't mean cramped, with the living room opening to the dining area, giving a spacious feeling to the layout. Here also is a warming fireplace, waiting to add cheer to chilly winter evenings. Two family bedrooms—or make one a comfortable study—share a full hall bath. The master bedroom suite is full of amenities, including a walk-in closet, a lavish bath and direct access to the rear covered patio. A two-car garage easily shelters the family fleet. Please specify basement or crawlspace foundation when ordering.

FLAGSTONE TERRACE

SITTING
8'-0" x 7'-8"

WIC

WINDOW SEAT

DINING
9'-0" x 9'-0"

KITCHEN
7'-6" x 8'-0"

NOOK
7'-0" x 6'-0"

MASTER BEDROOM
15'-4" x 12'-0"
VAULTED CEILING

FP

LIVING ROOM
18'-4" x 16'-6"
11'-6" TRAY CEILING

PANTRY

W
D

DRSG

BATH 1

WIC

BATH 2

DN

BEDROOM 3
10'-4" x 12'-8"

ENTRY

BEDROOM 2
11'-8" x 11'-4"
VAULTED CEILING

GARAGE
20'-8" x 21'-0"

DESIGN BY
©R.L. Pfotenhauer

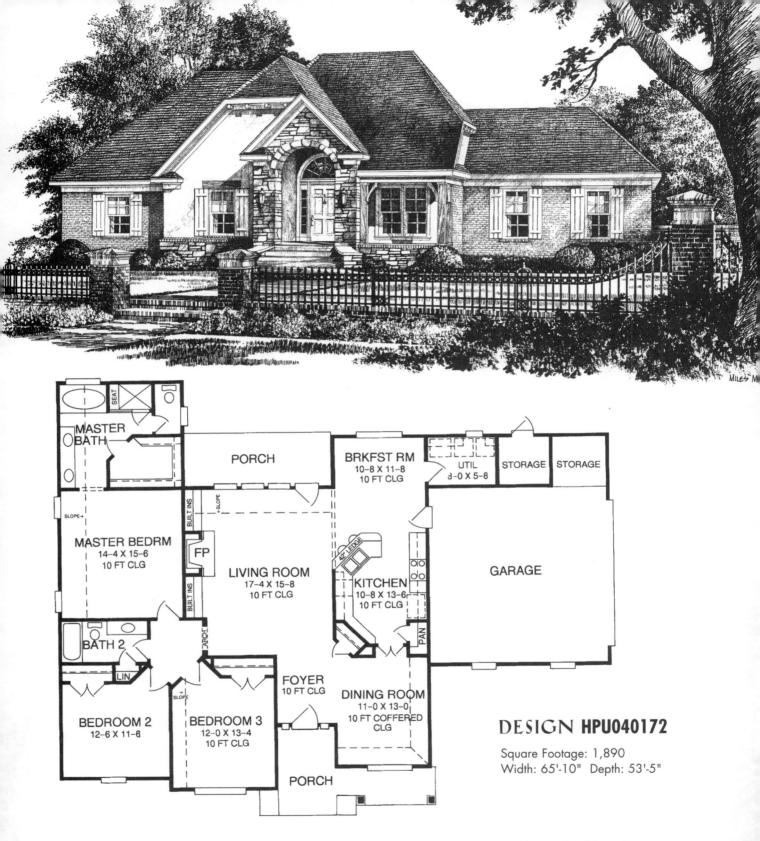

MASTER BATH

PORCH

BRKFST RM
10-8 X 11-8
10 FT CLG

UTIL
8-0 X 5-8

STORAGE

STORAGE

MASTER BEDRM
14-4 15-6
10 FT CLG

FP

LIVING ROOM
17-4 X 15-8
10 FT CLG

KITCHEN
10-8 X 13-6
10 FT CLG

GARAGE

BATH 2

LIN

FOYER
10 FT CLG

DINING ROOM
11-0 X 13-0
10 FT COFFERED CLG

BEDROOM 2
12-6 X 11-6

BEDROOM 3
12-0 X 13-4
10 FT CLG

PORCH

DESIGN HPU040172

Square Footage: 1,890
Width: 65'-10" Depth: 53'-5"

DESIGN BY
©Larry E. Belk Designs

This charming country home possesses a heart of gold. Wide views invite natural light and provide a sense of spaciousness in the living room. A fireplace with an extended hearth is framed by built-in bookcases and complemented by a sloped ceiling. A well-organized kitchen has wrapping counters and a serving ledge, which overlooks the breakfast area. Bright light fills the casual dining space through a wide window. The formal dining room has a coffered ceiling and enjoys easy service from the kitchen through double doors. The master suite contains a garden tub and a separate shower with a seat. Please specify crawlspace or slab foundation when ordering.

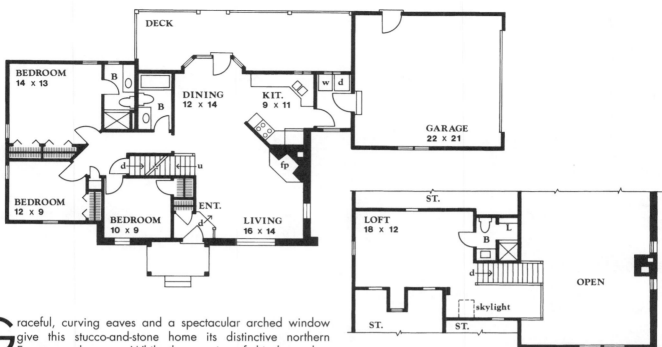

BEDROOM
14 x 13

B

DECK

DINING
12 x 14

KIT.
9 x 11

w d

GARAGE
22 x 21

BEDROOM
12 x 9

d

u

fp

BEDROOM
10 x 9

ENT.

d

LIVING
16 x 14

ST.

LOFT
18 x 12

L

B

d

OPEN

ST.

ST.

skylight

Graceful, curving eaves and a spectacular arched window give this stucco-and-stone home its distinctive northern European elegance. While the exterior of this home has abundant Old World charm, the interior is filled with contemporary amenities. From the entrance, an expansive open area comprised of the living room, dining room and kitchen—all with beam ceilings—provides a dramatic centerpiece. The angled bay from the dining room opens conveniently to the rear deck, furnishing options for dining alfresco. Sleeping quarters located on the left wing of the first floor include a master bedroom with a private bath. A full bath serves both family bedrooms and is readily accessible to guests. Upstairs, a spacious loft has its own bathroom and a balcony overlooking the living room.

DESIGN HPU040173

First Floor: 1,277 square feet
Second Floor: 378 square feet
Total: 1,655 square feet
Width: 74'-8" Depth: 42'-8"

DESIGN BY
©R.L. Pfotenhauer

DINING
10/6 X 12/0+

NOOK
13/10 X 8/4

OPT. FR.
DRS

15/0 X 9/0

DW

PAN REF

2 STORY
LIVING
13/0 X 14/0

FAMILY
13/10 X 20/8

DECK

DN
UP
DN

Though this home gives the impression of the Northwest, it will be the winner of any neighborhood. Craftsman style is evident both on the outside and the inside of this three-bedroom home. From the foyer, the two-story living room is just a couple of steps up and features a through-fireplace. The U-shaped kitchen has a cooktop work island, an adjacent nook and easy access to the formal dining room. A spacious family room shares the fireplace with the living room, is enhanced by built-ins and also offers a quiet deck for stargazing. The upstairs consists of two family bedrooms sharing a full bath and a vaulted master suite complete with a walk-in closet and sumptuous bath. A two-car, drive-under garage has plenty of room for storage. Please specify basement or slab foundation when ordering.

DESIGN BY
©Alan Mascord Design Associates, Inc.

BR. 3
11/0 X 10/8

BR. 2
11/0 X 10/0

SHELVES

DN

LOFT

FOYER
BELOW

LIVING
BELOW

LIN

VAULTED
MASTER
15/2 X 12/0

GARAGE
28/2 X 29/10

UP

DESIGN HPU040174

Main Floor: 1,106 square feet
Upper Floor: 872 square feet
Total: 1,978 square feet
Width: 38'-0" Depth: 35'-0"

DESIGN HPU040175

First Floor: 1,097 square feet
Second Floor: 807 square feet
Total: 1,904 square feet
Width: 40'-0" Depth: 45'-0"

The combination of rafter tails, stone-and-siding and gabled rooflines gives this home plenty of curb appeal. The Craftsman styling on this three-bedroom bungalow is highly attractive. Inside, enter a cozy vaulted den through double doors, just to the left of the foyer. A spacious, vaulted great room features a fireplace and is near the formal dining room, providing entertaining ease. The kitchen offers an octagonal island, a corner sink with a window, and a pantry. Up the angled staircase is the sleeping zone. Here two secondary bedrooms share a hall bath, while the master suite is enhanced with a private bath and a walk-in closet. The three-car garage easily shelters the family fleet.

DESIGN BY
©Alan Mascord Design Associates, Inc.

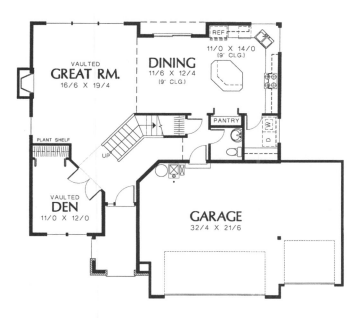

143

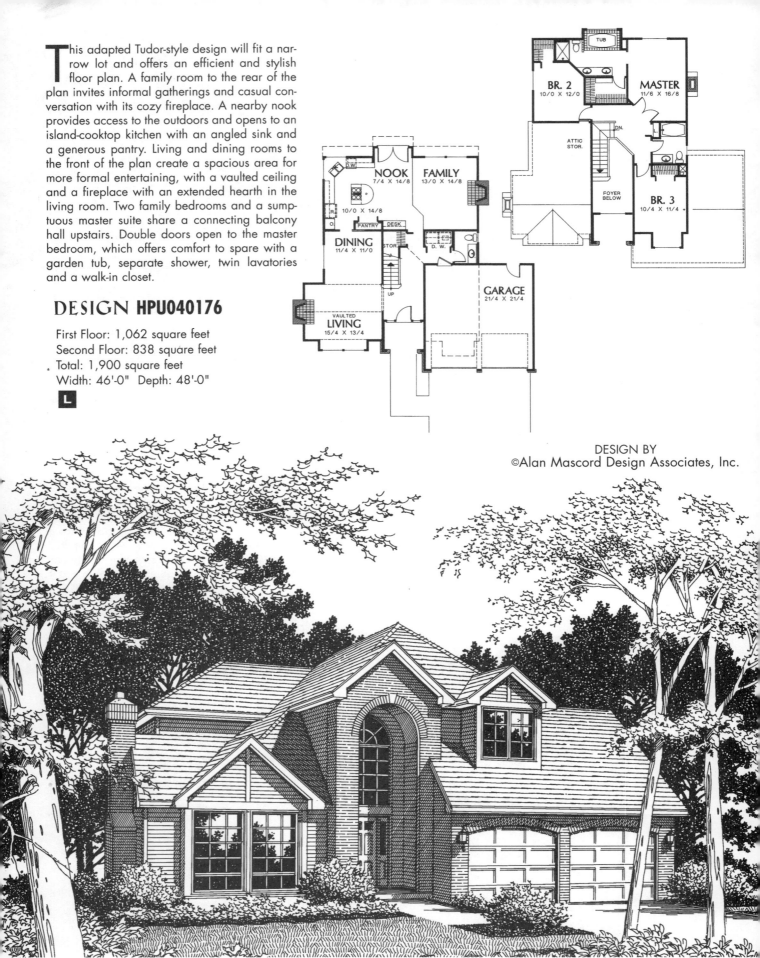

This adapted Tudor-style design will fit a narrow lot and offers an efficient and stylish floor plan. A family room to the rear of the plan invites informal gatherings and casual conversation with its cozy fireplace. A nearby nook provides access to the outdoors and opens to an island-cooktop kitchen with an angled sink and a generous pantry. Living and dining rooms to the front of the plan create a spacious area for more formal entertaining, with a vaulted ceiling and a fireplace with an extended hearth in the living room. Two family bedrooms and a sumptuous master suite share a connecting balcony hall upstairs. Double doors open to the master bedroom, which offers comfort to spare with a garden tub, separate shower, twin lavatories and a walk-in closet.

DESIGN **HPU040176**

First Floor: 1,062 square feet
Second Floor: 838 square feet
Total: 1,900 square feet
Width: 46'-0" Depth: 48'-0"

L

DESIGN BY
©Alan Mascord Design Associates, Inc.

A brick arch and a two-story bay window adorn the facade of this comfortable family home. Inside, the formal bayed living room and dining room combine to make entertaining a breeze. At the rear of the home, family life is easy with the open floor plan of the family room, nook and efficient kitchen. A fireplace graces the family room, and sliding glass doors access the outdoors from the nook. A powder room is conveniently located in the entry hall to make it easily accessible. Upstairs, three bedrooms include the master suite with a pampering bath. A full hall bath with twin vanities is shared by the family bedrooms. A bonus room is available for future development as a study, library or fourth bedroom.

DESIGN **HPU040177**

First Floor: 972 square feet
Second Floor: 843 square feet
Total: 1,815 square feet
Bonus Room: 180 square feet
Width: 45'-0" Depth: 37'-0"

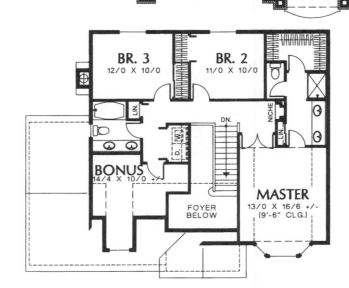

FAMILY
14/8 X 13/8

NOOK
9/8 X 13/8

10/8 X 11/2

D.W.

P. REF.

GARAGE
20/4 X 21/4 +/-

DINING
13/0 X 10/0

UP

LIVING
13/0 X 12/4 +/-

BR. 3
12/0 X 10/0

BR. 2
11/0 X 10/0

NICHE

LIN.

DN.

D. W.

LIN.

BONUS
14/4 X 10/0 +/-

FOYER
BELOW

MASTER
13/0 X 16/6 +/-
(9'-6" CLG.)

DESIGN BY
©Alan Mascord Design Associates, Inc.

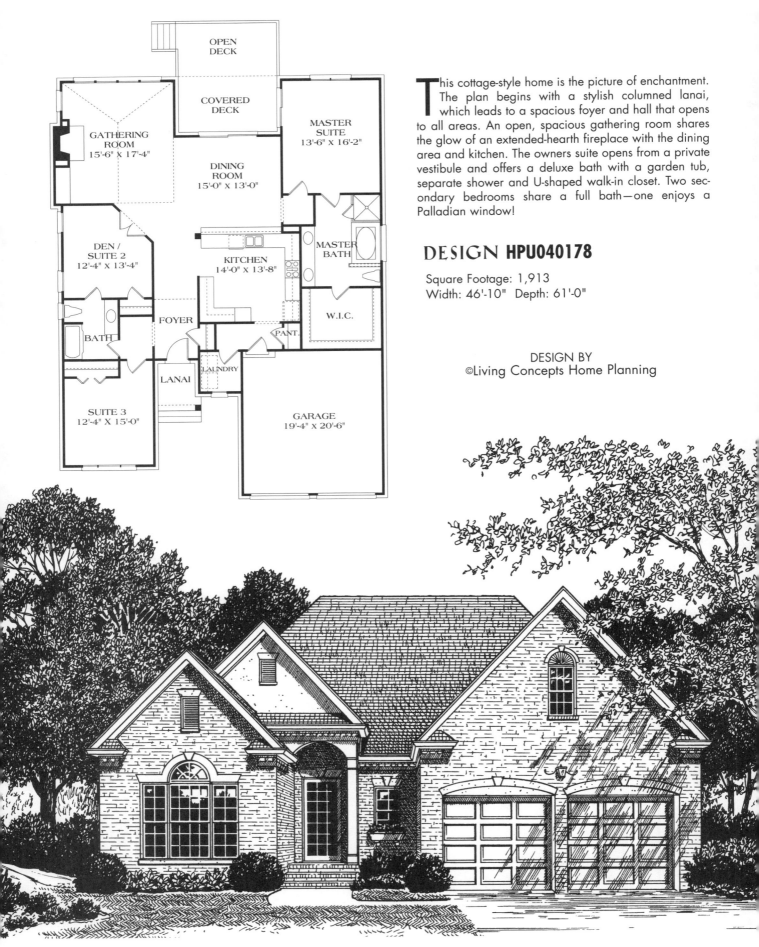

OPEN
DECK

COVERED
DECK

GATHERING
ROOM
15'-6" x 17'-4"

MASTER
SUITE
13'-6" X 16'-2"

DINING
ROOM
15'-0" X 13'-0"

DEN /
SUITE 2
12'-4" X 13'-4"

KITCHEN
14'-0" X 13'-8"

MASTER
BATH

BATH

FOYER

W.I.C.

PANT.

LANAI

LAUNDRY

SUITE 3
12'-4" X 15'-0"

GARAGE
19'-4" X 20'-6"

This cottage-style home is the picture of enchantment. The plan begins with a stylish columned lanai, which leads to a spacious foyer and hall that opens to all areas. An open, spacious gathering room shares the glow of an extended-hearth fireplace with the dining area and kitchen. The owners suite opens from a private vestibule and offers a deluxe bath with a garden tub, separate shower and U-shaped walk-in closet. Two secondary bedrooms share a full bath—one enjoys a Palladian window!

DESIGN HPU040178

Square Footage: 1,913
Width: 46'-10" Depth: 61'-0"

DESIGN BY
©Living Concepts Home Planning

A dramatic entry introduces this hillside design and offers an arched window over the door to add light to the foyer. A split staircase leads up to the main level of the home where there are formal living and dining rooms decorated with columns. A family room with a fireplace and built-in media center adjoins the island kitchen and breakfast nook at the rear. A door in the nook leads out to a rear deck. The master suite on the main level holds a walk-in closet and bath with a spa tub and separate shower. The lower level accesses the two-car garage and allows for two additional bedrooms and a full bath. A large storage space may also be used as a den, if you choose.

DESIGN BY
©Alan Mascord Design Associates, Inc.

DESIGN HPU040179

Main Floor: 1,278 square feet
Lower Floor: 698 square feet
Total: 1,976 square feet
Width: 40'-0" Depth: 42'-6"

DESIGN BY
©Living Concepts Home Planning

This open, airy design is one that seems much larger than it actually is. A large, two-story great room, which can be viewed from the balcony above, opens into the dining room. The roomy master suite boasts a terrific walk-in closet and bath with dual lavatories. A breakfast area that opens to a deck, and corner windows at the kitchen sink help bring the outdoors in. There's plenty of storage, including an ample pantry, a two-car garage and a bonus room that can double as a fourth suite. Special features include a plant ledge over the great room and an arched, copper dormer. Please specify slab or crawlspace foundation when ordering.

DECK/
TERRACE

BREAKFAST
8'-0" x 14'-6"

KITCHEN
10'-0" x 12'-0"

DINING
ROOM
11'-0" x 12'-0"

PANTRY

MASTER
SUITE
15'-0" x 12'-0"

W.I.C.

MASTER
BATH

LAUNDRY

GREAT ROOM
15'-0" x 19'-8"

UP

PDR.

GARAGE
20'-4" x 21'-0"

LOGGIA

STOR.

W.I.C.

SUITE 2
12'-0" x 12'-0"

SUITE 3/
OPT. LOFT
11'-0" x 12'-0"

W.I.C.

BALCONY

DN

LEDGE

BATH

BONUS ROOM
16'-6" x 16'-0"

OPEN
TO
BELOW

DESIGN HPU040180

First Floor: 1,383 square feet
Second Floor: 546 square feet
Total: 1,929 square feet
Bonus Room: 320 square feet
Width: 50'-6" Depth: 42'-10"

SHEER GENIUS

Comfortable homes that offer warm welcomes

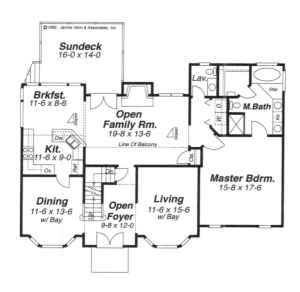

This French-style home is designed for a sloping lot, with the garage at basement level. The stone-and-stucco exterior is highlighted by interesting windows, corner quoins and a variety of gables. Inside, the two-story foyer is flanked by the formal living and dining rooms, both of which are lighted by bay windows. The family room features a fireplace and access to the sun deck. An efficient kitchen opens to a glass-walled breakfast room and provides a snack bar that serves the entire informal living area. Completing the first floor, the master suite includes a compartmented bath with a walk-in closet and twin vanities. Upstairs, three family bedrooms share a good-sized bath and views of much of the first floor.

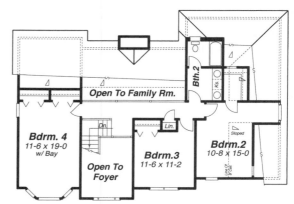

DESIGN HPU040181

First Floor: 1,560 square feet
Second Floor: 834 square feet
Total: 2,394 square feet
Width: 50'-0" Depth: 47'-0"

DESIGN BY
©Jannis Vann & Associates, Inc.

149

DESIGN HPU040183

Square Footage: 2,289
Width: 66'-0" Depth: 77'-0"

A striking facade with plenty of windows and column accents gives this home a regal appeal. Stucco works together with a handsome tiled roof to define a Mediterranean exterior. A see-through fireplace opens to the receiving room and graces the great room. The kitchen sits between the dining room and the great room and offers a cooktop island. The master suite provides a lounging area, a vaulted ceiling, two closets and a bath.

DESIGN BY
©Vaughn A. Lauban Designs

The dramatic entry with an arched opening leads to the comfortable interior of this delightful one-story home. Volume ceilings highlight the main living areas, which include a formal dining room and a great room with access to one of the verandas. In the turreted study, quiet time is assured. The master suite features a bath with a double-bowl vanity and a bumped-out whirlpool tub. The secondary bedrooms reside on the other side of the house.

DESIGN BY
©The Sater Design Collection

DESIGN HPU040182

Square Footage: 2,214
Width: 63'-0" Depth: 72'-0"

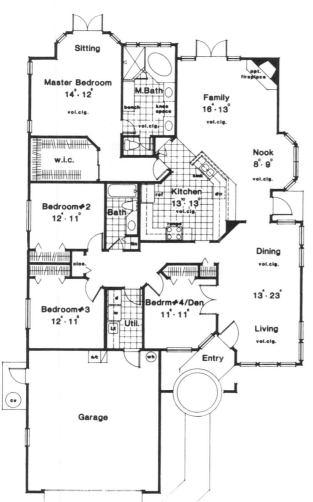

Sitting

Master Bedroom
14⁴·12⁸
vol.clg.

M.Bath
bench
knee space

Family
16⁴·13⁰
vol.clg.

opt. fireplace

w.i.c.

Nook
8⁰·9⁰
vol.clg.

Bedroom #2
12²·11⁰

Bath

Kitchen
13⁰·13⁰
vol.clg.

ref   dw

range

clos.

Dining
vol.clg.

13⁴·23

Bedroom #3
12²·11⁰

d
w

Bedrm #4/Den
11¹·11⁰

Util.

Living
vol.clg.

a.c.   wh

Entry

cu

Garage

Looking for plenty of bedrooms? This design offers four, including a grand master suite with a sitting room and private bath. Bedroom 4 may be used as a den; both the foyer and the main hall access this room. The central kitchen features a pass-through counter overlooking a breakfast nook. The nearby family room highlights a corner fireplace and double-door access to the rear yard. Formal living and dining rooms are offset to the front of the plan, but open to one another. All common areas have volume ceilings, as does the master bedroom and its bath. The laundry room connects the main house to the two-car garage.

DESIGN HPU040184

Square Footage: 2,202
Width: 45'-0" Depth: 77'-4"

DESIGN BY
©Lucia Custom Home Designers, Inc.

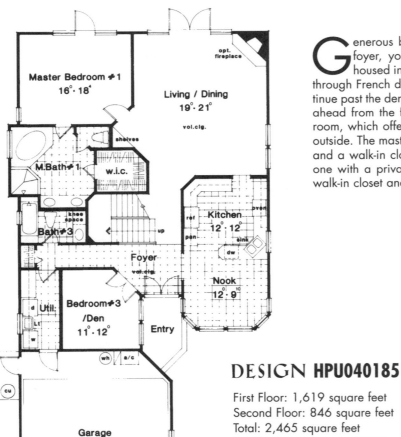

Generous bay windows give this home an opulent look. From the foyer, you can enter the kitchen and breakfast nook, which is housed in one of the wide bay windows. Or you can enter the den through French doors on the left—this could be a third bedroom. Or continue past the den to the laundry room and a hall bath. If you walk straight ahead from the foyer, you will end up in the combination living/dining room, which offers an optional corner fireplace and French doors to the outside. The master bedroom off this area includes a compartmented bath and a walk-in closet. The second floor houses another master suite—this one with a private balcony—and a secondary bedroom with a smaller walk-in closet and private bath.

DESIGN HPU040185

First Floor: 1,619 square feet
Second Floor: 846 square feet
Total: 2,465 square feet
Width: 37'-4" Depth: 69'-0"

DESIGN BY
©Lucia Custom Home Designers, Inc.

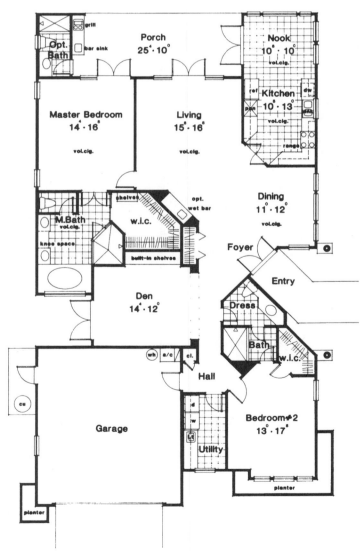

Born as sunny stucco and bred in warm-weather climates, this one-story, two-bedroom home is the perfect choice for starters or empty-nesters. The living room and dining room form an open area near the gourmet kitchen. An attached breakfast nook has a wall of glass for bright casual meals. Generous outdoor access includes double doors in the master bedroom, the living room, the den and the nook all leading to outdoor spaces. Other special features include an optional wet bar, an outdoor grill and sink, an optional pool bath and built-in shelves in the den.

DESIGN HPU040186

Square Footage: 2,150
Width: 42'-0" Depth: 75'-0"

DESIGN BY
©Lucia Custom Home Designers, Inc.

153

Three designs give options for the exterior of this home—all three come with the same floor plan. The entry leads into a small foyer, and opens to the living room and a two-story dining room. A powder room and a U-shaped stairway are on the way to the kitchen, which offers a large work island, walk-in pantry, breakfast nook and laundry room. The family room at the rear of the plan accesses the rear patio through sliding glass doors. The master bath features a double-bowl vanity, corner window tub and walk-in closet. Three second-floor bedrooms share a bath that has a double-bowl vanity. A fifth bedroom may be added over the dining room.

Optional 5th Bedroom

Alternate Elevation A

Alternate Elevation B

DESIGN HPU040187

First Floor: 1,514 square feet
Second Floor: 632 square feet
Total: 2,146 square feet
Width: 39'-4"   Depth: 53'-4"

DESIGN BY
©Lucia Custom Home Designers, Inc.

154

Modern gables define this plan's dramatic exterior. A covered front porch welcomes visitors into the foyer. To the left, the great room features a warming fireplace. The dining room is highlighted by a beautiful display of bayed windows. The kitchen opens to a breakfast area, which also features a bayed window area. This split-bedroom design allows for a private first-floor master bedroom, which includes its own private bath and walk-in closet. Throughout this plan, bay-window accents, a rear deck and a screened porch provide a fresh, indoor/outdoor livability. A two-car garage completes this floor. Bonus space on the second level makes this plan an intriguing option for the growing family.

DESIGN HPU040188

First Floor: 1,563 square feet
Second Floor: 736 square feet
Total: 2,299 square feet
Bonus Room: 280 square feet
Width: 44'-0" Depth: 72'-0"

L

DESIGN BY
©Home Planners

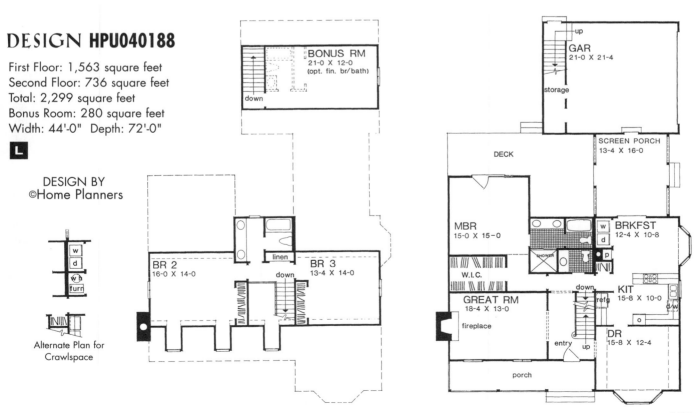

Alternate Plan for
Crawlspace

BONUS RM
21-0 X 12-0
(opt. fin. br/bath)

down

BR 2
16-0 X 14-0

linen

down

BR 3
13-4 X 14-0

up

GAR
21-0 X 21-4

storage

SCREEN PORCH
13-4 X 16-0

DECK

MBR
15-0 X 15-0

W.I.C.

GREAT RM
18-4 X 13-0

fireplace

entry up

down

w
d

BRKFST
12-4 X 10-8

SHOWER

KIT
15-8 X 10-0

DR
15-8 X 12-4

porch

L attice walls, pickets and horizontal siding complement a relaxed Key West design that's perfect for waterfront properties. The grand room with a fireplace, the dining room and Bedroom 2 open through French doors to the veranda. The master suite occupies the entire second floor and features access to a private balcony through double doors. This pampering suite also includes a spacious walk-in closet and a full bath with a whirlpool tub. Enclosed storage/bonus space and a garage are available on the lower level. This home is designed with a pier foundation.

DESIGN HPU040189

First Floor: 1,586 square feet
Second Floor: 601 square feet
Total: 2,187 square feet
Width: 50'-0" Depth: 44'-0"

DESIGN BY
©The Sater Design Collection

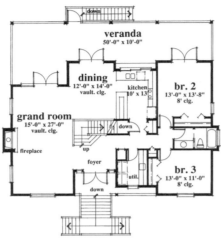

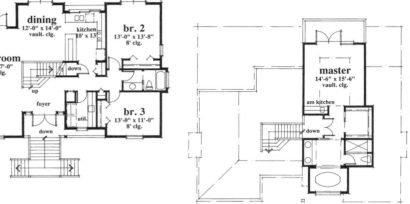

Lattice door panels, shutters, a balustrade and a metal roof add character to this delightful coastal home. Double doors flanking a fireplace open to the side sun deck from the spacious great room. Access to the rear veranda is also provided from this room. An adjacent dining room provides views of the rear grounds and space for formal and informal entertaining. The glassed-in nook shares space with the L-shaped kitchen containing a center work island. Bedrooms 2 and 3, a full bath and a utility room complete this floor. Upstairs, a sumptuous master suite awaits. Double doors extend to a private deck from the master bedroom. His and Hers walk-in closets lead the way to a grand bath featuring an arched whirlpool tub, a double-bowl vanity and a separate shower.

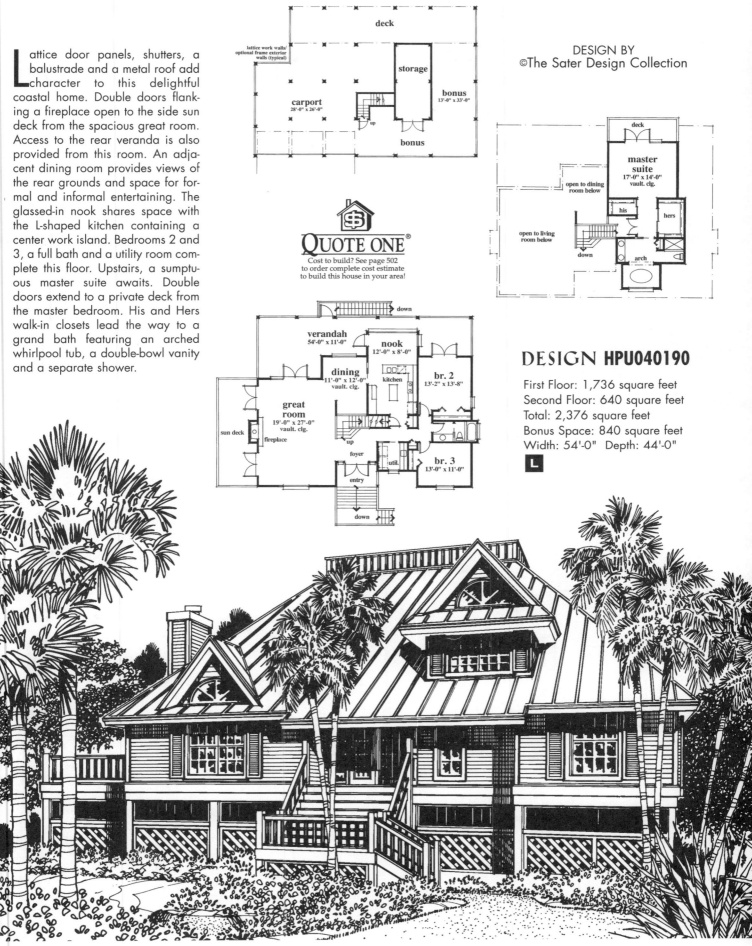

deck

lattice work walls/
optional frame exterior
walls (typical)

storage

carport
28'-0" x 26'-0"

bonus
13'-0" x 33'-0"

up

bonus

DESIGN BY
©The Sater Design Collection

deck

master
suite
17'-0" x 14'-0"
vault. clg.

open to dining
room below

his

hers

open to living
room below

down

arch

QUOTE ONE®

Cost to build? See page 502
to order complete cost estimate
to build this house in your area!

down

verandah
54'-0" x 11'-0"

nook
12'-0" x 8'-0"

dining
11'-0" x 12'-0"
vault. clg.

kitchen

br. 2
13'-2" x 13'-8"

great
room
19'-0" x 27'-0"
vault. clg.

sun deck

fireplace

up

foyer

util.

br. 3
13'-0" x 11'-0"

entry

down

DESIGN HPU040190

First Floor: 1,736 square feet
Second Floor: 640 square feet
Total: 2,376 square feet
Bonus Space: 840 square feet
Width: 54'-0"   Depth: 44'-0"

L

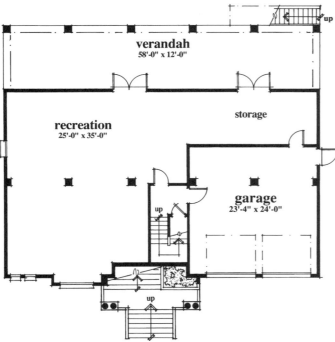

verandah
58'-0" x 12'-0"

recreation
25'-0" x 35'-0"

storage

up

garage
23'-4" x 24'-0"

up

up

DESIGN HPU040191

Square Footage: 2,190
Width: 58'-0" Depth: 54'-0"

DESIGN BY
©The Sater Design Collection

The dramatic arched entry of this Southampton-style cottage borrows freely from its Southern coastal past. The foyer and central hall open to the grand room. The kitchen is flanked by the dining room and morning nook, which opens to the lanai. On the left side of the plan, the master suite also accesses the lanai. Two walk-in closets, a compartmented bath with separate tub and shower and a double-bowl vanity complete this opulent retreat. The right side of the plan includes two secondary bedrooms and a full bath.

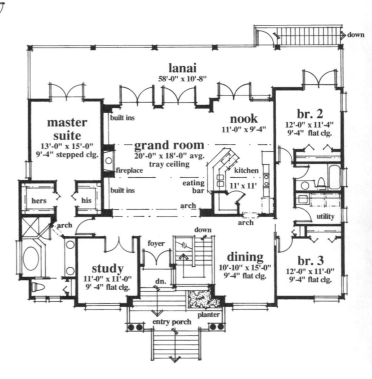

lanai
58'-0" x 10'-8"

built ins

nook
11'-0" x 9'-4"

br. 2
12'-0" x 11'-4"
9'-4" flat clg.

master suite
13'-0" x 15'-0"
9'-4" stepped clg.

grand room
20'-0" x 18'-0" avg.
tray ceiling

kitchen
11' x 11'

fireplace

built ins

hers

his

eating bar

arch

arch

utility

arch

down

foyer

dn.

dining
10'-10" x 15'-0"
9'-4" flat clg.

br. 3
12'-0" x 11'-0"
9'-4" flat clg.

study
11'-0" x 11'-0"
9'-4" flat clg.

planter

entry porch

A versatile swing room is a highlight of this compact and charming French-style home. Using the optional door to the entry, the swing room makes a perfect office, or it can be used as a bedroom or study. The king-size master suite is isolated for privacy and has a spacious bath and walk-in closet with passage to the utility room. The open and spacious living room features twelve-foot ceilings. Two secondary bedrooms offer walk-in closets and private baths. Please specify crawlspace or slab foundation when ordering.

DESIGN HPU040192

Square Footage: 2,200
Width: 56'-0" Depth: 74'-0"

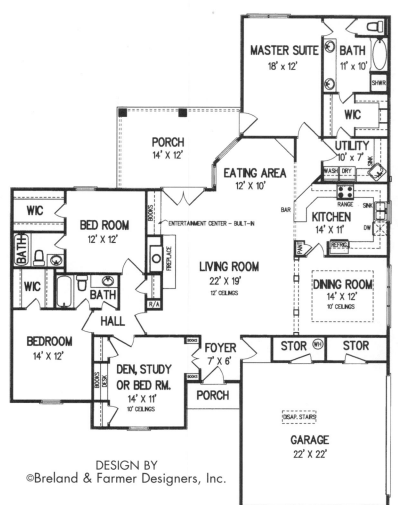

MASTER SUITE
18' x 12'

BATH
11' x 10'

SHWR

WIC

UTILITY
10' x 7'

WASH DRY

PORCH
14' X 12'

EATING AREA
12' x 10'

BAR

KITCHEN
14' x 11'

RANGE SINK

DW

WIC

BED ROOM
12' X 12'

BOOKS

ENTERTAINMENT CENTER – BUILT-IN

FIREPLACE

LIVING ROOM
22' X 19'
12' ceilings

PANT

REFRIG.

BATH

WIC

BATH

R/A

DINING ROOM
14' X 12'
10' ceilings

HALL

FOYER
7' X 6'

STOR WH STOR

BEDROOM
14' X 12'

BOOKS
DESK

DEN, STUDY
OR BED RM.
14' X 11'
10' ceilings

BOOKS

PORCH

DISAP. STAIRS

GARAGE
22' X 22'

DESIGN BY
©Breland & Farmer Designers, Inc.

159

Shuttered windows encompassing the breadth of this lovely home recall the easy-living feeling of the Southern Plantation style. Perfect for warm climates, this home includes a large rear porch, punctuated with skylights, that enlarges the capacity for entertaining. Two family bedrooms share a full bath and complement the master suite. The two-car garage has a compartmented storage area and is situated near the kitchen and laundry room. Please specify basement, crawlspace or slab foundation when ordering.

DESIGN BY
©Larry James & Associates, Inc.

Garage
20-4x21-4

M.Bath
17-8x10-6

Porch
22-0x12-0

1/2
Bath

Stor.
5-0x6-1

Master
Bedroom
19-2x13-7

Laun.
8-4x5-8

Greatroom
22-0x15-2

Kitchen
12-8x12-0

Bath

Bedroom
10-8x12-0

Bedroom
11-6x11-0

Foyer

Dining
11-6x13-6

Breakfast
12-8x9-10

Porch
30-8x6-0

Future
14-0x12-0

Future
29-4x16-0

Future
12-8x12-0

DESIGN HPU040193

Square Footage: 2,089
Bonus Space: 878 square feet
Width: 63'-10" Depth: 64'-7"

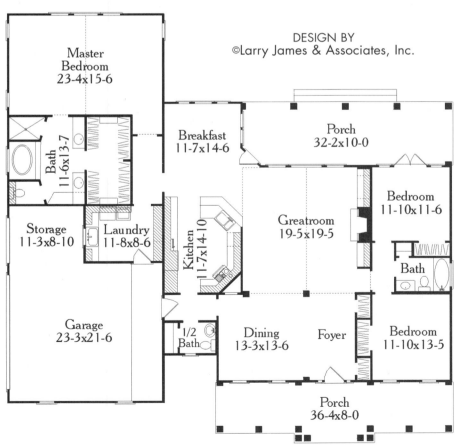

DESIGN BY
©Larry James & Associates, Inc.

Master Bedroom
23-4x15-6

Bath
11-6x13-7

Storage
11-3x8-10

Laundry
11-8x8-6

Garage
23-3x21-6

1/2
Bath

Breakfast
11-7x14-6

Kitchen
11-7x14-10

Greatroom
19-5x19-5

Dining
13-3x13-6

Foyer

Porch
32-2x10-0

Bedroom
11-10x11-6

Bath

Bedroom
11-10x13-5

Porch
36-4x8-0

Beyond this home's beautiful columned porch and keystone arches is a successful plan. Enter the foyer to find the formal dining room and two convenient closets. Straight ahead lies the great room, which includes a fireplace and built-ins. Between the spacious kitchen and the breakfast area is the hallway leading to the master bedroom. The private bath here provides convenience with dual vanities, a separate shower and an enormous walk-in closet. Two additional bedrooms to the far right of the plan share a full bath that includes a linen closet. The rear bedroom has French doors, which access the covered porch. Please specify crawl-space or slab foundation when ordering.

DESIGN HPU040194

Square Footage: 2,424
Width: 68'-2" Depth: 67'-6"

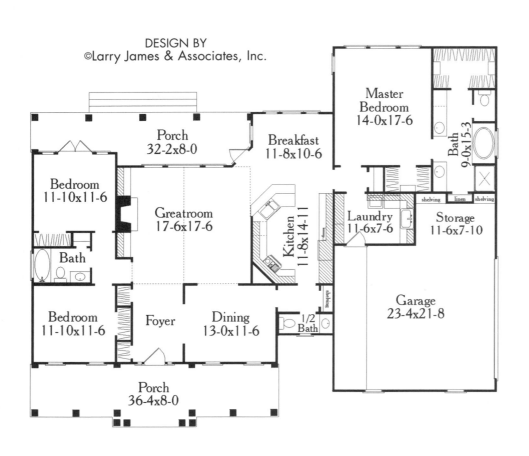

DESIGN BY
©Larry James & Associates, Inc.

Porch
32-2x8-0

Breakfast
11-8x10-6

Master
Bedroom
14-0x17-6

Bath
9-0x15-3

Bedroom
11-10x11-6

Greatroom
17-6x17-6

Kitchen
11-8x14-11

Bath

Laundry
11-6x7-6

shelving   linen   shelving

Storage
11-6x7-10

Bedroom
11-10x11-6

Foyer

Dining
13-0x11-6

1/2
Bath

shelving

Garage
23-4x21-8

Porch
36-4x8-0

Curb appeal abounds in this three-bedroom farmhouse with its columned porch, keystone lintel windows and stucco facade. A warming fireplace with adjacent built-ins in the great room can be viewed from the foyer and breakfast area. Light pours in from the rear porch with windows at every turn. Counter space abounds in this interesting kitchen adjoining the breakfast area. The private master suite enjoys a luxury bath with twin vanity sinks, a garden tub and separate shower. At the opposite end of the home, two secondary bedrooms share a bath. One features French-door access to the rear porch. Please specify basement, crawlspace or slab foundation when ordering.

DESIGN HPU040195

Square Footage: 2,046
Width: 68'-2" Depth: 57'-4"

This elegant, symmetrical home features a gabled porch complemented by columns. The breakfast room, adjacent to the kitchen, opens to a rear porch. The spacious great room provides a fireplace and a view of the patio. A lovely bayed window brightens the master bedroom, which includes a walk-in closet and a bath with a garden tub and a separate shower. Two secondary bedrooms each offer a private bath. A winding staircase leads to second-level future space. Please specify basement, crawlspace or slab foundation when ordering.

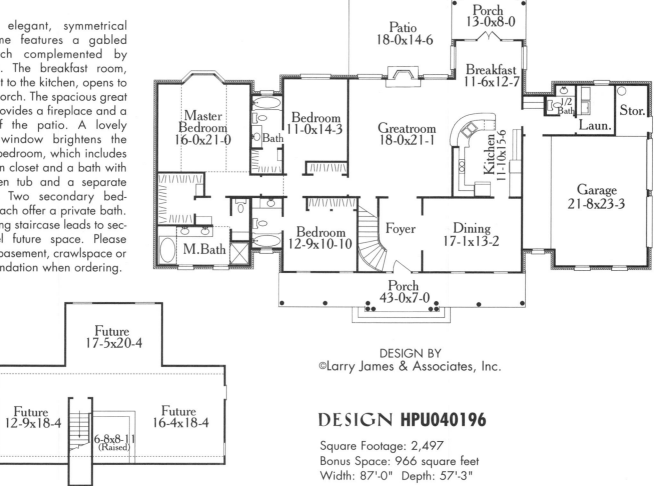

Patio 18-0x14-6

Porch 13-0x8-0

Breakfast 11-6x12-7

Master Bedroom 16-0x21-0

Bath

Bedroom 11-0x14-3

Greatroom 18-0x21-1

Kitchen 11-10x15-6

1/2 Bath

Laun.

Stor.

Garage 21-8x23-3

M.Bath

Bedroom 12-9x10-10

Foyer

Dining 17-1x13-2

Porch 43-0x7-0

Future 17-5x20-4

Future 12-9x18-4

6-8x8-11 (Raised)

Future 16-4x18-4

DESIGN BY
©Larry James & Associates, Inc.

DESIGN HPU040196

Square Footage: 2,497
Bonus Space: 966 square feet
Width: 87'-0" Depth: 57'-3"

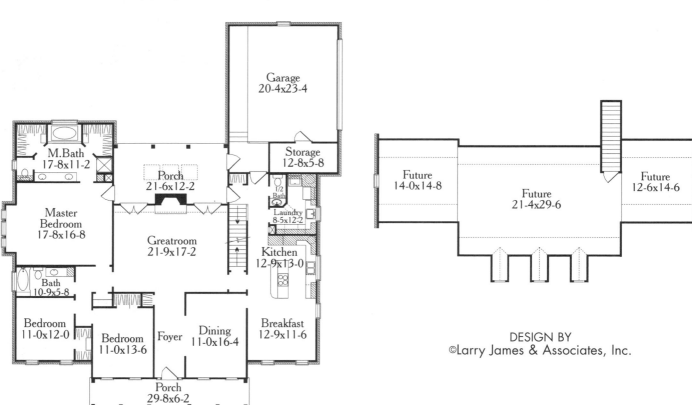

Garage
20-4x23-4

Storage
12-8x5-8

M.Bath
17-8x11-2

Porch
21-6x12-2

1/2
Bath

Laundry
8-5x12-2

Master
Bedroom
17-8x16-8

Greatroom
21-9x17-2

Kitchen
12-9x13-0

Bath
10-9x5-8

Bedroom
11-0x12-0

Bedroom
11-0x13-6

Foyer

Dining
11-0x16-4

Breakfast
12-9x11-6

Porch
29-8x6-2

Future
14-0x14-8

Future
21-4x29-6

Future
12-6x14-6

DESIGN BY
©Larry James & Associates, Inc.

Three dormers in a row bring charm while the porch colonnade adds elegance to this home. The dining room has plenty of room for formal gatherings and provides ease of service with the island kitchen close by. A bumped-out sitting bay, twin walk-in closets, dual vanities and a compartmented toilet highlight the spacious master suite. Please specify basement, crawlspace- or slab foundation when ordering.

DESIGN HPU040198

Square Footage: 2,410
Bonus Space: 1,123 square feet
Width: 64'-4"   Depth: 77'-4"

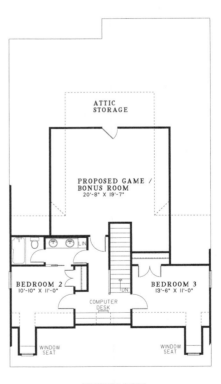

DESIGN BY
©Michael E. Nelson, Nelson Design Group, LLC

DESIGN HPU040199

First Floor: 1,698 square feet
Second Floor: 533 square feet
Total: 2,231 square feet
Bonus Room: 394 square feet
Width: 35'-4" Depth: 71'-6"

For the homeowner who wants luxury on a narrow lot, this design is the way. Walk into the formal spaces—a study with French doors and a dining room with shapely columns. From there, step into the voluminous kitchen with a hefty pantry and angled snack bar. The great room and breakfast room flow from this point into the rear master suite and garage. The secondary bedrooms are tucked away upstairs along with a large proposed game/bonus room. Please specify crawlspace or slab foundation when ordering.

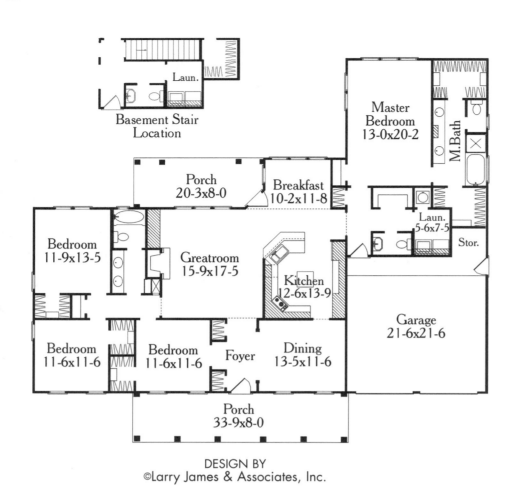

Basement Stair Location

Porch 20-3x8-0

Breakfast 10-2x11-8

Master Bedroom 13-0x20-2

M.Bath

Laun. 5-6x7-5

Stor.

Bedroom 11-9x13-5

Greatroom 15-9x17-5

Kitchen 12-6x13-9

Bedroom 11-6x11-6

Bedroom 11-6x11-6

Foyer

Dining 13-5x11-6

Garage 21-6x21-6

Porch 33-9x8-0

DESIGN BY
©Larry James & Associates, Inc.

Six columns and a steeply pitched roof lend elegance to this four-bedroom home. To the right of the foyer, the dining area sits conveniently near the efficient kitchen. The kitchen island and serving bar add plenty of work space to the food-preparation zone. Natural light will flood the breakfast nook through a ribbon of windows facing the rear yard. Escape to the relaxing master bedroom, with its luxurious bath set between His and Hers walk-in closets. The great room occupies the center of this L-shaped plan, and is complete with a warming fireplace and built-ins. Three family bedrooms enjoy private walk-in closets and share a fully appointed bath. Please specify basement, crawlspace or slab foundation when ordering.

DESIGN HPU040201

Square Footage: 2,267
Width: 71'-2" Depth: 62'-0"

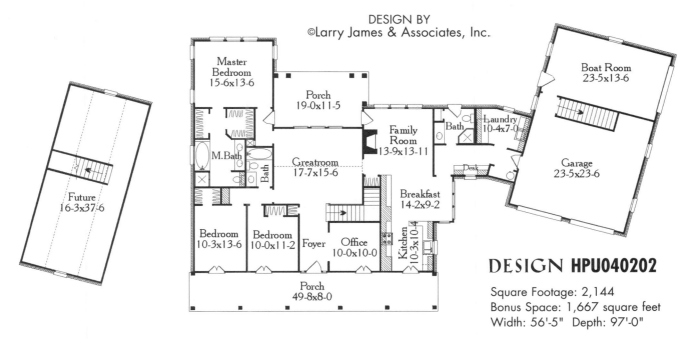

DESIGN BY
©Larry James & Associates, Inc.

Master Bedroom
15-6x13-6

Porch
19-0x11-5

Boat Room
23-5x13-6

M.Bath

Bath

Family Room
13-9x13-11

Laundry
10-4x7-0

Greatroom
17-7x15-6

Bath

Garage
23-5x23-6

Desk

Breakfast
14-2x9-2

Bedroom
10-3x13-6

Bedroom
10-0x11-2

Foyer

Office
10-0x10-0

Kitchen
10-3x10-4

Porch
49-8x8-0

Future
16-3x37-6

DESIGN HPU040202

Square Footage: 2,144
Bonus Space: 1,667 square feet
Width: 56'-5" Depth: 97'-0"

Future
36-5x25-0

Future
10-9x25-0

There is plenty of space to be developed on the second levels of both the house and the garage, making this an ideal country home. An office to the right of the foyer is another added bonus. The great room and family room are separated by a warming fireplace, and the family room accesses the rear porch. The wing bridging the garage and the central block houses a laundry room, a desk and a half-bath. The breakfast area features a bank of windows, while the kitchen, office and two family bedrooms each have French doors accessing the front porch. Please specify basement, crawlspace or slab foundation when ordering.

Welcome your family home to this wonderful four-bedroom cottage. Step through the entry door with its transom and sidelights to a well-lit foyer. A ribbon of windows greets the eye in the great room, and a warming fireplace spreads comfort. A pass-through window to the kitchen is an added convenience. The master suite enjoys a private wing, luxurious bath and His and Hers walk-in closets. On the opposite side of the plan, three secondary bedrooms—all with walk-in closets!—share a full bath. Please specify basement, crawlspace or slab foundation when ordering.

DESIGN BY
©Larry James & Associates, Inc.

DESIGN HPU040203

Square Footage: 2,093
Width: 71'-2" Depth: 56'-4"

Shutters, multi-pane glass windows and cross-hatched railing on the front porch make this a beautiful country cottage. To the left of the foyer is a roomy great room and a warming fireplace, framed by windows. To the right of the foyer, two family bedrooms feature walk-in closets and share a fully appointed bath. The efficient kitchen centers around a long island workstation and opens to the large dining/sitting room. The rear porch adds living space to view the outdoors. French doors, a fireplace and columns complete this three-bedroom design. Please specify basement, crawlspace or slab foundation when ordering.

DESIGN HPU040204

Square Footage: 2,053
Width: 57'-8" Depth: 71'-10"

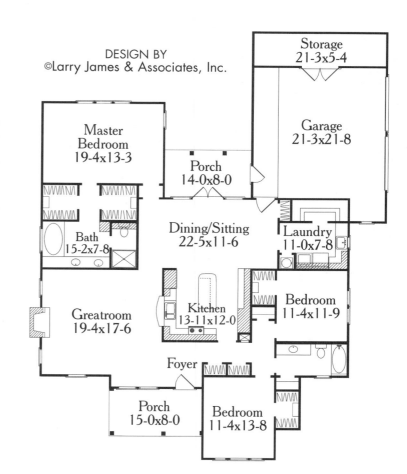

DESIGN BY
©Larry James & Associates, Inc.

Storage
21-3x5-4

Garage
21-3x21-8

Master
Bedroom
19-4x13-3

Porch
14-0x8-0

Dining/Sitting
22-5x11-6

Laundry
11-0x7-8

Bath
15-2x7-8

Greatroom
19-4x17-6

Kitchen
13-11x12-0

Bedroom
11-4x11-9

Foyer

Porch
15-0x8-0

Bedroom
11-4x13-8

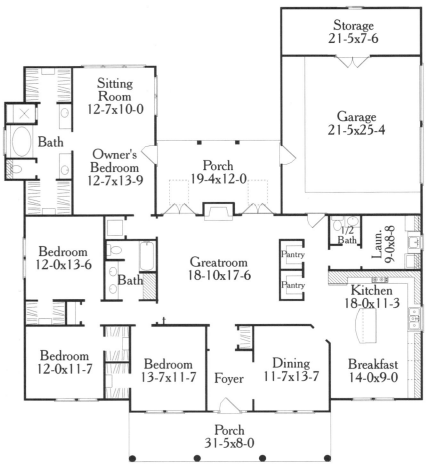

Storage
21-5x7-6

Garage
21-5x25-4

Sitting
Room
12-7x10-0

Bath

Owner's
Bedroom
12-7x13-9

Porch
19-4x12-0

1/2
Bath

Laun.
9-0x8-8

Bedroom
12-0x13-6

Bath

Greatroom
18-10x17-6

Pantry

Pantry

Kitchen
18-0x11-3

Bedroom
12-0x11-7

Bedroom
13-7x11-7

Foyer

Dining
11-7x13-7

Breakfast
14-0x9-0

Porch
31-5x8-0

This home boasts a well-laid-out design that promotes comfort and flow. The great room offers two sets of French doors to the rear porch, a fireplace, and a spacious layout perfect for entertaining. The open island kitchen shares an area with the breakfast room and connects to the dining room. The owners suite delights in a room-sized sitting area, His and Hers walk-in closets and vanities, a compartmented toilet, and a separate tub and shower. Please specify basement, crawlspace or slab foundation when ordering.

DESIGN HPU040205

Square Footage: 2,465
Width: 65'-1" Depth: 64'-2"

DESIGN BY
©Larry James & Associates, Inc.

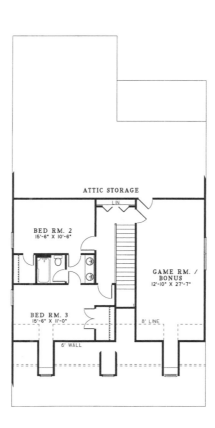

GARAGE
19'-4" X 20'-0"

GRILLING PORCH
16'-8" X 8'-0"

LIN.

D W

LAU

HANG ROD

MEDIA CENTER

GREAT RM.
10" BOXED CEILING
16'-8" X 14'-8"

M. BATH
8'-8" X 14'-8"

WHP TUB

8" COLUMNS

BREAKFAST AREA
16'-8" X 10'-0"

COMPUTER DESK

MASTER SUITE
10" BOXED CEILING
14'-7" X 13'-0"

PANTRY

REF.

DW

KITCHEN

RG

BATH

GUEST RM. / STUDY
12'-3" X 10'-0"

FOYER
7'-6" X 11'-0"

DINING RM.
13'-3" X 11'-0"

8" COLUMNS

COVERED PORCH
37'-0" X 8'-0"

ATTIC STORAGE

LIN

BED RM. 2
15'-6" X 10'-6"

GAME RM. / BONUS
12'-10" X 27'-7"

BED RM. 3
15'-6" X 11'-0"

8' LINE

6' WALL

DESIGN BY
©Michael E. Nelson, Nelson Design Group, LLC

This inviting country home includes a covered front porch with columns and railings, double-hung casement windows, wood and brick siding, and dormer windows. The formal dining room at the front of the house begins with an entrance flanked by two columns. The U-shaped kitchen has a pantry and a snack bar. A built-in computer desk lies adjacent to the breakfast room, and a box-ceilinged great room with a fireplace and media center sits at the back of the home. The master suite also has a boxed ceiling and a luxurious master bath with all of the amenities. Use the front bedroom as a study or guest room. On the second floor are two bedrooms, each with its own walk-in closet. The bonus room can be used as a game or hobby room, or as a spare bedroom. Please specify basement, crawlspace or slab foundation when ordering.

DESIGN HPU040206

First Floor: 1,713 square feet
Second Floor: 610 square feet
Total: 2,323 square feet
Bonus Room: 384 square feet
Width: 37'-0" Depth: 73'-0"

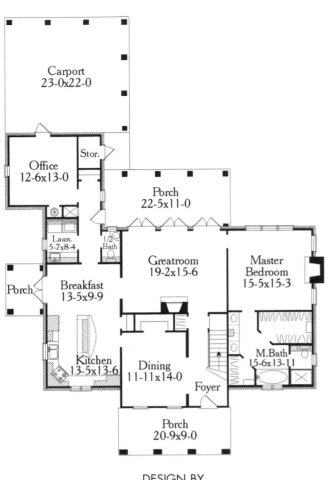

Carport
23-0x22-0

Office
12-6x13-0

Stor.

Laun.
5-7x8-4

1/2
Bath

Porch
22-5x11-0

Greatroom
19-2x15-6

Master
Bedroom
15-5x15-3

Porch

Breakfast
13-5x9-9

Kitchen
13-5x13-6

Dining
11-11x14-0

Foyer

M.Bath
15-6x13-11

Porch
20-9x9-0

DESIGN BY
©Larry James & Associates, Inc.

Bedroom
13-6x11-6

Bath

Bedroom
12-0x14-0

Open
to
Below

Balcony
20-9x9-0

Deep in the South, this home sets a country tone. This Southern Colonial design boasts decorative two-story columns and large windows that enhance the front porch and balcony. Enter through the foyer—notice that the formal dining room on the left connects to an island kitchen. The kitchen opens to a breakfast room, which accesses a side porch perfect for outdoor grilling. The great room features a warming fireplace and accesses a rear porch. The master bedroom also includes a fireplace, as well as a private bath with a whirlpool tub and a walk-in closet. A home office, laundry room and carport complete the first floor. Upstairs, two additional bedrooms share a full hall bath. One bedroom opens through two glass doors to a private balcony. Please specify crawlspace or slab foundation when ordering.

DESIGN HPU040207

First Floor: 1,663 square feet
Second Floor: 551 square feet
Total: 2,214 square feet
Width: 58'-10" Depth: 83'-7"

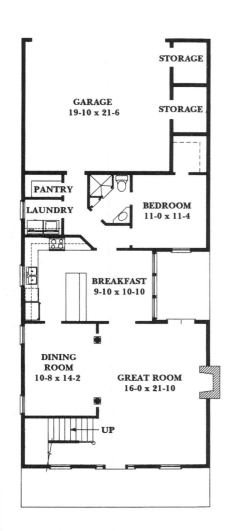

STORAGE

GARAGE
19-10 x 21-6

STORAGE

PANTRY

LAUNDRY

BEDROOM
11-0 x 11-4

BREAKFAST
9-10 x 10-10

DINING
ROOM
10-8 x 14-2

GREAT ROOM
16-0 x 21-10

UP

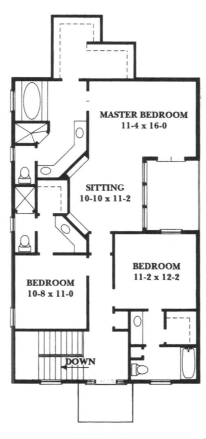

MASTER BEDROOM
11-4 x 16-0

SITTING
10-10 x 11-2

BEDROOM
11-2 x 12-2

BEDROOM
10-8 x 11-0

DOWN

DESIGN BY
©Authentic Historical Designs, Inc.

This stately home is striking in its simplicity and grandeur. Within, the high-ceilinged rooms retain the grandeur of the original homes of the late 19th Century. An expansive great room flows into a formal dining room, separated only by elegant interior columns. Beyond, a spacious kitchen features a snack bar and breakfast area, which overlooks the secluded courtyard. A downstairs bedroom can function as an office or cozy den.

DESIGN HPU040208

First Floor: 1,190 square feet
Second Floor: 1,220 square feet
Total: 2,410 square feet
Width: 30'-0" Depth: 72'-0"

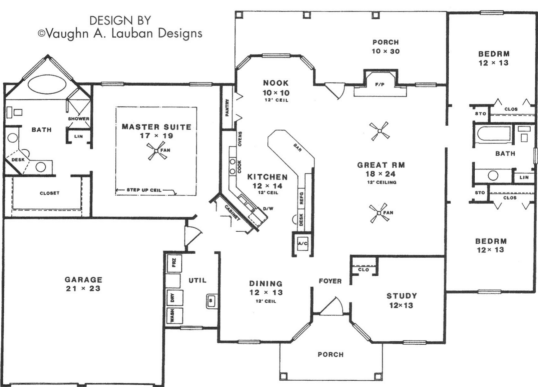

A striking facade with corner quoins and a two-story porch entry define a layout that marries elegance and comfort. With a defined but open dining room and convenient great room, the gourmet in the kitchen will be able to entertain while preparing the meal. The great room features a fireplace and rear-porch access, which makes this spot perfect for family gatherings and outdoor activities. Two secondary bedrooms share a full bath and enjoy plenty of closet and storage space. The master suite is bound to pamper the owner, with a step-up ceiling, spacious walk-in closet, dual vanities, bumped-out triangular tub space and separate shower.

DESIGN HPU040210

Square Footage: 2,256
Width: 72'-0" Depth: 52'-0"

The inspiration for this plan came directly from the 1878 edition of Bicknell's *Victorian Buildings*. At that time, the estimated building cost for this appealing residence was only $2,500. Though the cost of constructing this home has changed, its charm remains! Multiple windows brighten the living room, which opens to a small side porch. The kitchen boasts a walk-in pantry and adjoins a sunny breakfast area and a spacious keeping room with built-ins and a fireplace. The second floor features an inviting master suite with a relaxing bath that includes a raised corner tub. Three additional bedrooms, one with a walk-in closet, share a bath. The laundry area is conveniently close to the bedrooms.

DESIGN HPU040211

First Floor: 1,184 square feet
Second Floor: 1,093 square feet
Total: 2,277 square feet
Width: 28'-0"   Depth: 74'-0"

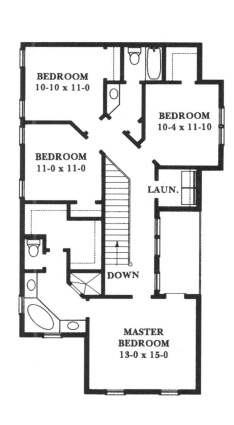

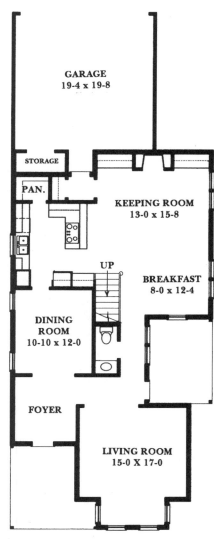

DESIGN BY
©Authentic Historical Designs, Inc.

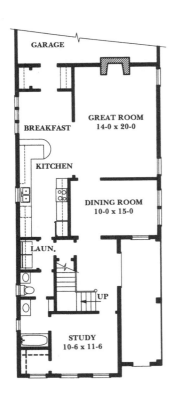

GARAGE

GREAT ROOM
14-0 x 20-0

BREAKFAST

KITCHEN

DINING ROOM
10-0 x 15-0

LAUN.

UP

STUDY
10-6 x 11-6

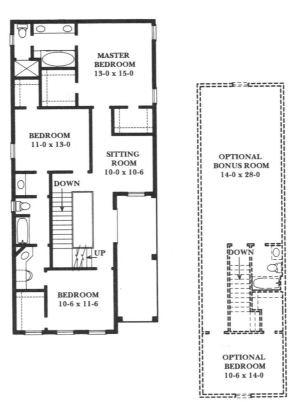

DESIGN BY
©Authentic Historical Designs, Inc.

MASTER
BEDROOM
13-0 x 15-0

BEDROOM
11-0 x 13-0

SITTING
ROOM
10-0 x 10-6

DOWN

UP

BEDROOM
10-6 x 11-6

OPTIONAL
BONUS ROOM
14-0 x 28-0

DOWN

OPTIONAL
BEDROOM
10-6 x 14-0

Distinctive design features of the Charleston single house make it a perfect candidate for the narrow urban lot. Since its narrow end faces the street and its two-story piazza faces the side yard, the plan affords its occupants much more privacy than a house with a front-facing porch. The street entry leads to a porch, providing a secluded, but graceful transition from the neighborhood. A grand foyer with an open stairwell opens to a formal dining room and the great room beyond. The front study could serve as an office or guest room. Bedrooms reside on the second floor—note the sitting room in the master suite. For more space, develop the bonus space on the upper level.

DESIGN HPU040212

First Floor: 1,227 square feet
Second Floor: 1,133 square feet
Total: 2,360 square feet
Bonus Room: 792 square feet
Width: 25'-0" Depth: 77'-0"

The romantic character of the hacienda is captured in this appealing residence. The barrel-tile roof, smooth stucco exterior and rope columns are other characteristics of the Spanish Colonial style. The front door is shielded from the weather; within, a foyer welcomes all who enter. The great room is generously sized; a downstairs guest room can also double as a study or office. A sunny dining room opens to a spacious kitchen with a large island and breakfast bar. Above, there is a sitting area large enough for a computer and desk area. A luxurious master suite privately accesses an upstairs deck. Note all the walk-in closets, which provide excellent storage spaces. The front bedroom also has walk-out access to the front balcony. Please specify basement or crawlspace foundation when ordering.

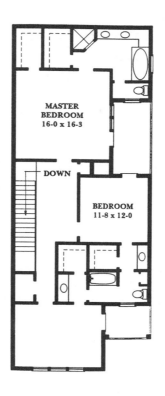

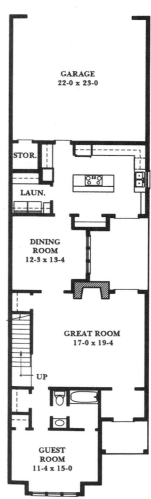

DESIGN HPU040213

First Floor: 1,247 square feet
Second Floor: 1,221 square feet
Total: 2,468 square feet
Width: 24'-0" Depth: 86'-0"

DESIGN BY
©Authentic Historical Designs, Inc.

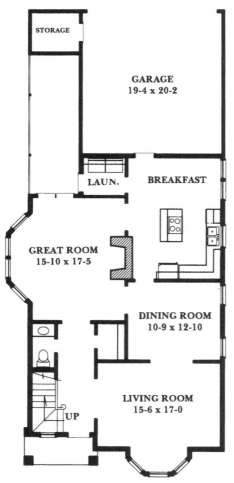

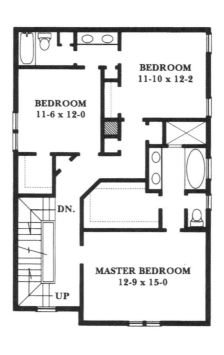

STORAGE

GARAGE
19-4 x 20-2

LAUN. | BREAKFAST

GREAT ROOM
15-10 x 17-5

DINING ROOM
10-9 x 12-10

LIVING ROOM
15-6 x 17-0

UP

BEDROOM
11-6 x 12-0

BEDROOM
11-10 x 12-2

DN.

MASTER BEDROOM
12-9 x 15-0

UP

DESIGN BY
©Authentic Historical Designs, Inc.

The facade of this enticing Victorian was taken from Bicknell's *Detail Cottage and Construction Architecture*, published in 1873, while the floor plan has been modified to suit modern lifestyles. The living room, with a lovely bay window, leads to the dining room. The great room, also with a bay window, opens to the covered side porch, and the island kitchen adjoins a sunlit breakfast area. An open staircase with an overlook leads to the family sleeping zone, composed of a master suite and two additional bedrooms. The master suite offers a large walk-in closet and a full bath with dual vanities; the two family bedrooms, one of which features a walk-in closet, share another full bath, this one with two linen closets.

DESIGN HPU040214

First Floor: 1,131 square feet
Second Floor: 1,038 square feet
Total: 2,169 square feet
Width: 30'-0" Depth: 66'-0"

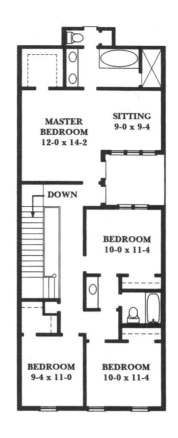

This timeless Georgian design will provide enduring approval. The expansive great room features a wood-burning fireplace and opens to a dining room of ample proportions with a niche under the stairs that can accommodate a small piano or desk. Serious cooks will appreciate the ample cabinet space, the pantry and the breakfast bar. A two-car garage completes the first floor. Upstairs, a luxurious master suite includes a sitting area, private bath and walk-in closet. Three additional family bedrooms share access to another full bath.

DESIGN HPU040215

First Floor: 940 square feet
Second Floor: 1,088 square feet
Total: 2,028 square feet
Width: 22'-0" Depth: 70'-0"

MASTER BEDROOM 12-0 x 14-2

SITTING 9-0 x 9-4

DOWN

BEDROOM 10-0 x 11-4

BEDROOM 9-4 x 11-0

BEDROOM 10-0 x 11-4

GARAGE 21-0 x 23-6

LAUN.

DINING ROOM 12-6 x 14-0

UP

GREAT ROOM 16-6 x 21-0

DESIGN BY
©Authentic Historical Designs, Inc.

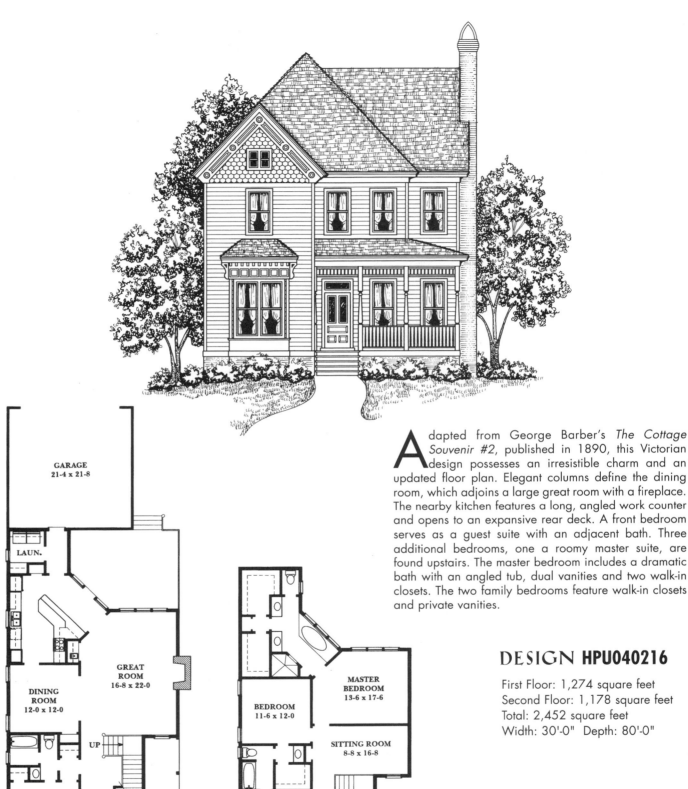

Adapted from George Barber's *The Cottage Souvenir #2*, published in 1890, this Victorian design possesses an irresistible charm and an updated floor plan. Elegant columns define the dining room, which adjoins a large great room with a fireplace. The nearby kitchen features a long, angled work counter and opens to an expansive rear deck. A front bedroom serves as a guest suite with an adjacent bath. Three additional bedrooms, one a roomy master suite, are found upstairs. The master bedroom includes a dramatic bath with an angled tub, dual vanities and two walk-in closets. The two family bedrooms feature walk-in closets and private vanities.

DESIGN HPU040216

First Floor: 1,274 square feet
Second Floor: 1,178 square feet
Total: 2,452 square feet
Width: 30'-0" Depth: 80'-0"

GARAGE
21-4 x 21-8

LAUN.

GREAT ROOM
16-8 x 22-0

DINING ROOM
12-0 x 12-0

UP

GUEST
11-0 x 12-0

MASTER BEDROOM
13-6 x 17-6

BEDROOM
11-6 x 12-0

SITTING ROOM
8-8 x 16-8

BEDROOM
11-6 x 12-0

DN

DESIGN BY
©Authentic Historical Designs, Inc.

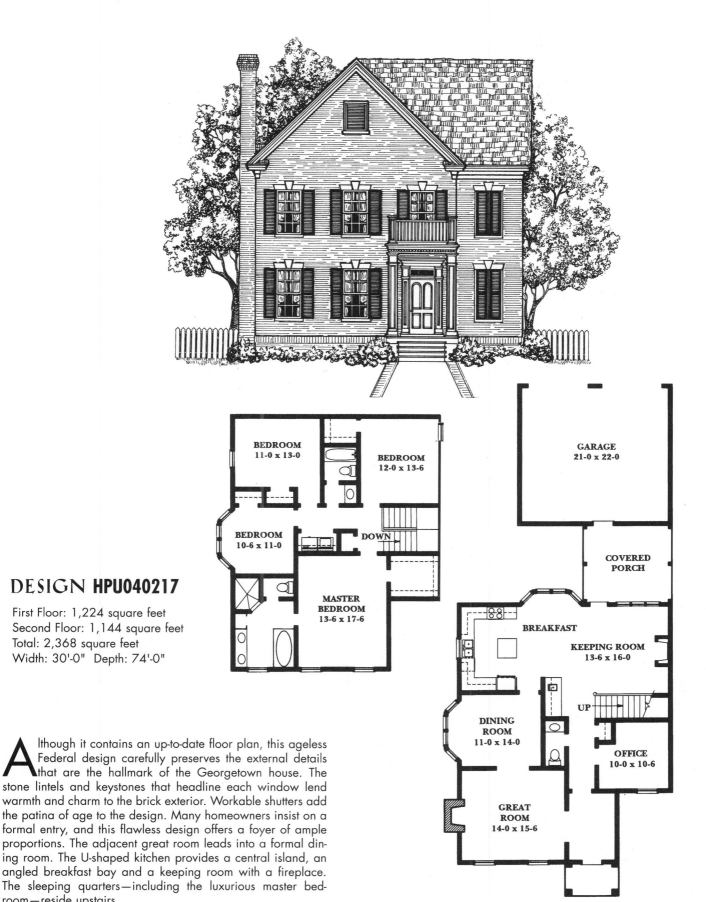

DESIGN HPU040217

First Floor: 1,224 square feet
Second Floor: 1,144 square feet
Total: 2,368 square feet
Width: 30'-0" Depth: 74'-0"

BEDROOM
11-0 x 13-0

BEDROOM
12-0 x 13-6

BEDROOM
10-6 x 11-0

DOWN

MASTER
BEDROOM
13-6 x 17-6

GARAGE
21-0 x 22-0

COVERED
PORCH

BREAKFAST

KEEPING ROOM
13-6 x 16-0

UP

DINING
ROOM
11-0 x 14-0

OFFICE
10-0 x 10-6

GREAT
ROOM
14-0 x 15-6

Although it contains an up-to-date floor plan, this ageless Federal design carefully preserves the external details that are the hallmark of the Georgetown house. The stone lintels and keystones that headline each window lend warmth and charm to the brick exterior. Workable shutters add the patina of age to the design. Many homeowners insist on a formal entry, and this flawless design offers a foyer of ample proportions. The adjacent great room leads into a formal dining room. The U-shaped kitchen provides a central island, an angled breakfast bay and a keeping room with a fireplace. The sleeping quarters—including the luxurious master bedroom—reside upstairs.

DESIGN BY
©Authentic Historical Designs, Inc.

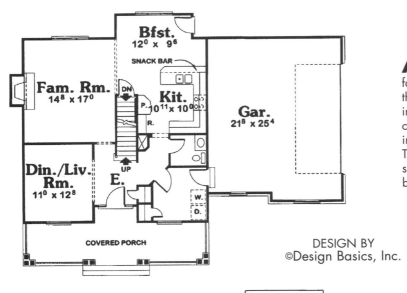

Bfst.
12⁰ x 9⁶

SNACK BAR

Fam. Rm.
14⁸ x 17⁰

Kit.
10¹¹ x 10⁰

DN

P.

R.

Gar.
21⁸ x 25⁴

Din./Liv. Rm.
11⁰ x 12⁸

E.

UP

W.

D.

COVERED PORCH

DESIGN BY
©Design Basics, Inc.

Br.2
11⁰ x 13⁸

LINEN

WHIRLPOOL

Mbr.
17⁸ x 14⁰

DN

Br.3
11⁰ x 12⁸

Br.4
10¹¹ x 12⁸

A gabled roof, shutters and the covered porch translate to traditional family living. Inside, the floor plan results in a convenient traffic pattern. The family room is removed from the wear-and-tear of through-traffic, while the placement of the formal dining/living room avoids kitchen clatter. A two-car garage completes the first floor. Upstairs, the master suite includes a private bath and generous walk-in closet. Three family bedrooms—one with a walk-in closet—share a bath that has a double vanity. Please specify basement or slab foundation when ordering.

DESIGN HPU040218

First Floor: 952 square feet
Second Floor: 1,272 square feet
Total: 2,224 square feet
Width: 52'-0" Depth: 34'-8"

DESIGNERS'INX

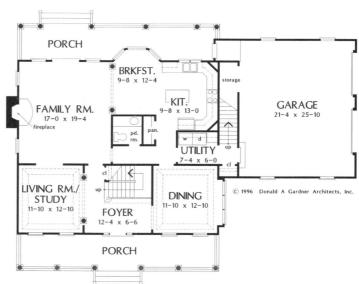

A large center gable with a Palladian window and a gently vaulted portico make this two-story home stand out from the typical farmhouse. A formal dining room and a living room/study, both highlighted by tray ceilings, flank the foyer, which leads into a spacious family room. Nine-foot ceilings add volume to the entire first floor, including the efficient kitchen with a center work island and large pantry. Upstairs, the gracious master suite features a tray ceiling, a generous walk-in closet, and a skylit bath with a double-bowl vanity, linen closet and garden tub. Three additional bedrooms share a full bath.

DESIGN BY
Donald A. Gardner Architects, Inc.

DESIGN HPU040219

First Floor: 1,299 square feet
Second Floor: 1,176 square feet
Total: 2,475 square feet
Bonus Room: 464 square feet
Width: 64'-8"   Depth: 47'-2"

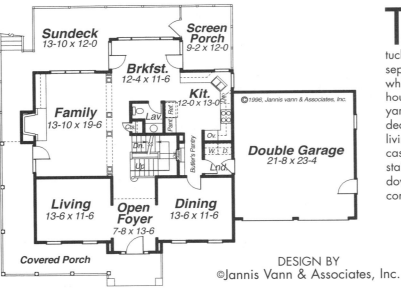

Sundeck
13-10 x 12-0

Screen Porch
9-2 x 12-0

Brkfst.
12-4 x 11-6

Kit.
12-0 x 13-0

©1996, Jannis vann & Associates, Inc.

Family
13-10 x 19-6

Lav.

Cts.

Pant. Ref.

Ov.

Butler's Pantry

W.D.

Dn.

Up

Lnd.

Double Garage
21-8 x 23-4

Living
13-6 x 11-6

Open Foyer
7-8 x 13-6

Dining
13-6 x 11-6

Covered Porch

DESIGN BY
©Jannis Vann & Associates, Inc.

This home is reminiscent of Main Street, USA with its classic features. The two-story foyer is flanked by the formal living and dining rooms, while the stairs are tucked back in the center of the house. Columns create a separation from the family room to the breakfast area, while keeping that open feeling across the entire rear of the house. Corner windows in the kitchen look into the side yard and rear screened porch. The porch leads to the rear deck, which also ties into the side porch, creating outdoor living on three sides of the house. As you ascend the staircase to the second floor, you will pass a lighted panel of stained glass on the landing, creating the illusion of a window wall. The second floor features four bedrooms and a compartmented hall bath.

DESIGN HPU040220

First Floor: 1,250 square feet
Second Floor: 1,166 square feet
Total: 2,416 square feet
Width: 64'-0" Depth: 52'-0"

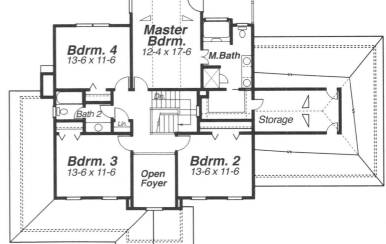

Sundeck
9-2 x 12-0

Bdrm. 4
13-6 x 11-6

Master Bdrm.
12-4 x 17-6

M.Bath

Bath 2

Lin.

Dn.

Storage

Bdrm. 3
13-6 x 11-6

Open Foyer

Bdrm. 2
13-6 x 11-6

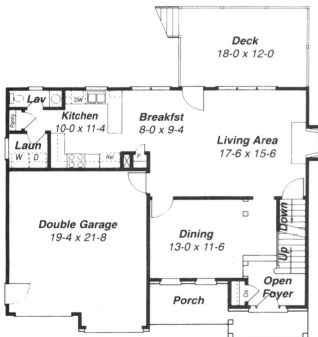

Deck
18-0 x 12-0

Kitchen
10-0 x 11-4

Breakfst
8-0 x 9-4

Lav

Pantry

Laun
W D

Ref

P

Living Area
17-6 x 15-6

Double Garage
19-4 x 21-8

Dining
13-0 x 11-6

Up Down

Cts

Open Foyer

Porch

The metal-roofed porch and multiple gables create added curb appeal to this traditional brick and siding design. Inside, a spacious living area flows into the breakfast room, which leads to the efficient kitchen with plenty of cabinets and counter space. The back deck is perfect for outdoor grilling or entertaining. A double garage completes the first floor. Upstairs, the three bedrooms feature a deluxe master suite, two family bedrooms that share a bath, and a loft available for a fourth bedroom, home office or play area. Please specify basement, crawlspace or slab foundation when ordering.

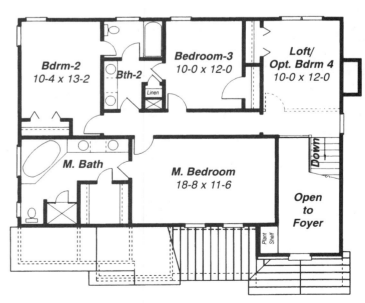

Bdrm-2
10-4 x 13-2

Bth-2

Linen

Bedroom-3
10-0 x 12-0

Loft/ Opt. Bdrm 4
10-0 x 12-0

M. Bath

M. Bedroom
18-8 x 11-6

Down

Open to Foyer

Plant Shelf

DESIGN HPU040221

First Floor: 905 square feet
Second Floor: 1,120 square feet
Total: 2,025 square feet
Width: 44'-4" Depth: 36'-5"

DESIGN BY
©Jannis Vann & Associates, Inc.

COVERED PORCH

MASTER
BEDRM
13⁴ x 18⁰

FAMILY
ROOM
15⁴ x 11⁶

LINEN

MASTER
BATH

BREAKFAST ROOM
15⁴ x 11⁸

DESK

WET
BAR

DINING
RM
13⁴ x 11⁰

KIT.
13⁰ x 11⁴

SINK

DW

5' HIGH SHELVES

UP DN

OPEN ABOVE

LIVING
RM
13⁴ x 11⁴

PDR

FOYER

COVERED PORCH

BEDRM
15⁴ x 11⁸

BEDRM
11⁶ x 11⁰

BATH

LINEN

DN

DESIGN BY
©Home Planners

This handsome bungalow is designed for easy living with a floor plan that puts the owner's comfort first. A quaint living and dining room is separated with a half-wall of built-in shelves. The large kitchen provides an open wet bar to the dining room and a snack bar to the combination breakfast/family room. The extra-large family room has sliding glass doors off the breakfast area and a door opening to the covered rear porch. The master suite offers privacy and convenience thanks to thoughtful first-floor planning. The two spacious bedrooms upstairs share a twin-basin bath.

DESIGN HPU040222

First Floor: 1,581 square feet
Second Floor: 592 square feet
Total: 2,173 square feet
Width: 35'-4" Depth: 66'-0"

Quote One®
Cost to build? See page 502
to order complete cost estimate
to build this house in your area!

Craftsman detailing adorns the exterior of this fine hillside home. Its cozy nature includes horizontal and shingle siding and a covered porch at the entry with a wide-based column. The great room is warmed by a hearth surrounded by built-ins. Columns define the dining room, which separates the great room and the U-shaped kitchen. A wide deck at the side of the home is accessed through the dining room or the great room. A cozy den sits at the back of this level and has double doors to the rear portion of the deck. Three bedrooms on the upper level include two family bedrooms with a shared full bath, and a master bedroom with a sitting area, private bath and walk-in closet. The lower level has space for a game room and a guest bedroom with a bath.

DESIGN HPU040223

First Floor: 1,158 square feet
Second Floor: 1,038 square feet
Total: 2,196 square feet
Bonus Space: 760 square feet
Width: 34'-6" Depth: 42'-0"

DESIGN BY
©Alan Mascord Design Associates, Inc.

187

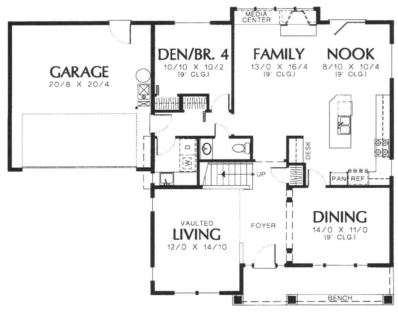

DESIGN HPU040225

First Floor: 1,300 square feet
Second Floor: 933 square feet
Total: 2,233 square feet
Width: 54'-0" Depth: 43'-0"

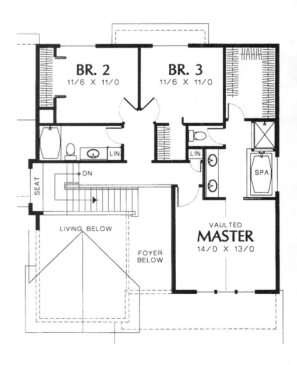

Subtle Craftsman style is evident in this three-bedroom home. From its rafter-tails poking out from under the roof overhang to the pillars supporting the shed roof over the porch, this attractive design is sure to be a favorite. Inside, there is room enough for all family pursuits. Formal entertaining is easy in the formal dining room, with a vaulted living room just across the hall for after-dinner conversations. Casual times will be fun in the family room, with a fireplace, built-in media center and nearby L-shaped kitchen and sunny nook. A den—or make it a fourth bedroom—completes this floor. Upstairs, two family bedrooms share a hall bath, while the vaulted master suite features a spacious private bath. Note also the large walk-in closet.

DESIGN BY
©Alan Mascord Design Associates, Inc.

188

NOOK
10/0 X 10/8
(9' CLG.)

FAMILY
13/2 X 15/0
(9' CLG.)

DINING
11/2 X 10/0
(9' CLG.)

9/10 X 10/4

RANGE

REF.

PAN.

TWO STORY
LIVING
15/2 X 17/8 +/-

UP

GARAGE
19/6 X 21/6

10/2 X 21/6

D

W

DEN
11/0 X 10/0
(11'-7" CLG.)

DESIGN HPU040226

First Floor: 1,255 square feet
Second Floor: 1,141 square feet
Total: 2,396 square feet
Width: 40'-0" Depth: 50'-0"

A two-story living room greets family and friends in this fine four-bedroom Craftsman home. A cozy den is isolated toward the front of the home, assuring privacy. The angled kitchen reigns in the center of the home, with easy access to the formal dining room, sunny nook and spacious family room. A fireplace in the family room promises warmth and welcome. The master bedroom, which includes a private bath with a spa tub and a walk-in closet, resides on the second floor. Three additional bedrooms share a full hall bath.

SPA TUB

BR. 2
10/2 X 11/0

MASTER
15/0 X 13/8

PLANT SHELF

LIN

BR. 3
10/6 X 10/8

LIVING RM. BELOW

DN

BR. 4
14/0 X 9/0+

FOYER
BELOW

PLANT SHELF

DEN
BELOW

DESIGN BY
©Alan Mascord Design Associates, Inc.

189

DESIGN HPU040227

Square Footage: 2,085
Width: 70'-0" Depth: 61'-0"

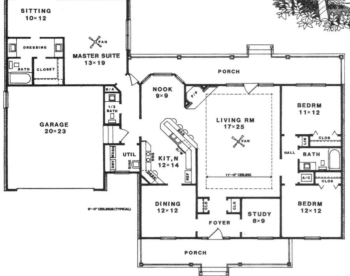

This traditional home offers a front covered porch to welcome family and friends. The foyer provides access to the study and dining room. A galley kitchen features a snack bar, built-in planning desk and a breakfast bay. The living room enjoys a corner fireplace and rear-porch access. The master suite boasts a bay sitting area, dressing area with dual vanities, and a walk-in closet. On the other side of the house, two family bedrooms share a full bath between them.

DESIGN BY
©Vaughn A. Lauban Designs

The facade of this home speaks of country lemonade and rocking chairs. The living room features a fireplace and front-porch views. The master suite enjoys its seclusion with a sumptuous bath and walk-in closet. An open dining room is reached through the living room and is served from the L-shaped island kitchen. A breakfast nook takes in the outdoors with an adjoining screened porch.

DESIGN BY
©Vaughn A. Lauban Designs

DESIGN HPU040228

First Floor: 1,677 square feet
Second Floor: 683 square feet
Total: 2,360 square feet
Width: 46'-0" Depth: 67'-0"

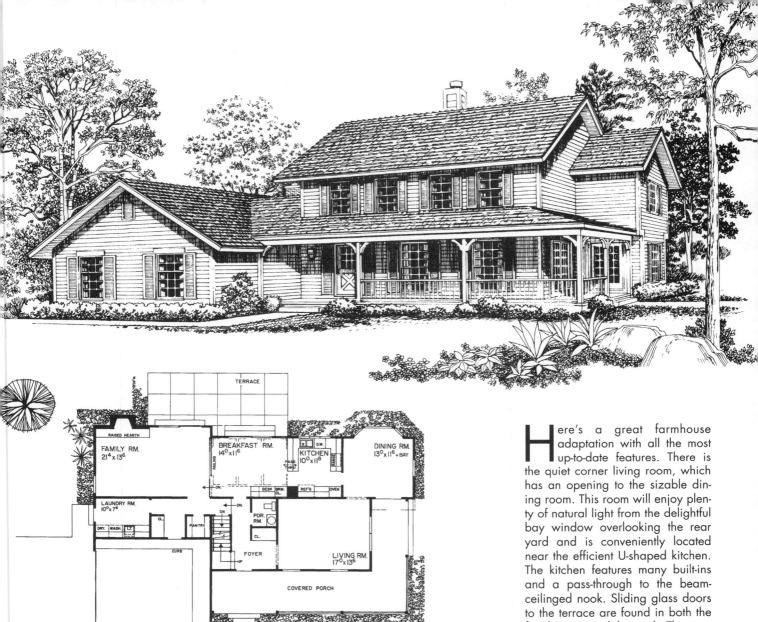

TERRACE

RAISED HEARTH

FAMILY RM.
21⁴ x 13⁶

BREAKFAST RM.
14⁰ x 11⁶

KITCHEN
10⁰ x 11⁸

DINING RM.
13⁰ x 11⁶ + BAY

LAUNDRY RM.
10⁰ x 7⁶

DESK BRM. CL. REF'D OVEN

DRY. WASH. CL.

PANTRY

PDR. RM.

CL.

FOYER

LIVING RM.
17⁰ x 13⁶

CURB

UP

GARAGE
21⁴ x 21⁸

COVERED PORCH

BEDROOM/
STUDY
11⁰ x 13²

VANITY

BATH DRESS. RM.

MASTER
BEDROOM
13⁰ x 13²

BATH

DESIGN BY
©Home Planners

DN.

UP TO
ATTIC

BEDROOM
10⁰ x 10⁶

BEDROOM
13⁰ x 10⁶

LIN.

CL.

ROOF

ROOF

DN

ATTIC 29⁴ x 26⁴
(HEADROOM 29⁴ x 10⁴)

ROOF

Quote One®

Cost to build? See page 502
to order complete cost estimate
to build this house in your area!

Here's a great farmhouse adaptation with all the most up-to-date features. There is the quiet corner living room, which has an opening to the sizable dining room. This room will enjoy plenty of natural light from the delightful bay window overlooking the rear yard and is conveniently located near the efficient U-shaped kitchen. The kitchen features many built-ins and a pass-through to the beam-ceilinged nook. Sliding glass doors to the terrace are found in both the family room and the nook. The service entrance to the garage is flanked by a clothes closet and a large, walk-in pantry. Recreational activities and hobbies can be pursued in the basement area. Four bedrooms and two baths are located on the second floor. The master bedroom includes a dressing room and double vanity.

DESIGN HPU040229

First Floor: 1,366 square feet
Second Floor: 969 square feet
Total: 2,335 square feet
Attic: 969 square feet
Width: 59'-6" Depth: 46'-0"

L **D**

Multi-pane windows, dormers, bay windows and a delightful covered porch provide a neighborly welcome into this delightful country cottage. The great room contains a fireplace, a cathedral ceiling and sliding glass doors with an arched window above to allow for natural illumination. A sun room with a hot tub leads to an adjacent deck. This space can also be reached from the master bath. The generous master suite is filled with amenities that include a walk-in closet and a spacious bath with a double-bowl vanity, shower and garden tub. Two additional bedrooms are located at the other end of the house for privacy. The garage is connected to the house by a breezeway.

DESIGN HPU040230

Square Footage: 2,021
Width: 67'-6" Depth: 67'-4"

DESIGN BY
Donald A. Gardner Architects, Inc.

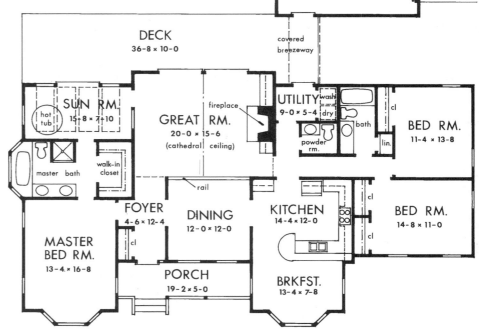

© 1985 Donald A. Gardner Architects, Inc.

© 1985 Donald A. Gardner Architects, Inc.

This brightly lit country home is enhanced by dormers and a welcoming entry porch. Inside the foyer, a formal living room leads to the dining room. The kitchen is conveniently set between the dining room and bayed breakfast nook. A laundry room and sewing room are set behind the two-car garage. The beam-ceilinged family room—the heart of the home—features a fireplace and access to a rear covered porch. The right side of the home is dedicated to the family's sleeping quarters. The beam-ceilinged master bedroom includes a spacious master bath and private access to the back porch. Three additional bedrooms share a full hall bath.

DESIGN HPU040231

Square Footage: 2,173
Width: 73'-4" Depth: 51'-4"

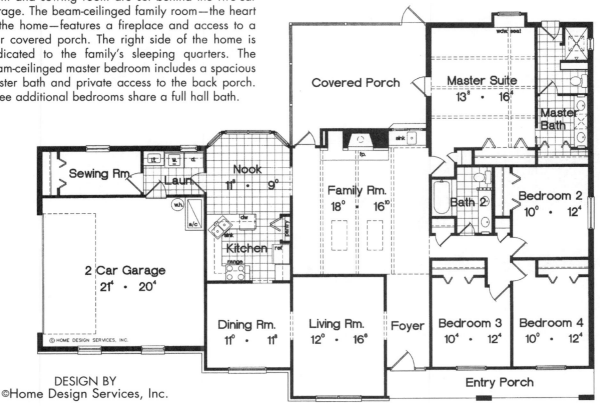

DESIGN BY
©Home Design Services, Inc.

193

DESIGN BY
©Michael E. Nelson, Nelson Design Group, LLC

DESIGN HPU040232

First Floor: 1,400 square feet
Second Floor: 644 square feet
Total: 2,044 square feet
Width: 42'-4" Depth: 40'-0"

This attractive two-story traditional home is filled with all the modern-day amenities. A columned front porch leads inside to the living room/office, which features a closet and book shelves. The master bedroom, which boasts two walk-in closets, accesses the living room/office through the master bath. On the other side of the home, the efficient kitchen features a raised bar, a pantry and open access to the dining room. The den boasts a warming fireplace, a built-in media center and a back door. Upstairs, dormers enhance two additional family bedrooms, which both feature walk-in closets and share access to a bath. Please specify basement, crawlspace or slab foundation when ordering.

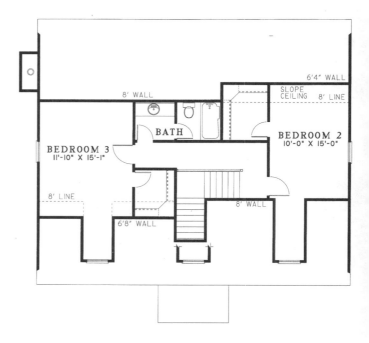

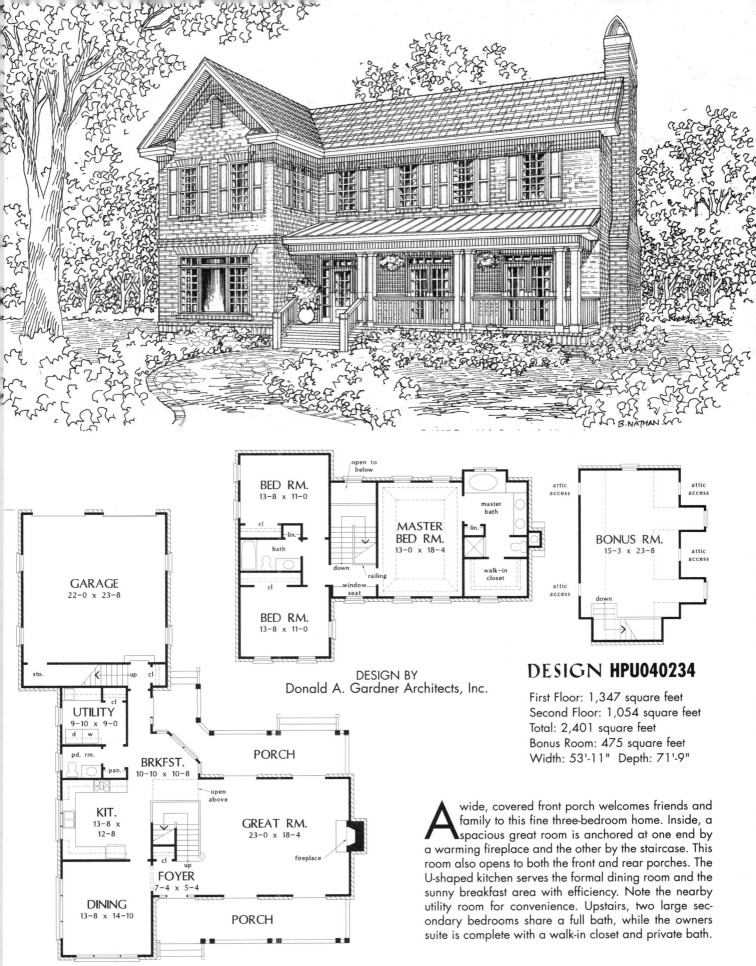

GARAGE
22-0 x 23-8

sto.

up   cl

cl

UTILITY
9-10 x 9-0

d   w

pd. rm.

pan.

BRKFST.
10-10 x 10-8

open
above

KIT.
13-8 x
12-8

cl   up

FOYER
7-4 x 5-4

DINING
13-8 x 14-10

PORCH

GREAT RM.
23-0 x 18-4

fireplace

PORCH

open to
below

BED RM.
13-8 x 11-0

cl

lin.

bath

cl

BED RM.
13-8 x 11-0

down

railing

window
seat

MASTER
BED RM.
13-0 x 18-4

master
bath

lin.

walk-in
closet

attic
access

attic
access

BONUS RM.
15-3 x 23-8

attic
access

attic
access

down

DESIGN BY
Donald A. Gardner Architects, Inc.

DESIGN HPU040234

First Floor: 1,347 square feet
Second Floor: 1,054 square feet
Total: 2,401 square feet
Bonus Room: 475 square feet
Width: 53'-11" Depth: 71'-9"

A wide, covered front porch welcomes friends and family to this fine three-bedroom home. Inside, a spacious great room is anchored at one end by a warming fireplace and the other by the staircase. This room also opens to both the front and rear porches. The U-shaped kitchen serves the formal dining room and the sunny breakfast area with efficiency. Note the nearby utility room for convenience. Upstairs, two large secondary bedrooms share a full bath, while the owners suite is complete with a walk-in closet and private bath.

B.NATHAN

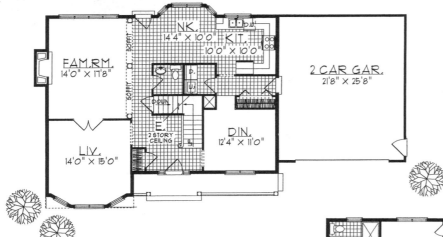

DESIGN HPU040235

First Floor: 1,228 square feet
Second Floor: 1,142 square feet
Total: 2,370 square feet
Bonus Room: 253 square feet
Width: 62'-0" Depth: 36'-0"

The front covered porch is perfect for reading the evening paper. Inside, the large kitchen has everything your family cook needs. The bayed nook has sliding glass doors, which open to the backyard. The family room contains a fireplace and large rear-facing windows. The formal living room sits off the foyer and has French doors, which can be open or closed for privacy. The formal dining room—off the foyer to the right—provides a perfect setting for holiday gatherings. Upstairs, the master bedroom boasts a tray ceiling, two closets and a private bath. The private bath includes a spa tub, shower and double vanity for couples on the go. The remaining bedrooms share a full bath.

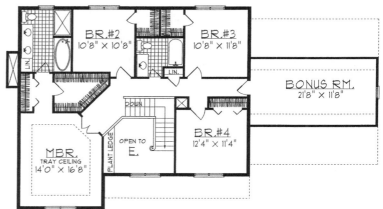

DESIGN BY
©Ahmann Design, Inc.

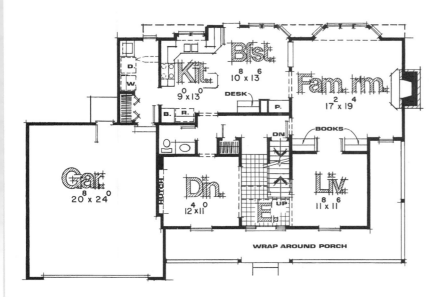

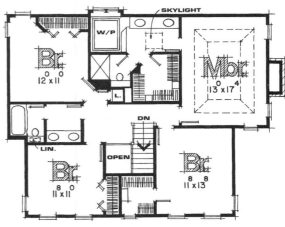

DESIGN HPU040236

First Floor: 1,188 square feet
Second Floor: 1,172 square feet
Total: 2,360 square feet
Width: 58'-0" Depth: 40'-0"

Beginning with the interest of a wraparound porch, there's a feeling of country charm in this two-story plan. Formal dining and living rooms, visible from the entry, offer ample space for gracious entertaining. The large family room is truly a place of warmth and welcome with its gorgeous bay window, fireplace and French doors to the living room. The kitchen, with an island counter, pantry and desk, makes cooking a delight. Upstairs, the secondary bedrooms share an efficient compartmented bath. The expansive master suite has its own luxury bath with a double vanity, whirlpool tub, walk-in closet and dressing area.

DESIGN BY
©Design Basics, Inc.

394 Donald A. Gardner Architects, Inc.

The grand foyer leads to a two-story great room with an extended-hearth fireplace and access to the rear deck and spa. Open planning allows the bayed breakfast nook and gourmet kitchen to enjoy the view of the fireplace, while the secluded formal dining room basks in natural light from two multi-pane windows. The master suite offers deck access and a bath that includes twin vanities and a windowed, whirlpool tub.

DESIGN HPU040238

First Floor: 1,499 square feet
Second Floor: 665 square feet
Total: 2,164 square feet
Bonus Room: 380 square feet
Width: 69'-8" Depth: 40'-6"

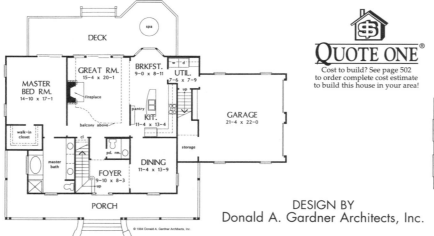

DECK

spa

GREAT RM.
15-4 x 20-1

BRKFST.
9-0 x 8-11

UTIL.
w · d

MASTER
BED RM.
14-10 x 17-1

fireplace

balcony above

pantry

KIT.
11-4 x 13-4

up

UTIL.
7-6 x 7-9

GARAGE
21-4 x 22-0

walk-in closet

master bath

cl

pd. rm.

storage

FOYER
9-10 x 8-3

DINING
11-4 x 13-9

up

PORCH

© 1994 Donald A. Gardner, Inc.

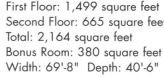
DESIGN BY
Donald A. Gardner Architects, Inc.

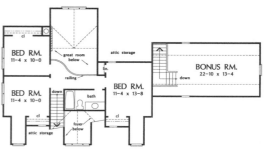

BED RM.
11-4 x 10-0

great room below

attic storage

lin.

BONUS RM.
22-10 x 13-4

down

BED RM.
11-4 x 10-0

railing

down

bath

BED RM.
11-4 x 13-8

cl

attic storage

foyer below

cl

DESIGN BY
©Home Planners

GARAGE
21⁰ x 22⁸

COVERED PORCH

RAILING

GREAT RM.
16² x 17⁴

LAUNDRY RM.

BREAKFAST RM.

MASTER SUITE
14⁰ x 15¹⁰

SITTING

KIT.
11 x 12⁸

FOYER

WALK-IN CLOSET

MASTER BATH

DINING
11⁸ x 14⁶

COVERED PORCH

RAILING

BEDRM
11² x 12⁰

BATH

BEDRM
11² x 12⁰

RAILING

DESIGN HPU040237

First Floor: 1,655 square feet
Second Floor: 515 square feet
Total: 2,170 square feet
Width: 68'-6" Depth: 66'-5"

L D

A peaked roof with a wide-arch decorative window provides a commanding entrance to this design. The foyer leads directly into the great room with a wall of windows facing the rear porch. The dining room with a bay window, the island kitchen and the breakfast room line up to provide maximum flexibility. The master suite offers a sitting area and a bath. Two bedrooms occupy the second floor.

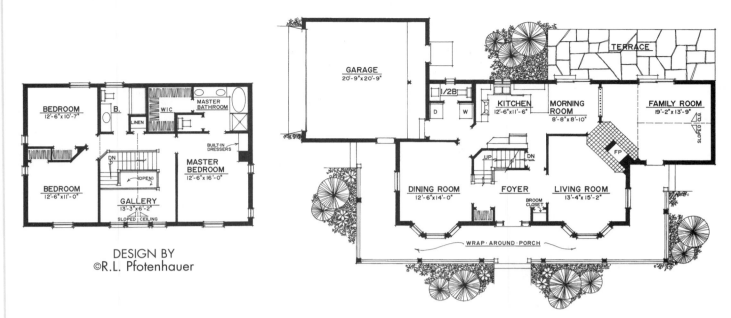

BEDROOM
12'-6"x10'-7"

B.

WIC

MASTER BATHROOM

LINEN

BUILT-IN DRESSERS

DN

(OPEN)

MASTER BEDROOM
12'-6"x16'-0"

BEDROOM
12'-6"x11'-0"

GALLERY
13'-3"x6'-2"

SLOPED CEILING

DESIGN BY
©R.L. Pfotenhauer

GARAGE
20'-9"x20'-9"

TERRACE

1/2B

D   W

KITCHEN
12'-6"x11'-6"

MORNING ROOM
8'-8"x8'-10"

FAMILY ROOM
19'-2"x13'-9"

SLOPED CLG

UP   DN

FP

DINING ROOM
12'-6"x14'-0"

FOYER

BROOM CLOSET

LIVING ROOM
13'-4"x15'-2"

WRAP·AROUND·PORCH

A covered wraparound porch welcomes you into this updated farmhouse. A traditional floor plan puts work and gathering areas downstairs and bedrooms upstairs. The living room and dining room stand at the front of the house, while the casual living areas at the back include the open kitchen with a breakfast nook and the family room with a double-facing fireplace shared with the living room. Close by is the half-bath and the laundry area. Sliding doors open from the family room and the breakfast nook to a terrace. Upstairs, the master bedroom has a walk-in closet and a bath with a separate tub and shower. Two more bedrooms share a second full bath.

DESIGN HPU040239

First Floor: 1,308 square feet
Second Floor: 992 square feet
Total: 2,300 square feet
Width: 70'-8" Depth: 42'-8"

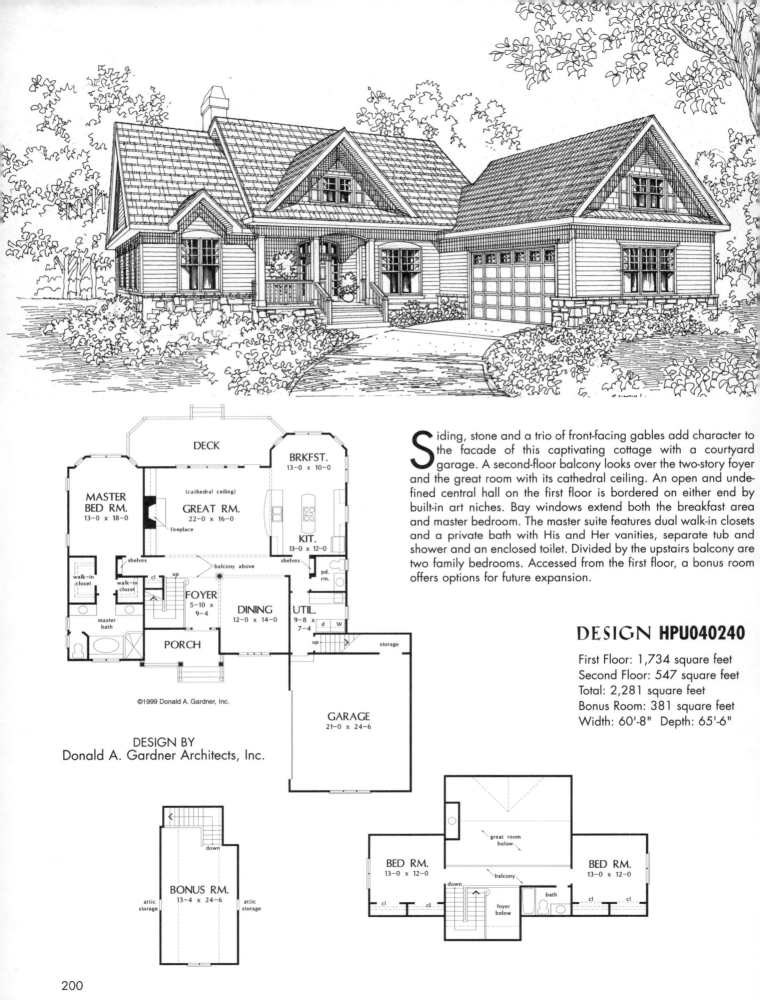

DECK

BRKFST.
13-0 x 10-0

MASTER
BED RM.
13-0 x 18-0

(cathedral ceiling)

GREAT RM.
22-0 x 16-0

fireplace

KIT.
13-0 x 12-0

shelves

walk-in
closet

shelves

pd.
rm.

walk-in
closet

cl

up

balcony above

FOYER
5-10 x
9-4

DINING
12-0 x 14-0

UTIL.
9-8 x
7-4

d w

master
bath

PORCH

up

storage

©1999 Donald A. Gardner, Inc.

GARAGE
21-0 x 24-6

DESIGN BY
Donald A. Gardner Architects, Inc.

S iding, stone and a trio of front-facing gables add character to the facade of this captivating cottage with a courtyard garage. A second-floor balcony looks over the two-story foyer and the great room with its cathedral ceiling. An open and undefined central hall on the first floor is bordered on either end by built-in art niches. Bay windows extend both the breakfast area and master bedroom. The master suite features dual walk-in closets and a private bath with His and Her vanities, separate tub and shower and an enclosed toilet. Divided by the upstairs balcony are two family bedrooms. Accessed from the first floor, a bonus room offers options for future expansion.

DESIGN HPU040240

First Floor: 1,734 square feet
Second Floor: 547 square feet
Total: 2,281 square feet
Bonus Room: 381 square feet
Width: 60'-8" Depth: 65'-6"

down

BONUS RM.
13-4 x 24-6

attic
storage

attic
storage

great room
below

BED RM.
13-0 x 12-0

balcony

BED RM.
13-0 x 12-0

cl

down

foyer
below

bath

cl

cl

Breakfast
12' x 10'4"

Master Bedroom
16'11" x 14'9"

Bath

walk-in closet

Dining Room
11'8" x 14'

Kitchen
13'3" x 10'

Laun.

Hall

Bath

Foyer

Great Room
17' x 18'8"

Two-car Garage
24'4" x 26'3"

Porch

DESIGN BY
©Studer Residential Designs, Inc.

This home is enhanced by a beautiful brick exterior. Inside, the foyer features a coat closet and opens to the great room. This room is brightened by a huge window overlooking the front yard and is warmed in the winter by a fireplace. The kitchen is conveniently set between the formal dining room and breakfast room, which accesses the rear property. Secluded on the first floor for privacy, the master bedroom includes a spacious walk-in closet and a private bath. The laundry room and a two-car garage complete this first floor. Upstairs, three additional family bedrooms share access to a full hall bath and a computer loft.

DESIGN HPU040241

First Floor: 1,540 square feet
Second Floor: 808 square feet
Total: 2,348 square feet
Width: 55'-8" Depth: 50'-8"

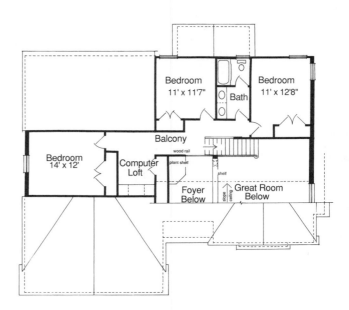

Bedroom
11' x 11'7"

Bath

Bedroom
11' x 12'8"

Balcony

wood rail

Bedroom
14' x 12'

Computer
Loft

plant shelf

shelf

Foyer
Below

Great Room
Below

DESIGN BY
Donald A. Gardner Architects, Inc.

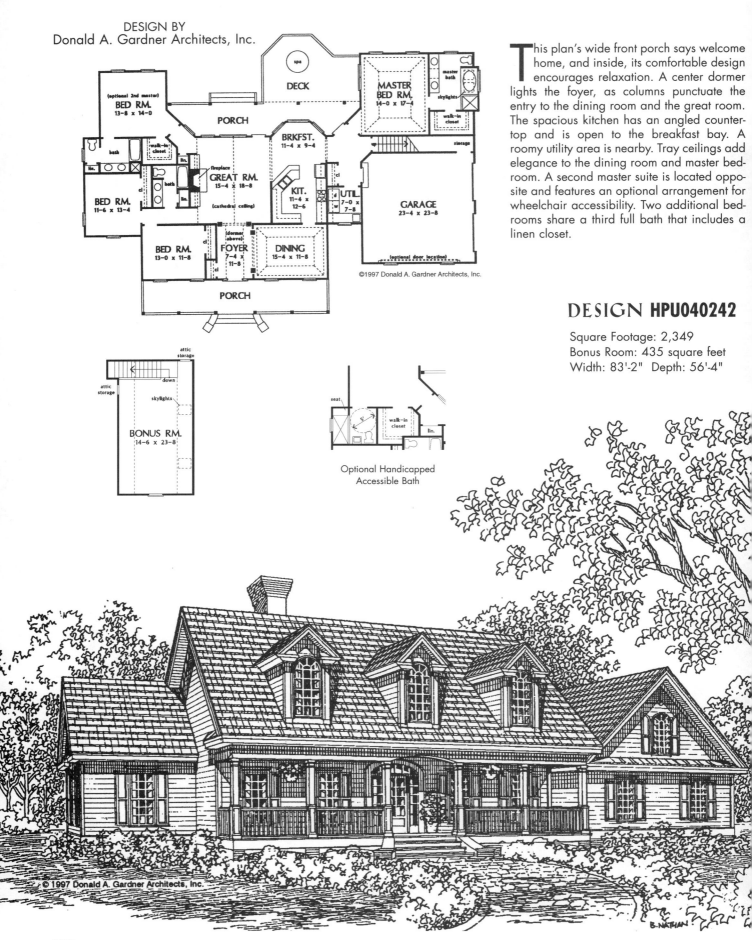

(optional 2nd master)
BED RM.
13-8 x 14-0

walk-in closet

bath

lin.

BED RM.
11-6 x 13-4

cl

bath

lin.

fireplace

GREAT RM.
15-4 x 18-8

(cathedral ceiling)

BED RM.
13-0 x 11-8

FOYER
7-4 x 11-8

(dormer above)

cl

cl

DINING
15-4 x 11-8

PORCH

spa

DECK

PORCH

BRKFST.
11-4 x 9-4

KIT.
11-4 x 12-6

UTIL.
7-0 x 7-8

cl

MASTER BED RM.
14-0 x 17-4

master bath

skylights

walk-in closet

up

storage

GARAGE
23-4 x 23-8

(optional door location)

©1997 Donald A. Gardner Architects, Inc.

attic storage

down

attic storage

skylights

BONUS RM.
14-6 x 23-8

seat

5'

walk-in closet

lin.

Optional Handicapped
Accessible Bath

This plan's wide front porch says welcome home, and inside, its comfortable design encourages relaxation. A center dormer lights the foyer, as columns punctuate the entry to the dining room and the great room. The spacious kitchen has an angled counter-top and is open to the breakfast bay. A roomy utility area is nearby. Tray ceilings add elegance to the dining room and master bedroom. A second master suite is located opposite and features an optional arrangement for wheelchair accessibility. Two additional bedrooms share a third full bath that includes a linen closet.

DESIGN HPU040242

Square Footage: 2,349
Bonus Room: 435 square feet
Width: 83'-2" Depth: 56'-4"

B. NATHAN

This board-and-batten farmhouse design carries down-home country charm with a dash of uptown New England flavor. Warm weather will invite friends and family out to the large, front covered porch to enjoy the outdoors. Just off the front entrance is a spacious living room that opens to the formal dining room, which enjoys a bay window and easy service from the U-shaped kitchen. The family room offers casual living space warmed by a raised-hearth fireplace and extended by double-door access to the rear terrace. The second floor houses two family bedrooms, which share a full bath, and a generous master suite with a walk-in closet and a private bath.

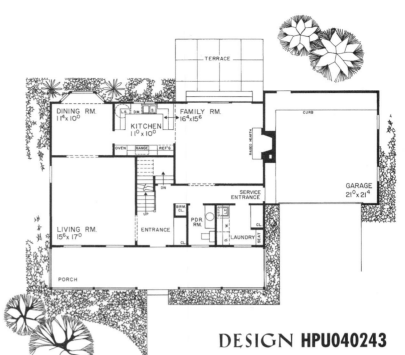

DESIGN BY
©Home Planners

Quote One®
Cost to build? See page 502
to order complete cost estimate
to build this house in your area!

DESIGN HPU040243

First Floor: 1,134 square feet
Second Floor: 874 square feet
Total: 2,008 square feet
Width: 61'-4" Depth: 38'-0"

L D

© 1993 Donald A. Gardner Architects, Inc.

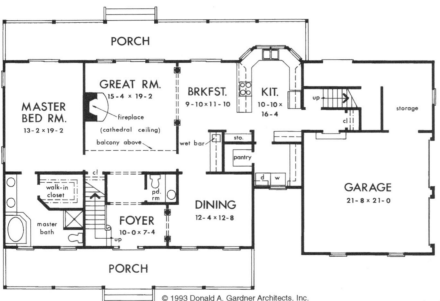

PORCH

GREAT RM.
15-4 x 19-2

BRKFST.
9-10 x 11-10

KIT.
10-10 x
16-4

up

storage

MASTER
BED RM.
13-2 x 19-2

fireplace
(cathedral ceiling)

balcony above

wet bar

sto.

pantry

walk-in
closet

cl

pd.
rm

d   w

DINING
12-4 x 12-8

GARAGE
21-8 x 21-0

master
bath

FOYER
10-0 x 7-4

up

PORCH

© 1993 Donald A. Gardner Architects, Inc.

This open country plan boasts front and rear covered porches and a bonus room for future expansion. The slope-ceilinged foyer has a Palladian window clerestory to let in natural light. The spacious great room presents a fireplace, cathedral ceiling and clerestory with arched windows. The second-floor balcony overlooks the great room. A U-shaped kitchen provides the ideal layout for food preparation. For flexibility, access is provided to the bonus room from both the first and second floors. The first-floor master bedroom features a bath with dual lavatories, a separate tub and shower and a walk-in closet. Two large bedrooms and a full bath are located on the second floor.

DESIGN HPU040245

First Floor: 1,632 square feet
Second Floor: 669 square feet
Total: 2,301 square feet
Bonus Room: 528 square feet
Width: 72'-6" Depth: 46'-10"

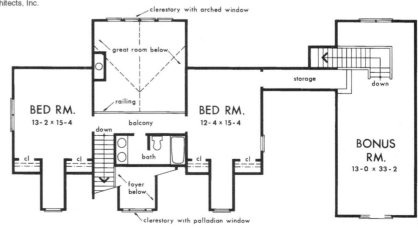

clerestory with arched window

great room below

railing

storage

down

BED RM.
13-2 x 15-4

balcony

down

BED RM.
12-4 x 15-4

BONUS
RM.
13-0 x 33-2

bath

cl

cl

cl

cl

foyer
below

clerestory with palladian window

DESIGN BY
Donald A. Gardner Architects, Inc.

QUOTE ONE®

Cost to build? See page 502
to order complete cost estimate
to build this house in your area!

GARAGE
22-4 x 21-4

DECK

spa

clerestory with arched window

(cathedral ceiling)
GREAT RM.
19-8 x 19-2

walk-in closet

skylight

master bath

cab.

fireplace

balcony above

covered breezeway

BRKFST.
9-8 x 10-6

UTIL.
8-0 x 9-4

d w

wet bar

pantry

KITCHEN
13-0 x 16-4

MASTER BED RM.
13-0 x 15-4

bath

cl

up

BED RM./ STUDY
12-0 x 11-0

FOYER
5-0 x 13-6

DINING
12-0 x 13-2

PORCH
30-4 x 8-0

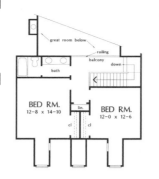

great room below

railing

balcony

down

bath

BED RM.
12-8 x 14-10

lin.

cl cl

BED RM.
12-0 x 12-6

DESIGN BY
Donald A. Gardner Architects, Inc.

DESIGN HPU040247

First Floor: 1,783 square feet
Second Floor: 611 square feet
Total: 2,394 square feet
Width: 70'-0" Depth: 79'-2"

Inside this lovely rustic design, an efficient family floor plan creates a relaxing ambience. The foyer opens to the dining room on the right, which connects to the kitchen. The great room is enhanced by a cathedral ceiling and features a fireplace. The master bedroom is placed on the first floor for extra privacy and includes a walk-in closet and master bath with a whirlpool tub. Upstairs, a second-floor balcony overlooks the great room.

Onlookers will delight in the symmetry of this facade's arched windows and dormers. The interior offers a great room with a cathedral ceiling. This open plan is also packed with the latest design features, including an island kitchen, wet bar, bedroom/study combo on the first floor and a gorgeous master suite with a spa-style bath. Upstairs, two family bedrooms share a compartmented hall bath.

DESIGN BY
Donald A. Gardner Architects, Inc.

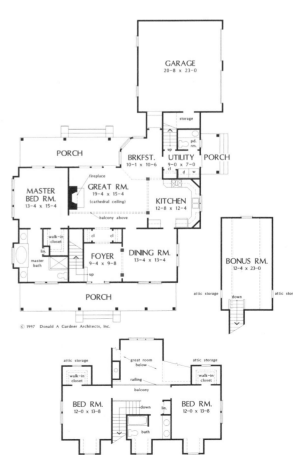

GARAGE
20-8 x 23-0

storage

pd. rm.

PORCH

BRKFST.
10-1 x 10-6

up

UTILITY
9-0 x 7-0

cl

d w

PORCH

fireplace

MASTER BED RM.
13-4 x 15-4

GREAT RM.
19-4 x 15-4
(cathedral ceiling)

KITCHEN
12-8 x 12-4

walk-in closet

cl cl

lin.

master bath

FOYER
9-4 x 9-8

up

DINING RM.
13-4 x 13-4

balcony above

PORCH

BONUS RM.
12-4 x 23-0

attic storage

down

attic storage

© 1997 Donald A Gardner Architects, Inc.

attic storage

walk-in closet

great room below

railing

balcony

attic storage

walk-in closet

BED RM.
12-0 x 13-8

down

lin.

bath

BED RM.
12-0 x 13-8

DESIGN HPU040246

First Floor: 1,467 square feet
Second Floor: 661 square feet
Total: 2,128 square feet
Bonus Room: 341 square feet
Width: 52'-2" Depth: 74'-0"

Traditional detailing such as the covered porch with a metal roof and brick steps gives this relaxed farmhouse extra finesse. A Palladian window, transoms over French doors, and large windows brighten the rooms, while nine-foot ceilings add volume and drama throughout the first floor. The master suite features a tray ceiling, and two second-floor bedrooms enjoy ample closet space and share a roomy bath.

DESIGN BY
Donald A. Gardner Architects, Inc.

PORCH

MASTER BED RM.
13-0 x 14-0

GREAT RM.
(two story)
19-0 x 19-2

fireplace

master bath

walk-in closet

up

FOYER
6-8 x 10-2
(two story)

DINING
12-0 x 12-8

KIT.
13-4 x 12-6

pantry

UTIL.
8-0 x 9-10

pd. rm.

BRKFST.
9-10 x 10-2

storage

GARAGE
21-0 x 24-6

PORCH

© 1995 Donald A Gardner Architects, Inc.

great room below

BED RM.
13-4 x 14-6

cl

sto. sto.

down

foyer below

BED RM.
12-0 x 12-8

walk-in closet

bath

lin.

skylights

BONUS RM.
21-0 x 14-8

attic storage

DESIGN HPU040249

First Floor: 1,561 square feet
Second Floor: 642 square feet
Total: 2,203 square feet
Bonus Room: 324 square feet
Width: 68'-0" Depth: 50'-4"

PORCH

GREAT RM.
(two story ceiling)
17-4 x 17-9

master bath

walk-in closet

walk-in closet

fireplace

MASTER BED RM.
13-0 x 13-8

pd. rm.

up

cl

FOYER
10-2 x 6-1

DINING
12-4 x 12-4

BRKFST.
11-0 x 13-10

pan.

KIT.
10-4 x 13-7

sto.

UTIL.
10-4 x 6-0

d

w

storage

PORCH

GARAGE
21-0 x 21-8

© 1997 Donald A. Gardner Architects, Inc.

great room below

BED RM.
11-0 x 12-8

cl

bath

lin.

down

foyer below

BED RM.
12-4 x 12-4

walk-in closet

attic storage

sto.

storage

down

attic storage

BONUS RM.
12-4 x 25-8

skylights

The grand foyer leads to a great room with a centered fireplace, a wall of windows and access to the rear porch. The breakfast room has its own door to the porch and shares its natural light with the kitchen. Twin walk-in closets introduce a lavish private bath in the master suite. Additional bedrooms reside on the second floor and share a full bath. A skylit bonus room offers extra storage space.

DESIGN HPU040248

First Floor: 1,489 square feet
Second Floor: 534 square feet
Total: 2,023 square feet
Bonus Room: 393 square feet
Width: 59'-4" Depth: 58'-7"

DESIGN BY
Donald A. Gardner Architects, Inc.

DESIGN HPU040250

Square Footage: 2,078
Bonus Room: 339 square feet
Width: 62'-2" Depth: 47'-8"

An enchanting L-shaped front porch lends charm and grace to this country home with dual dormers and gables. Bay windows expand both of the home's dining areas, while the great room and kitchen are amplified by a shared cathedral ceiling. The generous great room features a fireplace with flanking built-ins, skylights and access to a marvelous back porch. A cathedral ceiling enhances the master bedroom, which enjoys a large walk-in closet and luxurious bath. Two more bedrooms, one with a cathedral ceiling, share a generous hall bath that has a dual-sink vanity.

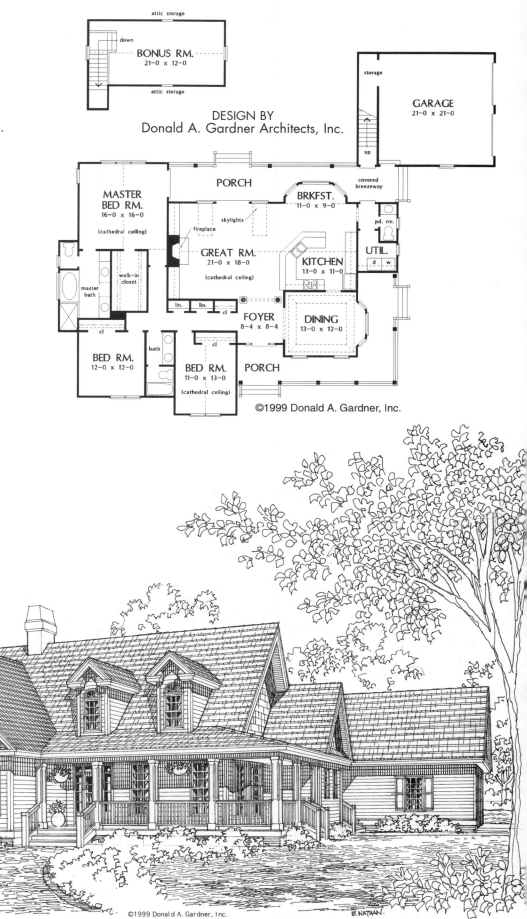

DESIGN BY
Donald A. Gardner Architects, Inc.

©1999 Donald A. Gardner, Inc.

©1999 Donald A. Gardner, Inc.

B. NATHAN

DESIGN HPU040251

Square Footage: 2,089
Bonus Room: 497 square feet
Width: 79'-0" Depth: 46'-0"

DESIGN BY
©Vaughn A. Lauban Designs

This country facade sports twin dormers, a bumped-out bay and gabled rooflines. Inside, the foyer invites you into either the dining room on the left or the study on the right. The great room features a fireplace and rear-porch access. A kitchen provides a breakfast bar, pantry and sink window. The master suite is secluded to the rear left of the plan and behind the garage for protection from street noise. Two family bedrooms share a full bath.

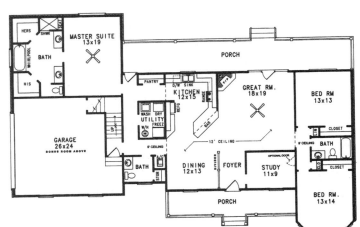

Twin dormers and a covered porch add to the relaxed country exterior of this home. The foyer opens to a study on the right and the dining room on the left. The galley-style kitchen services the dining room, breakfast nook and living room. The nook enjoys a bay window that overlooks the rear porch and yard. The master suite enjoys seclusion at the left rear of the home behind the two-car garage.

DESIGN BY
©Vaughn A. Lauban Designs

DESIGN HPU040252

Square Footage: 2,069
Width: 70'-0" Depth: 58'-8"

This quaint four-bedroom home with front and rear porches reinforces its beauty with arched windows and dormers. The pillared dining room opens on your right, while a study that could double as a guest room is available on your left. Straight ahead lies the massive great room with its cathedral ceiling, enchanting fireplace and access to the private rear porch and the deck with a spa and seat. Within steps of the dining room is the efficient kitchen and the sunny breakfast nook. The master suite enjoys a cathedral ceiling, rear-deck access and a master bath with a skylit whirlpool tub, walk-in closet and double vanity. Two additional bedrooms located at the opposite end of the house share a full bath that includes dual vanities.

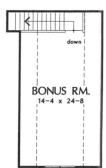

BONUS RM.
14-4 x 24-8

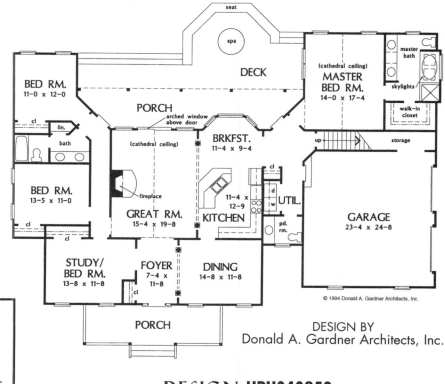

DESIGN BY
Donald A. Gardner Architects, Inc.

DESIGN HPU040253

Square Footage: 2,207
Bonus Room: 435 square feet
Width: 76'-1" Depth: 50'-0"

DESIGN HPU040254

Square Footage: 2,192
Bonus Room: 390 square feet
Width: 74'-10" Depth: 55'-8"

DESIGN BY
Donald A. Gardner Architects, Inc.

Exciting volumes and nine-foot ceilings add elegance to a comfortable and open plan. Sunlight fills the airy foyer from a vaulted dormer and streams into the great room. A dining room, delineated from the foyer by columns, features a tray ceiling. Family bedrooms share a full bath complete with a linen closet. The front bedroom doubles as a study for extra flexibility. The master bedroom suite sits to the left rear of the plan.

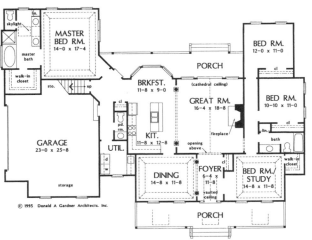

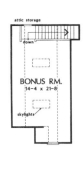

© 1994 Donald A. Gardner Architects, Inc.

DESIGN HPU040255

First Floor: 1,506 square feet
Second Floor: 513 square feet
Total: 2,019 square feet
Bonus Room: 397 square feet
Width: 65'-4" Depth: 67'-10"

DESIGN BY
Donald A. Gardner Architects, Inc.

With a casually elegant exterior, this three-bedroom farmhouse celebrates sunlight with a Palladian window dormer, a skylit screened porch and a rear arched window. The clerestory window in the two-story foyer throws natural light across the loft to the great room with a fireplace and a cathedral ceiling. The master suite is a calm retreat opening to the screened porch through a bay area. Two family bedrooms and a bonus room are located upstairs.

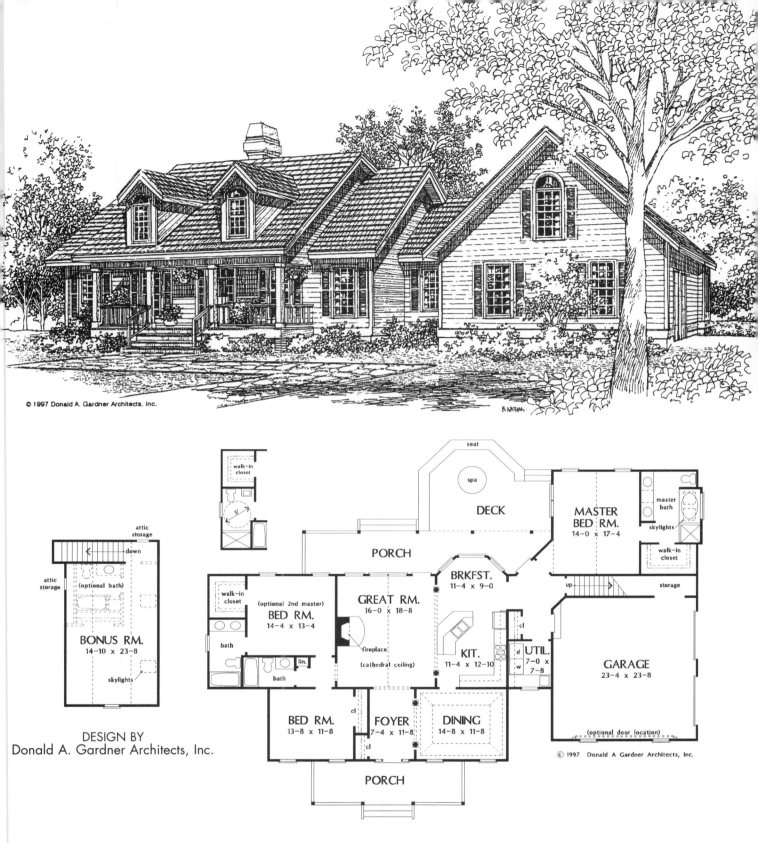

© 1997 Donald A. Gardner Architects, Inc.

B. NATHAN

attic storage
attic storage
down
(optional bath)
skylights

BONUS RM.
14-10 x 23-8

DESIGN BY
Donald A. Gardner Architects, Inc.

walk-in closet

walk-in closet

seat

spa

DECK

PORCH

MASTER BED RM.
14-0 x 17-4

master bath

skylights

walk-in closet

storage

up

BRKFST.
11-4 x 9-0

walk-in closet

bath

BED RM.
14-4 x 13-4
(optional 2nd master)

GREAT RM.
16-0 x 18-8

fireplace

(cathedral ceiling)

lin.

bath

KIT.
11-4 x 12-10

cl

UTIL.
7-0 x
7-8

d

w

GARAGE
23-4 x 23-8

BED RM.
13-8 x 11-8

cl

FOYER
7-4 x 11-8

cl

DINING
14-8 x 11-8

(optional door location)

© 1997 Donald A Gardner Architects, Inc.

PORCH

With its clean lines and symmetry, this home radiates grace and style. Inside, cathedral and tray ceilings add volume and elegance. The L-shaped kitchen includes an angled snack bar to the breakfast bay and great room. Secluded at the back of the house, the vaulted master suite includes a skylit bath. Of the two secondary bedrooms, one acts as a "second" master suite with its own private bath, and an alternate bath design creates a wheelchair-accessible option. The bonus room makes a great craft room, playroom, office or optional fourth bedroom with a bath. The two-car garage loads to the side.

DESIGN HPU040256

Square Footage: 2,057
Bonus Room: 444 square feet
Width: 80'-10" Depth: 61'-6"

DESIGN HPU040257

Square Footage: 2,042
Bonus Room: 475 square feet
Width: 75'-11" Depth: 56'-7"

DESIGN BY
Donald A. Gardner Architects, Inc.

A pleasing mixture of styles, this home combines a traditional brick veneer with an otherwise country home appearance. Built-ins flank the fireplace in the great room, while a soaring cathedral ceiling expands the room visually. The kitchen's angled counter opens the room to both the breakfast bay and great room. The screened porch is accessed from both the great room and the master suite.

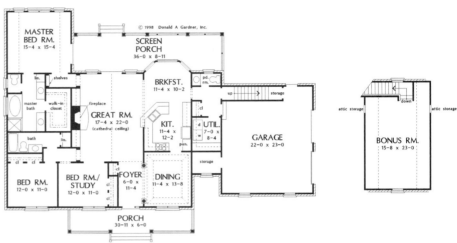

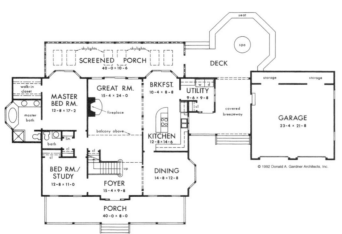

This farmhouse celebrates sunlight with a Palladian window dormer, a skylit screened porch and a rear arched window. The clerestory window in the foyer throws natural light across the loft to a great room with a fireplace and a cathedral ceiling. The central island kitchen and the breakfast area are open to the great room. The master suite is a calm retreat and opens to the screened porch through a bay area. Upstairs, a loft overlooking the great room connects two family bedrooms, each with a private bath.

QUOTE ONE®

Cost to build? See page 502
to order complete cost estimate
to build this house in your area!

DESIGN HPU040258

First Floor: 1,766 square feet
Second Floor: 670 square feet
Total: 2,436 square feet
Width: 93'-10" Depth: 62'-0"

DESIGN BY
Donald A. Gardner Architects, Inc.

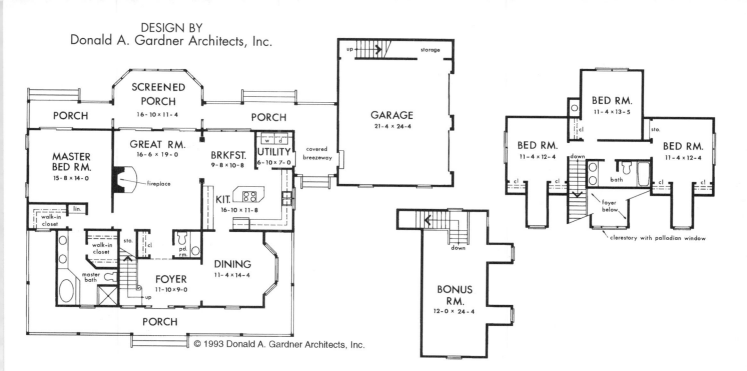

DESIGN BY
Donald A. Gardner Architects, Inc.

SCREENED PORCH
16-10 × 11-4

PORCH

GARAGE
21-4 × 24-4

up   storage

PORCH

MASTER BED RM.
15-8 × 14-0

GREAT RM.
16-6 × 19-0

fireplace

BRKFST.
9-8 × 10-8

UTILITY
6-10 × 7-0

w   d

covered breezeway

lin.

walk-in closet

KIT.
16-10 × 11-8

walk-in closet

sto.

cl

pd. rm.

DINING
11-4 × 14-4

master bath

FOYER
11-10 × 9-0

up

PORCH

down

BONUS RM.
12-0 × 24-4

BED RM.
11-4 × 13-5

cl

sto.

BED RM.
11-4 × 12-4

down

BED RM.
11-4 × 12-4

cl

cl

bath

cl

cl

foyer below

clerestory with palladian window

DESIGN HPU040259

First Floor: 1,585 square feet
Second Floor: 723 square feet
Total: 2,308 square feet
Bonus Room: 419 square feet
Width: 80'-4" Depth: 58'-0"

This complete farmhouse projects an exciting and comfortable feeling with its wraparound porch, arched windows and dormers. A Palladian window in the clerestory above the entrance foyer allows for an abundance of natural light. The large kitchen with a cooking island easily services the breakfast area and dining room. The generous great room with a fireplace offers access to the spacious screened porch for carefree outdoor living. The master bedroom suite, located on the first level for privacy and convenience, has a luxurious master bath. The second level allows for three bedrooms and a full bath. Don't miss the garage with a bonus room—both meet the main house via a covered breezeway.

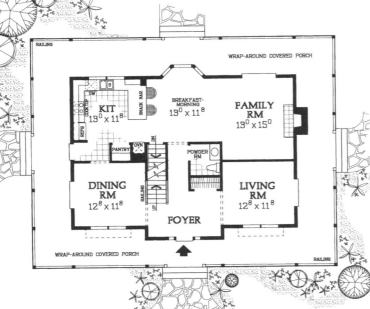

WRAP-AROUND COVERED PORCH

RAILING

KIT
13⁰ x 11⁸

BREAKFAST-
MORNING
13⁰ x 11⁸

SNACK BAR

FAMILY
RM
13⁰ x 15⁰

DW

REFR

COOK TOP

S

PANTRY

OVN

POWDER
RM

DINING
RM
12⁸ x 11⁸

RAILING

UP

DN

LIVING
RM
12⁸ x 11⁸

FOYER

WRAP-AROUND COVERED PORCH

RAILING

A menities fill this two-story country home, beginning with a full wraparound porch that offers access to each room on the first floor. Formal living and dining rooms border the central foyer, each with French-door access to the covered porch. At the rear of the first floor, a U-shaped kitchen, a bayed breakfast or morning room, and a large family room with a fireplace make up the living area. Upstairs, three family bedrooms share a centrally located utility room and a full hall bath that has dual sinks. The master suite features a box-bay window seat and a private bath with separate sinks and a walk-in closet. An additional half-bath on the first floor completes this exquisite design.

DESIGN HPU040260

First Floor: 1,160 square feet
Second Floor: 1,135 square feet
Total: 2,295 square feet
Width: 54'-0" Depth: 42'-0"

DESIGN BY
©Home Planners

QUOTE ONE®

Cost to build? See page 502
to order complete cost estimate
to build this house in your area!

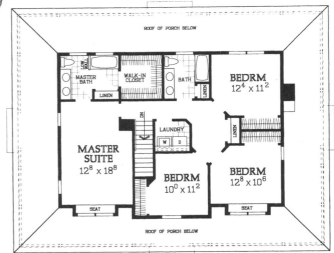

ROOF OF PORCH BELOW

MASTER
BATH

WALK-IN
CLOSET

BATH

LINEN

LINEN

BEDRM
12⁴ x 11²

LINEN

MASTER
SUITE
12⁸ x 18⁸

DN

LAUNDRY

W   D

BEDRM
12⁸ x 10⁶

SEAT

BEDRM
10⁰ x 11²

SEAT

ROOF OF PORCH BELOW

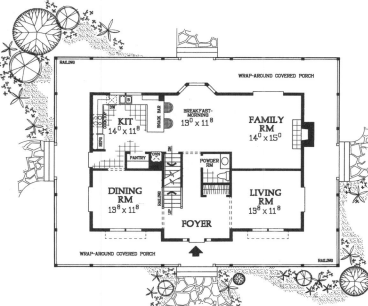

WRAP-AROUND COVERED PORCH

KIT
14⁰ x 11⁸

BREAKFAST-MORNING
13⁰ x 11⁸

SNACK BAR

FAMILY RM
14⁰ x 15⁰

PANTRY
OVN
POWDER RM

DINING RM
13⁸ x 11⁸

LIVING RM
13⁸ x 11⁸

FOYER

WRAP-AROUND COVERED PORCH

RAILING

DESIGN HPU040262

First Floor: 1,216 square feet
Second Floor: 1,191 square feet
Total: 2,407 square feet
Width: 56'-0" Depth: 42'-0"

L D

DESIGN BY
©Home Planners

Symmetrical gables and clapboard siding lend a Midwestern style to this prairies-and-plains farmhouse. A spacious foyer opens to formal rooms and leads to a casual living area with a tiled-hearth fireplace and a breakfast bay. The U-shaped kitchen enjoys an easy-care ceramic tile floor and a walk-in pantry. The second-floor sleeping quarters include a generous master suite with a window-seat dormer and a private bath with a whirlpool tub, walk-in closet, twin vanities and linen storage. Three family bedrooms share a full bath and a central hall that leads to additional storage and a laundry.

QUOTE ONE®
Cost to build? See page 502
to order complete cost estimate
to build this house in your area!

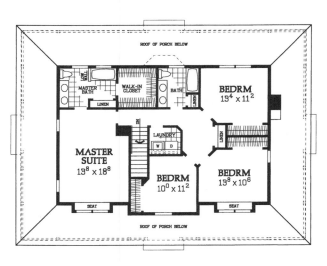

ROOF OF PORCH BELOW

MASTER BATH
WALK-IN CLOSET
BATH
LINEN
BEDRM
13⁴ x 11²

LAUNDRY
W D
LINEN

MASTER SUITE
13⁸ x 18⁸

BEDRM
10⁰ x 11²

BEDRM
13⁸ x 10⁶

SEAT

SEAT

ROOF OF PORCH BELOW

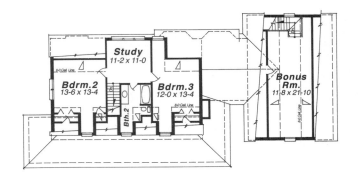

DESIGN HPU040264

First Floor: 1,362 square feet
Second Floor: 729 square feet
Total: 2,091 square feet
Bonus Room: 384 square feet
Width: 72'-0" Depth: 38'-0"

This design's open flow leads you through the living room to the dining room, where access through the bay opens to a sun deck. A kitchen connects to a bayed breakfast area. The master bedroom features a master bath suite with all the amenities. The second floor provides two spacious bedrooms with a shared study or computer room. Please specify basement, crawlspace or slab foundation when ordering.

Sundeck
16-8 x 14-0

Stor.
7-0 x 9-4

Laund.

Dining
13-0 x 13-6

Brkfst.
10-0 x 9-4

Lav.

M.Bath

Kit.
12-0 x 8-0

Double Garage
21-4 x 21-8

Master Bdrm.
13-6 x 17-0

Living Area
20-0 x 13-6

Foyer

Porch

© 1987, Jannis Vann & Associates, Inc.

DESIGN BY
©Jannis Vann & Associates, Inc.

Study
11-2 x 11-0

Bdrm.2
13-6 x 13-4

Bdrm.3
12-0 x 13-4

Bth.2

Bonus Rm.
11-8 x 21-10

DESIGN BY
©Home Planners

This classic farmhouse enjoys a wraparound porch that's perfect for enjoyment of the outdoors. The dining room is defined by graceful archways set off by decorative columns. The tiled kitchen has a center island counter with a snack bar. Two family bedrooms reside to the side of the plan; each enjoys private access to the covered porch. A secluded master suite features a sitting area with access to the rear terrace and spa.

DESIGN HPU040263

Square Footage: 2,090
Width: 84'-6" Depth: 64'-0"

L **D**

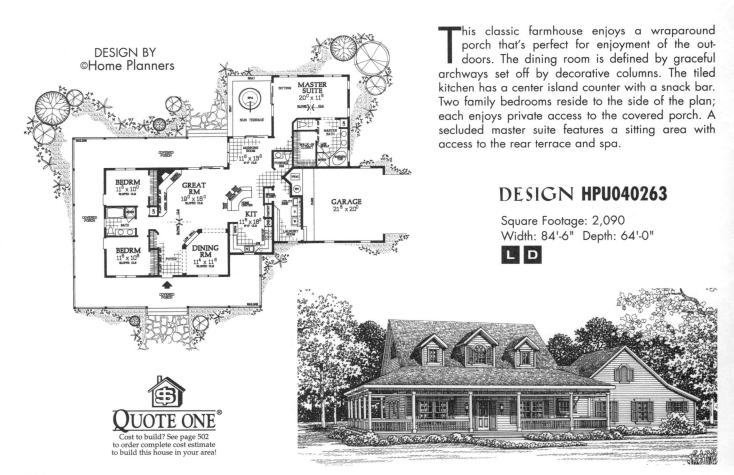

MASTER SUITE
20⁰ x 11⁵

SUN TERRACE

MORNING ROOM
11⁸ x 19⁸

MASTER BATH

COVERED PORCH

BEDRM
11⁸ x 10⁰

GREAT RM
19⁰ x 16⁰

KIT.
11⁸ x 18⁰

POWDER RM

UTILITY RM

GARAGE
21⁸ x 20⁰

BATH

BEDRM
11⁸ x 10⁸

DINING RM
11⁴ x 11⁸

FOYER

LAUNDRY ROOM

WALK-IN CLOSET

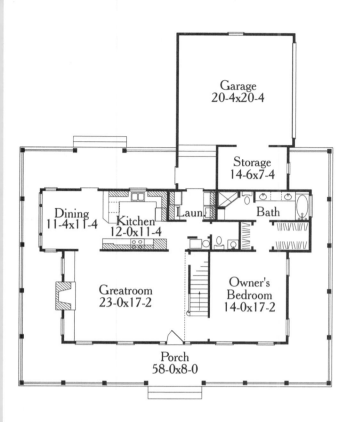

Garage
20-4x20-4

Storage
14-6x7-4

Dining
11-4x11-4

Kitchen
12-0x11-4

Laun.

Bath

Greatroom
23-0x17-2

Owner's
Bedroom
14-0x17-2

Porch
58-0x8-0

DESIGN BY
©Larry James & Associates, Inc.

Charming dormer windows and a wraparound porch make this country home a prize. The great room offers porch views and a fireplace to warm guests and family alike. The dining room features a bumped-out wall of windows and easy service from the nearby kitchen. The owners suite is pampered by a walk-in closet and lavish bath. Upstairs, two family bedrooms enjoy plenty of closet space and share a full bath. Please specify basement, crawlspace or slab foundation when ordering.

DESIGN HPU040265

First Floor: 1,339 square feet
Second Floor: 823 square feet
Total: 2,162 square feet
Width: 58'-0" Depth: 67'-2"

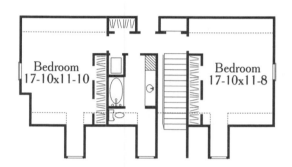

Bedroom
17-10x11-10

Bedroom
17-10x11-8

DESIGN HPU040267

First Floor: 1,526 square feet
Second Floor: 635 square feet
Total: 2,161 square feet
Bonus Room: 355 square feet
Width: 76'-4" Depth: 74'-2"

© 1992 Donald A. Gardner Architects, Inc.

Quote One®
Cost to build? See page 502
to order complete cost estimate
to build this house in your area!

Clerestory windows with arched tops enhance the exterior both front and back, as well as allowing natural light to penetrate into the foyer and the great room. A kitchen with an island counter and a breakfast area is open to the great room. The master suite includes a walk-in closet and a lush master bath. The second level contains two bedrooms sharing a full bath and a loft/study area over-looking the great room.

DESIGN BY
Donald A. Gardner Architects, Inc.

Spaciousness and lots of amenities earmark this design as a family favorite. The front wraparound porch leads to the foyer where a bedroom/study and dining room open. The central great room presents a warming fireplace, a cathedral ceiling and access to the rear porch. In the master suite, a walk-in closet and a private bath with a bumped-out tub are extra enhancements. Bonus space over the garage could become a home office.

© 1994 Donald A. Gardner Architects, Inc.

Quote One®
Cost to build? See page 502
to order complete cost estimate
to build this house in your area!

DESIGN HPU040266

First Floor: 1,841 square feet
Second Floor: 594 square feet
Total: 2,435 square feet
Bonus Room: 391 square feet
Width: 82'-2" Depth: 48'-10"

DESIGN BY
Donald A. Gardner Architects, Inc.

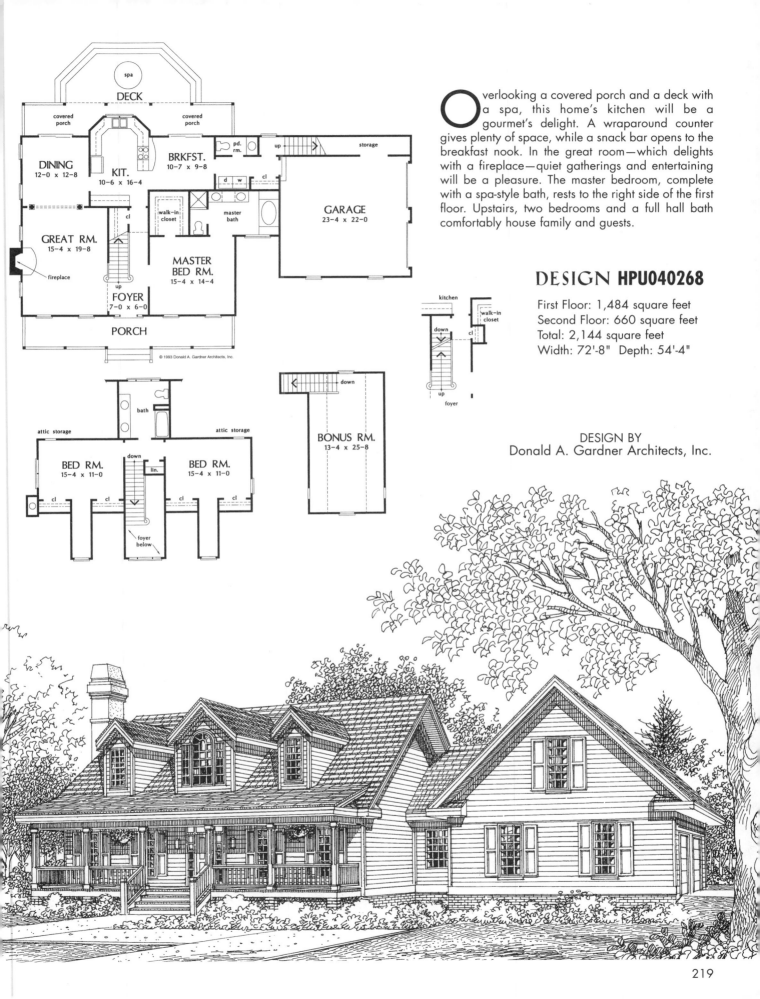

DECK

spa

covered porch · covered porch

DINING
12-0 x 12-8

KIT.
10-6 x 16-4

BRKFST.
10-7 x 9-8

pd. rm.

up

storage

d w cl

walk-in closet

master bath

GARAGE
23-4 x 22-0

GREAT RM.
15-4 x 19-8

fireplace

cl

MASTER BED RM.
15-4 x 14-4

up

FOYER
7-0 x 6-0

PORCH

© 1993 Donald A. Gardner Architects, Inc.

bath

attic storage

attic storage

BED RM.
15-4 x 11-0

down

lin.

BED RM.
15-4 x 11-0

cl cl cl cl

foyer below

down

BONUS RM.
13-4 x 25-8

kitchen

walk-in closet

down

cl

up

foyer

Overlooking a covered porch and a deck with a spa, this home's kitchen will be a gourmet's delight. A wraparound counter gives plenty of space, while a snack bar opens to the breakfast nook. In the great room—which delights with a fireplace—quiet gatherings and entertaining will be a pleasure. The master bedroom, complete with a spa-style bath, rests to the right side of the first floor. Upstairs, two bedrooms and a full hall bath comfortably house family and guests.

DESIGN HPU040268

First Floor: 1,484 square feet
Second Floor: 660 square feet
Total: 2,144 square feet
Width: 72'-8" Depth: 54'-4"

DESIGN BY
Donald A. Gardner Architects, Inc.

DESIGN HPU040269

First Floor: 1,756 square feet
Second Floor: 565 square feet
Total: 2,321 square feet
Width: 56'-8" Depth: 54'-4"

DESIGN BY
Donald A. Gardner Architects, Inc.

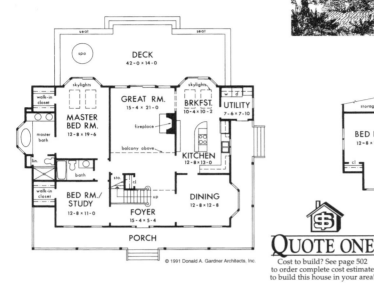

DECK
42-0 × 14-0

spa

seat   seat

skylights   skylights

walk-in
closet

GREAT RM.
15-4 × 21-0

BRKFST.
10-4 × 10-2

UTILITY
7-6 × 7-10

MASTER
BED RM.
12-8 × 19-6

fireplace

master
bath

balcony above

KITCHEN
12-8 × 13-0

lin.

bath

walk-in
closet

sto.   cl

BED RM./
STUDY
12-8 × 11-0

up

FOYER
15-4 × 5-4

DINING
12-8 × 12-8

PORCH

© 1991 Donald A. Gardner Architects, Inc.

clerestory with arched window

(cathedral ceiling)
great room below

storage   storage

railing

BED RM.
12-8 × 12-0

balcony

BED RM.
12-8 × 12-0

down

bath

cl   cl

foyer
below

clerestory with palladian window

QUOTE ONE®
Cost to build? See page 502
to order complete cost estimate
to build this house in your area!

A wraparound covered porch at the front and sides of this house and an open deck at the back provide plenty of outside living area. The spacious great room features a fireplace, cathedral ceiling and clerestory with an arched window. The first-floor master bedroom contains a generous closet and a bath with a garden tub, double-bowl vanity and shower. The second floor sports two bedrooms and a full bath with a double-bowl vanity.

DECK

seat

seat

spa

skylights

SUN RM.
16-2 × 8-10

GREAT RM.
15-4 × 21-0
(cathedral ceiling)
fireplace

BRKFST.
9-10 × 9-10

wash/dry

UTILITY
8-0 × 7-10

master bath

walk-in
closet

pass-thru

KITCHEN
12-8 × 13-0

balcony above

sto.   cl

pd.
rm.

MASTER
BED RM.
12-8 × 16-4

FOYER
11-10 × 7-2
(sloped ceiling)

up

DINING
14-8 × 12-8

PORCH

© 1990 Donald A. Gardner Architects, Inc.

clerestory with arched window

(cathedral ceiling)
great room below

storage   storage

railing

BED RM.
12-8 × 12-0

balcony

BED RM.
12-8 × 12-0

down

bath

cl   cl

foyer
below

clerestory with palladian window

QUOTE ONE®
Cost to build? See page 502
to order complete cost estimate
to build this house in your area!

A wraparound porch at the front and sides of this house and a deck with a built-in spa provide outside living area. The great room is appointed with a fireplace, cathedral ceiling and clerestory with an arched window. The kitchen is centrally located for maximum flexibility in layout and features a food-preparation island. Besides the first-floor master bedroom, which offers access to the sun room, there are two second-floor bedrooms that share a full bath.

DESIGN HPU040270

First Floor: 1,651 square feet
Second Floor: 567 square feet
Total: 2,218 square feet
Width: 55'-0" Depth: 53'-10"

DESIGN BY
Donald A. Gardner Architects, Inc.

© 1993 Donald A. Gardner Architects, Inc.

B. NATHAN

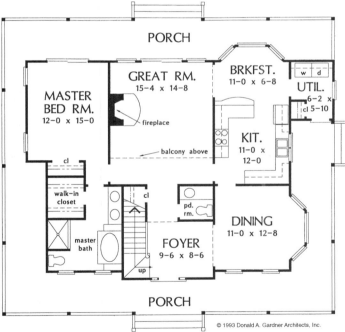

PORCH

GREAT RM.
15-4 x 14-8

BRKFST.
11-0 x 6-8

UTIL.
6-2 x
cl 5-10

w d

MASTER
BED RM.
12-0 x 15-0

fireplace

balcony above

KIT.
11-0 x
12-0

cl

walk-in
closet

cl

pd.
rm.

DINING
11-0 x 12-8

master
bath

FOYER
9-6 x 8-6

up

PORCH

© 1993 Donald A. Gardner Architects, Inc.

DESIGN HPU040271

First Floor: 1,346 square feet
Second Floor: 836 square feet
Total: 2,182 square feet
Width: 49'-5" Depth: 45'-4"

DESIGN BY
Donald A. Gardner Architects, Inc.

This classy, two-story home with a wraparound covered porch offers a dynamic open floor plan. The entrance foyer and the spacious great room both rise to two stories—a Palladian window at the second level floods these areas with natural light. The kitchen is centrally located for maximum flexibility in layout and, as an added feature, also has a breakfast bar. The large dining room delights with a bay window. The generous master suite has plenty of closet space as well as a bath with a whirlpool tub, a shower and a double-bowl vanity. On the second level, three bedrooms branch off the balcony that overlooks the great room. One large bedroom contains a private bath and a walk-in closet, while the other bedrooms share a full bath.

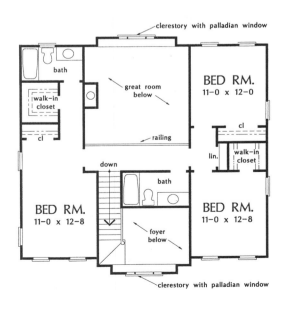

clerestory with palladian window

bath

walk-in
closet

cl

great room
below

BED RM.
11-0 x 12-0

cl

railing

lin.

walk-in
closet

down

bath

BED RM.
11-0 x 12-8

foyer
below

BED RM.
11-0 x 12-8

clerestory with palladian window

221

DESIGN HPU040272

First Floor: 1,471 square feet
Second Floor: 577 square feet
Total: 2,048 square feet
Bonus Room: 368 square feet
Width: 75'-5" Depth: 52'-0"

DESIGN BY
Donald A. Gardner Architects, Inc.

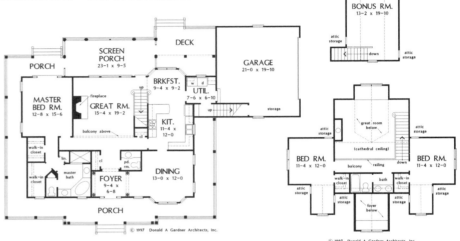

For the family that enjoys outdoor living, this wraparound porch that becomes a screened porch and then turns into a deck is the best of all worlds! At the front, the dining room features a bay window and mirrors the breakfast bay at the back, with the kitchen in between. On the opposite side of the plan, the master suite, with two walk-in closets and a deluxe bath, accesses the rear porch. Two family bedrooms share a full bath on the second floor.

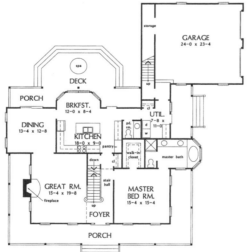

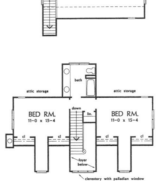

This charming farmhouse begins with a two-story entrance foyer with a Palladian window in a clerestory dormer above for natural light. The master suite, with its large walk-in closet, is on the first level for privacy and accessibility. The master bath includes a whirlpool tub, a shower and a double-bowl vanity. The second level has two bedrooms, a full bath and plenty of storage.

QUOTE ONE®

Cost to build? See page 502
to order complete cost estimate
to build this house in your area!

DESIGN HPU040273

First Floor: 1,537 square feet
Second Floor: 641 square feet
Total: 2,178 square feet
Bonus Room: 418 square feet
Width: 65'-8" Depth: 70'-0"

DESIGN BY
Donald A. Gardner Architects, Inc.

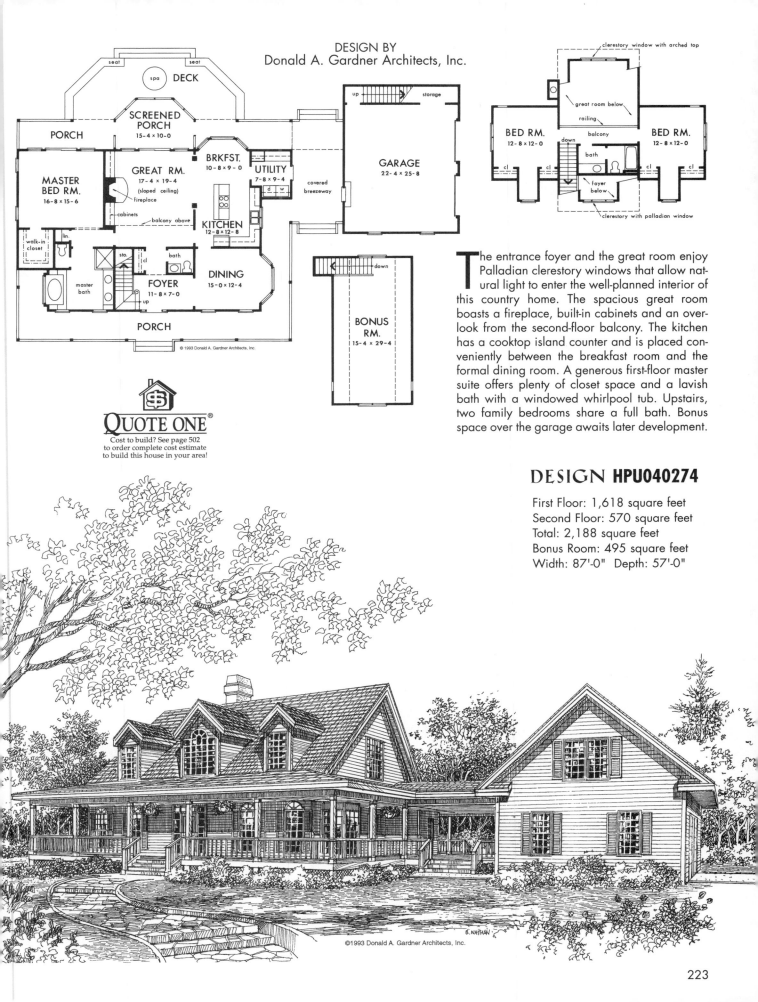

DECK

spa

seat   seat

SCREENED PORCH
15-4 × 10-0

PORCH

BRKFST.
10-8 × 9-0

UTILITY
7-8 × 9-4

GREAT RM.
17-4 × 19-4
(sloped ceiling)
fireplace

MASTER BED RM.
16-8 × 15-6

cabinets

balcony above

KITCHEN
12-8 × 12-8

walk-in closet

lin.

master bath

sto.

cl

bath

FOYER
11-8 × 7-0

up

DINING
15-0 × 12-4

PORCH

© 1993 Donald A. Gardner Architects, Inc.

up   storage

GARAGE
22-4 × 25-8

covered breezeway

down

BONUS RM.
15-4 × 29-4

clerestory window with arched top

great room below

railing

balcony

BED RM.
12-8 × 12-0

down

bath

BED RM.
12-8 × 12-0

cl   cl

cl   cl

foyer below

clerestory with palladian window

QUOTE ONE®
Cost to build? See page 502
to order complete cost estimate
to build this house in your area!

The entrance foyer and the great room enjoy Palladian clerestory windows that allow natural light to enter the well-planned interior of this country home. The spacious great room boasts a fireplace, built-in cabinets and an overlook from the second-floor balcony. The kitchen has a cooktop island counter and is placed conveniently between the breakfast room and the formal dining room. A generous first-floor master suite offers plenty of closet space and a lavish bath with a windowed whirlpool tub. Upstairs, two family bedrooms share a full bath. Bonus space over the garage awaits later development.

DESIGN HPU040274

First Floor: 1,618 square feet
Second Floor: 570 square feet
Total: 2,188 square feet
Bonus Room: 495 square feet
Width: 87'-0" Depth: 57'-0"

B. NATHAN

©1993 Donald A. Gardner Architects, Inc.

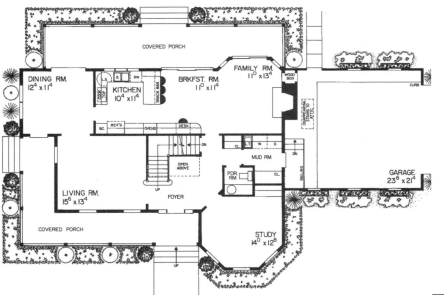

DESIGN HPU040275

First Floor: 1,269 square feet
Second Floor: 1,227 square feet
Total: 2,496 square feet
Width: 70'-0" Depth: 44'-5"

L

QUOTE ONE®
Cost to build? See page 502
to order complete cost estimate
to build this house in your area!

DESIGN BY
©Home Planners

The most popular feature of the Victorian house has always been its covered porches. The two finely detailed outdoor living spaces found on this home add much to formal and informal entertaining options. However, in addition to its wonderful Victorian facade, this home provides a myriad of interior features that cater to the active, growing family. Living and dining areas include a formal living room and dining room, a family room with fireplace, a study and a kitchen with an attached breakfast nook. The second floor contains three family bedrooms and a luxurious master suite with a whirlpool spa and His and Hers walk-in closets.

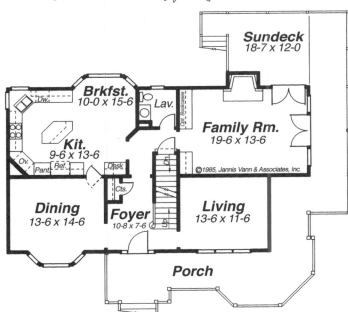

Sundeck
18-7 x 12-0

Brkfst.
10-0 x 15-6

Lav.

Family Rm.
19-6 x 13-6

Kit.
9-6 x 13-6

Opt. Bookcases

©1985, Jannis Vann & Associates, Inc.

Dining
13-6 x 14-6

Foyer
10-8 x 7-6

Living
13-6 x 11-6

Desk

Cts.

Pant.

Ref.

Ov.

Dw.

Porch

DESIGN BY
©Jannis Vann & Associates, Inc.

DESIGN HPU040276

First Floor: 1,155 square feet
Second Floor: 1,209 square feet
Total: 2,364 square feet
Width: 46'-0" Depth: 36'-8"

Victorian charm is displayed at its best with fish-scale siding, bay windows, a turret roof and gingerbread trim all featured on this design. The front porch features an expanded sitting area perfect for the porch swing or a table and chairs, as the porch roof wraps around the second-floor turret. Bay windows expand space in both the formal dining room and the breakfast area. The kitchen carries on the bay-window feel as the cabinets angle at the corners, creating a bright sink corner plus an angled island for extra work space. Outside living is enhanced by the deck that connects the rear deck with the front porch. The glass wall on the side of the family room floods the room with light. The second-floor turret creates a cozy sitting area in the master suite, which accesses a balcony. Three bedrooms share a hall bath located across from the second-floor laundry closet.

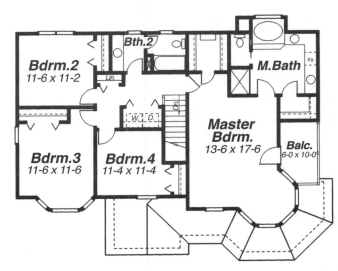

Bdrm.2
11-6 x 11-2

Bth.2

M.Bath

Bdrm.3
11-6 x 11-6

Bdrm.4
11-4 x 11-4

Master
Bdrm.
13-6 x 17-6

Balc.
6-0 x 10-0

W. D.

Lin.

Kls.

DESIGN HPU040277

First Floor: 1,186 square feet
Second Floor: 988 square feet
Total: 2,174 square feet
Width: 72'-4" Depth: 51'-2"

L D

DESIGN BY
©Home Planners

This Victorian-style exterior—a wraparound porch, mullion windows and turret-style bays—offers you a wonderful floor plan. Inside, an impressive tiled entry opens to the formal rooms, which nestle to the left side of the plan and enjoy natural light from an abundance of windows. More than just a pretty face, the turret houses a secluded study on the first floor and provides a sunny bay window for a family bedroom upstairs. The second-floor master suite boasts its own fireplace, a dressing area with a walk-in closet, and a lavish bath with a garden tub and twin vanities. The two-car garage offers space for a workshop or extra storage.

Victorian style is highly evident on this beautiful four-bedroom, two-story home. With fish-scale trim, a turret skirted by an octagonal porch, and varied window treatments, this home is a true winner. The interior continues with a cozy octagonal study, a spacious living room complete with a warming fireplace, a formal dining room that offers access to the rear porch, and a large efficient kitchen that shares a snack bar with the comfortable family room. The sleeping zone is contained upstairs and consists of three secondary bedrooms—one at the top of the tower—that shares a full hall bath, and a lavish master suite.

DESIGN HPU040278

First Floor: 1,186 square feet
Second Floor: 988 square feet
Total: 2,174 square feet
Width: 72'-0" Depth: 50'-10"

L D

DESIGN BY
©Home Planners

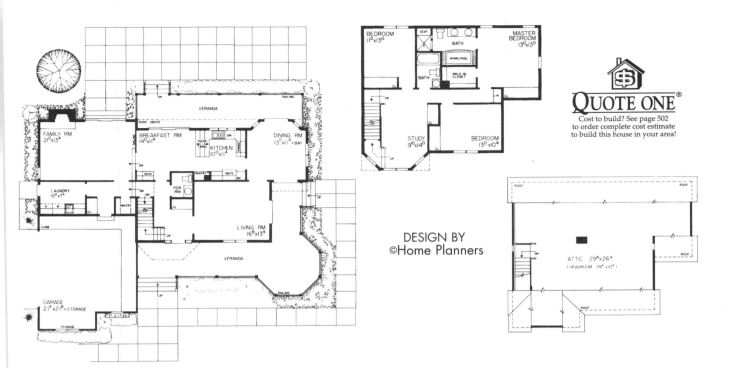

DESIGN BY
©Home Planners

DESIGN HPU040279

First Floor: 1,375 square feet
Second Floor: 1,016 square feet
Total: 2,391 square feet
Attic: 303 square feet
Width: 62'-7" Depth: 54'-0"

L

Covered porches, front and back, are a fine preview to the livable nature of this Victorian design. Living areas are defined in a family room with a fireplace, formal living and dining rooms, and a kitchen with a breakfast room. An ample laundry room, a garage with a storage area, and a powder room round out the first floor. Three second-floor bedrooms are joined by a study and two full baths. The master suite on this floor has two closets, including a spacious walk-in, as well as a relaxing bath with a tile-rimmed whirlpool tub and a separate shower with a seat.

DESIGN HPU040280

Square Footage: 2,250
Width: 84'-10" Depth: 62'-4"

DESIGN BY
Donald A. Gardner Architects, Inc.

A lovely courtyard precedes a grand French-door entry with an arched transom, while stone and stucco accent the exterior of this dignified Country French home. The foyer, great room and dining room feature stately eleven-foot ceilings, and interior columns mark boundaries for the great room and dining room. The spacious kitchen features a pass-through to the great room, where built-in shelves flank the fireplace. Cozy side decks and a large back porch add to the home's appeal. The master suite is magnificent with a double-door entry, an elegant tray ceiling, dual walk-in closets and an extravagant bath. Nearby, two additional bedrooms share their own hall bath.

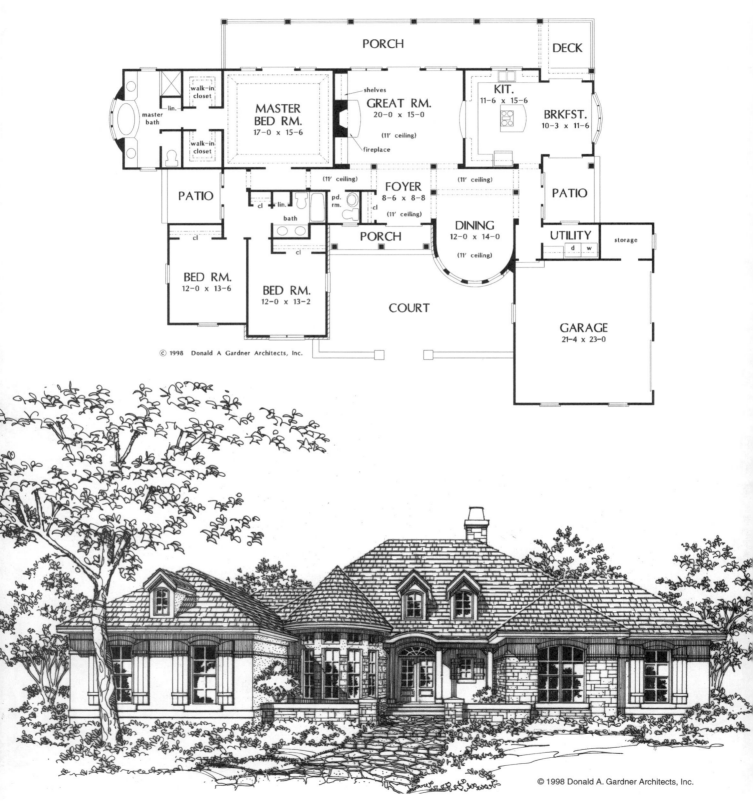

PORCH

DECK

walk-in closet

KIT.
11-6 x 15-6

master bath

lin.

MASTER
BED RM.
17-0 x 15-6

shelves

GREAT RM.
20-0 x 15-0

(11' ceiling)

fireplace

BRKFST.
10-3 x 11-6

walk-in closet

PATIO

(11' ceiling)

FOYER
8-6 x 8-8

(11' ceiling)

(11' ceiling)

PATIO

cl lin.

pd. rm.

cl

bath

UTILITY

d w

storage

cl

cl

BED RM.
12-0 x 13-6

PORCH

DINING
12-0 x 14-0

(11' ceiling)

BED RM.
12-0 x 13-2

COURT

GARAGE
21-4 x 23-0

© 1998 Donald A Gardner Architects, Inc.

© 1998 Donald A. Gardner Architects, Inc.

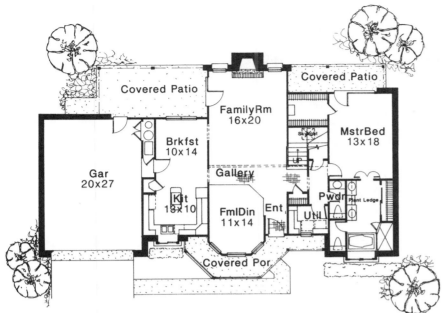

DESIGN HPU040281

First Floor: 1,572 square feet
Second Floor: 700 square feet
Total: 2,272 square feet
Bonus Room: 212 square feet
Width: 70'-0" Depth: 38'-5"

DESIGN BY
©Fillmore Design Group

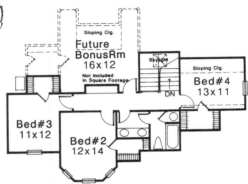

A charming porch wraps around the front of this farmhouse, whose entry opens to a formal dining room. Country and Victorian elements give this home a down-home feel. The island kitchen and sun-filled breakfast area are located nearby. The family room is warmed by a fireplace flanked by windows. Located for privacy, the first-floor master bedroom features its own covered patio and a private bath designed for relaxation. The second floor contains three family bedrooms—each with a walk-in closet—a full bath and a future bonus room.

DESIGN HPU040283

First Floor: 1,006 square feet
Second Floor: 1,099 square feet
Total: 2,105 square feet
Width: 47'-0" Depth: 43'-0"

DESIGN BY
©Design Basics, Inc.

This siding-and-brick traditional home focuses on the family. A charming covered porch welcomes guests, while inside, a formal dining area and great room with a fireplace are perfect for entertaining. A large efficient kitchen with an easy-access island and a bayed breakfast area is handy for those easy meals. Three family bedrooms and a comfortable master suite with a whirlpool bath and separate shower are located on the second floor. A loft area is a popular family retreat.

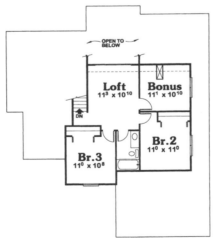

Brick and stone go hand-in-hand to create a pleasing exterior for this home. But the appeal doesn't remain only on the outside. The interior floor plan has many amenities and provides great traffic flow. The offset entry opens to a small hall and is distinguished by columns that separate it from the formal dining room. The great room boasts an eleven-foot ceiling and a corner fireplace. Just beyond is a U-shaped kitchen with an attached breakfast nook—note the snack counter that separates them. The master bedroom on the first floor features a private bath and walk-in closet. Family bedrooms on the second floor share a full bath. Bonus space and a loft area on the second floor expand its usefulness.

DESIGN HPU040282

First Floor: 1,457 square feet
Second Floor: 686 square feet
Total: 2,143 square feet
Bonus Room: 445 square feet
Width: 45'-4" Depth: 54'-0"

DESIGN BY
©Design Basics, Inc.

B. NATHAN

© 1992 Donald A. Gardner Architects, Inc.

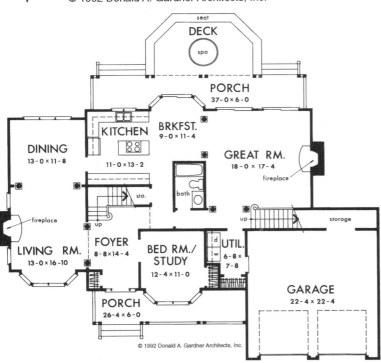

seat

DECK

spa

PORCH
37-0 × 6-0

KITCHEN
11-0 × 13-2

BRKFST.
9-0 × 11-4

GREAT RM.
18-0 × 17-4

fireplace

DINING
13-0 × 11-8

sto.

up

bath

LIVING RM.
13-0 × 16-10

fireplace

FOYER
8-8 × 14-4

**BED RM./
STUDY**
12-4 × 11-0

UTIL.
6-8 ×
7-8

d
w

up

storage

GARAGE
22-4 × 22-4

PORCH
26-4 × 6-0

© 1992 Donald A. Gardner Architects, Inc.

DESIGN HPU040284

First Floor: 1,569 square feet
Second Floor: 929 square feet
Total: 2,498 square feet
Bonus Room: 320 square feet
Width: 65'-8" Depth: 61'-4"

DESIGN BY
Donald A. Gardner Architects, Inc.

BED RM.
10-8 × 10-10

bath

master
bath

**MASTER
BED RM.**
13-8 × 17-4

down

linen

foyer
below

down

BED RM.
11-0 × 11-8

**BONUS
RM.**
12-4 × 22-4

This home's striking exterior is reinforced by its gables and arched glass window. The central foyer leads to all spaces in the home's open layout. Both the living room and great room boast fireplaces and round columns. The efficient U-shaped kitchen offers a cooking island for added luxury to serve both the dining room and breakfast area. The master bedroom holds a large walk-in closet and generous bath with a whirlpool tub, separate shower and double-bowl vanity. Two additional bedrooms share a full bath. A bedroom on the first level can easily double as a study.

DESIGN HPU040286

First Floor: 1,653 square feet
Second Floor: 700 square feet
Total: 2,353 square feet
Width: 54'-0" Depth: 50'-0"

DESIGN BY
©Design Basics, Inc.

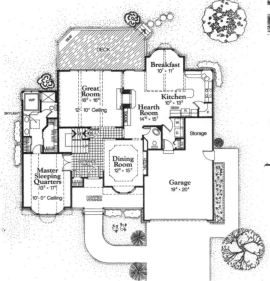

Beautiful arches and elaborate detail give the elevation of this four-bedroom, 1½-story home an unmistakable elegance. Inside, the floor plan is equally appealing. Note the formal dining room with a bay window, visible from the entrance hall. The large great room has a fireplace and a wall of windows with views of the rear property. A hearth room with a built-in bookcase adjoins the kitchen, which boasts a corner walk-in pantry and a spacious breakfast nook with a bay window. The first-floor master suite features His and Hers wardrobes, a large whirlpool tub and double lavatories. Upstairs, the family sleeping quarters share a full bath that includes compartmented sinks.

Elegant detail, a charming veranda and a tall brick chimney make a pleasing facade on this four-bedroom, two-story Victorian home. Yesterday's simpler lifestyle is reflected throughout this plan. From the large bayed parlor with its sloped ceiling to the sunken gathering room with a fireplace, there's plenty to appreciate about the floor plan. The L-shaped kitchen with its attached breakfast room has plenty of storage space and easily serves the dining room through a discreet doorway. Sleeping quarters include a master suite with a private dressing area and a whirlpool bath, and three family bedrooms arranged to share a hall bath.

DESIGN HPU040285

First Floor: 1,113 square feet
Second Floor: 965 square feet
Total: 2,078 square feet
Width: 46'-0" Depth: 41'-5"

DESIGN BY
©Design Basics, Inc.

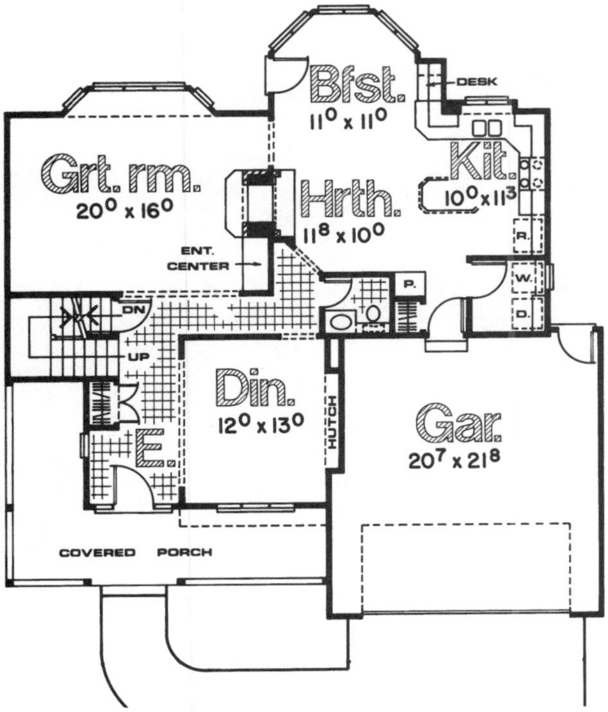

Bfst.
$11^{0} \times 11^{0}$
DESK
Grt. rm.
$20^{0} \times 16^{0}$
Kit.
$10^{0} \times 11^{3}$
Hrth.
$11^{8} \times 10^{0}$
ENT. CENTER
R.
W.
P.
D.
DN
UP
Din.
$12^{0} \times 13^{0}$
HUTCH
Gar.
$20^{7} \times 21^{8}$
E.
COVERED PORCH

Lap siding, special windows and a covered porch enhance the elevation of this popular style. The spacious two-story entry surveys the formal dining room with hutch space. An entertainment center, through-fireplace and bayed windows add appeal to the great room. Families will love the spacious kitchen with its breakfast and hearth room. Comfortable secondary bedrooms and a sumptuous master suite feature privacy by design. Bedroom 3 is highlighted by a half-round window, volume ceiling and double closets, while Bedroom 4 features a built-in desk. The master suite contains a vaulted ceiling, large walk-in closet, His and Hers vanities and an oval whirlpool tub.

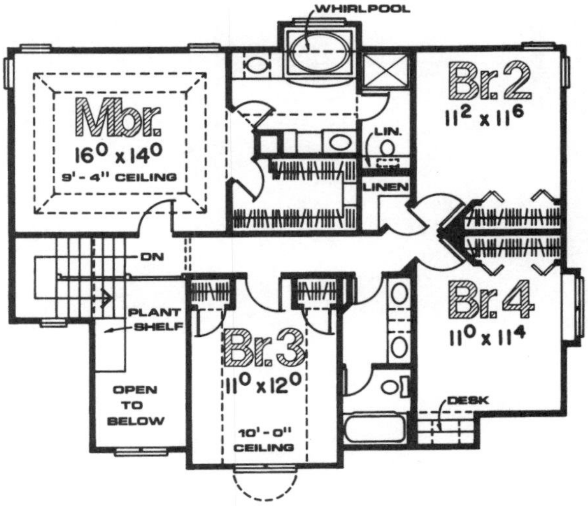

WHIRLPOOL
Mbr.
$16^{0} \times 14^{0}$
9' - 4" CEILING
LIN.
LINEN
Br. 2
$11^{2} \times 11^{6}$
DN
PLANT SHELF
OPEN TO BELOW
Br. 3
$11^{0} \times 12^{0}$
10' - 0" CEILING
Br. 4
$11^{0} \times 11^{4}$
DESK

DESIGN **HPU040287**

First Floor: 1,150 square feet
Second Floor: 1,120 square feet
Total: 2,270 square feet
Width: 46'-0" Depth: 48'-0"

DESIGN BY
©Design Basics, Inc.

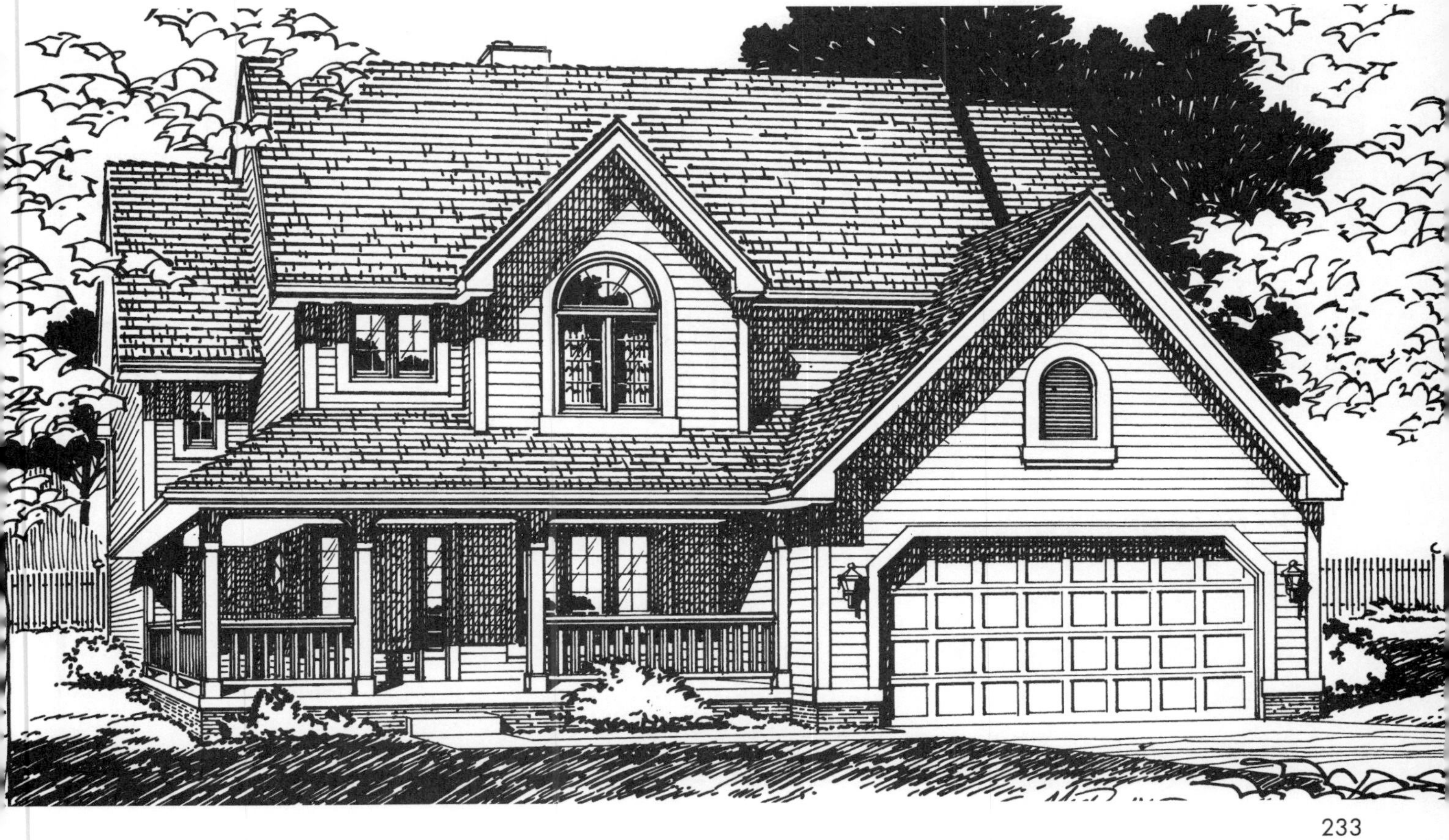

As attractive on the inside as it is on the outside, this hipped-roof design is sure to be a favorite for any growing family. A covered entry porch leads inside to an attractive living room and dining area. The efficient island kitchen is conveniently located near the two-car garage, the laundry room, the breakfast nook and the family room. The family room is warmed by a large fireplace. The master bedroom has private access through double doors to the rear porch, and also features a master bath with a walk-in closet. Two additional family bedrooms are located on the other side of the home. Bedroom 2 accesses a hall bath, and Bedroom 3 features its own private bath.

DESIGN HPU040288

Square Footage: 2,384
Width: 64'-0" Depth: 69'-4"

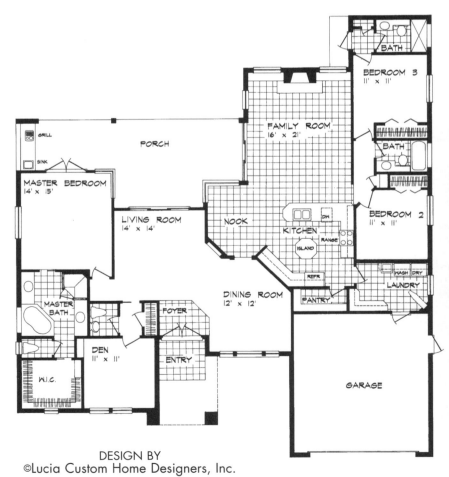

DESIGN BY
©Lucia Custom Home Designers, Inc.

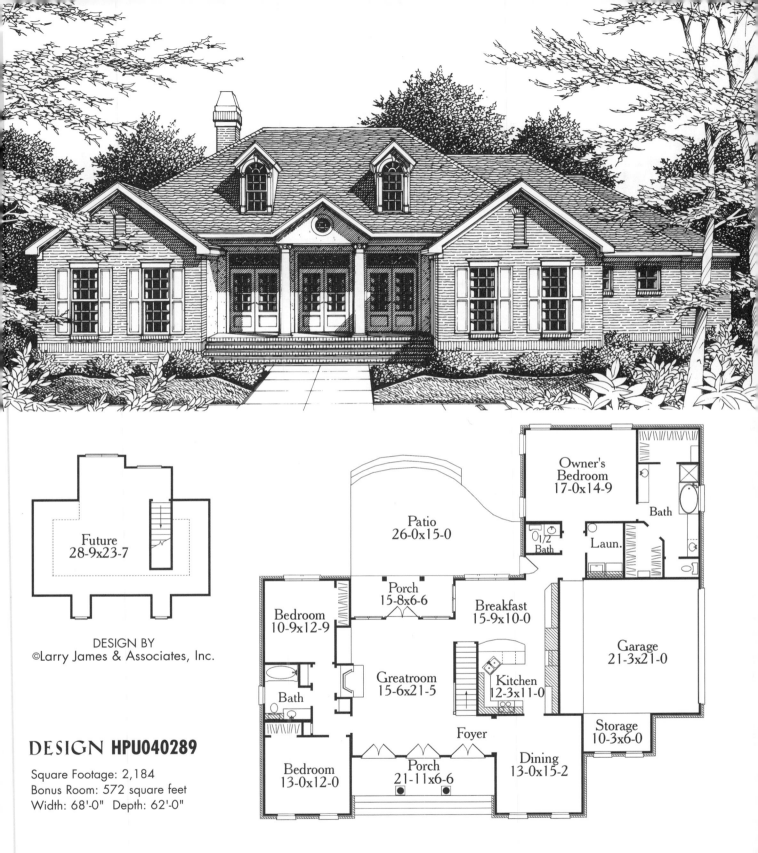

Future
28-9x23-7

DESIGN BY
©Larry James & Associates, Inc.

Owner's
Bedroom
17-0x14-9

Bath

Patio
26-0x15-0

Laun.

1/2
Bath

Porch
15-8x6-6

Breakfast
15-9x10-0

Garage
21-3x21-0

Bedroom
10-9x12-9

Greatroom
15-6x21-5

Kitchen
12-3x11-0

Bath

Storage
10-3x6-0

Foyer

DESIGN HPU040289

Square Footage: 2,184
Bonus Room: 572 square feet
Width: 68'-0" Depth: 62'-0"

Bedroom
13-0x12-0

Porch
21-11x6-6

Dining
13-0x15-2

The front porch is accented with stately columns and graceful full-length stairs. Three sets of French doors make the entry a stunning display of style. The great room features a central fireplace and rear-porch access. The breakfast room offers patio views and convenient kitchen service. The formal dining room, with the kitchen nearby, is perfect for entertaining guests. The secluded master suite enjoys two walk-in closets, a compartmented toilet, His and Hers vanities, and a separate tub and shower. Two secondary bedrooms, to the left of the great room, share a bath. Please specify basement, crawlspace or slab foundation when ordering.

Grt. rm.
15³ x 22⁰

Mbr.
13⁰ x 16⁰

Bfst.
11⁴ x 14⁰

Kit.
9⁰ x 14⁰

CATHEDRAL CEILING

10'-0" CLG.

SKYLIGHT

TRANSOMS

TRANSOMS

TRAPS

DESK

P.

W. D.

SNACK BAR

HUTCH

DN

UP

Din.
14⁰ x 11⁵

Gar.
30⁷ x 22⁷

WHIRL-POOL

COVERED PORCH

DESIGN HPU040291

First Floor: 1,505 square feet
Second Floor: 610 square feet
Total: 2,115 square feet
Width: 64'-0" Depth: 52'-0"

DESIGN BY
©Design Basics, Inc.

QUOTE ONE®
Cost to build? See page 502
to order complete cost estimate
to build this house in your area!

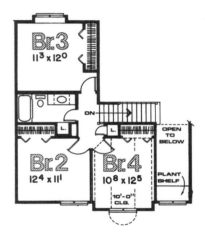

Br. 3
11³ x 12⁰

Br. 2
12⁴ x 11¹

Br. 4
10⁸ x 12⁵

10'-0" CLG.

DN

OPEN TO BELOW

PLANT SHELF

Farmhouse style is updated and improved by a high roofline and a central arched window. Many windows, lap siding and a covered porch give this elevation a welcoming country flair. The formal dining room with hutch space is conveniently located near the island kitchen. A main-floor laundry room with a sink is discreetly located next to the bright breakfast area with a desk and pantry. Highlighting the spacious great room are a raised-hearth fireplace, a cathedral ceiling and trapezoid windows. Special features in the master suite include a large dressing area with a double vanity, a skylight, a step-up corner whirlpool tub and a generous walk-in closet. Upstairs, the three secondary bedrooms are well separated from the master bedroom and share a hall bath.

PORCH

GREAT RM.
22-0 x 20-2

fireplace

shelves

DINING
12-0 x 14-0

MASTER
BED RM.
14-0 x 18-0

UTIL.
5-8 x
8-4

w
d

GALLERY
8-0 x 9-0

KITCHEN

BRKFST.
9-2 x 9-4

12-0 x 14-0

FOYER
12-8 x 10-0

down

niche

lin.

master
bath

bath

bath

lin.

lin.

cl

cl

cl

cl

walk-in
closet

PORCH

BED RM.
12-0 x 14-0

BED RM./
STUDY
12-0 x 14-0

DESIGN BY
Donald A. Gardner Architects, Inc.

An impressive hipped roof and unique, turret-style roofs top the two front bedrooms of this extraordinary coastal home. An arched window in an eyebrow dormer crowns the double-door front entrance. A remarkable foyer creates quite a first impression and leads into the generous great room via a distinctive gallery with columns and a tray ceiling. The great room, master bedroom and bath also boast tray ceilings—as well as numerous windows and back-porch access. The master bedroom not only provides a substantial amount of space in the walk-in closet, but also features a garden tub and roomy shower. A delightful bayed breakfast area complements the kitchen, and the island makes cooking much less crowded.

DESIGN HPU040292

Square Footage: 2,413
Width: 66'-4" Depth: 62'-10"

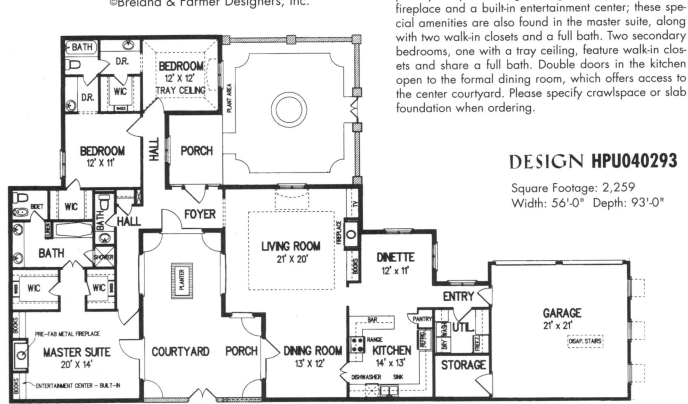

DESIGN BY
©Breland & Farmer Designers, Inc.

BEDROOM
12' X 12'
TRAY CEILING

BATH

D.R.

WIC

D.R.

SHOES

PLANT AREA

BEDROOM
12' X 11'

HALL

PORCH

BIDET

WIC

BATH

HALL

FOYER

LIVING ROOM
21' X 20'

FIREPLACE

TV

BOOKS

DINETTE
12' X 11'

ENTRY

BATH

SHOWER

BOOKS

WIC

WIC

PLANTER

PANTRY

BAR

UTIL.

GARAGE
21' X 21'

BOOKS

PRE-FAB METAL FIREPLACE

MASTER SUITE
20' X 14'

COURTYARD

PORCH

DINING ROOM
13' X 12'

RANGE

KITCHEN
14' X 13'

REFRIG.

DRY WASH

FREEZ.

DISAP. STAIRS

ENTERTAINMENT CENTER – BUILT-IN

DISHWASHER

SINK

STORAGE

Courtyards set the mood for this country cottage, beginning with the entry court. The narrow design of this three-bedroom plan makes it perfect for high-density areas where the owner still wants privacy. A spacious high-ceilinged living room offers a fireplace and a built-in entertainment center; these special amenities are also found in the master suite, along with two walk-in closets and a full bath. Two secondary bedrooms, one with a tray ceiling, feature walk-in closets and share a full bath. Double doors in the kitchen open to the formal dining room, which offers access to the center courtyard. Please specify crawlspace or slab foundation when ordering.

DESIGN HPU040293

Square Footage: 2,259
Width: 56'-0" Depth: 93'-0"

DESIGN HPU040294

First Floor: 1,150 square feet
Second Floor: 939 square feet
Total: 2,089 square feet
Width: 45'-10" Depth: 56'-5"

The exterior of this cottage has a distinctive European feel that will fit in almost anywhere. The combination of brick and stucco give it a country look, as do the stickwork detailing, the cupola and the massive chimneys. Formal living and dining rooms fill the right side of the plan, enhanced by a bay window, a fireplace and decorative columns. In addition to a second fireplace, the family room boasts two French doors to the side patio. The kitchen is L-shaped, with a cooktop island, a breakfast room and access to a rear patio. A laundry room and a half-bath are located off the family room. The second floor holds three bedrooms, including a master suite with a compartmented bath and two closets.

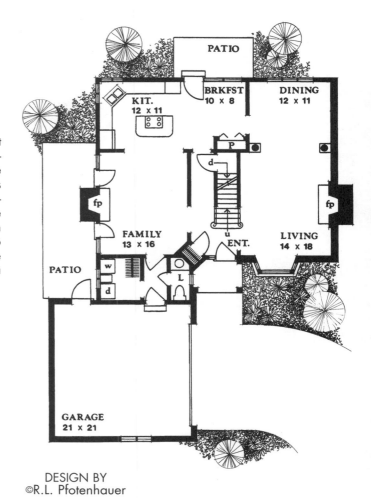

DESIGN BY
©R.L. Pfotenhauer

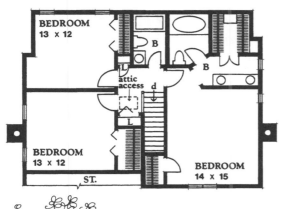

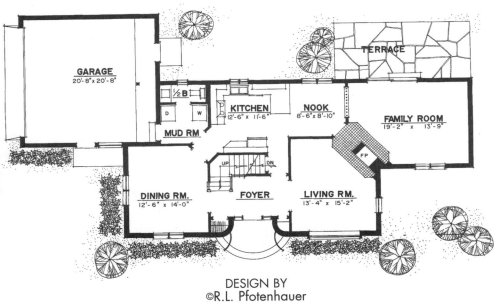

GARAGE
20'-8" x 20'-8"

½ B

KITCHEN
12'-6" x 11'-6"

NOOK
8'-6" x 8'-10"

TERRACE

FAMILY ROOM
19'-2" x 13'-9"

MUD RM

FP

DINING RM.
12'-6" x 14'-0"

FOYER

LIVING RM.
13'-4" x 15'-2"

DESIGN BY
©R.L. Pfotenhauer

BEDROOM
12'-6" x 10'-7"

BATH

LIN.

WIC

MR. BATH

BUILT-INS

BEDROOM
12'-6" x 11'-0"

DOWN

OPEN
TO
FOYER

MR. BEDROOM
13'-4" x 18'-4"

SHLV.

PLANTS

SHLV.

DESIGN HPU040295

First Floor: 1,159 square feet
Second Floor: 944 square feet
Total: 2,103 square feet
Width: 70'-8" Depth: 36'-0"

Shutters, a chimney, a railed semi-circular stoop and a weathervane combine to give this cottage its Old World charm. The openness and balance of the floor plan create simple comfort and livability. The centrally located L-shaped stairway rises from the two-story foyer, which is accented by a plant shelf and flanked by the formal living and dining rooms. Adjacent to the living room is a spacious family room with which it shares a through-fireplace. The kitchen, accessed from the dining room by an angled hall through double doors, is equipped with extra counter space and a bar to the breakfast room. The master bedroom is located at the top of the stairs and features double doors and a walk-in closet. Two secondary bedrooms upstairs share a full bath.

DESIGN HPU040296

First Floor: 1,132 square feet
Second Floor: 968 square feet
Total: 2,100 square feet
Width: 70'-6" Depth: 37'-1"

DESIGN BY
©R.L. Pfotenhauer

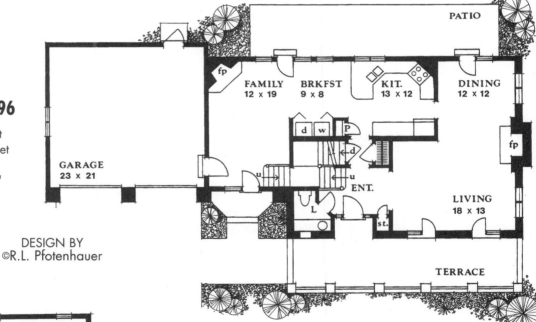

PATIO

GARAGE
23 x 21

FAMILY
12 x 19

BRKFST
9 x 8

KIT.
13 x 12

DINING
12 x 12

ENT.

LIVING
18 x 13

TERRACE

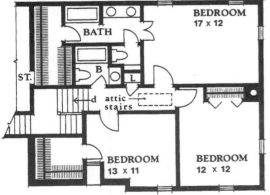

BEDROOM
17 x 12

BATH

ST.

attic
stairs

BEDROOM
13 x 11

BEDROOM
12 x 12

Brick and stucco, tall shutters and interesting roof details create a picturesque European-style cottage. A front terrace and a rear patio provide extra space for entertaining and relaxing, and the massive arch welcomes you in style. To the right of the entry, the formal living and dining rooms center on an imposing fireplace, one of two in the home. The other is in the family room, which offers a secondary front door as well as access to the patio. Casual meals will be enjoyed in the breakfast area, which is convenient to the kitchen. The master suite and two family bedrooms reside on the second floor; stairs lead to additional storage in the attic.

A stucco-and-brick facade declares the Old World influence used in this design. The steeply pitched roofline adds airiness to the interior spaces. The central entry opens to living spaces: a dining room on the left and the family room with fireplace on the right. The kitchen and breakfast nook are nearby. The kitchen features an island cooktop and a huge pantry. A door in the breakfast room leads out to the rear porch. The bedrooms include three family bedrooms—one of which could be used as a study—and a master suite. Note the double closets in the master bath.

DESIGN HPU040297

Square Footage: 2,322
Width: 68'-11" Depth: 74'-0"

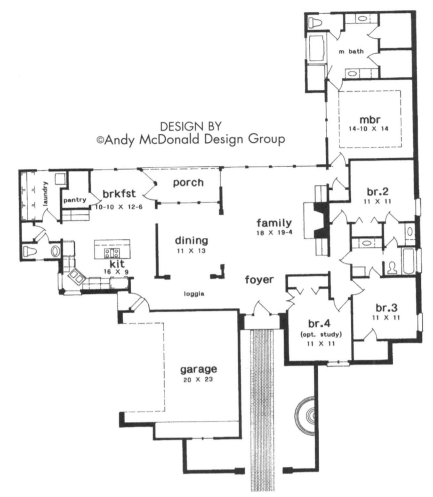

DESIGN BY
©Andy McDonald Design Group

NATURAL BEAUTY

Handsome styles, dramatic effects

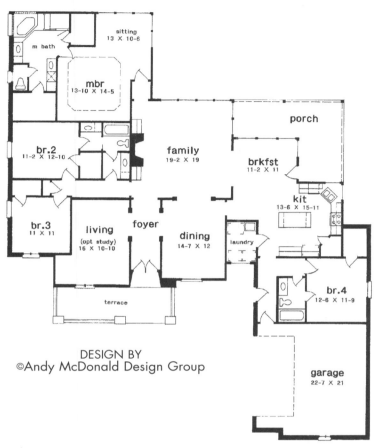

DESIGN BY
©Andy McDonald Design Group

In true French country style, this home begins with a fenced terrace that protects the double-door entry. The main foyer separates formal living and dining areas and leads back to a large family room with a fireplace and built-ins. The breakfast room overlooks a wrapping porch and opens to the island kitchen. Three bedrooms are found on the left side of the plan—two family bedrooms sharing a full bath and a master suite with a sitting area. A fourth bedroom is tucked behind the two-car garage and features a private bath.

DESIGN HPU040298

Square Footage: 2,678
Width: 69'-4" Depth: 84'-8"

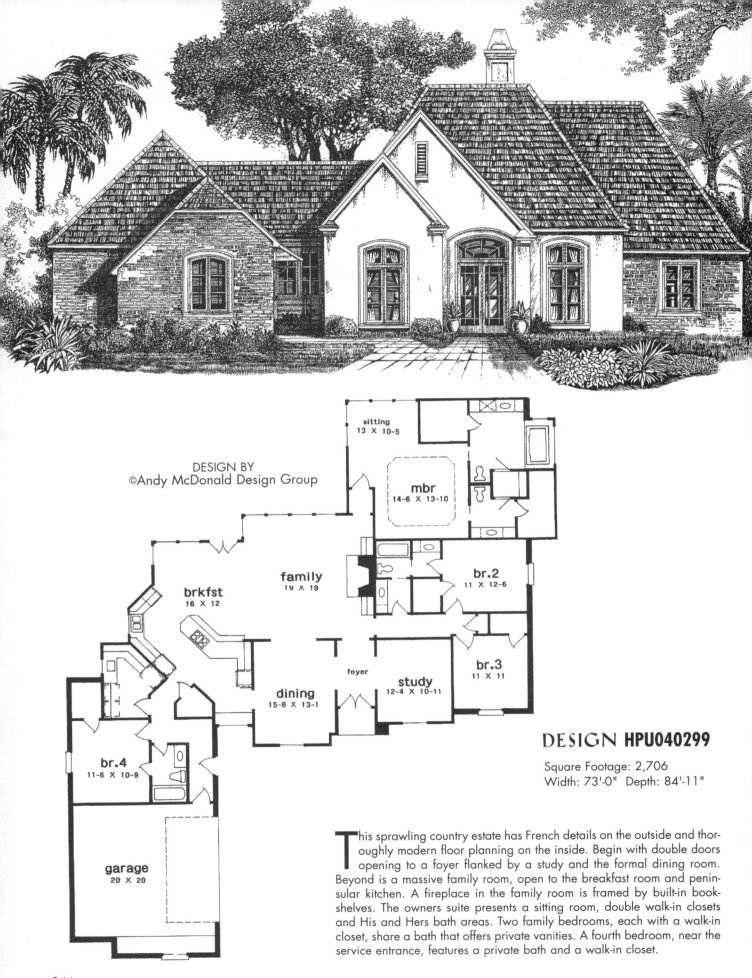

DESIGN BY
©Andy McDonald Design Group

sitting
13 X 10-5

mbr
14-6 X 13-10

family
19 X 19

brkfst
16 X 12

br.2
11 X 12-6

br.3
11 X 11

dining
15-8 X 13-1

foyer

study
12-4 X 10-11

br.4
11-6 X 10-9

garage
20 X 20

DESIGN HPU040299

Square Footage: 2,706
Width: 73'-0" Depth: 84'-11"

This sprawling country estate has French details on the outside and thoroughly modern floor planning on the inside. Begin with double doors opening to a foyer flanked by a study and the formal dining room. Beyond is a massive family room, open to the breakfast room and peninsular kitchen. A fireplace in the family room is framed by built-in bookshelves. The owners suite presents a sitting room, double walk-in closets and His and Hers bath areas. Two family bedrooms, each with a walk-in closet, share a bath that offers private vanities. A fourth bedroom, near the service entrance, features a private bath and a walk-in closet.

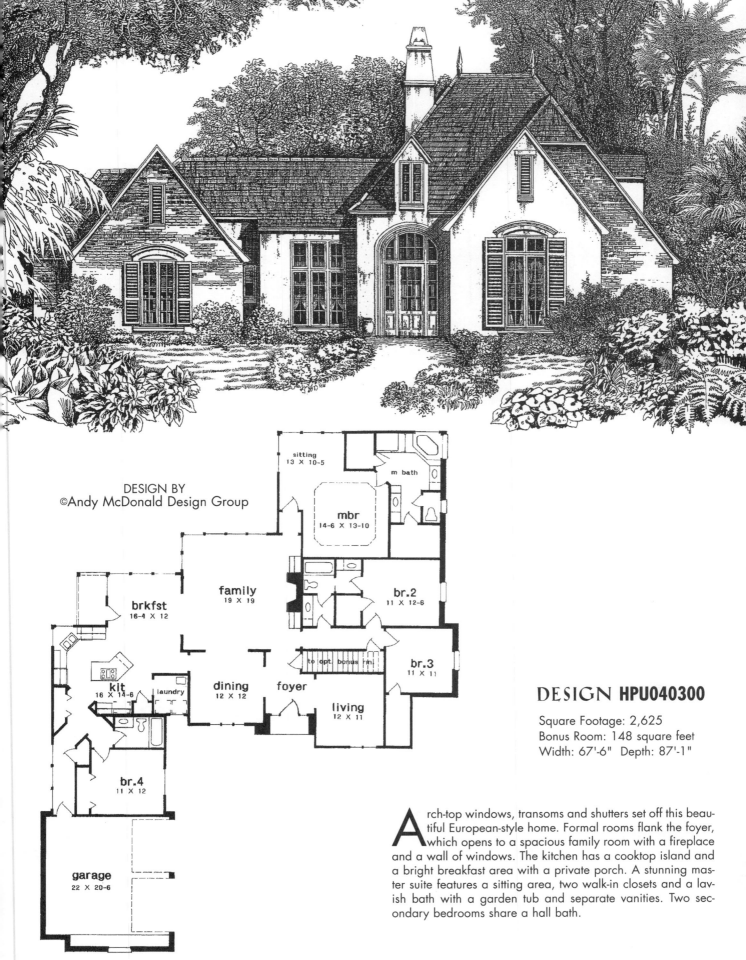

DESIGN BY
©Andy McDonald Design Group

sitting
13 X 10-5

m bath

mbr
14-6 X 13-10

family
19 X 19

brkfst
16-4 X 12

br.2
11 X 12-6

br.3
11 X 11

to opt. bonus rm.

kit
16 X 14-6

laundry

dining
12 X 12

foyer

living
12 X 11

br.4
11 X 12

garage
22 X 20-6

DESIGN HPU040300

Square Footage: 2,625
Bonus Room: 148 square feet
Width: 67'-6" Depth: 87'-1"

Arch-top windows, transoms and shutters set off this beautiful European-style home. Formal rooms flank the foyer, which opens to a spacious family room with a fireplace and a wall of windows. The kitchen has a cooktop island and a bright breakfast area with a private porch. A stunning master suite features a sitting area, two walk-in closets and a lavish bath with a garden tub and separate vanities. Two secondary bedrooms share a hall bath.

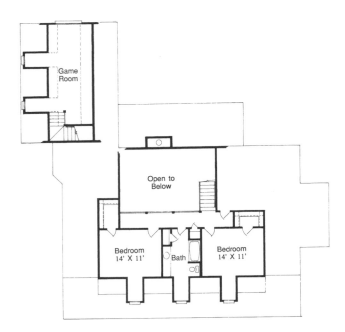

DESIGN HPU040301

First Floor: 1,977 square feet
Second Floor: 687 square feet
Total: 2,664 square feet
Width: 69'-6" Depth: 69'-9"

DESIGN BY
©Chatham Home Planning, Inc.

The game room above the garage of this four-bedroom, 1½-story Southern traditional home features a separate entrance and could make a convenient home office. The wraparound porch adds charm and function to the exterior. A formal dining room and a large family room with a fireplace and double doors to the rear-covered porch are accessed from the foyer. The master suite has a large offset bath with a corner tub, and across the hall is a second bedroom that could easily double as a study. Two additional bedrooms and a full bath are on the second level. Please specify crawlspace or slab foundation when ordering.

DESIGN HPU040302

First Floor: 2,155 square feet
Second Floor: 522 square feet
Total: 2,677 square feet
Width: 44'-0" Depth: 96'-2"

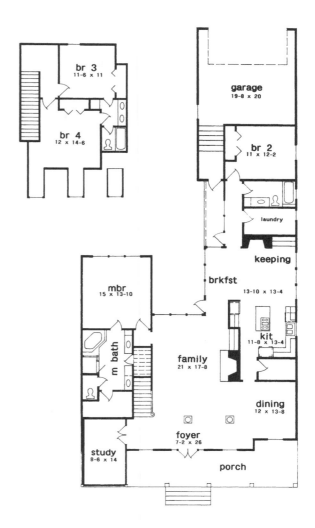

More than twice as long as it is wide, this plan presents a charming and deceptive facade. From the front gallery, the open family room provides a spacious area for gathering. To the side are a study and a master suite that includes a private bath. Behind the family room, you'll find a keeping room with a fireplace and built-in shelves, and a breakfast area that opens to the courtyard. A second bedroom and bath are located at the rear of the plan, while a third and fourth bedroom (sharing a bath) are on the second floor.

DESIGN BY
©Andy McDonald Design Group

DESIGN HPU040304

Square Footage: 2,607
Width: 75'-4" Depth: 81'-0"

This charming home has columned porches in both the front and back. To the left of the entry are the living and dining rooms, both defined by columns. The large open kitchen has a snack bar and breakfast area, and flows into the great room, which has a fireplace as the focal point. The bedrooms are grouped to the right, including two family bedrooms sharing a compartmented bath, and the master suite with a whirlpool tub. Please specify slab or crawlspace foundation when ordering.

DESIGN BY
©Michael E. Nelson,
Nelson Design Group, LLC

DESIGN HPU040303

First Floor: 1,976 square feet
Second Floor: 634 square feet
Total: 2,610 square feet
Width: 91'-10" Depth: 54'-0"

DESIGN BY
©Michael E. Nelson,
Nelson Design Group, LLC

This unique home is sure to be an eye-catcher on any property. The bungalow-type roof adds a bit of rustic flavor, with its overhang useful in keeping the sun from the windows. With the bedrooms separated from the main living areas, there is truly a sense of privacy achieved. The living areas include a great room with a fireplace, a studio area with deck access, a dining area and an efficient kitchen full of amenities. Here, the family gourmet will be pleased with tons of counter and cabinet space and a wall of pantry space. The sleeping structure is accessible via an enclosed bridge. Here one can either go up to the lavish master suite—complete with a private deck—or downstairs to a huge bedroom, also with a deck. Please specify crawlspace or pier foundation when ordering.

DESIGN HPU040305

First Floor: 1,623 square feet
Second Floor: 978 square feet
Total: 2,601 square feet
Width: 48'-0" Depth: 57'-0"

Offering a large wraparound porch, this fine two-story pier home is full of amenities. The living room has a warming fireplace and plenty of windows to enjoy the view. The galley kitchen features unique angles, with a large island/peninsula separating this room from the dining area. Two bedrooms share a bath and easy access to the laundry facilities. Upstairs, a lavish owners suite is complete with a detailed ceiling, a private covered porch, a walk-in closet and a pampering bath. A secondary bedroom—or make it a study—with a large walk-in closet finishes off this floor.

DESIGN BY
©Chatham Home Planning, Inc.

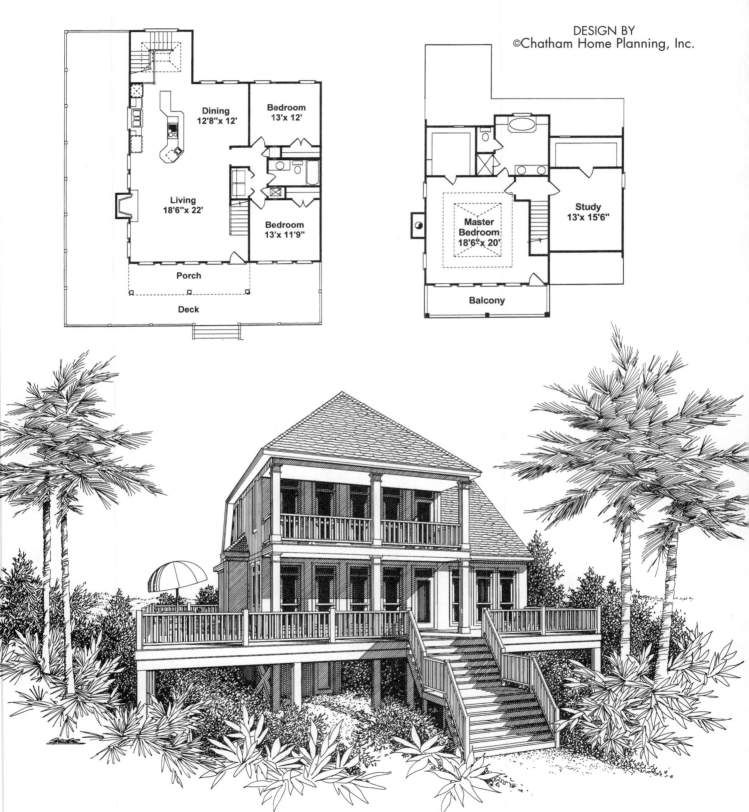

Dining
12'8"x 12'

Bedroom
13'x 12'

Living
18'6"x 22'

Bedroom
13'x 11'9"

Porch

Deck

Master
Bedroom
18'6"x 20'

Study
13'x 15'6"

Balcony

Storage
21-6x11-0

Garage
21-6x25-6

Porch
19-2x12-0

Master
Bedroom/
Sitting
Room
12-9x23-8

M.Bath
10-0x13-6

Laun.
9-0x8-7

1/2
Bath

Kitchen
18-0x11-6

Greatroom
19-1x17-5

Ht/
Ac

Bath

Bedroom
12-0x13-6

Breakfast
14-0x9-0

Dining
11-6x13-6

Foyer

Bedroom
11-6x13-6

Bedroom
12-0x11-7

Porch
31-5x8-0

A steeply pitched roof and transoms over multi-pane windows give this house great curb appeal. To the left of the foyer is the formal dining room with through access to the kitchen and breakfast area. A large island/snack bar adds plenty of counter space to the food-preparation area. Double French doors frame the fireplace in the great room, leading to the skylit covered porch at the rear of the home. The owners suite has a light-filled sitting room and luxurious bath with two walk-in closets, a garden tub and separate shower. At the front, three secondary bedrooms all have walk-in closets. Please specify basement, crawl-space or slab foundation when ordering.

DESIGN HPU040306

Square Footage: 2,555
Width: 66'-1" Depth: 77'-7"

Basement
Stair Location

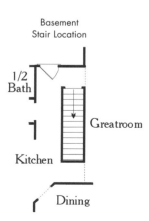

1/2
Bath

Greatroom

Kitchen

Dining

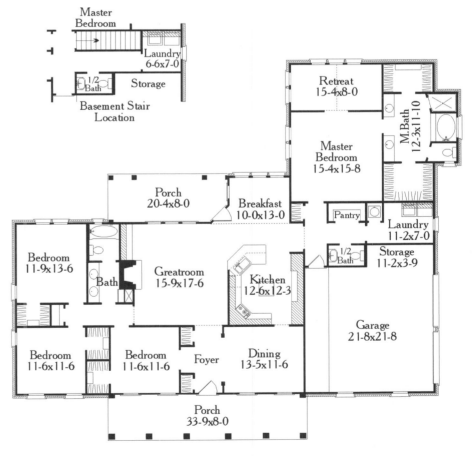

A porch full of columns gives a relaxing emphasis to this country home. To the right of the foyer, the dining area resides conveniently near the efficient kitchen. The kitchen island, walk-in pantry and serving bar add plenty of work space to the food-preparation zone. Natural light will flood the breakfast nook through a ribbon of windows facing the rear yard. Escape to the relaxing owners suite featuring a private sun room/retreat and a luxurious bath set between His and Hers walk-in closets. The great room at the center of this L-shaped plan is complete with a warming fireplace and built-ins. Three family bedrooms enjoy private walk-in closets and share a fully appointed bath. The two-car garage also has a storage area for family treasures. Please specify basement, crawlspace or slab foundation when ordering.

DESIGN HPU040307

Square Footage: 2,506
Width: 72'-2" Depth: 66'-4"

DESIGN BY
©Larry James & Associates, Inc.

251

DESIGN HPU040308

Square Footage: 2,585
Width: 66'-1" Depth: 77'-7"

Classical columns give the entrance of this floor plan a graceful appeal. The great room leads through two sets of double doors onto the rear porch. This porch can also be accessed by a door connected to the garage and another private door to the master bedroom. The master suite is brilliantly lit by multiple window views to the outdoors. Three additional bedrooms complete the family sleeping quarters. Please specify basement, crawlspace or slab foundation when ordering.

DESIGN BY
©Larry James & Associates, Inc.

DESIGN HPU040309

Square Footage: 2,570
Width: 73'-0" Depth: 71'-0"

This well-planned design offers the benefits of simplicity nicely embellished with well-chosen details. A gorgeous array of window accents provides an elegant facade with the eye-candy of natural light. The spacious great room is the centerpiece of the floor plan, with a fireplace set between built-ins. The sleeping quarters include an owners suite that offers a private study. Two secondary bedrooms share a full bath. Please specify basement, crawlspace or slab foundation when ordering.

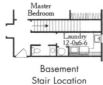

Basement
Stair Location

DESIGN BY
©Larry James & Associates, Inc.

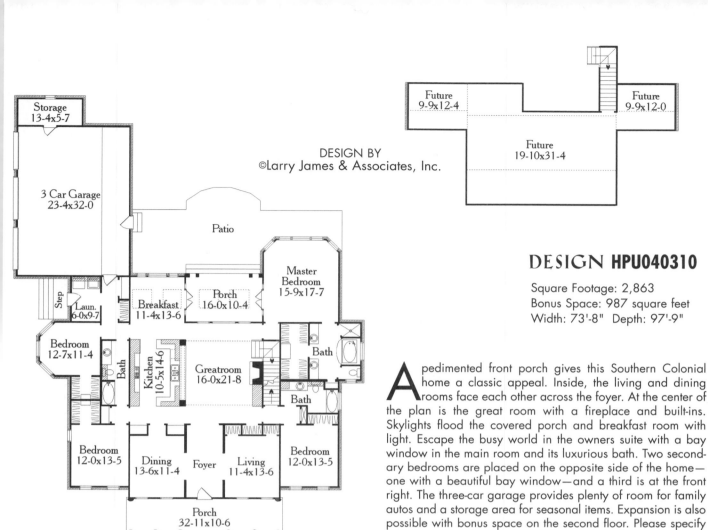

Storage
13-4x5-7

3 Car Garage
23-4x32-0

Patio

DESIGN BY
©Larry James & Associates, Inc.

Future
9-9x12-4

Future
9-9x12-0

Future
19-10x31-4

Step

Laun.
6-0x9-7

Breakfast
11-4x13-6

Porch
16-0x10-4

Master
Bedroom
15-9x17-7

Bedroom
12-7x11-4

Bath

Kitchen
10-5x14-6

Greatroom
16-0x21-8

Bath

Bath

Bedroom
12-0x13-5

Dining
13-6x11-4

Foyer

Living
11-4x13-6

Bedroom
12-0x13-5

Porch
32-11x10-6

DESIGN HPU040310

Square Footage: 2,863
Bonus Space: 987 square feet
Width: 73'-8" Depth: 97'-9"

A pedimented front porch gives this Southern Colonial home a classic appeal. Inside, the living and dining rooms face each other across the foyer. At the center of the plan is the great room with a fireplace and built-ins. Skylights flood the covered porch and breakfast room with light. Escape the busy world in the owners suite with a bay window in the main room and its luxurious bath. Two secondary bedrooms are placed on the opposite side of the home— one with a beautiful bay window—and a third is at the front right. The three-car garage provides plenty of room for family autos and a storage area for seasonal items. Expansion is also possible with bonus space on the second floor. Please specify basement, crawlspace or slab foundation when ordering.

NOOK
9/8 X 10/6
(9' CLG.)

FAMILY
16/2 X 15/6
(9' CLG.)

MASTER
13/0 X 15/2
(9' CLG.)

SPA

SHELVES

13/0 X 11/6

REF PAN

UP

STOR

D W

STOR
9/10 X 7/4

VAULTED
DINING
13/0 X 11/2

GARAGE
21/4 X 20/8

DEN
10/0 X 10/6
(9' CLG.)

OPTIONAL FIREPLACE

VAULTED
LIVING
13/0 X 15/0

DESIGN HPU040311

First Floor: 1,769 square feet
Second Floor: 893 square feet
Total: 2,662 square feet
Width: 50'-0" Depth: 50'-0"

DESIGN BY
©Alan Mascord Design Associates, Inc.

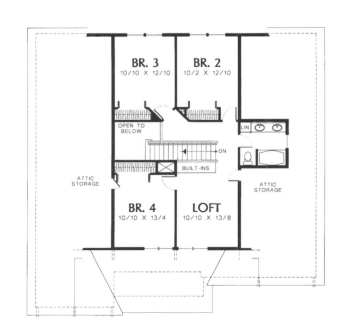

BR. 3
10/10 X 12/10

BR. 2
10/2 X 12/10

OPEN TO
BELOW

LIN

ATTIC
STORAGE

BUILT-INS

DN

ATTIC
STORAGE

BR. 4
10/10 X 13/4

LOFT
10/10 X 13/8

Shingles, gables, window detail and rafter tails all combine to give this home plenty of curb appeal. The entrance opens right next to the vaulted living and dining area, with a cozy den to the right. The unique kitchen features a peninsula, pantry and easy access to the formal dining room and sunny nook. The nearby family room is warmed by a corner fireplace. Located on the first floor for privacy, the master bedroom suite is complete with a walk-in closet—with built-in shelves—and a pampering bath. The second floor consists of three family bedrooms sharing a full bath and an open study loft with built-ins.

Shingles and stone combine to present a highly attractive facade on this spacious three-bedroom home. The Craftsman-style influence is very evident and adds charm. The two-story foyer is flanked by a large, yet cozy, den on the right and on the left, beyond the staircase, is the formal dining room with built-ins. The vaulted great room also offers built-ins, as well as a fireplace. The U-shaped kitchen will surely please the gourmet of the family with its planning desk, corner sink, cooktop island and plenty of counter and cabinet space. The vaulted master suite is complete with a plant shelf, a walk-in closet and a lavish bath. Two secondary bedrooms make up the sleeping zone upstairs, each with a walk-in closet and having access to the full bath. A large bonus room is available for use as a guest suite.

DESIGN HPU040312

First Floor: 2,005 square feet
Second Floor: 689 square feet
Total: 2,694 square feet
Bonus Room: 356 square feet
Width: 68'-0"   Depth: 73'-6"

DESIGN BY
©Alan Mascord Design Associates, Inc.

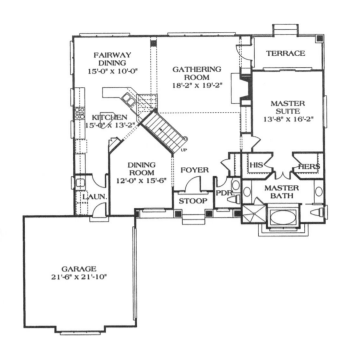

DESIGN HPU040313

First Floor: 1,662 square feet
Second Floor: 882 square feet
Total: 2,544 square feet
Width: 59'-0" Depth: 59'-6"

Gables, rafter tails, pillars supporting the shed roof over the porch, and window detailing all bring the flavor of Craftsman styling to your neighborhood with a touch of grace. This spacious home has a place for everyone. The angled kitchen, with a work island, peninsular sink and plenty of counter and cabinet space, will offer the family many a gourmet treat. The spacious gathering room offers a warming fireplace, built-ins and access to a rear terrace. Filled with amenities, the first-floor master suite is designed to pamper. Upstairs, two suites, each with a private bath, share an open area known as the linkside retreat. Here, access is available to a small veranda, perfect for watching sunsets.

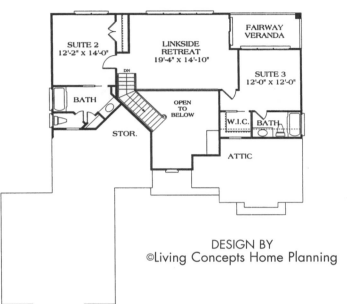

DESIGN BY
©Living Concepts Home Planning

With rustic rafter tails, sturdy pillars and a siding-and-shingle facade, this welcoming bungalow offers plenty of curb appeal. Inside, the formal dining room is to the left of the foyer, and gives easy access to the angled kitchen. A spacious gathering room offers a fireplace, built-ins, a gorgeous wall of windows and access to a covered terrace. Located on the first floor for privacy, the owners suite is lavish with its amenities. Upstairs, two suites offer private baths and share a linkside retreat that includes a covered veranda.

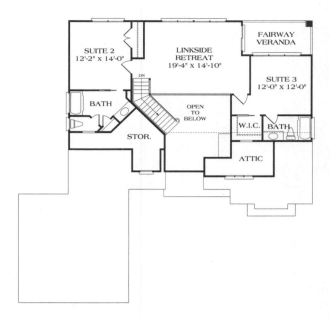

DESIGN HPU040314

First Floor: 1,661 square feet
Second Floor: 882 square feet
Total: 2,543 square feet
Width: 59'-0" Depth: 58'-11"

DESIGN BY
©Living Concepts Home Planning

DESIGN HPU040315

First Floor: 1,326 square feet
Second Floor: 1,257 square feet
Total: 2,583 square feet
Width: 30'-0" Depth: 78'-0"

DESIGN BY
©Authentic Historical Designs, Inc.

The steeply pitched pavilion roof is a distinctive feature that identifies this house as a classic French design. Inside, a long foyer ushers visitors into a generous great room, which is separated from the kitchen by a wide cased opening. An L-shaped breakfast bar provides a place for a quick snack. The computer room/office off the great room could be eliminated and used as a breakfast area. Above, a lavish master suite has separate His and Hers walk-in closets and an oversized shower. Please specify basement or crawlspace foundation when ordering.

DESIGN HPU040316

First Floor: 1,767 square feet
Second Floor: 1,079 square feet
Total: 2,846 square feet
Width: 30'-0" Depth: 82'-0"

DESIGN BY
©Authentic Historical Designs, Inc.

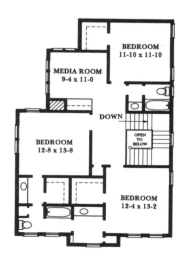

With its formal symmetry, balanced proportion and classical detailing, this Georgian design will maintain its appeal for those who value timeless architecture. Once inside, its open floor plan will entice those who realize that modern families enjoy a different lifestyle. The entrance is open to a spacious great room and formal dining room. The column-encircled stairway wraps itself around a built-in wet bar, with easy access to kitchen, dining and living areas of the home. Yet, even though the plan is very open, there are many private spaces provided. There is a computer/desk area between the kitchen and the first-floor master suite. This roomy master suite contains a secluded and separate sitting area. Note the convenient location of the walk-in closet. A second-floor media room will provide additional living space.

At the turn of the century, the growing number of railroads and automobiles made suburban living possible as an alternative to living in the city. The bungalow home was America's first response to the need for affordable single-family housing in these first new suburbs. The gently pitched street-facing gable is a dominant characteristic of the bungalow style, as well as its wide overhanging roof, deep porch and simplified interior. A century later, our updated version of the bungalow is well-suited to the needs of modern families. It provides a wide-open family room, with a large keeping room and breakfast room, as well as a separate living room and dining room. Easy access to the long side porch provides additional living space. Upstairs, four bedrooms, each with walk-in closets, provide ample space for a busy family. Please specify basement or crawlspace foundation when ordering.

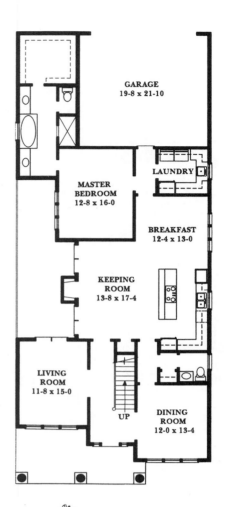

DESIGN HPU040317

First Floor: 1,718 square feet
Second Floor: 1,021 square feet
Total: 2,739 square feet
Width: 33'-0" Depth: 80'-0"

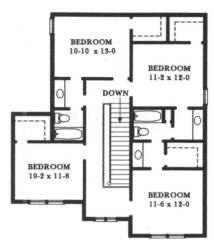

DESIGN BY
©Authentic Historical Designs, Inc.

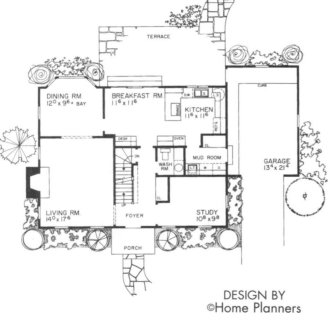

DESIGN BY
©Home Planners

The facade of this three-story, pitch-roofed house has a symmetrical placement of windows and a restrained but elegant central entrance. The central hall, or foyer, expands midway through the house to a family kitchen. Off the foyer are two rooms—a living room with a fireplace and a study. Three bedrooms are housed on the second floor, including a deluxe master suite with a pampering bath. The windowed third-floor attic can be used as a study and a studio.

DESIGN HPU040319

First Floor: 1,023 square feet
Second Floor: 1,008 square feet
Third Floor: 476 square feet
Total: 2,507 square feet
Width: 49'-8" Depth: 32'-0"

L **D**

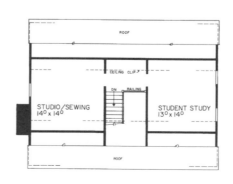

Cost to build? See page 502 to order complete cost estimate to build this house in your area!

260

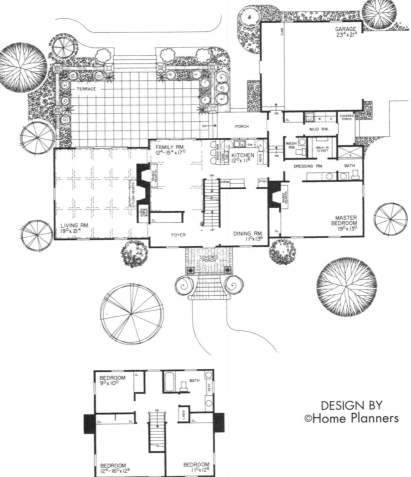

Two one-story wings flank the two-story center section of this design, which echoes the architectural forms of 18th-Century Tidewater Virginia. The left wing offers a spacious living room, perfect for entertaining guests and for family events; the right wing houses the master bedroom suite, service area and garage. The heart of the home provides casual living with the kitchen, dining room and family room. Upstairs, three family bedrooms—one is perfect for a nursery or game room—share a full hall bath that includes twin vanities.

DESIGN HPU040320

First Floor: 1,827 square feet
Second Floor: 697 square feet
Total: 2,524 square feet
Width: 72'-0" Depth: 54'-0"

DESIGN BY
©Home Planners

DESIGN HPU040322

First Floor: 1,581 square feet
Second Floor: 1,344 square feet
Total: 2,925 square feet
Width: 74'-0" Depth: 46'-0"

L D

DESIGN BY
©Home Planners

Here's a traditional farmhouse design that's made for down-home hospitality, casual conversation and the good grace of pleasant company. The star attractions are the large covered porch and terrace, perfectly relaxing gathering points for family and friends. Inside, the design is truly a hard worker: separate living and family rooms, each with its own fireplace; a formal dining room; a large kitchen and breakfast area with bay windows; a private study; a workshop and a mudroom. The second floor contains a spacious master suite with twin closets and three family bedrooms that share a full bath.

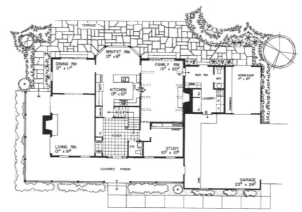

Quote One®
Cost to build? See page 502 to order complete cost estimate to build this house in your area!

A beautiful covered porch wraps around the welcoming entrance of this country home. Sunlit, bayed areas at the rear of the plan—in the great room and breakfast nook—illuminate this efficient family floor plan. Upstairs, the pampering master suite is enhanced by a fireplace, a volume ceiling and double doors, which lead to a private sun deck. Three family bedrooms share a full hall bath.

DESIGN HPU040321

First Floor: 1,267 square feet
Second Floor: 1,327 square feet
Total: 2,594 square feet
Width: 58'-8" Depth: 38'-0"

DESIGN BY
©Home Design Services, Inc.

DESIGN HPU040323

First Floor: 1,286 square feet
Second Floor: 1,675 square feet
Total: 2,961 square feet
Width: 35'-0" Depth: 64'-0"

The Southern plantation comes to mind when looking at this two-story home complete with a porch and terrace. Formal elegance is the order of the day as you enter the foyer flanked by the living and dining rooms. The family room features a full window wall overlooking the deck, which is also accessible from the rear entry of the garage. Corner cabinets house the sink and surface unit, keeping everything within a few steps of each other. Rear stairs lead to the master suite, located over the garage, providing privacy from the rest of the second floor. Four additional bedrooms—one with its own private bath—are also on the second floor. Please specify basement or slab foundation when ordering.

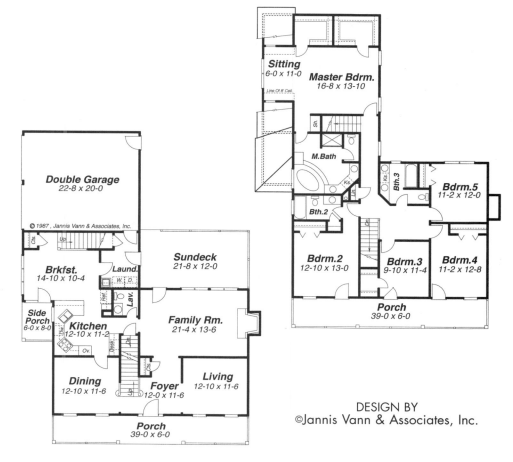

Double Garage
22-8 x 20-0

© 1987, Jannis Vann & Associates, Inc.

Brkfst.
14-10 x 10-4

Laund.

Sundeck
21-8 x 12-0

Side Porch
6-0 x 8-0

Kitchen
12-10 x 11-2

Family Rm.
21-4 x 13-6

Dining
12-10 x 11-6

Foyer
12-0 x 11-6

Living
12-10 x 11-6

Porch
39-0 x 6-0

Sitting
6-0 x 11-0

Master Bdrm.
16-8 13-10

M.Bath

Bth.2

Bth.3

Bdrm.5
11-2 x 12-0

Bdrm.2
12-10 x 13-0

Bdrm.3
9-10 x 11-4

Bdrm.4
11-2 x 12-8

Porch
39-0 x 6-0

DESIGN BY
©Jannis Vann & Associates, Inc.

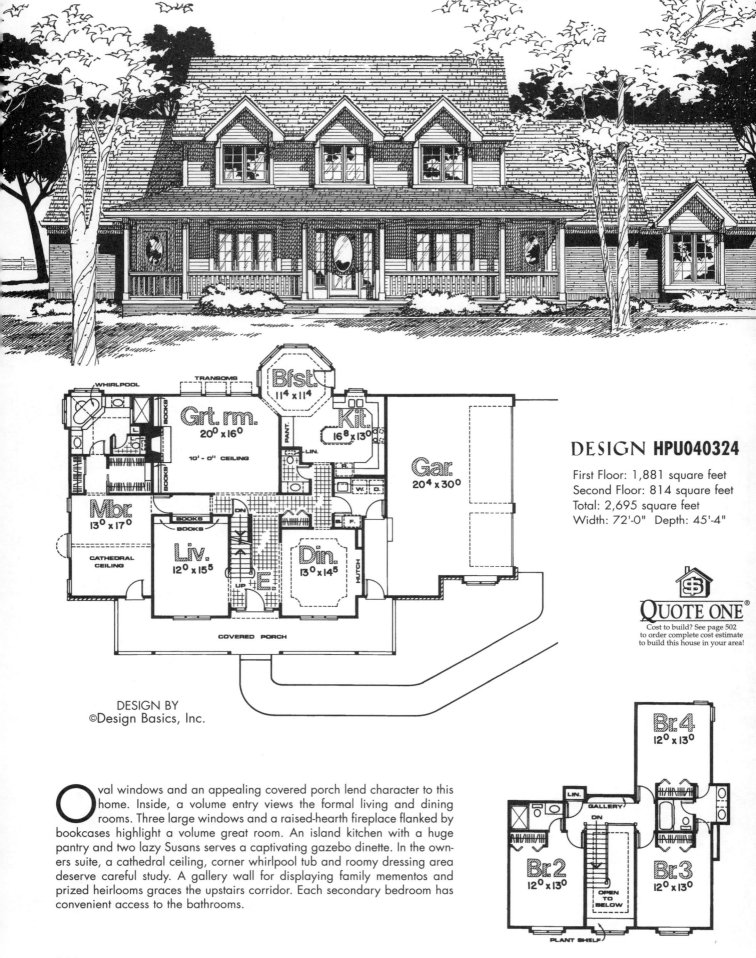

DESIGN HPU040324

First Floor: 1,881 square feet
Second Floor: 814 square feet
Total: 2,695 square feet
Width: 72'-0" Depth: 45'-4"

QUOTE ONE®

Cost to build? See page 502
to order complete cost estimate
to build this house in your area!

DESIGN BY
©Design Basics, Inc.

Oval windows and an appealing covered porch lend character to this home. Inside, a volume entry views the formal living and dining rooms. Three large windows and a raised-hearth fireplace flanked by bookcases highlight a volume great room. An island kitchen with a huge pantry and two lazy Susans serves a captivating gazebo dinette. In the owners suite, a cathedral ceiling, corner whirlpool tub and roomy dressing area deserve careful study. A gallery wall for displaying family mementos and prized heirlooms graces the upstairs corridor. Each secondary bedroom has convenient access to the bathrooms.

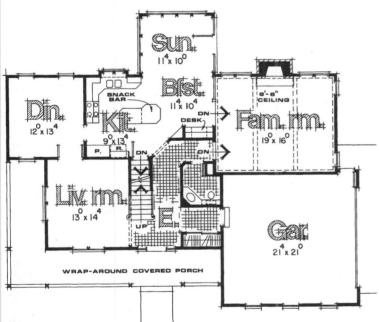

Here's the luxury you've been looking for—from the wraparound covered front porch to the bright sun room off the breakfast room. A sunken family room with a fireplace serves everyday casual gatherings, while the more formal living and dining rooms are reserved for special entertaining situations. The kitchen has a central island with a snack bar and is located most conveniently for serving and cleaning up. Upstairs are four bedrooms, one a lovely master suite with French doors to the pirvate bath and a whirlpool tub with a dramatic bay window. A double vanity in the shared bath easily serves the three family bedrooms.

DESIGN HPU040325

First Floor: 1,322 square feet
Second Floor: 1,272 square feet
Total: 2,594 square feet
Width: 56'-0" Depth: 48'-0"

Quote One®

Cost to build? See page 502
to order complete cost estimate
to build this house in your area!

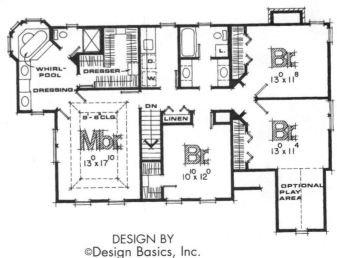

DESIGN BY
©Design Basics, Inc.

265

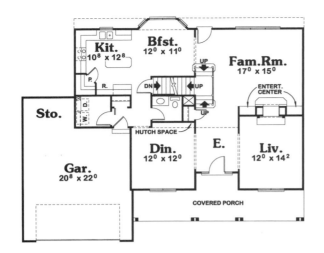

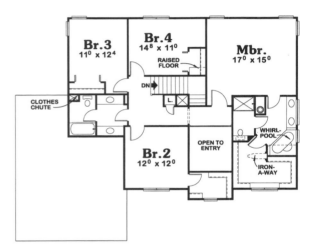

DESIGN HPU040326

First Floor: 1,266 square feet
Second Floor: 1,292 square feet
Total: 2,558 square feet
Bonus Room: 531 square feet
Width: 54'-0" Depth: 44'-0"

DESIGN BY
©Design Basics, Inc.

This classic American two-story home borrows details from farmhouse, Craftsman and Colonial styles to add up to a beautiful facade. The covered front porch is a lovely introduction to both formal and informal living spaces on the interior. The living room features a see-through fireplace to the family room and is complemented by a formal dining room with hutch space. The U-shaped island kitchen and bayed breakfast nook combine to form an open area for casual dining. A stairway to the second level boasts twin accesses—in the foyer and in the family room. Four bedrooms are situated on the second floor. They include three family bedrooms with a shared bath and walk-in closets. The master suite has a private bath with a whirlpool tub, separate shower, fold-away iron and huge walk-in closet.

Finials, scalloped shingles and a covered front porch with spiderweb trim enhance the exterior of this home. Inside, the formal living and dining rooms flank the foyer; the dining room offers space for a hutch or china cabinet. The family room, accessed by double doors in the living room, includes a fireplace and a wall of windows. The snug island kitchen serves a breakfast bay that opens to the backyard. Upstairs, a tray ceiling adds drama to the owners suite, which features a full bath with double vanities and a whirlpool tub. All three of the secondary bedrooms include walk-in closets and access a full hall bath.

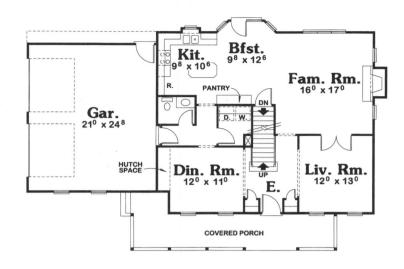

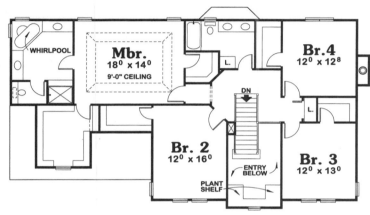

DESIGN HPU040327

First Floor: 1,120 square feet
Second Floor: 1,411 square feet
Total: 2,531 square feet
Width: 57'-4"   Depth: 33'-0"

DESIGN BY
©Design Basics, Inc.

267

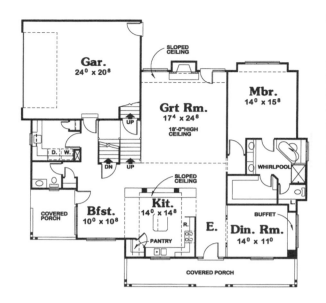

This home's fine window detailing, two front porches and rafter tails lend the feel of true Craftsman styling. The airiness of the kitchen is enhanced with openings to the second floor, entry and breakfast area. A built-in buffet and two half-railings warmly welcome passersby into the formal dining room. A tall ceiling in the great room is further dramatized when viewed from an open railing on the second floor. Also of interest in this room is the fireplace centered on the outside wall. A computer area on the second floor accompanies the second-floor bedrooms as a homework area. A large storage area accessed from the mid-level staircase landing offers a place for a playroom. Note the first-floor master suite with its lavish bath.

DESIGN HPU040328

First Floor: 1,823 square feet
Second Floor: 858 square feet
Total: 2,681 square feet
Width: 56'-8" Depth: 50'-8"

DESIGN BY
©Design Basics, Inc.

It's hard to beat the charm of this country home, which features bright bays of windows in the dining room and breakfast nook, plus a shady covered front porch. The kitchen with its cooktop island is convenient to both formal and casual dining areas. The spacious living room offers a fireplace, built-in bookshelves and access to the rear patio. The rest of the main floor is granted to the master suite, which includes a double-vanity bath with an oval tub and a separate shower. Two of the three family bedrooms upstairs have dormers.

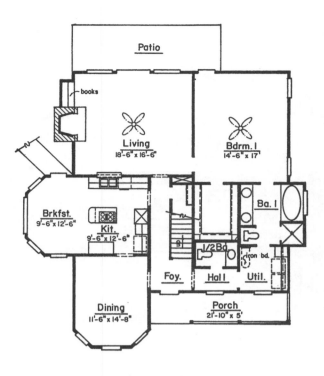

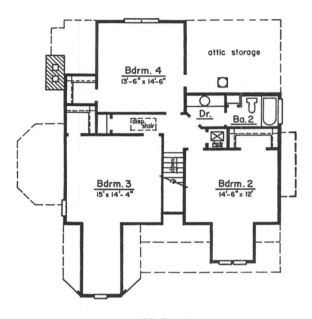

DESIGN BY
©Chatham Home Planning, Inc.

DESIGN HPU040329

First Floor: 1,499 square feet
Second Floor: 1,012 square feet
Total: 2,511 square feet
Width: 41'-6" Depth: 45'-0"

269

DESIGN HPU040331

Square Footage: 2,519
Width: 75'-0" Depth: 59'-0"

DESIGN BY
©Vaughn A. Lauban Designs

Porch railing, siding and twin dormered windows reflect the easy-on-the-eyes quality of country style. Walk inside to discover a very comfortable floor plan that serves family or friends well. The foyer boasts two coat closets, with the dining room to the left and the study to the right. The galley-style kitchen functions as the hub of the home, able to handle the dining room, breakfast nook and living room without fuss. The owners suite revels in its privacy with features like twin walk-in closets, a bayed tub, separate shower and dual vanities. Three family bedrooms are situated at the right of the plan. Two bedrooms share a compartmented bath, while the third enjoys its own full bath.

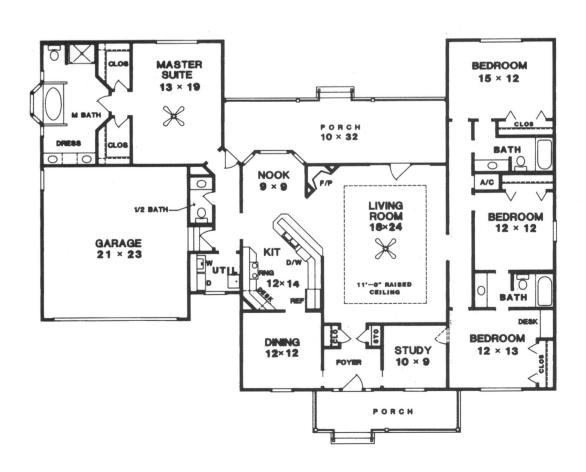

Graceful French doors and tall, shuttered windows combined with a sprawling country front porch give this charming home its unique appeal. Nine-foot ceilings expand the main floor. Walk through the elegant foyer to a grand living area, with a centered fireplace and built-in bookcase. This living space opens to the rear covered porch. The private master suite with a walk-in closet features a luxurious bath with a separate shower and compartmented toilet. A guest room (or make it a study) also has access to a full bath. Just off the formal dining area is a gourmet kitchen with an island cooktop counter. A bay-windowed breakfast area adds informal eating space. Two second-floor family bedrooms share an expansive full bath, just off the balcony hallway, and boast private dressing areas and walk-in closets. Please specify crawlspace or slab foundation when ordering.

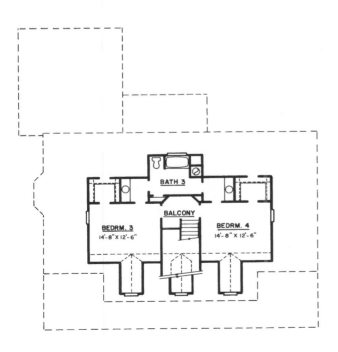

DESIGN HPU040332

First Floor: 1,916 square feet
Second Floor: 749 square feet
Total: 2,665 square feet
Width: 63'-0" Depth: 63'-9"

DESIGN BY
©Chatham Home Planning, Inc.

DESIGN HPU040333

First Floor: 1,614 square feet
Second Floor: 892 square feet
Total: 2,506 square feet
Bonus Room: 341 square feet
Width: 71'-10" Depth: 50'-0"

DESIGN BY
Donald A. Gardner Architects, Inc.

At the front of this farmhouse design, the master suite includes a sitting bay, two walk-in closets, a door to the front porch and a compartmented bath with a double-bowl vanity. The formal dining room is in the second bay, also with a door to the front porch. Access to the rear porch is from the great room, which is open under a balcony to the breakfast room. On the second floor, three family bedrooms share a bath that has a double-bowl vanity. One of the family bedrooms offers a walk-in closet. A bonus room over the garage could be used as a study or game room.

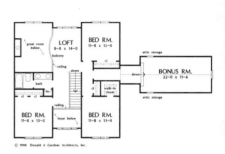

DESIGN BY
Donald A. Gardner Architects, Inc.

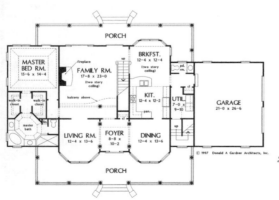

Filled with the charm of farmhouse details, such as twin dormers and bay windows, this design begins with a classic covered porch. The entry leads to a foyer flanked by columns that separate it from the formal dining and living rooms. The U-shaped kitchen separates the dining room from the bayed breakfast room. The first-floor owners suite features a bedroom with a tray ceiling and a luxurious private bath.

DESIGN HPU040334

First Floor: 1,914 square feet
Second Floor: 597 square feet
Total: 2,511 square feet
Bonus Room: 487 square feet
Width: 79'-2" Depth: 51'-6"

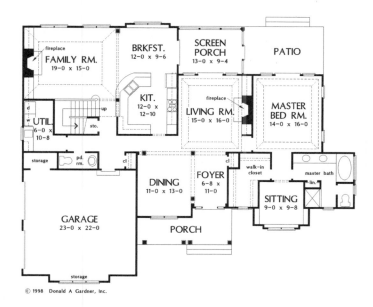

© 1998 Donald A Gardner, Inc.

This charming country-style plan includes a screened porch that opens from the breakfast nook and living room. Entertaining is simple with the dining room and living room convenient to each other. Both the formal living room and the cozy family room have a fireplace. A private homeowner's wing features a rambling master suite with a lavish bath featuring a separate tub and shower, dual vanities, a spacious walk-in closet and a private sitting room for quiet moments. Two secondary bedrooms, a full bath and a bonus room reside upstairs.

DESIGN HPU040335

First Floor: 2,010 square feet
Second Floor: 600 square feet
Total: 2,610 square feet
Bonus Room: 378 square feet
Width: 68'-2" Depth: 54'-8"

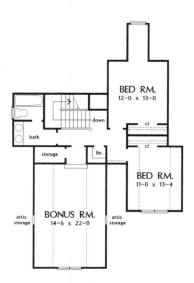

DESIGN BY
Donald A. Gardner Architects, Inc.

DESIGN HPU040336

First Floor: 1,463 square feet
Second Floor: 1,244 square feet
Total: 2,707 square feet
Bonus Room: 300 square feet
Width: 53'-0" Depth: 66'-0"

DESIGN BY
Donald A. Gardner Architects, Inc.

A stunning combination of country and traditional exterior elements forms an exciting facade for this four-bedroom home. Generous formal and informal living areas create great spaces for entertaining large parties as well as intimate gatherings. Fireplaces add warmth to both the living room and the great room, while front and back porches expand living space outside. All four bedrooms are located on the second floor, which features a marvelous balcony overlooking the foyer. The owners suite boasts a tray ceiling, two walk-in closets and a luxurious private bath.

©1999 Donald A. Gardner, Inc.

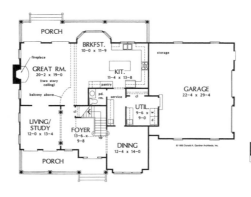

QUOTE ONE®
Cost to build? See page 502
to order complete cost estimate
to build this house in your area!

Here's an upscale country home with down-home comfort. The two-story great room is warmed by a rounded-hearth fireplace. French doors brighten the formal living room, while wide counters, a food-preparation island and a bayed breakfast nook create a dreamy kitchen area. The second floor includes a master suite, two bedrooms that share a full bath, and a skylit bonus room. The master suite boasts a sitting area and a private bath with twin vanities and a whirlpool tub.

DESIGN HPU040337

First Floor: 1,484 square feet
Second Floor: 1,061 square feet
Total: 2,545 square feet
Bonus Room: 486 square feet
Width: 66'-10" Depth: 47'-8"

DESIGN BY
Donald A. Gardner Architects, Inc.

© 1995 Donald A. Gardner Architects, Inc.

With two covered porches to encourage outdoor living, multi-pane windows and an open lay-out, this farmhouse has plenty to offer. Columns define the living room/study area. The family room is accented by a fireplace and has access to the rear porch. An adjacent sunny, bayed breakfast room is convenient to the oversized island kitchen. Four bed-rooms upstairs include a deluxe master suite with a lush bath and walk-in closet. Three family bedrooms have plenty of storage space and share a full hall bath.

DESIGN HPU040338

First Floor: 1,483 square feet
Second Floor: 1,349 square feet
Total: 2,832 square feet
Bonus Room: 486 square feet
Width: 66'-10" Depth: 47'-8"

QUOTE ONE®
Cost to build? See page 502
to order complete cost estimate
to build this house in your area!

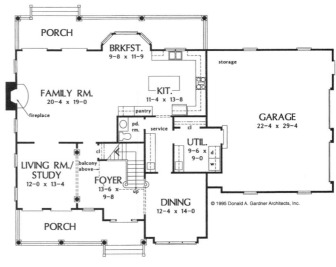

PORCH

BRKFST.
9-8 x 11-9

storage

FAMILY RM.
20-4 x 19-0

KIT.
11-4 x 13-8

GARAGE
22-4 x 29-4

fireplace

pantry

pd. rm.

service

cl

UTIL.
9-6 x 9-0

d / w

LIVING RM./STUDY
12-0 x 13-4

balcony above

cl

FOYER
13-6 x 9-8

up

DINING
12-4 x 14-0

© 1995 Donald A. Gardner Architects, Inc.

PORCH

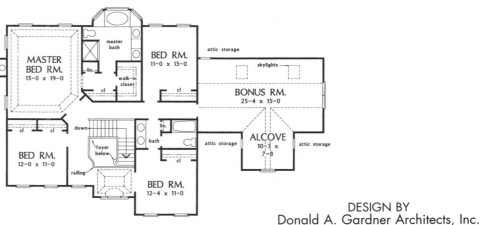

master bath

MASTER BED RM.
15-0 x 19-0

BED RM.
11-0 x 13-0

attic storage

skylights

lin.

walk-in closet

BONUS RM.
25-4 x 15-0

cl

cl

cl

down

BED RM.
12-0 x 11-0

foyer below

lin.

bath

attic storage

ALCOVE
10-3 x 7-8

attic storage

railing

BED RM.
12-4 x 11-0

cl

DESIGN BY
Donald A. Gardner Architects, Inc.

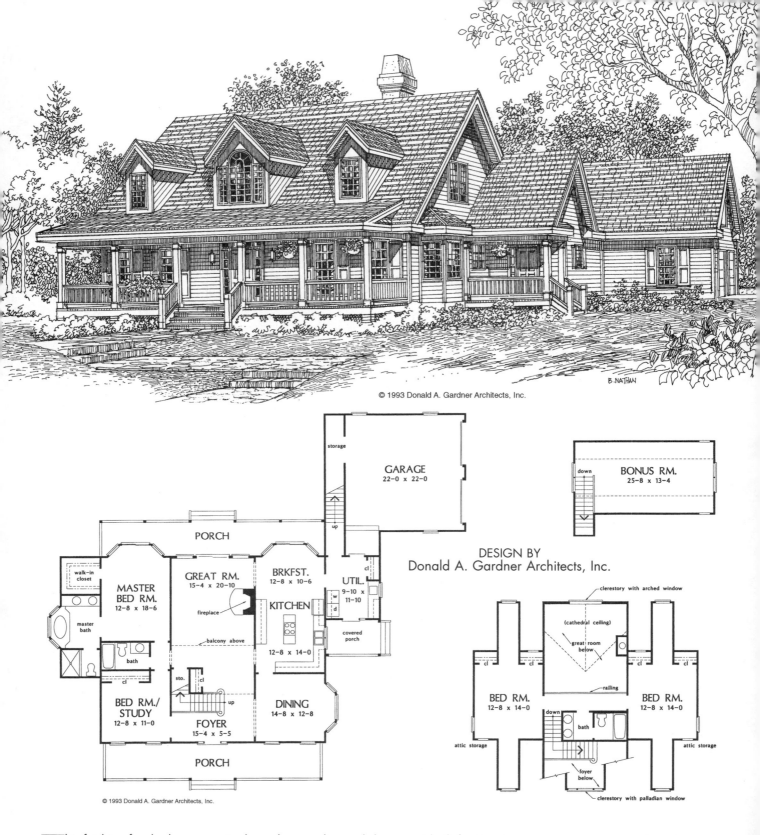

© 1993 Donald A. Gardner Architects, Inc.

B. NATHAN

GARAGE 22-0 x 22-0

storage

up

BONUS RM. 25-8 x 13-4

down

DESIGN BY
Donald A. Gardner Architects, Inc.

walk-in closet

MASTER BED RM. 12-8 x 18-6

master bath

bath

cl

BED RM./ STUDY 12-8 x 11-0

PORCH

GREAT RM. 15-4 x 20-10

fireplace

balcony above

sto.

cl

up

FOYER 15-4 x 5-5

KITCHEN

12-8 x 14-0

BRKFST. 12-8 x 10-6

UTIL. 9-10 x 11-10

w d

cl

covered porch

DINING 14-8 x 12-8

PORCH

clerestory with arched window

(cathedral ceiling)

great room below

railing

cl cl cl cl

BED RM. 12-8 x 14-0

BED RM. 12-8 x 14-0

attic storage

down

bath

attic storage

foyer below

clerestory with palladian window

© 1993 Donald A. Gardner Architects, Inc.

This fetching four-bedroom country home has porches and dormers at both front and rear to offer a welcoming touch. The spacious great room enjoys a large fireplace, a cathedral ceiling and an arched clerestory window. An efficient kitchen is centrally located in order to provide service to the dining room and bayed breakfast area and includes a cooktop island. The expansive owners suite is located on the first floor with a generous walk-in closet and a luxurious private bath. A front bedroom would make a lovely study or guest room. The second level is highlighted by a balcony hall that leads to two family bedrooms sharing a full bath.

DESIGN HPU040339

First Floor: 1,871 square feet
Second Floor: 731 square feet
Total: 2,602 square feet
Bonus Room: 402 square feet
Width: 77'-6" Depth: 70'-0"

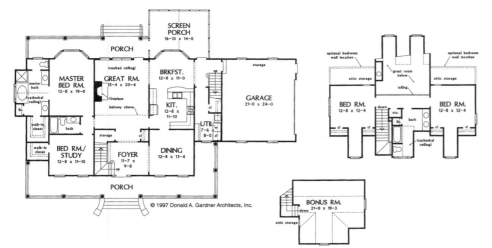

© 1997 Donald A. Gardner Architects, Inc.

This farmhouse offers an inviting wraparound porch for comfort and three gabled dormers for style. The foyer leads to a generous great room with an extended-hearth fireplace, a cathedral ceiling and access to the back covered porch. The first-floor master suite enjoys a sunny bay window and features a private bath. Upstairs, two family bedrooms share an elegant bath that has a cathedral ceiling.

DESIGN HPU040340

First Floor: 1,939 square feet
Second Floor: 657 square feet
Total: 2,596 square feet
Bonus Room: 386 square feet
Width: 80'-10" Depth: 55'-8"

DESIGN BY
Donald A. Gardner Architects, Inc.

DESIGN HPU040341

First Floor: 1,907 square feet
Second Floor: 656 square feet
Total: 2,563 square feet
Bonus Room: 467 square feet
Width: 89'-10" Depth: 53'-4"

DESIGN BY
Donald A. Gardner Architects, Inc.

Sunny bay windows splash this favorite farmhouse with style, and create a charming facade that's set off by an old-fashioned country porch. Inside, the two-story foyer opens to a formal dining room and to a study, which could be used as a guest suite. The casual living area enjoys a fireplace with an extended hearth and access to an expansive screened porch. The sensational master suite offers a walk-in closet and a bath with a bumped-out bay tub, twin vanities and a separate shower. The two family bedrooms share a full bath upstairs.

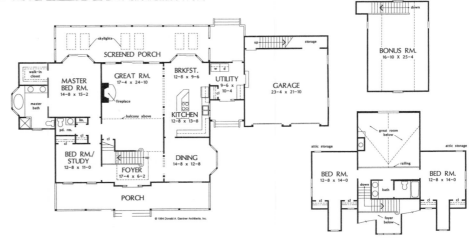

© 1994 Donald A. Gardner Architects, Inc.

DESIGN HPU040342

First Floor: 1,357 square feet
Second Floor: 1,204 square feet
Total: 2,561 square feet
Width: 80'-0" Depth: 57'-0"

DESIGN BY
Donald A. Gardner Architects, Inc.

QUOTE ONE®
Cost to build? See page 502
to order complete cost estimate
to build this house in your area!

This grand farmhouse features a double-gabled roof, a Palladian window and an intricately detailed brick chimney. The living room opens to the foyer for formal entertaining, while the family room offers a fireplace, wet bar and direct access to the porch. The lavish kitchen boasts a cooking island and serves the dining room, breakfast nook and porch. The master suite on the second level has a large walk-in closet and a master bath with a whirlpool tub, separate shower and double-bowl vanity. Three additional bedrooms share a full bath.

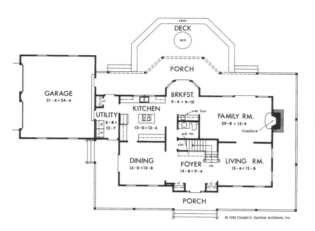

A wraparound covered porch at the front and sides of this home and the open deck with a spa and seating provide plenty of outside living area. A central great room features a vaulted ceiling, fireplace and clerestory windows above. The loft/study on the second floor overlooks this gathering area. Besides a formal dining room, kitchen, breakfast room and sun room on the first floor, there is also a generous owners suite with a garden tub. Three second-floor bedrooms complete the sleeping accommodations.

DESIGN HPU040343

First Floor: 1,734 square feet
Second Floor: 943 square feet
Total: 2,677 square feet
Width: 55'-0" Depth: 59'-10"

DESIGN BY
Donald A. Gardner Architects, Inc.

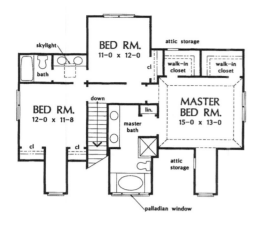

skylight

BED RM.
11-0 x 12-0

attic storage

bath

walk-in closet

walk-in closet

cl

down

BED RM.
12-0 x 11-8

lin.

master bath

MASTER BED RM.
15-0 x 13-0

cl

cl

attic storage

palladian window

DESIGN HPU040344

First Floor: 1,576 square feet
Second Floor: 947 square feet
Total: 2,523 square feet
Bonus Room: 405 square feet
Width: 71'-4" Depth: 66'-0"

Enjoy balmy breezes as you relax on the wrap-around porch of this delightful country farmhouse. The foyer introduces a dining room to the right and a bedroom or study to the left. The expansive great room—with its cozy fireplace—has direct access to the rear porch. Columns define the kitchen and breakfast area. The house gourmet will enjoy preparing meals at the island cooktop, which also allows for additional eating space. A built-in pantry and a desk are additional popular features in the well-planned kitchen/breakfast room combination. A powder room and a utility room are located nearby. The master bedroom features a tray ceiling and a luxurious bath. Two additional bedrooms share a skylit bath.

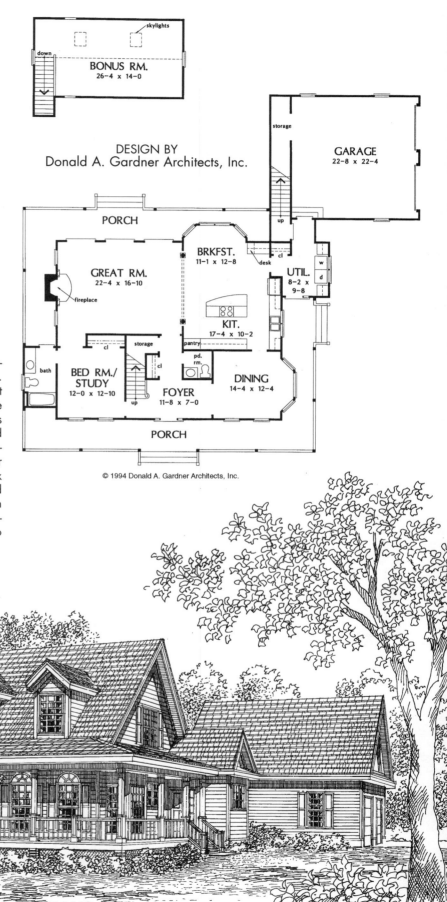

skylights

down

BONUS RM.
26-4 x 14-0

DESIGN BY
Donald A. Gardner Architects, Inc.

storage

GARAGE
22-8 x 22-4

PORCH
PORCH

up

GREAT RM.
22-4 x 16-10

fireplace

BRKFST.
11-1 x 12-8

desk

cl

UTIL.
8-2 x 9-8

w
d

KIT.
17-4 x 10-2

pantry

cl

storage

pd. rm.

BED RM./ STUDY
12-0 x 12-10

bath

cl

up

FOYER
11-8 x 7-0

DINING
14-4 x 12-4

PORCH

B. NATHAN.

DESIGN HPU040346

First Floor: 1,878 square feet
Second Floor: 739 square feet
Total: 2,617 square feet
Bonus Room: 383 square feet
Width: 79'-8" Depth: 73'-4"

DESIGN BY
Donald A. Gardner Architects, Inc.

This is Southern farmhouse living at its finest. From its wraparound porch and dormer windows to its open and spacious floor plan, this home allows families to live in comfort and style. Illuminating the vaulted foyer is an arched clerestory window within the large center dormer. A cathedral ceiling crowns the generous great room, while the kitchen with a center work island offers easy service to the great room by way of a convenient pass-through. The master suite leaves nothing to chance with screened-porch access and a splendid bath with an oversized walk-in closet. The first floor bedroom/study, with its own entrance, makes an ideal home office or guest room, and two more bedrooms located upstairs are separated by a balcony overlooking the great room.

Classic country character complements this home, complete with rustic stone corners, a covered front porch and interesting gables. The entry opens to the formal living areas that include a large dining room to the right, and straight ahead to a spacious living room warmed by a fireplace. A gallery leads the way to the efficient kitchen enhanced with a snack bar and large pantry. Casual meals can be enjoyed overlooking the covered veranda and rear grounds from the connecting breakfast room. The other side of the gallery accesses the luxurious owners suite and three second bedrooms—all with walk-in closets. The opulent owners suite enjoys a private covered porch in the rear of the plan.

DESIGN HPU040345

First Floor: 2,539 square feet
Second Floor: 170 square feet
Total: 2,709 square feet
Bonus Room: 469 square feet
Width: 98'-0" Depth: 53'-11"

DESIGN BY
©Fillmore Design Group

A wraparound porch makes this unique Victorian farmhouse stand out with style and grace, as does the lovely detailing of this plan. This design is versatile enough to accommodate either a small or large family. The entry is flanked on the left side by a large kitchen/breakfast area with an island, and on the right side by a parlor/music room. The family room is enhanced with a bar ledge, fireplace and built-in entertainment center. The owners suite has access to a covered deck. The upstairs level is shared by three bedrooms, two full baths and a bonus room.

DESIGN BY
©Fillmore Design Group

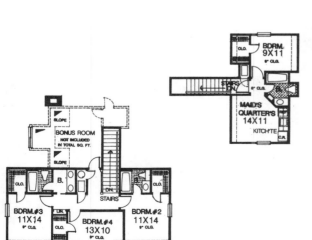

DESIGN **HPU040347**

First Floor: 2,023 square feet
Second Floor: 749 square feet
Total: 2,772 square feet
Apartment: 448 square feet
Width: 77'-2" Depth: 57'-11"

DESIGN HPU040348

First Floor: 1,379 square feet
Second Floor: 1,304 square feet
Total: 2,683 square feet
Width: 54'-8" Depth: 61'-4"

DESIGN BY
©Home Design Services, Inc.

Spectacular Victorian details offer the romantic look of a bygone era. A wrap-around porch, fish-scaling, turrets and intricate woodwork are just the beginning of this fine home. Inside, the living and dining areas are open and provide an excellent space for entertaining. With the breakfast nook tucked into a windowed bay, the kitchen serves up plenty of cabinet and counter space for the family gourmet. The nearby family room will be a favorite spot for casual evenings with friends. A den/study enjoys a quiet front bay with front-porch views. Three family bedrooms share a bath, while the master bedroom enjoys lush accommodations.

DESIGN HPU040349

First Floor: 1,794 square feet
Second Floor: 743 square feet
Total: 2,537 square feet
Bonus Room: 245 square feet
Width: 66'-0" Depth: 56'-0"

DESIGN BY
©Design Basics, Inc.

From the veranda, you can enter this home through the front entry or through the sun room. The family and sun-room combination is the high point of this design. The adjacent kitchen features a walk-in pantry and a breakfast area that opens to the back porch. A bay window highlights the first-floor master bedroom, and both the bedroom and its private bath are warmed by a through-fireplace. On the second floor, three bedrooms share a bath that has a double-bowl vanity. A balcony overlooks the family room below. There's optional attic storage plus storage space in the two-car garage. Please specify basement or slab foundation when ordering.

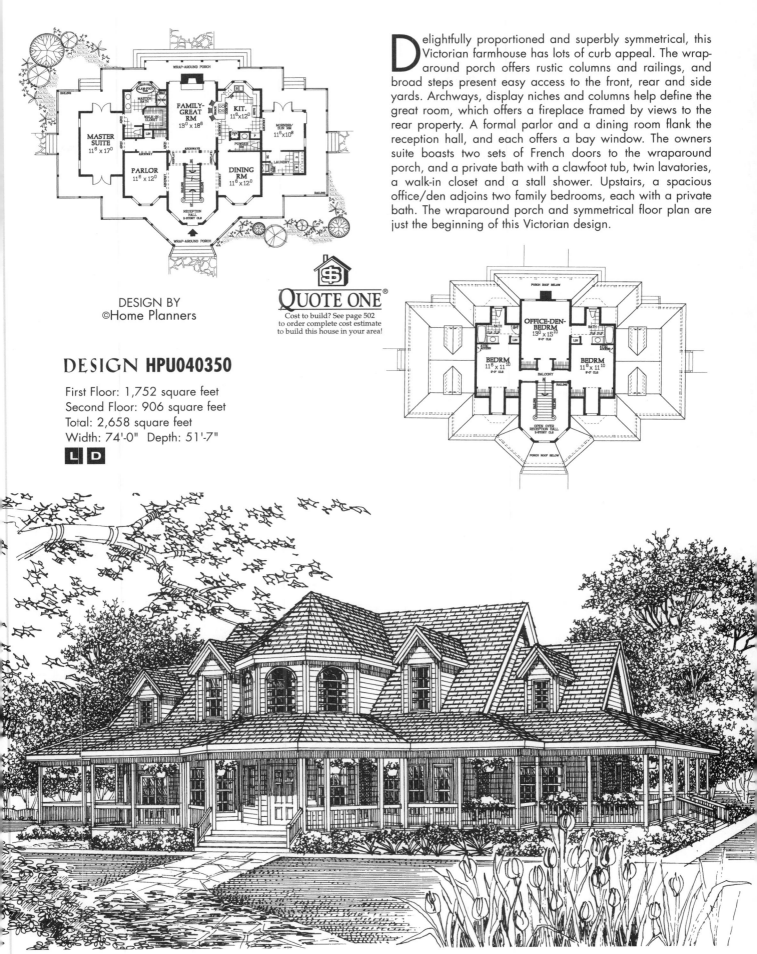

Delightfully proportioned and superbly symmetrical, this Victorian farmhouse has lots of curb appeal. The wraparound porch offers rustic columns and railings, and broad steps present easy access to the front, rear and side yards. Archways, display niches and columns help define the great room, which offers a fireplace framed by views to the rear property. A formal parlor and a dining room flank the reception hall, and each offers a bay window. The owners suite boasts two sets of French doors to the wraparound porch, and a private bath with a clawfoot tub, twin lavatories, a walk-in closet and a stall shower. Upstairs, a spacious office/den adjoins two family bedrooms, each with a private bath. The wraparound porch and symmetrical floor plan are just the beginning of this Victorian design.

DESIGN BY
©Home Planners

QUOTE ONE®
Cost to build? See page 502
to order complete cost estimate
to build this house in your area!

DESIGN HPU040350

First Floor: 1,752 square feet
Second Floor: 906 square feet
Total: 2,658 square feet
Width: 74'-0" Depth: 51'-7"

L D

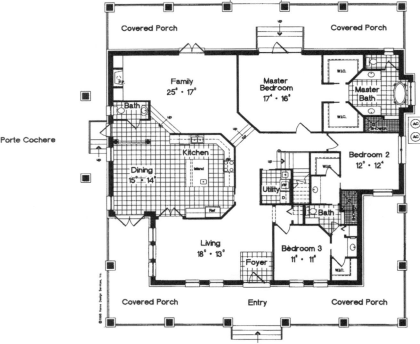

Covered Porch

Covered Porch

Family
25⁰ · 17⁰

Master
Bedroom
17⁴ · 16⁰

W.I.C.

Master
Bath

Bath

Porte Cochere

Kitchen

Dining
15⁰ · 14⁰

Island

Bedroom 2
12⁰ · 12⁴

W.I.C.

Utility

Bath

Living
18⁰ · 13⁰

Foyer

Bedroom 3
11⁴ · 11⁴

W.I.C.

Covered Porch

Entry

Covered Porch

DESIGN **HPU040351**

Square footage: 2,842
Bonus Space: 1,172 square feet
Width: 91'-0" Depth: 69'-4"

DESIGN BY
©Home Design Services, Inc.

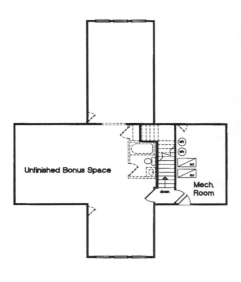

Unfinished Bonus Space

Mech.
Room

A cozy wraparound porch hugs the exterior of this quaint country home. Inside, a spacious island kitchen/dining area is connected to a sunken family room. The master bedroom privately accesses the rear porch and features a master bath with two walk-in closets and a bumped out whirlpool tub. Two additional family bedrooms are available, plus an unfinished bonus area with an optional bath.

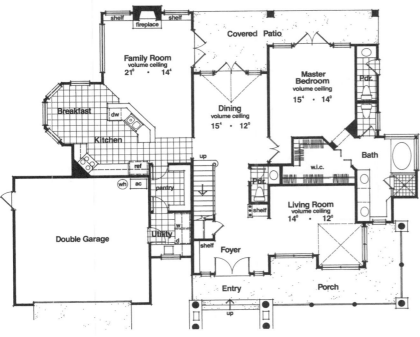

Family Room
volume ceiling
21⁰ · 14⁴

shelf | fireplace | shelf

Breakfast

Kitchen

dw

ref

wh | ac

pantry

Double Garage

Utility

w
d

shelf

Foyer

up

Entry

up

Covered Patio

Dining
volume ceiling
15⁴ · 12⁰

Master Bedroom
volume ceiling
15⁴ · 14⁰

Pdr.

Bath

w.i.c.

Pdr.

shelf

Living Room
volume ceiling
14⁰ · 12⁰

Porch

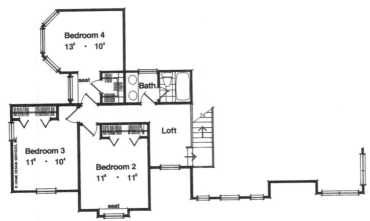

Bedroom 4
13⁰ · 10⁴

seat

Bath

Bedroom 3
11⁸ · 10⁴

Loft

Bedroom 2
11⁸ · 11⁰

seat

Expansive interior space, a porch and a patio are found in this country-style plan. Front-to-back views begin at the double doors that open to the foyer and extend through the dining room to the covered patio. To the right, the foyer spreads into the living room, which opens to a tower. The pass-through kitchen is linked to the sunny bayed breakfast area and has a large walk-through pantry near-by. The family room includes a fire-place flanked by windows and built-in shelves. French doors provide access to the covered patio from the family room, the dining room, and the master bedroom. A lower-level master bedroom includes a private full bath a walk-in closet, double van-ity and spa tub. Three additional bed-rooms and a loft are located upstairs.

DESIGN HPU040353

First Floor: 1,820 square feet
Second Floor: 700 square feet
Total: 2,520 square feet
Width: 67'-0" Depth: 55'-3"

DESIGN BY
©Home Design Services, Inc.

DESIGN HPU040355

Square Footage: 2,758
Width: 81'-4" Depth: 76'-0"

L **D**

DESIGN BY
©Home Planners

This comfortable traditional home offers plenty of modern livability. A clutter room off the two-car garage is an ideal space for a workbench, sewing or hobbies. Across the hall one finds a media room, the perfect place for a stereo, VCR and more. A spacious country kitchen to the right of the greenhouse (great for fresh herbs) is a cozy gathering place for family and friends, as well as a convenient work area. Both the formal living room, with its friendly fireplace, and the dining room provide access to the rear grounds. A spacious, amenity-filled master suite features His and Hers walk-in closets, a relaxing whirlpool tub and access to the rear terrace. Two large secondary bedrooms share a full bath.

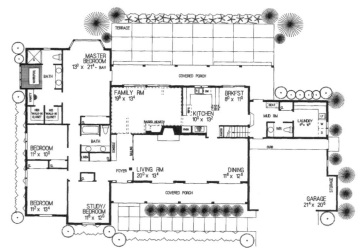

Covered porches to the front and rear will be the envy of the neighborhood when this house is built. The interior plan meets family needs perfectly in well-zoned areas: a sleeping wing with four bedrooms and two baths, a living zone with formal and informal gathering space, and a work zone with a U-shaped kitchen and laundry with a powder room. The two-car garage has a huge storage area.

DESIGN HPU040354

Square Footage: 2,549
Width: 88'-8" Depth: 53'-6"

L

DESIGN BY
©Home Planners

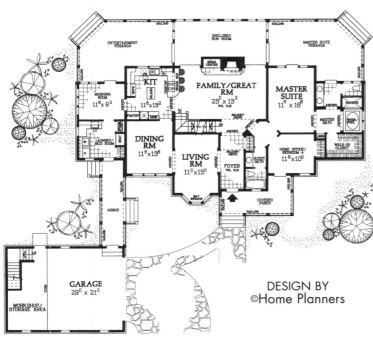

Varying roof planes, gables and dormers help create the unique character of this house. Inside, the family/great room gains attention with its high ceiling, fireplace/media-center wall, view of the upstairs balcony and French doors to the sun room. In the U-shaped kitchen, an island work surface, a planning desk and pantry are added conveniences. The spacious owners suite can function with the home office, library or private sitting room. Its direct access to the huge raised veranda provides an ideal private outdoor haven for relaxation. The second floor highlights two bedrooms and a bath. Bonus space can be found above the garage with its workshop area and stairway to a second-floor storage or multi-purpose room.

DESIGN BY
©Home Planners

DESIGN HPU040356

First Floor: 1,969 square feet
Second Floor: 660 square feet
Total: 2,629 square feet
Bonus Room: 360 square feet
Width: 90'-8" Depth: 80'-4"

L **D**

QUOTE ONE®
Cost to build? See page 502
to order complete cost estimate
to build this house in your area!

DESIGN BY
©Larry James & Associates, Inc.

Walk-in Closet

M.Bath

Master
Bedroom
17-10x15-6

Porch
13-0x10-0

Breakfast
11-5x14-0

Greatroom
17-3x19-6

Bedroom
15-6x11-6

Storage
8-2x9-10

Laun.
7-5x9-10

1/2
Bath

Bath

Garage
21-0x26-0

Kitchen
11-5x12-0

Foyer

Bedroom
11-7x13-6

Dining
11-5x15-2

Bedroom
11-5x13-6

DESIGN HPU040358

Square Footage: 2,670
Width: 70'-6" Depth: 72'-4"

A lovely brick facade is decorated with shutters, arched and straight lintels and a transom with side-lights on the entry of this comforting cottage. At the center of the house, the great room holds a fireplace sided with built-ins. Four bedrooms and lots of storage give this house long-lasting appeal with any family. Please specify crawlspace or slab foundation when ordering.

DINING
12-0 x 15-6

PORCH

MASTER
BED RM.
14-0 x 18-0

PORCH

fireplace

BRKFST.
9-8 x 10-0

KITCHEN
12-0 x 15-0

GREAT RM.
22-0 x 18-8
(cathedral ceiling)

walk-in
closet

walk-in
closet

UTIL.
5-8 x
6-8

pantry

storage

railing

down

FOYER
6-8 x
10-0

pd.
rm.

cl

master
bath

seat

GARAGE
21-8 x 23-4

PORCH

storage

PATIO

BED RM.
11-6 x 13-4

wet bar

fireplace

BED RM.
13-6 x 11-0

REC. RM.
19-8 x 18-8

bath

cl

cl

lin.

bath

cl

up

sto.

A rched windows and arches in the covered front porch complement the gabled peaks on the facade of this stylish Craftsman home with a stone-and-siding exterior and partial, finished walkout basement. Designed for sloping lots, this home positions its common living areas and master suite on the main floor and a generous recreation room and two family bedrooms on the lower level. An exciting cathedral ceiling expands the foyer and great room, while the dining room and master bedroom and bath enjoy elegant tray ceilings. With a bay window and back-porch access, the master suite boasts dual walk-ins and a luxurious bath.

DESIGN HPU040357

Main Level: 1,725 square feet
Lower Level: 1,090 square feet
Total: 2,815 square feet
Width: 59'-0" Depth: 59'-4"

DESIGN BY
Donald A. Gardner Architects, Inc.

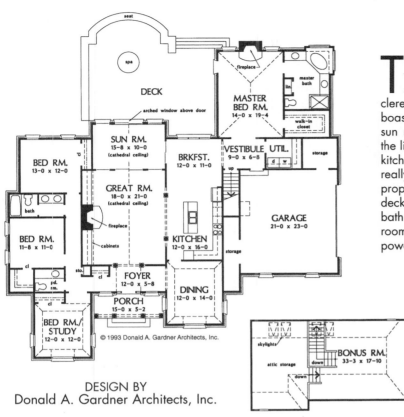

This home's personality is reflected in charming arch-top windows, set off with keystones and decorative shutters. A columned foyer enjoys natural light from a clerestory window, and opens to the great room, which boasts a cathedral ceiling and sliding glass doors to the sun room. An extended-hearth fireplace adds warmth to the living area. Open planning allows the nearby gourmet kitchen to share the glow of the hearth. The breakfast room really lets the sunshine in with a triple window to the rear property. The master suite offers private access to the rear deck with a spa, and features a cozy fireplace, a relaxing bath and a generous walk-in closet. Three family bedrooms—or make one a study—share a full bath and a powder room on the other side of the plan.

DESIGN HPU040359

Square Footage: 2,663
Bonus Room: 653 square feet
Width: 72'-7" Depth: 78'-0"

DESIGN BY
Donald A. Gardner Architects, Inc.

© 1993 Donald A. Gardner Architects, Inc.

© 1993 Donald A. Gardner Architects, Inc.

DESIGN HPU040361

First Floor: 1,870 square feet
Second Floor: 767 square feet
Total: 2,637 square feet
Width: 59'-4" Depth: 61'-4"

DESIGN BY
©Design Basics, Inc.

This charming facade sports a winning combination of brick and siding, set off by many lovely windows. An arched portico leads to a comfortable interior that's both traditional and casual. The great room opens to a spacious breakfast area with a side porch. The kitchen also serves the formal dining room, which offers a convenient powder room nearby. Upstairs, three secondary bedrooms share a bath that includes two lavatories.

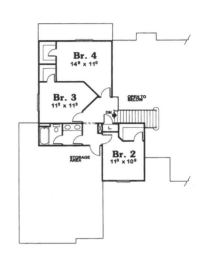

Multiple gables, shuttered windows and a covered front porch define the exterior of this farmhouse. The luxury-filled interior includes a great room that shares a through-fireplace with the hearth room, which offers a built-in entertainment center and bookshelves. A nearby breakfast bay opens to a small covered porch. The island kitchen boasts a walk-in pantry and easy access to the formal dining room. The owners suite provides a sitting room with built-in bookshelves, a large walk-in closet and an opulent bath with a whirlpool tub and double vanities. A full bath serves three secondary bedrooms upstairs, one of which features a walk-in closet. Please specify basement or block foundation when ordering.

DESIGN HPU040360

First Floor: 1,955 square feet
Second Floor: 660 square feet
Total: 2,615 square feet
Width: 60'-0" Depth: 60'-4"

DESIGN BY
©Design Basics, Inc.

DESIGN HPU040362

First Floor: 1,304 square feet
Second Floor: 1,504 square feet
Total: 2,808 square feet
Bonus Room: 209 square feet
Width: 48'-0" Depth: 46'-0"

DESIGN BY
©Design Basics, Inc.

French country accents highlight the exterior of this spacious, traditional home. The foyer opens to an interesting hall that partly encircles the octagonal living room. The family room opens from one end of the hallway, and the master suite is reached through the opposite end. The dining room, open to the foyer, is just off the kitchen and breakfast room. The laundry room, with access to outside and to the garage, completes this floor. Upstairs, two bedrooms offer walk-in closets and share a compartmented bath. An unfinished bonus room could be used for storage.

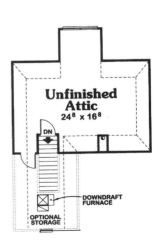

DESIGN BY
©Fillmore Design Group

DESIGN HPU040363

Square Footage: 2,858
Width: 89'-7" Depth: 68'-4"

Multiple front gables, multi-pane windows and a recessed entry make up the front exterior of this attractive home. Ten-foot ceilings are featured throughout the sprawling main living areas. A massive fireplace and built-in bookshelves or entertainment units distinguish the spacious family room. The area containing the open kitchen and breakfast room boasts a large bay window facing the patio. The master bedroom suite features a luxurious bath and walk-in closet, plus an adjacent wood-paneled study.

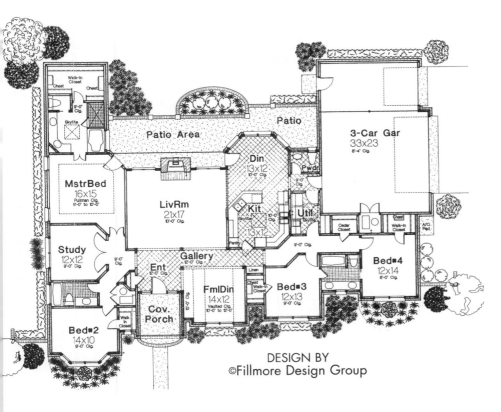

Patio Area

Walk-In Closet

Chest
Chest

Skylite

MstrBed
16x15
Pullman Clg.
11'-0" to 10'-0"

LivRm
21x17
11'-0" Clg.

Din
13x12
11'-0" Clg.

Patio

Pwdr

3-Car Gar
33x23
8'-4" Clg.

Study
12x12
9'-0" Clg.

Kit
13x12
Skylite

Util.
Skylite

Cedar
Closet

Chest

Walk-In
Closet

A/C.
Pad.

9'-0" Clg.

Gallery

Ent
Clg.

Linen

Chest
Walk-In
Closet

Bed#4
12x14
8'-0" Clg.

Cov.
Porch

FmlDin
14x12
Vaulted Clg.
10'-0" to 12'-0"

Bed#3
12x13
9'-0" Clg.

Bed#2
14x10
9'-0" Clg.

Walk
In
Closet

DESIGN BY
©Fillmore Design Group

A brick archway covers the front porch of this European-style home, creating a truly grand entrance. Situated beyond the entry, the living room takes center stage with a fireplace flanked by tall windows overlooking the backyard. To the right is a bayed eating area reserved for casual meals and an efficient kitchen. Steps away is the formal dining room for holidays and special occasions. Skillful planning creates flexibility for the owners suite. If you wish, use Bedroom 2 as a secondary bedroom or guest room, with the adjacent study accessible to everyone. Or if you prefer, combine the owners suite with the study and use it as a private retreat with Bedroom 2 as a nursery, creating a wing that provides complete privacy. Completing this clever plan are two family bedrooms—each with a walk-in closet—a powder room and a utility room.

DESIGN HPU040364

Square Footage: 2,696
Width: 80'-0" Depth: 64'-1"

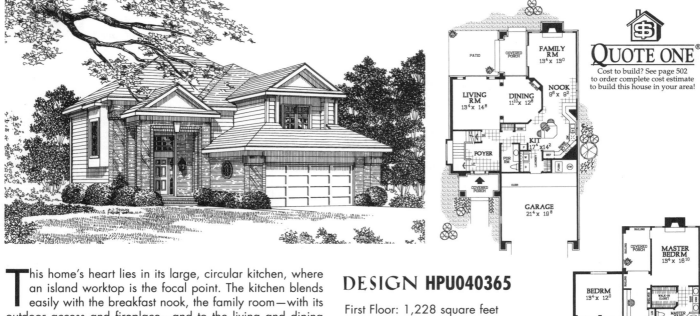

Cost to build? See page 502
to order complete cost estimate
to build this house in your area!

This home's heart lies in its large, circular kitchen, where an island worktop is the focal point. The kitchen blends easily with the breakfast nook, the family room—with its outdoor access and fireplace—and to the living and dining areas. Both rooms provide access to the backyard via sliding glass doors. Upstairs, three family bedrooms share a full bath and a handy writing desk—big enough for a computer. Also located on the second floor is the master bedroom, which features a fireplace and a splendid bath. A deck with room to relax completes this floor.

DESIGN HPU040365

First Floor: 1,228 square feet
Second Floor: 1,285 square feet
Total: 2,513 square feet
Width: 36'-8" Depth: 66'-2"

DESIGN BY
©Home Planners

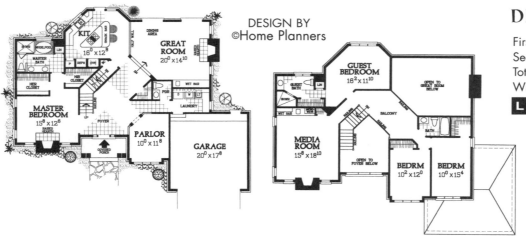

DESIGN BY
©Home Planners

DESIGN HPU040366

First Floor: 1,620 square feet
Second Floor: 1,266 square feet
Total: 2,886 square feet
Width: 60'-4" Depth: 48'-8"

L D

Cost to build? See page 502
to order complete cost estimate
to build this house in your area!

Massive chimneys and large-pane windows in a variety of shapes add interest to the exterior of this elegant home. A parlor to the right of the foyer is optimally located for formal gatherings, but most of the family's activities will take place in the sunken great room, with its dining area, raised-hearth fireplace and wet bar. The second floor offers a well-appointed guest suite with a large bath, two family bedrooms and a media room with a fireplace.

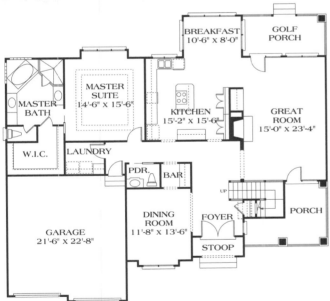

DESIGN HPU040367

First Floor: 1,825 square feet
Second Floor: 842 square feet
Total: 2,667 square feet
Width: 59'-0" Depth: 54'-6"

DESIGN BY
©Living Concepts Home Planning

Stone and siding lend a rustic nature to this traditional home. A covered stoop is enhanced by a graceful arch and a glass-paneled entry. A formal dining room is served by a gourmet kitchen through a butler's pantry with a wet bar. The great room provides a fireplace and a French door to a golf porch. An angled tub and an oversized shower highlight the master bath, while a box-bay window and a tray ceiling enhance the homeowner's bedroom. Each of the second-floor suites has a generous bath. The loft overlooks the great room.

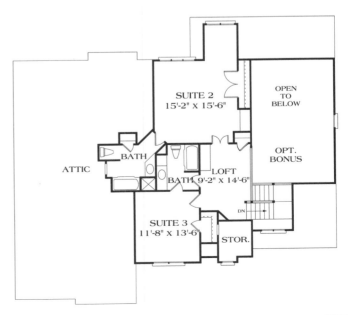

A brick exterior, cast-stone trim and corner quoins make up this attractive single-living-area design. The large living area opens to the kitchen/breakfast room, all with ten-foot ceilings. A large bay window enhances the breakfast room with a full glass door to the covered patio. A large master suite with vaulted ceilings features a luxurious master bath with double lavatories and an oversized walk-in closet.

DESIGN HPU040368

Square Footage: 2,504
Width: 65'-0" Depth: 59'-10"

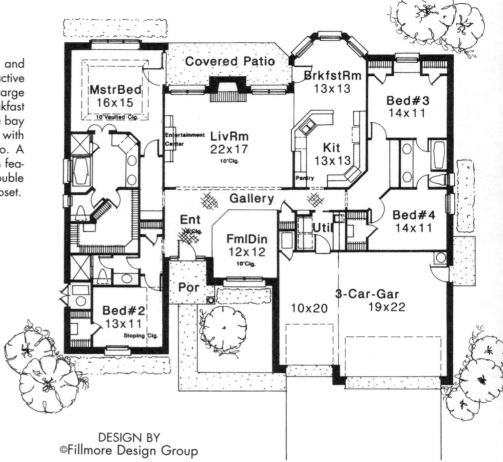

Covered Patio

MstrBed
16 x 15
10' Vaulted Clg.

BrkfstRm
13 x 13

Bed#3
14 x 11

LivRm
22 x 17
10' Clg.

Entertainment Center

Kit
13 x 13

Pantry

Gallery

Ent
10' Clg.

FmlDin
12 x 12
10' Clg.

Util

Bed#4
14 x 11

Por

10 x 20

3-Car-Gar
19 x 22

Bed#2
13 x 11
Sloping Clg.

DESIGN BY
©Fillmore Design Group

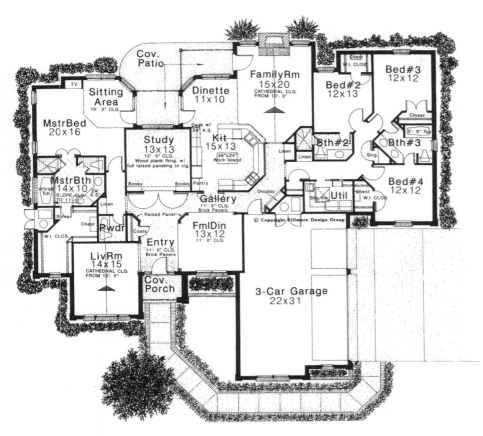

Cov. Patio

Sitting Area
10'-0" CLG.

TV

MstrBed
20x16

MstrBth
14x10
SLOPE CLG.
TO 11'-0"

Whirlpl Tub
24" K.S.

Linen

Chest

W.I. CLOS.

Shlvs.

Pwdr

Coats

LivRm
14x15
CATHEDRAL CLG.
FROM 10'-0"

Cov. Porch

Entry
11'-0" CLG.
Brick Pavers

Study
13x13
12'-0" CLG.
Wood plank flrng. w/
full raised paneling to clg.

Books   Books

Desk w/
24" K.S.

Kit
15x13
48"x24"
Work Island

Pantry

Raised Panel

Gallery
11'-0" CLG.
Brick Pavers

FmlDin
13x12
11'-0" CLG.

Dinette
11x10

FamilyRm
15x20
CATHEDRAL CLG.
FROM 10'-0"

Linen

Display

Bth#2

Linen

Bed#2
12x13

Chest
W.I. CLOS.

Bed#3
12x12

Closet

5'-0" Tub

Bth#3

Strg.

Bed#4
12x12

Sky-lite

Util

Chest W.I. CLOS.

© Copyright Fillmore Design Group

3-Car Garage
22x31

Varying rooflines, a stately brick exterior and classic window treatment accentuate the beauty of this traditional one-story home. Inside, formal living areas flank the entry—living room to the left and dining room to the right—presenting a fine introduction. Double French doors provide an elegant entrance to the centrally located study. To the right, you will find the casual living areas: a U-shaped kitchen, a dinette and a large family room with a cathedral ceiling. Three secondary bedrooms and two full baths complete this side of the plan. Tucked behind the living room is the owners suite. Amenities enhancing this private getaway include a sitting area with built-in space for a TV, a huge walk-in closet, and a private bath with a whirlpool tub and a separate shower.

DESIGN HPU040370

Square Footage: 2,985
Width: 80'-0" Depth: 68'-0"

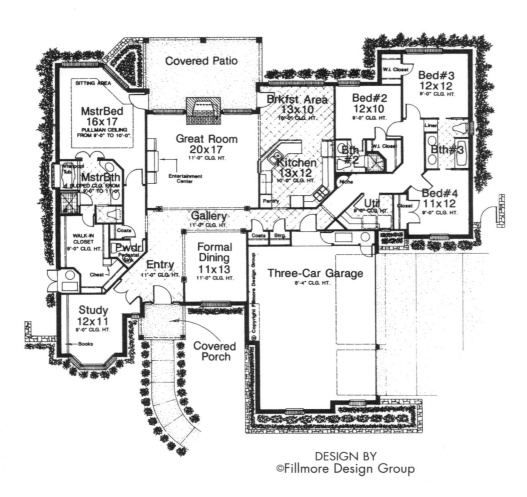

Covered Patio

SITTING AREA

MstrBed
16 x 17
PULLMAN CEILING
FROM 9'-0" TO 10'-0".

Great Room
20 x 17
11'-0" CLG. HT.

Entertainment
Center

Brkfst Area
13 x 10
10'-0" CLG. HT.

Bed#3
12 x 12
9'-0" CLG. HT.

Bed#2
12 x 10
9'-0" CLG. HT.

W.I. Closet

Whirlpool
Tub

MstrBth
SLOPED CLG. FROM
8'-0" TO 11'-0"

Kitchen
13 x 12
10'-0" CLG. HT.

Bth
#2

W.I. Closet

Linen

Bth#3

Niche

Bed#4
11 x 12
9'-0" CLG. HT.

Closet

WALK-IN
CLOSET
9'-0" CLG. HT.

Coats

Pantry

Pwdr
Pedestal

Gallery
11'-0" CLG. HT.

Util
9'-0" CLG. HT.

Coats

Strg

Chest

Entry

Formal
Dining
11 x 13
11'-0" CLG. HT.

Three-Car Garage
8'-4" CLG. HT.

© Copyright Fillmore Design Group

Study
12 x 11
9'-0" CLG. HT.

Books

Covered
Porch

DESIGN BY
©Fillmore Design Group

With a solid exterior of rough cedar and stone, this new French country design will stand the test of time. A wood-paneled study on the front features a large bay window. The heart of the house is found in a large, open great room with a built-in entertainment center. The spacious master bedroom features a corner reading area and access to an adjacent covered patio. A three-car garage and three additional bedrooms complete this generous family home.

DESIGN HPU040371

Square Footage: 2,590
Width: 73'-6" Depth: 64'-10"

Interesting angles and creative detailing characterize the exterior of this brick cottage. The island kitchen opens to an informal dining area with access to two covered patios. Formal rooms are closer to the front door for ease in entertaining. Sleeping quarters include two family bedrooms to the right of the plan and another bedroom, which could be used as a study, on the left. The left wing is home to a lavish owners suite.

DESIGN HPU040373

Square Footage: 2,526
Width: 64'-0" Depth: 81'-7"

DESIGN BY
©Fillmore Design Group

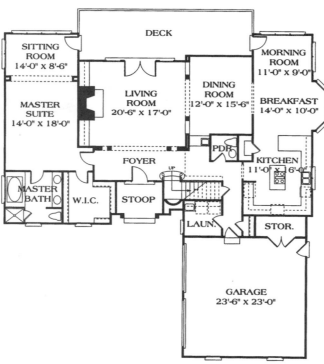

A gallery-style foyer leads to all areas of the plan, both formal and casual. The morning room is enhanced with five windows and access to the rear deck. A well-planned gourmet kitchen has an island cooktop counter, a walk-in pantry and a breakfast area with a bay window. Walls of glass brighten the sitting room, which provides French-door access to the deck. Upper-level sleeping quarters include two family bedrooms, which share a full bath that contains linen storage.

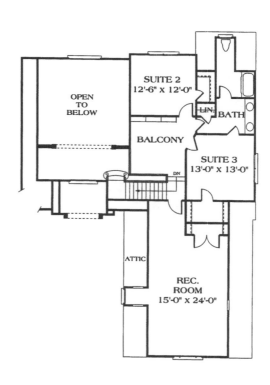

DESIGN HPU040374

First Floor: 2,100 square feet
Second Floor: 756 square feet
Total: 2,856 square feet
Bonus Room: 482 square feet
Width: 63'-5" Depth: 65'-8"

DESIGN BY
©Living Concepts Home Planning

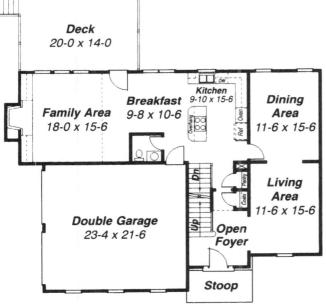

Deck
20-0 x 14-0

Family Area
18-0 x 15-6

Breakfast
9-8 x 10-6

Kitchen
9-10 x 15-6

Dining Area
11-6 x 15-6

Double Garage
23-4 x 21-6

Dn

Coats

Pantry

Up

Living Area
11-6 x 15-6

Open Foyer

Stoop

DESIGN HPU040375

First Floor: 1,183 square feet
Second Floor: 1,571 square feet
Total: 2,754 square feet
Width: 52'-4" Depth: 38'-0"

DESIGN BY
©Jannis Vann & Associates, Inc.

Classic quoins and multi-pane windows dress up this perfect blend of stone and stucco, which creates a fresh look for French country style. A glass-paneled door and clerestory window bathe the two-story foyer in natural light. The formal living and dining areas are set apart on one side of the plan. A family room enjoys a centered fireplace flanked by built-in bookcases and is conveniently open to the breakfast area, kitchen and sun deck outside. Upstairs, a tray ceiling highlights the master suite, which offers a bath and generous walk-in closet. Two family bedrooms share a full bath; a third bedroom and a loft, or fifth bedroom, share a third full bath.

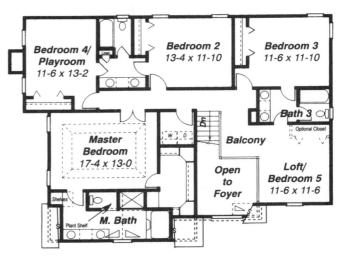

Bedroom 4/ Playroom
11-6 x 13-2

Bedroom 2
13-4 x 11-10

Bedroom 3
11-6 x 11-10

Bath 3

Optional Closet

Master Bedroom
17-4 x 13-0

Balcony

Open to Foyer

Loft/ Bedroom 5
11-6 x 11-6

Shelves

Plant Shelf

M. Bath

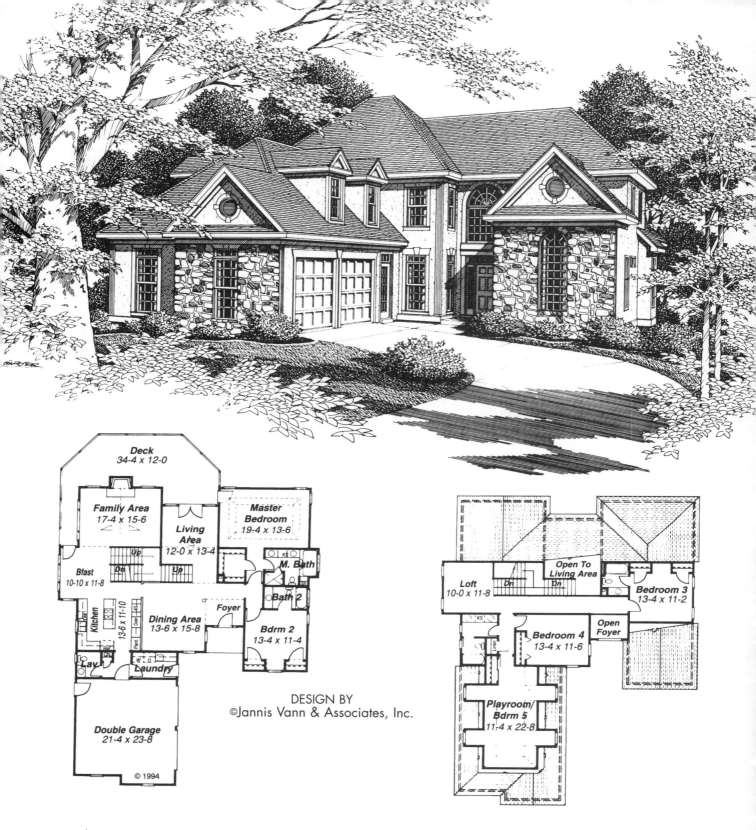

Deck
34-4 x 12-0

Family Area
17-4 x 15-6

Living Area
12-0 x 13-4

Master Bedroom
19-4 x 13-6

Bfast
10-10 x 11-8

Up

Dn

Up

M. Bath

Bath 2

Kitchen
13-6 x 11-10

Dining Area
13-6 x 15-8

Foyer

Bdrm 2
13-4 x 11-4

Lav

Laundry

Double Garage
21-4 x 23-8

© 1994

DESIGN BY
©Jannis Vann & Associates, Inc.

Loft
10-0 x 11-8

Open To Living Area

Dn

Dn

Bedroom 3
13-4 x 11-2

Bedroom 4
13-4 x 11-6

Open Foyer

Playroom/ Bdrm 5
11-4 x 22-8

An L-shaped plan and fine brick-and-siding detail present a home that is sure to please. The floor plan is designed to accommodate both formal and informal entertaining, with the formal dining and living rooms perfect for dinner parties. Toward the rear, a spacious family room offers a fireplace for cheery, casual get-togethers. A guest suite is located to the right of the foyer, near the lavish master suite. The second floor consists of two bedrooms—one with its own bath—a loft and a huge playroom over the garage.

DESIGN HPU040376

First Floor: 2,055 square feet
Second Floor: 898 square feet
Total: 2,953 square feet
Bonus Room: 358 square feet
Width: 56'-0" Depth: 80'-0"

A combination of stacked river stone and cedar shakes gives warmth and character to this English country facade. A vaulted ceiling adds height and spaciousness to the great room, which opens to the dining room for effortless entertaining. A fireplace and a built-in wet bar are welcome additions to the area, as is easy access to a covered deck. A side door near the kitchen opens to a breezeway leading to the garage. A study with a fireplace is a quiet spot, conveniently close to the master suite, which boasts a deluxe bath and a private door to the deck. A guest suite is located to the left of the foyer, where stairs lead up to the second floor and two more bedroom suites. There's plenty of storage on this level, as well as a loft that can serve many purposes.

DESIGN **HPU040377**

First Floor: 2,122 square feet
Second Floor: 719 square feet
Total: 2,841 square feet
Bonus Room: 535 square feet
Width: 117'-0" Depth: 57'-2"

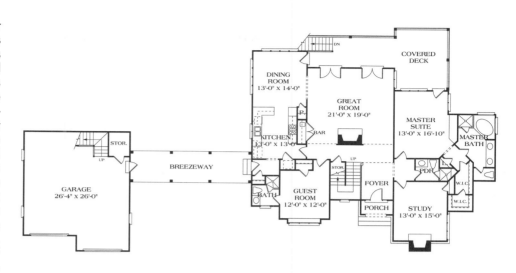

DESIGN BY
©Living Concepts Home Planning

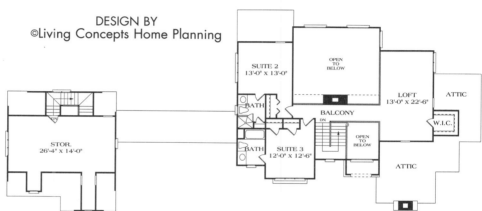

303

This home is designed to be a homeowner's dream come true. A formal living area opens from the gallery foyer through graceful arches and looks out to the veranda, which hosts an outdoor grill and service counter, perfect for outdoor entertaining. The leisure room offers a private veranda, a cabana bath and a wet bar just off the gourmet kitchen. Walls of windows and a bayed breakfast nook let in natural light and set a bright tone for this area. The master suite opens to the rear property through French doors, and boasts a lavish bath with a corner whirlpool tub that overlooks a private garden. An art niche off the gallery hall, a private dressing area and a secluded study complement the master suite. Two family bedrooms occupy the opposite wing of the plan, and share a full bath and private hall.

DESIGN HPU040378

Square Footage: 2,978
Width: 84'-0" Depth: 90'-0"

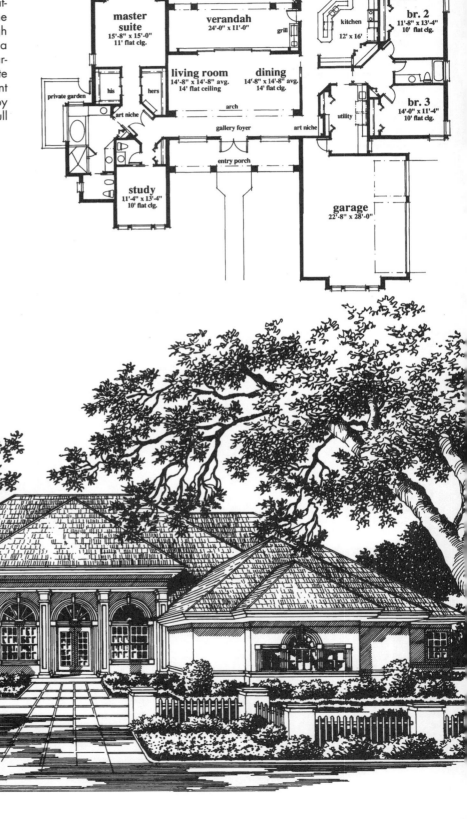

DESIGN BY
©The Sater Design Collection

verandah

leisure
17'-0" x 18'-4"
10' flat ceiling

nook
10'-0" x 10'-0"
10' flat clg.

wet bar

lanai

master
suite
15'-8" x 15'-0"
11' flat clg.

verandah
24'-0" x 11'-0"

grill

kitchen
12' x 16'

br. 2
11'-8" x 13'-4"
10' flat clg.

private garden

his

hers

art niche

living room
14'-8" x 14'-8" avg.
14' flat ceiling

dining
14'-8" x 14'-8" avg.
14' flat clg.

arch

utility

br. 3
14'-0" x 11'-4"
10' flat clg.

gallery foyer

art niche

entry porch

study
11'-4" x 13'-4"
10' flat clg.

garage
22'-8" x 28'-0"

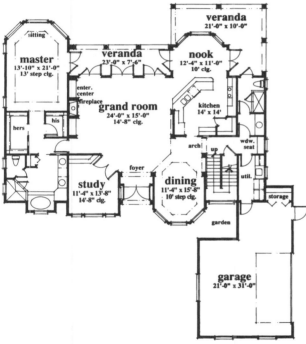

DESIGN HPU040379

First Floor: 2,181 square feet
Second Floor: 710 square feet
Total: 2,891 square feet
Width: 66'-4" Depth: 79'-0"

DESIGN BY
©The Sater Design Collection

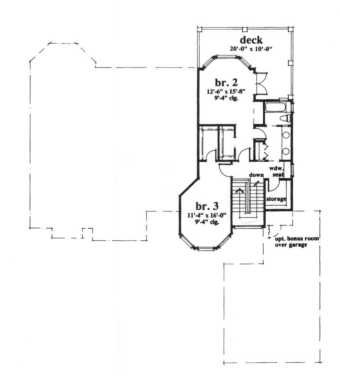

An arched, covered porch presents fine double doors leading to a spacious foyer in this decidedly European home. A two-story tower contains an elegant formal dining room on the first floor and a spacious bedroom on the second floor. The grand room is aptly named with a fireplace, a built-in entertainment center and three sets of doors opening onto the veranda. A large kitchen is ready to please the gourmet of the family with a big walk-in pantry and a sunny, bay-windowed eating nook. The secluded master suite is luxury in itself. A bay-windowed sitting area, access to the rear veranda, His and Hers walk-in closets and a lavish bath are all set to pamper you. Upstairs, two bedrooms, both with walk-in closets, share a full hall bath that includes twin vanities. Please specify basement or slab foundation when ordering.

DESIGN HPU040380

First Floor: 1,920 square feet
Second Floor: 912 square feet
Total: 2,832 square feet
Width: 70'-0"   Depth: 40'-0"

DESIGN BY
©Archival Designs, Inc.

The impressive facade of this classic design previews an elegant floor plan. To the left of the large foyer, French doors open to a study filled with natural light. The open dining room, to the right of the foyer, is defined by a single column. To the rear of the plan, the living room/den and kitchen—with a bowed breakfast area—provide space for the family to gather. Also at the rear of the plan, a guest room features its own bath and private access to the outside through a garage entrance. On the left side of the plan, the master suite offers a walk-in closet, a luxurious bath and private access to the study. Upstairs, two bedrooms—each with a private compartmented vanity—share a bath. Bookshelves line the library loft, which is lighted by three skylights.

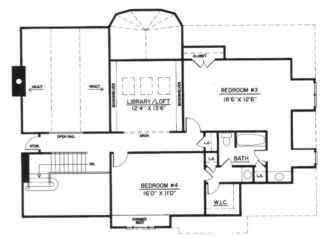

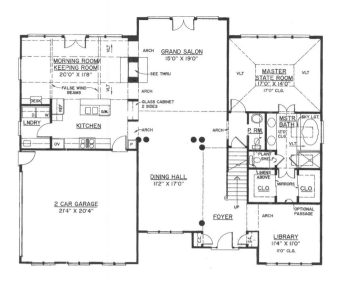

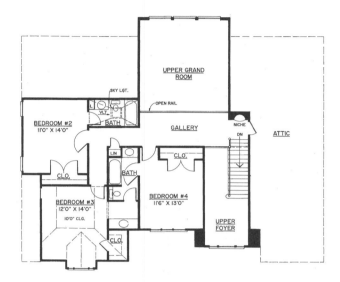

Nested, hipped gables create a dramatic effect in this beautiful two-story brick home. The arched doorway is echoed in the triple clerestory window that lights the two-story foyer. Columns decorate the formal dining room, which is open to the two-story grand room with fireplace. The master suite is located downstairs for privacy, while upstairs, three secondary bedrooms are joined by a gallery overlooking the grand room.

DESIGN HPU040381

First Floor: 1,809 square feet
Second Floor: 898 square feet
Total: 2,707 square feet
Width: 54'-4"   Depth: 46'-0"

DESIGN BY
©Archival Designs, Inc.

307

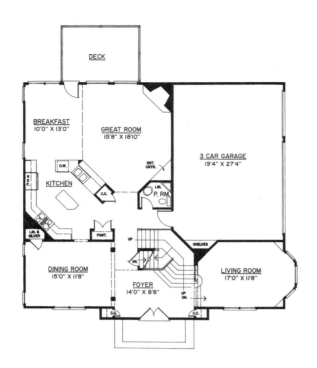

BREAKFAST
10'0" X 13'0"

GREAT ROOM
15'8" X 18'10"

3 CAR GARAGE
19'4" X 27'4"

DECK

KITCHEN

ENT.
CNTR.

P. RM.

DINING ROOM
15'0" X 11'8"

FOYER
14'0" X 8'8"

LIVING ROOM
17'0" X 11'8"

PANT.

UP

SHELVES

If ever a home was designed with a Fifth Avenue address in mind, this is it. The grand entry opens to a wide foyer that presents two coat closets and angled stairs to the second floor. Through a pair of columns to the left, enter the dining room. Or go to the right into the formal living room that has an elegant bay window. The angled kitchen opens to the breakfast room and two-story great room. Stairs to the second floor go up to the wide loft that overlooks the great room. The laundry room on this floor serves the three family bedrooms with their two baths and the master suite.

HERS

UPPER GREAT
ROOM

LAUN.

CLO.

BEDROOM #4
13'0" X 13'0"

M. BA.

BATH

BEDROOM #3
12'4" X 11'0"

LOFT

BEDROOM #2
13'4" X 11'0"

M. BEDROOM
15'4" X 17'4"

UPPER FOYER

BATH

DESIGN HPU040382

First Floor: 1,332 square feet
Second Floor: 1,331 square feet
Total: 2,663 square feet
Width: 48'-0"   Depth: 42'-0"

DESIGN BY
©Archival Designs, Inc.

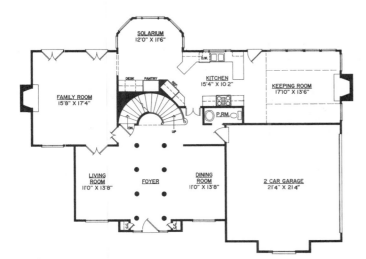

DESIGN HPU040383

First Floor: 1,431 square feet
Second Floor: 1,519 square feet
Total: 2,950 square feet
Width: 60'-0" Depth: 44'-0"

DESIGN BY
©Archival Designs, Inc.

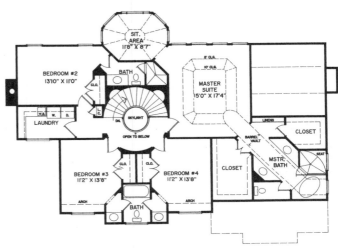

Stunning stucco detailing, attractive gabled rooflines and an elegant, arched entrance are elements of traditional style that dress up this fine four-bedroom home. Inside, columns define a graceful foyer and separate the formal dining room and formal living room. The spacious family room, off to the left, features a warming fireplace and direct access to the rear grounds. A solarium is near the efficient kitchen, providing a warm and sunny place to relax. The keeping room is another gathering spot that will surely be a favorite of your family. Talk about lavish! When it comes to the master suite, the home-owner will have a hard time leaving this wonderful room. Two walk-in closets, a separate octagonal sitting room and a fabulous bath are sure to please.

DESIGN HPU040385

First Floor: 1,465 square feet
Second Floor: 1,349 square feet
Total: 2,814 square feet
Bonus Room: 319 square feet
Width: 72'-4" Depth: 38'-4"

DESIGN BY
©Jannis Vann & Associates, Inc.

A massive arch guards the entrance to this French-style stucco home, its keystone accent repeated over the windows in several different combinations. Inside, symmetrical dining and living rooms flank the two-story foyer. A swinging door leads from the dining room to the island kitchen, which offers a choice of a snack bar or a breakfast nook for casual meals. The laundry room and a powder room are nearby. A sunken family room boasts a fireplace and access to a sun deck that stretches across the rear of the house. The second floor offers four bedrooms, including a deluxe master suite. Please specify basement, crawlspace or slab foundation when ordering.

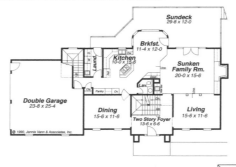

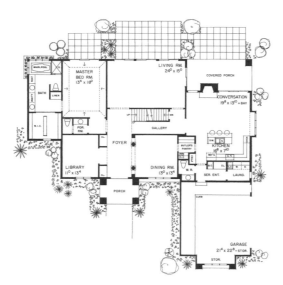

QUOTE ONE®
Cost to build? See page 502
to order complete cost estimate
to build this house in your area!

This home will keep even the most active family from feeling cramped. Adjacent to the kitchen is a conversation area with additional access to the covered porch, a snack bar, fireplace and a window bay. A butler's pantry leads to the formal dining room. Placed conveniently on the first floor, the master suite features a roomy bath with a huge walk-in closet and dual vanities. Two large bedrooms are found on the second floor.

DESIGN HPU040384

First Floor: 2,328 square feet
Second Floor: 603 square feet
Total: 2,931 square feet
Width: 69'-4" Depth: 66'-0"

L D

DESIGN BY
©Home Planners

Intricate details make the most of this lovely one-story design. Besides the living room/dining room area to the rear, there is a large conversation area with a fireplace and plenty of windows. The kitchen is separated from living areas by an angled snack-bar counter. Three bedrooms grace the right side of the plan. The master suite features a tray ceiling and sliding glass doors to the rear terrace. The dressing area is graced by His and Hers walk-in closets, a double-bowl lavatory and a compartmented toilet. The shower area is highlighted with glass block and is sunken down one step. A garden whirlpool tub finishes off this area.

DESIGN HPU040386

Square Footage: 2,916
Width: 77'-10" Depth: 73'-10"

L **D**

DESIGN BY
©Home Planners

QUOTE ONE®
Cost to build? See page 502
to order complete cost estimate
to build this house in your area!

311

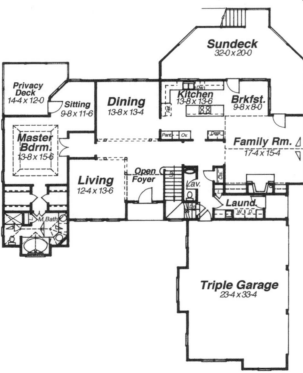

Sundeck
32-0 x 20-0

Privacy Deck
14-4 x 12-0

Sitting
9-8 x 11-6

Dining
13-8 x 13-4

Kitchen
13-8 x 13-6

Brkfst.
9-8 x 8-0

Master Bdrm.
13-8 x 15-6

Pant. Ov.

Family Rm.
17-4 x 15-4

Open Foyer

Living
12-4 x 13-6

Lav.

Laund.
W D

M. Bath

Triple Garage
23-4 x 33-4

Arches and gables contrast and complement in a recurring theme on this impressive French exterior. Note particularly the clerestory window over the foyer. Formal living and dining rooms open off the foyer, providing a large area for entertaining. A sun deck expands outdoor living possibilities, with access from the breakfast room and the family room. A fireplace in the family room spreads cheer throughout the informal area. To the left of the plan, the master wing includes a deluxe bath, two walk-in closets and a sitting room with access to a privacy deck. The second floor offers three bedrooms, two baths and a bonus room for future use.

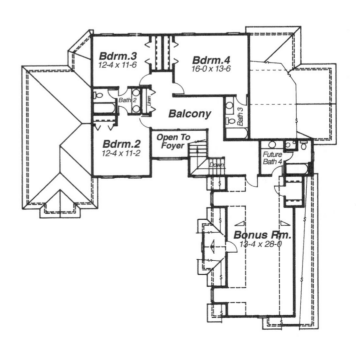

Bdrm.3
12-4 x 11-6

Bdrm.4
16-0 x 13-6

Bath 2

Balcony

Bath 3

Bdrm.2
12-4 x 11-2

Open To Foyer

Future Bath 4

Down

Bonus Rm.
13-4 x 28-0

DESIGN HPU040387

First Floor: 1,967 square feet
Second Floor: 1,014 square feet
Total: 2,981 square feet
Bonus Room: 607 square feet
Width: 66'-0" Depth: 65'-8"

DESIGN BY
©Jannis Vann & Associates, Inc.

Visual delight in this European-style home includes a high, hipped roof, multipane windows and a glass entry with a transom. Formal elegance is captured in the two-story living area featuring a warming fireplace and deck entry. The open space of the kitchen and breakfast area is well accented by a bay window. One family bedroom with a full bath resides on the first floor; the remaining two bedrooms and luxurious master suite are located on the second floor.

DESIGN HPU040388

First Floor: 1,268 square feet
Second Floor: 1,333 square feet
Total: 2,601 square feet
Width: 50'-0" Depth: 50'-4"

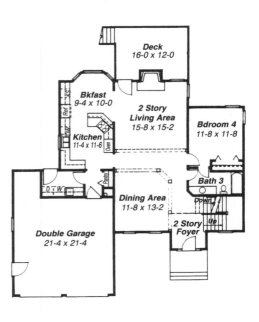

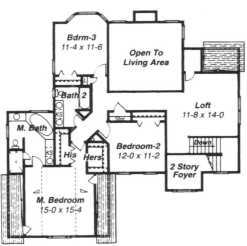

DESIGN BY
©Jannis Vann & Associates, Inc.

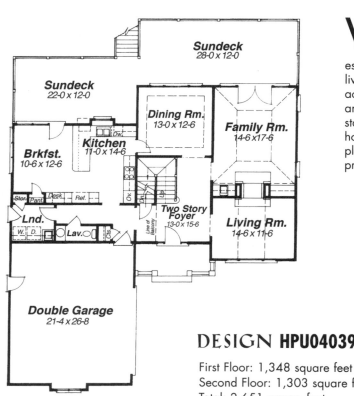

With the wonderful sun deck across the back of this home, you won't have to move to the Mediterranean to get your fill of sunshine. The stucco exterior, keystone arches and hipped roof add to the European flavor of the design. The living room opens off the two-story foyer, which also provides access to the family room and the dining room. A through-fireplace and built-ins separate and enhance the family and living rooms. A stairway in the two-story foyer leads to the second floor, which houses three family bedrooms and a master suite that's sure to please with a whirlpool tub, twin vanities, two closets and a small private balcony.

DESIGN HPU040390

First Floor: 1,348 square feet
Second Floor: 1,303 square feet
Total: 2,651 square feet
Width: 50'-0" Depth: 67'-0"

DESIGN BY
©Jannis Vann & Associates, Inc.

Ornate European exterior detailing creates a unique and timeless design in this fabulous French country classic home. Inside the house are open formal areas for living and dining. The kitchen, featuring a cooktop/utility island and built-in pantry, opens into the breakfast area and a cozy keeping den. The enormous walk-in closet in the master retreat allows access from both the bedroom and the bath. The bath itself offers the convenience of dual vanities. Upstairs, a balcony that overlooks the gathering room leads to two additional suites and a bonus room over the garage. A private courtyard at the rear of the house adds privacy to family outdoor living.

DESIGN HPU040391

First Floor: 2,061 square feet
Second Floor: 695 square feet
Total: 2,756 square feet
Bonus Room: 377 square feet
Width: 55'-0" Depth: 79'-10"

DESIGN BY
©Living Concepts Home Planning

DESIGN HPU040392

First Floor: 2,051 square feet
Second Floor: 749 square feet
Total: 2,800 square feet
Width: 50'-0" Depth: 74'-0"

At only 50 feet in width, this fabulous design will fit anywhere! From the moment you enter the home from the foyer, this floor plan explodes in every direction with huge living spaces. Flanking the foyer are the living and dining rooms, and the visual impact of the staircase is breathtaking. Two-story ceilings adorn the huge family room with double-stacked glass walls. Sunlight floods the breakfast nook, and the kitchen is a gourmet's dream, complete with cooking island and loads of overhead cabinets. Tray ceilings grace the owners suite, which also offers a well-designed private bath. Here, a large soaking tub, doorless shower, private toilet chamber and a huge walk-in closet are sure to please. Upstairs, two oversized bedrooms and a loft space—perfect for the home computer—share a full bath.

DESIGN BY
©Home Design Services, Inc.

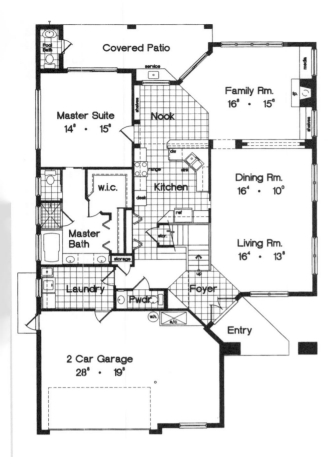

DESIGN HPU040393

First Floor: 1,844 square feet
Second Floor: 1,017 square feet
Total: 2,861 square feet
Width: 45'-0" Depth: 67'-8"

DESIGN BY
©Home Design Services, Inc.

The excitement begins upon entering the foyer of this home, where an impressive staircase is its focal point. From there you view the formal spaces of the living and dining room with vaulted ceilings. Passing through an archway, you enter the family room with its impressive media/fireplace wall. Just off the nook is a sliding glass door to the covered patio, where a wet bar can be found as well as a pool bath. The kitchen is a gourmet's dream, with loads of pantry storage and a planning desk. A built-in wall of shelves and arches just off the nook welcome you to the master wing. The suite is generously sized and has a wonderful wall of high transom glass, as well as sliding glass doors to the patio. The second floor is impressive with three large bedrooms, two of which share a bath, and one bedroom with a private bath.

DESIGN HPU040395

Square Footage: 2,718
Width: 63'-8" Depth: 64'-4"

DESIGN BY
©Home Design Services, Inc.

Here's an exciting contemporary design that's more than just a pretty face. A tiled foyer leads to an open family room with a volume ceiling and a wall of glass that brings in a sense of the outdoors. The master wing provides a guest suite, complete with its own full bath. An oversized spa-style tub highlights the homeowner's retreat, which includes a generous walk-in closet, a soaking tub enclosed in a curved wall of glass block, and a tray ceiling in the bedroom. The kitchen features a walk-in pantry and a mitered-glass nook for casual meals. Three secondary bedrooms share a cabana bath, which opens to the covered patio.

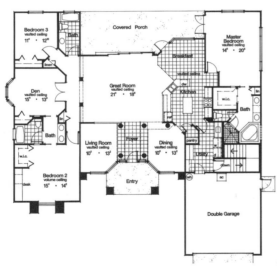

A walkout basement adds to the total living space of this one-of-a-kind hillside home. The entry is flanked by the formal living and dining rooms and then opens to a massive great room with a covered porch beyond. The kitchen and breakfast nook are open to the great room; the kitchen features an island work center. Two family bedrooms and a den are on the left side of the plan. Bedroom 3 has a private bath. The den is a focal point, seen through arches and double doors from the great room. The master suite is on the right side and has a walk-in closet, porch access and sumptuous bath.

DESIGN HPU040394

Square Footage: 2,742
Width: 66'-8" Depth: 67'-0"

DESIGN BY
©Home Design Services, Inc.

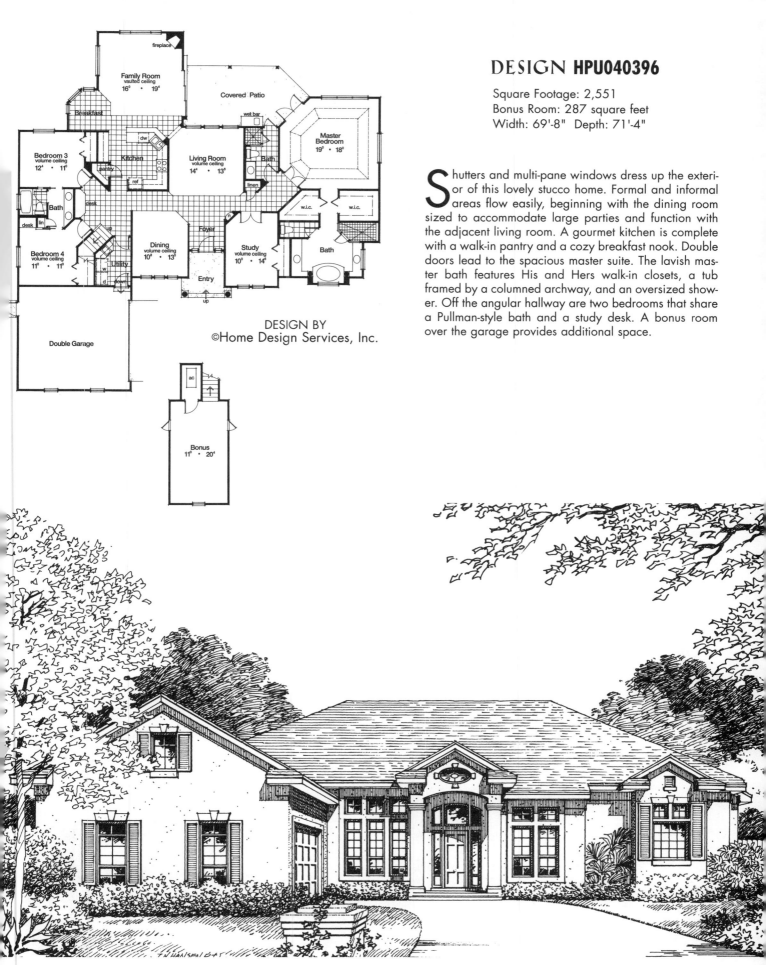

DESIGN HPU040396

Square Footage: 2,551
Bonus Room: 287 square feet
Width: 69'-8"   Depth: 71'-4"

Shutters and multi-pane windows dress up the exterior of this lovely stucco home. Formal and informal areas flow easily, beginning with the dining room sized to accommodate large parties and function with the adjacent living room. A gourmet kitchen is complete with a walk-in pantry and a cozy breakfast nook. Double doors lead to the spacious master suite. The lavish master bath features His and Hers walk-in closets, a tub framed by a columned archway, and an oversized shower. Off the angular hallway are two bedrooms that share a Pullman-style bath and a study desk. A bonus room over the garage provides additional space.

DESIGN BY
©Home Design Services, Inc.

DESIGN HPU040398

Square Footage: 2,962
Width: 70'-0" Depth: 76'-0"

DESIGN BY
©Home Design Services, Inc.

Enter the formal foyer of this home and you are greeted with a traditional split living-room/dining-room layout. But the family room is where the real living takes place. It expands onto the outdoor living space, which features a summer kitchen. The ultimate master suite contains coffered ceilings, a "boomerang" vanity and angular mirrors that reflect the bayed soaking tub and shower. Efficient use of space creates a huge closet with little dead center space.

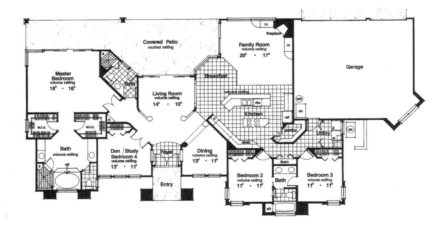

The angles in this home create unlimited views and spaces that appear larger. Majestic columns of brick add warmth to a striking elevation. Inside, the foyer commands special perspective on living areas including the living room, dining room and den. The island kitchen serves the breakfast nook and the family room. A large pantry provides ample space for food storage. Nearby, in the owners suite, mitered glass and a private bath set the tone for simple luxury. Two secondary bedrooms share privacy and quiet at the front of the house. The den may also convert to a fourth bedroom, if desired.

DESIGN HPU040397

Square Footage: 2,597
Width: 96'-6" Depth: 50'-0"

DESIGN BY
©Home Design Services, Inc.

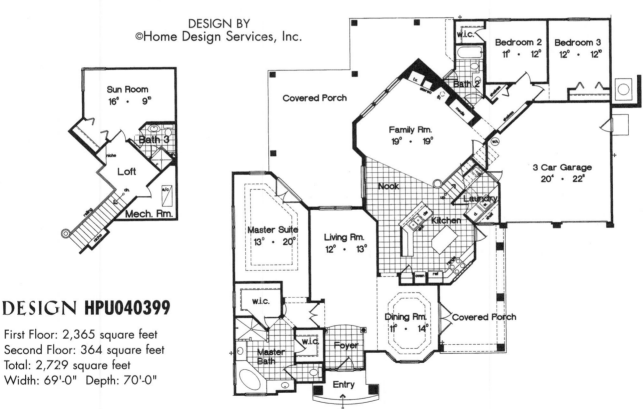

Sun Room
16⁰ • 9⁰

Bath 3

niche

Loft

Mech. Rm.

Covered Porch

w.i.c.

Bedroom 2
11⁰ • 12⁰

Bedroom 3
12⁰ • 12⁰

Bath 2

Family Rm.
19⁰ • 19⁰

3 Car Garage
20⁴ • 22⁸

Nook

Laundry

Master Suite
13⁰ • 20⁰

Living Rm.
12⁰ • 13⁰

Kitchen

DESIGN HPU040399

First Floor: 2,365 square feet
Second Floor: 364 square feet
Total: 2,729 square feet
Width: 69'-0" Depth: 70'-0"

w.i.c.

Master Bath

w.i.c.

Foyer

Dining Rm.
11⁰ • 14⁰

Covered Porch

Entry

up

The columned foyer welcomes you into a series of spaces that reach out in all directions. The living room has a spectacular view of the huge covered patio area that's perfect for summer entertaining. The dining room has a tray ceiling and French doors that lead to a covered porch. A secluded owners suite affords great views through French doors and also has a tray ceiling. The private master bath is complete with His and Hers walk-in closets and a soaking tub. The family wing combines an island kitchen, nook and family gathering space, with the built-in media/fireplace wall the center of attention. Two secondary bedrooms share a bath. A staircase overlooking the family room takes you up to the sun room complete with a full bath, making this a very desirable kids' space.

DESIGN HPU040401

Square Footage: 2,656
Width: 92'-0" Depth: 69'-0"

DESIGN BY
©Home Design Services, Inc.

A graceful design sets this charming home apart from the ordinary and transcends the commonplace. From the foyer, the dining room branches off the sunny living room, setting a lovely backdrop for entertaining. Casual living is the focus in the oversized family room, where sliding doors open to the patio and the eat-in, gourmet kitchen is open for easy conversation. Two family bedrooms and a cabana bath are just off the family room. The master suite has a cozy fireplace in the sitting area, twin closets and a compartmented bath. A large covered patio adds to the living area.

Q uoins and keystone accents lend a French country flavor to this stucco exterior, but brick contrasts and a glass-paneled entry give it a fresh face. A tiled foyer leads to a gracefully curved gallery hall. The heart of the plan is the vaulted living room, which overlooks the covered patio and rear grounds, but friends may want to gather in the family room, where a centered fireplace offers cozy niches. A gourmet kitchen is designed to handle casual meals as well as planned occasions, with a service kitchen on the patio for outdoor events.

DESIGN HPU040400

Square Footage: 2,931
Width: 70'-8" Depth: 83'-0"

DESIGN BY
©Home Design Services, Inc.

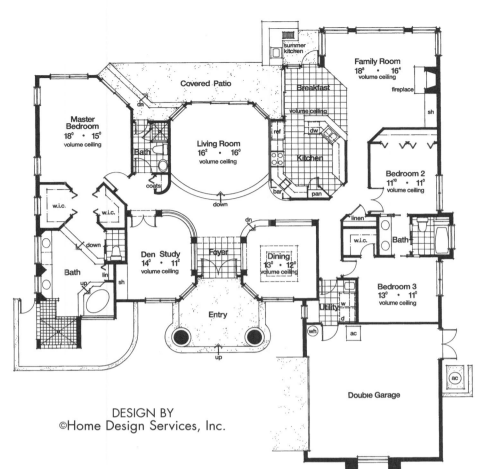

Covered Patio

Master Bedroom
18⁰ • 15⁰
volume ceiling

summer kitchen

Family Room
18⁸ • 16⁴
volume ceiling

fireplace

Breakfast
volume ceiling

sh

Bath

Living Room
16² • 16⁰
volume ceiling

ref

dw

Kitchen

w.i.c.

w.i.c.

coats

Bedroom 2
11¹⁰ • 11⁰
volume ceiling

down

bar

pan

linen

Bath

down

Den Study
14⁰ • 11²
volume ceiling

Foyer

Dining
13⁰ • 12⁰
volume ceiling

Bath

up

lin

sh

w.i.c.

Entry

Bedroom 3
13⁰ • 11⁰
volume ceiling

Utility

w

d

wh

ac

up

ac

Double Garage

DESIGN BY
©Home Design Services, Inc.

DESIGN HPU040402

Square Footage: 2,636
Width: 68'-8" Depth: 76'-0"

A towering entry welcomes you to the foyer of this soaring contemporary design. Interior glass walls give openness to the den/study, and mirror the arches to the formal dining room. The sunken living room has a bayed window wall, which views the patio. The master-suite wing also holds the den/study, which can access the powder room/patio bath. Sliding glass doors from the master suite access the patio. The master bath features dual closets, a sunken vanity/bath area and a doorless shower. The family wing holds the gourmet kitchen, nook and family room with a fireplace.

DESIGN HPU040403

First Floor: 2,249 square feet
Second Floor: 620 square feet
Total: 2,869 square feet
Bonus Room: 308 square feet
Width: 69'-6" Depth: 52'-0"

DESIGN BY
Donald A. Gardner Architects, Inc.

An impressive two-story entrance welcomes you to this stately home. Massive chimneys and pillars and varying rooflines add interest to the stucco exterior. The foyer, lighted by a clerestory window, opens to the formal living and dining room. The living room—which could also serve as a study—features a fireplace, as does the family room. Both rooms access the patio. The L-shaped island kitchen opens to a bay-windowed breakfast nook, which is echoed by the sitting area in the master suite. A room next to the kitchen could serve as a bedroom or a home office. The second floor contains two family bedrooms plus a bonus room for future expansion.

This stucco home contrasts gently curved arches with gables, and uses large multi-pane windows to flood the interior with natural light. Square pillars form an impressive entry, leading to a two-story foyer. The living room is set apart from the informal area of the house, and could serve as a cozy study instead. The back patio can be reached from both the breakfast nook and the family room, which features a cathedral ceiling and a fireplace. The owners suite offers two walk-in closets and a bath with twin vanities, garden tub and separate shower.

DESIGN HPU040404

First Floor: 1,904 square feet
Second Floor: 645 square feet
Total: 2,549 square feet
Bonus Room: 434 square feet
Width: 71'-2" Depth: 45'-8"

DESIGN BY
Donald A. Gardner Architects, Inc.

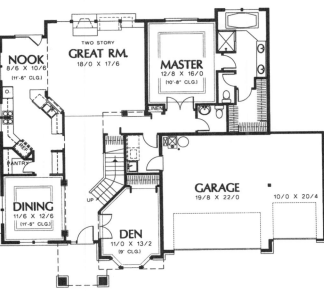

NOOK
8/6 X 10/6
(11'-6" CLG.)

TWO STORY
GREAT RM.
18/0 X 17/6

MASTER
12/8 X 16/0
(10'-8" CLG.)

LINEN

PANTRY

DINING
11/6 X 12/6
(11'-8" CLG.)

UP

GARAGE
19/8 X 22/0   10/0 X 20/4

DEN
11/0 X 13/2
(9' CLG.)

Square columns flank the entry to this contemporary three-bedroom home. The two-story great room provides a fireplace and a wall of windows. A formal dining room, located at the front of the plan, offers a tray ceiling and works well with the kitchen. A bayed den is available for quiet study. The owners suite is located on the first floor for privacy and features many amenities. Upstairs, two family bedrooms share a full bath.

DESIGN HPU040405

First Floor: 1,818 square feet
Second Floor: 698 square feet
Total: 2,516 square feet
Width: 50'-0" Depth: 53'-0"

DESIGN BY
©Alan Mascord Design Associates, Inc.

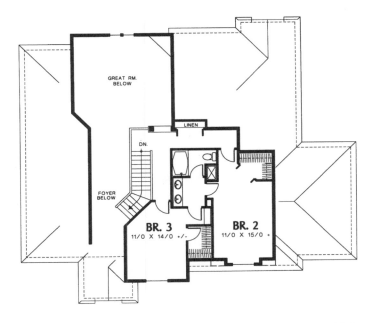

GREAT RM.
BELOW

LINEN

DN.

FOYER
BELOW

BR. 3
11/0 X 14/0 +/-

BR. 2
11/0 X 15/0

DESIGN HPU040407

Square Footage: 2,529
Width: 78'-2" Depth: 50'-2"

DESIGN BY
©R.L. Pfotenhauer

This charming home attracts notice with a beautiful facade including corner quoins, a symmetrical design and a lovely roofline. The floor plan provides comfortable livability. A central great room connects to the breakfast room and galley-style kitchen. A formal dining room, just off the foyer, has a huge wall of windows for elegant dining. A complementary room to the left of the foyer serves as a den or guest bedroom as needed. The owners bedroom features a tray ceiling and wonderfully appointed bath. A family bedroom to the front of the plan has a vaulted ceiling. The plan is completed by a screened porch in the rear.

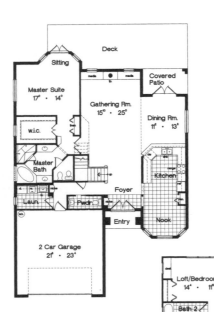

DESIGN HPU040406

First Floor: 1,698 square feet
Second Floor: 848 square feet
Total: 2,546 square feet
Width: 44'-0" Depth: 64'-8"

DESIGN BY
©Home Design Services, Inc.

The gathering room is the heart of this design, and all other spaces move from its core. The large kitchen with a sunny, bayed nook is bathed in light through walls of glass, while the formal dining room has French doors that open onto a private patio. The hub of family activity is the gathering room. It comes complete with a fireplace media wall, which soars two stories with niches and glass transoms. The master suite features a bay-windowed sitting area with a view to the deck area. The bath boasts loads of closet space, and His and Hers vanities flank a soaking tub and shower.

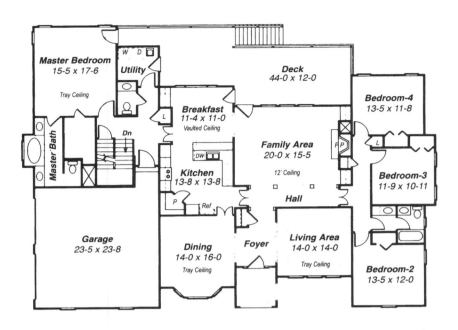

Master Bedroom
15-5 x 17-6
Tray Ceiling

Utility
W D

Master Bath

Dn

Breakfast
11-4 x 11-0
Vaulted Ceiling

Kitchen
13-8 x 13-8
DW

P Ref

Deck
44-0 x 12-0

Family Area
20-0 x 15-5
12' Ceiling

Bedroom-4
13-5 x 11-8

Hall

Bedroom-3
11-9 x 10-11

Garage
23-5 x 23-8

Dining
14-0 x 16-0
Tray Ceiling

Foyer

Living Area
14-0 x 14-0
Tray Ceiling

Bedroom-2
13-5 x 12-0

DESIGN BY
©Jannis Vann & Associates, Inc.

Inside this stylish stucco home, elegant columns separate front-facing, formal living and dining areas from rear-facing, informal living areas. The family room features a twelve-foot ceiling, a fireplace and a door leading to an expansive deck. The kitchen, breakfast room and family room flow together for entertaining ease. Bedrooms are separated for privacy. The secondary bedrooms share a full bath. The secluded master suite features a tray ceiling, large walk-in closet and bumped-out tub with dual vanities.

DESIGN HPU040408

Square Footage: 2,720
Width: 78'-0" Depth: 56'-0"

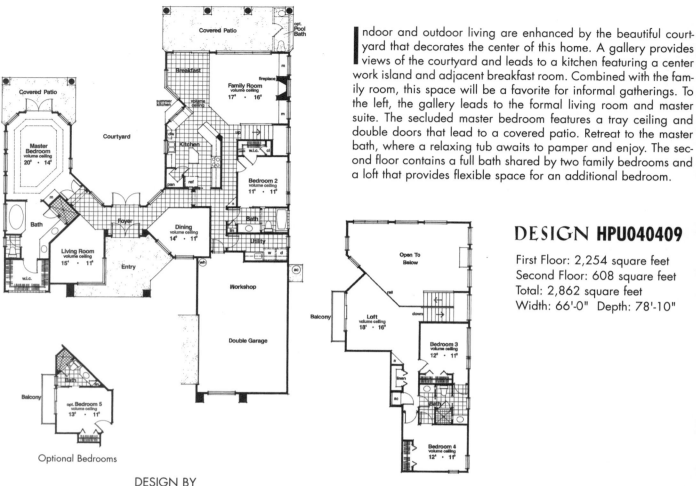

DESIGN BY
©Home Design Services, Inc.

Indoor and outdoor living are enhanced by the beautiful courtyard that decorates the center of this home. A gallery provides views of the courtyard and leads to a kitchen featuring a center work island and adjacent breakfast room. Combined with the family room, this space will be a favorite for informal gatherings. To the left, the gallery leads to the formal living room and master suite. The secluded master bedroom features a tray ceiling and double doors that lead to a covered patio. Retreat to the master bath, where a relaxing tub awaits to pamper and enjoy. The second floor contains a full bath shared by two family bedrooms and a loft that provides flexible space for an additional bedroom.

DESIGN HPU040409

First Floor: 2,254 square feet
Second Floor: 608 square feet
Total: 2,862 square feet
Width: 66'-0"   Depth: 78'-10"

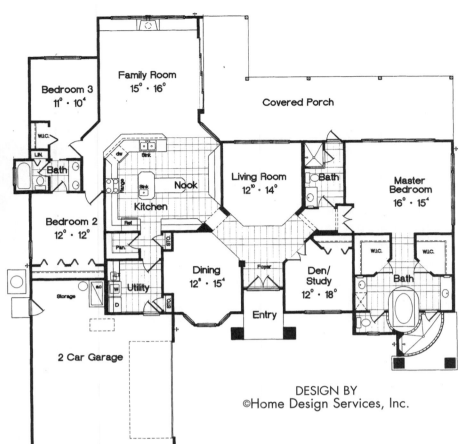

Bedroom 3
11° · 10⁴

Family Room
15° · 16°

Covered Porch

W.I.C.

LIN.

Bath

Nook

Sink

dw

Sink

Kitchen

Living Room
12° · 14°

Bath

Master
Bedroom
16° · 15⁴

Bedroom 2
12° · 12°

Ref

Pan.

STO.

W.I.C.

W.I.C.

Utility

W

AC

D

Dining
12⁸ · 15⁴

Foyer

Den/
Study
12° · 18°

Bath

STO.

Storage

Entry

2 Car Garage

DESIGN BY
©Home Design Services, Inc.

rand Palladian windows create a classic look for this sensational stucco home. A magnificent view from the living room provides unlimited vistas of the rear grounds through a wall of glass, with the nearby dining room completing the formal area. The kitchen, breakfast nook and family room comprise the family wing, coming together to create the perfect place for casual gatherings. Two secondary bedrooms share a bath and provide complete privacy to the master suite, located on the opposite side of the plan. The master bedroom sets the mood for relaxation, and the lavish master bath pampers with a sumptuous soaking tub flanked by a step-down shower and compartmented toilet. Bonus space may be completed at a later date to accommodate additional space requirements.

DESIGN HPU040411

Square Footage: 2,530
Width: 71'-10" Depth: 72'-8"

J.N. HANSEN S.D.G.

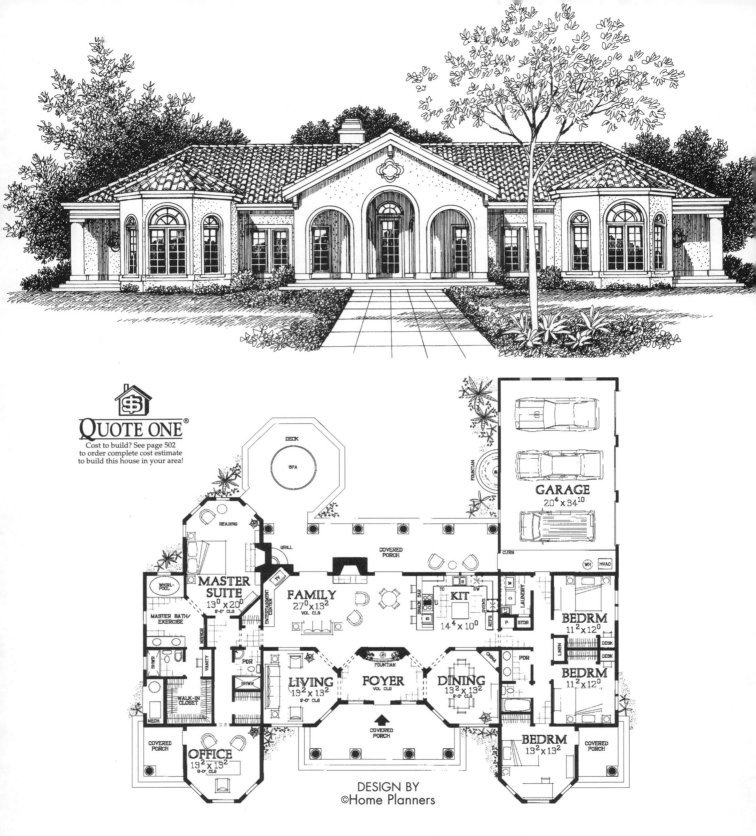

DESIGN BY
©Home Planners

Besides great curb appeal, this home has a wonderful floor plan. The foyer features a fountain that greets visitors and leads to a formal dining room on the right and a living room on the left. A large family room at the rear has a built-in entertainment center and a fireplace. The U-shaped kitchen is perfectly located for servicing all living and dining areas. To the right of the plan, away from the central entertaining spaces, are three family bedrooms sharing a full bath. On the left side, with solitude and comfort for the owners suite are a large sitting area, an office and an amenity-filled bath. Outside the owners suite is a deck with a spa.

DESIGN HPU040412

Square Footage: 2,831
Width: 84'-0" Depth: 77'-0"

DESIGN BY
©Home Planners

Quote One®

Cost to build? See page 502
to order complete cost estimate
to build this house in your area!

Exposed rafter tails, arched porch detailing, massive paneled front doors and stucco exterior walls enhance the western character of this U-shaped ranch house. Double doors open to a spacious, slope-ceilinged art gallery. The quiet sleeping zone is comprised of an entire wing. The extra room at the front of this wing may be used for a den or an office. The family dining and kitchen activities are located at the opposite end of the plan. Indoor-outdoor living relationships are outstanding. The large, open courtyard is akin to the fabled Greek atrium. It is accessible from each of the zones and functions with a covered arbor, which looks out over the rear landscape. The master suite has a generous sitting area, a walk-in closet, twin lavatories, a whirlpool tub and a stall shower.

DESIGN HPU040413

Square Footage: 2,539
Width: 75'-2" Depth: 68'-8"

L

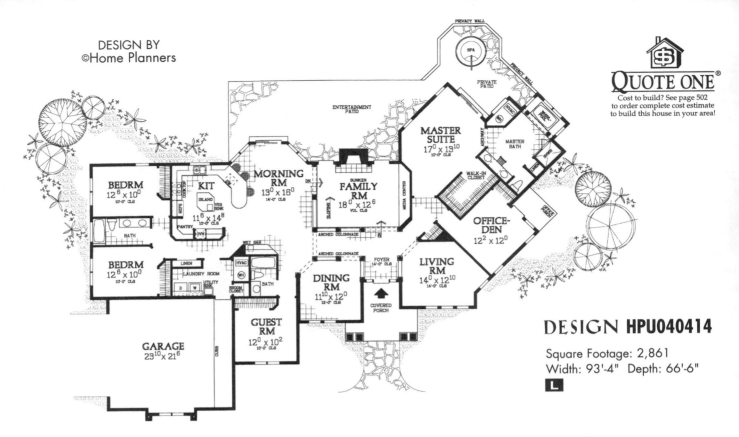

Quote ONE®
Cost to build? See page 502
to order complete cost estimate
to build this house in your area!

DESIGN HPU040414

Square Footage: 2,861
Width: 93'-4" Depth: 66'-6"

L

Double columns and an arched entry create a grand entrance to this elegant one-story home. Inside, arched colonnades add grace and definition to the formal living and dining rooms, as well as the family room. The master suite occupies a separate wing, providing a private retreat. Treat yourself to luxury in the master bath, which includes a bumped-out whirlpool tub, a separate shower and twin vanities. An office/den located nearby easily converts to a nursery. A snack bar provides space for quick meals and separates the island kitchen from the bay-windowed morning room. Three additional bedrooms—one a guest room with an adjacent bath—share two baths.

TIMELESS ELEGANCE

Graceful designs with a new perspective

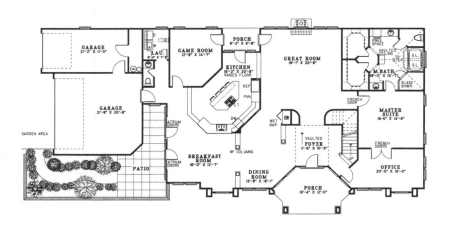

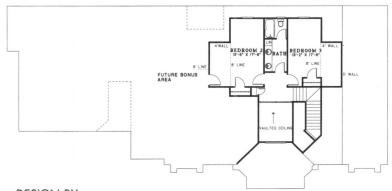

DESIGN BY
©Michael E. Nelson,
Nelson Design Group, LLC

This three-bedroom house was designed to fulfill a passion for windows and columns. Inside, the foyer streams with light from the sunburst transom over the door. To the right is an office with French-door access to the master suite. A sumptuous bath adorns the master suite, complete with His and Hers closets, a glass shower, a garden tub with two skylights and twin-vanity sinks. The great room features a fireplace and views of the rear yard. Columns lend elegant detail to the dining room and separate it from the nearby breakfast room. Beautiful atrium doors in the breakfast room allow views of the side patio. The kitchen and game room feature access to a rear porch, perfect for an outdoor grill. Two bedrooms share a full bath on the second level. Expansion is possible on the second floor. Please specify basement, crawlspace or slab foundation when ordering.

DESIGN HPU040415

First Floor: 2,634 square feet
Second Floor: 757 square feet
Total: 3,391 square feet
Width: 95'-0" Depth: 47'-9"

DESIGN HPU040416

Square Footage: 3,477
Width: 95'-0" Depth: 88'-8"

L

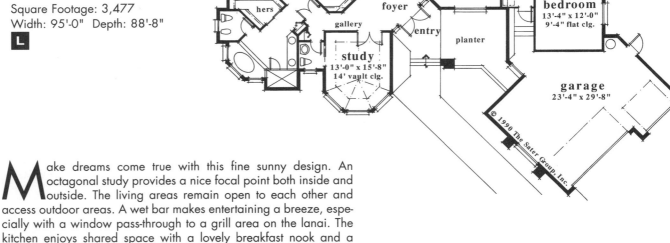

built ins
fireplace

lanai

leisure
23'-0" x 17'-8"
12'-6" flat clg.

nook
10'-8" x 10'-8"
12' step clg.

lanai
30'-0" x 10'-0"

grill

kitchen

bedroom
13'-4" x 13'-8"
9'-4" flat clg.

master
suite
17'-0" x 20'-4"
14' flat clg.

living
15'-0" x 17'-2"
14' flat clg.

wetbar

gallery

am kitchen

2 view fireplace

dining
17'-0" x 13'-0"
14' flat clg.

utility

bedroom
13'-4" x 12'-0"
9'-4" flat clg.

his

hers

foyer

gallery

entry

planter

study
13'-0" x 15'-8"
14' vault clg.

garage
23'-4" x 29'-8"

© 1990 The Sater Group, Inc.

Make dreams come true with this fine sunny design. An octagonal study provides a nice focal point both inside and outside. The living areas remain open to each other and access outdoor areas. A wet bar makes entertaining a breeze, especially with a window pass-through to a grill area on the lanai. The kitchen enjoys shared space with a lovely breakfast nook and a bright leisure room. Two bedrooms are located near the family living center. In the master bedroom suite, luxury abounds with a two-way fireplace, a morning kitchen, two walk-in closets and a compartmented bath. Another full bath accommodates a pool area.

DESIGN BY
©The Sater Design Collection

DESIGN HPU040417

Square Footage: 3,273
Width: 71'-4"
Depth: 77'-0"

This house is in a class all its own. The entry gives way to an impressive living room with a dining room and study radiating from it. The master bedroom suite rests to one side of the plan and includes His and Hers walk-in closets and a luxury bath. A second full bath leads from the sitting area to the outdoors. At the other side of the house, informal living areas open with a kitchen, a breakfast nook and a family leisure area. Two bedrooms here share a full bath and will provide ample space for children or guests.

DESIGN BY
©The Sater Design Collection

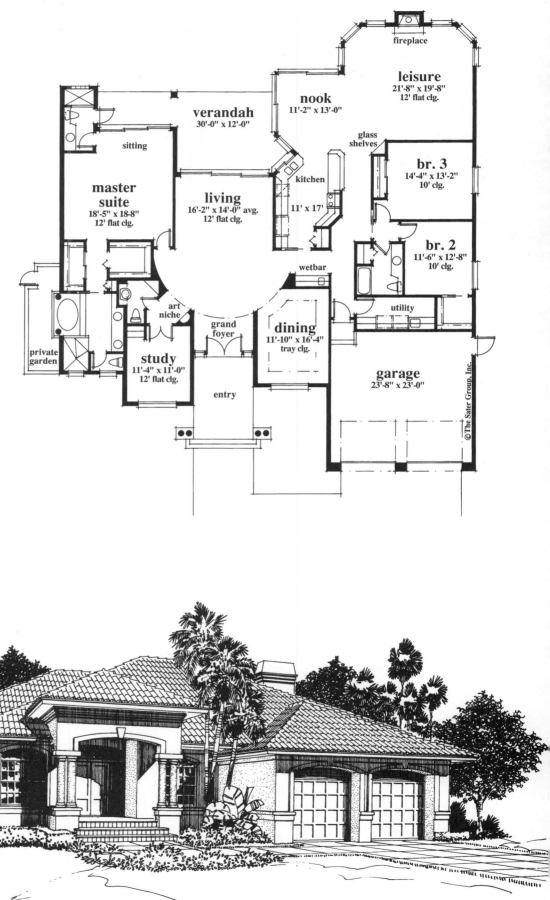

verandah
30'-0" x 12'-0"

sitting

nook
11'-2" x 13'-0"

fireplace

leisure
21'-8" x 19'-8"
12' flat clg.

glass shelves

br. 3
14'-4" x 13'-2"
10' clg.

master suite
18'-5" x 18'-8"
12' flat clg.

living
16'-2" x 14'-0" avg.
12' flat clg.

kitchen
11' x 17'

br. 2
11'-6" x 12'-8"
10' clg.

wetbar

utility

art niche

grand foyer

dining
11'-10" x 16'-4"
tray clg.

private garden

study
11'-4" x 11'-0"
12' flat clg.

entry

garage
23'-8" x 23'-0"

©The Sater Group, Inc.

335

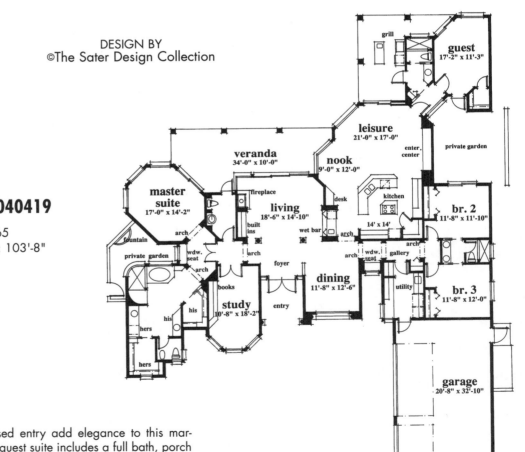

DESIGN HPU040419

Square Footage: 3,265
Width: 80'-0" Depth: 103'-8"

A turret study and a raised entry add elegance to this marvelous stucco home. A guest suite includes a full bath, porch access and a private garden entry, making it perfect for use as an in-law suite. Secondary bedrooms share a full bath. The owners suite has a foyer with a window seat overlooking another private garden and fountain area; the private owners bath holds dual closets, a garden tub and a walk-in shower with curved glass.

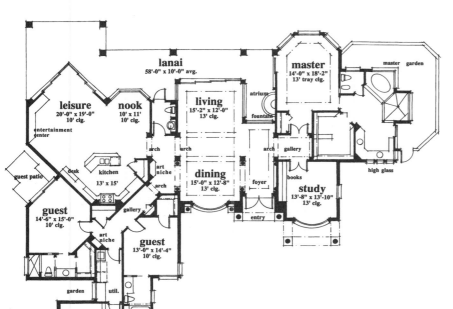

lanai
58'-0" x 10'-0" avg.

leisure
20'-0" x 19'-0"
10' clg.

entertainment
center

nook
10' x 11'
10' clg.

living
15'-2" x 12'-0"
13' clg.

atrium

fountain

master
14'-0" x 18'-2"
13' tray clg.

master garden

guest patio

desk

kitchen
13' x 15'

arch

art
niche

arch

dining
15'-0" x 12'-8"
13' clg.

arch

gallery

books

high glass

guest
14'-6" x 15'-0"
10' clg.

art
niche

gallery

guest
13'-0" x 14'-4"
10' clg.

foyer

entry

study
13'-8" x 13'-10"
13' clg.

garden

util.

garage
22'-0" x 32'-0"

DESIGN HPU040420

Square Footage: 3,244
Width: 90'-0" Depth: 105'-0"

A high, hipped roof and contemporary fanlight windows set the tone for this elegant plan. The grand foyer opens to the formal dining and living rooms that are set apart with arches, highlighted with art niches and framed with walls of windows. Featuring a gourmet kitchen, breakfast nook and leisure room with a built-in entertainment center, the living area has full view of and access to the lanai. Secondary bedrooms are privately situated through a gallery hall, and both include private baths and walk-in closets. The main wing houses a full study and an owners suite with a private garden.

DESIGN BY
©The Sater Design Collection

337

S and-finished stucco, distinctive columns and oversized circle-top windows grace this luxurious three-bedroom home. A sunken living room features a two-sided gas fireplace that it shares with the formal dining room. The family room is also sunken and shares a two-sided fireplace with an indoor spa and a glazed roof overhead. Two secondary bedrooms and a master suite are on the second floor. The master suite enjoys a through-fireplace between the bath and the bedroom.

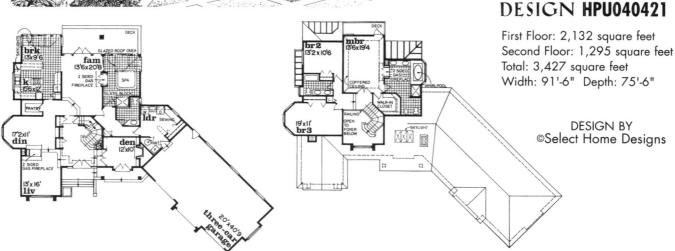

DESIGN HPU040421

First Floor: 2,132 square feet
Second Floor: 1,295 square feet
Total: 3,427 square feet
Width: 91'-6" Depth: 75'-6"

DESIGN BY
©Select Home Designs

T his award-winning design has been recognized for its innovative use of space while continuing to keep family living areas combined for maximum enjoyment. The formal spaces separate the master suite and den/study from family space. The master retreat contains a master bath with His and Hers vanities, a private toilet room and walk-in closet. The perfect touch in this two-story design is the placement of two bedrooms downstairs with two extra bedrooms on the second floor.

DESIGN BY
©Home Design Services, Inc.

DESIGN HPU040422

First Floor: 2,624 square feet
Second Floor: 540 square feet
Total: 3,164 square feet
Width: 66'-0" Depth: 83'-0"

Varying rooflines, arches and corner quoins adorn the facade of this magnificent home. A porte cochere creates a stunning prelude to the double-door entry. A wet bar serves the sunken living room and overlooks the pool area. The dining room has a tray ceiling and is located near the gourmet kitchen with its preparation island and angled counter. A guest room opens off the living room. The generous family room, warmed by a fireplace, opens to the screened patio. The master bedroom has a sitting room and a fireplace that's set into an angled wall. Its luxurious bath includes a step-up tub. Upstairs, two bedrooms share the oversized balcony and nearby observation room.

DESIGN **HPU040423**

First Floor: 2,669 square feet
Second Floor: 621 square feet
Total: 3,290 square feet
Width: 78'-0" Depth: 84'-6"

DESIGN BY
©Home Design Services, Inc.

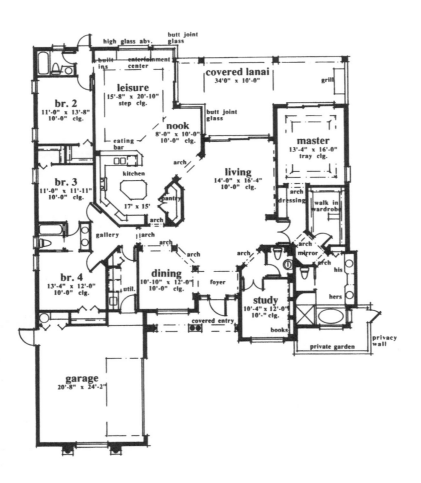

Filled with luxury and special amenities, this stucco beauty offers the best in upscale living. A recessed entry opens to the formal areas: a living room and dining room separated by columns and an arch. For more casual times, look to the leisure room near the island kitchen and nook. A covered lanai lies just outside the living room and the leisure room. The master suite is separated from the three family bedrooms. It contains outstanding closet space and a fine bath with a garden tub. A nearby study has the use of a half-bath. Note that Bedroom 2 has a private bath.

DESIGN HPU040424

Square Footage: 3,036
Width: 63'-10" Depth: 84'-0"

DESIGN BY
©The Sater Design Collection

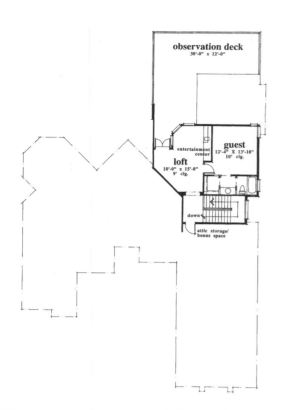

DESIGN BY
©The Sater Design Collection

Two guest suites—one on each floor—enhance the interior of this magnificent stucco home. A grand entrance provides passage to a foyer that opens to the study on the left, the formal dining room on the right and the formal living room straight ahead. The casual living area combines a kitchen with an island cooktop, a sun-filled breakfast nook and a spacious leisure room. Arched openings lead into the owners bedroom and a lavish bath that enjoys a private garden. The second-floor guest suite includes a loft and a large observation deck.

DESIGN HPU040425

First Floor: 2,894 square feet
Second Floor: 568 square feet
Total: 3,462 square feet
Width: 67'-0" Depth: 102'-0"

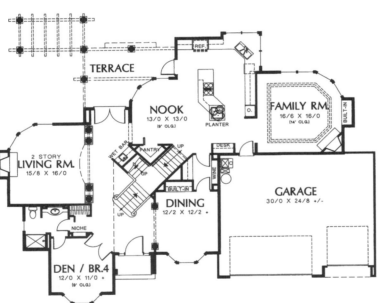

This stucco exterior with shutters and keystone lintels over the entry and windows lends a fresh European charm to this four-bedroom home. A great area for formal entertaining, the two-story living room pleases with its columns, large windows and fireplace. A wet bar furthers the ambience here. Double doors open to a terrace. Informal living takes off in the breakfast nook, kitchen and family room. The upstairs master suite enjoys lots of privacy and a luxurious bath with twin-vanity sinks, a walk-in closet, spa tub and separate shower. The second-floor stairway is exquisite, with three flights joining into one landing and space for plants.

DESIGN HPU040426

First Floor: 1,920 square feet
Second Floor: 1,552 square feet
Total: 3,472 square feet
Bonus Room: 252 square feet
Width: 72'-0" Depth: 55'-0"

L

DESIGN BY
©Alan Mascord Design
Associates, Inc.

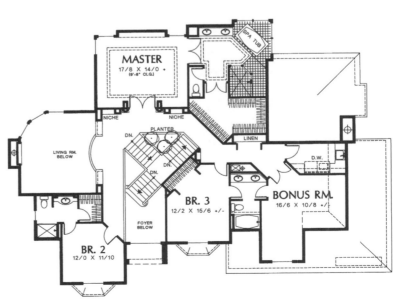

If you have a lot that slopes slightly to the front, this design will accommodate with a garage that is sunken from the main house. The entry is opulent and inviting and opens to a den with a bay window on the left and a formal living room with a fireplace on the right. The family room connects directly to the kitchen and features another fireplace. Three family bedrooms join the master suite on the second floor.

DESIGN HPU040428

First Floor: 1,740 square feet
Second Floor: 1,477 square feet
Total: 3,217 square feet
Bonus Room: 382 square feet
Width: 63'-0" Depth: 52'-0"

DESIGN BY
©Alan Mascord Design
Associates, Inc.

Formal entertaining occurs in the front of this home where the living room, dining room, butler's pantry and powder room are located, while the family enjoys the den and vaulted family room at the rear. The family room features a fireplace, built-in shelves and access to the rear yard. Upstairs, the master suite offers a walk-in closet, a luxurious bath and its own fireplace. Two secondary bedrooms share a compartmented bath and a vaulted loft.

DESIGN BY
©Alan Mascord Design
Associates, Inc.

DESIGN HPU040427

First Floor: 1,698 square feet
Second Floor: 1,644 square feet
Total: 3,342 square feet
Width: 56'-0" Depth: 54'-6"

DESIGN HPU040429

First Floor: 2,375 square feet
Second Floor: 762 square feet
Total: 3,137 square feet
Width: 73'-0" Depth: 64'-6"

L

DESIGN BY
©Alan Mascord Design
Associates, Inc.

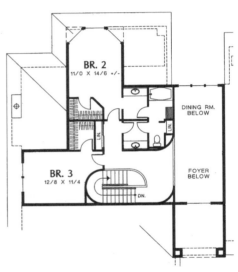

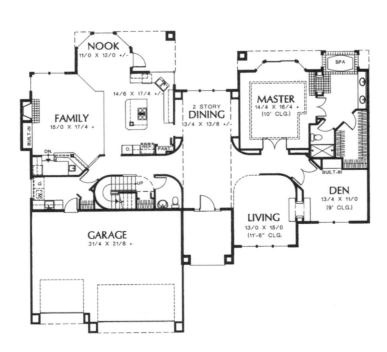

Clean lines, a hipped roof and a high, recessed entry define this sleek, contemporary home. Inside, curved lines add a twist to the well-designed floor plan. For informal entertaining, gather in the multi-windowed family room with its step-down wet bar and warming fireplace. The open kitchen will delight everyone with its center cooktop island, a corner sink and an adjacent breakfast nook. A formal dining room enjoys views of the rear grounds and separates the informal living area from the master wing. Enter the grand master suite through double doors and take special note of the see-through fireplace between the bedroom and bath. A large walk-in closet, a relaxing spa and dual vanities complete the master bath. An additional see-through fireplace is located between the living room and den. Upstairs, two family bedrooms (each with walk-in closets) share a full bath.

DESIGN **HPU040430**

Main Level: 2,300 square feet
Lower Level: 1,114 square feet
Total: 3,414 square feet
Width: 56'-0" Depth: 61'-6"

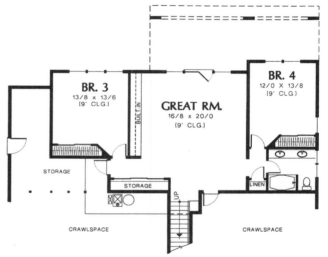

DESIGN BY
©Alan Mascord Design
Associates, Inc.

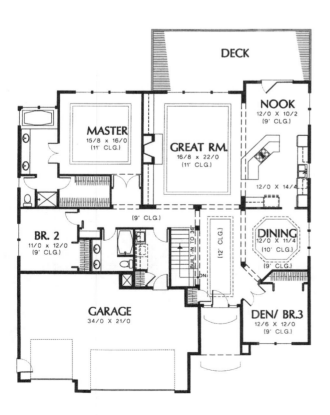

Looking for all the world like a one-story plan, this elegant hillside design has a surprise on the lower level. The main level is reached through an arched, recessed entry that opens to a twelve-foot ceiling. The formal dining room is on the right, next to a cozy den or Bedroom 3. Columns decorate the hall and separate it from the dining room and great room, which contains a tray ceiling and a fireplace flanked by built-ins. The breakfast nook and kitchen are just steps away, on the left. Lower-level space includes another great room with built-ins and two family bedrooms sharing a full bath.

A private guest suite, loft and large bonus room on the second floor enhance the floor plan of this magnificent brick home. A dormered entry featuring a large Palladian window opens the two-story foyer to the dining room on the left. A sunken living area framed by columns is located at the rear of the house. This fire-warmed family space flows into the kitchen and bayed breakfast area opening out to a rear deck. A master suite features a walk-in closet and lavish private bath. Two family bedrooms share a full bath to complete the first floor.

DESIGN BY
©Jannis Vann & Associates, Inc.

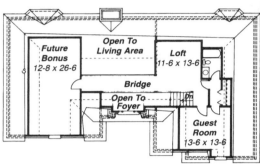

DESIGN HPU040431

First Floor: 2,697 square feet
Second Floor: 360 square feet
Total: 3,057 square feet
Width: 64'-10" Depth: 41'-2"

DESIGN HPU040432

First Floor: 2,469 square feet
Second Floor: 1,025 square feet
Total: 3,494 square feet
Width: 67'-8" Depth: 74'-2"

Cost to build? See page 502
to order complete cost estimate
to build this house in your area!

A lovely double arch gives this European-style home a commanding presence. Once inside, a two-story foyer provides an open view directly through the formal living room to the rear grounds beyond. The private owners suite features dual sinks, twin walk-in closets, a corner garden tub and a separate shower. A second bedroom and a full bath are located nearby. Please specify basement, crawlspace or slab foundation when ordering.

DESIGN BY
©Larry E. Belk Designs

Flower boxes, arches and multi-pane windows all combine to create the elegant facade of this four-bedroom home. Inside, the two-story foyer has a formal dining room to its right and leads to a two-story living room that is filled with light. An efficient kitchen has a bayed breakfast room and shares a snack bar with a cozy family room. Located on the first floor for privacy, the master suite is graced with a luxurious bath. Upstairs, three secondary bedrooms share two full baths and have access to a large game room. For future growth, there is an expandable area accessed through the game room. Please specify basement, crawlspace or slab foundation when ordering.

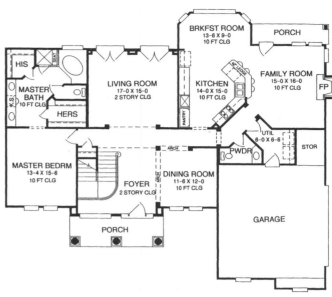

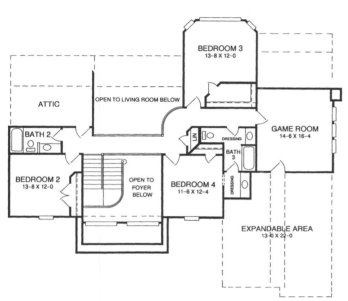

DESIGN HPU040433

First Floor: 1,919 square feet
Second Floor: 1,190 square feet
Total: 3,109 square feet
Width: 64'-6"   Depth: 55'-10"

DESIGN BY
©Larry E. Belk Designs

This country estate is bedecked with all the details that pronounce its French origins. The roofline, in particular, is an outstanding feature and allows high ceilings for interior spaces. Gathering areas are varied and large. They include a study, family room and keeping room. A large porch to the rear can be reached through the breakfast room or the master-suite sitting area. All three bedrooms have walk-in closets.

DESIGN BY
©Andy McDonald Design Group

DESIGN HPU040435

Square Footage: 3,032
Width: 73'-0" Depth: 87'-8"

DESIGN HPU040434

Square Footage: 3,230
Width: 94'-8" Depth: 88'-5"

A mini-estate with French country details, this home preserves the beauty of historical design without sacrificing modern convenience. Through double doors, the floor plan opens from a central foyer flanked by a dining room and a study. The family room offers windows overlooking the rear yard and a fireplace. The owners bedroom suite features a sitting room and bath fit for royalty. A smaller family bedroom has a full bath nearby. A third bedroom also enjoys a full bath.

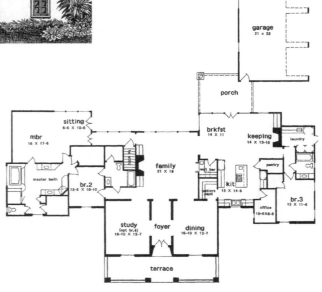

DESIGN BY
©Andy McDonald Design Group

DESIGN HPU040436

First Floor: 2,297 square feet
Second Floor: 977 square feet
Total: 3,274 square feet
Width: 67'-7" Depth: 98'-9"

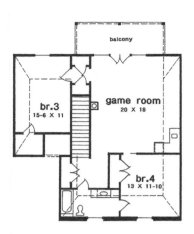

DESIGN BY
©Andy McDonald Design Group

This comfortable French cottage is perfect to raise a family. Inside, the dining room is ready for easy entertaining with access to the front courtyard through a French door or via the foyer door. Nearby, warm up by the family-room fireplace, or watch nature unfold outside through a ribbon of windows. The kitchen enjoys an island workstation and a pantry. Adjoining the kitchen are a keeping room and a breakfast nook. A secondary bedroom with a private bath—perfect as guest quarters—has access to the keeping room. The owners wing ensures luxury and privacy, featuring a fireplace in the bedroom. Upstairs, two additional bedrooms share a bath and access to the game room.

E uropean charm is written all over the facade of this lovely home. A paneled entry, a delicate balustrade and a hipped roof announce a thoughtful plan with an open interior and room to grow. A center island in the kitchen features a cooktop and space for food preparation. Privately located on the first floor, the master suite enjoys a luxurious bath. Three family bedrooms share a full bath on the second level.

DESIGN HPU040437

First Floor: 2,542 square feet
Second Floor: 909 square feet
Total: 3,451 square feet
Width: 74'-0" Depth: 84'-11"

DESIGN BY
©Andy McDonald Design Group

DESIGN HPU040438

Square Footage: 3,039
Width: 73'-8" Depth: 93'-3"

DESIGN BY
©Andy McDonald Design Group

A welcoming double-door glass entrance leads to a home reminiscent of a villa. The side-facing garage visually enlarges the home and provides extra storage at the back. Two fireplaces, in the keeping room and the family room, are a cozy touch. The smaller bedroom located near the luxurious master bedroom could be used for a home office. Two more bedrooms are found on the other side of the plan.

This grand French manor begins with the ultimate in privacy—a walled entry courtyard. Enter the home through double doors in the foyer, or in the study. The family room overlooks the courtyard and is open to the formal dining area. A keeping room, breakfast room and island kitchen form one large informal area to the back of the home. The keeping room has access to another walled courtyard. A large storage area separates the garage from the house. Bedrooms 3 and 4—and an optional Bedroom 5—on the second level share a full bath.

DESIGN **HPU040439**

First Floor: 2,556 square feet
Second Floor: 605 square feet
Total: 3,161 square feet
Width: 64'-4" Depth: 106'-8"

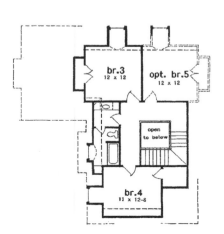

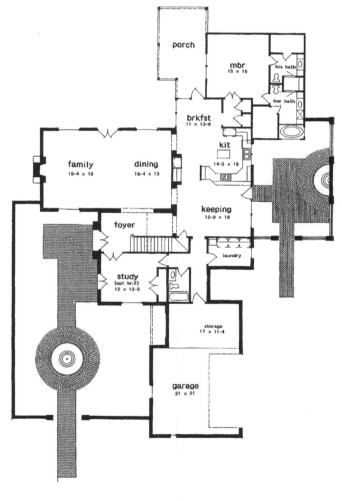

DESIGN BY
©Andy McDonald Design Group

351

DESIGN HPU040440

First Floor: 2,719 square feet
Second Floor: 618 square feet
Total: 3,337 square feet
Width: 47'-6" Depth: 119'-7"

ooks are deceiving in this narrow design that enjoys plenty of room despite its small appearance. The living room opens from the front portico and accesses a covered porch to the rear overlooking the courtyard. A staircase from the family room leads up to two family bedrooms that share a bath but have separate vanities. Open to the family room, the kitchen provides a walk-in pantry, cooktop island and window sink. The study and master bedroom are to the rear of the plan.

DESIGN BY
©Andy McDonald Design Group

A steeply pitched French-style roof and an Italian-inspired, arched, double-door entry create an exterior with international interest. Inside is a thoroughly modern floor plan designed for active families. Upstairs, two family bedrooms share a bathroom. Each has a private vanity area. The children's den is an ideal place to play or study. An additional bedroom upstairs is a space-expanding option in this home. Downstairs, the island kitchen opens to the breakfast nook and keeping room. A nearby family room and dining room combination separates the casual areas from the master bedroom and another bedroom or a study.

DESIGN BY
©Andy McDonald Design Group

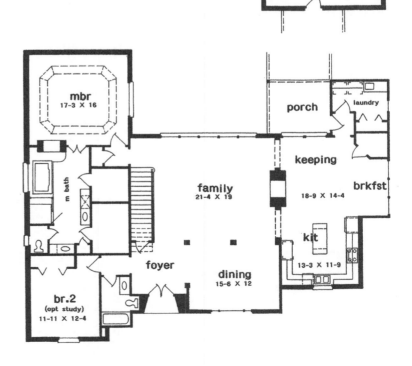

DESIGN HPU040441

First Floor: 2,345 square feet
Second Floor: 663 square feet
Total: 3,008 square feet
Bonus Room: 194 square feet
Width: 62'-10" Depth: 80'-11"

This charming home will have you hooked at first sight. An arch soffit invites guests to the great room. Enjoy the fireplace, built-in cabinets and enormous arched window overlooking the backyard from the great room. The kitchen provides a great use of space with a built-in desk, island and walk-in pantry. The master bedroom features built-in cabinets with French doors that open to the private bathroom.

DESIGN HPU040443

First Floor: 2,508 square feet
Second Floor: 960 square feet
Total: 3,468 square feet
Width: 79'-8" Depth: 70'-0"

DESIGN BY
©Ahmann Design, Inc.

You are sure to fall in love with what this traditional French Country two-story design has to offer. The great room offers a fireplace surrounded by built-in cabinets, a two-story ceiling and striking arched windows. The study will provide you with a corner of the house to yourself with a view out the front and side. The master bedroom enjoys plenty of space and walk-in closets. The master bathroom features a welcoming arch over the bathtub and large shower.

DESIGN BY
©Ahmann Design, Inc.

DESIGN HPU040442

First Floor: 2,514 square feet
Second Floor: 975 square feet
Total: 3,489 square feet
Width: 74'-8" Depth: 64'-8"

An attractive facade and amenity-filled interior make this home a showplace both outside and in. Immediately off the two-story foyer is the living room and formal dining room, both with interesting ceiling details, and the quiet library with built-in bookcases. The enormous gourmet kitchen features a large island work counter/snack bar, pantry, desk and gazebo breakfast room. Just steps away is the spacious family room with a grand fireplace and windows overlooking the backyard. Upstairs are three family bedrooms served by two baths and a luxurious master suite with a bay-windowed sitting room, detailed ceiling and skylit bath with a whirlpool tub.

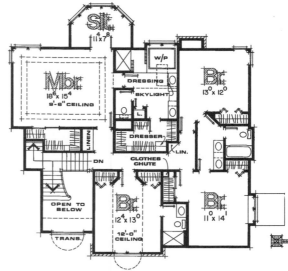

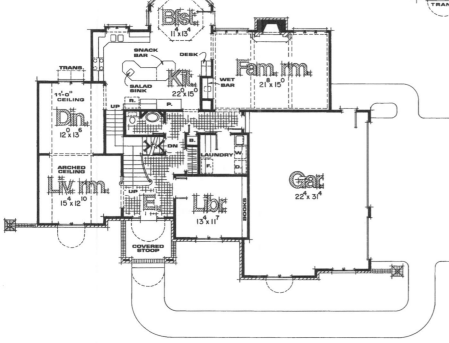

DESIGN HPU040444

First Floor: 1,709 square feet
Second Floor: 1,597 square feet
Total: 3,306 square feet
Width: 62'-0" Depth: 55'-4"

DESIGN BY
©Design Basics, Inc.

DESIGN HPU040446

First Floor: 1,916 square feet
Second Floor: 1,256 square feet
Total: 3,172 square feet
Width: 59'-8" Depth: 60'-10"

DESIGN BY
©Living Concepts Home Planning

This home begins with a recessed cove entry and foyer open to an expanse of living area with views of the deck beyond. The living room features a fireplace with built-in bookcases on either side. The first-floor master suite has a walk-in closet and double vanity. The kitchen with a pantry is adjacent to a breakfast nook with a bay window and a formal dining room. On the second floor, two additional bedrooms share a bath and a recreation room.

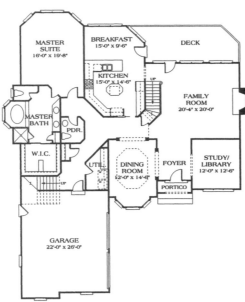

DESIGN BY
©Living Concepts Home Planning

DESIGN HPU040445

First Floor: 2,264 square feet
Second Floor: 1,018 square feet
Total: 3,282 square feet
Bonus Room: 349 square feet
Width: 62'-8" Depth: 76'-4"

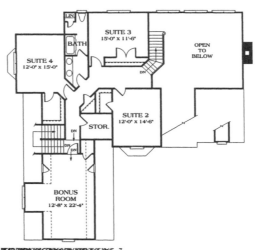

Stunning formal rooms highlight the front of this traditional design. An open foyer leads to a sizable family room, which provides a fireplace. The central gourmet kitchen serves an elegant dining room as well as a breakfast area bright with windows. The master wing features a garden tub, separate shower and double-bowl vanity. Upstairs, three additional bedrooms share a full bath and a hall that leads to a sizable bonus room.

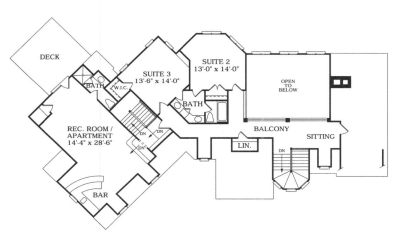

If you've ever dreamed of living in a castle, this could be the home for you. Can't you just see Rapunzel leaning from one of those stepped windows in the turret? The stone-and-stucco exterior could easily come from the French countryside. The interior is also fit for royalty, from the formal dining room to the multi-purpose grand room to the comfortable sitting area off the kitchen. The owners suite has its own fireplace, two walk-in closets and a compartmented bath with dual vanities and a garden tub. Two stairways lead to the second floor. One, housed in the turret, leads to a sitting area and a balcony overlooking the grand room. The balcony leads to two more bedrooms and a recreation room (or apartment) with a deck.

DESIGN HPU040447

First Floor: 2,351 square feet
Second Floor: 866 square feet
Total: 3,217 square feet
Width: 113'-7" Depth: 57'-5"

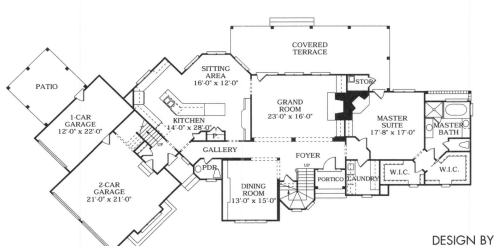

DESIGN BY
©Living Concepts Home Planning

357

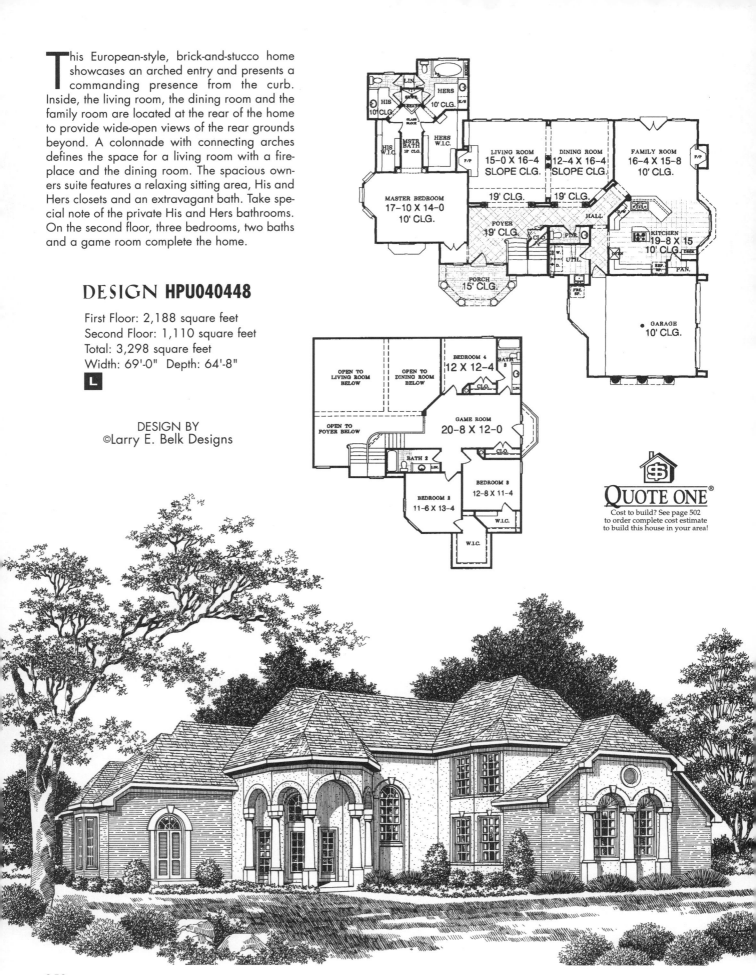

This European-style, brick-and-stucco home showcases an arched entry and presents a commanding presence from the curb. Inside, the living room, the dining room and the family room are located at the rear of the home to provide wide-open views of the rear grounds beyond. A colonnade with connecting arches defines the space for a living room with a fireplace and the dining room. The spacious owners suite features a relaxing sitting area, His and Hers closets and an extravagant bath. Take special note of the private His and Hers bathrooms. On the second floor, three bedrooms, two baths and a game room complete the home.

DESIGN HPU040448

First Floor: 2,188 square feet
Second Floor: 1,110 square feet
Total: 3,298 square feet
Width: 69'-0" Depth: 64'-8"

L

DESIGN BY
©Larry E. Belk Designs

QUOTE ONE®
Cost to build? See page 502
to order complete cost estimate
to build this house in your area!

An almost cathedral-like presence dominates this palatial facade. Its thick tower and the pointed glass above the front door inspire reverence. The floor plan is anything but church-austere, however. No luxury was left out. The large family room hosts both formal and informal gatherings and connects to the sheltered breakfast room and island kitchen. A bayed dining room rises to the more formal occasion. A master suite that you might have designed for yourself is secluded on the main level. Three family bedrooms are joined by a game room upstairs.

KITCHEN
12'-8" X 18'-4"

PANTRY
10' CH

UTILITY

DOWN TO BASEMENT

F W D

Optional Basement
Stair Location

PORCH

BREAKFAST
12'-0" X 10'-0"
10' CH

MASTER BEDROOM
19'-4" X 15'-4"
10' CH

FP

FAMILY ROOM
15'-4" X 19'-4"
10' CH

KITCHEN
12'-8" X 18'-4"

UP

PANTRY

10' CH

W.I.C.

HALL

UTILITY

F W D

3-CAR GARAGE
27'-2" X 21'-0"
10' CH

WHIRLPOOL

MASTER
BATH
10' CH

PWDR

UP

W.I.C.

LIN

STUDY
11'-0" X 11'-0"
12' CH

ENTRY
20' CH

PORCH

DINING ROOM
13'-0" X 15'-4"
10' CH

STORAGE

SUN DECK

BEDROOM 3
14'-0" X 12'-4"
9' CH

GAME ROOM
15'-0" X 19'-8"
9' CH

W.I.C.

BATH

W.I.C.

LIN

BEDROOM 4
13'-4" X 11'-4"
9' CH

DN

BATH

HALL

DN

OPEN TO BELOW

W.I.C.

BEDROOM 2
13'-0" X 13'-4"
9' CH

DESIGN HPU040449

First Floor: 2,117 square feet
Second Floor: 1,206 square feet
Total: 3,323 square feet
Width: 83'-11" Depth: 56'-11"

DESIGN BY
©Design Basics, Inc.

The informal ambience of English Tudor style is reflected in this European mini-estate. A brick, stucco and half-timber exterior, combined with shake shingles on a roof with dramatically curved eaves, provide the appropriate finish materials. Add to this the multi-pane windows and a pigeonnaire on the garage, and the beauty of this Old World-style home is complete. Elegance prevails inside as well, beginning with the wide entry gallery and continuing through the spacious living room, beam-ceilinged dining room, kitchen and morning room. The main-level master suite enjoys a quiet study nearby for reflective moments. Designed for a rear sloping lot, this home includes a lower-level game room, two bedrooms, a full bath and lots of storage space.

DESIGN BY
©R.L. Pfotenhauer

DESIGN HPU040450

Main Level: 2,087 square feet
Lower Level: 1,027 square feet
Total: 3,114 square feet
Width: 107'-2" Depth: 71'-9"

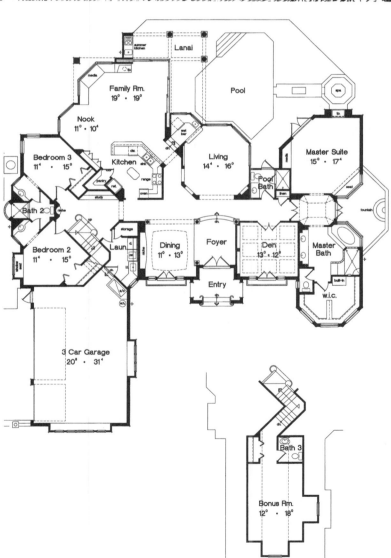

DESIGN HPU040451

Square Footage: 3,064
Bonus Room: 366 square feet
Width: 79'-6" Depth: 91'-0"

From a more graceful era, this 1½-story estate evokes the sense of quiet refinement. Exquisite exterior detailing makes it a one-of-a-kind. Inside are distinctive treatments that make the floor plan unique and functional. The central foyer is enhanced with columns that define the dining room and formal living room. A beam ceiling complements the den. An indulgent master suite includes a private garden with a fountain, pool access, a large walk-in closet and a fireplace to the outdoor spa. Family bedrooms share an unusual compartmented bath. The kitchen and family room are completed with a breakfast nook. Pool access and a lanai with a summer kitchen make this area a natural for casual lifestyles. A bonus area over the garage can become a home office or game room.

DESIGN BY
©Home Design Services, Inc.

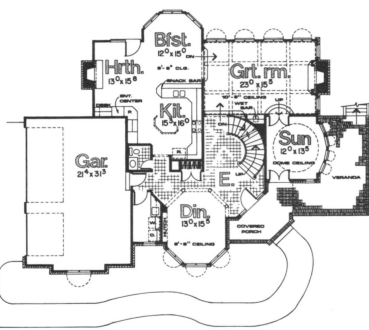

DESIGN BY
©Design Basics, Inc.

DESIGN HPU040452

First Floor: 1,719 square feet
Second Floor: 1,688 square feet
Total: 3,407 square feet
Width: 62'-0" Depth: 55'-4"

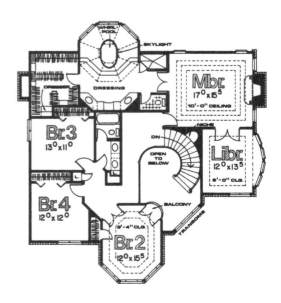

Two-story bays, luminous windows and brick details embellish this stately, traditional castle. Wouldn't you love to call it home? Inside, the soaring foyer is angled to provide impressive views of the spectacular curving staircase and columns that define the octagonal dining room. Although hard to choose, this home's most outstanding feature may be the sun room, which is crowned with a dome ceiling and lit with a display of bowed windows. This room gives access to the multi-windowed great room and an expansive veranda. A cozy hearth room, a breakfast room and an oversized kitchen complete the casual living area. The sumptuous master suite features a fireplace, a library and an opulent master bath with a gazebo ceiling and a skylight above the magnificent whirlpool tub. Three secondary bedrooms, one with a dramatic French-door balcony overlooking the foyer, and a full hall bath complete the second floor.

This two-story home features the old-fashioned look of a turn-of-the-century home mixed with a modern design. A courtyard is beautifully decorated with a combination of brick and stone for a traditional look. The great room has a two-story ceiling with a fireplace. The nook is open to the kitchen with a magnificent wood deck in front, and a screened porch to the right, ideal for enjoying the beautiful outdoor weather. The master suite has a wonderful bathroom, complete with a hot tub. Upstairs you'll appreciate the view of both the foyer and family room below as you cross the hall to any of the three bedrooms. You'll also enjoy the three-and-a-half-car garage, just right for your automobiles and recreational vehicles.

DESIGN HPU040453

First Floor: 2,224 square feet
Second Floor: 885 square feet
Total: 3,109 square feet
Width: 91'-8" Depth: 66'-8"

DESIGN BY
©Ahmann Design, Inc.

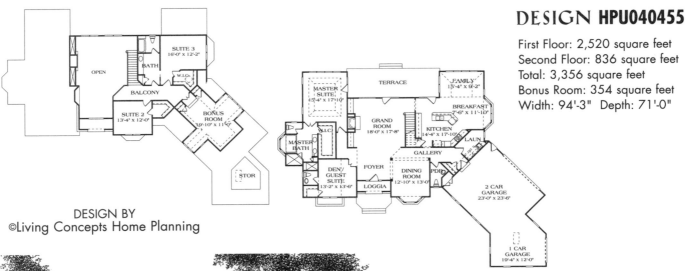

DESIGN HPU040455

First Floor: 2,520 square feet
Second Floor: 836 square feet
Total: 3,356 square feet
Bonus Room: 354 square feet
Width: 94'-3" Depth: 71'-0"

DESIGN BY
©Living Concepts Home Planning

This stunning stucco exterior is enhanced by corner quoins and a two-story recessed entry accented with decorative stonework. The grand room and formal dining room form a large open area warmed by a fireplace and brightened by a metal-roofed bay window in front and windows and doors overlooking the rear terrace. Upstairs, two family bedrooms share a compartmented bath and a balcony overlook. A bonus room offers room for later expansion.

DESIGN HPU040454

First Floor: 2,398 square feet
Second Floor: 657 square feet
Total: 3,055 square feet
Bonus Room: 374 square feet
Width: 72'-8" Depth: 69'-1"

DESIGN BY
©Living Concepts Home Planning

European formality meets a bold American spirit in this splendid transitional plan. The library features a sloped ceiling and an arched window, and would make an excellent home office or guest suite. The deluxe owners suite uses defining columns between the bedroom and the lavish bath. Two secondary bedrooms share a bath upstairs. Please specify basement or crawlspace foundation when ordering.

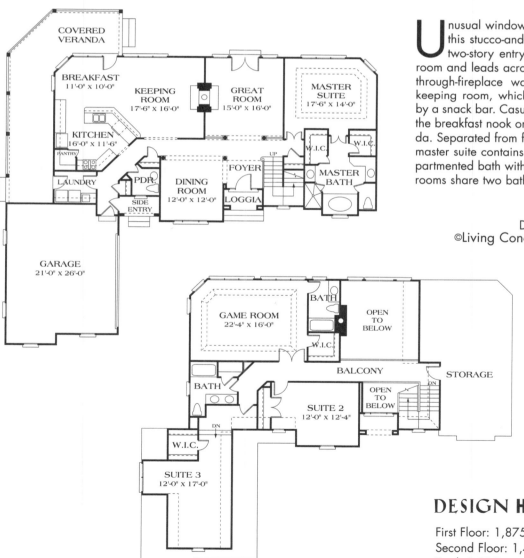

COVERED VERANDA

BREAKFAST
11'-0" x 10'-0"

KEEPING ROOM
17'-6" x 16'-0"

GREAT ROOM
15'-0" x 16'-0"

MASTER SUITE
17'-6" x 14'-0"

KITCHEN
16'-0" x 11'-6"

PANTRY

W.I.C.

W.I.C.

LAUNDRY

PDR.

FOYER

MASTER BATH

SIDE ENTRY

DINING ROOM
12'-0" x 12'-0"

UP

LOGGIA

GARAGE
21'-0" x 26'-0"

Unusual window treatments are a nice touch on this stucco-and-stone exterior. Inside the grand two-story entry, the foyer opens to the dining room and leads across the hall to the great room. A through-fireplace warms the great room and the keeping room, which is separated from the kitchen by a snack bar. Casual meals can also be enjoyed in the breakfast nook or taken out to the covered veranda. Separated from family bedrooms for privacy, the master suite contains two walk-in closets and a compartmented bath with two vanities. Two upstairs bedrooms share two baths and a game room.

DESIGN BY
©Living Concepts Home Planning

GAME ROOM
22'-4" x 16'-0"

BATH

OPEN TO BELOW

W.I.C.

BALCONY

STORAGE

BATH

OPEN TO BELOW

DN

SUITE 2
12'-0" x 12'-4"

DN

W.I.C.

SUITE 3
12'-0" x 17'-0"

DESIGN HPU040456

First Floor: 1,875 square feet
Second Floor: 1,440 square feet
Total: 3,315 square feet
Width: 71'-4" Depth: 66'-4"

DESIGN HPU040457

First Floor: 2,085 square feet
Second Floor: 1,234 square feet
Total: 3,319 square feet
Bonus Room: 323 square feet
Width: 63'-10" Depth: 62'-11"

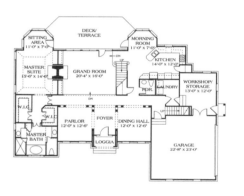

A grand two-story entry, echoed on the garage, and a prominent chimney provide vertical accents to this massive stucco-and-stone home. A gallery hall follows the outline of the sunken grand room, which features a fireplace and access to a deck. Bedrooms include a guest suite on the first floor, a manor-sized master suite and two family bedrooms.

Designed for active lifestyles, this home caters to homeowners who enjoy dinner guests, privacy, luxurious surroundings and open spaces. The foyer, parlor and dining hall are defined by sets of columns. The grand room opens to the deck/terrace, which is also accessed from the sitting area and morning room. The left wing of the plan is dominated by the owners suite with its sitting bay, fireplace, two walk-in closets and compartmented bath.

DESIGN HPU040458

First Floor: 2,198 square feet
Second Floor: 1,028 square feet
Total: 3,226 square feet
Bonus Room: 466 square feet
Width: 72'-8" Depth: 56'-6"

DECK

MASTER SUITE
16'-0" x 18'-0"

GATHERING ROOM
17'-0" x 18'-6"

BREAKFAST
12'-2" x 8'-0"

KITCHEN
12'-2" x 13'-0"

PANT.

REF.

W.I.C.

MASTER BATH

PDR.

FOYER

DINING ROOM
12'-2" x 13'-6"

UP.

LIN.

LAUNDRY

LOGGIA

GARAGE
21'-6" x 21'-0"

DESIGN BY
©Living Concepts Home Planning

SUITE 3
18'-6" x 14'-0"

OPEN TO BELOW

SUITE 4
12'-2" x 12'-6"

CLOS.

BATH

LIN.

BALCONY

CLOS.

LIN.

BATH

SUITE 2
13'-0" x 14'-0"

DN

OPEN TO BELOW

CLOS.

CLOS.

CLOS.

PDR.

ATTIC

BONUS ROOM
13'-2" x 18'-6"

ATTIC

ATTIC

DESIGN HPU040459

First Floor: 1,846 square feet
Second Floor: 1,249 square feet
Total: 3,095 square feet
Bonus Room: 394 square feet
Width: 52'-2" Depth: 66'-2"

A striking cove entrance sets the tone for this well-planned, two-story traditional design. Inside, the foyer leads directly into the imposing gathering room, open to the second floor, with double-door access to the large rear deck. To the right, the efficient kitchen is nestled between a formal dining room and breakfast nook. The master bedroom suite has a garden bath and large walk-in closet, plus direct access to the deck. Three additional bedrooms are arranged upstairs off the long balcony overlooking the gathering room. Two full baths and a large bonus room with a half-bath are also on this level.

DINING RM.
13'-8"x15'-2"

KITCHEN
14'-10"x 13'-0"

COUNTER

NOOK
12'-0"x13'-0"
(+ BAY)

FAMILY ROOM
20'-10"x15'-0"
(VAULTED CEILING)

FP

BOOKS

BOOKS

RAIL

FLAGSTONE TERRACE

PANTRY

OVEN BC

DN

W D

UTILITY

FP

LIVING ROOM
19'-4"x 13'-8"

ENTRY
12'-3"x13'-0"

PR

STUDY
13'-8"x11'-0"
(+ BAY)

GARAGE
23'-4"x31'-8"

DESIGN HPU040460

First Floor: 1,853 square feet
Second Floor: 1,342 square feet
Total: 3,195 square feet
Width: 68'-3" Depth: 50'-8"

DESIGN BY
©R.L. Pfotenhauer

BEDROOM 3
12'-0"x 12'-9"

BEDROOM 2
12'-5"x 11'-6"

SHWR

SHELVES

MR. BATH
& DRSG

GLASS BLOCKS

WH'POOL
TUB

BATH 2

SH.

WIC

LINENS

SH.

WIC

BEDROOM 4
13'-8"x11'-6"

DN

(OPEN TO
ENTRY)

MR BEDROOM
13'-8"x19'-2"
(VAULTED CEILING)

The repetition of cornice returns and brick arches creates an appealing pattern, while numerous windows add an airy feel. A spacious family room with a fireplace and built-in shelves occupies the right side of the plan. To the left of the family room, the L-shaped kitchen with a cooktop island serves both formal and informal dining areas. Light will stream through the bay window in the breakfast nook. Upstairs, the owners suite provides two walk-in closets and a whirlpool tub. Also on the second floor, three family bedrooms share a full bath.

T his brick two-story home makes an elegant statement with a full-facade entry, columns and keystone lintels. Inside, the two-story foyer greets guests with a formal dining room defined with columns. To the left of the foyer, double doors lead to the private library, and a short hallway nearby accesses the master suite. This suite enjoys its own private wing, with a striking bay-window view of the rear gardens and a lavish bathroom. The kitchen and breakfast room enjoy another bay-window view of the backyard, at the right of the plan. On the second floor, three secondary bedrooms, two full baths and a bonus room complete this design.

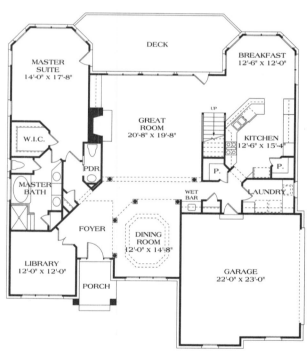

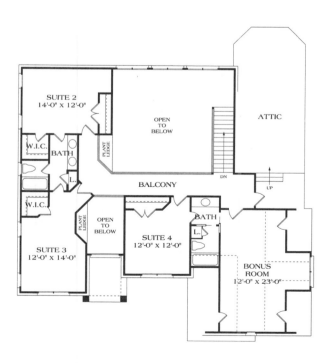

DESIGN HPU040461

First Floor: 2,048 square feet
Second Floor: 1,081 square feet
Total: 3,129 square feet
Bonus Room: 332 square feet
Width: 55'-0" Depth: 61'-8"

DESIGN BY
©Living Concepts Home Planning

369

DESIGN HPU040462

First Floor: 2,461 square feet
Second Floor: 1,019 square feet
Total: 3,480 square feet
Width: 74'-0" Depth: 79'-6"

DESIGN BY
©Design Basics, Inc.

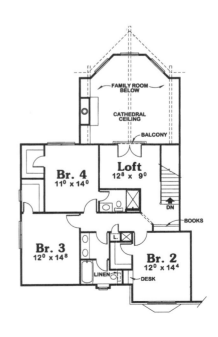

A bay window, an arched entry and a single-story turret display the elegance shown throughout this plan. An elevated entry gives a view of the dining room past an open railing. French doors centered in the great room lead outside, and a second set of French doors opens to the family room, where twin entertainment centers encase the fireplace. An atrium door opens from this room to the outdoors. The functional kitchen offers a large cooktop island and snack bar and views the adjacent breakfast room through three arched openings. The owners suite, with a private bath in the turret, occupies the right side of the plan. A loft on the second floor works well as a computer center and features double doors that open to overlook the family room below. One secondary bedroom has a private bath, while two bedrooms share a bath.

Multi-pane windows and a massive arched entry welcome you to this attractive brick home. Inside, the foyer leads directly to the family room, with its eye-catching corner fireplace. Perfect for formal entertaining as well as family relaxing, this room is convenient to both the dining room at the front and the sunny bayed breakfast nook at the rear of the plan. The roomy patio will be a popular gathering place for guests and family alike. The island kitchen is ideally situated to serve all areas of the home. For privacy, a guest suite is set by itself to the left of the house, and a quiet study may be found at the front. Upstairs, the master suite beckons, with lots of windows, a massive walk-in closet and a pampering bath. Three family bedrooms and an unfinished area complete the plan. Please specify crawlspace or slab foundation when ordering.

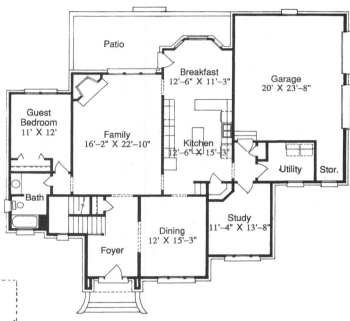

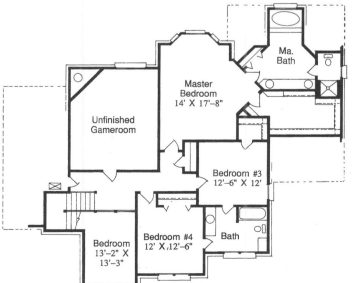

DESIGN HPU040463

First Floor: 1,775 square feet
Second Floor: 1,345 square feet
Total: 3,120 square feet
Bonus Room: 262 square feet
Width: 62'-4" Depth: 54'-10"

DESIGN BY
©Chatham Home Planning, Inc.

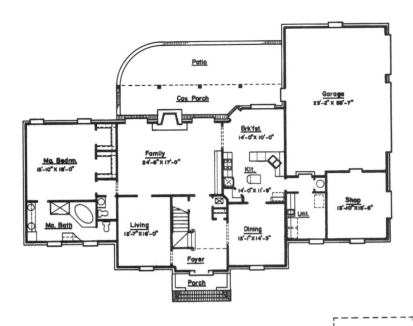

Luxury is highly evident in this fine brick mansion. The master bedroom suite is one example of this, with its two walk-in closets, huge bedroom area and lavish bath. Another example of luxury is the four secondary bedrooms upstairs, with access to a private study. Take note of the spacious family room, complete with a fireplace and access to the rear covered patio. The island kitchen is sure to please, serving with ease the formal dining room or the sunny breakfast room. The three-car garage will easily shelter the family fleet.

DESIGN HPU040464

First Floor: 2,190 square feet
Second Floor: 1,418 square feet
Total: 3,608 square feet
Width: 84'-10" Depth: 61'-10"

DESIGN BY
©Chatham Home Planning, Inc.

This stunning stucco mansion, with corner quoins and an elegant entrance, is sure to be a family favorite. The two-story foyer is flanked by the formal living and dining rooms and presents a graceful staircase to the upper level. A sunken family room features a fireplace and direct access to the rear sun deck. Light flows from bay windows into the breakfast room. Upstairs, a lavish master suite waits to pamper the homeowner, while three secondary bedrooms share two baths and access to a huge bonus room. Please specify basement, crawlspace or slab foundation when ordering.

DESIGN BY
©Jannis Vann & Associates, Inc.

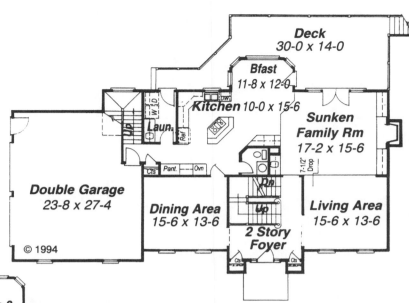

Deck
30-0 x 14-0

Bfast
11-8 x 12-0

Kitchen 10-0 x 15-6

Sunken Family Rm
17-2 x 15-6

Laun.

Double Garage
23-8 x 27-4

© 1994

Dining Area
15-6 x 13-6

2 Story Foyer

Living Area
15-6 x 13-6

7-1/2" Drop

Pant. Ovn

Bdrm 2
11-4 x 15-6

Bdrm-3
11-4 x 11-6

Bath 2

M. Bath

Bonus Room
14-4 x 27-4

Bath 3

Bdrm-4
13-2 x 13-6

2 Story Foyer

Master Bedroom
15-6 x 17-6

DESIGN HPU040465

First Floor: 1,553 square feet
Second Floor: 1,477 square feet
Total: 3,030 square feet
Bonus Room: 397 square feet
Width: 72'-4" Depth: 48'-0"

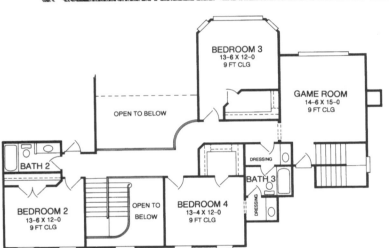

BEDROOM 3
13-6 X 12-0
9 FT CLG

GAME ROOM
14-6 X 15-0
9 FT CLG

OPEN TO BELOW

BATH 2

DRESSING

BATH 3

BEDROOM 2
13-6 X 12-0
9 FT CLG

OPEN TO BELOW

BEDROOM 4
13-4 X 12-0
9 FT CLG

DRESSING

DESIGN HPU040466

First Floor: 2,055 square feet
Second Floor: 1,229 square feet
Total: 3,284 square feet
Width: 65'-0" Depth: 60'-10"

Colonial character mingles with country charm and Greek Revival elegance in this roomy four-bedroom home. A two-story foyer cheerfully introduces the elegant dining room with its tray ceiling. Across from the foyer, the light-filled living room features twin French doors accessing the rear yard. Located on the first floor, the master suite enjoys a luxury bathroom with a garden tub, a separate shower, His and Hers walk-in closets and twin vanity sinks. The kitchen, break-fast room and family room share an open area and access to a powder room near the garage. The second level includes three secondary bed-rooms, two bathrooms and a game room.

DESIGN BY
©Larry E. Belk Designs

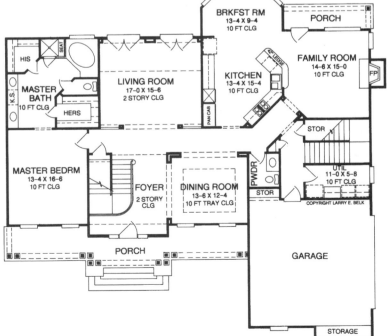

BRKFST RM
13-4 X 9-4
10 FT CLG

PORCH

HIS

SEAT

MASTER
BATH
10 FT CLG

K.S.

HERS

LIVING ROOM
17-0 X 15-6
2 STORY CLG

KITCHEN
13-4 X 15-4
10 FT CLG

FAMILY ROOM
14-6 X 15-0
10 FT CLG

FP

PAN CAB

STOR

MASTER BEDRM
13-4 X 16-6
10 FT CLG

FOYER
2 STORY
CLG

DINING ROOM
13-6 X 12-4
10 FT TRAY CLG

PWDR

STOR

UTIL
11-0 X 5-8
10 FT CLG

COPYRIGHT LARRY E. BELK

PORCH

GARAGE

STORAGE

This two-story brick home is reminiscent of an early American design. From the efficiency of the extraordinary floor plan to the elegance of the custom trims and wood details, this home's timeless value is artistically showcased. The flow of the first floor creates ease of entertaining guests in the formal living room and dining room areas, while a comfortable and inviting atmosphere for family enjoyment exists in the kitchen and spacious hearth room. A fireplace, built-in entertainment center and custom wood ceiling treatment help to create a warm, cozy effect. Wood rails and newel posts decorate the stairs leading to a separate wing on the mid-level, offering children's bedrooms and a computer space. Continuing to the upper level, the master bedroom suite with its sitting area, fireplace and deluxe bath/dressing room combine to create a fabulous retreat.

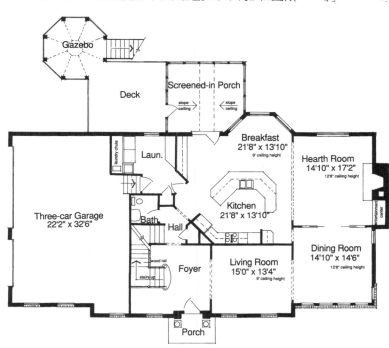

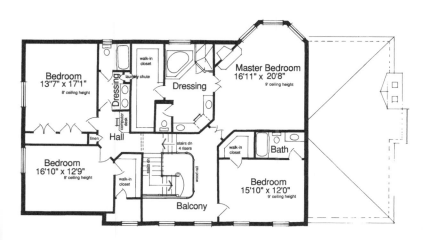

DESIGN HPU040467

First Floor: 1,666 square feet
Second Floor: 1,779 square feet
Total: 3,445 square feet
Width: 71'-8" Depth: 38'-10"

DESIGN BY
©Studer Residential Designs, Inc.

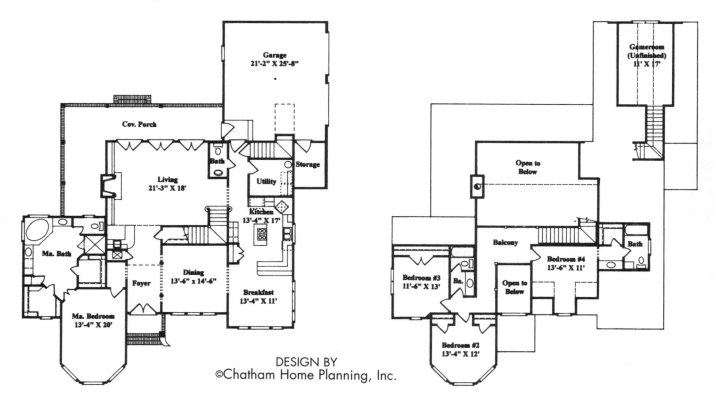

DESIGN BY
©Chatham Home Planning, Inc.

A graceful tower enhances the facade of this delightful four-bedroom home. Once inside, columns define the formal dining room, while directly ahead is the spacious living room, complete with a fireplace and built-ins. The kitchen enjoys an island cooktop and a window over the sink. Light streams into both the kitchen and breakfast room from numerous windows. Luxury can be found in abundance in the master suite. Here, two walk-in closets, a separate tub and shower, and two vanities wait to pamper the homeowner. Upstairs is the sleeping zone, which includes three bedrooms—one with its own bath.

DESIGN HPU040468

First Floor: 2,095 square feet
Second Floor: 928 square feet
Total: 3,023 square feet
Bonus Room: 223 square feet
Width: 66'-0" Depth: 76'-3"

DESIGN HPU040469

First Floor: 1,812 square feet
Second Floor: 1,300 square feet
Total: 3,112 square feet
Width: 35'-0" Depth: 88'-0"

DESIGN BY
©Authentic Historical Designs, Inc.

Characteristics of Greek Revival architecture enliven the exterior of this four-bedroom home. The dining-room entrance is framed by a pair of square columns. The foyer leads to a large great room and also to a cozy keeping room off the kitchen. The kitchen has a large walk-in pantry and a sunny breakfast area that looks out onto a private courtyard. The downstairs master suite is tucked quietly away from the noise of family life. On the second level, a large sitting room and activity area overlooks the kitchen below, enabling the family cook to stay involved in the family fun. Three family bedrooms and two full bathrooms complete this floor.

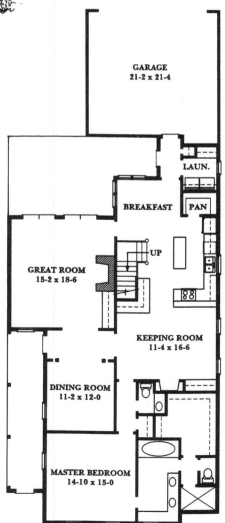

GARAGE
21-2 x 21-4

LAUN.

BREAKFAST   PAN

GREAT ROOM
15-2 x 18-6

UP

KEEPING ROOM
11-4 x 16-6

DINING ROOM
11-2 x 12-0

MASTER BEDROOM
14-10 x 15-0

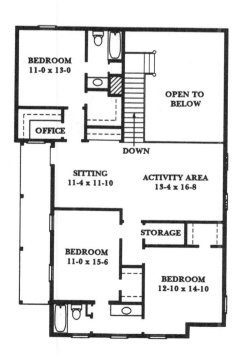

BEDROOM
11-0 x 13-0

OPEN TO
BELOW

OFFICE

DOWN

SITTING
11-4 x 11-10

ACTIVITY AREA
13-4 x 16-8

STORAGE

BEDROOM
11-0 x 15-6

BEDROOM
12-10 x 14-10

This grand Georgian home has a double-door entry topped by a beautiful arched window. Inside, the foyer opens to the two-story living room, which has a wide bow window overlooking the rear property. Double doors open to a study warmed by a fireplace. The kitchen features a walk-in pantry and serves both the formal dining room and the breakfast area, which adjoins the bright keeping room. The owners suite, secluded on the first floor, is large and opulent. Three more bedrooms and two baths are upstairs for family and friends.

DESIGN HPU040470

First Floor: 2,253 square feet
Second Floor: 890 square feet
Total: 3,143 square feet
Width: 61'-6" Depth: 64'-0"

DESIGN BY
©Archival Designs, Inc.

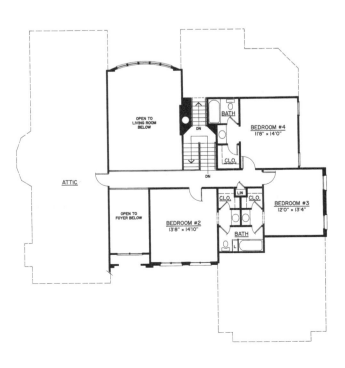

What better way to start—or even to end—your day than in the beautiful octagonal breakfast room within this masterful design? It opens to a curved island kitchen, with plenty of room for even the messiest of cooks and to the cozy family room, which provides access, via French doors, to the outside and shares a fireplace with the front parlor. A formal dining room and a powder room complete the fist floor. On the second floor, the master bedroom offers a romantic octagonal design, as well as a fireplace in the large sitting area. It also includes a luxurious master bath with twin walk-in closets. Two family bedrooms with walk-in closets share a full bath, while another bedroom features its own private bath.

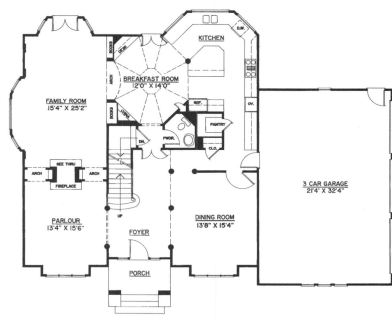

DESIGN HPU040471

First Floor: 1,597 square feet
Second Floor: 1,859 square feet
Total: 3,456 square feet
Width: 62'-0" Depth: 46'-0"

DESIGN BY
©Archival Designs, Inc.

DESIGN HPU040472

First Floor: 1,768 square feet
Second Floor: 1,436 square feet
Total: 3,204 square feet
Width: 77'-8" Depth: 64'-8"

DESIGN BY
©Ahmann Design, Inc.

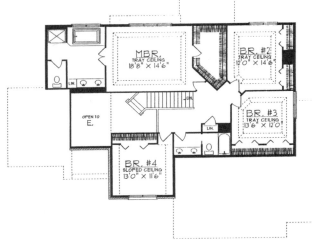

This exquisite, luxurious, brick two-story home is filled with dramatic amenities. You are welcomed by a uniquely shaped foyer that has ceilings that extend two stories. There is a formal living and dining room that flows into the amazing entryway. Double doors access the study. The kitchen is every chef's dream; it is spacious and well-designed, and it features a center island and nook where you can venture to the screened porch through splendid French doors. The family room is cozy and comfortable. The fireplace is surrounded by beautifully constructed built-in cabinets. A mud/laundry room is just off the garage. The second floor has three bedrooms and a master suite—all have detailed ceiling designs. There is a full bath with a double vanity, a whirlpool tub and a walk-in shower in the master suite.

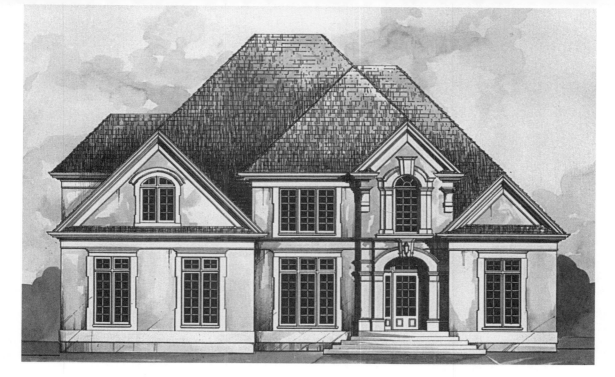

This narrow-lot design would be ideal for a golf course or lakeside lot. Inside the arched entry, the formal dining room is separated from the foyer and the massive grand room by decorative pillars. At the end of the day, the family will enjoy gathering in the cozy keeping room with its fireplace and easy access to the large island kitchen and the sunny gazebo-style breakfast room. The owners suite is located on the first floor for privacy and features a uniquely designed bedroom and a luxurious bath with His and Hers walk-in closets. Your family portraits and favorite art treasures will be well displayed along the upstairs gallery, which shares space with three family bedrooms and two full baths.

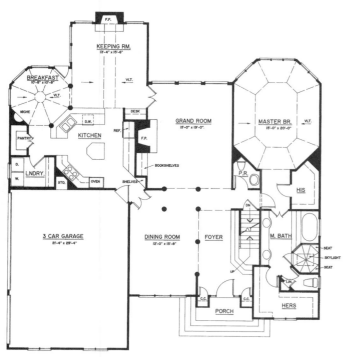

DESIGN HPU040473

First Floor: 2,032 square feet
Second Floor: 1,028 square feet
Total: 3,060 square feet
Unfinished Basement:
2,032 square feet
Width: 55'-8" Depth: 62'-0"

DESIGN BY
©Archival Designs, Inc.

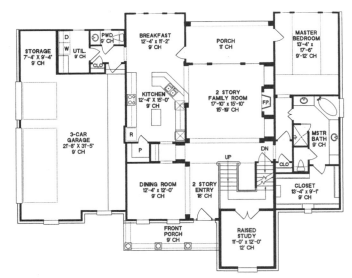

The charm of this French country home begins with the hipped roof, brick facade and the arched and circle windows of the exterior. Upon entering, you will find a formal dining room to your left, which connects to the kitchen via a butler's pantry. A breakfast nook to the rear of the plan has views of the backyard and access to a half-bath and the utility room. At the center of the home is a beautiful two-story family room with a fireplace and access to the rear porch. The owners suite also accesses this porch and finds privacy on the right side of the first floor. The owners bath has a compartmented toilet, twin vanities and a huge walk-in closet. A raised study is found at the first landing of the staircase, which then continues up to three secondary bedrooms and two more baths.

DESIGN HPU040474

First Floor: 2,060 square feet
Second Floor: 1,020 square feet
Total: 3,080 square feet
Bonus Room: 459 square feet
Width: 68'-3" Depth: 55'-9"

DESIGN BY
©Design Basics, Inc.

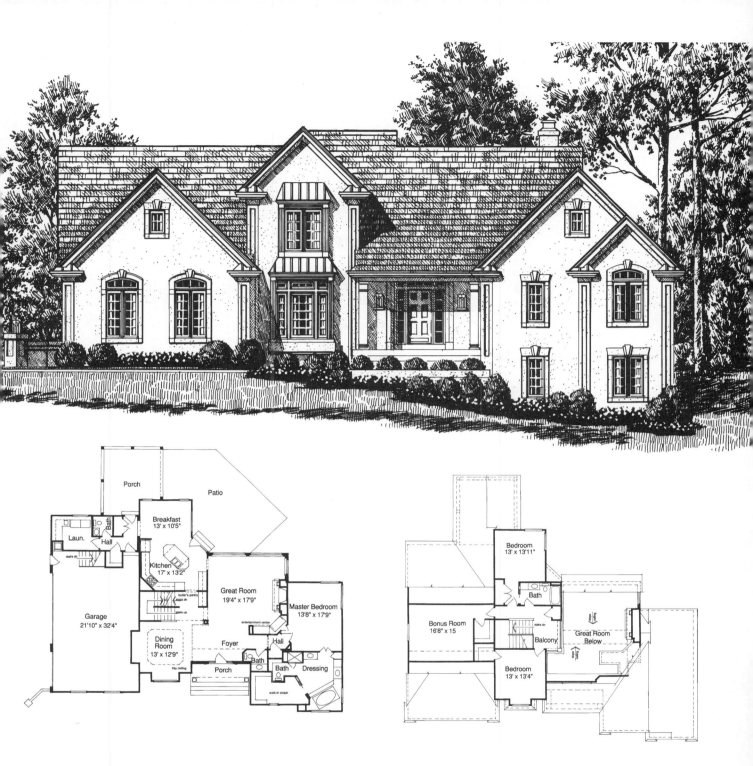

Multiple gables, a box window and easy maintenance combine to create a dramatic appearance for this two-story European classic home. The excitement of the great room begins with a wall of windows across the rear, a sloped ceiling and built-in entertainment cabinet. The kitchen offers an angled island that parallels the French doors and large breakfast room. The dining-room ceiling has a raised center section, and a furniture alcove is added for extra roominess. The luxury and convenience of the first-floor master bedroom suite is highlighted by His and Hers vanities, a separate shower and whirlpool tub. The second floor provides a private retreat for a guest suite and a bonus room offering the option of a fourth bedroom, library or hobby room. A balcony provides a panoramic view of the great room and foyer. The rear of this home is stepped for privacy and boasts a clever use of windows.

DESIGN HPU040475

First Floor: 2,192 square feet
Second Floor: 654 square feet
Total: 2,846 square feet
Bonus Room: 325 square feet
Width: 75'-0" Depth: 70'-0"

DESIGN BY
©Studer Residential Designs, Inc.

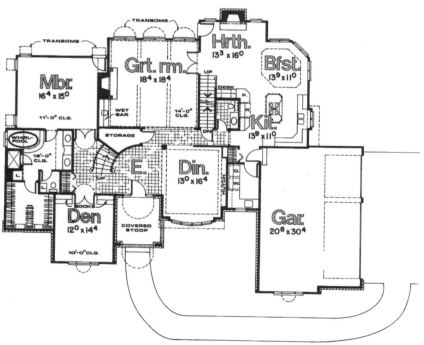

DESIGN HPU040476

First Floor: 2,252 square feet
Second Floor: 920 square feet
Total: 3,172 square feet
Width: 73'-4"   Depth: 57'-4"

A curving staircase graces the entry to this beautiful home and hints at the wealth of amenities found in the floor plan. Besides an oversized great room with a fireplace and arched windows, there's a cozy hearth room with its own fireplace. The gourmet kitchen has a work island and breakfast area. A secluded den contains bookcases and an arched transom above double doors. The master bedroom is on the first floor, thoughtfully separated from three family bedrooms upstairs. Bedrooms 2 and 4 share a full bath, while Bedroom 3 has its own private bath. Note the informal stair to the second floor originating in the hearth room.

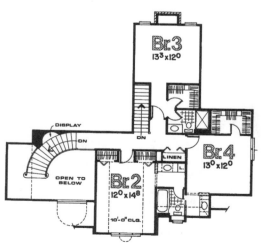

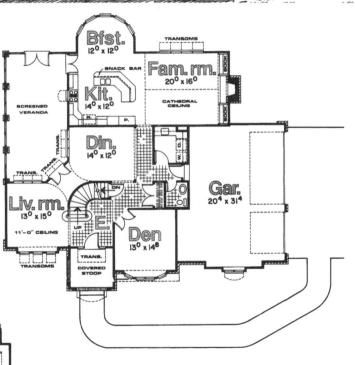

DESIGN HPU040477

First Floor: 1,631 square feet
Second Floor: 1,426 square feet
Total: 3,057 square feet
Width: 60'-0" Depth: 58'-0"

DESIGN BY
©Design Basics, Inc.

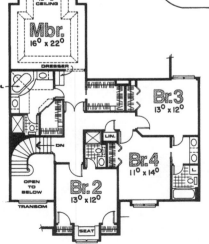

Stucco accents and graceful window treatments enhance the facade of this elegant two-story home. Inside, the two-story foyer is flanked by a formal living room on the left and a bay-windowed den on the right. The large, efficient kitchen easily serves a beautiful breakfast room and a comfortable family room. Note the cathedral ceiling, transom windows, built-in bookcases and warming fireplace in the family room. Upstairs, two secondary bedrooms share a full bath while a third has its own and can be used as a guest suite. The deluxe master suite is sure to please with its detailed ceiling, bayed sitting area, built-in dresser, two walk-in closets and luxurious bath.

DESIGN HPU040478

First Floor: 2,672 square feet
Second Floor: 687 square feet
Total: 3,359 square feet
Bonus Room: 522 square feet
Width: 72'-6" Depth: 64'-5"

DESIGN BY
Donald A. Gardner Architects, Inc.

Abrick exterior mixed with cedar shakes creates an intriguing facade for this four-bedroom home with its dramatic hipped roof and dual chimneys. This home features formal living and dining rooms as well as a more casual family room and breakfast area. The living room is vaulted and overlooked by a second-floor balcony. A bedroom/study and the master suite are located on the first floor, while the second floor features two more bedrooms and a bonus room.

DESIGN HPU040479

First Floor: 2,372 square feet
Second Floor: 1,111 square feet
Total: 3,483 square feet
Bonus Room: 394 square feet
Width: 85'-4" Depth: 51'-3"

DESIGN BY
Donald A. Gardner Architects, Inc.

An exquisite brick exterior wraps this stately traditional home in luxury. An impressive two-story ceiling with clerestory dormers amplifies the great room with a fireplace, built-ins and access to the back porch. Topped with a tray ceiling, the master suite enjoys back-porch access, dual walk-ins and a luxurious bath. Upstairs, a balcony overlooks the foyer and great room. Two upstairs bedrooms feature vaulted ceilings, while a third boasts a private bath.

NK.
13'0" X 12'0"

WOOD DECK
19'6" X 13'8"

EATING BAR

DW

FAM.
2-STORY CLG.
19'10" X 14'8"

KIT.
12'0" X 11'8"

BUILT-IN CAB.

BUILT-IN CAB.

3 CAR GAR.
23'4" X 42'4"

UP   DN

BOOK SHELVES

DIN.
13'4" X 14'8"

E.
2-STORY CLG.

LIV.
12'0" X 14'0"

This brick two-story home has an ideal set-up for family or formal gatherings. When entering this home, you are greeted by a two-story foyer and a striking open staircase to the upper level. There are double doors just off the foyer to the formal living room. The formal dining room is spacious and a perfect place to serve holiday meals. The family room is astonishing with its two-story ceilings, fireplace and built-in cabinet. You can venture to the second level by either of the two staircases. There are four bedrooms on this level, which includes a cathedral-ceilinged master suite. The master bath offers a walk-in shower with a seat and double vanity.

DESIGN HPU040480

First Floor: 1,559 square feet
Second Floor: 1,713 square feet
Total: 3,272 square feet
Width: 64'-0" Depth: 54'-0"

DESIGN BY
©Ahmann Design, Inc.

MBR.
CATHEDRAL CEILING
13'0" X 17'10"

BR. #2
11'8" X 14'4"

OPEN TO
FAM.

SEAT

LIN.

LIN.

BR. #3
14'0" X 12'4"

OPEN TO
E.

BR. #4
12'0" X 12'4"

LIN.

DESIGN HPU040482

First Floor: 2,157 square feet
Second Floor: 956 square feet
Total: 3,113 square feet
Width: 71'-0" Depth: 62'-0"

Stucco, siding, shutters and class—all combine here to give this home plenty of curb appeal. A two-story foyer leads through an arched soffit to the formal living room on the left and offers a formal dining room to the right. A master bedroom suite is designed to pamper, with a large walk-in closet and a lavish, private bath. Upstairs, three family bedrooms share a large hall bath and a handy loft, good for studying, reading or computer work.

DESIGN BY
©Ahmann Design, Inc.

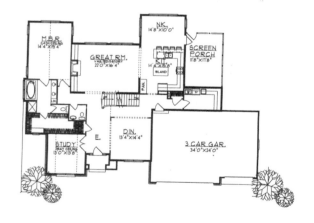

DESIGN HPU040481

First Floor: 2,174 square feet
Second Floor: 877 square feet
Total: 3,051 square feet
Width: 76'-0" Depth: 56'-0"

DESIGN BY
©Ahmann Design, Inc.

The two-story French country home will welcome you, and the amount of space in this home will give you plenty of room to grow. From the entry, the French doors open to a study with a tray ceiling. The great room with a two-story ceiling, fireplace, built-in shelves and stunning windows that overlook the backyard will amaze you. Also on the main floor of this home is a spectacular master bedroom.

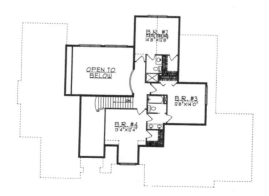

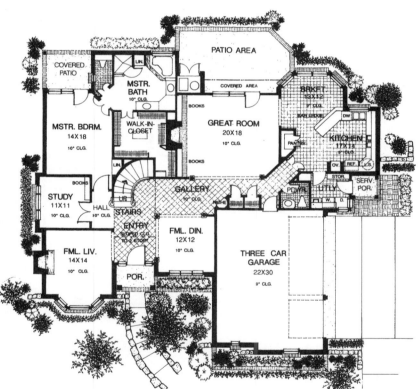

DESIGN BY
©Fillmore Design Group

H ere's a cottage that would have provided plenty of room for Goldilocks AND the three bears! Wonderful rooflines top a brick exterior with cedar and stone accents—and lots of English country charm. Stone wing walls extend the front profile, and a cedar hood tops the large bay window. The two-story entry reveals a graceful curving staircase and opens to the formal living and dining rooms. Fireplaces are found in the living room as well as the great room, which also boasts built-in bookcases and access to the rear patio. The kitchen and breakfast room add to the informal area and include a snack bar. A private patio is part of the owners suite, which also offers an intriguing corner tub, twin vanities, a large walk-in closet and a nearby study. Three family bedrooms and a bonus room comprise the second floor.

DESIGN HPU040483

First Floor: 2,438 square feet
Second Floor: 882 square feet
Total: 3,320 square feet
Width: 70'-0"   Depth: 63'-2"

Glass-filled, hipped dormers and corner quoins lend this four-bedroom home great curb appeal. Skylights illuminate the vaulted foyer and curved staircase. The formal dining room has a niche for a buffet and French doors leading to the rear deck. Decorative columns help define the living room, which offers a fireplace. A quiet den provides a bay window and a nearby full bath. The gourmet kitchen overlooks the family room, which has a hearth. A luxurious master suite and three secondary bedrooms fill the second floor.

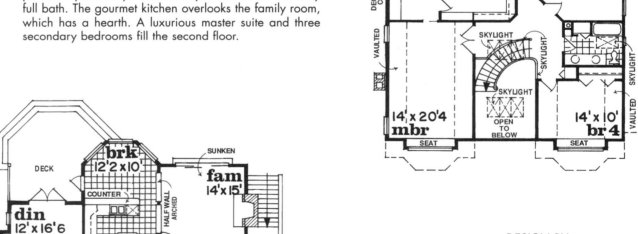

DESIGN BY
©Select Home Designs

DESIGN HPU040484

First Floor: 1,725 square feet
Second Floor: 1,364 square feet
Total: 3,089 square feet
Width: 64'-4" Depth: 50'-4"

Decorative columns and gently curving arches welcome guests to this comfortable, brick, two-story home. Convenience is a hallmark within, with a second-floor laundry room for the three family bedrooms and a full-size stackable washer and dryer between the master bath and one of two walk-in closets. Continuing to put the homeowner first, this plan also features multiple built-ins and storage options. The great room features a beam ceiling, warming fireplace, entertainment center and built-in shelving. A tray ceiling adorns the master bedroom. The master bath is luxurious with a whirlpool tub and separate glass shower. Please specify basement, crawlspace or slab foundation when ordering.

DESIGN BY
©Michael E. Nelson,
Nelson Design Group, LLC

DESIGN HPU040485

First Floor: 1,974 square feet
Second Floor: 1,396 square feet
Total: 3,370 square feet
Width: 63'-0" Depth: 50'-4"

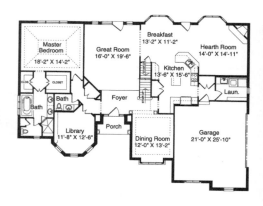

This gorgeous home combines fine exterior detailing with an exciting, functional floor plan. Three bay windows provide light and dimension to favorite family gathering areas. Columns define the formal dining room that enjoys easy access to the kitchen. An island, large pantry and wrap-around counter make cooking fun. The master bedroom pampers, while a second-floor balcony and three additional bedrooms complete this spectacular home.

DESIGN HPU040487

First Floor: 2,233 square feet
Second Floor: 853 square feet
Total: 3,086 square feet
Width: 67'-4" Depth: 50'-4"

DESIGN BY
©Studer Residential Designs, Inc.

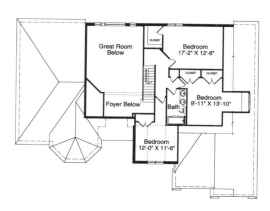

DESIGN HPU040486

First Floor: 1,597 square feet
Second Floor: 1,859 square feet
Total: 3,456 square feet
Width: 62'-0" Depth: 46'-0"

DESIGN BY
©Michael E. Nelson,
Nelson Design Group, LLC

Quoins, keystone lintels and a Palladian window denote European influence in this charming, brick, four-bedroom home. A beautiful built-in media center and shelving system surrounds the fireplace in the great room. French doors in the great room access the grilling porch, extending the livable space outdoors. A bay window lights the master bedroom, and the sumptuous bath with its whirlpool tub adds elegance. Three secondary bedrooms featuring walk-in closets are located upstairs and share a full bath. Please specify basement or crawlspace foundation when ordering.

Plenty of amenities are available within the brick-and-siding exterior of this two-story home. The covered porch invites guests and owners to relax and contemplate the scenery. The foyer elegantly invites guests to dinner in the formal dining room. Conveniently nearby, the kitchen has plenty of counter space, a snack bar and a walk-in pantry. The keeping room—complete with a corner fireplace—and the light-filled breakfast room provide plenty of informal eating and relaxing space around the kitchen. The great room also features a corner fireplace. Luxury is the keyword of the master suite. Adorned with a boxed ceiling and warmed by a gas fireplace with built-ins, the master suite enjoys a bath with a whirlpool tub and separate glass shower, His and Hers walk-in closets, and dual-vanity sinks. The second floor features a game room with built-ins around a window seat and two family bedrooms sharing a full bath. Please specify basement, crawlspace or slab foundation when ordering.

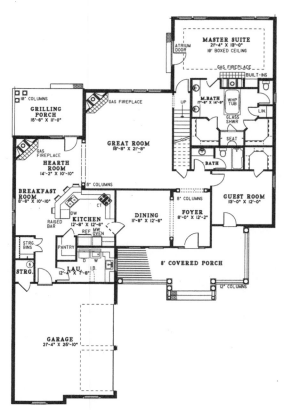

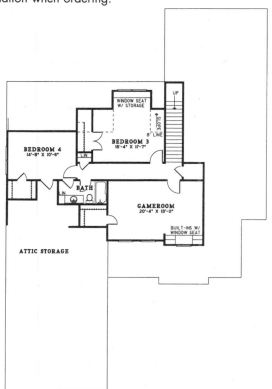

DESIGN HPU040488

First Floor: 2,257 square feet
Second Floor: 949 square feet
Total: 3,206 square feet
Width: 56'-0" Depth: 85'-7"

DESIGN BY
©Michael E. Nelson,
Nelson Design Group, LLC

Designed with your growing family in mind, this spacious two-story design is sure to be the home for you. The two-story entryway leads to the airy kitchen and breakfast nook. The kitchen, with a rectangular island for preparing and enjoying meals, looks into the family room. With a two-story ceiling and built-in cabinets surrounding the fireplace, the family room is ideal for family gatherings. A formal dining room and living room provide the perfect atmosphere for entertaining. Upstairs, the master bedroom has a generous walk-in closet and a master bath, complete with a spa tub and dual vanity. Three additional bedrooms share a full bath. Other amenities include a main-floor powder room and laundry room, which allows access to the three-car garage.

DESIGN HPU040489

First Floor: 1,746 square feet
Second Floor: 1,473 square feet
Total: 3,219 square feet
Width: 59'-0"   Depth: 54'-0"

DESIGN BY
©Ahmann Design, Inc.

DESIGN HPU040491

First Floor: 2,096 square feet
Second Floor: 1,062 square feet
Total: 3,158 square feet
Width: 48'-0" Depth: 56'-0"

DESIGN BY
©Ahmann Design, Inc.

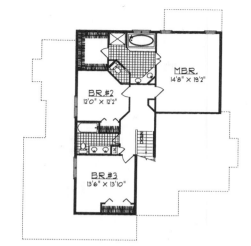

This two-story home features an eye-catching combination of brick and siding. Upon entering the foyer, you will take pleasure in the wide-open space the house provides. The copious feel of the living, family and dining rooms is great for social gatherings or comfortable nights around the fireplace. Upstairs, you'll find the spacious master bedroom with a large bathroom and walk-in closet.

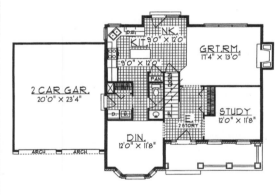

The two-story entryway leads to the cozy great room. Complete with a fireplace, the great room opens into the kitchen. The kitchen, with wraparound counters and a center island, is adjacent to the nook. A separate formal dining room is perfect for entertaining. Upstairs, the master bedroom has a cathedral ceiling and provides a private retreat, full bath and a roomy walk-in closet. Three additional bedrooms share a full bath.

DESIGN HPU040490

First Floor: 995 square feet
Second Floor: 1,125 square feet
Finished Basement:
995 square feet
Total: 3,115 square feet
Width: 56'-4" Depth: 35'-8"

DESIGN BY
©Ahmann Design, Inc.

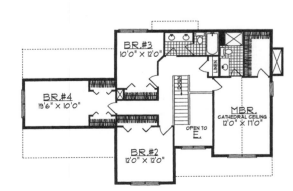

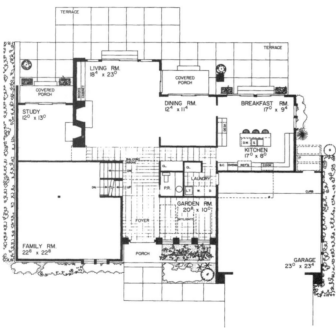

This attractive split-level contemporary home includes a skylit garden room just off the foyer. Note the large, sunken family room, great for entertaining a crowd. The living room features a fireplace with built-in shelves and access to the rear gardens. The study enjoys a cozy fireplace and a private covered porch. The gourmet kitchen enjoys a roomy island snack bar and a sunny breakfast room. The second floor includes the master bedroom with a whirlpool bath and walk-in closet, and two family bedrooms sharing a full bath.

DESIGN HPU040492

Main Level: 2,070 square feet
Upper Level: 1,320 square feet
Total: 3,390 square feet
Width: 68'-4" Depth: 52'-4"

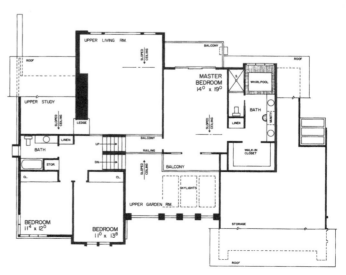

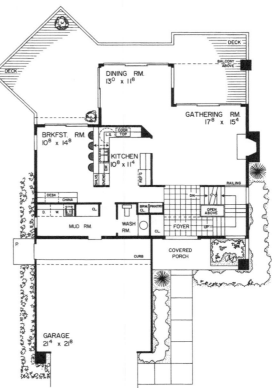

DESIGN HPU040493

Main Level: 1,096 square feet
Upper Level: 1,115 square feet
Lower Level: 1,104 square feet
Total: 3,315 square feet
Width: 40'-0" Depth: 58'-0"

L

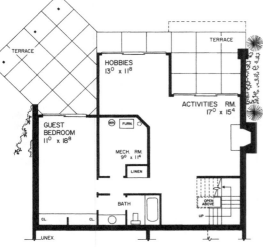

DESIGN BY
©Home Planners

A splendidly symmetrical design, this clean-lined, open-planned contemporary home is a great place for the outdoor-minded. The gathering room—with a fireplace—dining room and breakfast room all lead out to a deck off the main level. Similarly, the lower-level activity room—with another fireplace—hobby room and guest bedroom contain separate doors to the backyard terrace. Upstairs are three bedrooms, including a suite with a through-fireplace, private balcony, walk-in closet, dressing room and whirlpool tub.

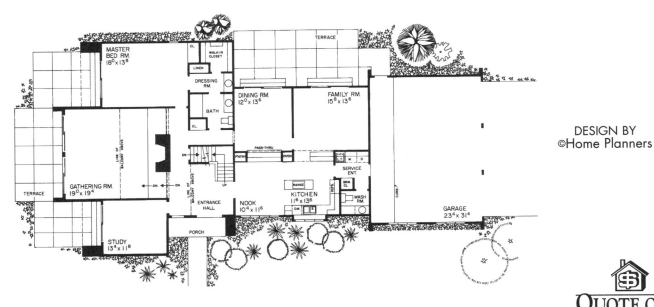

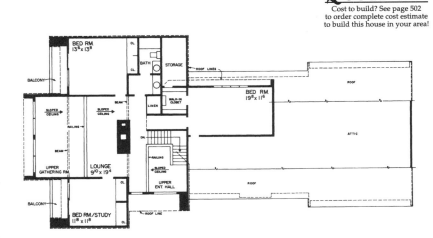

DESIGN BY
©Home Planners

DESIGN HPU040494

First Floor: 2,132 square feet
Second Floor: 1,156 square feet
Total: 3,288 square feet
Width: 90'-0" Depth: 46'-0"

L **D**

This beautifully designed two-story home provides an eye-catching exterior. The floor plan is a perfect complement. The front kitchen features an island range, adjacent breakfast nook and pass-through to a formal dining room. The master suite offers a spacious walk-in closet and dressing room. The side terrace can be reached from the master suite, the gathering room and the study. The second floor contains three bedrooms and storage space galore. The center lounge offers a sloped ceiling and skylight.

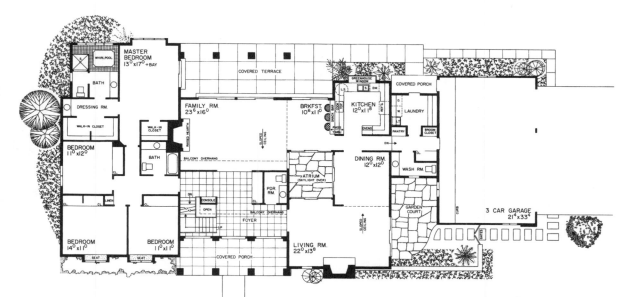

This lavish modern design has it all, including an upper lounge, family room and foyer. A front-facing living room with its own fireplace looks out upon a side garden court and the centrally located atrium. A large, efficient kitchen with snack-bar service to the breakfast room also enjoys its own greenhouse window. The sleeping area is situated at one end of the house downstairs to ensure privacy and relaxation. Here, a deluxe owners suite features a soothing whirlpool tub, dressing area and an abundance of walk-in closets. Three secondary bedrooms, two with window seats, share a full bath.

DESIGN **HPU040495**

First Floor: 3,173 square feet
Second Floor: 267 square feet
Total: 3,440 square feet
Width: 105'-0" Depth: 52'-8"

DESIGN BY
©Home Planners

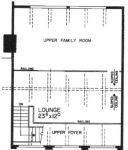

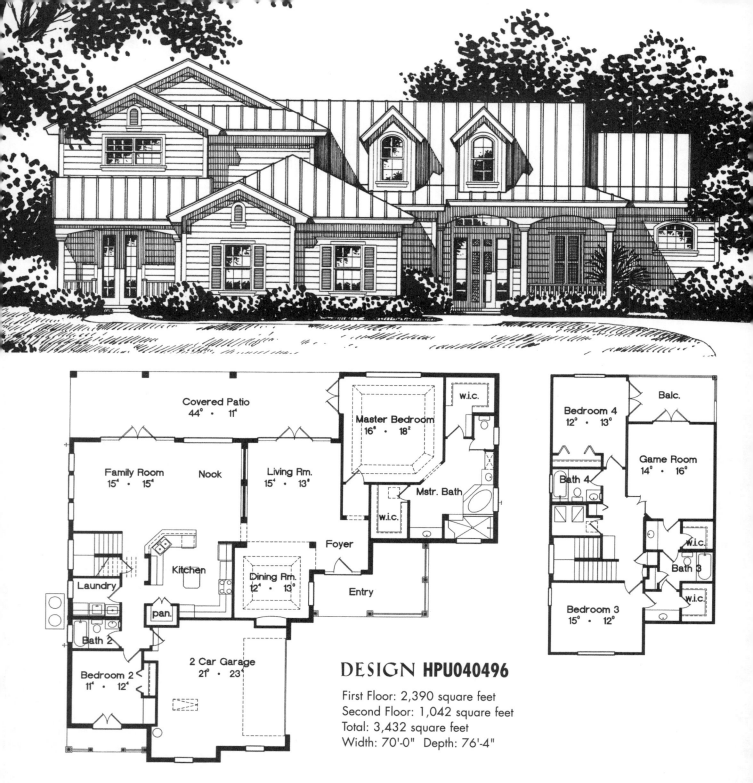

Covered Patio
44⁰ · 11⁴

Master Bedroom
16⁸ · 18²

w.i.c.

Mstr. Bath

w.i.c.

Family Room
15⁴ · 15⁴

Nook

Living Rm.
15⁴ · 13⁸

Kitchen

Foyer

Laundry

Dining Rm.
12⁴ · 13⁰

pan.

Entry

Bath 2

Bedroom 2
11⁴ · 12⁴

2 Car Garage
21⁰ · 23¹

Bedroom 4
12⁰ · 13⁰

Balc.

Game Room
14⁰ · 16⁰

Bath 4

w.i.c.

Bath 3

w.i.c.

Bedroom 3
15⁰ · 12⁰

DESIGN HPU040496

First Floor: 2,390 square feet
Second Floor: 1,042 square feet
Total: 3,432 square feet
Width: 70'-0" Depth: 76'-4"

DESIGN BY
©Home Design Services, Inc.

A two-story farmhouse with a wraparound front porch and plenty of natural light welcomes you into this graceful, four-bedroom country classic. The large kitchen featuring a center island with a counter and a roomy breakfast area opens to the large great room for easy entertaining. There are plenty of interior architectural effects, with columns, arches and niches to punctuate the interior spaces. A separate dining room provides formality to this elegant home. The owners suite, privately situated on the first floor, features separate double vanities, a garden whirlpool tub and separate walk-around shower. A second bedroom on the main level would be a great guest room or maid's quarters with a private bath and direct access to the garage. Bedrooms 3 and 4 are tucked upstairs with a game room and two full baths.

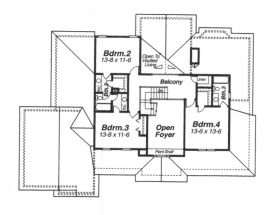

A combination of brick and siding and a raised metal porch roof create a stately look. This plan features the master bedroom on the main level, but also enjoys an optional fifth bedroom/library, allowing guests to remain on the first floor while three other bedrooms share the second floor. A dramatic entry features a two-story foyer looking past the U-shaped stairs into a vaulted living area with a dramatic rear window. The master suite enjoys a fireplace and bay-windowed sitting area, along with dual closets and vanities.

DESIGN HPU040497

First Floor: 2,047 square feet
Second Floor: 1,011 square feet
Total: 3,058 square feet
Width: 69'-8" Depth: 56'-5"

DESIGN BY
©Jannis Vann & Associates, Inc.

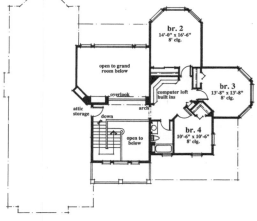

This romantic farmhouse, with its open living spaces and covered porches, is designed with gracious family living in mind. The grand room takes center stage with rear-porch access, a corner fireplace, a built-in media center and a pass-through to the kitchen. The master suite is lavishly appointed with a spa-style bath and a sitting area. Upstairs, a computer loft with built-ins serves as a common area to the three family bedrooms. Please specify basement or slab foundation when ordering.

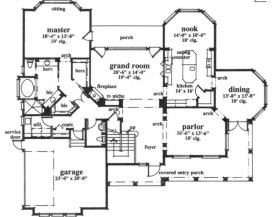

DESIGN HPU040498

First Floor: 2,240 square feet
Second Floor: 943 square feet
Total: 3,183 square feet
Width: 69'-8" Depth: 61'-10"

DESIGN BY
©The Sater Design Collection

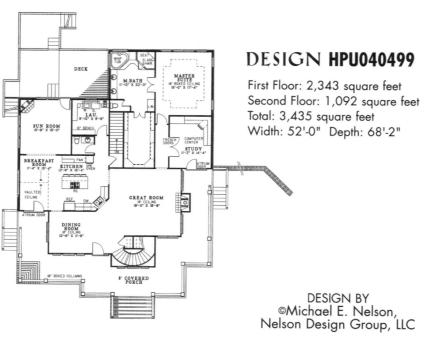

DESIGN HPU040499

First Floor: 2,343 square feet
Second Floor: 1,092 square feet
Total: 3,435 square feet
Width: 52'-0" Depth: 68'-2"

DESIGN BY
©Michael E. Nelson,
Nelson Design Group, LLC

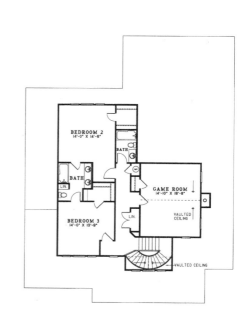

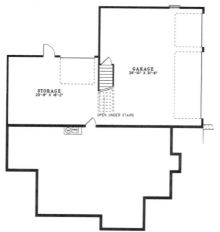

A wraparound porch and a Palladian window lend grace and charm to this three-bedroom farmhouse. Enjoy a moment of quiet contemplation on the front porch, or go inside to enjoy a warming fire in the great room. The open dining room and great room create a perfect entertainment area, with easy access to the kitchen—including a pass-through over the kitchen sink. The kitchen features a large island/snack bar. The nearby breakfast room has a vaulted ceiling, atrium-door access to the front porch and a view of the sun room. This room includes a corner fireplace, light-filled windows and access to the rear deck. A built-in computer center allows plenty of work space in the study. The master suite contains luxury amenities, such as a glass shower, whirlpool bathtub, walk-in closet and boxed ceiling. Two family bedrooms, two full bathrooms and a game room reside on the second level. Please specify basement, crawlspace or slab foundation when ordering.

With equally appealing front and side entrances, a charming Victorian facade invites entry to this stunning home. The foyer showcases the characteristic winding staircase and opens to the large great room with a masonry fireplace. An enormous kitchen features a cooktop island and a breakfast bar large enough to seat four. A lovely bay window distinguishes the nearby dining room. The master suite with a masonry fireplace is located on the first floor. The amenity-filled master bath features double vanities, a whirlpool tub, a separate shower and a gigantic walk-in closet with an additional cedar closet. The second floor contains two bedrooms—one with access to the outdoor balcony on the side of the home. The third floor is completely expandable. Please specify crawlspace or slab foundation when ordering.

DESIGN HPU040500

First Floor: 2,194 square feet
Second Floor: 870 square feet
Total: 3,064 square feet
Bonus Room: 251 square feet
Width: 50'-11" Depth: 91'-2"

L

DESIGN BY
©Larry E. Belk Designs

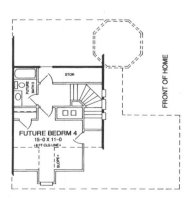

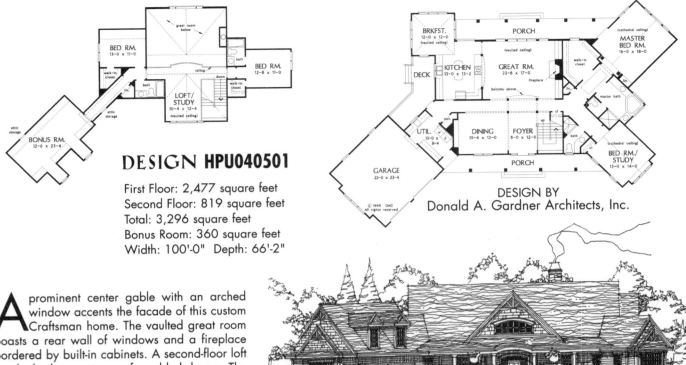

DESIGN HPU040501

First Floor: 2,477 square feet
Second Floor: 819 square feet
Total: 3,296 square feet
Bonus Room: 360 square feet
Width: 100'-0" Depth: 66'-2"

DESIGN BY
Donald A. Gardner Architects, Inc.

A prominent center gable with an arched window accents the facade of this custom Craftsman home. The vaulted great room boasts a rear wall of windows and a fireplace bordered by built-in cabinets. A second-floor loft overlooks the great room for added drama. The master suite is completely secluded and enjoys a cathedral ceiling and a luxurious bath. The home includes three additional bedrooms and baths as well as a vaulted loft/study and bonus room.

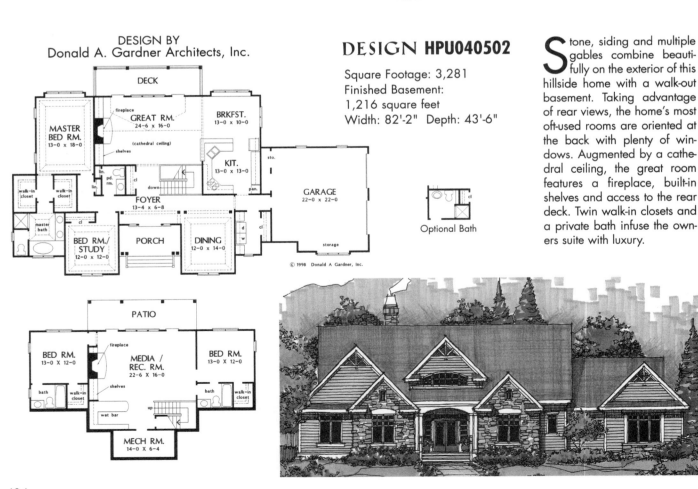

DESIGN BY
Donald A. Gardner Architects, Inc.

DESIGN HPU040502

Square Footage: 3,281
Finished Basement:
1,216 square feet
Width: 82'-2" Depth: 43'-6"

Optional Bath

S tone, siding and multiple gables combine beautifully on the exterior of this hillside home with a walk-out basement. Taking advantage of rear views, the home's most oft-used rooms are oriented at the back with plenty of windows. Augmented by a cathedral ceiling, the great room features a fireplace, built-in shelves and access to the rear deck. Twin walk-in closets and a private bath infuse the owners suite with luxury.

DESIGN HPU040503

First Floor: 2,755 square feet
Second Floor: 735 square feet
Total: 3,490 square feet
Bonus Room: 481 square feet
Width: 92'-6" Depth: 69'-10"

DESIGN BY
Donald A. Gardner Architects, Inc.

PORCH

PATIO

PORCH

FAMILY RM.
16-0 x 22-0
(cathedral ceiling)

BRKFST.
9-4 x 9-0

SITTING
9-0 x 9-0

MASTER
BED RM.
18-0 x 14-0
(cathedral ceiling)

fireplace

shelves

fireplace

fireplace

shelves

walk-in
closet

lin.

KIT.
16-0 x 15-4

LIVING RM.
18-0 x 15-10
(cathedral ceiling)

shelves

cl

pantry

lin.

cl

master
bath

pd.
rm.

UTIL
8-0 x
8-4

cl

FOYER
10-8 x 8-0

(two story
ceiling)

shelves

walk-in
closet

DINING
12-0 x 14-0

STUDY
12-0 x 14-4

d
w

GARAGE
22-0 x 23-0

PORCH

storage

© 1998 Donald A Gardner, Inc.

Dormers, gables with wood brackets, a double-door entry and a stone-and-siding exterior lend charm and sophistication to this Craftsman estate. Cathedral ceilings and fireplaces are standard in the living room, family room and main bedroom, while the living room, family room and study feature built-in bookshelves. The spacious kitchen with an island stovetop and walk-in pantry opens completely to the family room and breakfast area. The master suite excels with a private sitting room, access to its own porch, two oversized walk-in closets and a lavish bath. Overlooking both foyer and living room, the second-floor balcony connects two bedrooms, a library and a bonus room.

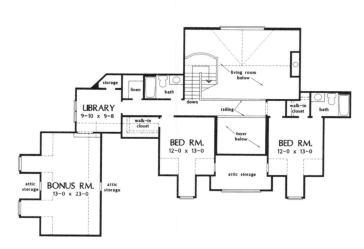

living room
below

storage

LIBRARY
9-10 x 9-8

linen

bath

down

railing

walk-in
closet

bath

walk-in
closet

walk-in
closet

BED RM.
12-0 x 13-0

foyer
below

BED RM.
12-0 x 13-0

attic
storage

BONUS RM.
13-0 x 23-0

attic
storage

attic storage

This four-bedroom design, though it has the quaint exterior of an older home, has all the features of modern-day life. A spacious den with a fireplace and rear-porch access provides the perfect gathering spot for quiet times; for more formal occasions, a living room and dining room are available. To the rear of the plan, a cozy bedroom with a roomy closet and porch access adjoins a full bath. The owners suite includes a walk-in closet and an opulent bath with a garden tub. Upstairs, two additional bedrooms feature private baths, walk-in closets and built-in bookshelves. A slope-ceilinged multi-purpose room—perhaps a game room, computer room or home office—completes the plan. Please specify crawlspace or slab foundation when ordering.

DESIGN BY
©Breland & Farmer Designers, Inc.

DESIGN HPU040504

First Floor: 1,925 square feet
Second Floor: 1,134 square feet
Total: 3,059 square feet
Width: 78'-0"   Depth: 52'-0"

DESIGN HPU040505

First Floor: 2,042 square feet
Second Floor: 1,099 square feet
Total: 3,141 square feet
Width: 66'-0" Depth: 44'-6"

DESIGN BY
©Select Home Designs

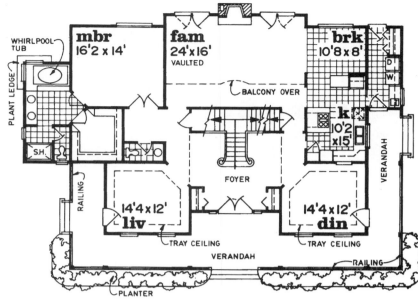

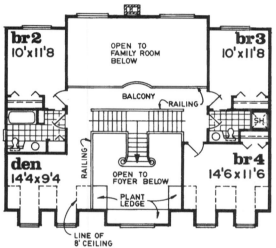

A wide, wrapping veranda graces the front of this design and is accessed from the living room and the dining room, as well as double doors at the entry. Both the living and dining rooms have tray ceilings. The family room is vaulted and has a cozy fireplace as its focal point. To either side of the fireplace are double doors to the rear yard. The kitchen has a center cooking island, spacious counters and a pass-through to the dining room. The breakfast room serves for casual occasions. The main-floor master suite features a lavish master bath with a roomy walk-in closet, whirlpool spa and twin vanity. A den or media center is found on the second floor with three family bedrooms and two full baths.

DESIGN HPU040507

First Floor: 2,033 square feet
Second Floor: 1,116 square feet
Total: 3,149 square feet
Width: 71'-0" Depth: 56'-0"

DESIGN BY
©Chatham Home Planning, Inc.

Tall columns march along the raised porch of this Southern-style home and frame a grand two-story foyer. In the great room, the fireplace stands between French doors leading to the rear porch and deck. The outstanding owners bedroom suite features a sitting room, a private porch and deck and a corner bath with a whirlpool tub. Upstairs a hall balcony connects three additional bedrooms and two full baths. Please specify crawlspace or slab foundation when ordering.

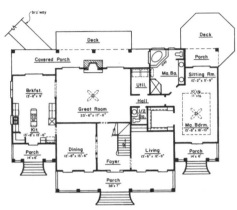

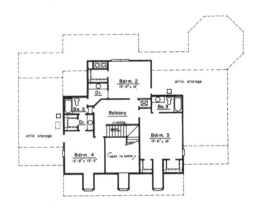

DESIGN HPU040506

Square Footage: 3,084
Bonus Room: 868 square feet
Width: 74'-0" Depth: 72'-0"

DESIGN BY
©Vaughn A. Lauban Designs

A gracious colonnade and three distinctive dormers set high on the roof give this home an elegant but homey appeal. Columns that separate and distinguish formal spaces flank the double-door entry. This home enjoys a split floor plan that allows for a secluded owners suite with pleasing appointments to the bath and bedroom. A guest suite or study can be found at the front left of the plan. Two additional bedrooms share a hall bath.

There's curb appeal galore in this stylish traditional home. Dormer windows extend gracefully from the steep roofline. A large front porch provides a comfortable retreat. Practical as well, this home provides storage space off the garage and in the attic. A game room upstairs, a computer alcove with a built-in desk under one of the dormer windows, and a downstairs study are functional for a variety of lifestyles. Three bedrooms—four if the study is used as a bedroom—three bathrooms and a powder room, and a terrific kitchen open to the hearth room and breakfast room, with a built-in entertainment center, complete this fabulous plan. Please specify basement, crawlspace or slab foundation when ordering.

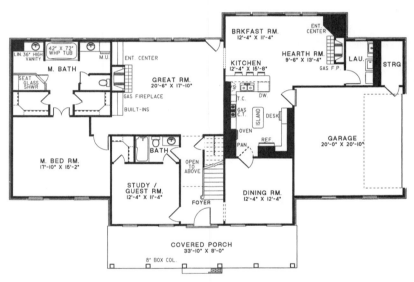

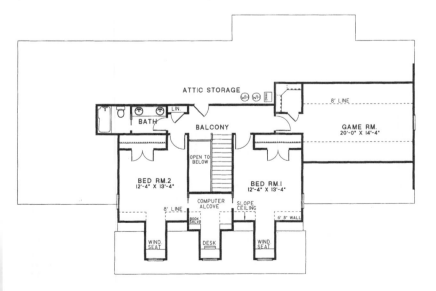

DESIGN HPU040508

First Floor: 1,977 square feet
Second Floor: 1,098 square feet
Total: 3,075 square feet
Width: 72'-4" Depth: 48'-4"

DESIGN BY
©Michael E. Nelson,
Nelson Design Group, LLC

DESIGN HPU040509

First Floor: 2,357 square feet
Second Floor: 995 square feet
Total: 3,352 square feet
Bonus Room: 545 square feet
Width: 95'-4" Depth: 54'-10"

DESIGN BY
Donald A. Gardner Architects, Inc.

From the two-story foyer with a Palladian clerestory window and a graceful stairway to the large great room with a cathedral ceiling and curved balcony, impressive spaces prevail in this open plan. The master suite, privately located at the opposite end of the first floor, features a sitting bay, an extra-large walk-in closet and a bath with every possible luxury. Three bedrooms and two full baths reside on the second floor.

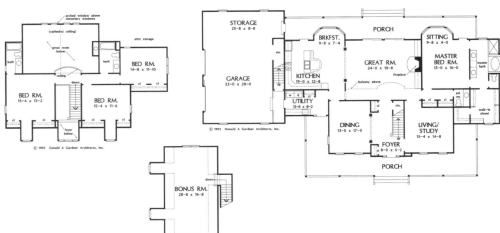

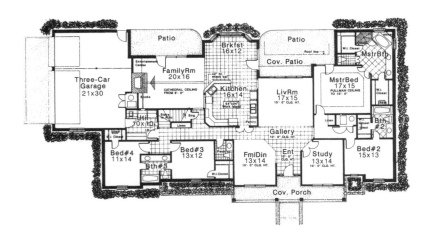

A distinctive exterior, a cathedral ceiling in the large family room, and room to expand make this country contemporary home a good choice. A study and formal dining room flank the entryway; three family bedrooms are across the front. The master suite offers plenty of seclusion, and a stairway leads to a future upstairs area.

DESIGN HPU040510

Square Footage: 3,270
Width: 101'-0" Depth: 48'-0"

DESIGN BY
©Fillmore Design Group

The definition of a transitional home is that it has space that can be converted as the family grows or as it moves out and less space is needed. This home is a perfect example. From its foyer, a study/bedroom opens to the left and features access to a bath. Another area worth noting is the basement. The rooms here can be used as either a garage/storage area and a bedroom, office or hobby room. As for the rest of the house, amenities abound in the master suite, efficient kitchen and hobby room off of the garage. Please specify crawlspace or slab foundation when ordering.

DESIGN BY
©Michael E. Nelson,
Nelson Design Group, LLC

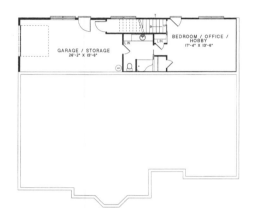

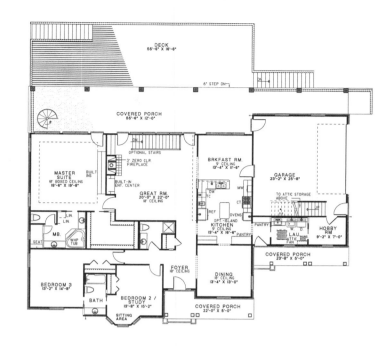

DESIGN HPU040511

Main Level: 2,650 square feet
Lower Level: 409 square feet
Total: 3,059 square feet
Width: 79'-0" Depth: 77'-8"

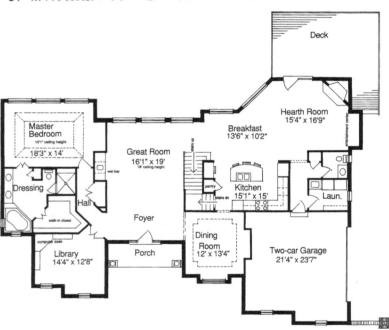

The splendor of this exciting two-story home begins with the solid brick exterior, multiple gables and soft wood trim. High ceilings in the foyer and great room showcase the wall of windows across the rear. The dining room is topped with a tray ceiling, and an alcove provides added space to display formal furniture. An expansive gourmet kitchen, island with seating, large breakfast area and cozy hearth room provide for today's active family lifestyles. From the garage, a hallway offers an orderly and quiet entry. Built-ins for a home computer and bookshelves are shown in the library. Relax and enjoy the master bedroom suite with its many luxurious amenities, including an exciting ceiling treatment and an expansive use of windows. The balcony of the second floor provides a dramatic view to the great room and leads to three additional bedrooms, creating a spectacular family-size home.

DESIGN HPU040512

First Floor: 2,297 square feet
Second Floor: 830 square feet
Total: 3,127 square feet
Width: 74'-8" Depth: 53'-0"

DESIGN BY
©Studer Residential Designs, Inc.

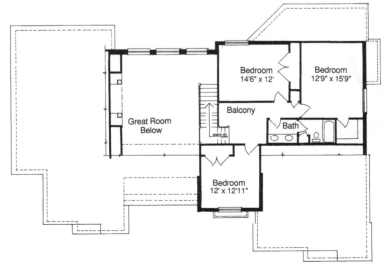

DESIGN HPU040513

Square Footage: 3,034
Width: 81'-4" Depth: 66'-8"

DESIGN BY
©Ahmann Design, Inc.

Truly a house one can call home—from its shingled and gabled exterior to its highly efficient interior—this design is sure to please. Stairs near the foyer lead to an optional finished basement. Directly ahead is an arched-ceiling great room, complete with a through-fireplace, built-in cabinets and a wall of windows. A lavish master bedroom suite offers two walk-in closets and a private bath. Two secondary bedrooms share a full bath.

Multiple gables, a boxed window and a brick-and-stone exterior combine to create an exciting front on this beautiful two-story home. A dramatic fireplace, sloped ceiling and built-in entertainment cabinet decorate the fashionable great room. The first-floor master bedroom with its tray ceiling, super bath and walk-in closet pampers homeowners with its size and luxury. Split stairs lead to a second-floor balcony that overlooks the great room for a dramatic effect. Three additional bedrooms top this spectacular home.

DESIGN HPU040514

First Floor: 2,181 square feet
Second Floor: 1,072 square feet
Total: 3,253 square feet
Width: 75'-0" Depth: 56'-9"

DESIGN BY
©Studer Residential Designs, Inc.

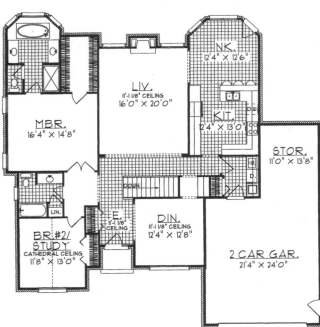

This four-bedroom brick home offers something extra special—though it looks like a ranch home, it's a two-story in reality! Designed for a hillside lot, this home offers two bedrooms, with bay windows, and a cozy recreation room with a fireplace on its lower level. On the main level, a formal dining room is at the front of the home, while the U-shaped kitchen easily serves the bayed nook via snack bar. A spacious living room warms those cool evenings with a fireplace. The lavish master suite comes complete with a walk-in closet and deluxe private bath. A secondary bedroom—or make it a study—finishes out this floor.

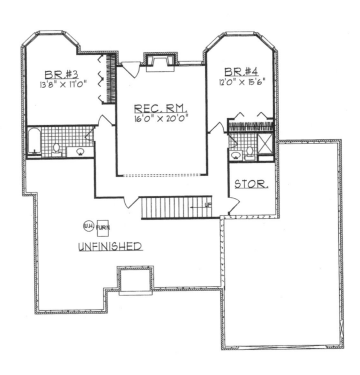

DESIGN HPU040515

Main Level: 1,930 square feet
Lower Level: 1,121 square feet
Total: 3,051 square feet
Width: 57'-0" Depth: 58'-10"

DESIGN BY
©Ahmann Design, Inc.

414

A delightful mix of styles combine to give this home plenty of curb appeal. From the foyer, a study, formal dining room and spacious great room are accessible. The gourmet of the family will enjoy the kitchen, with its work surface/snack-bar island and tons of counter and cabinet space. Two bedrooms are located on the right side of the home, each offering a walk-in closet and a private bath. The deluxe master bedroom suite is lavish in its amenities, which include a large walk-in closet, a fireplace and a sumptuous bath. Note the huge game room and extra bedroom over the garage—perfect for an in-law suite. Please specify basement, crawlspace or slab foundation when ordering.

DESIGN HPU040516

First Floor: 2,633 square feet
Second Floor: 752 square feet
Total: 3,385 square feet
Width: 75'-2" Depth: 89'-6"

DESIGN BY
©Michael E. Nelson,
Nelson Design Group, LLC

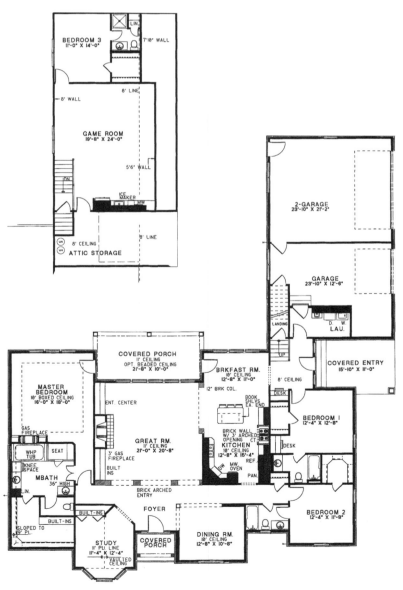

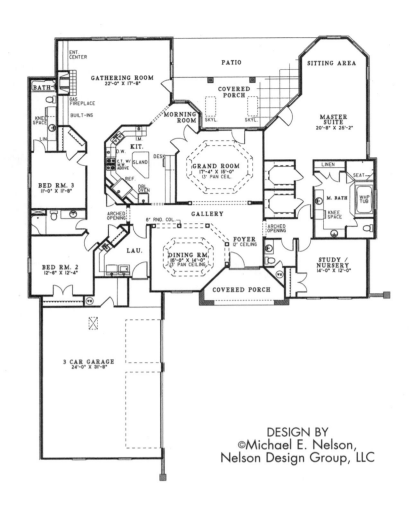

GATHERING ROOM
22'-0" X 17'-8"

ENT.
CENTER

BATH

KNEE
SPACE

GAS
FIREPLACE

BUILT-INS

LIN

BED RM. 3
11'-0" X 11'-8"

MORNING
ROOM

KIT.

D.W.

C.T. W/
M.W.
ABOVE

ISLAND

DESK

REF.

DBL.
OVEN

ARCHED
OPENING

LAU.

BED RM. 2
12'-8" X 12'-4"

PATIO

COVERED
PORCH

SKYL.   SKYL.

GRAND ROOM
17'-4" X 15'-0"
13' PAN CEIL.

GALLERY

8" RND. COL.

DINING RM.
15'-0" X 14'-0"
13' PAN CEILING

FOYER
12' CEILING

ARCHED
OPENING

COVERED PORCH

SITTING AREA

MASTER
SUITE
20'-8" X 25'-2"

LINEN

SEAT

M. BATH

KNEE
SPACE

WHP
TUB

STUDY /
NURSERY
14'-0" X 12'-0"

3 CAR GARAGE
24'-0" X 31'-8"

DESIGN BY
©Michael E. Nelson,
Nelson Design Group, LLC

Gently curving arches and a grand covered porch liven up the facade of this palatial home. The foyer is flanked by columns defining the formal dining room and arched openings to other areas of the home. The grand room is situated beneath a thirteen-foot pan ceiling. Doors lead to the morning room and the rear skylit porch. The morning room enjoys spectacular views of the patio and separates the modern kitchen from the gathering room. Complete with built-in entertainment facilities and a gas fireplace, the family will be drawn to this warm room. Two family bedrooms are located nearby. The other side of the home holds the fantastic owners suite and the study/nursery. The suite features patio access, a roomy sitting area with bay windows, His and Hers walk-in closets and a luxurious private bath. A three-car garage with a storage room caps this design. Please specify crawlspace or slab foundation when ordering.

DESIGN HPU040517

Square Footage: 3,124
Width: 70'-0" Depth: 88'-2"

DESIGN BY
©Studer Residential Designs, Inc.

DESIGN HPU040518

First Floor: 3,087 square feet
Second Floor: 1,037 square feet
Total: 4,124 square feet
Width: 92'-2" Depth: 70'-10"

An elegant front porch, columns inside and out, various ceiling treatments and decorative windows create a spectacular home. An open floor plan provides large formal and informal spaces. The island kitchen with extensive counter space offers easy access to the formal dining and breakfast areas. Located for privacy, the impressive master bedroom suite showcases a deluxe dressing room with a whirlpool tub, dual vanities, an oversized shower and a walk-in closet. A library is located near the master bedroom. Split stairs are positioned for family convenience and lead to three bedrooms, each with a large walk-in closet and private access to a bath. A three-car garage and full basement complete this exciting showplace.

DESIGN HPU040519

Main Level: 3,570 square feet
Lower Level: 2,367 square feet
Total: 5,937 square feet
Width: 84'-6" Depth: 69'-4"

The stone-and-brick exterior with multiple gables and a side-entry garage create a design that will attract many passersby. The gourmet kitchen with an island and a snack bar combine with the spacious breakfast room and hearth room to create a warm and friendly atmosphere for family living. The luxurious master bedroom with a sitting area and fireplace is complemented by a deluxe dressing room and walk-in closet.

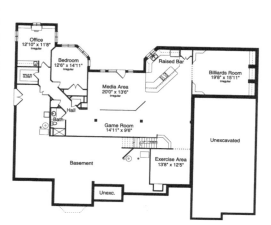

DESIGN BY
©Studer Residential Designs, Inc.

A brick-and-stone exterior with a tower and recessed entry creates a strong, solid look for this enchanting home. The large foyer introduces the great room with its beam ceiling and tall windows. The master bedroom with a sloped ceiling and spacious dressing area offers a relaxing retreat. Split stairs located for family convenience introduce the spectacular lower level, which is home to a wine room, exercise room, wet bar and two additional bedrooms.

DESIGN HPU040520

Main Level: 2,562 square feet
Lower Level: 1,955 square feet
Total: 4,517 square feet
Width: 75'-8" Depth: 70'-6"

DESIGN BY
©Studer Residential Designs, Inc.

This exciting ranch-style home offers a floor plan to accommodate the lifestyle of a busy homeowner. The main floor offers a large open great room and formal dining room framed with an eleven-foot ceiling. A large kitchen with an island provides roominess for the cook and cook's helper. Pampering the homeowner with its luxury, the master bedroom suite has a coffered ceiling and deluxe dressing room. Two additional bedrooms and a first-floor laundry provide everything needed for comfortable living. The option of creating additional living space is available in the walkout basement.

DESIGN BY
©Studer Residential Designs, Inc.

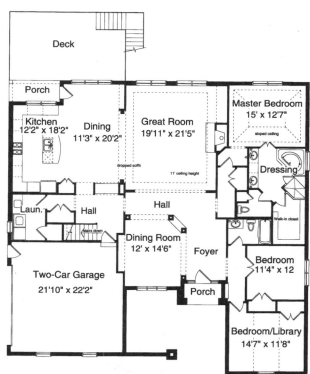

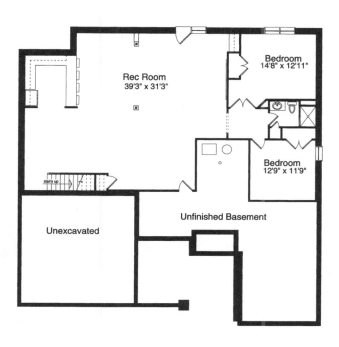

DESIGN HPU040521

Main Level: 2,469 square feet
Lower Level: 1,671 square feet
Total: 4,140 square feet
Width: 59'-0"   Depth: 59'-6"

DESIGN HPU040523

First Floor: 3,364 square feet
Second Floor: 1,198 square feet
Total: 4,562 square feet
Width: 98'-6" Depth: 61'-5"

DESIGN BY
©Studer Residential Designs, Inc.

The richness of natural stone and brick set the tone for the warmth and charm of this transitional home. A deluxe bath and a dressing area with a walk-in closet complement the owners suite. The library retreat boasts built-in bookshelves and a fourteen-foot ceiling. A dramatic view greets you at the second-floor balcony. Two family bedrooms share a tandem bath that includes separate vanities, and a third bedroom holds a private bath.

DESIGN HPU040522

Main Level: 2,766 square feet
Lower Level: 1,882 square feet
Total: 4,648 square feet
Width: 81'-10" Depth: 50'-8"

DESIGN BY
©Studer Residential Designs, Inc.

A popular brick-and-stone exterior provides the rich, solid look to this beautiful home. Pampering the homeowner with its luxury, the master bedroom suite provides a deluxe bath with a whirlpool tub, separate shower, double-bowl vanity and spacious walk-in closet. Two bedroom suites on the lower level provide inviting accommodations for overnight guests or returning college students.

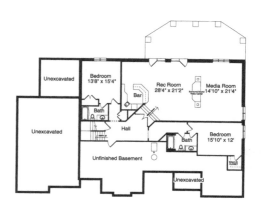

The combination of stucco, stacked stone and brick adds texture and character to this French country home. The foyer offers views to the study, dining room and living room. Double French doors open to the study with built-in bookcases and a window seat overlooking the rear deck. The breakfast room, family room and spacious kitchen make a nice backdrop for family living. The master suite is enhanced by a raised, corner fireplace and a bath with an exercise room. Upstairs, two family bedrooms—or make one an office—and a full bath are balanced by a large game room.

DESIGN BY
©Larry E. Belk Designs

DESIGN HPU040524

First Floor: 3,328 square feet
Second Floor: 868 square feet
Total: 4,196 square feet
Width: 108'-2" Depth: 61'-6"

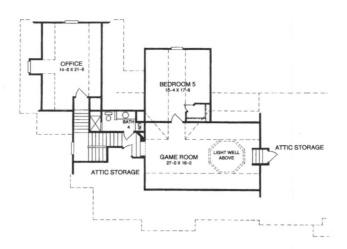

DESIGN HPU040525

First Floor: 5,152 square feet
Second Floor: 726 square feet
Total: 5,878 square feet
Width: 146'-7" Depth: 106'-7"

From the master bedroom suite to the detached four-car garage, this design will delight even the most discerning palates. While the formal living and dining rooms bid greeting as you enter, the impressive great room, with its cathedral ceiling, raised-hearth fireplace and veranda access, will take your breath away. A gallery hall leads to the kitchen and the family sleeping wing on the right and to the study, guest suite and master suite on the left. The large island kitchen, with its sunny breakfast nook, will be a gourmet's delight. The master suite includes a bayed sitting area, a dual fireplace shared with the study, and a luxurious bath. Each additional bedroom features its own bath and sitting area. Upstairs is a massive recreation room with a sunlit studio area and a bridge leading to an attic over the garage.

DESIGN BY
©Fillmore Design Group

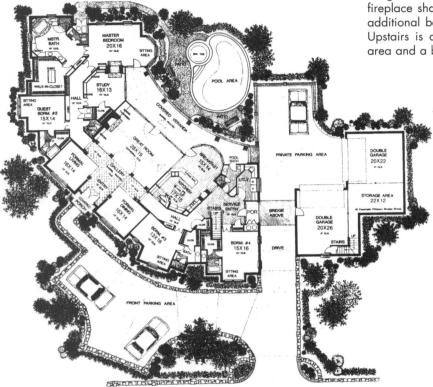

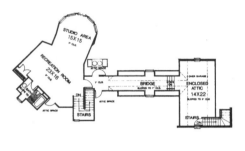

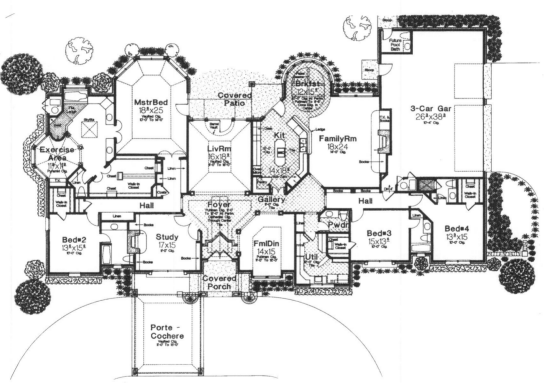

The hipped-roof, French-country exterior and porte-cochere entrance are just the beginning of this unique and impressive design. An unusual Pullman ceiling graces the foyer as it leads to the formal dining room on the right, to the study with a fireplace on the left and straight ahead to the formal living room with its covered patio access. A gallery directs you to the island kitchen with its abundant counter space and adjacent sun-filled breakfast bay. On the left side of the home, a spectacular master suite will become your favorite haven and the envy of your guests. The master bedroom includes a coffered ceiling, a bayed sitting area and patio access. The master bath features a large doorless shower, a separate exercise room and a huge walk-in closet with built-in chests. All of the family bedrooms offer private baths and walk-in closets.

DESIGN BY
©Fillmore Design Group

DESIGN HPU040526

Square Footage: 4,615
Width: 109'-10" Depth: 89'-4"

nteresting window treatments highlight this stone-and-shake facade, but don't overlook the columned porch to the left of the portico. Arches outline the formal dining room and the family room, both of which are convenient to the island kitchen. Household chores are made easier by the placement of a pantry, a powder room, a laundry room and an office between the kitchen and entrances to the side porch and the garage. If your goal is relaxing, the breakfast room, screened porch and covered deck are also nearby. The pampering owners suite is to the left of the main level, with three more bedrooms and a recreation room on the lower level. A bonus room above the garage receives natural light from a dormer window.

DESIGN BY
©Living Concepts Home Planning

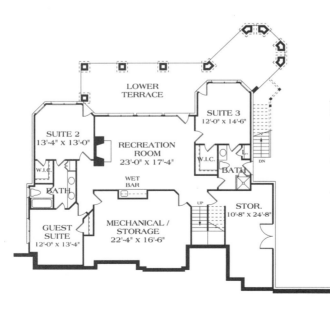

DESIGN **HPU040527**

Main Level: 2,213 square feet
Lower Level: 1,333 square feet
Total: 3,546 square feet
Bonus Room: 430 square feet
Width: 67'-2" Depth: 93'-1"

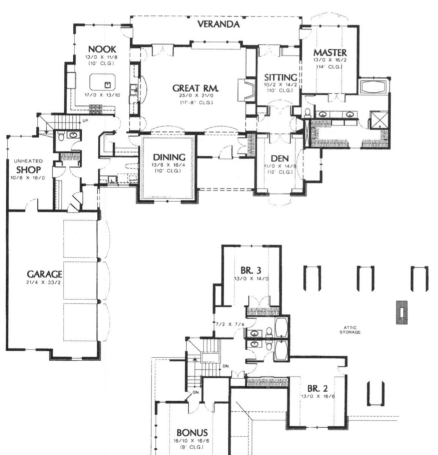

DESIGN HPU040528

First Floor: 2,698 square feet
Second Floor: 819 square feet
Total: 3,517 square feet
Bonus Room: 370 square feet
Width: 90'-6" Depth: 84'-0"

DESIGN BY
©Alan Mascord Design
Associates, Inc.

If you've ever traveled the European countryside, past rolling hills that range in hue from apple-green to deep, rich emerald, you may have come upon a home much like this one. Stone accents combined with stucco, and shutters that frame multi-pane windows add a touch of charm that introduces the marvelous floor plan found inside. The foyer opens onto a great room that offers a panoramic view of the veranda and beyond. To the left, you'll find a formal dining room; to the right, a quiet den. Just steps away resides the sitting room that introduces the grand master suite. A kitchen with a nook, laundry room and large shop area complete the first floor. The second floor contains two family bedrooms, two full baths and a bonus room.

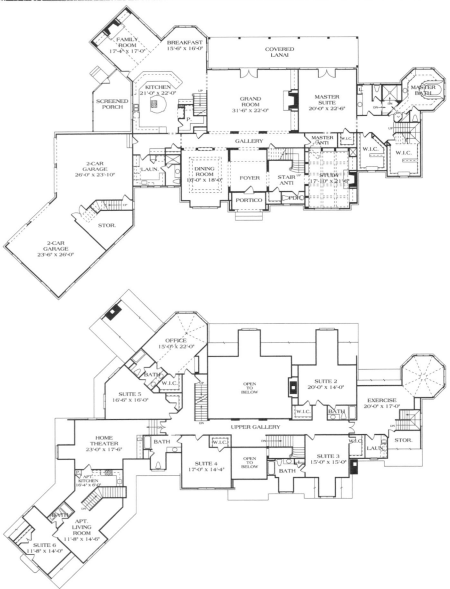

DESIGN BY
©Living Concepts Home Planning

Gables, varied rooflines, interesting dormers, arched windows, a recessed entry—the detailing on this stone manor is exquisite! The foyer opens through arches to the formal dining room, an elegant stair hall and the grand room, with its fireplace, built-ins and French doors to the lanai. The informal zone includes a kitchen with an oversized work island and pantry, a breakfast nook and a family room with a fireplace and its own screened porch. An anteroom outside the master suite gives the homeowners added privacy and allows the option of a private entrance to the study. The master bath is loaded with extras, including a stairway to the upstairs exercise room. The second floor also offers a home theater and a home office, as well as four bedroom suites and a mother-in-law or maid's apartment. Note that there are four sets of stairs to aid in the traffic flow and a laundry room on each level.

DESIGN HPU040529

First Floor: 5,200 square feet
Second Floor: 4,177 square feet
Total: 9,377 square feet
Width: 155'-9" Depth: 107'-11"

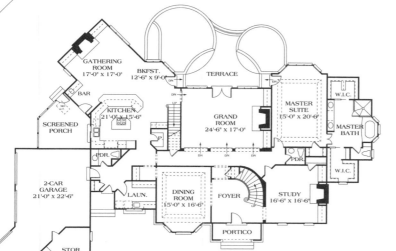

A stone-accented entrance welcomes you to this impressive French country estate. A sunken grand room combines with a bay-windowed dining room to create the formal living area. French doors open out to a multi-level terrace that links formal and informal areas and the master suite. A screened porch off the gathering room has a pass-through window from the kitchen to facilitate warm-weather dining. The master wing includes a study with a fireplace as well as a bayed sitting area and an amenity-laden bath. Two of the four bedrooms have private baths, while the others have separate dressing and vanity areas within a shared bath. A recreation room with a corner bar completes the plan.

DESIGN HPU040530

First Floor: 3,387 square feet
Second Floor: 1,799 square feet
Total: 5,186 square feet
Bonus Room: 379 square feet
Width: 110'-10" Depth: 84'-6"

DESIGN BY
©Living Concepts Home Planning

427

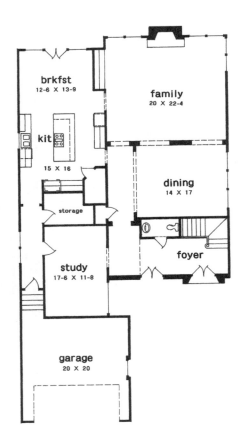

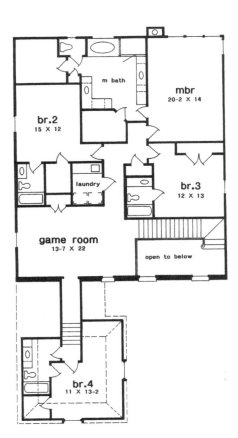

brkfst
12-6 X 13-9

family
20 X 22-4

kit
15 X 16

dining
14 X 17

storage

study
17-6 X 11-8

foyer

garage
20 X 20

m bath

br.2
15 X 12

mbr
20-2 X 14

laundry

br.3
12 X 13

game room
13-7 X 22

open to below

br.4
11 X 13-2

DESIGN BY
©Andy McDonald Design Group

A garage-top bedroom may be the perfect place for your teenager, offering privacy, a separate bathroom, a large walk-in closet and a view out of two arched dormer windows. There are plenty of great spaces for children and adults in this elegant home. A downstairs study and an upstairs game room are two extras that set this home apart. Four bedrooms each have a private bathroom, with an additional powder room located downstairs. Notice that there is lots of extra storage space in this home and that the laundry room is conveniently located near the cluster of bedrooms. An ideal home for growing families, for those who have frequent overnight guests or for use as a bed and breakfast, it offers true versatility with elegant styling.

DESIGN HPU040531

First Floor: 1,909 square feet
Second Floor: 1,992 square feet
Total: 3,901 square feet
Bonus Room: 299 square feet
Width: 39'-9" Depth: 76'-10"

PORCH

LIVING ROOM
18'-0" x 20'-0"
VAULTED CEILING

FP

MASTER BEDROOM
19'-0" x 18'-0"
VAULTED CEILING

WIC

FP

KITCHEN
15'-0" x 14'-0"

DN

PORCH

FAMILY ENTRY

LAV.

W D

LAUNDRY

MORNING ROOM
12'-0" x 16'-0"

UP

DN

MASTER BATH
14'-4" x 15'-0"

WET BAR

LAV.

PANTRY

FP

DN

WIC   WIC

UP

ENTRY FOYER

DINING ROOM
17'-0" x 14'-0"

FAMILY ROOM
16'-0" x 16'-0"

THREE CAR GARAGE
23'-0" x 30'-0"

LIBRARY
14'-0" x 18'-0"

VAULTED CEILING

PORCH

PORCH

DESIGN BY
©R.L. Pfotenhauer

DESIGN HPU040532

First Floor: 3,182 square feet
Second Floor: 1,190 square feet
Total: 4,372 square feet
Bonus Room: 486 square feet
Width: 104'-0" Depth: 60'-0"

In the Pays Basque region of rural France, you can find finished farmhouses such as this beauty. The steeply pitched roof drains water quickly, and the curved eaves push the water away from the wall, protecting the stucco. The two-story entry is graced with a beautiful curved stair, opening to a two-story living room with a vaulted ceiling. To the right is a formal dining room and to the left, a finely detailed library with a vaulted ceiling and an impressive arched window. The private master bedroom, with its vaulted ceiling, king-size bath and huge walk-in closets, will never go out of style. The second floor has two bedrooms with their own bathrooms and a bonus room for future use. Note the second stair that is convenient to the informal areas.

OPEN TO BELOW

BEDROOM
13'-0" x 16'-0"

BATH

DN

BONUS ROOM
13'-0" X 30'-0"

BALCONY

UPPER HALL

LINEN

WIC

DN

BATH

OPEN TO BELOW

BEDROOM
14'-0" x 13'-0"

429

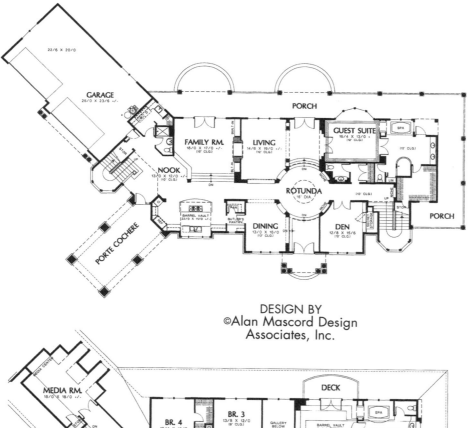

DESIGN BY
©Alan Mascord Design
Associates, Inc.

If it's space you desire, with a classy facade to further enhance it, this is the home for you! Inside, the foyer is flanked by a cozy den to the right and a formal dining room to the left. A lavish guest suite is loaded with amenities and is near the formal living room. The spacious kitchen will please any gourmet, with a cooktop island, walk-in pantry and a nearby sunken family room. Here, a fireplace, shared by the formal living room, will add warmth and charm to any gathering. Upstairs, two large bedrooms—each with walk-in closets and private lavatories—share a bath. A media room is just down the hall and is great for reading, studying or watching movies. The sumptuous master suite is designed to pamper, with such amenities as a walk-in closet, private deck, huge shower and separate spa tub. Note the tremendous amount of storage in the four-car garage.

DESIGN HPU040533

First Floor: 3,620 square feet
Second Floor: 2,440 square feet
Total: 6,060 square feet
Width: 139'-6" Depth: 91'-1"

DESIGN HPU040534

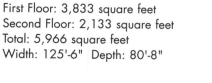

First Floor: 3,833 square feet
Second Floor: 2,133 square feet
Total: 5,966 square feet
Width: 125'-6"   Depth: 80'-8"

Stucco and stone details and multiple gables give this home a distinctive exterior. The striking glass-walled turret houses an elegant, octagonal, two-story living room with a fireplace. The dining room, across the foyer, is accessible to the gourmet kitchen through a butler's pantry. The kitchen opens to the large family room and a breakfast nook with access to a covered porch. The master suite takes up the left wing of the house with its bumped-out garden tub, room-sized walk-in closet and private covered porch. Two staircases—a beautifully curved one in the foyer and one in the family room—lead upstairs, where three bedrooms share two baths along with an exercise room and a large bonus room over the garage.

DESIGN BY
©Alan Mascord Design
Associates, Inc.

431

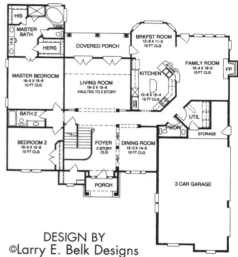

DESIGN HPU040535

First Floor: 2,518 square feet
Second Floor: 1,013 square feet
Total: 3,531 square feet
Bonus Room: 192 square feet
Width: 67'-8" Depth: 74'-2"

Old World charm gives this design its universal appeal. The mixture of stone and brick on the exterior elevation gives the home a warm, inviting feel. Inside, an up-to-date floor plan has it all. Two living areas provide space for both formal and informal entertaining. The kitchen and breakfast room are open to the large family room. The owners suite and a secondary bedroom are located on the first floor. The second bedroom makes a great nursery, study or convenient guest bedroom. Upstairs, bedrooms 3 and 4 share a large bath, with private dressing areas. Please specify basement, crawlspace or slab foundation when ordering.

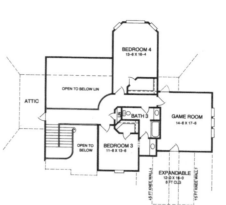

DESIGN BY
©Larry E. Belk Designs

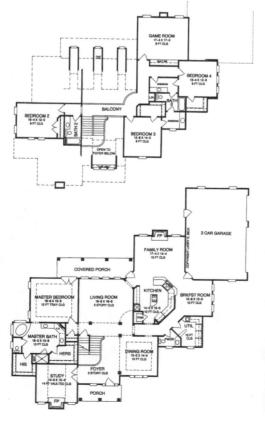

DESIGN HPU040536

First Floor: 2,666 square feet
Second Floor: 1,471 square feet
Total: 4,137 square feet
Width: 82'-2" Depth: 79'-10"

DESIGN BY
©Larry E. Belk Designs

A brick exterior, interesting window dressings and a multitude of rooflines lend this house eye appeal. Inside, a two-story foyer illuminates with natural light and leads past columns to the formal dining room and living room. To the left of the plan, the tray-ceilinged master bedroom enjoys private access to the rear porch, and features a luxurious bath. The second level includes three family bedrooms, two full baths and a game room.

DESIGN BY
©Larry E. Belk Designs

DESIGN HPU040537

First Floor: 3,261 square feet
Second Floor: 1,920 square feet
Total: 5,181 square feet
Bonus Room: 710 square feet
Width: 86'-2" Depth: 66'-10"

Elegantly styled in the French country tradition, this home features a well-thought-out floor plan with all the amenities. A large dining room and a study open off the two-story grand foyer that showcases a lovely flared staircase. A covered patio is accessed from the large formal living room. A more informal family room is conveniently located off the kitchen and breakfast room. The roomy master suite includes a sitting area, a luxurious private bath and its own entrance to the study. The second floor can be reached from the formal front stair or a well-placed rear staircase. Three large bedrooms and a game room are located upstairs. Bedrooms 3 and 4 feature private dressing areas and a shared bath. Bedroom 2 shares a bath with the game room. The walkout basement can be expanded to provide more living space. Please specify basement or crawlspace foundation when ordering.

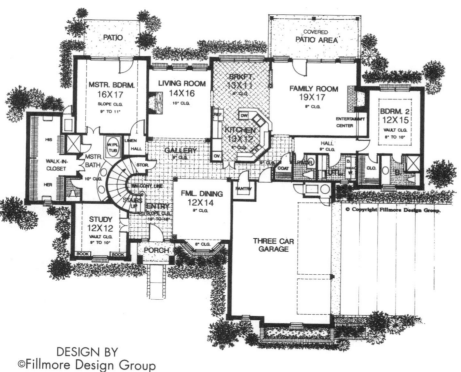

DESIGN BY
©Fillmore Design Group

DESIGN HPU040538

First Floor: 2,778 square feet
Second Floor: 931 square feet
Total: 3,709 square feet
Bonus Room: 1,405 square feet
Width: 86'-0" Depth: 60'-1"

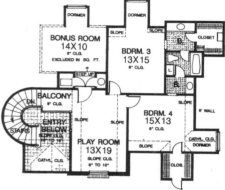

This brick-and-stone combination features a country-fresh look with a contemporary interior floor plan. Step into the gallery, and directly to your left is the sweeping staircase; to the right, you will find a large kitchen and breakfast area. The family room is enhanced with an entertainment center, fireplace and access to the rear patio. The first-floor master suite boasts a sumptuous bath. Along with two bedrooms, the second floor holds a playroom and a bonus room.

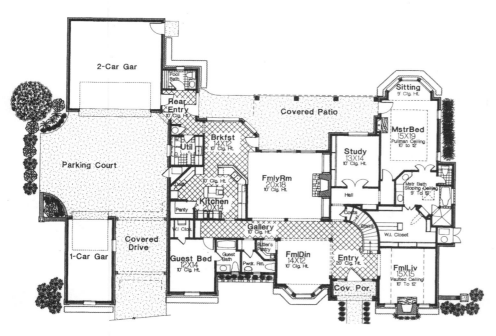

DESIGN HPU040539

First Floor: 3,248 square feet
Second Floor: 1,426 square feet
Total: 4,674 square feet
Width: 99'-10"   Depth: 74'-10"

DESIGN BY
©Fillmore Design Group

Multiple rooflines, a stone, brick and siding facade and an absolutely grand entrance combine to give this home the look of luxury. A striking family room showcases a beautiful fireplace framed with built-ins. The nearby breakfast room streams with light and accesses the rear patio. The kitchen features an island workstation, walk-in pantry and plenty of counter space. A guest suite is available on the first floor, perfect for when elderly members of the family visit. The master suite, also on the first floor, enjoys easy access to a large study, a bayed sitting room and a luxurious bath. Private baths are also included for each of the upstairs bedrooms.

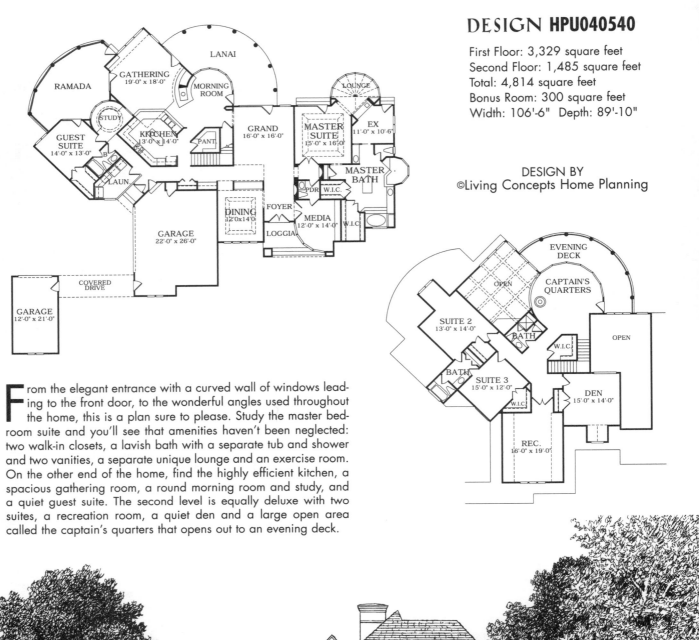

DESIGN HPU040540

First Floor: 3,329 square feet
Second Floor: 1,485 square feet
Total: 4,814 square feet
Bonus Room: 300 square feet
Width: 106'-6" Depth: 89'-10"

DESIGN BY
©Living Concepts Home Planning

From the elegant entrance with a curved wall of windows leading to the front door, to the wonderful angles used throughout the home, this is a plan sure to please. Study the master bedroom suite and you'll see that amenities haven't been neglected: two walk-in closets, a lavish bath with a separate tub and shower and two vanities, a separate unique lounge and an exercise room. On the other end of the home, find the highly efficient kitchen, a spacious gathering room, a round morning room and study, and a quiet guest suite. The second level is equally deluxe with two suites, a recreation room, a quiet den and a large open area called the captain's quarters that opens out to an evening deck.

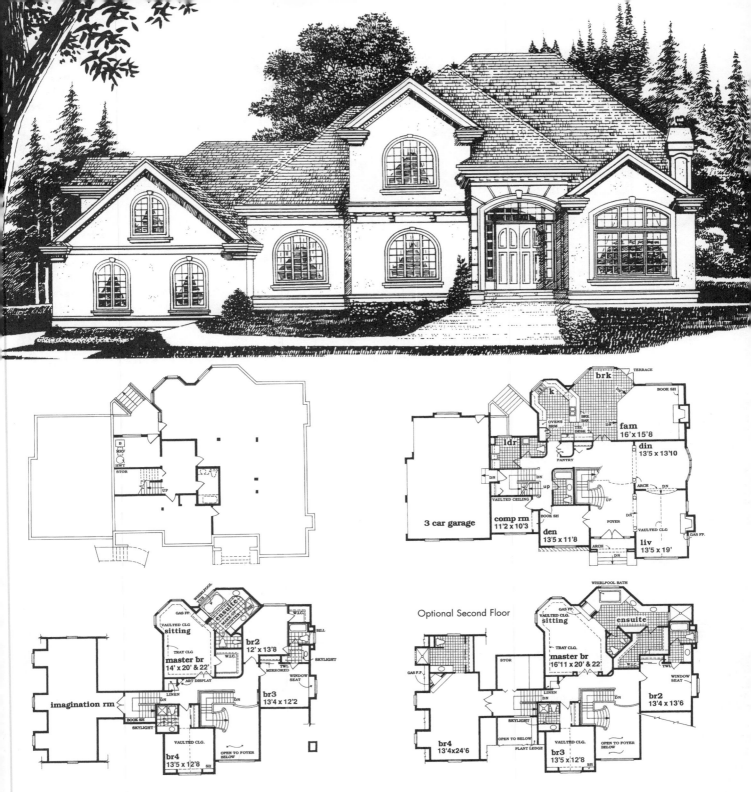

F inished in brick, with an elegant entry, this dramatic two-story home is the essence of luxury. Double doors open to a foyer with a sunken living room on the right and a den on the left. An archway leads to the formal dining room, mirroring the curved window in the living room and the bowed window in the dining room. The den and nearby computer room have use of a full bath—making them handy as extra guest rooms when needed. The family room, like the living room, is sunken and warmed by a hearth, but also has built-in bookcases. A snack-bar counter separates the U-shaped kitchen from the light-filled breakfast room. The second floor can be configured in two different ways. Both allow for a gigantic master suite with His and Hers vanities, an oversized shower, a walk-in closet and a sitting area.

DESIGN HPU040541

First Floor: 2,403 square feet
Second Floor: 1,684 square feet
Total: 4,087 square feet
Bonus Room: 644 square feet
Width: 77'-10" Depth: 55'-8"

DESIGN BY
©Select Home Designs

437

A graceful column and a multitude of windows define the entrance to this fine two-story home. Inside, a two-story foyer opens to a formal dining room on the left and directly ahead to the formal living room—complete with a warming fireplace. A cozy den, with a built-in desk and built-in cabinets, would work well as a home office. The spacious family room, with a second fireplace, built-in cabinets and snack bar into the kitchen, will be a favorite gathering place for your family. The homeowner will surely love the master bedroom suite on the second floor. Sunken down two steps, with two walk-in closets, a corner whirlpool tub, separate shower stall and two individual lavatories, this suite is designed to pamper. Three secondary bedrooms, two full baths and a bonus room complete this floor.

DESIGN BY
©Ahmann Design, Inc.

DESIGN HPU040543

First Floor: 1,931 square feet
Second Floor: 1,580 square feet
Total: 3,511 square feet
Bonus Room: 439 square feet
Width: 90'-3" Depth: 65'-8"

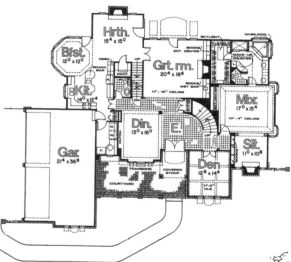

The stone facade of this traditional design evokes images of a quieter life, a life of harmony and comfortable luxury. The owners suite offers privacy on the first floor and features a sitting room with bookshelves, two walk-in closets and a private bath with a corner whirlpool tub. Three family bedrooms, each with a walk-in closet, and two baths make up the second floor.

QUOTE ONE®
Cost to build? See page 502
to order complete cost estimate
to build this house in your area!

DESIGN HPU040542

First Floor: 2,603 square feet
Second Floor: 1,020 square feet
Total: 3,623 square feet
Width: 76'-8" Depth: 68'-0"

DESIGN BY
©Design Basics, Inc.

Keystone lintels, an arched transom over the entry and sidelights spell classic design for this four-bedroom home. The tiled foyer offers entry to any room you choose, whether it be the secluded den with its built-in bookshelves, the formal dining room, the formal living room with its fireplace, wet bar and wall of windows, or the spacious rear family and kitchen area with its sunny breakfast nook. The owners suite offers privacy on the first floor and features a sitting room with bookshelves, two walk-in closets and a private bath with a corner whirlpool tub. Upstairs, two family bedrooms share a bath and enjoy separate vanities. A third family bedroom features its own full bath and a built-in window seat in a box-bay window. Note the four-car garage with plenty of room for the family fleet.

DESIGN BY
©Design Basics, Inc.

DESIGN HPU040544

First Floor: 2,813 square feet
Second Floor: 1,091 square feet
Total: 3,904 square feet
Width: 85'-5" Depth: 74'-8"

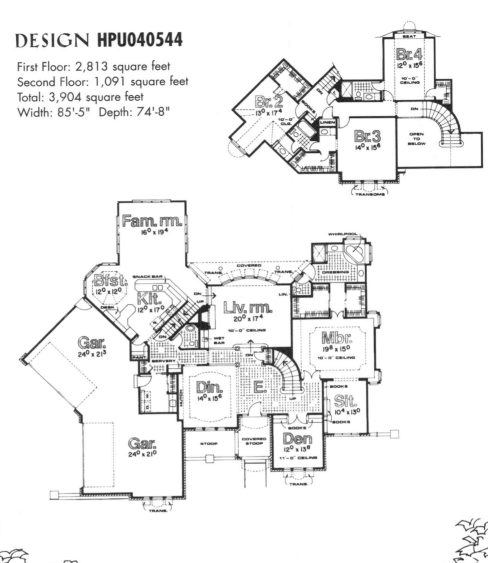

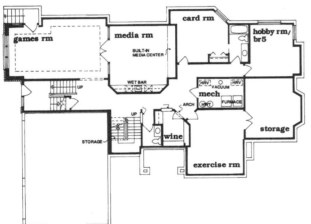

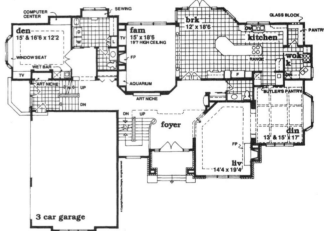

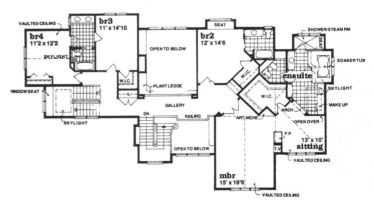

This grand, two-story European home is adorned with a facade of stucco and brick, meticulously appointed with details for gracious living. Guests enter through a portico to find a stately, two-story foyer. The formal living room features a tray ceiling and fireplace and is joined by a charming dining room with a large bay window. A butler's pantry joins the dining room to the gourmet kitchen, which holds a separate wok kitchen, an island work center and a breakfast room with double doors leading to the rear patio. The nearby family room enjoys a built-in aquarium, media center and fireplace. A den with a tray ceiling, window seat and built-in computer center is tucked in a corner for privacy. Served by two separate staircases, the second floor features a spectacular owners suite with a separate sitting room, an oversized closet and a bath with a shower/steam room and spa tub.

DESIGN BY
©Select Home Designs

PLAN HPU040545

First Floor: 2,596 square feet
Second Floor: 2,233 square feet
Total: 4,829 square feet
Basement: 2,012 square feet
Width: 81'-0" Depth: 61'-0"

QUOTE ONE®
Cost to build? See page 502
to order complete cost estimate
to build this house in your area!

This stunning traditional exterior combines brick and stucco for a dramatic look. Tray ceilings add architectural interest to both the living and dining rooms; the living room is further graced by a fireplace. Double doors off the vaulted foyer provide access to a den—or make it a guest room, if you wish. The kitchen is spacious and boasts a cooking island and an adjoining sunny breakfast room. A private media room is accessible from the family room through double French doors. The second floor features a large master bedroom with an enormous walk-in closet, a two-sided gas fireplace and an extensive luxury master bath. Three family bedrooms—one with a private bath—and a skylit bonus room over the garage complete the upper level.

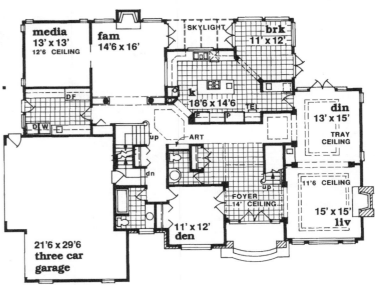

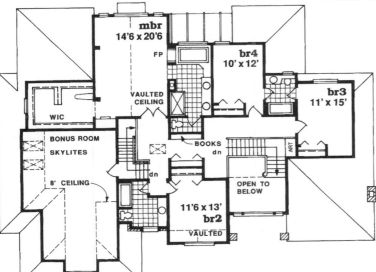

DESIGN HPU040546

First Floor: 2,389 square feet
Second Floor: 1,712 square feet
Total: 4,101 square feet
Bonus Room: 497 square feet
Width: 72'-0" Depth: 54'-0"

DESIGN BY
©Select Home Designs

441

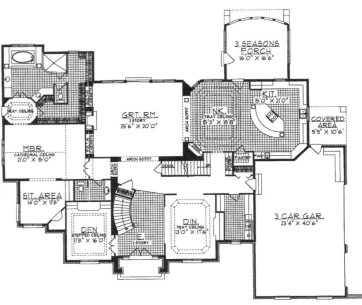

Lavish, grand and luxurious—these words apply to this beautiful brick mansion with its expansive entrance. Inside, the two-story foyer leads to a formal dining room on the right and a cozy den with built-ins on the left. A curving staircase points the way to the upper level and the balcony overlooking the foyer and the great room. The huge kitchen is sure to please the gourmet of the family. It includes a large cooktop island with a snack bar, a walk-in pantry, plenty of counter and cabinet space, an adjacent nook and access to the three-seasons porch. Lavish is the word for the owners suite, which includes among its many amenities a separate sitting area with a fireplace. Upstairs, each bedroom has a walk-in closet and private bath. The bonus room is available for future expansion and features a full bath and large closet.

DESIGN HPU040547

First Floor: 3,536 square feet
Second Floor: 1,690 square feet
Total: 5,226 square feet
Bonus Room: 546 square feet
Width: 89'-8" Depth: 76'-0"

DESIGN BY
©Ahmann Design, Inc.

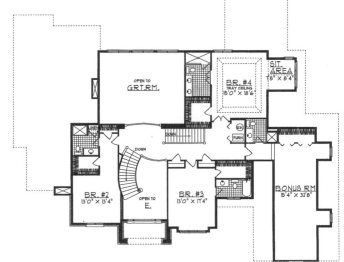

Multi-pane windows glimmer with sunlight, and corner quoins lend an established air to this five-bedroom plan. The foyer of this traditional-style home features a curved staircase. Amenities on the main floor include a sewing room, a separate wok kitchen and a butler's pantry. The kitchen boasts a walk-in pantry, expansive counter space and an island stove. On the second floor, the expansive master bedroom hosts a dramatic double-door entry and a large master bath. Three family bedrooms and two full baths complete this level. The basement enjoys a media room, a game room equipped with a fireplace, an exercise room, a storage area and a fifth bedroom with a bath.

DESIGN BY
©Select Home Designs

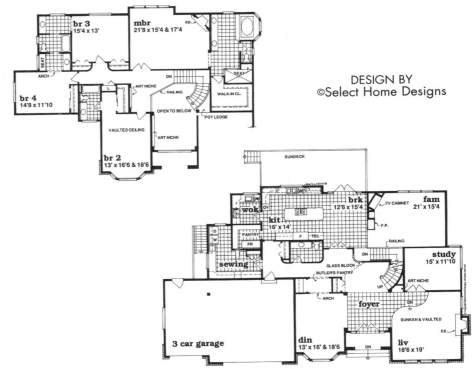

DESIGN HPU040548

First Floor: 2,555 square feet
Second Floor: 1,975 square feet
Total: 4,530 square feet
Width: 81'-8" Depth: 50'-4"

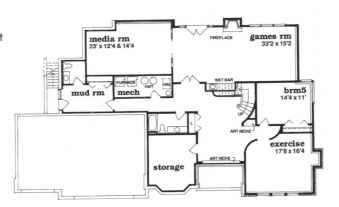

DESIGN BY
©Alan Mascord Design
Associates, Inc.

DESIGN HPU040549

First Floor: 2,813 square feet
Second Floor: 1,058 square feet
Total: 3,871 square feet
Width: 83'-0" Depth: 61'-0"

For an extra-luxurious hillside home, with unfinished space on the lower level, look no farther than this grand design. The main and upper levels have spacious living and sleeping areas, a service kitchen for the formal dining room, a den and gourmet kitchen. Two family bedrooms with a shared bath sit on the main level, while the master suite has the entire upper floor to itself. The master bath features twin vanity sinks, an oversized tub and a separate shower. The lower level holds the three-car garage, game room, shop and a full bath. Please specify basement or crawlspace foundation when ordering.

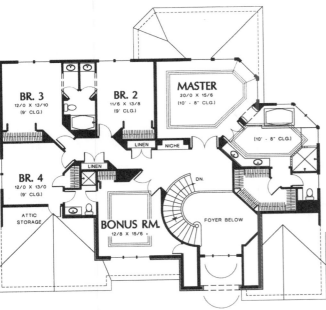

This grand traditional manor greets you with a two-story entry topped with a Palladian window. Inside, a beautiful curved staircase leads up to the sleeping quarters. The great room, the dining room and the breakfast nook provide plenty of windows. The open floor plan lets the kitchen serve every room with ease. A guest room with a full bath is tucked away in the back, while a study offers a private retreat at the front. The luxurious master suite features a bath with two sinks, a compartmented toilet and a large soaking tub.

DESIGN HPU040550

First Floor: 2,141 square feet
Second Floor: 1,724 square feet
Total: 3,865 square feet
Bonus Room: 249 square feet
Width: 64'-0" Depth: 59'-0"

DESIGN BY
©Alan Mascord Design
Associates, Inc.

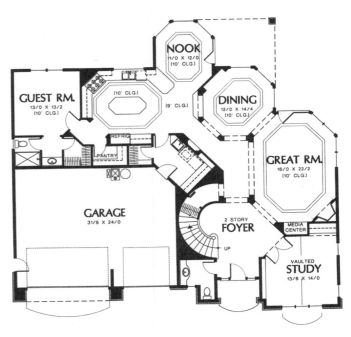

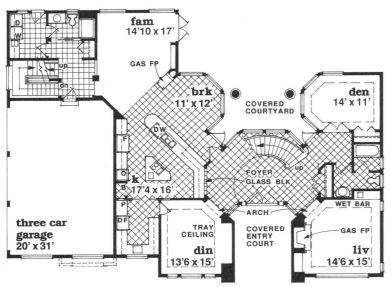

fam
14'10 x 17'

GAS FP

brk
11' x 12'

COVERED
COURTYARD

den
14' x 11'

up

k
17'4 x 16'

F

DW

O

B

P

DF

FOYER
GLASS BLK

up

WET BAR

ARCH

**three car
garage**
20' x 31'

TRAY
CEILING

din
13'6 x 15'

COVERED
ENTRY
COURT

GAS FP

liv
14'6 x 15'

D

W

up

dn

DESIGN **HPU040551**

First Floor: 2,240 square feet
Second Floor: 1,979 square feet
Total: 4,219 square feet
Width: 72'-0" Depth: 54'-6"

DESIGN BY
©Select Home Designs

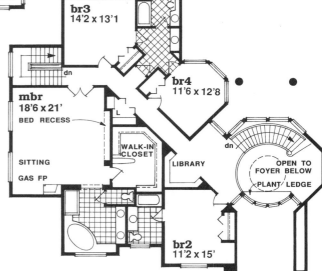

br3
14'2 x 13'1

dn

br4
11'6 x 12'8

mbr
18'6 x 21'

BED RECESS

SITTING

GAS FP

L

WALK-IN
CLOSET

LIBRARY

dn

OPEN TO
FOYER BELOW

PLANT LEDGE

br2
11'2 x 15'

Enjoy regal splendor in a superbly detailed four-bedroom home. The entrance foyer creates a dramatic welcome with its curved staircase accented by a bayed wall of glass. This comfortable living room includes a gas fireplace and convenient wet bar. Featuring an innovative design, the kitchen boasts a triangular cooking island and an angled counter with a large seating area. A large bayed breakfast area is connected to the spacious family room by a double-sided gas fireplace. This beautiful, covered rear courtyard is framed with glass on three sides. The luxurious powder room with an adjoining bath is easily accessed by both the den and living room. The secondary rear stairs permit informal access to Bedrooms 3 and 4.

DESIGN HPU040552

First Floor: 2,006 square feet
Second Floor: 1,799 square feet
Total: 3,805 square feet
Width: 71'-8" Depth: 54'-2"

DESIGN BY
©Select Home Designs

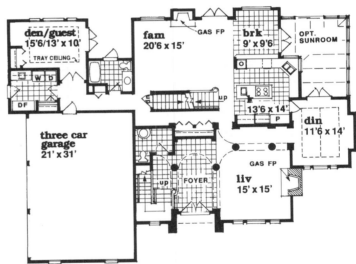

den/guest
15'6/13' x 10'
TRAY CEILING

W D

DF

three car
garage
21' x 31'

fam
20'6 x 15'

GAS FP

brk
9' x 9'6

OPT.
SUNROOM

13'6 x 14'

din
11'6 x 14'

up

GAS FP

FOYER

liv
15' x 15'

up

P

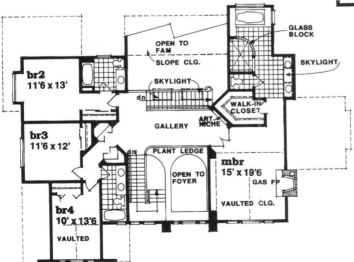

OPEN TO
FAM
SLOPE CLG.

GLASS
BLOCK

SKYLIGHT

br2
11'6 x 13'

SKYLIGHT

dn

WALK-IN
CLOSET

br3
11'6 x 12'

GALLERY

ART
NICHE

dn

PLANT LEDGE

mbr
15' x 19'6

GAS FP

OPEN TO
FOYER

br4
10' x 13'6

VAULTED CLG.

VAULTED

This beautifully detailed, luxurious four-bedroom home has an exterior of traditional brick. The two-story foyer opens to an impressive colonnade, creating a dramatic entry to this exclusive home. The pillars visually separate the living room, main foyer and hallway. The spacious kitchen, with a center cooking island, offers a large breakfast bar and corner sink overlooking the optional sun room. A private den or guest room with an adjacent full bath has rear access through double French doors. A railed gallery open to the vaulted family room and main foyer creates privacy for the master bedroom retreat. The elegant master bath features a skylit twin vanity, a large shower, a soaking tub and a compartmented toilet. A secondary rear stair provides access to the three family bedrooms.

This stately brick home offers a magnificent elevation from every angle, with a particularly impressive arched portico. The entry hall is highlighted by a majestic staircase ascending to an elegant balcony. The spacious formal dining room includes two built-in china cabinets and is easily reached from the living room with its cheery fireplace and attractive window seat. Between them is a handsomely appointed den with floor-to-ceiling cabinetry, a window seat and a spider-beam ceiling. An expansive gourmet kitchen with a walk-in pantry and an island cooktop/snack bar opens into a distinctive family room featuring a built-in rolltop desk, an entertainment center and a raised-hearth fireplace. The nearby breakfast nook offers panoramic views to the outside. Upstairs, a lavish master suite includes a sitting room with a fireplace framed by bookcases, a two-person whirlpool bath and two walk-in closets. Two of the family bedrooms feature flip-top window seats for added storage.

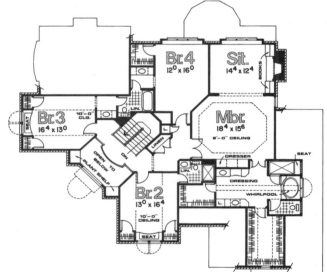

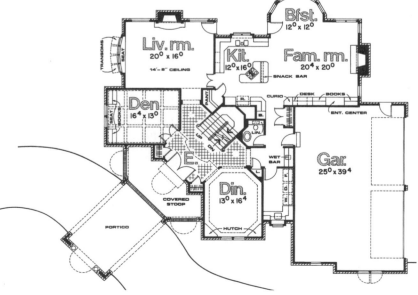

DESIGN HPU040553

First Floor: 2,040 square feet
Second Floor: 1,952 square feet
Total: 3,992 square feet
Width: 68'-0" Depth: 66'-0"

DESIGN BY
©Design Basics, Inc.

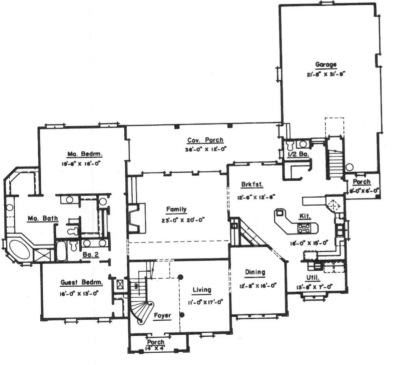

The vertical line of the two-story entrance is emphasized by stone quoins and echoed in the tall windows across the front of this impressive stucco home. The foyer, dominated by a graceful stairway, opens through decorative columns to the formal living and dining rooms. The family cook will appreciate the efficient kitchen, with its angled island cooktop and serving bar, walk-in pantry and sunny breakfast nook. A fireplace and built-in shelves are the focal point of the spacious family room, from which gatherings can easily spill out onto the rear covered porch. Two bedroom suites complete the first floor—a guest room with a private bath and a sumptuous master suite with access to the back porch and a pampering bath. Upstairs, two family bedrooms share a compartmented bath and a reading loft. A game room over the garage is reached by a separate staircase. Please specify crawlspace or slab foundation when ordering.

DESIGN HPU040554

First Floor: 3,002 square feet
Second Floor: 1,418 square feet
Total: 4,420 square feet
Width: 87'-10" Depth: 82'-0"

DESIGN BY
©Chatham Home Planning, Inc.

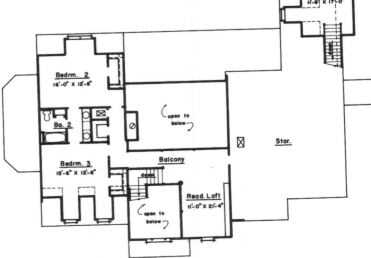

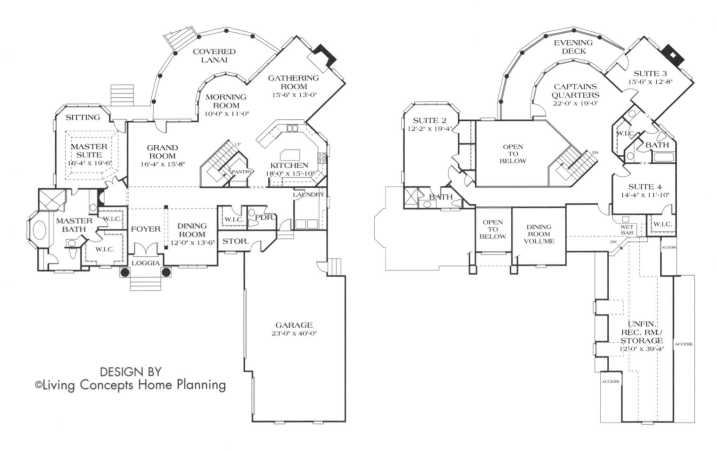

SITTING

MASTER SUITE
16'-4" x 19'-6"

COVERED LANAI

MORNING ROOM
10'-0" x 11'-0"

GATHERING ROOM
15'-6" x 13'-0"

GRAND ROOM
16'-4" x 15'-8"

UP

PANTRY

KITCHEN
18'-0" x 15'-10"

W.I.C.

MASTER BATH

W.I.C.

FOYER

W.I.C.

DINING ROOM
12'-0" x 13'-6"

W.I.C.

PDR.

LAUNDRY

STOR.

LOGGIA

GARAGE
23'-0" x 40'-0"

DESIGN BY
©Living Concepts Home Planning

EVENING DECK

CAPTAINS QUARTERS
22'-0" x 19'-0"

SUITE 3
15'-6" x 12'-8"

SUITE 2
12'-2" x 19'-4"

OPEN TO BELOW

W.I.C.

BATH

BATH

DN

SUITE 4
14'-4" x 11'-10"

OPEN TO BELOW

DINING ROOM VOLUME

WET BAR

DN

W.I.C.

ACCESS

UNFIN. REC. RM./ STORAGE
12'-0" x 39'-4"

ACCESS

ACCESS

Double columns flank a raised loggia that leads to a beautiful two-story foyer. Flanking this elegance to the right is a formal dining room. Straight ahead, under a balcony and defined by yet more pillars, is the spacious grand room. A bow-windowed morning room and a gathering room feature a full view of the rear lanai and beyond. The owners bedroom suite is lavish with its amenities, which include a bayed sitting area, direct access to the rear terrace, a walk-in closet and a sumptuous bath.

DESIGN HPU040555

First Floor: 2,547 square feet
Second Floor: 1,637 square feet
Total: 4,184 square feet
Bonus Room: 802 square feet
Width: 74'-0" Depth: 95'-6"

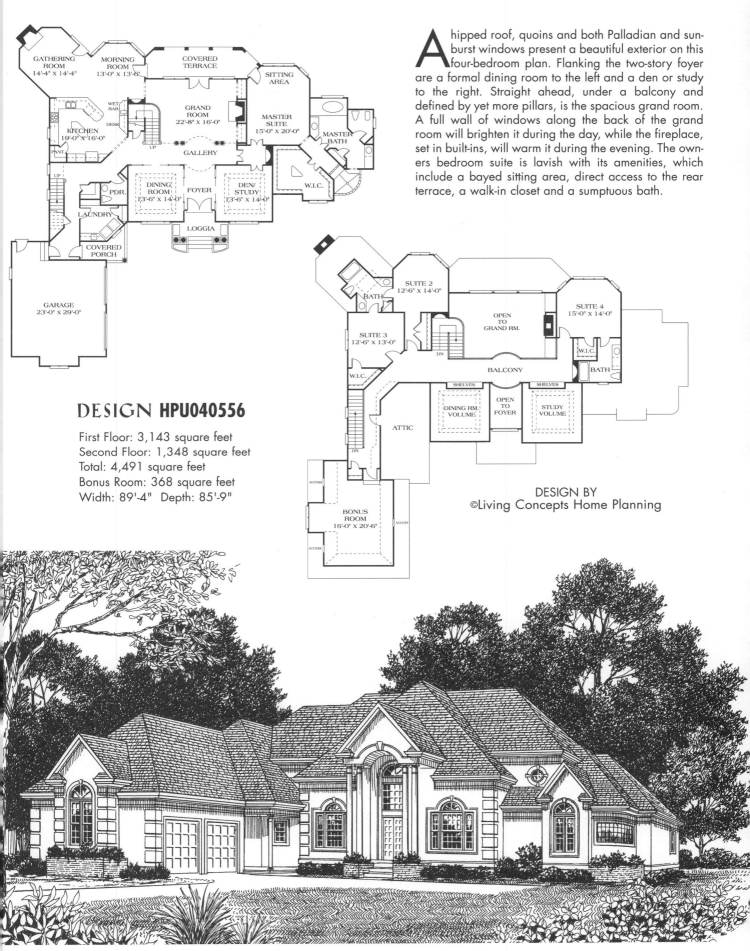

GATHERING ROOM
14'-4" x 14'-4"

MORNING ROOM
13'-0" x 13'-6"

COVERED TERRACE

SITTING AREA

WET BAR

GRAND ROOM
22'-8" x 16'-0"

MASTER SUITE
15'-0" x 20'-0"

DESK

KITCHEN
19'-0" x 16'-0"

UP

GALLERY

MASTER BATH

PANT.

UP

PDR.

DINING ROOM
13'-6" x 14'-0"

FOYER

DEN/ STUDY
13'-6" x 14'-0"

W.I.C.

LAUNDRY

LOGGIA

COVERED PORCH

GARAGE
23'-0" x 29'-0"

DESIGN HPU040556

First Floor: 3,143 square feet
Second Floor: 1,348 square feet
Total: 4,491 square feet
Bonus Room: 368 square feet
Width: 89'-4" Depth: 85'-9"

BATH

SUITE 2
12'-6" x 14'-0"

OPEN TO GRAND RM.

SUITE 4
15'-0" x 14'-0"

SUITE 3
12'-6" x 13'-0"

W.I.C.

DN

BALCONY

W.I.C.

BATH

W.I.C.

SHELVES

SHELVES

ATTIC

DINING RM. VOLUME

OPEN TO FOYER

STUDY VOLUME

DN

ACCESS

BONUS ROOM
16'-0" x 20'-6"

ACCESS

ACCESS

DESIGN BY
©Living Concepts Home Planning

A hipped roof, quoins and both Palladian and sunburst windows present a beautiful exterior on this four-bedroom plan. Flanking the two-story foyer are a formal dining room to the left and a den or study to the right. Straight ahead, under a balcony and defined by yet more pillars, is the spacious grand room. A full wall of windows along the back of the grand room will brighten it during the day, while the fireplace, set in built-ins, will warm it during the evening. The owners bedroom suite is lavish with its amenities, which include a bayed sitting area, direct access to the rear terrace, a walk-in closet and a sumptuous bath.

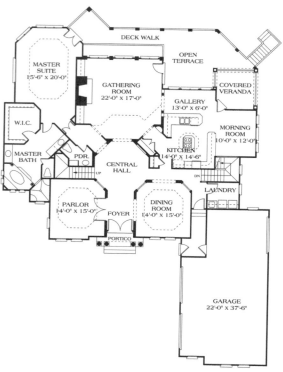

Grand elegance is highly evident on the facade of this four-bedroom, two-story home. Note the details on the entrance portico—double columns, a balcony and a pediment. The elegance continues inside as seen with the formal dining room and formal parlor, which flank the foyer. An octagonal central hall leads to all other areas: a spacious gathering room, an island kitchen with an adjacent gallery and morning room, and a master bedroom suite. Upstairs, three large bedrooms—each with walk-in closets—share two full baths, access to a sitting area for reading, and a study area, which is perfect for the family computer.

DESIGN HPU040557

First Floor: 2,716 square feet
Second Floor: 1,457 square feet
Total: 4,173 square feet
Basement: 1,290 square feet
Width: 69'-6" Depth: 101'-0"

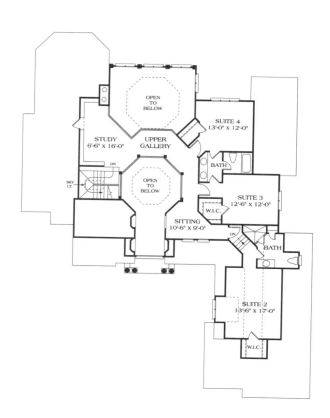

DESIGN BY
©Living Concepts Home Planning

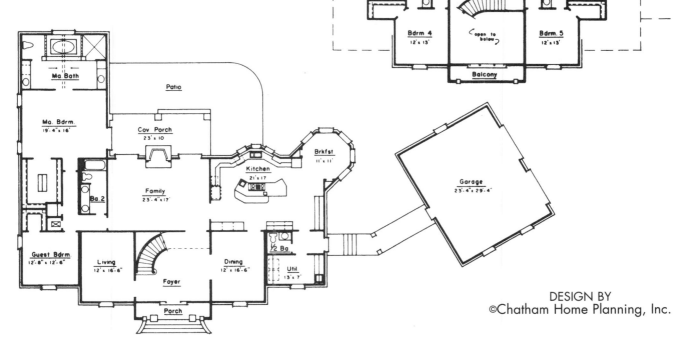

From the columned front porch to the curved patio in back, this house is filled with elegance and style. The foyer, featuring a graceful curving staircase, opens to the formal living and dining rooms. The focal point of the large family room is its fireplace, but windows will beckon you to the covered porch and patio outside. Multiple windows also highlight the kitchen, with its large work island, and the round breakfast room. The owners suite is in a private wing and has a large walk-in closet, an amenity-laden bath and its own entrance to the back porch. A nearby guest room could serve as a study or a library. Please specify slab or crawlspace foundation when ordering.

DESIGN HPU040558

First Floor: 3,117 square feet
Second Floor: 1,411 square feet
Total: 4,528 square feet
Width: 76'-10" Depth: 68'-10"

DESIGN BY
©Chatham Home Planning, Inc.

DESIGN HPU040559

First Floor: 1,741 square feet
Second Floor: 1,884 square feet
Total: 3,625 square feet
Width: 61'-9" Depth: 48'-10"

DESIGN BY
©Living Concepts Home Planning

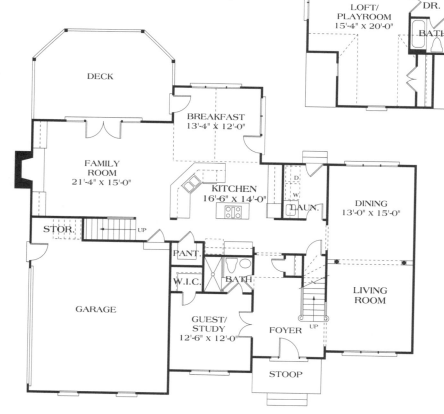

SUITE 3
14'-0" X 12'-6"

BATH

DR.

SUITE 2
13'-8" X 12'-2"

MASTER
SUITE
20'-6" X 14'-0"

DN

UP

BALCONY

DN

W.I.C.   W.I.C.

LOFT/
PLAYROOM
15'-4" X 20'-0"

DR.

LIN.

MASTER
BATH

BATH

SUITE 4
12'-8" X 14'-0"

OPEN
TO
BELOW

DECK

BREAKFAST
13'-4" X 12'-0"

FAMILY
ROOM
21'-4" X 15'-0"

KITCHEN
16'-6" X 14'-0"

D.
W.

LAUN.

DINING
13'-0" X 15'-0"

STOR.   UP

PANT.

W.I.C.   BATH

GUEST/
STUDY
12'-6" X 12'-0"

FOYER   UP

LIVING
ROOM

GARAGE

STOOP

Corner quoins, gabled rooflines and attractive shutters give this four-bedroom home plenty of curb appeal. Inside, the floor plan is designed for entertaining. For formal occasions, there is the living/dining room combination, separated by graceful columns. Casual gatherings will be welcomed in the spacious family room, which features a fireplace, built-ins and direct access to the rear deck. A sunny breakfast room is easily served by the efficient kitchen. A guest/study with a walk-in closet and a full bath complete this level. Upstairs, three bedrooms share two baths and access to a large playroom/loft. The master bedroom suite is sure to please with a tray ceiling, two walk-in closets and a luxurious bath.

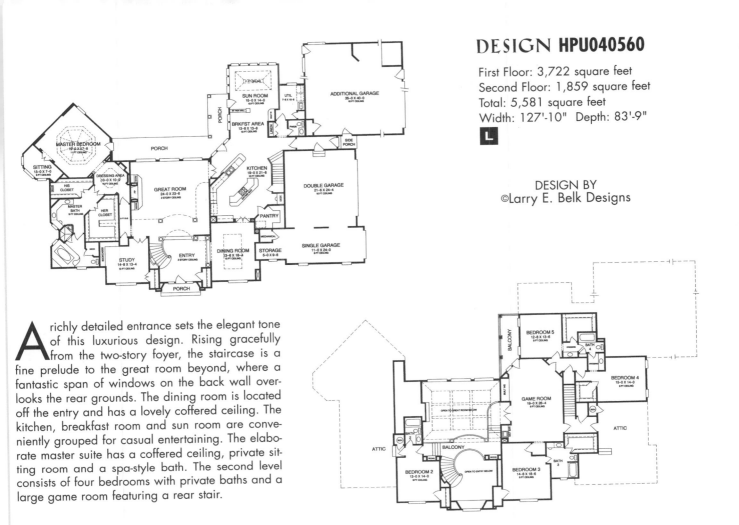

DESIGN HPU040560

First Floor: 3,722 square feet
Second Floor: 1,859 square feet
Total: 5,581 square feet
Width: 127'-10" Depth: 83'-9"

L

DESIGN BY
©Larry E. Belk Designs

A richly detailed entrance sets the elegant tone of this luxurious design. Rising gracefully from the two-story foyer, the staircase is a fine prelude to the great room beyond, where a fantastic span of windows on the back wall overlooks the rear grounds. The dining room is located off the entry and has a lovely coffered ceiling. The kitchen, breakfast room and sun room are conveniently grouped for casual entertaining. The elaborate master suite has a coffered ceiling, private sitting room and a spa-style bath. The second level consists of four bedrooms with private baths and a large game room featuring a rear stair.

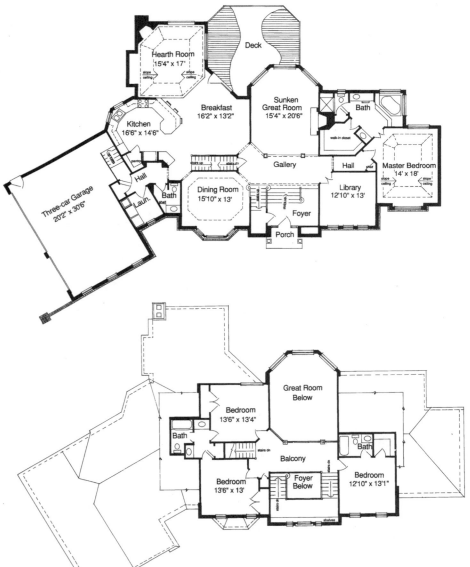

Hearth Room
15'4" x 17'

Deck

Breakfast
16'2" x 13'2"

Sunken
Great Room
15'4" x 20'6"

Bath

Kitchen
16'6" x 14'6"

walk-in closet

Master Bedroom
14' x 18'

Hall

Gallery

Hall

Three-car Garage
20'2" x 30'6"

Bath

Laun.

Dining Room
15'10" x 13'

Library
12'10" x 13'

Foyer

Porch

Bedroom
13'6" x 13'4"

Great Room
Below

Bath

Bath

stairs dn

Balcony

Bedroom
13'6" x 13'

Foyer
Below

Bedroom
12'10" x 13'1"

shelves

The diversity and strength of the exterior of this home reflects the excitement of the interior styling. Stairs in the foyer lead to a first-floor gallery, providing a panoramic view of the sunken great room. The two-story ceiling, along with the dramatic, rear-wall window arrangement and the elegantly faced fireplace, elevate this home into a phenomenal showplace. An extravagant kitchen/breakfast area with counter seating and a spacious pantry flows easily to the cozy hearth room. A second fireplace, furniture alcove, exciting ceiling treatment and multiple windows enhance the enjoyment of this family gathering place. Located on the first floor and positioned for privacy, an expansive master bedroom suite provides luxury, spaciousness and relaxation for the homeowner. Rounding out the first floor are the formal dining room and a private library/retreat. Three large bedrooms, two baths, service stairs to the kitchen and a balcony with a dramatic view of the great room top this exciting home.

DESIGN HPU040561

First Floor: 2,710 square feet
Second Floor: 964 square feet
Total: 3,674 square feet
Width: 101'-0" Depth: 68'-8"

DESIGN BY
©Studer Residential Designs, Inc.

As one approaches this magnificent estate, he/she will be transformed back in time to the land of gentry. The opulence extends from the circular stairway that floats in front of the grand salon and floor-to-ceiling windows. The dining hall can easily seat twelve with additional furnishings. There is also a butler's pantry on the way to the oversized, octagonal kitchen, with a vaulted family room, vaulted breakfast area and an open stairway to the basement and second floor. To the left of the foyer is a master suite with all the finest appointments expected in a large home, from built-in dressers, cedar closets, study access, fireplace, built-ins and a massive column area over the bed. The second floor has a large stateroom with a sitting room and bath. Two additional staterooms feature private baths.

DESIGN HPU040562

First Floor: 3,102 square feet
Second Floor: 1,487 square feet
Total: 4,589 square feet
Bonus Room: 786 square feet
Width: 106'-0" Depth: 56'-6"

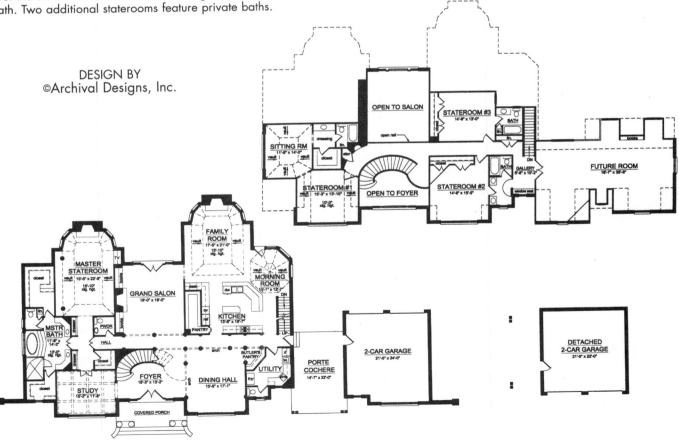

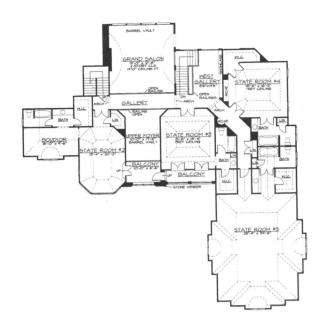

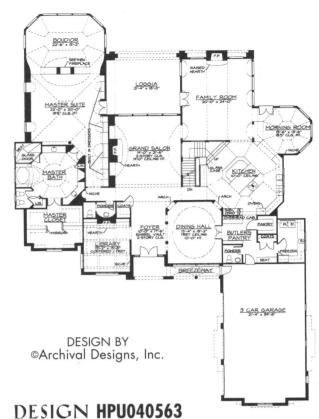

DESIGN HPU040563

First Floor: 4,508 square feet
Second Floor: 3,322 square feet
Total: 7,830 square feet
Width: 83'-0" Depth: 116'-0"

A stone-and-siding exterior, spires and interesting window details add to the elegance of this four-bedroom mansion. A keeping room with a pass-through to the kitchen and a fireplace with a built-in wood box, and a formal dining room with a fireplace on the first floor allow plenty of social possibilities. Separate guest quarters with a full bath, a lounge area and an upstairs studio, which is connected to the main house by a gallery, further enhance this home's livability. Four bedrooms with two full baths are found on the second floor, including the master suite with a fireplace.

DESIGN HPU040564

First Floor: 1,950 square feet
Second Floor: 1,680 square feet
Total: 3,630 square feet
Width: 77'-0" Depth: 52'-0"

DESIGN BY
©Archival Designs, Inc.

Interesting windows and rooflines give a unique character to this stucco facade. European influences are unmistakable. The study is highlighted by a beam ceiling, built-ins and floor-to-ceiling windows. The grand room is to the left of the plan and includes a bayed sitting area and a fireplace. Another bay window brightens the breakfast room, which is found between the island kitchen and a den with a second fireplace. The living room and a grand stair hall complete the first floor. The elegant stairway leads up to three family bedrooms and a sumptuous master suite.

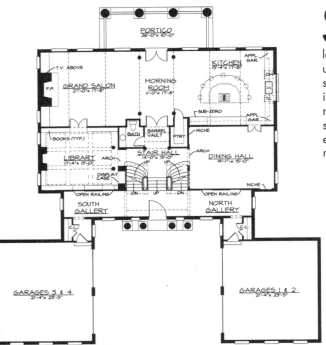

Simply elegant, with dignified details, this beautiful home is reminiscent of English estate homes. Two double garages flank a columned front door and are attached to the main floor by galleries leading to the entry foyer. Here a double staircase leads upstairs and encourages a view beyond the morning room, grand salon and rear portico. The gourmet kitchen has a uniquely styled island counter with a cooktop. For formal meals, the dining hall is nearby. The elaborate master suite and three staterooms reside on the second level. The master bedroom features a circular shape and enjoys access to a private lanai, a through-fireplace to the master bedroom, and numerous alcoves and built-in amenities.

DESIGN BY
©Archival Designs, Inc.

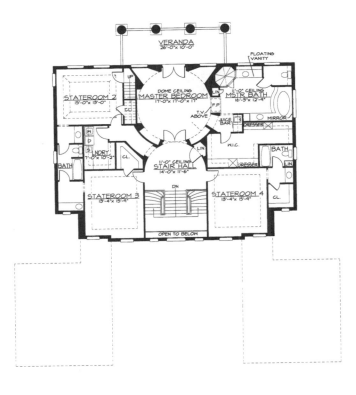

DESIGN HPU040565

First Floor: 2,175 square feet
Second Floor: 1,927 square feet
Total: 4,102 square feet
Basement: 1,927 square feet
Width: 74'-0" Depth: 82'-0"

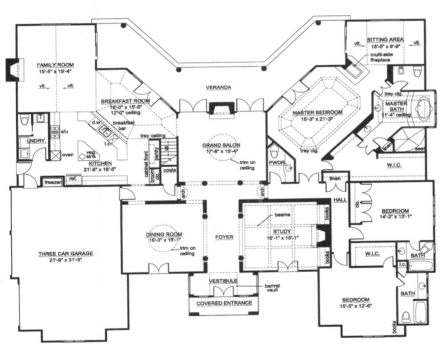

The his Neoclassical home has plenty to offer! The elegant entrance is flanked by a formal dining room on the left and a beam-ceilinged study—complete with a fireplace—on the right. An angled kitchen is sure to please with a work island, plenty of counter and cabinet space, and a snack counter that it shares with the sunny breakfast room. A family room with a second fireplace is nearby. The lavish master suite features many amenities, including a huge walk-in closet, a three-sided fireplace and a lavish bath. Two secondary bedrooms have private baths. Finish the second-floor bonus space to create an office, a play room and a full bath. A three-car garage easily shelters the family fleet.

DESIGN BY
©Archival Designs, Inc.

DESIGN HPU040566

Square Footage: 3,823
Bonus Space: 1,018 square feet
Width: 80'-6" Depth: 70'-8"

461

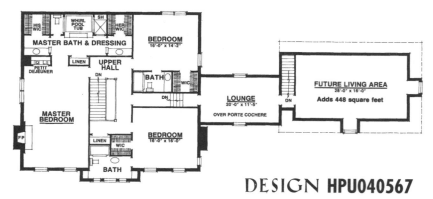

DESIGN HPU040567

First Floor: 1,789 square feet
Second Floor: 2,060 square feet
Total: 3,849 square feet
Bonus Room: 448 square feet
Width: 101'-0" Depth: 56'-2"

DESIGN BY
©R.L. Pfotenhauer

An abundance of amenities graces this two-story traditional design. Fireplaces warm both the formal dining room and the parlor, which connects to the large family room, also with a fireplace and an optional bookcase. The L-shaped kitchen, with its multi-purpose island, shares space with a cozy morning room. On the second floor, two family bedrooms feature walk-in closets and private baths, while the master bedroom features a fourth fireplace, a *petit dejeuner*, or kitchenette, and a His and Hers master bath with a whirlpool tub. A lounge located above the porte cochere will become a favorite getaway spot.

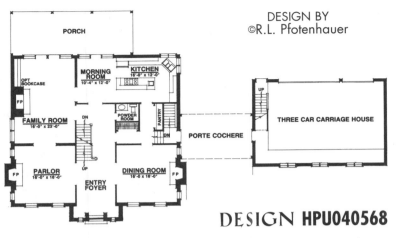

DESIGN BY
©R.L. Pfotenhauer

PORCH

MORNING ROOM 10'-4" x 12'-0"

KITCHEN 16'-0" x 12'-0"

OPT BOOKCASE

FP

FAMILY ROOM 16'-0" x 23'-0"

POWDER ROOM

PANTRY

DN

THREE CAR CARRIAGE HOUSE

UP

PORTE COCHERE

DN

PARLOR 16'-0" x 16'-0"

FP

DINING ROOM 16-0 x 16'-0"

FP

ENTRY FOYER

UP

DESIGN HPU040568

First Floor: 1,760 square feet
Second Floor: 2,001 square feet
Total: 3,761 square feet
Bonus Room: 448 square feet
Width: 99'-1" Depth: 57'-9"

HIS WIC

WHIRL POOL TUB

SH

HER WIC

MASTER BATH & DRESSING

BEDROOM 16'-0" x 14'-2"

LINEN

UPPER HALL

PETIT DEJEUNER

BATH

WIC

DN

FUTURE LIVING AREA 26'-0" x 16'-0"
Adds 448 square feet

DN

MASTER BEDROOM

DN

LOUNGE 20'-0" x 11'-5"
OVER PORTE COCHERE

FP

LINEN

WIC

BEDROOM 16'-0" x 16'-0"

BATH

WH

F

UTILITY ROOM 42'-0" x 16'-3"

W D

UP

BATH

BEDROOM/GUEST 16'-0" x 21'-0"

UP

TAP ROOM

STOR

RECREATION

FP

Stately gentility is a most appropriate phrase for this dignified Georgian design. The brick finish on the exterior is further enhanced by the cut-stone trim and the twin brick chimneys venting the multiple fireplaces. The large formal entry is an elegant setting for the four-foot-wide main stair—only one of three stairs that gives this home a well-thought-out traffic pattern. This home has all of the amenities that the most discerning homeowner could want. Note the generous family room, the island kitchen and the adjoining rear porch for comfortable informal living. The second floor has one of the most luxurious master suites. It features His and Hers dressing areas, a fireplace and even a *petit dejeuner* for late night snacks. Don't overlook the possibilities for the future living spaces in the lower level and over the carriage house.

A two-story entry with striking columns and a pediment combine with a hipped roof to showcase this Neoclassical design. The dining room is conveniently near the entry foyer, perfect for formal entertainment. A beautiful wall of built-ins—including a media center—surrounding the fireplace adorns the great room. The kitchen is loaded with counter space, a built-in computer center, a walk-in pantry and a snack bar. The hearth room features a warming fireplace and access to the grilling porch. To the right of the plan, a guest room with a full bath, and a luxurious master suite enjoy privacy from entertainment zones. Indulge yourself with this sumptuous bath with His and Hers walk-in closets and a whirlpool tub and separate shower. A curved staircase leads to the second level and its three family bedrooms—or transform one into a game room.

DESIGN HPU040569

First Floor: 2,782 square feet
Second Floor: 1,173 square feet
Total: 3,955 square feet
Width: 82'-0" Depth: 58'-10"

DESIGN BY
©Michael E. Nelson,
Nelson Design Group, LLC

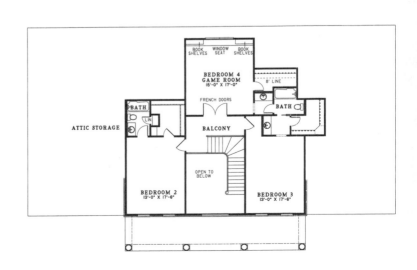

DESIGN **HPU040570**

First Floor: 4,528 square feet
Second Floor: 3,590 square feet
Finished Basement:
2,992 square feet
Total: 11,110 square feet
Width: 138'-2" Depth: 80'-10"

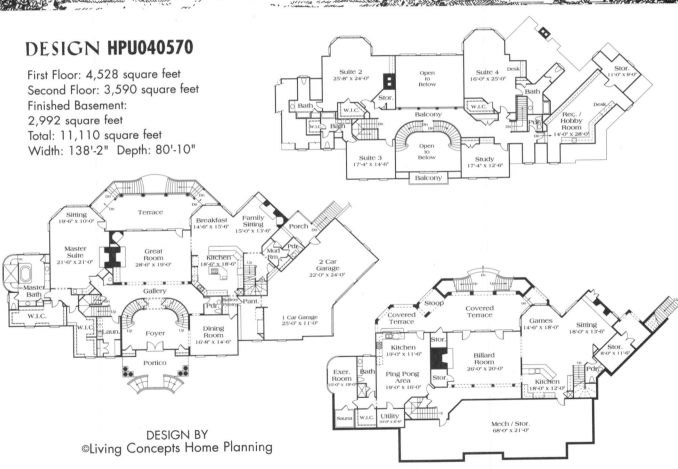

DESIGN BY
©Living Concepts Home Planning

If you're looking for a home that fits a sloping lot, yet retains a strength and character that matches that of our Colonial forefathers, you need look no further. The front elevation reflects a traditional style that incorporates design elements of an earlier period. However, the floor plan and the rear elevation provide a contemporary twist. Beyond the portico, you'll enter a two-story foyer framed by twin curving staircases. Straight ahead, a spacious great room separates the private owners suite to the left, and the formal dining room, kitchen, breakfast room and family/sitting room to the right. The second floor contains three suites—two with bay windows—three-and-a-half baths, a study and a recreation room. The basement sports a billiard room, two kitchens, an exercise room, a full bath, a game room and a sitting room.

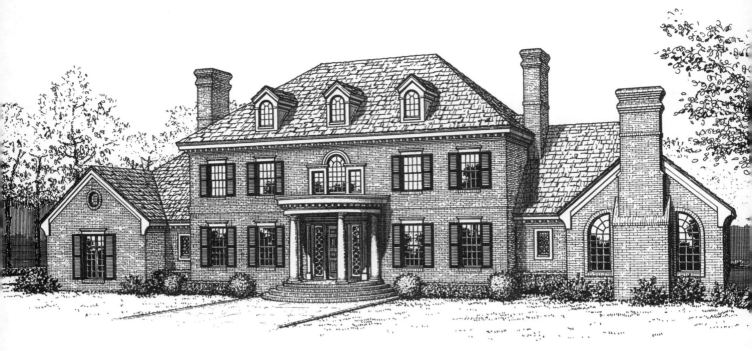

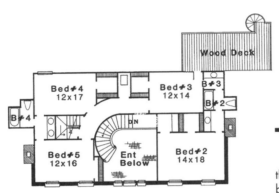

Bed #4
12x17

Bed #3
12x14

B #4

B #3

B #2

DN

Bed #5
12x16

Ent Below

Bed #2
14x18

Wood Deck

DESIGN HPU040571

First Floor: 3,294 square feet
Second Floor: 1,300 square feet
Total: 4,594 square feet
Width: 106'-10" Depth: 52'-10"

The charm of the Old South is designed into this stately Federal manor. A round entry portico leads to the two-story foyer with a circular staircase. The formal living room, dining room and family room each feature a distinctive fireplace; the latter is also highlighted by a built-in entertainment center, walk-in wet bar, beamed cathedral ceiling, and access to a rear covered patio. Impressive ten-foot ceilings grace the entire first floor. The secluded master suite has a vaulted ceiling, three walk-in closets and patio access. Four additional bedrooms on the second floor share adjoining baths.

DESIGN BY
©Fillmore Design Group

Pool

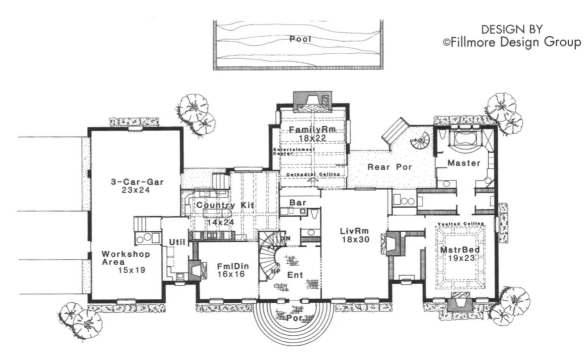

3-Car-Gar
23x24

Workshop Area
15x19

Util

Country Kit
14x24

FmlDin
16x16

Ent

FamilyRm
18x22

Entertainment Center

Cathedral Ceiling

Bar

DN

UP

LivRm
18x30

Rear Por

Master

Vaulted Ceiling

MstrBed
19x23

Por

DESIGN HPU040572

First Floor: 3,599 square feet
Second Floor: 1,621 square feet
Total: 5,220 square feet
Width: 108'-10" Depth: 53'-10"

DESIGN BY
©Fillmore Design Group

A grand facade detailed with brick corner quoins, stucco flourishes, arched windows and an elegant entrance presents this home and preludes the amenities inside. A spacious foyer is accented by a curving stair and flanked by a formal living room and a formal dining room. For cozy times, a through-fireplace is located between a large family room and a quiet study. The master suite is designed to pamper, with two walk-in closets (one is absolutely huge), a two-sided fireplace sharing its heat with a bayed sitting area and the bedroom, and a lavish master bath filled with attractive amenities. Upstairs, three secondary bedrooms each have a private bath and walk-in closet. Also on this level is a spacious recreation room, perfect for a game room or children's playroom.

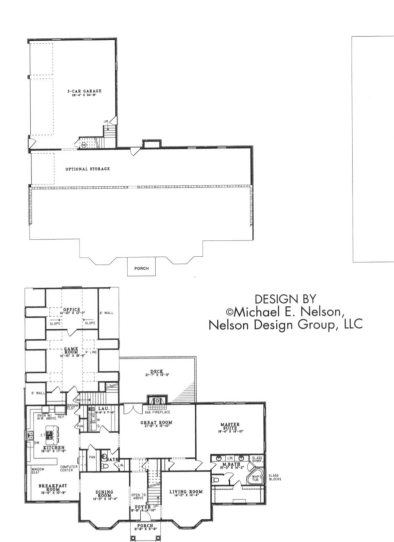

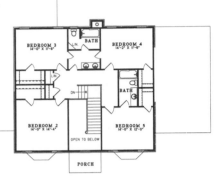

DESIGN HPU040573

First Floor: 3,209 square feet
Second Floor: 1,192 square feet
Total: 4,401 square feet
Width: 68'-8" Depth: 76'-0"

DESIGN BY
©Michael E. Nelson,
Nelson Design Group, LLC

This two-story home has French flair on the exterior and modern comforts inside. The entry leads to the dining and living rooms at the front of the house, each enjoying a bay-window view of the front yard. The central great room features a fireplace framed with windows on each side. Escape to the secluded master suite with its luxurious bath, including a glass shower and separate whirlpool tub. To the left of the plan is a spacious kitchen with an island/snack bar, large pantry spaces, a built-in computer center and an adjoining breakfast room. Four secondary bedrooms and two full bathrooms complete the second floor. Please specify crawlspace, basement or slab foundation when ordering.

A graceful Palladian-style entry with fluted, two-story columns commands charm and respect for this Georgian homestead. Inside, a marble entry provides a traditional circular stairway and balcony. To the left lies an inviting living room and a family room that includes a fireplace and atrium doors leading to the deck area and beyond. The large kitchen, formal dining room with bay window, bar area and expansive sun room provide more than enough space for entertaining guests. An exercise room is featured for family fun and health. A luxurious master suite is positioned at the rear for seclusion, while a guest suite can be found just to the front. Five family bedrooms complete the second floor.

DESIGN HPU040574

First Floor: 4,082 square feet
Second Floor: 1,745 square feet
Total: 5,827 square feet
Width: 101'-7" Depth: 73'-0"

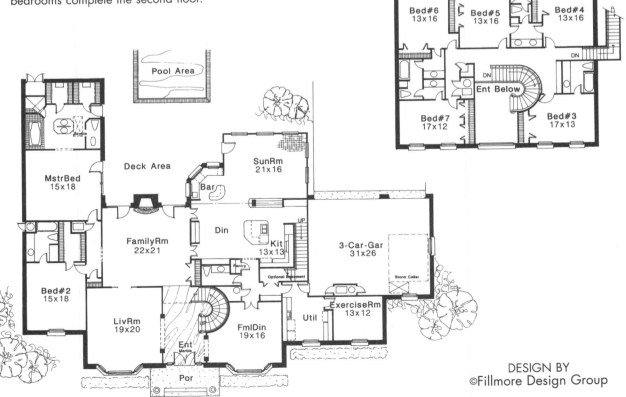

DESIGN BY
©Fillmore Design Group

469

DESIGN HPU040575

First Floor: 3,300 square feet
Second Floor: 1,170 square feet
Total: 4,470 square feet
Width: 87'-0" Depth: 82'-0"

The gracious exterior of this classic European-style home is accentuated by dual boxed windows, dramatically curved stairs and a glassed entry decorated with tall columns. A grand foyer showcases the dining room and great room, which offers a fireplace and French doors opening to a rear terrace. A gourmet kitchen adjoins the breakfast room, also open to the terrace; just beyond, a corner fireplace warms the hearth room. The luxurious owners suite provides a spacious walk-in closet and an opulent bath. Upstairs, a balcony overlooks the foyer and gallery. Three secondary bedrooms all provide walk-in closets; one offers a private bath.

DESIGN BY
©Studer Residential Designs, Inc.

Finished in brick veneer, this stately home has presence and a sense of permanence. The two-level entry opens to a bright foyer with a circular stair. On the right the living room features a box-bay window; on the left is a dining room with another box-bay window. The island kitchen, with a walk-in pantry and abundant counter space, easily serves the dining room. A breakfast room adjoins the kitchen and has a window seat and veranda access. It spills into the sunken family room with a fireplace. On the main floor, the master suite boasts a cozy sitting area, two walk-in closets and a master bath with a whirlpool spa and twin vanities. Each family bedroom has a spacious closet. A playroom on the second floor is graced by a coffered ceiling and a walk-in storage closet.

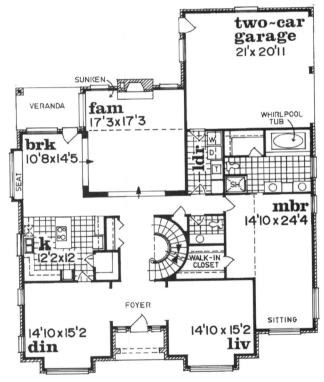

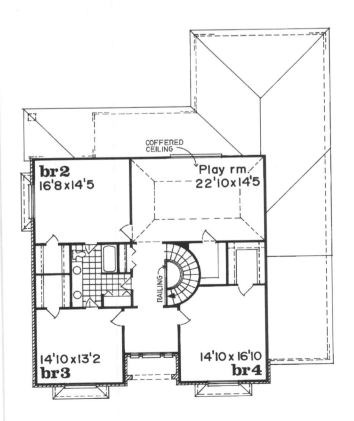

DESIGN HPU040576

First Floor: 2,177 square feet
Second Floor: 1,633 square feet
Total: 3,810 square feet
Width: 52'-0" Depth: 65'-0"

DESIGN BY
©Select Home Designs

DESIGN HPU040577

First Floor: 2,094 square feet
Second Floor: 2,169 square feet
Total: 4,263 square feet
Width: 76'-0" Depth: 70'-0"

DESIGN BY
©Studer Residential Designs, Inc.

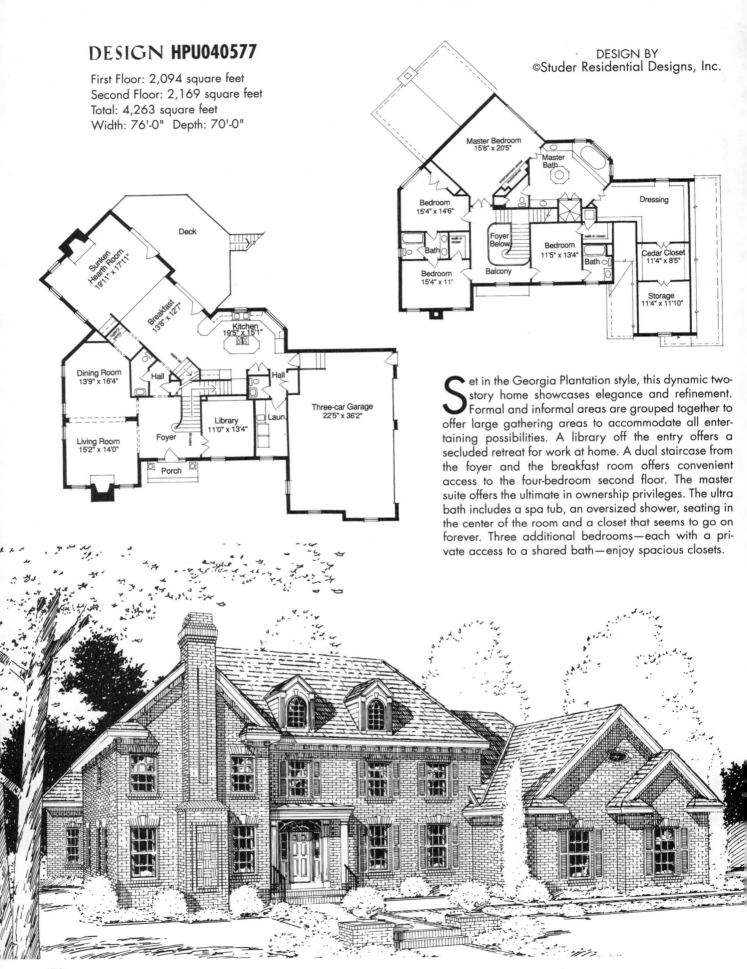

Master Bedroom 15'8" x 20'5"

Master Bath

Dressing

Bedroom 15'4" x 14'6"

Foyer Below

Bedroom 11'5" x 13'4"

Cedar Closet 11'4" x 8'5"

Bath

walk-in closet

walk-in closet

Bath

Bedroom 15'4" x 11'

Balcony

Storage 11'4" x 11'10"

Deck

Sunken Hearth Room 19'11" x 17'11"

Breakfast 13'8" x 12'7"

Kitchen 19'5" x 15'1"

Dining Room 13'9" x 16'4"

Hall

Hall

Laun.

Three-car Garage 22'5" x 36'2"

Library 11'0" x 13'4"

Foyer

Living Room 15'2" x 14'0"

Porch

Set in the Georgia Plantation style, this dynamic two-story home showcases elegance and refinement. Formal and informal areas are grouped together to offer large gathering areas to accommodate all entertaining possibilities. A library off the entry offers a secluded retreat for work at home. A dual staircase from the foyer and the breakfast room offers convenient access to the four-bedroom second floor. The master suite offers the ultimate in ownership privileges. The ultra bath includes a spa tub, an oversized shower, seating in the center of the room and a closet that seems to go on forever. Three additional bedrooms—each with a private access to a shared bath—enjoy spacious closets.

ountry meets traditional in this splendid design. A covered front porch offers a place to enjoy the sunrise or place a porch swing. Gables, brick, stone and dormers bring out a comfortable appeal. With the formal areas flanking the foyer, an open flow is established between the column-accented dining room and the library with its distinguished beam ceiling. The two-story great room features a wall of windows looking out to the rear grounds. On the left, the gourmet kitchen serves up casual and formal meals to the breakfast and hearth rooms with the dining room just steps away. The master bedroom enjoys a sitting area with an array of view-catching windows, a spacious dressing area and an accommodating walk-in closet. Three family bedrooms—one with a private bath—complete the second level.

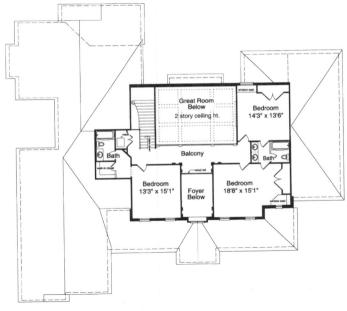

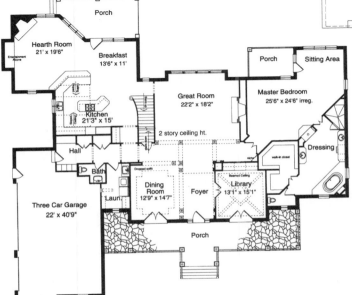

DESIGN HPU040578

First Floor: 3,414 square feet
Second Floor: 1,238 square feet
Total: 4,652 square feet
Width: 90'-6" Depth: 78'-9"

DESIGN BY
©Studer Residential Designs, Inc.

473

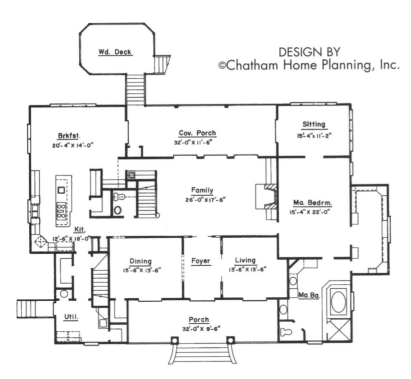

DESIGN BY
©Chatham Home Planning, Inc.

DESIGN HPU040579

First Floor: 3,045 square feet
Second Floor: 1,174 square feet
Total: 4,219 square feet
Width: 77'-0" Depth: 53'-0"

From its large front porch to its rear porch and deck, this lavish farmhouse bids welcome. The foyer offers entrance to both the formal living and dining rooms and opens into the heart of the home—the spacious family room, with its central fireplace and rear-yard access. A well-equipped kitchen features a desk, an island cooktop and a large breakfast area with views to the outside. The master bedroom boasts a separate sitting room, a huge walk-in closet and a luxurious bath with separate sinks and a whirlpool tub. All three of the upstairs family bedrooms include a walk-in closet and, while Bedrooms 3 and 4 share a full hall bath that includes dual sinks, Bedroom 2 features its own bath.

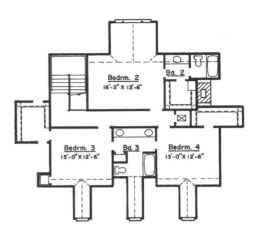

Dormer windows complement classic square columns on this country estate home, gently flavored with a Southern-style facade. A two-story foyer opens to traditional rooms. Two columns announce the living room, which has a warming hearth. The formal dining room opens to the back covered porch, decked out with decorative columns. The first-floor master suite has His and Hers walk-in closets, an oversized shower, a whirlpool tub and a windowed water closet, plus its own door to the covered porch. A well-appointed kitchen features a corner walk-in pantry and opens to a double-bay family room and breakfast area. Upstairs, each of two family bedrooms has a private vanity. A gallery hall leads past a study/computer room— with two window seats—to a sizable recreation area that offers a tower-room bay.

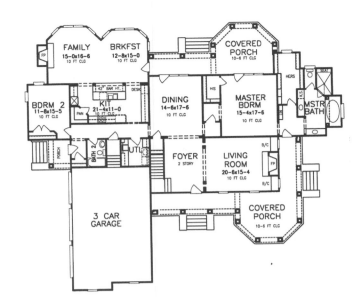

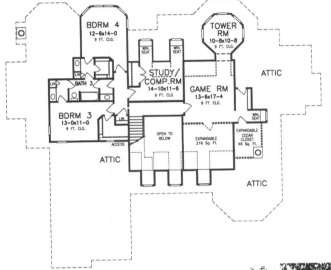

DESIGNHPU040580

First Floor: 2,687 square feet
Second Floor: 1,630 square feet
Total: 4,317 square feet
Bonus Room: 216 square feet
Width: 87'-1" Depth: 76'-7"

DESIGN BY
©Larry E. Belk Designs

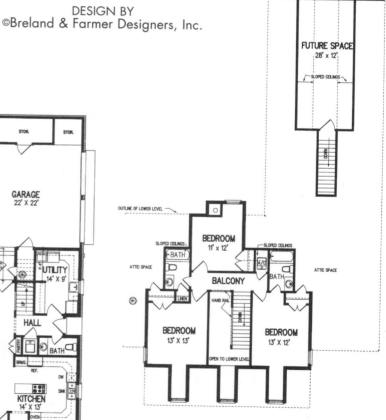

Three classic dormers welcome you home. A covered porch and gabled roof offer country comfort. A formal dining room and informal eating area are located only steps away from the fully appointed kitchen. A spacious family room features a fireplace and a built-in entertainment center. The utility room is large enough to handle standard needs; there is even room for a hobby space. For those needing a home office, the bonus space with stairs accessed by an outside entrance is perfect for clients or customers. If it is to be used for a game room, noise will not be a factor because of its isolated location over the garage. The master suite boasts a large sitting area complete with a built-in entertainment center. Three large bedrooms and two full baths are located on the upper level. Please specify basement, crawlspace or slab foundation when ordering.

DESIGN BY
©Breland & Farmer Designers, Inc.

DESIGN HPU040581

First Floor: 2,702 square feet
Second Floor: 810 square feet
Total: 3,512 square feet
Bonus Room: 336 square feet
Width: 62'-0" Depth: 86'-0"

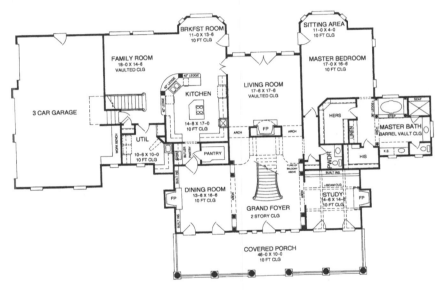

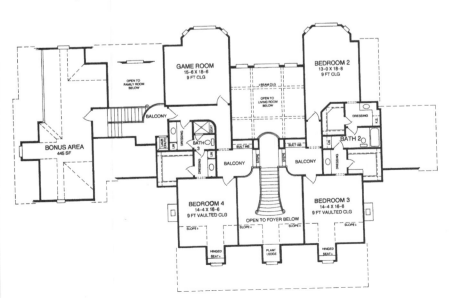

Reminiscent of the grand homes of the Old South, this elegantly appointed home is a beauty inside and out. A centerpiece stair rises gracefully from the two-story grand foyer and features Romeo-balcony overlooks to the foyer and living room. The kitchen, breakfast room and family room provide open space for the gathering of family and friends. The beam-ceilinged study and the dining room flank the grand foyer and each includes a fireplace. The master suite features a cozy sitting area and a luxury master bath with His and Hers vanities and walk-in closets. Three large bedrooms and a game room complete the second floor. Baths are efficiently designed with private dressing areas to give each bedroom a private bath. A large expandable area is available at the top of the rear stair.

DESIGN HPU040582

First Floor: 3,170 square feet
Second Floor: 1,914 square feet
Total: 5,084 square feet
Bonus Room: 445 square feet
Width: 100'-10" Depth: 65'-5"

DESIGN BY
©Larry E. Belk Designs

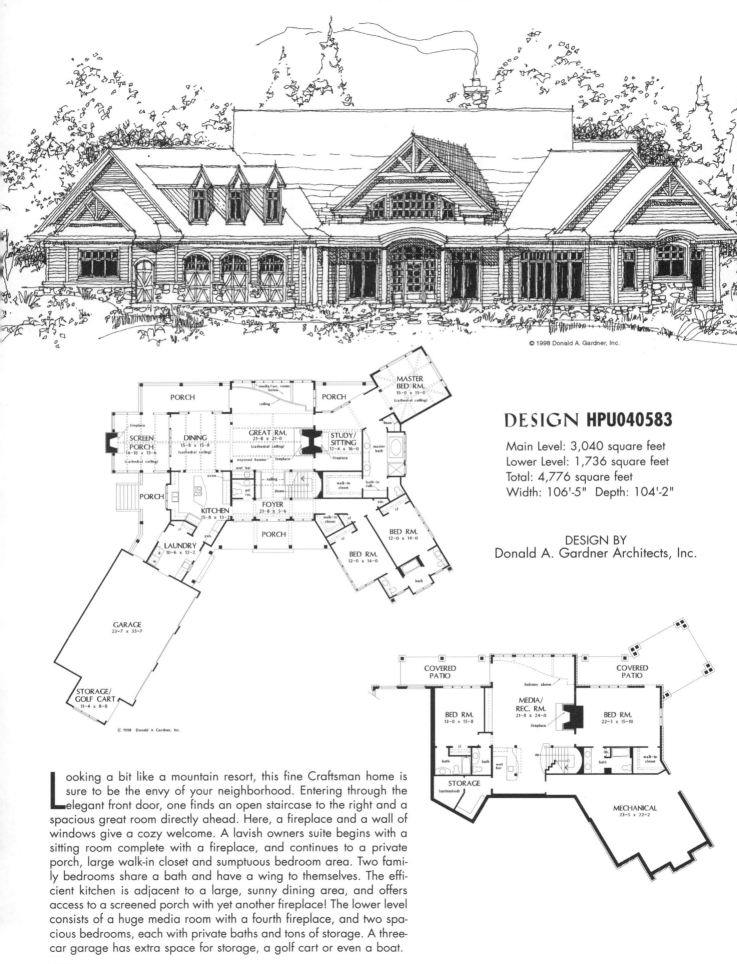

© 1998 Donald A. Gardner, Inc.

PORCH

MASTER
BED RM.
15-0 x 15-0
(cathedral ceiling)

media/rec. room
below.

PORCH

linen

SCREEN
PORCH
14-10 x 15-6
(cathedral ceiling)

fireplace

DINING
15-8 x 15-8
(cathedral ceiling)

GREAT RM.
21-8 x 21-0
(cathedral ceiling)

STUDY/
SITTING
12-4 x 16-0

master
bath

fireplace

exposed beams   fireplace

oven

wet bar

railing

walk-in
closet

built-in
cab.

PORCH

KITCHEN
15-8 x 13-2

pd.
rm.

railing

down

cl.

FOYER
21-8 x 5-6

PORCH

walk-in
closet

cl

BED RM.
12-0 x 14-0

LAUNDRY
10-6 x 12-2

cl

pan.

BED RM.
12-0 x 14-0

bath

GARAGE
23-7 x 35-7

STORAGE/
GOLF CART
11-4 x 8-0

© 1998 Donald A Gardner, Inc.

DESIGN HPU040583

Main Level: 3,040 square feet
Lower Level: 1,736 square feet
Total: 4,776 square feet
Width: 106'-5"   Depth: 104'-2"

DESIGN BY
Donald A. Gardner Architects, Inc.

COVERED
PATIO

balcony above

COVERED
PATIO

BED RM.
13-0 x 15-8

MEDIA/
REC. RM.
21-8 x 24-0

fireplace

BED RM.
22-3 x 15-10

cl

bath

bath

wet
bar

up

lin.

bath

walk-in
closet

STORAGE
(unfinished)

MECHANICAL
23-5 x 22-2

Looking a bit like a mountain resort, this fine Craftsman home is sure to be the envy of your neighborhood. Entering through the elegant front door, one finds an open staircase to the right and a spacious great room directly ahead. Here, a fireplace and a wall of windows give a cozy welcome. A lavish owners suite begins with a sitting room complete with a fireplace, and continues to a private porch, large walk-in closet and sumptuous bedroom area. Two family bedrooms share a bath and have a wing to themselves. The efficient kitchen is adjacent to a large, sunny dining area, and offers access to a screened porch with yet another fireplace! The lower level consists of a huge media room with a fourth fireplace, and two spacious bedrooms, each with private baths and tons of storage. A three-car garage has extra space for storage, a golf cart or even a boat.

This extraordinary four-bedroom estate features gables with decorative wood brackets, arched windows and a stone-and-siding facade for undeniable Craftsman character. At the heart of the home, a magnificent cathedral ceiling adds space and stature to the impressive great room, which accesses both back porches. Sharing the great room's cathedral ceiling, a loft makes an excellent reading nook. Tray ceilings adorn the dining room and library/media room, while all four bedrooms enjoy cathedral ceilings. A sizable kitchen is open to a large gathering room for ultimate family togetherness. The master suite features back-porch access, a lavish private bath and an oversized walk-in closet. A spacious bonus room is located over the three-car garage for further expansion.

DESIGN BY
Donald A. Gardner Architects, Inc.

DESIGN HPU040584

First Floor: 3,555 square feet
Second Floor: 250 square feet
Total: 3,805 square feet
Bonus Room: 490 square feet
Width: 99'-8"   Depth: 78'-8"

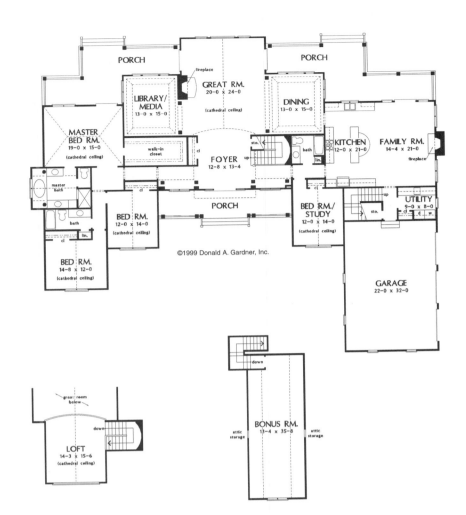

©1999 Donald A. Gardner, Inc.

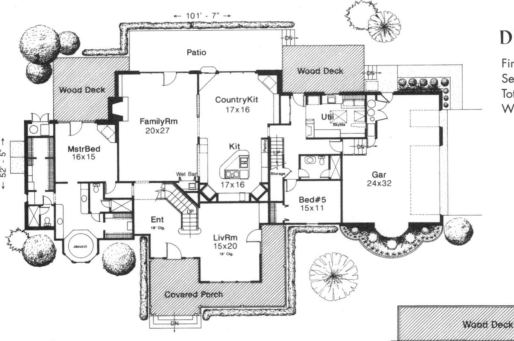

DESIGN HPU040585

First Floor: 3,073 square feet
Second Floor: 1,230 square feet
Total: 4,303 square feet
Width: 101'-7" Depth: 52'-5"

This large Victorian two-story home with brick and shingle siding has two unique bay windows with conical roofs and a covered porch. The expansive kitchen and country kitchen areas look to the rear patio, as does the family room, complete with a fireplace and wet bar. The owners suite access-es a private wood deck and is enhanced with two large walk-in closets, as well as a whirlpool tub. Two separate staircases lead upstairs to the sleeping quarters. Three bedrooms reside on the second floor; they share a full bath and a wood deck. A balcony looks down to the entry below.

DESIGN BY
©Fillmore Design Group

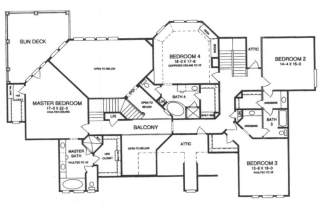

DESIGN HPU040586

First Floor: 3,359 square feet
Second Floor: 2,174 square feet
Total: 5,533 square feet
Width: 96'-5" Depth: 85'-6"

L

DESIGN BY
©Larry E. Belk Designs

A truly unique luxury home, this farmhouse has all the amenities. The fantastic covered porch surrounds three sides of the home and provides a wonderful area for outdoor living. A two-story foyer angles to draw the eye through double arches to the elegant living room with a fireplace flanked by built-ins and an area for the grand piano. The kitchen, breakfast room and family room join for casual living. Also on the first level are a home office, a game room and a cozy study. Upstairs, the master bedroom is luxuriously appointed and opens to a private sun deck. Three family bedrooms each have walk-in closets and private bath access.

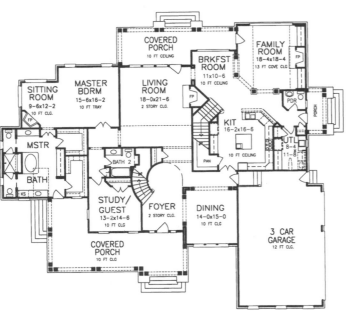

Timeless sophistication characterizes this lovely home designed for entertaining and family. A roomy wraparound front porch opens to the dramatic two-story foyer with a gracefully curved front stair. The large dining room and living room, with a beam ceiling and a striking two-story window wall, welcome all to this sensational home. The kitchen, breakfast room and family room are open to one another. A series of decorative columns defines the family room. The owners suite boasts a cozy sitting room with a corner fireplace. The private bath features His and Hers baths. Upstairs are two bedrooms, each with a private bath. A grand entryway welcomes visitors into this ageless wonder.

DESIGN HPU040587

First Floor: 3,219 square feet
Second Floor: 1,202 square feet
Total: 4,421 square feet
Width: 86'-1" Depth: 76'-10"

DESIGN BY
©Larry E. Belk Designs

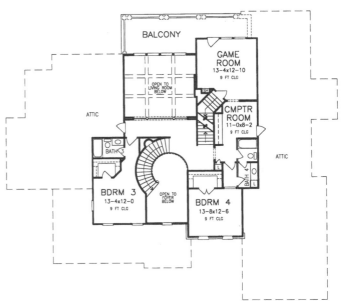

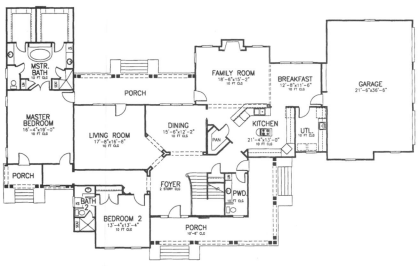

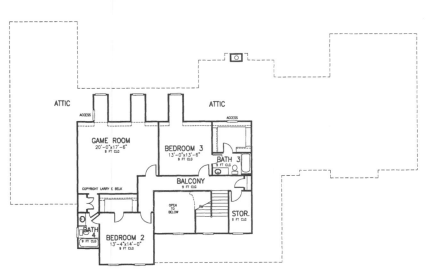

Brick and fieldstone adorn this two-story, four-bedroom home. A wraparound covered porch offers shelter from the elements and ushers you into a two-story foyer. Arches and columns separate the formal living and dining rooms, while the kitchen presents interesting angles and opens into the spacious family room via a snack bar. Note the direct access to the rear covered porch from the living room as well as from the family room. A secondary bedroom resides on the first floor and could be used as a guest suite or a cozy den. The master suite is sure to please with its many amenities, which include two walk-in closets, a lavish bath and access to a private porch. Upstairs, two family bedrooms are complete with private baths and large walk-in closets. A game room finishes this floor.

DESIGN HPU040588

First Floor: 2,931 square feet
Second Floor: 1,319 square feet
Total: 4,250 square feet
Width: 103'-7" Depth: 63'-9"

DESIGN BY
©Larry E. Belk Designs

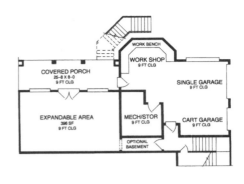

DESIGN HPU040589

First Floor: 3,413 square feet
Second Floor: 2,076 square feet
Total: 5,489 square feet
Bonus Room: 430 square feet
Width: 90'-6" Depth: 63'-6"

DESIGN BY
©Larry E. Belk Designs

Classic design combined with dynamite interiors make this executive home a real gem. Inside, a free-floating curved staircase rises majestically to the second floor. The enormous living room, great for formal entertaining, features a dramatic two-story window wall. The family room, breakfast room and kitchen are conveniently grouped. A large pantry and a companion butler's pantry serve both the dining room and kitchen. Privately located, the master suite includes a sitting area and sumptuous master bath. The second floor includes Bedroom 2, which has a private bath. Bedrooms 3 and 4 share a bath that includes two private dressing areas. A large game room is accessed from a rear stair.

A distinctively French flair is the hallmark of this European-styled home. Inside, the two-story foyer provides views to the huge great room beyond. A well-placed study off the foyer provides an area for that much-used home office. The kitchen, breakfast room and sun room are adjacent to lend a spacious feel. The great room is visible from this area through decorative arches. A roomy utility room receives laundry from a chute above. A nearby built-in bench and desk help organize the rear entry of the home. The master suite includes a roomy sitting area and a lovely master bath with a centerpiece whirlpool tub flanked by half-columns. Upstairs, Bedrooms 2 and 3 share a bath that includes private dressing areas. An enormous game room is located upstairs and is reached by the convenient rear stair. Please specify crawlspace or slab foundation when ordering.

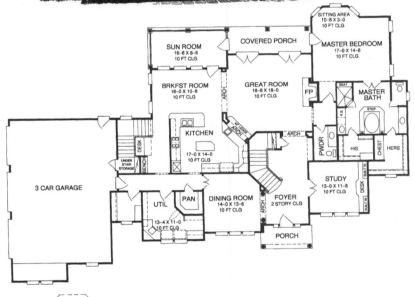

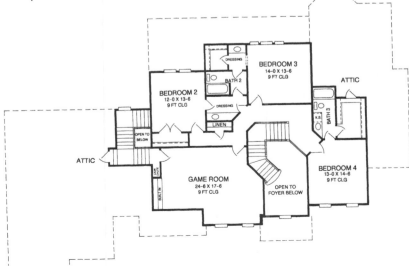

DESIGN HPU040590

First Floor: 2,608 square feet
Second Floor: 1,432 square feet
Total: 4,040 square feet
Width: 89'-10" Depth: 63'-8"

DESIGN BY
©Larry E. Belk Designs

This home speaks of luxury and practicality and is abundant in attractive qualities. A study and dining room flank the foyer, while the great room offers a warming fireplace and double-French-door access to the rear yard straight back. A butler's pantry acts as a helpful buffer between the kitchen and the columned dining room. Double bays at the rear of the home form the keeping room and the breakfast room on one side and the owners bedroom on the other. Three family bedrooms and two baths grace the second floor. A game room is perfect for casual family-time. Please specify basement or slab foundation when ordering.

DESIGN HPU040591

First Floor: 2,639 square feet
Second Floor: 1,625 square feet
Total: 4,264 square feet
Width: 73'-8"   Depth: 58'-6"

L

DESIGN BY
©Larry E. Belk Designs

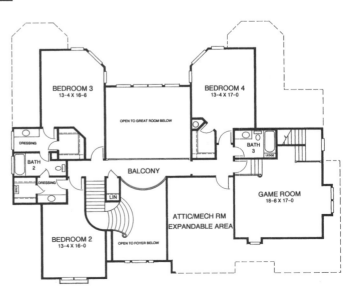

An impressive entry, multi-pane windows and mock balconies combine to give this facade an elegance of which to be proud. The grand foyer showcases a stunning staircase and is flanked by a formal dining room to the right and a cozy study to the left. The elegant sunken living room is graced by a fireplace, a wondrous piano bay, and a vaulted ceiling. The openness of the sunny breakfast room and the family room make casual entertaining a breeze. Located on the first floor for privacy, the master bedroom suite is lavish with its luxuries. A bayed sitting area encourages early morning repose, while the bath revels in pampering you. Upstairs, three bedrooms share two full baths and have access to a large game room over the three-car garage. Please specify crawlspace or slab foundation when ordering.

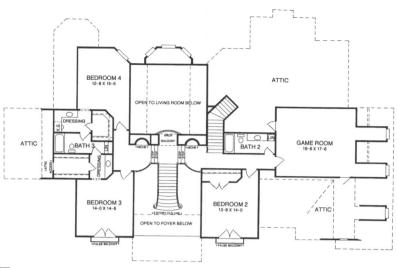

DESIGN HPU040592

First Floor: 3,264 square feet
Second Floor: 1,671 square feet
Total: 4,935 square feet
Width: 96'-10" Depth: 65'-1"

DESIGN BY
©Larry E. Belk Designs

DESIGN HPU040593

First Floor: 2,470 square feet
Second Floor: 1,360 square feet
Total: 3,830 square feet
Width: 77'-4" Depth: 59'-8"

DESIGN BY
©Lucia Custom Home
Designers, Inc.

This design so well embraces the outdoors, it's almost difficult to distinguish where inside living areas end and outdoor spaces begin. Notice, for instance, the delightful dining garden, snuggled in between the formal dining room and the garage. Above it is a balcony adorning Bedroom 5. The family room has a curved glass view of the covered porch to the rear of the home; the living room echoes this option to the front. Even the dining room and master bedroom utilize curved glass accents. There is no lack of room in this design, either. Five bedrooms include a gallant master suite. Plus, the cozy study can become a guest bedroom as it is near a full bath. The second-level loft is a great place for quiet study or reading.

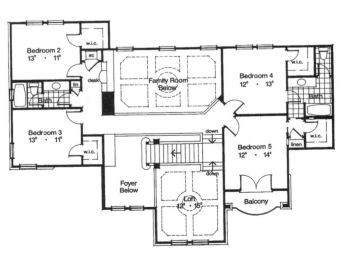

Blend the best elements of Spanish Colonial and contemporary design, and the result is an estate such as this. There are two ways to enter: through the main entry that separates the study and the dining room, or through the courtyard entry that leads directly into the eat-in kitchen. The living room is assigned columns and has a lovely gallery leading to the rear lanai. The family room is snug. It is a gateway to a private patio with a summer kitchen. A guest bedroom and master suite complete this level. The second floor holds three family bedrooms and access to two balconies (one with a near-by wet bar). Bonus space features a light-filled tower—make this hobby or study space.

DESIGN HPU040594

First Floor: 3,566 square feet
Second Floor: 1,196 square feet
Total: 4,762 square feet
Bonus Room: 479 square feet
Width: 85'-0" Depth: 81'-4"

DESIGN BY
©Lucia Custom Home
Designers, Inc.

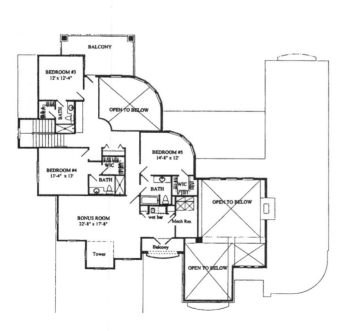

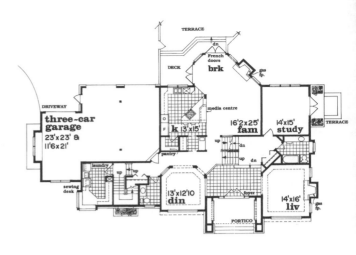

Three full levels of livability are contained within the floor plan of this design. The main level features formal living and dining areas, a family room with a vaulted ceiling, a breakfast nook and a study with a private terrace. The three-car garage is on this level and opens to the back of the plan. The upper level holds the bedrooms—three family bedrooms and a master suite. Bedroom 4 has a private bath, as does the master suite. Lower-level livability includes a game room, a home theater and an exercise area, plus a wine cellar for your private collection. A terrace at this level opens off the game room. Two large storage areas will be welcome.

DESIGN HPU040595

Main Level: 2,201 square feet
Upper Level: 2,034 square feet
Lower Level: 1,882 square feet
Total: 6,117 square feet
Width: 82'-6" Depth: 55'-8"

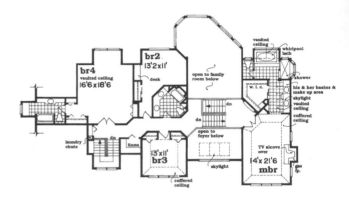

DESIGN BY
©Select Home Designs

T his unusual stucco-and-siding design opens with a grand portico to a foyer containing a volume ceiling that extends to the living room. A multi-pane transom lights the foyer and the open staircase beyond. The living room has a fireplace and then proceeds up a few steps to the dining room with a coffered ceiling and butler's pantry, which connects it to the gourmet kitchen. Cooks will love the wet bar in the butler's pantry, the walk-in food pantry, a wine cooler, a built-in desk and the center island with a cooktop and salad sink. The attached hearth room has the requisite fireplace and three sets of French doors to the covered porch. The family room sports a coffered ceiling and fireplace flanked by French doors. The second floor boasts four bedrooms, including a master suite with a tray ceiling, covered deck and lavish bath. Two full baths serve the family bedrooms and a bonus room that might be used as an additional bedroom or hobby space.

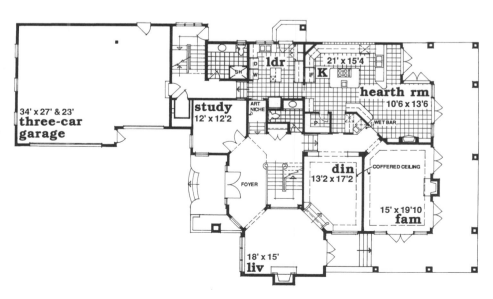

DESIGN HPU040596

First Floor: 2,473 square feet
Second Floor: 2,686 square feet
Total: 5,159 square feet
Width: 57'-8" Depth: 103'-6"

DESIGN BY
©Select Home Designs

491

This elegant exterior blends a classical look with a contemporary feel. Corner quoins and round columns highlight the front elevation. The formal living room, complete with a fireplace and a wet bar, and the formal dining room access the lanai through three pairs of French doors. The well-appointed kitchen features an island prep sink, a walk-in pantry and a desk. The secondary bedrooms are full guest suites, located away from the private owner's wing. The master suite has enormous His and Hers closets, built-ins, a wet bar and a three-sided fireplace that separates the sitting room and the bedroom. The luxurious bath features a stunning, rounded glass-block shower and a whirlpool tub.

DESIGN BY
©The Sater Design Collection

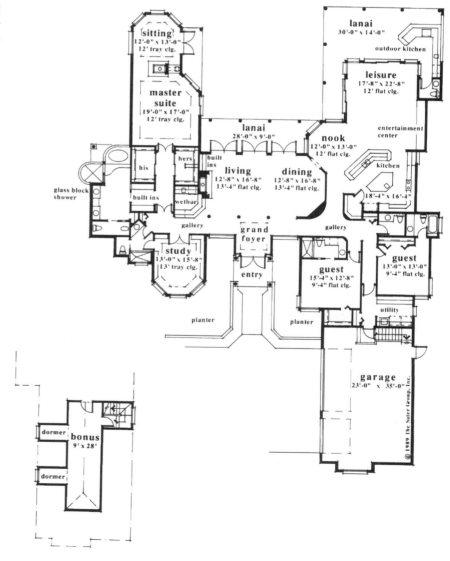

DESIGN HPU040597

Square Footage: 3,896
Bonus Room: 356 square feet
Width: 90'-0" Depth: 120'-8"

L

This grand traditional home offers an elegant, welcoming residence for the homeowner with luxury in mind. The grand foyer opens to a wonderful display of casual and formal living areas. Beyond the foyer, the spacious living room provides views of the rear grounds and opens to the veranda and rear yard through three pairs of French doors. An arched galley hall leads past the formal dining room to the family areas where casual get-togethers are enjoyed. Here, an ample gourmet kitchen easily serves the nook and the leisure room. The owners wing consists of a study or home office, and a grand master suite with an indulgent bath, offering the ultimate in comfort. The upper level contains three secondary bedrooms—each with a walk-in closet—and two with a private balcony. Please specify basement or slab foundation when ordering.

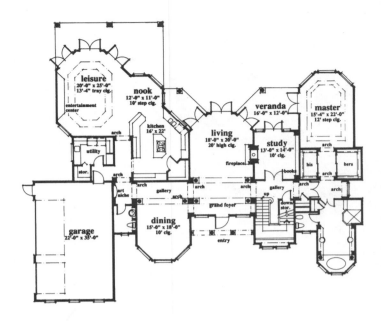

DESIGN HPU040598

First Floor: 3,546 square feet
Second Floor: 1,213 square feet
Total: 4,759 square feet
Width: 95'-4" Depth: 83'-0"

DESIGN BY
©The Sater Design Collection

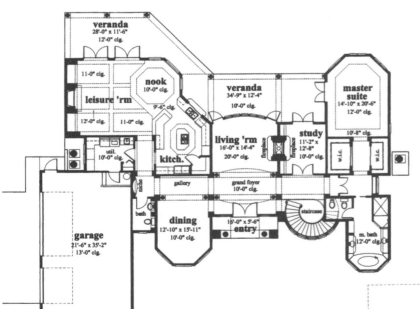

DESIGN HPU040599

First Floor: 2,841 square feet
Second Floor: 1,052 square feet
Total: 3,893 square feet
Width: 85'-0" Depth: 76'-8"

DESIGN BY
©The Sater Design Collection

This luxurious plan assures elegant living. A turret, two-story bay windows and plenty of arched glass impart a graceful style to the exterior, while rich amenities furnish contentment within. A grand foyer decked with columns introduces the living room, which boasts a curve of glass windows viewing the rear gardens. A through-fireplace is shared by the study and living room. The master suite fills the entire right section of the design and enjoys a tray ceiling, two walk-in closets, a separate shower and a garden tub set in a bay window. Informal entertainment will be a breeze with the leisure room, which adjoins the kitchen and breakfast nook and opens to a rear veranda. At the top of a lavish curving staircase are two family bedrooms sharing a full bath and a guest suite with a private deck.

DESIGN HPU040600

First Floor: 4,760 square feet
Second Floor: 1,552 square feet
Total: 6,312 square feet
Width: 98'-0" Depth: 103'-8"

 L

As beautiful from the rear as from the front, this home features a spectacular blend of arch-top windows, French doors and balusters. Dramatic two-story ceilings and tray details add custom spaciousness. An impressive, informal leisure room has a sixteen-foot tray ceiling, an entertainment center and a grand ale bar. The large, gourmet kitchen is well appointed and easily serves the nook and formal dining room. The master suite has a large bedroom and a bayed sitting area. His and Hers vanities and walk-in closets and a curved, glass-block shower are highlights in the bath. The staircase leads to the deluxe secondary guest suites, two of which have observation decks to the rear and each with their own full baths.

DESIGN BY
©The Sater Design Collection

Cost to build? See page 502
to order complete cost estimate
to build this house in your area!

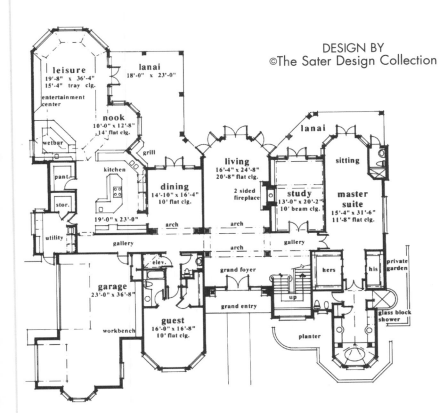

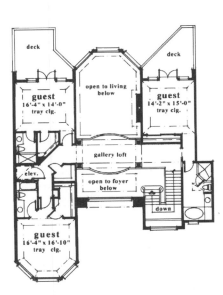

ontemporary styling coupled with traditional finishes of brick and stucco make this home a stand-out that caters to the discriminating few. The entry, with a two-story ceiling, steps down into an enormous great room with a see-through fireplace. A formal living room is open from the entry and begins one wing of the home. The bedroom wing provides three bedrooms, each with a large amenity-filled bath, as well as a study area and a recreation room. The opposite wing houses the dining room, kitchen, breakfast room and two more bedrooms. The kitchen offers a curved window overlooking the side yard and a cooktop island with a vegetable sink. A stair leads to a loft overlooking the great room and entry.

DESIGN BY
©Larry E. Belk Designs

DESIGN **HPU040601**

First Floor: 5,183 square feet
Second Floor: 238 square feet
Total: 5,421 square feet
Width: 93'-5" Depth: 113'-0"

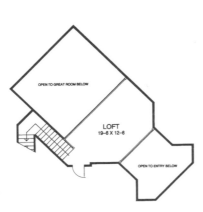

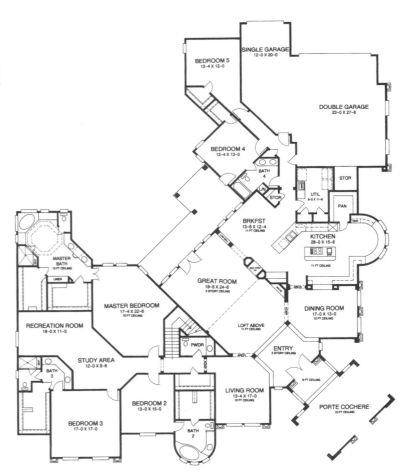

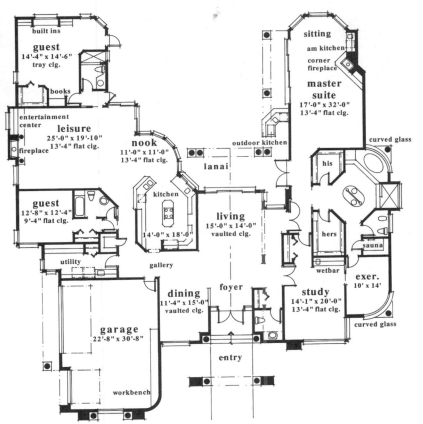

guest
14'-4" x 14'-6"
tray clg.

built ins

books

entertainment
center

leisure
25'-0" x 19'-10"
13'-4" flat clg.

fireplace

nook
11'-0" x 11'-0"
13'-4" flat clg.

lanai

sitting

am kitchen

corner
fireplace

master
suite
17'-0" x 32'-0"
13'-4" flat clg.

outdoor kitchen

curved glass

his

guest
12'-8" x 12'-4"
9'-4" flat clg.

kitchen

14'-0" x 18'-0"

living
15'-0" x 14'-0"
vaulted clg.

hers

sauna

utility

gallery

wetbar

exer.
10' x 14'

dining
11'-4" x 15'-0"
vaulted clg.

foyer

study
14'-1" x 20'-0"
13'-4" flat clg.

garage
22'-8" x 30'-8"

curved glass

entry

workbench

A free-standing entryway is the focal point of this luxurious residence. It has an arch motif that is carried through to the rear using a gabled roof and a vaulted ceiling from the foyer out to the lanai. High ceilings are found throughout the home, creating a spacious atmosphere. The kitchen, which features a cooktop island and plenty of counter space, opens to the leisure area with a handy snack bar. Two guest suites with private baths are just off this casual living area. The master wing is truly pampering, stretching the entire length of the home. The suite has a large sitting area, a corner fireplace and a morning kitchen. The bath features an island vanity, a raised tub with a curved glass wall overlooking a private garden, a sauna and separate closets. An exercise room has a curved glass wall and a pocket door to the study, where a wet bar is ready to serve up refreshment.

DESIGN HPU040602

Square Footage: 4,565
Width: 88'-0" Depth: 95'-0"

L

DESIGN BY
©The Sater Design Collection

PLANS ONLINE

*A new Web site, **www.eplans.com**, provides a way for you to*

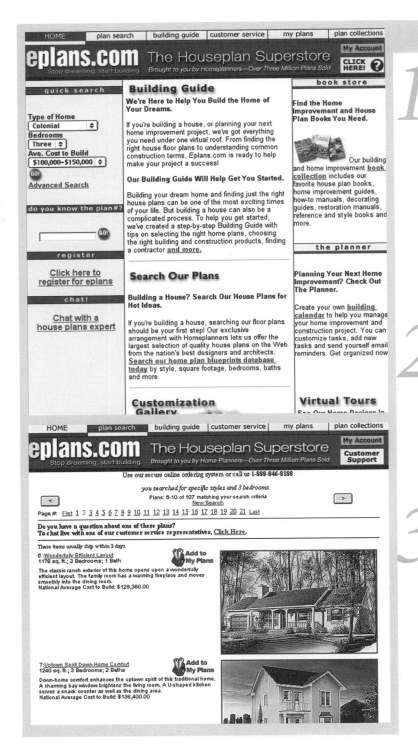

THE EPLANS SITE

1 SEARCH FOR PLANS

The heart of the site is the Plan Search feature that offers an extensive database of plans for your consideration. Do a simplified search by style, number of bedrooms and approximate cost to build in order to find appropriate homes in your range. Or, choose a more advanced search that includes choices for square footage, number of floors, number of bedrooms and baths, width and depth, style, amenities, garage size and, if you prefer, a specified designer.

Either way, you gain access to a selection of homes that meets your specifications, allowing you to easily make comparisons. The site shows front perspectives as well as detailed floor plans for each of your choices. You can even look at enlarged versions of the drawings to make more serious analyses.

2 SAVE FAVORITE PLANS

As you're doing your searches, you can save favorite plans to a personal portfolio called My Plans so that you can easily recall them for future reference and review. This feature stores summary information for each of the plans you select and allows you to review details of the plan quickly without having to re-search or re-browse. You can even compare plans, deleting those that don't measure up and keeping those that appeal, so you can narrow down your search more quickly.

3 PURCHASE PLANS

Once you've made your final choice, you can proceed to purchase your plan, either by checking out through our secure online ordering process or by calling the toll-free number offered in the site. If you choose to check out online, you'll receive information about foundation options for your chosen plan, plus other helpful products such as a building cost estimator to help you gauge costs to build the plan in your zip code area, a materials list specific to your plan, color and line renderings of the plan, and mirror and full reverses. Information relating to all of these products can also be reviewed with a customer service representative if you choose to order by phone.

search for home plans that is as simple as pointing and clicking.

also on the EPLANS site...

VIRTUAL TOURS

In order to help you more completely visualize the homes as built, eplans offers virtual tours of a select group of homes. Showing both interior and exterior features of the homes, the virtual tour gives you a complete vision of how the floor plans for the home will look when completed. All you have to do is choose a home in the Virtual Tour gallery, then click on an exterior or interior view. The view pops up and immediately begins a slow 360° rotation to give you the complete picture. Special buttons allow you to stop the rotation anywhere you like, reverse the action, or move it up or down, and zoom in on a particular element. There's even a large-screen version to allow you to review the home in greater detail.

CUSTOMIZATION GALLERY

For a special group of plans, a customization option allows you to try out building product selections to see which looks the best and to compare styles, colors, and textures. You'll start with an eplans design rendering and then be given options for such elements as roofing, columns, siding, and trim, among others. A diverse grouping of materials and color options is available in each product category. As you choose each option, it will appear on the rendering, allowing you to mix and match options and try out various design ideas. When you're satisfied with your choices, you can enlarge the view, print it out or save it in your personalized Home Project Folder for future reference.

The eplans site is convenient and contains not only the best home plans in the business, but also a host of other features and services. Like Home Planners handy books and magazines, it speaks your language in user-friendly fashion.

In fact, if you want or need more help, there is a Live Person, real-time chat opportunity available with one of our customer service representatives right on the site to answer questions and help you make plans selections.

Let Us Show You Our Home Blueprint Package.

Building a home? Planning a home? Our Blueprint Package has nearly everything you need to get the job done right, whether you're working on your own or with help from an architect, designer, builder or subcontractors. Each Blueprint Package is the result of many hours of work by licensed architects or professional designers.

QUALITY

Hundreds of hours of painstaking effort have gone into the development of your blueprint set. Each home has been quality-checked by professionals to insure accuracy and buildability.

VALUE

Because we sell in volume, you can buy professional quality blueprints at a fraction of their development cost. With our plans, your dream home design costs only a few hundred dollars, not the thousands of dollars that architects charge.

SERVICE

Once you've chosen your favorite home plan, you'll receive fast, efficient service whether you choose to mail or fax your order to us or call us toll free at 1-800-521-6797. For customer service, call toll free 1-888-690-1116.

SATISFACTION

Over 50 years of service to satisfied home plan buyers provide us unparalleled experience and knowledge in producing quality blueprints.

ORDER TOLL FREE
1-800-521-6797

After you've looked over our Blueprint Package and Important Extras on the following pages, simply mail the order form on page 511 or call toll free on our Blueprint Hotline: 1-800-521-6797. We're ready and eager to serve you. For customer service, call toll free 1-888-690-1116.

Each set of blueprints is an interrelated collection of detail sheets which includes components such as floor plans, interior and exterior elevations, dimensions, cross-sections, diagrams and notations. These sheets show exactly how your house is to be built.

AMONG THE SHEETS INCLUDED MAY BE:

FRONTAL SHEET

This artist's sketch of the exterior of the house gives you an idea of how the house will look when built and landscaped. Large floor plans show all levels of the house and provide an overview of your new home's livability, as well as a handy reference for deciding on furniture placement.

FOUNDATION PLANS

This sheet shows the foundation layout including support walls, excavated and unexcavated areas, if any, and foundation notes. If slab construction rather than basement, the plan shows footings and details for a monolithic slab. This page, or another in the set, may include a sample plot plan for locating your house on a building site.

DETAILED FLOOR PLANS

These plans show the layout of each floor of the house. Rooms and interior spaces are carefully dimensioned and keys are given for cross-section details provided later in the plans. The positions of electrical outlets and switches are shown.

HOUSE CROSS-SECTIONS

Large-scale views show sections or cut-aways of the foundation, interior walls, exterior walls, floors, stairways and roof details. Additional cross-sections may show important changes in floor, ceiling or roof heights or the relationship of one level to another. Extremely valuable for construction, these sections show exactly how the various parts of the house fit together.

INTERIOR ELEVATIONS

Many of our drawings show the design and placement of kitchen and bathroom cabinets, laundry areas, fireplaces, bookcases and other built-ins. Little "extras," such as mantelpiece and wainscoting drawings, plus molding sections, provide details that give your home that custom touch.

EXTERIOR ELEVATIONS

These drawings show the front, rear and sides of your house and give necessary notes on exterior materials and finishes. Particular attention is given to cornice detail, brick and stone accents or other finish items that make your home unique.

SAMPLE PACKAGE

FRONTAL SHEET

FOUNDATION PLANS

DETAILED FLOOR PLANS

EXTERIOR ELEVATIONS

INTERIOR ELEVATIONS

HOUSE CROSS-SECTIONS

IMPORTANT EXTRAS TO DO THE JOB RIGHT!

INTRODUCING EIGHT IMPORTANT PLANNING AND CONSTRUCTION AIDS DEVELOPED BY OUR PROFESSIONALS TO HELP YOU SUCCEED IN YOUR HOME-BUILDING PROJECT

MATERIALS LIST

(Note: Because of the diversity of local building codes, our Materials List does not include mechanical materials.)

For many of the designs in our portfolio, we offer a customized materials take-off that is invaluable in planning and estimating the cost of your new home. This Materials List outlines the quantity, type and size of materials needed to build your house (with the exception of mechanical system items). Included are framing lumber, windows and doors, kitchen and bath cabinetry, rough and finish hardware, and much more. This handy list helps you or your builder cost out materials and serves as a reference sheet when you're compiling bids. A Materials List cannot be ordered before blueprints are ordered.

SPECIFICATION OUTLINE

This valuable 16-page document is critical to building your house correctly. Designed to be filled in by you or your builder, this book lists 166 stages or items crucial to the building process. It provides a comprehensive review of the construction process and helps in choosing materials. When combined with the blueprints, a signed contract, and a schedule, it becomes a legal document and record for the building of your home.

QUOTE ONE®

SUMMARY COST REPORT / MATERIALS COST REPORT

A new service for estimating the cost of building select designs, the Quote One® system is available in two separate stages: The Summary Cost Report and the Materials Cost Report.

The **Summary Cost Report** is the first stage in the package and shows the total cost per square foot for your chosen home in your zip-code area and then breaks that cost down into various categories showing the costs for building materials, labor and installation. The report includes three grades: Budget, Standard and Custom. These reports allow you to evaluate your building budget and compare the costs of building a variety of homes in your area.

Make even more informed decisions about your home-building project with the second phase of our package, our **Materials Cost Report.** This tool is invaluable in planning and estimating the cost of your new home. The material and installation (labor and equipment) cost is shown for each of over 1,000 line items provided in the Materials List (Standard grade), which is included when you purchase this estimating tool. It allows you to determine building costs for your specific zip-code area and for your chosen home design. Space is allowed for additional estimates from contractors and subcontractors, such as for mechanical materials, which are not included in our packages. This invaluable tool includes a Materials List. For most plans, a Materials Cost Report cannot be ordered before blueprints are ordered. Call for details. In addition, ask about our Home Planners Estimating Package.

The Quote One® program is continually updated with new plans. If you are interested in a plan that is not indicated as Quote One® please call and ask our sales reps. They will be happy to verify the status for you. To order these invaluable reports, use the order form on page 511 or call 1-800-521-6797.

502

CONSTRUCTION INFORMATION

If you want to know more about techniques—and deal more confidently with subcontractors—we offer these useful sheets. Each set is an excellent tool that will add to your understanding of these technical subjects. These helpful details provide general construction information and are not specific to any single plan.

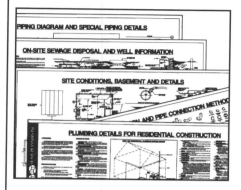

PLUMBING

The Blueprint Package includes locations for all the plumbing fixtures, including sinks, lavatories, tubs, showers, toilets, laundry trays and water heaters. However, if you want to know more about the complete plumbing system, these Plumbing Details will prove very useful. Prepared to meet requirements of the National Plumbing Code, these fact-filled sheets give general information on pipe schedules, fittings, sump-pump details, water-softener hookups, septic system details and much more. Sheets also include a glossary of terms.

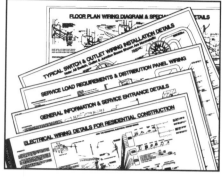

ELECTRICAL

The locations for every electrical switch, plug and outlet are shown in your Blueprint Package. However, these Electrical Details go further to take the mystery out of household electrical systems. Prepared to meet requirements of the National Electrical Code, these comprehensive drawings come packed with helpful information, including wire sizing, switch-installation schematics, cable-routing details, appliance wattage, doorbell hookups, typical service panel circuitry and much more. A glossary of terms is also included.

CONSTRUCTION

The Blueprint Package contains everything an experienced builder needs to construct a particular house. However, it doesn't show all the ways that houses can be built, nor does it explain alternate construction methods. To help you understand how your house will be built—and offer additional techniques—this set of Construction Details depicts the materials and methods used to build foundations, fireplaces, walls, floors and roofs. Where appropriate, the drawings show acceptable alternatives.

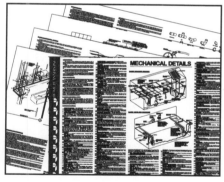

MECHANICAL

These Mechanical Details contain fundamental principles and useful data that will help you make informed decisions and communicate with subcontractors about heating and cooling systems. Drawings contain instructions and samples that allow you to make simple load calculations, and preliminary sizing and costing analysis. Covered are today's most commonly used systems from heat pumps to solar fuel systems. The package is filled with illustrations and diagrams to help you visualize components and how they relate to one another.

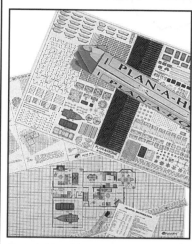

THE FINISHING TOUCHES...

THE DECK BLUEPRINT PACKAGE

Many of the homes in this book can be enhanced with a professionally designed Home Planners Deck Plan. Those home plans highlighted with a **D** have a matching Deck Plan, sold separately, which includes a Deck Plan Frontal Sheet, Deck Framing and Floor Plans, Deck Elevations and a Deck Materials List. A Standard Deck Details Package, also available, provides all the how-to information necessary for building *any* deck. Our Complete Deck Building Package contains one set of Custom Deck Plans of your choice, plus one set of Standard Deck Building Details, all for one low price. Our plans and details are carefully prepared in an easy-to-understand format that will guide you through every stage of your deck-building project. This page contains a sampling of six different Deck layouts (and a front-yard landscape) to match your favorite house. See page 506 for prices and ordering information.

EUROPEAN-FLAIR HOME
Landscape OLA088

WEEKEND-ENTERTAINER DECK
Deck ODA013

CENTER-VIEW DECK
Deck ODA015

KITCHEN-EXTENDER DECK
Deck ODA016

SPLIT-LEVEL ACTIVITY DECK
Deck ODA018

TRI-LEVEL DECK WITH GRILL
Deck ODA020

CONTEMPORARY LEISURE DECK
Deck ODA021

THE LANDSCAPE BLUEPRINT PACKAGE

For the homes marked with an **L** in this book, Home Planners has created a front-yard Landscape Plan that matches or is complementary in design to the house plan. These comprehensive blueprint packages include a Frontal Sheet, Plan View, Regionalized Plant & Materials List, a sheet on Planting and Maintaining Your Landscape, Zone Maps and Plant Size and Description Guide. These plans will help you achieve professional results, adding value and enjoyment to your property for years to come. Each set of blueprints is a full 18" x 24" in size with clear, complete instructions and easy-to-read type. Six of the forty front-yard Landscape Plans to match your favorite house are shown below.

Regional Order Map

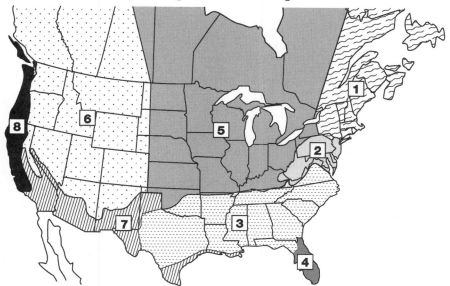

Most of the Landscape Plans shown on these pages are available with a Plant & Materials List adapted by horticultural experts to 8 different regions of the country. Please specify the Geographic Region when ordering your plan. See pages 506-509 for prices, ordering information and regional availability.

Region	1	Northeast
Region	2	Mid-Atlantic
Region	3	Deep South
Region	4	Florida & Gulf Coast
Region	5	Midwest
Region	6	Rocky Mountains
Region	7	Southern California & Desert Southwest
Region	8	Northern California & Pacific Northwest

CAPE COD COTTAGE
Landscape OLA003

GAMBREL-ROOF COLONIAL
Landscape OLA004

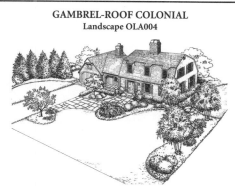

CENTER-HALL COLONIAL
Landscape OLA005

CLASSIC NEW ENGLAND COLONIAL
Landscape OLA006

COUNTRY-STYLE FARMHOUSE
Landscape OLA008

TRADITIONAL SPLIT-LEVEL
Landscape OLA029

PRICE SCHEDULE & PLANS INDEX

HOUSE BLUEPRINT PRICE SCHEDULE

Prices guaranteed through December 31, 2001

TIERS	1-SET STUDY PACKAGE	4-SET BUILDING PACKAGE	8-SET BUILDING PACKAGE	1-SET REPRODUCIBLE	HOME CUSTOMIZER® PACKAGE
P1	$20	$50	$90	$140	N/A
P2	$40	$70	$110	$160	N/A
P3	$60	$90	$130	$180	N/A
P4	$80	$110	$150	$200	N/A
P5	$100	$130	$170	$230	N/A
P6	$120	$150	$190	$250	N/A
A1	$420	$460	$520	$625	$680
A2	$460	$500	$560	$685	$740
A3	$500	$540	$600	$745	$800
A4	$540	$580	$640	$805	$860
C1	$585	$625	$685	$870	$925
C2	$625	$665	$725	$930	$985
C3	$675	$715	$775	$980	$1035
C4	$725	$765	$825	$1030	$1085
L1	$785	$825	$885	$1090	$1145
L2	$835	$875	$935	$1140	$1195
L3	$935	$975	$1035	$1240	$1295
L4	$1035	$1075	$1135	$1340	$1395

OPTIONS FOR PLANS IN TIERS A1–L4

Additional Identical Blueprints in same order for "A1–L4" price plans ....$50 per set

Reverse Blueprints (mirror image) with 4- or 8-set order for "A1–L4" price plans ....$50 fee per order

Specification Outlines ....$10 each

Materials Lists for "A1–C3" price plans ....$60 each

Materials Lists for "C4–L4" price plans ....$70 each

OPTIONS FOR PLANS IN TIERS P1–P6

Additional Identical Blueprints in same order for "P1–P6" price plans ....$10 per set

Reverse Blueprints (mirror image) for "P1–P6" price plans ....$10 per set

1 Set of Deck Construction Details ....$14.95 each

Deck Construction Package ....add $10 to Building Package price
(includes 1 set of "P1–P6" price plans, plus
1 set Standard Deck Construction Details)

1 Set of Gazebo Construction Details ....$14.95 each

Gazebo Construction Package ....add $10 to Building Package price
(includes 1 set of "P1–P6" price plans, plus
1 set Standard Gazebo Construction Details)

IMPORTANT NOTES

The 1-set study package is marked "not for construction."
Prices for 4- or 8-set Building Packages honored only at time of original order. Some basement foundations carry a $225 surcharge. Right-reading reverse blueprints, if available, will incur a $165 surcharge.

INDEX

To use the Index below, refer to the design number listed in numerical order (a helpful page reference is also given). Note the price index letter and refer to the House Blueprint Price Schedule above for the cost of one, four or eight sets of blueprints or the cost of a reproducible drawing. Additional prices are shown for identical and reverse blueprint sets, as well as a very useful Materials List for some of the plans. Also note in the Index below those plans that have matching or complementary Deck Plans or Landscape Plans. Refer to the schedules above for prices of these plans. All plans in this publication are customizable. However, only Home Planners

plans can be customized with the Home Planners Home Customizer® Package. These plans are indicated below with the letter "Y." See page 511 for more information. The letter "Y" also identifies plans that are part of our Quote One® estimating service and those that offer Materials Lists. See page 502 for more information.

To Order: Fill in and send the order form on page 511—or call toll free 1-800-521-6797 or 520-297-8200. FAX: 1-800-224-6699 or 520-544-3086

DESIGN	PRICE	PAGE	MATERIALS LIST	CUSTOMIZABLE	QUOTE ONE	DECK	DECK PRICE	LANDSCAPE	LANDSCAPE PRICE	REGIONS
HPU040004	A1	4	Y							
HPU040005	A2	5								
HPU040006	A1	6								
HPU040007	A1	7	Y							
HPU040008	A2	8								
HPU040009	A2	9b								
HPU040010	C2	9a	Y							
HPU040011	A1	10								
HPU040012	A4	11	Y							
HPU040013	A2	12a								
HPU040014	A3	12b	Y							
HPU040015	A2	13								
HPU040016	A2	14b	Y							
HPU040017	A2	14a	Y							
HPU040018	A2	15	Y							
HPU040019	A2	16	Y							
HPU040020	A1	17	Y							
HPU040021	A2	18b								
HPU040022	A2	18a								
HPU040023	A1	19								
HPU040024	A1	20								
HPU040025	A1	21								
HPU040026	A4	22	Y							
HPU040027	A2	23								
HPU040028	A2	24b	Y							
HPU040029	A2	24a	Y							
HPU040030	A4	25								
HPU040031	A2	26								
HPU040032	A2	27								
HPU040033	A2	28								
HPU040034	A2	29	Y							
HPU040035	A4	30a								
HPU040036	A4	30b								
HPU040037	A4	31								
HPU040038	A3	32	Y							
HPU040039	A2	33	Y							
HPU040040	A2	34	Y							
HPU040041	A2	35	Y							
HPU040042	A4	36								
HPU040043	A4	37								
HPU040044	A2	38	Y							
HPU040045	A2	39	Y							
HPU040047	A2	40b	Y							
HPU040048	A2	40a	Y							
HPU040049	A2	41								
HPU040050	A2	42	Y							
HPU040051	A2	43								
HPU040052	A2	44a	Y							
HPU040053	A2	44b	Y							
HPU040054	A2	45	Y							
HPU040055	A2	46b	Y							
HPU040056	A2	46a	Y							
HPU040057	A2	47	Y					Y		
HPU040058	A2	48	Y							

DESIGN	PRICE	PAGE	MATERIALS LIST	CUSTOMIZABLE	QUOTE ONE	DECK	DECK PRICE	LANDSCAPE	LANDSCAPE PRICE	REGIONS
HPU040059	A2	49	Y							
HPU040060	A2	50	Y							
HPU040061	A2	51a	Y							
HPU040062	A2	51b	Y							
HPU040063	A2	52a								
HPU040064	A2	52b	Y							
HPU040065	A2	53	Y							
HPU040066	A2	54a								
HPU040067	A3	54b								
HPU040068	A3	55								
HPU040069	A2	56b								
HPU040070	A3	56a								
HPU040071	A2	57								
HPU040072	A3	58a								
HPU040073	A2	58b	Y							
HPU040074	A3	59	Y							
HPU040075	A2	60a								
HPU040076	A4	60b								
HPU040077	A2	61	Y							
HPU040078	A4	62	Y							
HPU040079	A3	63								
HPU040080	A3	64a								
HPU040081	A3	64b								
HPU040082	A3	65	Y							
HPU040083	A3	67								
HPU040084	A3	67								
HPU040085	A4	68								
HPU040086	A4	69								
HPU040087	A3	70								
HPU040088	A3	71								
HPU040089	A3	72b								
HPU040090	A4	72a								
HPU040091	A4	73						OLA024	P4	123568
HPU040092	A4	74								
HPU040093	A4	75								
HPU040094	A3	76								
HPU040095	A3	77								
HPU040096	A3	78								
HPU040097	A3	79								
HPU040098	A3	80								
HPU040099	A3	81								
HPU040101	A3	82	Y							
HPU040102	A3	83								
HPU040103	A4	84								
HPU040104	A3	85								
HPU040105	A3	86								
HPU040106	A4	87	Y	Y	Y			OLA024	P4	123568
HPU040107	A4	88	Y							
HPU040108	A3	89	Y							
HPU040109	A3	90								
HPU040110	C1	91								
HPU040111	A3	92								
HPU040112	C1	93								
HPU040113	A3	95	Y							
HPU040114	A3	94	Y							
HPU040115	A3	95	Y							
HPU040116	A4	96a								
HPU040117	A3	96b								
HPU040118	A3	97								
HPU040119	A3	98	Y					OLA001	P3	123568
HPU040120	A3	99								
HPU040121	A4	100								
HPU040122	A3	101								
HPU040123	C1	102								
HPU040124	A4	103	Y							
HPU040125	A3	104b	Y							
HPU040126	A3	104a	Y							
HPU040127	A3	105	Y							
HPU040128	A3	106b	Y							
HPU040129	A3	106a								
HPU040130	A3	107	Y							
HPU040131	A3	108b								
HPU040132	A3	108a								
HPU040133	A3	109								
HPU040134	A4	110b								
HPU040135	A3	110a			Y					
HPU040136	A3	111			Y					
HPU040137	A3	112b	Y							
HPU040138	A3	112a	Y							
HPU040139	A3	113	Y							
HPU040140	A3	114	Y					OLA001	P3	123568
HPU040141	A3	115	Y					OLA001	P3	123568
HPU040142	C3	116b	Y							
HPU040143	A3	116a								
HPU040144	A3	117								
HPU040145	A3	118	Y							
HPU040146	A2	119								
HPU040147	A3	120a	Y							
HPU040148	A3	120b	Y							

DESIGN	PRICE	PAGE	MATERIALS LIST	CUSTOMIZABLE	QUOTE ONE	DECK	DECK PRICE	LANDSCAPE	LANDSCAPE PRICE	REGIONS
HPU040149	A4	121	Y							
HPU040150	A3	122b	Y							
HPU040151	A3	122a								
HPU040152	A3	123			Y					
HPU040153	A3	124a								
HPU040154	A3	124b	Y							
HPU040155	A3	125								
HPU040156	A3	126	Y							
HPU040157	C2	127								
HPU040158	A3	128								
HPU040159	A3	129								
HPU040160	A3	130	Y		Y			OLA001	P3	123568
HPU040161	A3	131						OLA004	P3	123568
HPU040162	A3	132						OLA004	P3	123568
HPU040163	A3	133	Y		Y			OLA005	P3	123568
HPU040164	A3	134b								
HPU040165	A3	134a								
HPU040166	A4	135								
HPU040167	A4	136b								
HPU040168	A4	136a								
HPU040169	A4	137								
HPU040170	A3	138	Y							
HPU040171	A3	139								
HPU040172	A4	140								
HPU040173	A3	141								
HPU040174	A3	142								
HPU040175	A3	143	Y							
HPU040176	A3	144	Y					OLA001	P3	123568
HPU040177	A3	145	Y							
HPU040178	A3	146								
HPU040179	A3	147	Y							
HPU040180	A3	148								
HPU040181	A4	149								
HPU040182	C1	150b						OLA012	P3	12345678
HPU040183	A4	150a	Y							
HPU040184	A4	151								
HPU040185	A4	152								
HPU040186	A4	153								
HPU040187	A4	154								
HPU040188	C1	155	Y		Y			OLA025	P3	123568
HPU040189	A4	156								
HPU040190	C2	157	Y		Y			OLA024	P4	123568
HPU040191	A4	158								
HPU040192	A4	159	Y							
HPU040193	A4	160	Y							
HPU040194	C2	161	Y							
HPU040195	A4	162	Y							
HPU040196	C2	163	Y							
HPU040198	C2	164	Y							
HPU040199	A4	165								
HPU040201	A4	166	Y							
HPU040202	A4	167	Y							
HPU040203	A4	168	Y							
HPU040204	A4	169	Y							
HPU040205	C2	170	Y							
HPU040206	A4	171								
HPU040207	A4	172	Y							
HPU040208	A4	173								
HPU040210	A4	174	Y							
HPU040211	A4	175			Y					
HPU040212	A4	176								
HPU040213	A4	177								
HPU040214	A4	178			Y					
HPU040215	A4	179								
HPU040216	A4	180			Y					
HPU040217	A4	181								
HPU040218	C1	182	Y							
HPU040219	A4	183	Y							
HPU040220	C1	184	Y		Y					
HPU040221	A4	185								
HPU040222	C2	186	Y	Y	Y					
HPU040223	A4	187								
HPU040225	A4	188								
HPU040226	A4	189	Y							
HPU040227	A4	190a								
HPU040228	A4	190b								
HPU040229	C1	191	Y	Y	Y	ODA001	P2	OLA001	P3	123568
HPU040230	A4	192	Y							
HPU040231	A3	193	Y							
HPU040232	A4	194	Y							
HPU040234	A4	195	Y							
HPU040235	A4	196								
HPU040236	C1	197	Y							
HPU040237	C1	198b	Y	Y	Y	ODA011	P2	OLA008	P4	1234568
HPU040238	A4	198a	Y		Y					
HPU040239	A4	199								
HPU040240	A4	200	Y							
HPU040241	A4	201								
HPU040242	A4	202	Y							

DESIGN	PRICE	PAGE	MATERIALS LIST	CUSTOMIZABLE	QUOTE ONE	DECK	DECK PRICE	LANDSCAPE	LANDSCAPE PRICE	REGIONS
HPU040243	A4	203	Y	Y	Y	ODA014	P2	OLA008	P4	1234568
HPU040245	A4	204	Y		Y					
HPU040246	A4	205b	Y							
HPU040247	A4	205a	Y							
HPU040248	A4	206b	Y							
HPU040249	A4	206a	Y							
HPU040250	A4	207	Y							
HPU040251	A4	208a	Y							
HPU040252	A4	208b	Y							
HPU040253	A4	209	Y		Y					
HPU040254	A4	210a	Y							
HPU040255	A4	210b	Y							
HPU040256	A4	211	Y							
HPU040257	A4	212a	Y							
HPU040258	A4	212b	Y		Y					
HPU040259	A4	213	Y							
HPU040260	C1	214	Y	Y	Y					
HPU040262	C1	215	Y	Y	Y	ODA012	P3	OLA010	P3	1234568
HPU040263	C1	216b	Y	Y	Y	ODA012	P3	OLA010	P3	1234568
HPU040264	A4	216a	Y							
HPU040265	A4	217	Y							
HPU040266	A4	218b	Y		Y					
HPU040267	A4	218a	Y		Y					
HPU040268	A4	219	Y							
HPU040269	A4	220a	Y		Y					
HPU040270	A4	220b	Y		Y					
HPU040271	A4	221	Y							
HPU040272	A4	222a								
HPU040273	A4	222b	Y		Y					
HPU040274	A4	223	Y		Y					
HPU040275	A4	224	Y	Y	Y			OLA024	P4	123568
HPU040276	A4	225	Y	Y						
HPU040277	A4	226a	Y	Y		ODA011	P2	OLA025	P3	123568
HPU040278	C1	226b	Y	Y	Y	ODA011	P2	OLA088	P4	12345678
HPU040279	C1	227	Y	Y	Y			OLA010	P3	1234568
HPU040280	A4	228	Y							
HPU040281	C1	229								
HPU040282	C1	230b	Y							
HPU040283	C1	230a								
HPU040284	A4	231	Y							
HPU040285	C1	232b	Y							
HPU040286	C1	232a	Y		Y					
HPU040287	C1	233	Y							
HPU040288	A4	234								
HPU040289	A4	235	Y							
HPU040291	C1	236	Y		Y					
HPU040292	A4	237	Y							
HPU040293	A4	238	Y							
HPU040294	A4	239								
HPU040295	A4	240								
HPU040296	A4	241								
HPU040297	C1	242								
HPU040298	C1	243								
HPU040299	C1	244								
HPU040300	C1	245								
HPU040301	C1	246								
HPU040302	C3	247								
HPU040303	C1	248b								
HPU040304	C1	248a								
HPU040305	C1	249								
HPU040306	C2	250			Y					
HPU040307	C2	251			Y					
HPU040308	C2	252a			Y					
HPU040309	C2	252b			Y					
HPU040310	C2	253			Y					
HPU040311	C1	254			Y					
HPU040312	C1	255								
HPU040313	C3	256								
HPU040314	C3	257								
HPU040315	C1	258a								
HPU040316	C1	258b								
HPU040317	C1	259								
HPU040319	C2	260	Y	Y	Y	ODA014	P2	OLA006	P3	123568
HPU040320	C2	261	Y	Y				OLA017	P3	123568
HPU040321	C1	262b	Y							
HPU040322	C2	262a	Y	Y	Y	ODA015	P2	OLA008	P4	1234568
HPU040323	C1	263			Y					
HPU040324	C2	264			Y					
HPU040325	C2	265	Y		Y					
HPU040326	C2	266	Y							
HPU040327	C3	267			Y					
HPU040328	C1	268			Y					
HPU040329	C1	269								
HPU040331	A4	270			Y					
HPU040332	C1	271			Y					
HPU040333	C1	272a			Y					
HPU040334	C1	272b			Y					
HPU040335	C1	273			Y					
HPU040336	C1	274a			Y					
HPU040337	C1	274b	Y		Y					
HPU040338	C1	275	Y		Y					
HPU040339	C1	276	Y							
HPU040340	C1	277a	Y							
HPU040341	C1	277b	Y							
HPU040342	C1	278a	Y		Y					
HPU040343	C1	278b	Y							
HPU040344	C1	279								
HPU040345	C3	280b								
HPU040346	C1	280a	Y							
HPU040347	C1	281								
HPU040348	C1	282a			Y					
HPU040349	C1	282b	Y							
HPU040350	C2	283	Y	Y	Y	ODA012	P3	OLA024	P4	123568
HPU040351	C2	284			Y					
HPU040353	C1	285								
HPU040354	C2	286b	Y		Y			OLA001	P3	123568
HPU040355	C2	286a	Y		Y	ODA015	P2	OLA013	P4	12345678
HPU040356	C2	287	Y	Y	Y	ODA011	P2	OLA025	P3	123568
HPU040357	C1	288b	Y							
HPU040358	C2	288a	Y							
HPU040359	C1	289	Y							
HPU040360	C2	290b								
HPU040361	C2	290a	Y							
HPU040362	C1	291	Y							
HPU040363	C2	292								
HPU040364	C2	293								
HPU040365	C2	294a	Y	Y	Y					
HPU040366	C3	294b	Y	Y	Y	ODA016	P2	OLA021	P3	123568
HPU040367	C3	295								
HPU040368	A4	296								
HPU040370	C2	297								
HPU040371	C2	298								
HPU040373	C2	299								
HPU040374	C3	300								
HPU040375	C1	301	Y							
HPU040376	C1	302								
HPU040377	C3	303								
HPU040378	C2	304	Y							
HPU040379	C2	305	Y							
HPU040380	C1	306								
HPU040381	C1	307								
HPU040382	C1	308								
HPU040383	C1	309								
HPU040384	C2	310b	Y	Y	Y	ODA006	P2	OLA004	P3	123568
HPU040385	C1	310a								
HPU040386	C2	311	Y	Y	Y	ODA012	P3	OLA018	P3	12345678
HPU040387	C1	312								
HPU040388	C1	313								
HPU040390	C1	314								
HPU040391	C1	315								
HPU040392	C1	316								
HPU040393	C1	317								
HPU040394	C1	318b								
HPU040395	C1	318a								
HPU040396	C2	319								
HPU040397	C2	320b								
HPU040398	A4	320a								
HPU040399	C1	321								
HPU040400	C1	322b								
HPU040401	C2	322a								
HPU040402	C1	323								
HPU040403	C1	324a	Y							
HPU040404	C1	324b	Y							
HPU040405	C1	325								
HPU040406	C1	326b								
HPU040407	C1	326a								
HPU040408	C1	327								
HPU040409	C2	328								
HPU040411	C2	329								
HPU040412	C2	330	Y	Y	Y			OLA015	P4	123568
HPU040413	C2	331	Y	Y	Y			OLA038	P3	7
HPU040414	C2	332	Y	Y	Y			OLA016	P4	1234568
HPU040415	C1	333			Y					
HPU040416	C3	334	Y		Y			OLA001	P3	123568
HPU040417	C1	335						OLA017	P3	123568
HPU040419	C3	336								
HPU040420	C2	337								
HPU040421	C2	338a	Y							
HPU040422	C2	338b								
HPU040423	C2	339								
HPU040424	C2	340								
HPU040425	C3	341								
HPU040426	C2	342	Y					OLA004	P3	123568
HPU040427	C2	343b								
HPU040428	C2	343a								
HPU040429	C2	344	Y					OLA001	P3	123568
HPU040430	C2	345								
HPU040431	C2	346a								

DESIGN	PRICE	PAGE	MATERIALS LIST	CUSTOMIZABLE	QUOTE ONE	DECK	DECK PRICE	LANDSCAPE	LANDSCAPE PRICE	REGIONS
HPU040432	C3	346b	Y		Y			OLA008	P4	1234568
HPU040433	C3	347								
HPU040434	C2	348b								
HPU040435	C3	348a								
HPU040436	C3	349								
HPU040437	C2	350a								
HPU040438	C3	350b								
HPU040439	C3	351								
HPU040440	C2	352								
HPU040441	C3	353								
HPU040442	C2	354b								
HPU040443	C2	354a								
HPU040444	C3	355	Y							
HPU040445	C2	356b								
HPU040446	C2	356a								
HPU040447	C3	357								
HPU040448	C2	358	Y		Y			OLA008	P4	1234568
HPU040449	C3	359	Y							
HPU040450	C2	360								
HPU040451	C3	361								
HPU040452	C2	362	Y							
HPU040453	C2	363								
HPU040454	C2	364b								
HPU040455	C2	364a								
HPU040456	C2	365								
HPU040457	C2	366a								
HPU040458	C2	366b								
HPU040459	C2	367								
HPU040460	C2	368								
HPU040461	C4	369								
HPU040462	C2	370	Y							
HPU040463	C2	371	Y							
HPU040464	C4	372								
HPU040465	C2	373	Y							
HPU040466	C2	374								
HPU040467	C2	375								
HPU040468	C3	376								
HPU040469	C2	377								
HPU040470	C2	378								
HPU040471	C2	379								
HPU040472	C2	380								
HPU040473	C2	381								
HPU040474	C4	382	Y		Y					
HPU040475	C2	383								
HPU040476	C2	384	Y							
HPU040477	C3	385	Y							
HPU040478	C3	386a	Y							
HPU040479	C3	386b	Y							
HPU040480	C2	387								
HPU040481	C2	388b								
HPU040482	C2	388a								
HPU040483	C3	389								
HPU040484	C2	390	Y							
HPU040485	C2	391								
HPU040486	C1	392b								
HPU040487	C2	392a								
HPU040488	C2	393	Y							
HPU040489	C2	394								
HPU040490	C2	395b								
HPU040491	C2	395a								
HPU040492	C2	396	Y		Y			OLA030	P3	12345678
HPU040493	C3	397	Y		Y			OLA030	P3	12345678
HPU040494	C3	398	Y	Y	Y	ODA022	P3	OLA031	P4	12345678
HPU040495	C3	399	Y	Y	Y					
HPU040496	C2	400			Y					
HPU040497	C2	401a			Y					
HPU040498	C2	401b								
HPU040499	C2	402								
HPU040500	C2	403						OLA004	P3	123568
HPU040501	C3	404a	Y							
HPU040502	C3	404b	Y							
HPU040503	C3	405	Y							
HPU040504	C2	406	Y							
HPU040505	C2	407	Y							
HPU040506	C2	408b	Y							
HPU040507	C2	408a								
HPU040508	C2	409								
HPU040509	C3	410a	Y							
HPU040510	C3	410b								
HPU040511	C2	411								
HPU040512	C2	412								
HPU040513	C2	413a								
HPU040514	C2	413b								
HPU040515	C2	414								
HPU040516	C2	415								
HPU040517	C2	416								
HPU040518	C4	417								
HPU040519	C3	418a								
HPU040520	C4	418b			Y					
HPU040521	C1	419								
HPU040522	C3	420b								
HPU040523	C4	420a								
HPU040524	L1	421								
HPU040525	L2	422								
HPU040526	L1	423								
HPU040527	L1	424								
HPU040528	C3	425								
HPU040529	L4	426								
HPU040530	L3	427								
HPU040531	C4	428								
HPU040532	C4	429								
HPU040533	L2	430			Y					
HPU040534	L1	431								
HPU040535	C3	432a								
HPU040536	C4	432b								
HPU040537	L1	433								
HPU040538	C3	434								
HPU040539	C4	435								
HPU040540	L2	436								
HPU040541	L1	437	Y							
HPU040542	C4	438b	Y		Y					
HPU040543	C3	438a								
HPU040544	C4	439	Y							
HPU040545	L1	440	Y		Y					
HPU040546	C4	441	Y							
HPU040547	L1	442								
HPU040548	L1	443								
HPU040549	C3	444								
HPU040550	C3	445	Y							
HPU040551	C4	446	Y							
HPU040552	C4	447	Y							
HPU040553	C4	448	Y							
HPU040554	C4	449								
HPU040555	L2	450								
HPU040556	C4	451								
HPU040557	L1	452								
HPU040558	C4	453								
HPU040559	C3	454								
HPU040560	L1	455						OLA017	P3	123568
HPU040561	C3	456								
HPU040562	C4	457								
HPU040563	L3	458								
HPU040564	C3	459								
HPU040565	L2	460								
HPU040566	C3	461								
HPU040567	C3	462								
HPU040568	C3	463								
HPU040569	C3	464			Y					
HPU040570	L4	465								
HPU040571	L1	466	Y							
HPU040572	L1	467								
HPU040573	C4	468	Y							
HPU040574	L2	469								
HPU040575	C4	470								
HPU040576	C3	471	Y							
HPU040577	C4	472								
HPU040578	C4	473								
HPU040579	C4	474								
HPU040580	C4	475								
HPU040581	C2	476	Y							
HPU040582	L1	477								
HPU040583	L1	478	Y							
HPU040584	C3	479	Y							
HPU040585	C4	480								
HPU040586	L1	481	Y					OLA017	P3	123568
HPU040587	L1	482								
HPU040588	C4	483								
HPU040589	L1	484								
HPU040590	C4	485						OLA008	P4	1234568
HPU040591	L1	486								
HPU040592	L1	487								
HPU040593	L1	488								
HPU040594	L1	489								
HPU040595	C4	490								
HPU040596	L1	491	Y					OLA017	P3	123568
HPU040597	C4	492						OLA017	P3	123568
HPU040598	L2	493	Y							
HPU040599	L1	494			Y			OLA008	P4	1234568
HPU040600	L4	495	Y		Y			OLA008	P4	1234568
HPU040601	L1	496						OLA008	P4	1234568
HPU040602	C4	497	Y							

BEFORE YOU ORDER...

BEFORE FILLING OUT THE COUPON AT RIGHT OR CALLING US ON OUR TOLL-FREE BLUEPRINT HOTLINE, YOU MAY WANT TO LEARN MORE ABOUT OUR SERVICES AND PRODUCTS. HERE'S SOME INFORMATION YOU WILL FIND HELPFUL.

OUR EXCHANGE POLICY

Since blueprints are printed in response to your order, we cannot honor requests for refunds. However, we will exchange your entire first order for an equal or greater number of blueprints within our plan collection within 90 days of the original order. The entire content of your original order must be returned to our offices before an exchange will be processed. If the returned blueprints look used, redlined or copied, we will not honor your exchange. Fees for exchanging your blueprints are as follows: 20% of the amount of the original order...*plus* the difference in cost if exchanging for a design in a higher price bracket or *less* the difference in cost if exchanging for a design in lower price bracket. **(Reproducible blueprints are not exchangeable.)** Please add $25 for postage and handling via Regular Service; $35 via Priority Service; $45 via Express Service. Shipping and handling charges are not refundable.

ABOUT REVERSE BLUEPRINTS

If you want to build in reverse of the plan as shown, we will include any number of reverse blueprints (mirror image) from a 4- or 8-set package for an additional fee of $50. Although lettering and dimensions will appear backward, reverses will be a useful aid if you decide to flop the plan.

REVISING, MODIFYING AND CUSTOMIZING PLANS

The wide variety of designs available in this publication allows you to select ideas and concepts for a home to fit your building site and match your family's needs, wants and budget. Like many homeowners who buy these plans, you and your builder, architect or engineer may want to make changes to them. Some changes may be made by your builder, but we recommend that most changes be made by a licensed architect or engineer. If you need to make alterations to a design that is customizable, you need only order our Home Customizer® Package to get you started. As set forth below, we cannot assume any responsibility for blueprints which have been changed, whether by you, your builder or by professionals selected by you or referred to you by us, because such individuals are outside our supervision and control.

ARCHITECTURAL AND ENGINEERING SEALS

Some cities and states are now requiring that a licensed architect or engineer review and "seal" a blueprint, or officially approve it, prior to construction due to concerns over energy costs, safety and other factors. Prior to application for a building permit or the start of actual construction, we strongly advise that you consult your local building official who can tell you if such a review is required.

ABOUT THE DESIGNS

The architects and designers whose work appears in this publication are among America's leading residential designers. Each plan was designed to meet the requirements of a nationally recognized model building code in effect at the time and place the plan was drawn. Because national building codes change from time to time, plans may not comply with any such code at the time they are sold to a customer. In addition, building officials may not accept these plans as final construction documents of record as the plans may need to be modified and additional drawings and details added to suit local conditions and requirements. We strongly advise that purchasers consult a licensed architect or engineer, and their local building official, before starting any construction related to these plans.

LOCAL BUILDING CODES AND ZONING REQUIREMENTS

At the time of creation, our plans are drawn to specifications published by the Building Officials and Code Administrators (BOCA) International, Inc.; the Southern Building Code Congress (SBCCI) International, Inc.; the International Conference of Building Officials (ICBO); or the Council of American Building Officials (CABO). Our plans are designed to meet or exceed na-

tional building standards. Because of the great differences in geography and climate throughout the United States and Canada, each state, county and municipality has its own building codes, zone requirements, ordinances and building regulations. Your plan may need to be modified to comply with local requirements regarding snow loads, energy codes, soil and seismic conditions and a wide range of other matters. In addition, you may need to obtain permits or inspections from local governments before and in the course of construction. Prior to using blueprints ordered from us, we strongly advise that you consult a licensed architect or engineer—and speak with your local building official—before applying for any permit or beginning construction. We authorize the use of our blueprints on the express condition that you strictly comply with all local building codes, zoning requirements and other applicable laws, regulations, ordinances and requirements. **Notice: Plans for homes to be built in Nevada must be re-drawn by a Nevada-registered professional. Consult your building official for more information on this subject.**

FOUNDATION AND EXTERIOR WALL CHANGES

Depending on your specific climate or regional building practices, you may wish to change a full basement to a slab or crawlspace foundation. Most professional contractors and builders can easily adapt your plans to alternate foundation types. Likewise, most can easily change 2x4 wall construction to 2x6, or vice versa.

DISCLAIMER

We and the designers we work with have put substantial care and effort into the creation of our blueprints. However, because we cannot provide on-site consultation, supervision and control over actual construction, and because of the great variance in local building requirements, building practices and soil, seismic, weather and other conditions, WE CANNOT MAKE ANY WARRANTY, EXPRESS OR IMPLIED, WITH RESPECT TO THE CONTENT OR USE OF OUR BLUEPRINTS, INCLUDING BUT NOT LIMITED TO ANY WARRANTY OF MERCHANTABILITY OR OF FITNESS FOR A PARTICULAR PURPOSE.

TERMS AND CONDITIONS

These designs are protected under the terms of United States Copyright Law and may not be copied or reproduced in any way, by any means, unless you have purchased Sepias or Reproducibles which clearly indicate your right to copy or reproduce. We authorize the use of your chosen design as an aid in the construction of one single family home only. You may not use this design to build a second or multiple dwellings without purchasing another blueprint or blueprints or paying additional design fees.

HOW MANY BLUEPRINTS DO YOU NEED?

A single set of blueprints is sufficient to study a home in greater detail. However, if you are planning to obtain cost estimates from a contractor or subcontractors—or if you are planning to build immediately—you will need more sets. Because additional sets are cheaper when ordered in quantity with the original order, make sure you order enough blueprints to satisfy all requirements. The following checklist will help you determine how many you need:

__ Owner

__ Builder (generally requires at least three sets; one as a legal document, one to use during inspections, and at least one to give to subcontractors)

__ Local Building Department (often requires two sets)

__ Mortgage Lender (usually one set for a conventional loan; three sets for FHA or VA loans)

__ TOTAL NUMBER OF SETS

Have You Seen Our Newest Designs?

At least 50 of our latest creations are featured in each edition of our New Design Portfolio. You may have received a copy with your latest purchase by mail. If not, or if you purchased this book from a local retailer, just return the coupon below for your FREE copy. Make sure you consider the very latest of what Home Planners has to offer.

Yes! Please send my FREE copy of your latest New Design Portfolio.

Offer good to U.S. shipping address only.

Name _____

Address_____

City_____ State _____ Zip _____

HOME PLANNERS, LLC
Wholly owned by Hanley-Wood, LLC
3275 WEST INA ROAD, SUITE 110
TUCSON, ARIZONA 85741

Order Form Key

| HPT18 |

ORDER FORM

The Home Customizer®

"This house is perfect...if only the family room were two feet wider." Sound familiar? In response to the numerous requests for this type of modification, Home Planners has developed **The Home Customizer® Package**. This exclusive package offers our top-of-the-line materials to make it easy for anyone, anywhere to customize any Home Planners design to fit their needs. Check the index on page 506-509 for those plans which are customizable.

Some of the changes you can make to any of our plans include:

- exterior elevation changes
- kitchen and bath modifications
- roof, wall and foundation changes
- room additions and more!

The Home Customizer® Package includes everything you'll need to make the necessary changes to your favorite Home Planners design. The package includes:

- instruction book with examples
- architectural scale and clear work film
- erasable red marker and removable correction tape
- ¼"-scale furniture cutouts
- 1 set reproducible drawings
- 1 set study blueprints for communicating changes to your design professional
- a copyright release letter so you can make copies as you need them
- referral letter with the name, address and telephone number of the professional in your region who is trained in modifying Home Planners designs efficiently and inexpensively.

The Home Customizer® Package will not only save you 25% to 75% of the cost of drawing the plans from scratch with an architect or engineer, it will also give you the flexibility to have your changes and modifications made by our referral network or by the professional of your choice. Now it's even easier and more affordable to have the custom home you've always wanted.

☎ ORDER TOLL FREE!
FOR INFORMATION ABOUT ANY OF OUR SERVICES OR TO ORDER CALL

1-800-521-6797 OR 520-297-8200
Browse our website:
www.eplans.com

BLUEPRINTS ARE NOT REFUNDABLE
EXCHANGES ONLY

FOR CUSTOMER SERVICE,
CALL TOLL FREE **1-888-690-1116.**

HOME PLANNERS, LLC wholly owned by Hanley-Wood, LLC
3275 WEST INA ROAD, SUITE 110 • TUCSON, ARIZONA • 85741

THE BASIC BLUEPRINT PACKAGE
Rush me the following (please refer to the Plans Index and Price Schedule in this section):
___Set(s) of blueprints for plan number(s) _____. $_____
___Set(s) of reproducibles for plan number(s) _____. $_____
___Home Customizer® Package for plan(s)_____. $_____
___Additional identical blueprints (standard or reverse) in same order @ $50 per set. $_____
___Reverse blueprints @ $50 fee per order. Right-reading reverse @ $165 surcharge $_____

IMPORTANT EXTRAS
Rush me the following:
___Materials List: $60 (Must be purchased with Blueprint set.) Add $10 for Schedule C4–L4 plans. $_____
___**Quote One®** Summary Cost Report @ $29.95 for one, $14.95 for each additional,
for plans _____ $_____
Building location: City _____ Zip Code _____
___**Quote One®** Materials Cost Report @ $120 Schedules P1–C3; $130 Schedules C4–L4,
for plan_____(Must be purchased with Blueprints set.) $_____
Building location: City _____ Zip Code _____
___Specification Outlines @ $10 each. $_____
___Detail Sets @ $14.95 each; any two $22.95; any three $29.95; all four for $39.95 (save $19.85). $_____
___❏ Plumbing ❏ Electrical ❏ Construction ❏ Mechanical
___Plan-A-Home® @ $29.95 each. $_____

DECK BLUEPRINTS
(Please refer to the Plans Index and Price Schedule in this section)
___Set(s) of Deck Plan _____. $_____
___Additional identical blueprints in same order @ $10 per set. $_____
___Reverse blueprints @ $10 per set. $_____
___Set of Standard Deck Details @ $14.95 per set. $_____
___Set of Complete Deck Construction Package (Best Buy!) Add $10 to Building Package
Includes Custom Deck Plan _____ Plus Standard Deck Details

LANDSCAPE BLUEPRINTS
(Please refer to the Plans Index and Price Schedule in this section)
___Set(s) of Landscape Plan _____. $_____
___Additional identical blueprints in same order @ $10 per set. $_____
___Reverse blueprints @ $10 per set. $_____
Please indicate the appropriate region of the country for Plant & Material List.
(See map on page 505): Region _____

POSTAGE AND HANDLING	1–3 sets	4+ sets
Signature is required for all deliveries. **DELIVERY** No CODs (Requires street address—No P.O. Boxes)		
•Regular Service (Allow 7–10 business days delivery)	❏ $20.00	❏ $25.00
•Priority (Allow 4–5 business days delivery)	❏ $25.00	❏ $35.00
•Express (Allow 3 business days delivery)	❏ $35.00	❏ $45.00
OVERSEAS DELIVERY	fax, phone or mail for quote	

Note: All delivery times are from date Blueprint Package is shipped.

POSTAGE (From box above) $_____
SUBTOTAL $_____
SALES TAX (AZ & MI residents, please add appropriate state and local sales tax.) $_____
TOTAL (Subtotal and tax) $_____

YOUR ADDRESS (please print)
Name _____

Street_____

City _____State_____Zip _____

Daytime telephone number (_____) _____

FOR CREDIT CARD ORDERS ONLY
Credit card number _____ Exp. Date: (M/Y) _____
Check one ❏ Visa ❏ MasterCard ❏ Discover Card ❏ American Express

Signature_____
Please check appropriate box: ❏ Licensed Builder-Contractor ❏ Homeowner

☎ ORDER TOLL FREE!
1-800-521-6797 or 520-297-8200

Order Form Key

HPT18

Design HPU040219

OVER 3 MILLION BLUEPRINTS SOLD

"We instructed our builder to follow the plans including all of the many details which make this house so elegant…Our home is a fine example of the results one can achieve by purchasing and following the plans which you offer…Everyone who has seen it has assured us that it belongs in 'a picture book.' I truly mean it when I say that my home 'is a DREAM HOUSE.' "

S.P.
Anderson, SC

"We have had a steady stream of visitors, many of whom tell us this is the most beautiful home they've seen. Everyone is amazed at the layout and remarks on how unique it is. Our real estate attorney, who is a Chicago dweller and who deals with highly valued properties, told me this is the only suburban home he has seen that he would want to live in."

W. & P.S.
Flossmoor, IL

"Your blueprints saved us a great deal of money. I acted as the general contractor and we did a lot of the work ourselves. We probably built it for half the cost! We are thinking about more plans for another home. I purchased a competitor's book but my husband wants only your plans!"

K.M.
Grovetown, GA

"We are very happy with the product of our efforts. The neighbors and passersby appreciate what we have created. We have had many people stop by to discuss our house and kindly praise it as being the nicest house in our area of new construction. We have even had one person stop and make us an unsolicited offer to buy the house for much more than we have invested in it."

K. & L.S.
Bolingbrook, IL

"The traffic going past our house is unbelievable. On several occasions, we have heard that it is the 'prettiest house in Batvia.' Also, when meeting someone new and mentioning what street we live on, quite often we're told, 'Oh, you're the one in the yellow house with the wrap-around porch! I love it!' "

A.W.
Batvia, NY

"I have been involved in the building trades my entire life…Since building our home we have built two other homes for other families. Their plans from local professional architects were not nearly as good as yours. For that reason we are ordering additional plan books from you."

T.F.
Kingston, WA

"The blueprints we received from you were of excellent quality and provided us with exactly what we needed to get our successful home-building project underway. We appreciate your invaluable role in our home-building effort."

T.A.
Concord, TN